CW00793686

Mastering HR Management with SAP® ERP HCM

SAP PRESS is a joint initiative of SAP and Galileo Press. The know-how offered by SAP specialists combined with the expertise of the Galileo Press publishing house offers the reader expert books in the field. SAP PRESS features first-hand information and expert advice, and provides useful skills for professional decision-making.

SAP PRESS offers a variety of books on technical and business related topics for the SAP user. For further information, please visit our website: *www.sap-press.com*.

Gallardo
Configuring and Using CATS
2008, 162 pp.
978-1-59229-232-5

Schaer
Time Management with SAP ERP HCM
2009, 579 pp.
978-1-59229-229-5

Masters/Kotsakis
Implementing Employee and Manager Self-Services in SAP ERP HCM
2008, 431 pp.
978-1-59229-188-5

Gillet
Integrating CATS
2009, 232 pp.
978-1-59229-260-8

Sven Ringling, Jörg Edinger, Janet McClurg

Mastering HR Management with SAP® ERP HCM

Bonn • Boston

ISBN 978-1-59229-278-3

2nd Edition, updated and revised

German Edition published 2007 by Galileo Press, Bonn, Germany.

Galileo Press is named after the Italian physicist, mathematician and philosopher Galileo Galilei (1564–1642). He is known as one of the founders of modern science and an advocate of our contemporary, heliocentric worldview. His words *Eppur si muove* (And yet it moves) have become legendary. The Galileo Press logo depicts Jupiter orbited by the four Galilean moons, which were discovered by Galileo in 1610.

Editor Frank Paschen
English Edition Editor Jenifer Niles
Translation Lemoine International, Inc., Salt Lake City, UT
Copy Editor Michael Beady
Cover Design Jill Winitzer
Layout Design Vera Brauner
Production Editor Kelly O'Callaghan
Typesetting Publishers' Design and Production Services, Inc.
Printed and bound in Canada

Contents at a Glance

Contents

Invitation

Yes, that's correct and not a misprint. You may expect a "Preface" here. Because acknowledgments of all parties involved in this book are contained in Appendix E, Authors, and the "instructions" of this book can be found in the next chapter, we would like to extend an invitation. An invitation for what?

Our invitation to you to:

- Exchange your thoughts and ideas with other readers and the authors. For this purpose, Galileo Press offers an online forum exclusively covering the topics of this book. *We invite you to discuss!*
- The online offer also includes process examples and additional information in electronic format. *We invite you to download!*
- As an additional service, we also provide all readers of this book with a free-of-charge email newsletter focusing on SAP ERP HCM, which is supplemented with up-to-date topics of personnel management. Simply subscribe online at *www.admanus.de/english-newsletter*, where you can read previous editions in the newsletter archive and convince yourself of their quality. For your HR-IT strategy, HCM strategy and decisions around HR shared service and outsourcing, please refer to this newsletter: *www.iproconhcm.co.uk/NL*. Both newsletters are published every two months and can be unsubscribed at any time. *We invite you to stay informed!*
- Throughout this book, you will find examples in which system options are used to support the processes differently than originally intended. Personnel management in SAP ERP HCM provides you with a multitude of options that cannot be described within the scope of this book. Familiarize with the structures and functions of the system and discover options of how you can meet your requirements beyond the default scenarios. *We invite you to innovate!*

Of course, this invitation is also extended to all female readers. To simplify reading, all gender-specific pronouns used in this text, such as *user, employee*, etc. are masculine. This is due to practical reasons and no offense to our female readers is either intended or implied.

In this chapter, we will discuss the goal of this book, the scope of the content, who can benefit from the book, and what's new in this edition.

1 Goal of this Book

SAP ERP HCM is a very extensive topic, and many people are interested in it for different reasons. But, as we all know, "the jack-of-all-trades is a master of none," so we distinguish our book by limiting the scope of this book and giving you useful tips for the areas we cover.

1.1 Scope of the Content

The book describes SAP ERP HCM based on Release ERP 6.0. But users of older releases as of 4.6C can utilize this book to a large extent. As was the case with R/3 Enterprise, SAP ERP will be continuously developed through small updates (support packages), new additional developments, and larger annual supplements, while at the same time ensuring the validity of the essential statements made in this book.

The processes discussed in this book are detailed in such a way that the functional scope and the basic properties of SAP ERP HCM are clearly identified for the respective process. Furthermore, Customizing—that is, the customer-specific system configuration—is exemplified at central points. In general, we have placed more emphasis on understanding the overall concept and relationships than on detailed descriptions of customizing tables.

For readers who haven't used the system in their daily work, we have provided numerous screenshots from the system. These should help illustrate the information provided in this book and thus make it more tangible.

Even using abstract descriptions, without too many details, and avoiding a screenshot gallery that shows each and every potentially relevant screen, SAP ERP HCM is too voluminous a topic to treat entirely in one single book. For this reason, the book focuses on the administrative processes and avoids dealing with matters related to the system basis or programming. Personnel planning and development is described in a separate book by the same authors, which was also published by SAP PRESS. In that book, we draw a line of separation between the parts that SAP formerly referred to as PA and PD. Although no longer officially used, there are still reasons for making this distinction. There is a difference in the technical implementation, which is also reflected in the system configuration. Further, in the administrative processes considered, the focus is on technology and processes, while the implementation of personnel planning and development is almost entirely decided on the process-definition side. Moreover, travel management is not considered at all.

While Chapters 9 and 10 (Payroll and Benefits administration) focus on the US in terms of legislation, readers from other countries can still benefit from both chapters as they explain the general setup of those processes in SAP HCM.

Another important element of the book is the visualization of process examples. These enable a much better understanding of the processes and their IT support than a purely textual description would. These process examples are available online in file format at *http://www.iprocon.com/book-process* — use the password *innovation.*

1.2 Release Names

Even though most people still use the term Human Resources (HR), within this book we use HCM or SAP ERP HCM, which is the official terminology of this SAP system.

With regard to the name of the first two ERP releases there was some confusion. Whereas the first versions were officially called mySAP ERP 2004 and mySAP ERP 2005, the new releases provided by SAP AG as of 2005 no longer include the prefix "my." In the meantime, the year dates have been replaced as well so that you now should use "mySAP ERP 2004" and "SAP ERP 6.0." Until now, however, "SAP ERP 5.0" has been used as a synonym of "mySAP ERP 2004," and "SAP ERP 2005" as a synonym of "SAP ERP 6.0." In the future, the new denomination should establish itself, and the next version will be officially called "SAP ERP 7.0."

1.3 Target Groups

The following target audiences will find useful information in this book:

- *Decision makers in HR, Information Technology (IT),* and *organizational departments* will gain a critical overview of the SAP ERP HCM functionalities. They will also develop a feeling for the basic strengths and weaknesses and the cost drivers.
- *Project managers* are provided with the most important integration aspects and success factors that are critical for the implementation.
- *Members of implementation project teams, consultants,* and *those responsible for customizing* will find many tips for each process. In this context, basic functionalities are described in more detail so that employees who are just assuming these roles will receive appropriate guidelines for getting started. For advanced users, the book contains many recommendations that don't go into too much detail. It is more important to understand the basic direction of each process or project.
- *Interested users* who would like to see beyond the borders of their specific activities, and key users who are also responsible for the continued development of the system, will get a good overview of the various interactions and develop a better understanding of how the system works.
- *Programmers* who work close to the application in the SAP ERP HCM environment will find the contents of this book very helpful in facilitating communication with the user departments and the review of technical concepts.
- *Students or other interested parties* who are just learning about personnel management will develop true insight into the practice of HR and its IT implementation with SAP ERP HCM. The book's topics represent important functions of a personnel department and indicate where problems can occur. It is especially for this target group that the book provides business-related background information.

1.4 Working with this Book

You can read the individual chapters of this book in any sequence. For readers who are less familiar with SAP ERP HCM, however, we recommend that you read Chapter 4, "Personnel Administration," before proceeding with the other chapters.

In addition, over time you should also get an overview of all processes, not simply the process or processes for which you are responsible or in which you work. A basic understanding of the additional context is absolutely beneficial for working in highly integrated processes.

The detailed descriptions of various customizing activities can be skipped according to your personal preferences.

Once again, we would like to remind you that the process models described in this book are also available online (see Invitation). These can be customized to individual requirements and are therefore suitable for internal presentations or training.

1.5 New in this Edition

Compared to the previous edition, this edition provides a lot of new and changed content, which is worth reading. These changes can be found in the chapter structure, the number of pages, and the enhanced team of authors.

You can expect the following innovations:

- All chapters took into account both new project experience and feedback from readers.
- For all chapters it was checked whether additions were necessary with regard to SAP ERP 6.0 or new solutions. Unfortunately, you cannot always make a clear distinction between different release statuses. Many innovations of SAP ERP 6.0 are provided as predeliveries or as HR support packages for older releases. SAP ERP itself is not as static as you are used to in previous releases; different components may have different release cycles. The newsletter of the enhanced team of authors (see Invitation) informs readers about changes.
- The restructuring particularly applies to Chapter 2, "Overview of SAP ERP HCM," which now includes portal basics, whereas the content of the former Chapter 13, "Role-Based Portal Solution," has been updated, enhanced, and distributed over the entire book. As a result, portal-based applications are no longer considered in an isolated manner, but are integrated with the respective processes.
- Chapter 4, "Personnel Administration," now includes many enhancements for portal applications, including Employee Interaction Center (EIC).

- Chapter 6, "E-Recruiting," was completely revised and considerably enhanced. Because there are some customers who will still work with "traditional" recruitment, Chapter 7, "Traditional Recruitment," was also revised; however, it now follows E-Recruiting.
- Chapter 8, "Time Management," was supplemented with Web applications.
- Chapter 9, "Payroll," was enhanced with some aspects of Customizing, particularly with regard to the remuneration statement with HR Forms.
- Chapter 11, "HR Reporting," was abridged in favor of other topics, because SAP PRESS published *HR Reporting with SAP* to cover this topic thoroughly.
- Chapter 12, "QA/Internal Control System," was enhanced with a stronger focus on internal control systems.

SAP ERP HCM is an extensive, powerful package for supporting the processes of personnel management. In addition, the ability to integrate it with the logistics and accounting processes, along with the options of the SAP NetWeaver Portal within the framework of the total SAP Business Suite solution are among its many strengths.

2 Overview of SAP ERP HCM

In the following sections, we will detail the historical development of the current SAP ERP HCM solution in the context of the overall solution and the various HCM components. Then, we will describe the role-based user interfaces, particularly those provided in SAP NetWeaver Portal.

2.1 Incorporation of HCM into SAP ERP and SAP Business Suite

Until recently, SAP was primarily associated with one single system—R/3. The term *System R/3* stands for *Real-time System 3* and is founded in the development history of this software. For a long time, R/3 and its predecessors were *the* software of SAP AG and were used as synonyms for *SAP* or *SAP system*.

In addition to a multitude of industry-specific processes, R/3 is organized into the following main areas:

- Accounting
- Logistics
- Personnel management
- Basic system/Web Application Server (Web AS)

Gradually, more products were added (e.g., Business Information Warehouse, or BIW, at an early stage) that now form the SAP ERP system in combination with the further development of R/3 modules.

SAP NetWeaver 3 is the technical platform that combines numerous cross-process components that can then be used in various business applications (e.g., HCM or accounting). The most important applications include:

- SAP NetWeaver AS (the former Web AS or successor to the R/3 Basis system)
- SAP NetWeaver Business Intelligence (BI) (successor to BW)
- SAP NetWeaver Exchange Infrastructure (XI) (provides open interfaces to other systems)
- SAP NetWeaver Portal (combines different applications in role-based views, which users can access via a Web interface; see Section 2.3)

Usually, multiple SAP NetWeaver systems are installed in a productive system landscape, for example, one system as the basis for SAP ERP, another one for the portal (see Section 2.4), and further systems for other applications of SAP Business Suite. In addition to SAP ERP, SAP Business Suite also comprises the following solutions:

- SAP Customer Relationship Management (CRM)
- SAP Product Lifecycle Management (PLM)
- SAP Supply Chain Management (SCM)
- SAP Supplier Relationship Management (SRM)

From SAP R/3 to SAP ERP: Evolution instead of revolution

Due to the omission of the familiar name R/3, many people consider the switch to SAP ERP as a considerable change. In fact, the development is more evolutionary than revolutionary—particularly if you examine it from the point of view of the HCM application. You are provided with many new functions and user interfaces, but in most cases you can continue to use the old functions after upgrading to SAP ERP and gradually switch over as required.

You cannot view the processes of personnel management in isolation because they are inherently integrated with the other R/3 processes. Figure 2.1 displays the elements of SAP ERP in a Solution Map. End-User Service Delivery particularly summarizes the self-service interfaces of the portal.

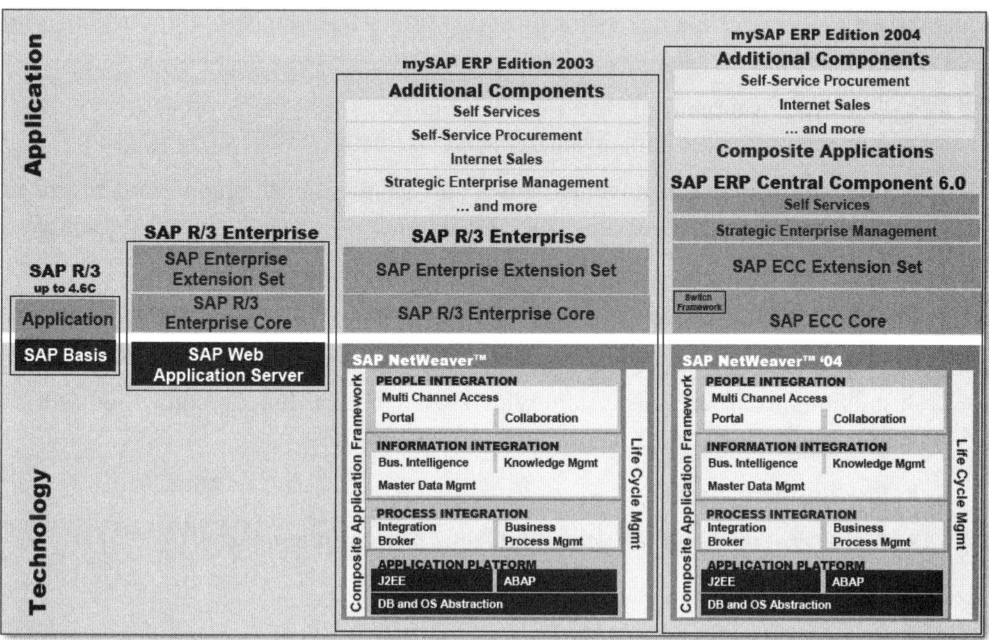

Figure 2.1 Solution Map for SAP ERP

The important integration aspects relevant to the processes described in this book are the following:

- Posting of payroll results and travel cost accounting in financial accounting (FI) and cost accounting (CO)
- Integration with the payment programs of FI
- Assignment of cost centers and other cost units from CO into the personnel master data
- Incorporation of the organizational structure of organizational management into the accounting structure
- Accounting for services, cost distribution, or foreign services (purchasing or Materials Management – MM) from time management
- Validation of various fields (e.g., company car or loan) against a facility number in asset accounting

- Generation of time tickets for incentive wages from logistics (Production Planning—PP)
- Cross-Application Time Sheet (CATS): Connection of many processes in which employees' time is kept, evaluated, and calculated
- Integration between travel expenses and payment entitlement with regard to taxable reimbursement amounts and statement of per diems on the employment tax card
- Use of selected personnel master data in other components, particularly SAP Environmental Health & Safety (EH&S)

Just as important are the system-wide cross-sectional functionalities into which Human Resources (HR) is incorporated. They include:

- SAP Business Workflow
- BI as a cross-process reporting and control environment
- Role concept
- Development environment
- SAP Business Workplace
- Archiving
- Portal environment
- Interfaces to external systems (XI)

2.2 Components of Personnel Management with the SAP System

Initially, we want to present the components of personnel management in R/3 release 4.7 (R/3 Enterprise). On one hand, this makes it easier for those who have not yet switched to SAP ERP. On the other hand, this "old" structure can still be found in the menu and the implementation guide (IMG) of SAP ERP 6.0. In various respects, this structure better reflects reality than the new terms that follow. The latter rather illustrate the direction of further development and suggest a more comprehensive integration between different processes than is currently available.

2.2.1 Components of Personnel Management in SAP R/3 Enterprise

The important processes of personnel work are supported. The following form the basis:

- Personnel administration, including a complete personnel master data maintenance and administration
- Organizational management for flexible mapping of the organizational structure of the company and classification of employees

Additional personnel management processes in R/3 are:

- **Recruitment**
  Managing vacancies, job advertisements, selection, and correspondence
- **Personnel Time Management**
  Maintenance and evaluation of time data, managing time accounts, creating input for payroll
- **Incentive Wages**
  Piece rate and premium wages for workers
- **Payroll**
  Calculation of gross and net salaries, payment, reporting to authorities, posting to the Financials component
- **Benefits**
  Pension plans, insurance, and other benefits in compliance with the specific rules of each country
- **Travel Management (this component was a part of HR initially but was moved to financials and then to corporate services)**
  Planning of trips, procurement of tickets, etc., request and approval processes, settlement and posting to financial accounting
- **Training and Event Management**
  Event catalogue, organizing events and resource planning, management of attendees, correspondence, billing and activity allocation
- **Personnel Development**
  Skill management, career and succession planning, appraisals, development plans
- **Compensation Management**
  Compensation planning for individual employees and groups, budgeting, policies, benchmarking, job pricing

- **Personnel Cost Planning**
  Planning of costs based on basic pay master data, organizational management, payroll results, and payroll simulation
- **Shift Planning**
  Managing the optimal workforce deployment based on requirements and shift plans

All of these components and their integration into other processes are available in R/3 without having to install additional components.

Other essential components used in personnel management, but can be installed as independent systems include:

- E-Recruiting
- Learning Solution (learning platform including E-Learning)
- BIW (reporting)

2.2.2 Structure of SAP ERP HCM

SAP ERP HCM (release 6.0) is subdivided into three parts: talent management, workforce process management, and workforce deployment. Most of the processes described in this book can be found in workforce process management. In the following lists, these processes are indicated in *italics*.

Talent Management

Talent management includes the recruitment, development, and retention of employees required for the enterprise to succeed and comprises the following processes:

- E-Recruiting
- Career planning
- Succession planning
- Development planning and further training
- Performance management (objective setting and appraisals)
- Enterprise Compensation Planning and cost planning

Workforce Process Management

Workforce process management deals with the administrative processes of personnel management and includes:

- Personnel administration (master data management)
- Organizational management
- Benefits
- Payroll
- Time management
- Management of Global Employees (Expatriates) and Concurrent Employment
- HCM Processes and Forms (a purely technical component that provides portal-based flows for supporting different SAP ERP HCM processes)

Workforce Deployment

Workforce deployment plans and controls the deployment of employees. SAP provides the following components:

- Project resource planning
- Resource and program management
- Retail planning

This subdivision is rather random to some extent and experience has shown that the denominations change faster than the content. For example, the assignment of cost planning is not entirely clear in this pattern (although there is an integration link that can be used to create budget amounts using Personnel Cost Planning and then you can transfer them to budgets in Enterprise Compensation Management). Ultimately, it is most important to know the individual components and their interactions, which will be described in the following chapters. The classification into categories is of secondary importance.

2.2.3 A Basis for Other Processes in this Book

An indispensable basis for the use of the processes described in this book is personnel administration, in which personnel master data is maintained. This is described in more detail in Chapter 4, "Personnel Administration." Another indispensable factor is the correct configuration of the basis system (SAP NetWeaver). For more information about this configuration you should consider the relevant publications from SAP PRESS on NetWeaver.

It is highly recommended that you implement the organizational management component, at least in a simple, pragmatic form (see Chapter 5, "Organizational Management in SAP ERP HCM").

The other processes, for which integration exists (e.g., FI, CO), don't necessarily have to be supported within the SAP ERP solution. You are also provided with interfaces to third-party systems; however, they result in higher level of effort in an implementation.

2.3 Roles in SAP ERP HCM

With the role concept SAP is distancing itself from its previous focus on technical entities and structures. Instead, everything is now oriented toward the user and his daily tasks. Roles can be tailored to one specific user group and enable users to work efficiently, particularly inexperienced users, who usually only use a small set of functionalities.

2.3.1 General Remarks

The sheer scope of the functions provided by SAP's HCM processes is considerable, and the inexperienced user is sure to feel overwhelmed. Added to this is the fact that, from the user's viewpoint, it often takes too many mouse-clicks to get to the required functionalities. Refocusing the concept of the system on user roles represents a clear improvement in terms of efficiency and user acceptance.

The fact that roles combine the Easy Access menu and authorizations provides the user with wonderfully useful options that he should not neglect to use. The Payroll menu and its benefits deserve particular mention. Imagine that staff in the payroll department of an American enterprise, for example, needs only the payroll simulation, the remuneration statement, and some reports. Figure 2.2 shows the menu path to the posting run execution (that is, how the function is accessed without the use of the role concept). A suitably designed role, on the other hand, makes accessing this function much easier, as shown in Figure 2.3.

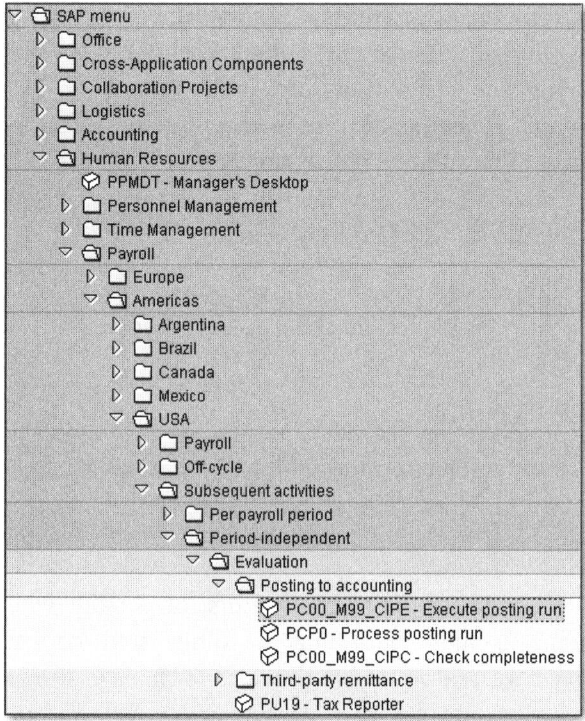

Figure 2.2 Long-Winded Access Without Role Menu

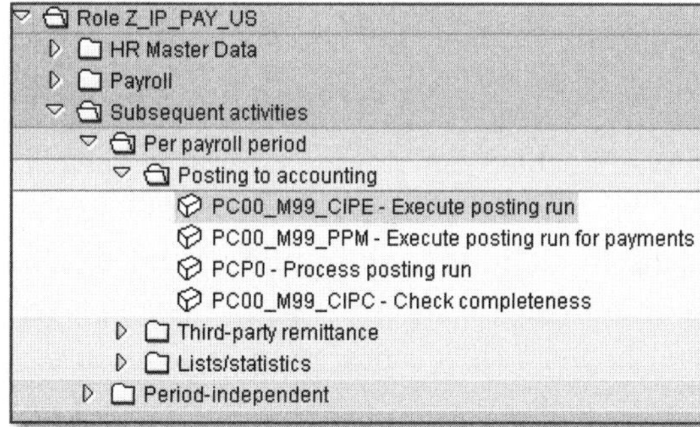

Figure 2.3 Efficient Access via User-specific Role

The orientation of SAP ERP around user roles does not stop at role-specific menus. More and more applications within the system can be tailored to the individual user. In fact, this was already the case in older releases — see the examples of actions and infotype menus given in Chapter 4. User-specific elements were further extended in release 4.6C and beyond. Also, various scenarios bundle together the typical functionalities of specific roles in to one interface. A time administrator, for example, has an interface that is specially tailored to his requirements and enables him to perform exactly the activities he needs to perform in his daily work. The Manager's Desktop provided similar functions for managers who required information about their team members. The Internet Transaction Server (ITS)–based () Employee Self-Service (ESS) (see section 2.4.1) and particularly the portal concept (see section 2.4) went even further than this when they were first introduced.

In SAP ERP, roles not only control the design of menus and user interfaces. Roles as technical objects are particularly responsible for checking access authorizations.[1]

2.3.2 Selected Roles in SAP ERP HCM

The following sections introduce some selected roles within SAP ERP HCM.

Time Administrator

The Time Manager's Workplace provides time administrators, or persons who are responsible for central time management, with functions similar to those that the employee area of the Manager's Desktop (MDT) provides to managers. It is accessed via the menu path Human Resources • Time Management • Administration • Time Manager's Workplace. For detailed information on the Time Manager's Workplace, see Chapter 8, "Time Management."

Employees in ESS

ESS component provides very useful Web-enabled functions that improve the efficiency and quality of HR management. Simply put, it allows employees to display and maintain their own personal data. In addition, you can be provided with evaluations that go beyond the data of individual employees (e.g., the employee directory or Who's Who described in Chapter 4. ESS is described in detail in section 2.4.

Managers

In many enterprises, when managers need information about their employees, it is often still provided to them in paper form. Electronic lists created using any of the

1 See also Martin Esch, Anja Junold: *Authorizations in SAP ERP HCM*, Boston 2008.

Office products are not much better, because—like paper lists—they are up-to-date only to the time of creation and do not allow for any interactivity (for example, a manager may have an overview list but may want to see detailed information for one particular item in the list).

However, many managers find it too time-consuming to access the information directly in the HR information system that is used in their enterprise. This may be because the various pieces of information are stored in any number of different locations, and besides HR data, the manager may also require access to workflow data or cost center data.

The MDT (see Section 2.5) and the Manager Self-Service (MSS) (see Section 2.4.6) in SAP ERP HCM are designed to address these needs. Using Organizational Management data, the system "knows" which employees are assigned to which manager. The tasks that each manager can perform in the system are set in Customizing.

HR Business Partner

Non-centrally working employees, who support the personnel function in the business units on site, but who assume administrative maintenance work in the system only to a limited extent, are provided with a specially tailored, Web-based interface (see Section 4.5.6) that is available for the role HR Administrator in the HR Administrative Services component.

Employees in Personnel Service Centers

The Employee Interaction Center (EIC) provides role-specific access (see Section 4.5.7 in Chapter 4) for first-level support in personnel service centers, which are organized similarly to call centers.

2.3.3 Critical Success Factors

A description of how to create roles and composite roles, including the relevant authorizations, is beyond the scope of this book. In the following, we simply provide some recommendations that you should keep in mind in regard to enterprise-specific role concepts:

- In the process of defining roles, all of the relevant information about the roles and their tasks must be made available. For this to be possible, the users must be intensively involved in the process, especially if the system in question is a decentralized one.

- Role-specific menus are strongly recommended to really support the end users in their daily work.
- Use the options available to you for structuring the role concept in a modular way using composite roles.
- It is worthwhile displaying the structure of work centers, tasks, and task blocks in your department and those of dispersed users in overview form first, and only then dealing with the details of assigning authorizations.
- If multiple systems are in use, centralized user administration is the best option.
- First, compile a suitable menu for each role. Then, based on this, the profile generator creates a proposal for the access authorizations. This proposal is usually very good, but critically evaluate it anyway after filling in the empty fields. An intensive test is essential, due to the complexity of this topic.

2.4 ESS/MSS and the Portal

Modern Information Technology (IT) systems provide users with a convenient, Web-based access. Usually, this considerably improves the processes. This section provides an overview of the options provided by SAP for this purpose and their complexity.

Enterprises require that a modern IT system supports them in facilitating their processes. This usually means that integration gaps and different processors must be avoided. The number of required process steps should also be reduced. If possible, the processes should be completed in the location they started. This means that simple transactions are transferred to the end users. For example, if an employee forgets the clock-out entry at the time-recording terminal, this shouldn't require him to fill in a form the next day and send it to the HR department via internal mail where it is recorded by the person responsible. It would rather be preferable if the employee could supplement the missing clock-out entry in the system himself. Because this doesn't constitute his main task, the system must be easy to use and intuitive without any training. It should also be ensured that the entire process doesn't fail because the employee forgot his user name and/or password.

ESS is a key component if employees are to integrate with administrative HR processes. However, this is not about relieving the HR department from simple administrative tasks. Frequently, these processes are unnecessarily complex and consequently expensive, as you can see in the example mentioned earlier. Information is recorded several times—in a form and in the system. This results in an additional error source and may initiate another correction process that is even more complex. You should also not underestimate the possible frustration potential involved in unnecessarily complex processes.

The objectives and benefits of ESS can be summarized as follows:

- Accelerating the processes
- Increasing the quality
- Reducing the costs
- Higher motivation and satisfaction

HR departments have to change or already have changed in such a way that a majority of the requests submitted to the department are no longer processed by highly qualified employees (see Figure 2.4). This provides the free space required to deal with strategically important topics.

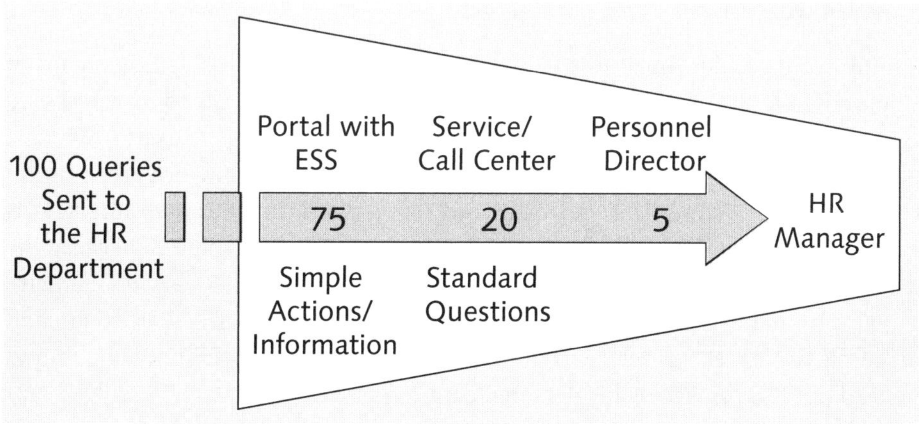

Figure 2.4 Organizational Model of the HR Service Center

The following sections briefly introduce you to the technical interrelations for Web-based user interfaces in ESS and MSS. Usually, people responsible for HCM don't have to be able to answer these technical questions in detail. It is more important that they can *ask* the right questions when they have discussions with technically oriented IT employees or consultants. If you consider the following sections to be too technically oriented, you can also find information about ESS and MSS from the application point of view in the following chapters.

2.4.1 ESS with SAP

SAP has provided ESS as a solution for many years. There are already some solution proposals for the following two major problems:

- easy, intuitively operable user interface (not SAP GUI!)
- no additional user name and password that could be forgotten

ESS is operated via a Web interface, that is, you work in a web browser. Here, the benefit is that many employees are already familiar with the user interface and its operation (Internet). Furthermore, this considerably facilitates the distribution of software, which must be available on every workplace computer that is supposed to access ESS. Web browsers are standard equipment of every workplace computer. The problem becomes apparent if you consider how to install an SAP GUI with a data volume of approximately 650MB on 10,000 workplace computers that are distributed over different geographical locations. Then, this SAP GUI must be provided with patches at regular intervals.

The problem of additional user names and passwords can be solved by means of single sign-on (SSO). Users are provided with authorizations that control access to specific data. In the case of ESS, access is normally granted to the users' own data only. An SSO solution, however, ensures that the user and password are identical to the already-existing user and password for network logon, for example. It is even possible that the users don't have to log on when they call ESS because the data for the network logon is used in the background. This is very convenient, but also bears the risk of personal data being accessed very easily. For example, if an employee leaves his desk without locking the computer, everyone who knows how to call ESS can access his personal data.

2.4.2 Web Architecture

To understand the various technologies available for SAP ERP and their interrelations, it is best to take a look at the chronological development of ESS.

In older releases beginning with 3.1 there was no direct connection between web browsers and the SAP system. For this purpose, you required additional software — the ITS. It translates between the SAP system and the Web browser (see Figure 2.5).

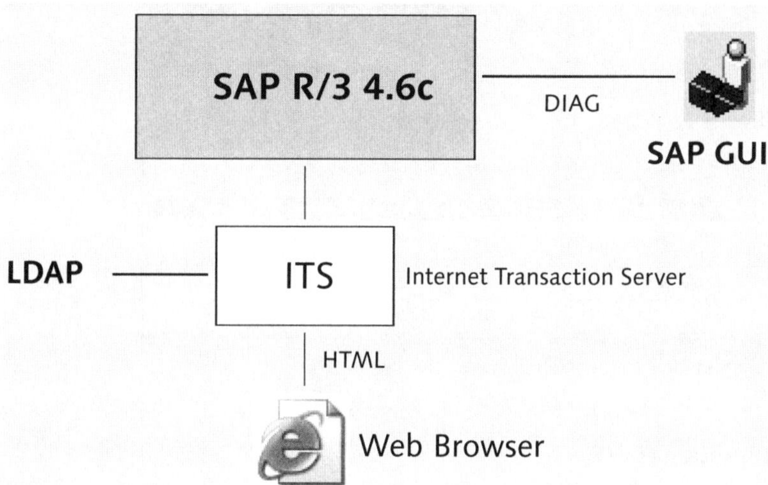

Figure 2.5 Web Architecture for 4.6

For this purpose, three different technologies were provided for implementing Internet services.

Web GUI

This is the simplest, but also most unaesthetic implementation option. It hardly involves any additional development work to use SAP GUI applications in ESS. However, the user-friendliness leaves a lot to be desired. ITS assumes the task to replicate an SAP GUI in the web browser, that is, it translates a transaction in HTML. As a result, the user interface known from SAP GUI is available in the web browser. That's how the ITS-based ESS scenario for travel expenses (Transaction TRIP) was implemented (see Figure 2.6), for example. This was presumably done because SAP GUI Transaction TRIP already provides a user interface that is not typical for most transactions. Here, HTML elements are used in the SAP GUI already.

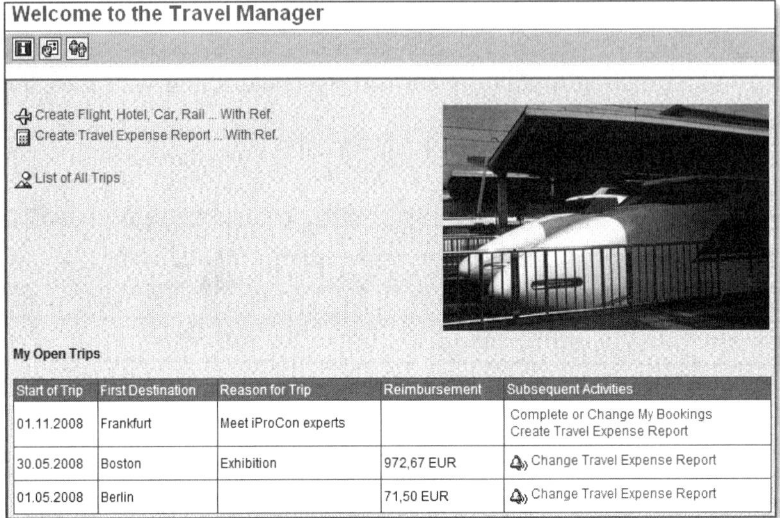

Figure 2.6 Transaction TRIP in the Web Browser

Easy Web Transaction (EWT)

EWTs are SAP transactions whose interface design was optimized for web browsers. EWTs can be created and processed in the development environment of SAP ERP (Transaction SE80). Then, they are published to ITS. An EWT usually contains only some SAP GUI elements, such as the menu bar and the transaction fields. As a result, its layout is very similar to typical Web interfaces (see Figure 2.7).

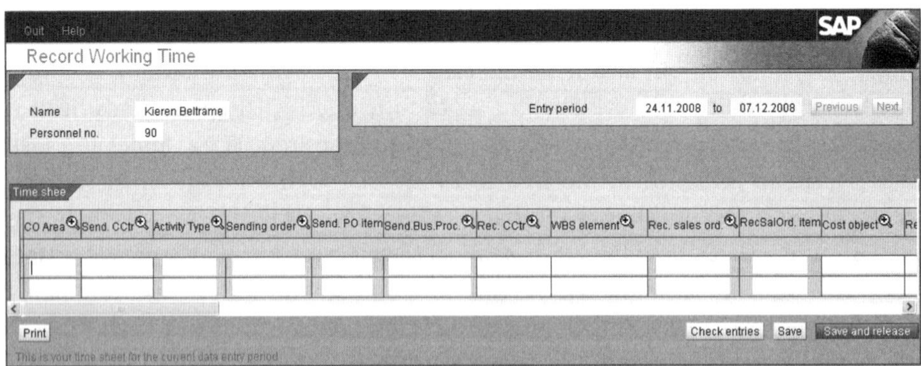

Figure 2.7 Transaction CATW-EWT in the Web Browser

Flow Logic

Internet services, which have been implemented in Flow Logic (in Transaction SE80; analog to EWTs), comprise one or more HTML pages that are enhanced with a very simple script language to call function modules in SAP R/3. The layout can be designed according to your own requirements (see Figure 2.8, right hand side). Note, however, that flow logic can only be used with ECC 5.0 and below.

In addition, the ITS provides a Lightweight Direct Access Protocol (LDAP) interface via which the validity of the entered user data (user name and password) can be checked by a third-party system. For example, this third-party system can be a Microsoft Active Directory that is also used to check the network logon. This ensures that the same user name and password can be used for the network and ITS logon (SSO). For this kind of authentication, the password assigned in the SAP system is irrelevant and not checked. Only the authorizations assigned to the user ID are read.

The ESS menu based on ITS is displayed in Figure 2.8.

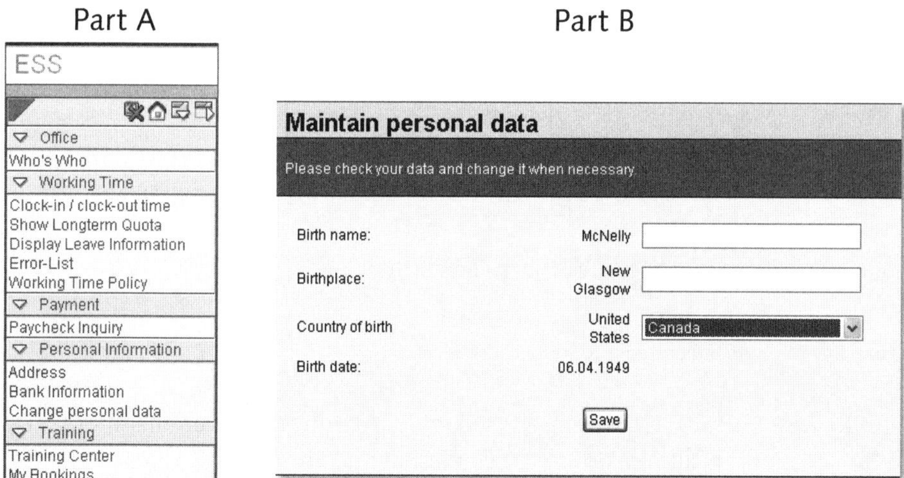

Figure 2.8 ESS Menu Based on ITS

With Release 4.7, SAP created a Web interface directly to the R/3 system for the first time (see Figure 2.9). The technology of Business Server Pages (BSP) was provided. BSPs usually consist of HTML pages with ABAP source code as the script language. In addition, BSPs can be analyzed using the debugger; this considerably reduces the development times compared to Internet services.

However, the standard ESS services still require the ITS. Web interfaces to more recent components were no longer implemented as Internet services, but as BSPs (e.g., the detail planning of the new cost planning, the Objective Setting and Appraisals component, and E-Recruiting). It is generally possible to mix these two technologies. For example, BSP for detail planning of the new cost planning can be integrated with the ITS-based ESS menu. SSO settings in the R/3 system and the ITS ensured that the user ID and the password no longer has to be entered when calling the detail planning.

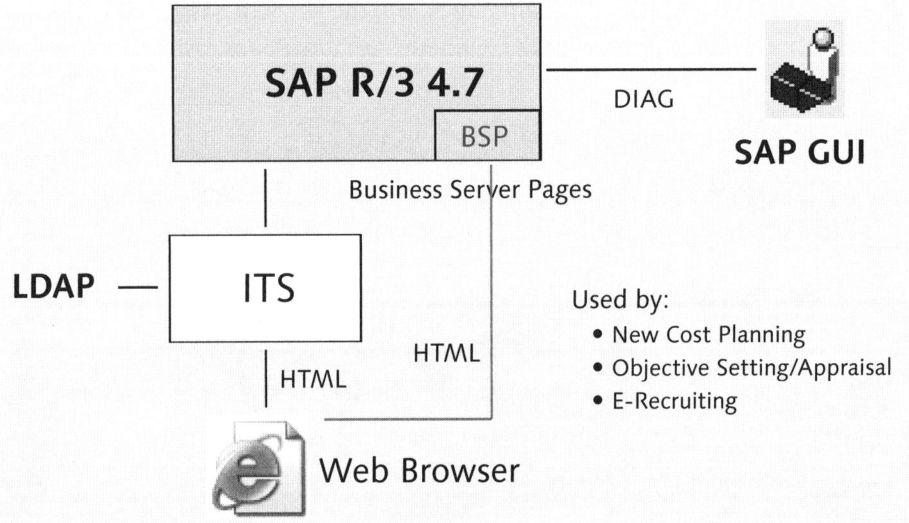

Figure 2.9 Web Architecture for R/3 Enterprise (4.7)

With Release ERP 5.0, ITS was integrated with SAP ERP. However, the internal ITS no longer supports all functions of the external ITS. For example, the internal ITS can't execute Internet services that are based on Flow Logic (nor is the LDAP interface supported any longer). Up to and including ERP 5.0 you can use an external ITS in addition to the internal ITS, which is no longer possible as of ERP 6.0. This means that you can't use Flow Logic applications as of ERP 6.0 any longer. However, they can be transferred to BSPs with relatively little effort.

With ERP 5.0, Web Dynpro for Java was delivered as another Web interface technology. The entire ESS in the SAP standard was re-programmed based on Web Dynpro for Java, whereas the old standard applications based on ITS were still available as alternatives. This means that the ESS scenarios are now presented as you are accustomed to with the Internet (see Figure 2.11). However, this result requires a totally new and more complex architecture (see Figure 2.10).

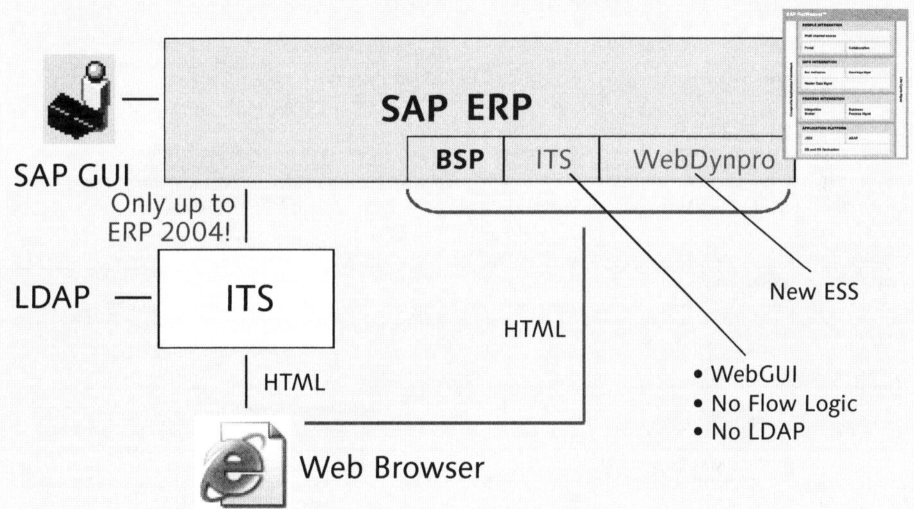

Figure 2.10 Web Architecture in SAP ERP

The interface of the new ESS is based on Web Dynpro for Java, that is, you require a Java stack (a second server). However, this is only the interface. The entire business logic is implemented in the SAP ERP HCM backend that is still based on an ABAP stack.

For the menu (Session Management) and SSO you require the SAP NetWeaver Portal that is based on the Java stack as well. Basically, you can adjust the portal settings in such a way that you are only provided with the menu for ESS. So this would be the new edition of the old ITS-based ESS (see Figures 2.11 and 2.12). For this minimum design, the term *portal* would be too common and ESS portal or employee portal would be better here.

However, SAP NetWeaver Portal provides a wide range of functions which allow it to live up to requirements expected of a portal. Take a look at the SAP Developer Network to get an idea of the efficiency (see *sdn.sap.com*).

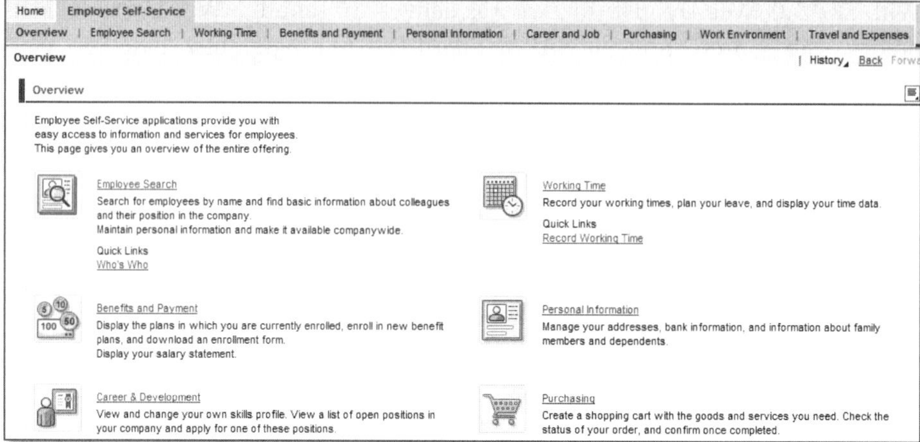

Figure 2.11 ESS Applications in the Portal

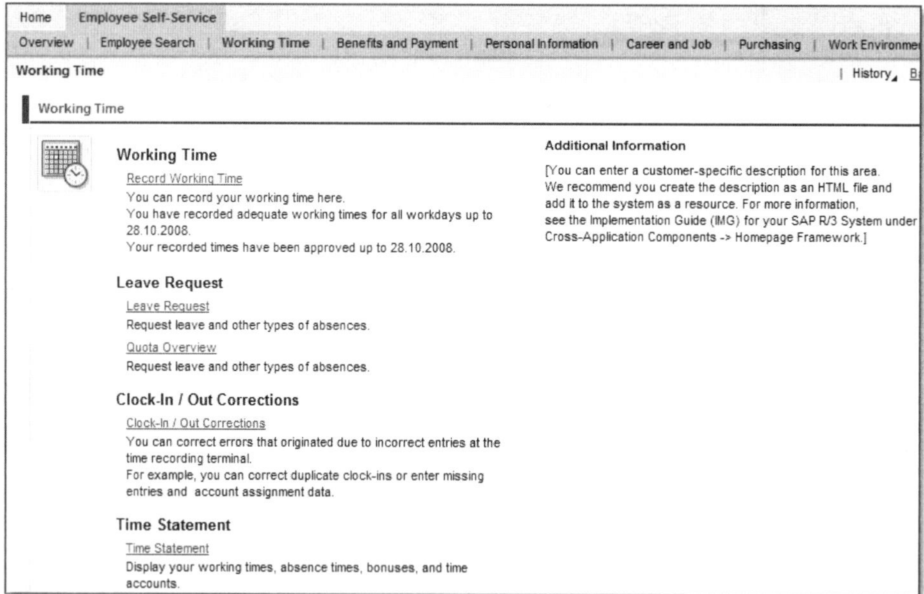

Figure 2.12 ESS Time Management in the Portal (Not All Scenarios Displayed Here Are SAP Standard)

2.4.3 SSO in the New ESS

Java stacks and ABAP stacks both use their own database and they cannot access the other's respective database. Consequently, the Java stack has its own user administration — the User Management Engine (UME). Because both SAP NetWeaver

Portal and Web Dynpro for Java are based on the Java stack and because these components provide the interface for the users, you must establish the user ID to be used for logging on.

Java stack's UME can handle different operating modes between which you can't switch as required. In one operating mode, for example, you can also use the user administration of the ABAP stack (see Figure 2.13). All user IDs that are created in the ABAP stack are then automatically available in the Java stack and consequently for logging on to SAP NetWeaver Portal. You can also set UME to use an LDAP interface analog to the external ITS. By doing so, all user IDs from an Active Directory (the network logon) would be available. And if a trust setting is created between the Java stack and the ABAP stack via a certificate, the password is no longer checked in the SAP ERP HCM backend.

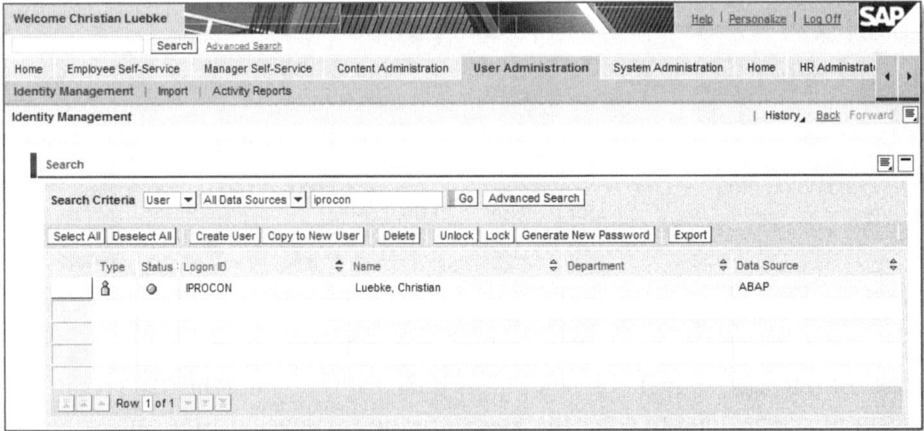

Figure 2.13 UME Uses the User Administration of the ABAP Stack

2.4.4 Authorizations in the Portal

Authorizations must always be checked in the backend system. In the portal, you are only provided with the menu entries. The respective backend system (in the case of ESS usually SAP ERP HCM) decides whether they may be executed. If an employee is provided with the menu entry for ESS in the portal, although the respective user ID does not exist in the SAP HCM backend system, the SAP HCM backend system displays an error message when calling the entry.

To ensure that you don't have to assign a menu to each user ID in SAP NetWeaver Portal, you can use groups. Depending on the UME settings, the groups are either transferred from the Active Directory (see Figure 2.14) or from the user administration in the ABAP stack. These groups are then assigned to corresponding menus.

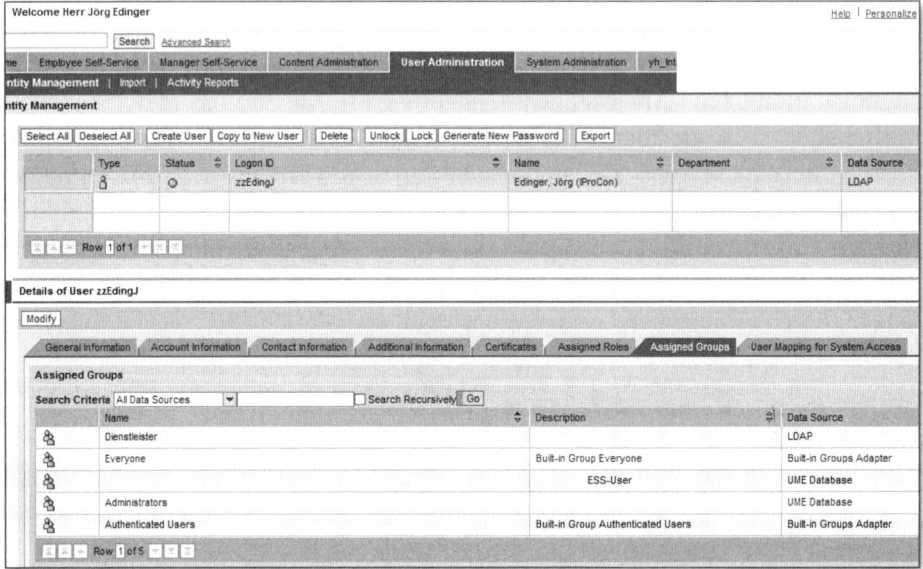

Figure 2.14 Group Information about the User from the LDAP

2.4.5 ESS

An employee can only access ESS in the SAP ERP HCM backend, if his user ID is connected to a personnel number. This is done by using Infotype 0105 (Communication), where you can enter the user ID in the employee master data.

The web browser communicates with two systems in terms of ESS. Here, the menu is provided by SAP NetWeaver Portal (Java stack). However, the lower part (see Figure 2.15) is provided by the HCM backend. The advantage of this is that you can adapt this area dynamically at runtime depending on the logged-on employees. For example, employees in different countries can be provided with different ESS services without having to assign a different role. Only the HCM backend can fulfill this task because the employee master data is available only here.

The Homepage Framework defines the design of the HCM backend in the ESS area of SAP NetWeaver Portal. Here you must make adaptations to add additional ESS services or to remove those not required. Moreover, you must make service-specific settings for the individual ESS services (IMG path Personnel Management • Employee Self-Service • Service-specific Settings).

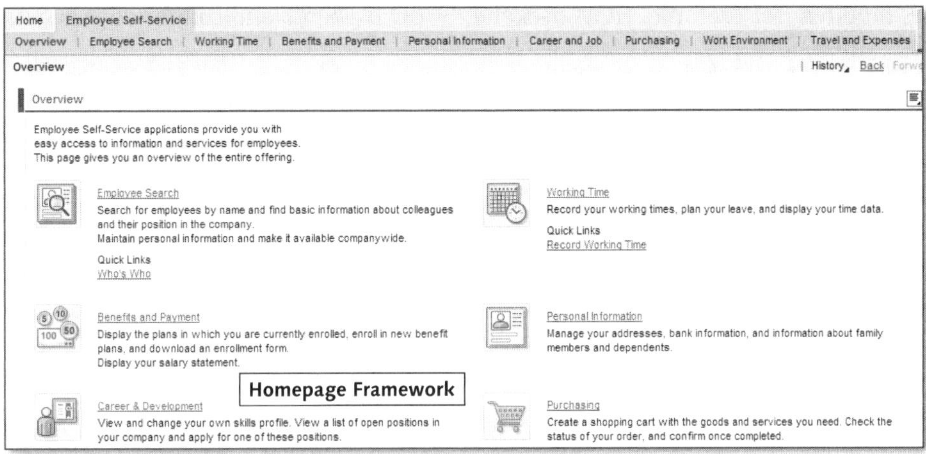

Figure 2.15 Homepage Framework

The Homepage Framework is not used exclusively for ESS. It rather accesses E-Recruiting, for example (see Chapter 6, "E-Recruiting"). You can find a detailed documentation on this topic in IMG under Personnel Management • Employee Self-Service • General Settings • Homepage for Self-Services. At this point, we would like to add that the Homepage Framework supports a wide range of service types and can therefore be used universally. In addition to Web Dynpro for Java or for ABAP applications, you can also call BSPs, ITS services, portal pages, and URLs. Moreover, the Homepage Framework is release dependent with regard to ESS. All default SAP entries for SAP ERP 6.0 are assigned the ending _2005. In future versions, the ESS homepage framework is supposed to be replaced by a menu purely based on the portal role, similar to MSS today.

Refer to the corresponding chapters of this book to find application examples for ESS in the various processes.

2.4.6 MSS

For managers, it becomes increasingly important that their work processes are not slowed down and that they can obtain information beyond the usual business hours without requiring complex processes (the right piece of information at the right time). This can only be ensured if the managers can directly access the relevant information via a system.

MSS focuses on the two main work areas, employee management and budget management (see Figure 2.16). Here, information is collected from various systems as required (for example, HCM backend, FI/CO backend, and connected Business Warehouse (BW) systems).

A prerequisite for the use of MSS in the system is that the employee is a manager, that is, he must be assigned to a chief position in the Organizational Management component of SAP HCM.

In contrast to ESS, the Homepage Framework is not used here. The worksets (menu) are defined via the portal roles. You can make service-specific settings in the IMG under INTEGRATION WITH OTHER SAP COMPONENTS • BUSINESS PACKAGES/ FUNCTIONAL PACKAGES • MANAGER SELF-SERVICE.

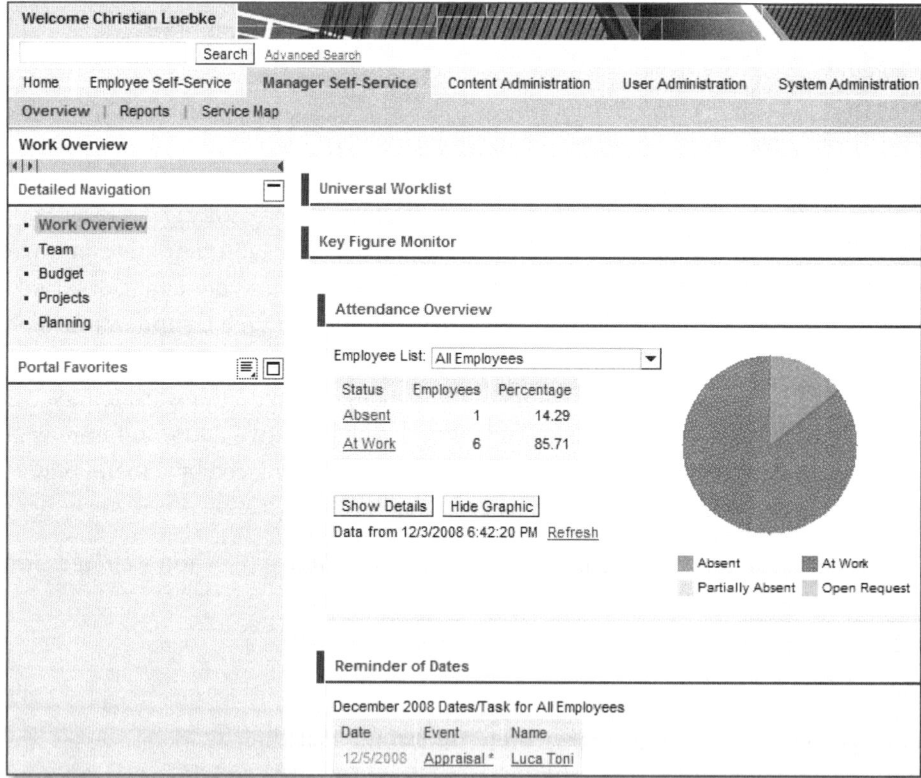

Figure 2.16 MSS Initial Screen

Refer to the corresponding chapters of this book to find application examples for MSS in the various processes.

2.4.7 Critical Success Factors for the Use of Portal Applications

- The infrastructure has become very complex due to high flexibility. Without detailed knowledge of the architecture it is difficult to detect errors. Only in rare cases do the installations work immediately. This is usually due to the fact that some parts of the infrastructure already exist and that the additionally required components must be added. A completely new installation, however, hardly causes any problems.
- There is no clear distinction between basis and application anymore and the boundaries have become blurred. To implement a functioning ESS, the teams of basis and application must work together closely.
- The patch statuses of the systems concerned are extremely important. Only certain patch constellations ensure a functioning system. This is due to the fact that the actual application is distributed to multiple systems.
- The topic of SSO is often underestimated. Here, you must make fundamental decisions for the entire enterprise. It is not an isolated topic.
- Due to the fact that it is no longer a system, but rather a composite, it is essential that a load test is implemented for the entire system to recognize bottlenecks in due time.
- Managers and employees may not always be enthusiastic about changes that are connected with the support of HR processes through Self-Services just because there are new technical options that are integrated in nice-looking Internet interfaces. The technical challenges may appear complex—but the necessary change management may constitute an even bigger problem and should not be ignored. Above all, it is important that all parties involved recognize the benefits and do not consider the changeover as a saving measure of the HR department at the expense of all other employees.

2.5 Manager's Desktop

The MDT does not have a Web-based interface and is therefore less user-friendly than MSS. Nevertheless, it is suitable for enterprises, which don't use portals (yet), to provide their managers with a simplified and easy-to-manage access to the data of their employees. MDT is completely integrated with the SAP ERP HCM system and can therefore be implemented independently without having to consider the effects on enterprise-wide systems and processes. This fact and the relatively low implementation effort ensure that it is often used as an interim solution until the enterprise's portal becomes available. Because MDT is a pure HCM component, we want to describe it in more detail here.

The tasks assumed by managers can be divided into the following areas:

- **Own employees**
  Evaluations, approvals, employee appraisals, employee development
- **Organization**
  Report, organizational changes, and related items
- **Costs and budget**
  Cost center information, headcount planning, budget management
- **Recruitment**
  Evaluations, decisions, and related actions
- **Customer-specific functions**
  Incorporating additional information and services

2.5.1 The User Interface

The MDT is divided into two main areas (see Figure 2.17). The left-hand side contains the functions or theme categories that the manager can execute. The right-hand side contains the objects used to execute functions. For example, the HR administration area on the left contains the function for calling a list of all employees with anniversaries of years of service. An object is selected to perform the call; for example, an organizational unit or a person is selected on the right-hand side, and then assigned to the required function by Drag & Drop.

The main points in the initial screen and in the MDT—such as employee, organization, costs, and budget—are called theme categories. These categories are themselves divided into individual subcategories, such as reports, education and training, employee appraisals, and personnel development (see Figure 2.17).

Figure 2.18 shows an example of very comprehensive functionalities for each of a manager's employees. The names of the employees are displayed on the right-hand side of the screen in accordance with the organizational structure. The left-hand side of the screen contains an Explorer bar with the functions that can be executed for each employee.

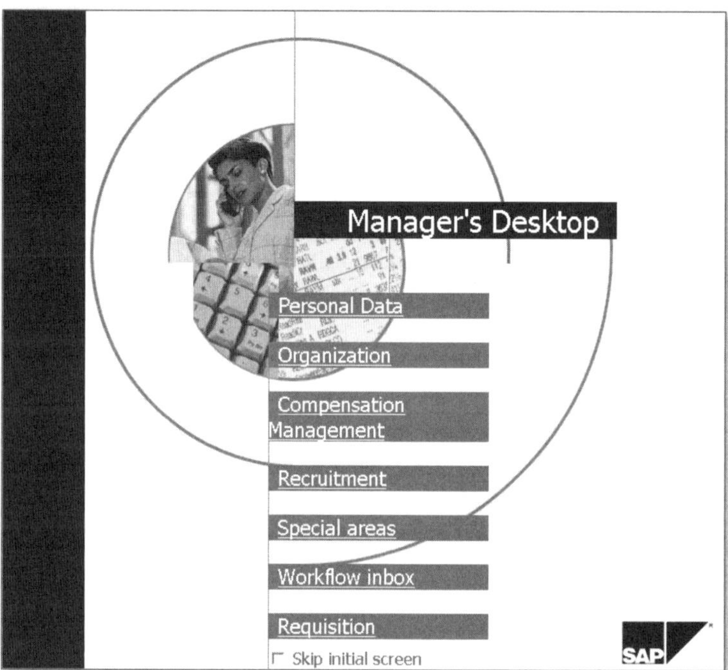

Figure 2.17 MDT Initial Screen

2.5.2 Adjustment Options

By selecting your own background image for the MDT initial screen you can change its design. You can also make other adjustments in the Customizing settings by selecting the IMG path PERSONNEL MANAGEMENT • MANAGER'S DESKTOP • CUSTOMER ADJUSTMENT • DEFINE SCENARIO-SPECIFIC SETTINGS.

Scenarios

Scenario is the term used to refer to all of the applications that are available to the user within the MDT. If you want to make modifications to standard scenarios, you should do so using the action DEFINE STANDARD SCENARIO, as modifications made in any other way may be deleted when the system is updated (support package imports). However, we recommend that you copy a standard scenario rather than modify it as this allows you to define all settings specifically for the scenario in question.

Besides naming your scenario, one of the first things you have to do is define its evaluation path. In the evaluation path, you specify how the system will identify the employees that are subordinate to a particular manager. By default, these are all of the employees who belong either directly or indirectly to the organizational unit that the manager is in charge of (chief position).

The initial screen of the MDT provides an overview of all of the available categories. If you check the Skip initial screen box, the initial screen is no longer displayed when you call up the MDT and you go straight to the theme category and tab that first appears in Customizing (see Figure 2.18).

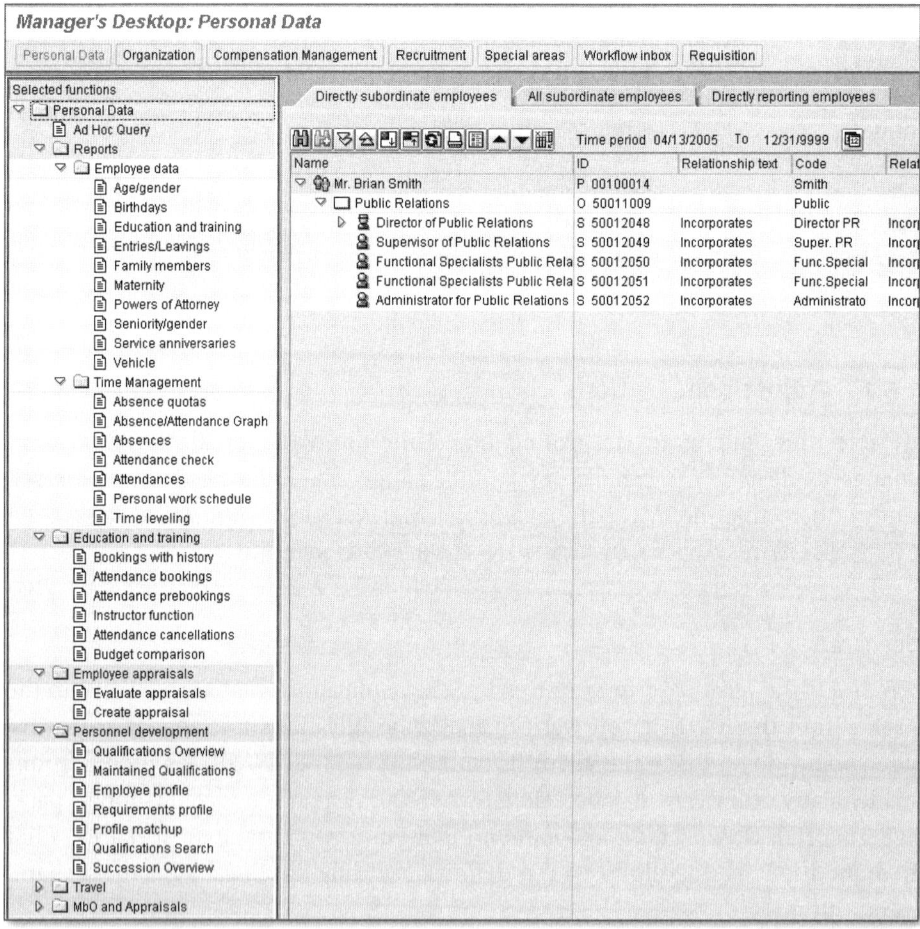

Figure 2.18 The MDT Interface

The Hide virtual root option prevents the manager, as the root of the organizational structure, from being displayed. This option is not activated in Figure 2.19, which is why the manager Brian Smith is shown as the root of the Personal Data organizational units.

The Reorganization not permitted option (see Figure 2.19) enables the user to specify that the manager who uses the MDT may not execute any organizational changes by means of Drag & Drop inside his area of responsibility. This also means that the Reorganization subcategory in the function tree of the Organization topic category is no longer displayed. Finally, the Referenced scenario field allows you to document which scenario was used as a template for the newly created scenario.

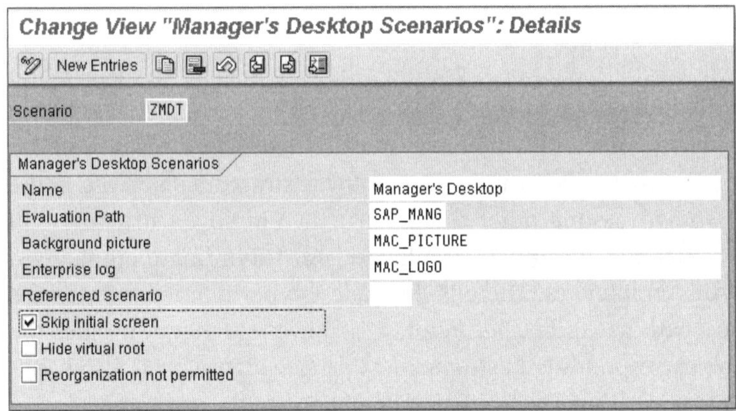

Figure 2.19 Define MDT Scenario

This also means that the new scenario automatically inherits all of the entries of the referenced scenario from tables T77MWBFCH (scenario-specific settings), T77MWBD (views of organizational structure), and T77MWBK (views per category).

The scenario is now completely defined. The name of the scenario (ZMDT in the example) has to be entered in the user's user parameters (SAP menu SYSTEM • USER PROFILE • OWN DATA). The user parameter is MWB_SCEN. Make absolutely sure that the scenario is entered in uppercase letters (see Figure 2.20).

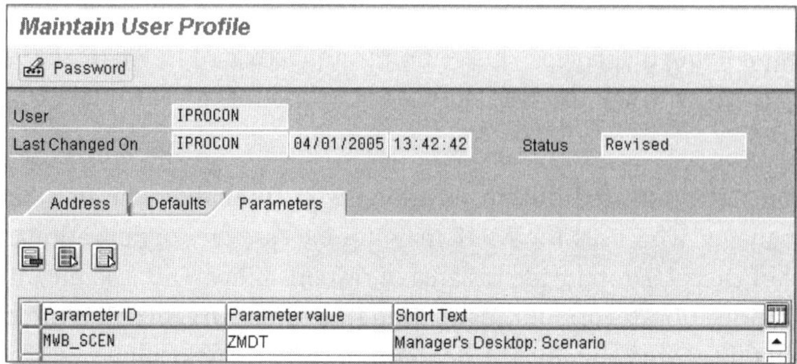

Figure 2.20 User Parameter MWB_SCEN

Views

Once you have defined the scenario(s), you then have to specify the *Views*. You use an evaluation path (IMG PERSONNEL MANAGEMENT • MANAGER'S DESKTOP • CUSTOMER ADJUSTMENTS • DETERMINE VIEWS OF ORGANIZATIONAL STRUCTURE) to define which views are used to determine the employee structure displayed in the MDT. Figure 2.21 shows, among other things, that the employee structure will contain the views Directly subordinate employees, All subordinate employees, and Directly reporting employees. There is thus one tab per defined view in the MDT. An evaluation path has to be specified for each of these views. Besides the evaluation path, the corresponding Customizing table (see Figure 2.21) also specifies the order of the tabs. Alternatively, instead of specifying the start object in the evaluation path, you can specify a function module for identifying the start object in the Start object function field.

Scenario	Eval.path	Nu...	Evaluation path text	Seq...	Icon name	Column g...	Start object functi...	Start object
ZMDT	MDTDIREC	0	Directly reporting employees	3	ICON_EMPLOYEE	MDT_ORGS		
ZMDT	MDTSBES	0	Directly subordinate employees	1	ICON_EMPLOYEE	MDT_ORGS		
ZMDT	MDTSBESX	0	All subordinate employees	2	ICON_EMPLOYEE	MDT_ORGS		

Figure 2.21 Defining the Views of the Organizational Structure

You can use the IMG path PERSONNEL MANAGEMENT • MANAGER'S DESKTOP • CUSTOMER ADJUSTMENTS • DETERMINE VIEWS PER CATEGORY to make the views defined in the previous step available for each category (such as employee, organization, costs and budgets, and so on) in the organizational structure. You do this using the action Composite Definition of views (evaluation paths) (see Figure 2.22) and not the action Determine views (evaluation paths) per category, as the latter entry is SAP specific it will be overwritten when the next patch is imported.

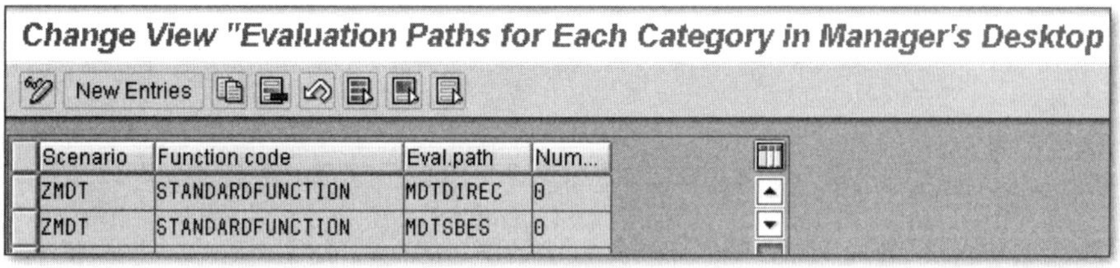

Change View "Evaluation Paths for Each Category in Manager's Desktop

Scenario	Function code	Eval.path	Num...
ZMDT	STANDARDFUNCTION	MDTDIREC	0
ZMDT	STANDARDFUNCTION	MDTSBES	0

Figure 2.22 Defining Views per Category

Note that only entries of categories in the Function code field with the function code type HOME have an effect in this table. Before you make any entries, use table T77MWBFCD (see Figure 2.23) to find out which function code has the type HOME. In our example, the function code STANDARDFUNCTION is used for employees. The definition of this function code specifies that only the views MDTDIREC (directly reporting employees) and MDTSBES (directly subordinate employees) are to be made available. Now that we have made these Customizing changes, if someone selects the theme category Employees in the MDT, he will see only two tabs for the view of the organizational structure.

Display View "Function Codes for Manager's Desktop": Overview

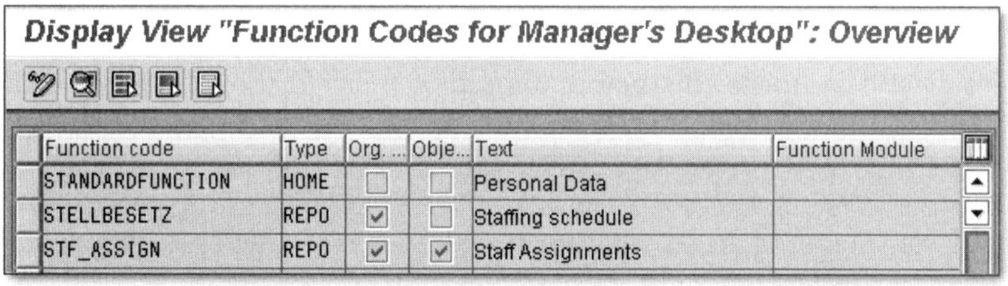

Function code	Type	Org. ...	Obje...	Text	Function Module
STANDARDFUNCTION	HOME	☐	☐	Personal Data	
STELLBESETZ	REPO	☑	☐	Staffing schedule	
STF_ASSIGN	REPO	☑	☑	Staff Assignments	

Figure 2.23 View of Table T77MWBFCD

Figure 2.24 summarizes the connection between the views of the organizational structure and the allocation of these views to theme categories.

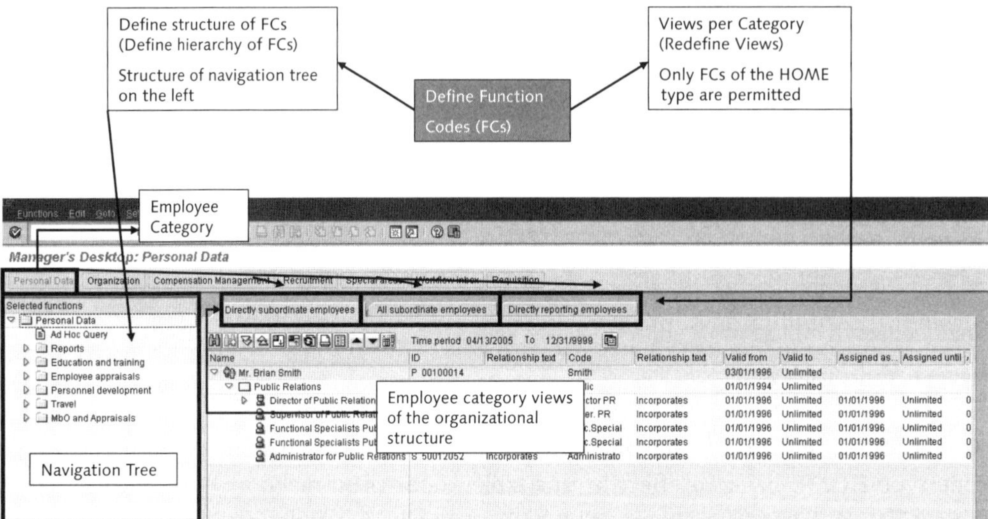

Figure 2.24 Connection Between Function Codes, Views, and Navigation Tree

Function Codes

Function codes are objects that represent different types of data.. Some examples of function codes are of the type HOME, representing root nodes, or categories and function codes of the type REPO, representing reports. Let us concentrate initially on function codes of the type HOME, to which we have already assigned various views. If you want to define new function codes of this type, to use them as categories, you have to do this before allocating them to the views. To open the Customizing for function codes (see Figure 2.25) use the IMG path PERSONNEL MANAGEMENT • MANAGER'S DESKTOP • ENHANCEMENT OF FUNCTION CODES.

An important consideration in creating function codes is the type, as this determines whether you are dealing with a node, a subnode, report, or another executable object. The types HOME and NODE indicate nodes that are used to create the hierarchy. HOME is superordinate to the type NODE. Besides specifying the type of a function code, you can also specify whether the function is based on the organizational structure (as is usually the case) or whether it is executed in an object-specific manner, or both.

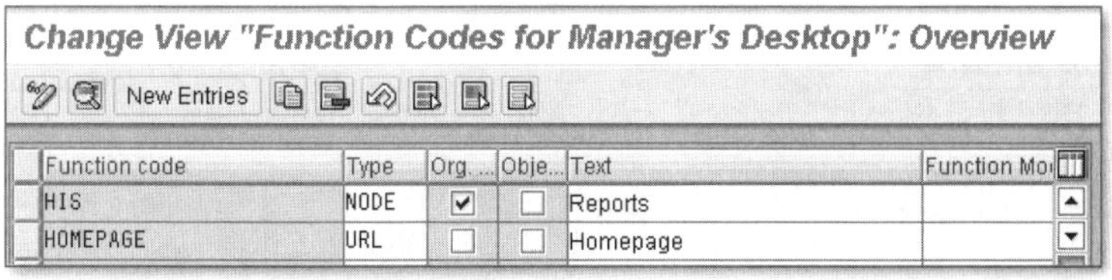

Change View "Function Codes for Manager's Desktop": Overview

New Entries

Function code	Type	Org. ...	Obje...	Text	Function Mo
HIS	NODE	☑	☐	Reports	
HOMEPAGE	URL	☐	☐	Homepage	

Figure 2.25 Table for Defining Function Codes

Set the Organizational structure-based flag for all function codes that are used with organization objects (including persons). If this flag is set for at least one executable node in a category, selecting the relevant button causes parts of the organizational structure to be displayed directly in the right-hand area of the screen. If, on the other hand, this flag is not set for any executable node, selecting the relevant theme category causes the first function to be started immediately. For example, this flag is set for the function code HIS, because the reports under this node are used for employee data and thus for organizational objects. If a theme category contains only URLs (that is, links to Internet or intranet sites); for example, calling this category causes the HTML page that is connected to the first URL to be displayed directly.

If, on the other hand, a function code is set object type specific—something that is possible only for reports and function modules—then this report can be executed only on one level, for example, the organizational unit level. If a function code is object specific, you have to specify the object type for which the function can be executed. The path you use to do this is Personnel Management • Manager's Desktop • Extend Function Codes • Define Object Type-Specific Function Codes.

One more customizing option that we would like to show you at this point is the enhancement of the function code structure. This option allows you, among other things, to integrate your own reports into the MDT. You can extend the hierarchy of the theme categories using the Customizing path Personnel Management • Manager's Desktop • Extend Function Codes • Define Structure of Function Codes. The Customizing settings shown in Figure 2.25 assign their own hierarchy of function codes in the user's own MDT scenario to the structure of the Employee category. Figure 2.26 juxtaposes the settings with their associated functions, to further clarify how the hierarchy of function codes works.

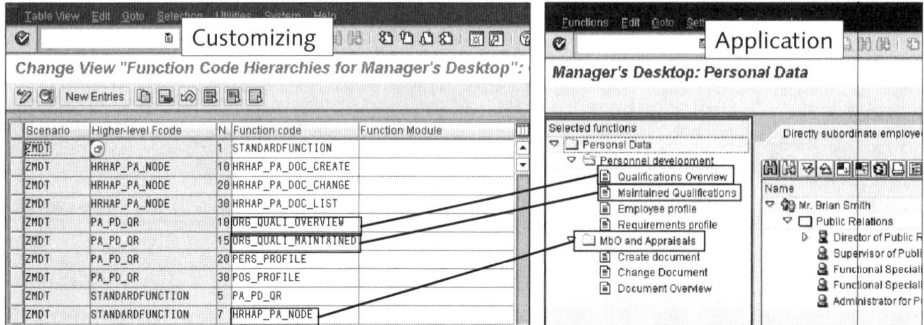

Figure 2.26 Connections Between Customizing Settings and Their Associated Functions in the MDT Interface

The function code structure is thus the last step in defining the navigation tree in the left-hand part of the MDT screen. Both the scope and the sequence of the function codes are specified in this step. If you leave the Higher-level Fcode field empty, specify the sequence number in the Sequence field, and enter a function code of the type HOME, a new node representing a category is created in the navigation tree. The relevant entry is then made in the Higher-level Fcode for any subnodes of this node.

Reports that are called inside the MDT never start with a selection screen. Instead, a variant of a report is always called. The variant name is stored in the function code table. If you do still want to display selection screens for certain reports, you have to modify the system accordingly. One option is to create a customer-specific Customizing table for the function codes that are called by means of a selection screen, to define the number of reports that will be called by this method. A prerequisite for this is that the function module RH_MWB_FCODE_EXECUTE has been adjusted accordingly.

Any other settings that need to be made via the MDT Customizing should be listed as follows, for the sake of completeness:

- Special settings for headcount planning (quota planning)
- Definitions of special workflows for using the SAP Business Workflow

The MDT also enables you to call reports from other systems. For example, managers are very likely to want to start HR reports, FI and CO reports, and to do so from one central point (that is, from the MDT), even though HR and FI/CO systems are often separate systems. We shall now briefly describe how to incorporate reports from distributed systems into the MDT.

When calling Accounting reports, you do so using function codes of the type RWRP from a view that also displays the cost centers of the structure (see Figure 2.27). However, when customizing the function codes (see Figure 2.28), you enter the abbreviation of the report group name from table T803VP, and not the ABAP name, in the program name field. This ensures that the correct report is selected, given that the ABAP name that is used in Report Writer reports in the development system is not the same as the name in the production system. The system standard contains a Remote Function Call (RFC) scenario for calling programs in other systems. The Application Linking and Enabling (ALE) Customizing is automatically checked in this scenario. If, for example, you have set up the cost centers that are assigned in HCM to be checked with those in the CO system, the system also calls up the reports via the RFC destination stored in the respective ALE scenario.

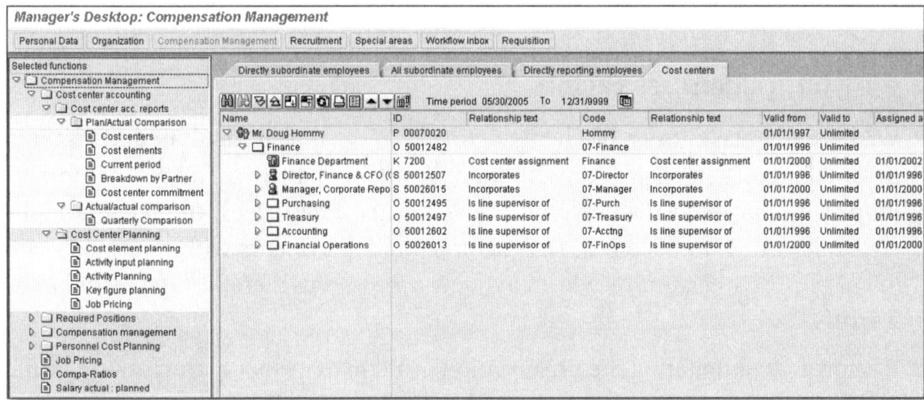

Figure 2.27 Cost-Center View of the Organizational Structure

Function code	Type	Org. ...	Obje...	Text	Function M...	Progra...	Transaction
RWPLANACT	NODE	☐	☐	Plan/Actual Comparison			
RWREP1AIP	RWRP	☑	☐	Cost elements		1AIP	
RWREP1OAB	RWRP	☑	☐	Cost center commitment		1OAB	
RWREP1SHK	RWRP	☑	☐	Breakdown by Partner		1SHK	
RWREP1SIP	RWRP	☑	☐	Cost centers		1SIP	
RWREP1SLK	RWRP	☑	☐	Current period		1SLK	
RWREP1SQU	RWRP	☑	☐	Quarterly Comparison		1SQU	

Figure 2.28 Defining Function Codes

Our experience shows that the existing standard functionality for calling reports in other systems is often too inflexible in practice, in terms of the following points:

- Insufficient time frame available for selection
- No way of setting restrictions by cost type (except in fixed variants)
- No way of calling all kinds of reports

However, these problems are not insurmountable; some extra development in the form of a customer-specific RFC can solve them. You can include the required code in a function module, which in turn can be specified in the definition of the function codes (see Figure 2.28).

In these scenarios, you need to pay particular attention to the issue of target system authorizations, especially because only static cost-center authorizations can be assigned, and thus a considerable number of roles may be the result. However, as before, additional customer-specific development may be the answer to this problem.

2.5.3 Critical Success Factors

- Management tasks must be clearly defined. This can be difficult in departments with temporary managers or with more than one manager. The more information that is made available about the associated employees, the more complicated the situation becomes. For example, in departments with more than one manager, the question of who may view whose remuneration details is problematic.
- The process of updating the organizational and management structures in terms of Organizational Management must be clearly defined and should ensure that the structures are always up-to-date. Otherwise, functions will not be available to the employees who need them or will be only partially available, and the system will quickly lose acceptance among the employees.
- It is particularly important to involve the workers' council, if appropriate for your country, in the implementation process. Such bodies often have objections, as they are wary of unrestricted reporting functions and their potential for uncontrolled use by management.
- Start off with a small range of functions that is restricted to pure reporting.

- Ensure that competent contact persons are available for technical and content-related questions in the rollout phase. A step-by-step rollout may be required.
- Ensure also that management supports the total replacement of paper-based procedures with reports in the MDT. You must avoid a situation where, at the request of some managers, paper-based procedures run in parallel to electronic procedures (except for a short transitory phase).
- Take into account the realities in each department. In some cases, some tasks may be delegated to assistants. In this case, special roles will have to be created that do not contain any critical data or functions.
- Authorizations for MDT users should be largely similar to those of an employee with access to Transaction PA30, to avoid potential errors in calling reports from the very beginning.

Project management certainly doesn't need to be redefined; however, an SAP ERP HCM implementation project contains very specific requirements, so we will discuss these specific project management issues in this chapter.

3 SAP ERP HCM Projects

This chapter outlines the specific characteristics of an SAP ERP HCM project and considers the structure of such a project, the available resources, and critical success factors.

3.1 Structure of an SAP ERP HCM Project

In the following sections, we particularly focus on the alternatives for the project scope and the typical project phases involved in an SAP ERP HCM project.

3.1.1 Project Scope

Depending on the given prerequisites, there are many useful possibilities to define the scope of an initial implementation. To this end, we assume that the goal is to implement the main processes described in this book:

- Personnel Administration
- Recruitment (if applicable, as E-Recruiting)
- Time management (depending on the industry and remuneration model, including incentive wages)
- Payroll
- Company pension plan (depending on the country and company-specific requirements)
- Personnel controlling (in so far as it is based on the processes listed here)
- Quality Assurance of the processes implemented

In addition, the following questions arise:

1. Must all of these processes be implemented on the same key date?
2. Are additional supplemental processes required?

The second question can clearly be answered "yes," based on the experience of many projects. As a rule of thumb, in a company with more than 1,000 employees, organizational management should be integrated from the beginning. Also, the latest SAP HCM development offerings are based on the foundation of the Organizational Management component. This makes it possible to map the actual organizational structure as a basis for reports on daily business, personnel controlling, and authorizations. Integrating organizational management later on tends to increase the costs significantly.

With the exception of recruitment, all of the previously mentioned processes are strongly dependent on each other. Therefore, if possible, they should also be implemented together. The alternative would be to build very complex temporary interfaces to legacy systems to bridge the times between the individual implementations. It is better to reserve this effort for the implementation itself. Consider also that if the process is mapped continuously for most users, no navigation between the different systems is necessary. An implementation at different dates should therefore only occur if the existing capacities do not permit any other solution or if it is a very comprehensive implementation (as a rule of thumb, with a project runtime of more than one year) — but you must still consider whether a rollout of individual subsidiaries would be the better solution to control a project.

Recruitment — ideally based on E-Recruiting for a new implementation, because the old recruitment solution of SAP is no longer being further developed — can be implemented in a second step (e.g., together with personnel development). However, it should be integrated in the design phase when establishing the company structure and the organizational structure. Although the recommended approaches described here provide a common best-practice approach to SAP HCM implementation, each company's unique requirements and business drivers will ultimately determine the components included in a total or phased implementation approach.

We will now also comment on the processes we haven't referred to yet:

For some project scopes, *Travel Management* could be implemented in the first step, especially if integration to SAP HCM Payroll is required.

If *Shift Planning* is required, you must check for every specific case whether this process is possible in legacy systems without any complex interface to Time Management in SAP ERP HCM.

Personnel Cost Planning and *Compensation Management* are dependent on Organizational Management and Personnel Administration, and to a lesser degree, Payroll. You must also check here how complex an interface is required from the SAP ERP HCM system to a legacy system. When starting the payroll on January 1 in a particular year, you should implement both of these components for the next subsequent planning round, i.e., usually in September or October.

Employee and *Manager Self-Services* (ESS and MSS) are applications that have a largely decentralized effect. To ensure the stability of the processes and to respond to requests from decentralized users in the personnel department, an implementation is recommended if the central processes are stable and if the users in the personnel department have constructed a secure system. Because self-services have become a matter of course, you usually cannot omit already-known services when you switch from an older release or a non-SAP system to SAP ERP HCM, and the portal applications must be integrated with the project scope right from the start. In this case, you must pay special attention to testing the self-services, particularly with regard to stability, performance, and user friendliness. If you plan a new implementation of self-services, the change process must be planned well for the employees and managers. For example, the first services should provide a clearly identifiable benefit for the users to avoid the impression that the project was exclusively about reducing work for the Human Resources (HR) department.

In general, for an SAP ERP HCM implementation the basic principle applies that the project risk is considerably reduced if the project is divided into clear phases that also have real deliverables and accountability. A planned project runtime of more than a year without a visible result is risky and often leads to delayed timelines and higher implementation costs.

In companies with group structures, the implementation in a pilot area with subsequent phased rollout is one approach to consider. In the SAP ERP HCM processes described here, this depends mostly on the situation and conditions of the company. If payroll itself must be implemented centrally for all areas, the phased rollout concept is difficult to implement. A phased rollout can work more easily with components such as ESS, Manager's Desktop (MDT), travel management, or recruitment.

3.1.2 Project Phases (ASAP)

The *Accelerated SAP (ASAP) concept* is used here to separate the project phases. ASAP is both a comprehensive tool to support an SAP implementation and it is a methodology. As a tool, ASAP has been successfully integrated with SAP Solution Manager. Solution Manager is a platform providing the tool, content, and gateway to create, operate, manage, and monitor your SAP solutions, from planning and implementation and beyond. The ASAP roadmap described here is still in use, however. While you can certainly check whether it makes sense to use the Solution Manager with regard to the specific requirements, the methodology in ASAP is generally accepted. There are, however, obvious differences in the names of the phases and their content at the details level. Figure 3.1 illustrates the *ASAP roadmap* that delineates the project phases of an SAP project.

In the following sections we describe the individual phases. Here we partly deviate from the detail statements of the ASAP concept, primarily because we cannot basically assume the use of ASAP tools.

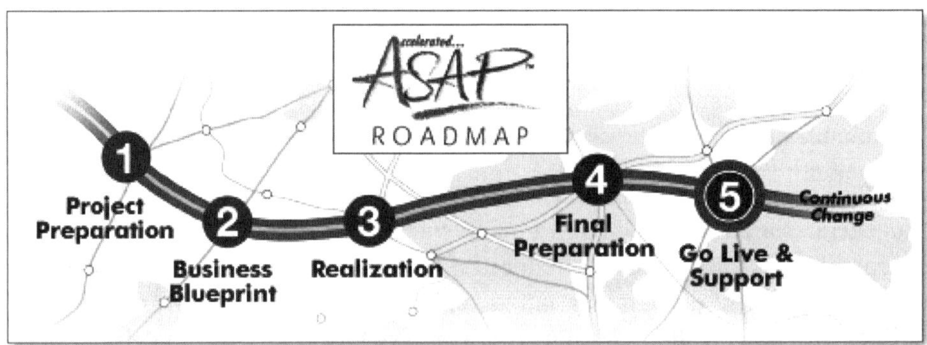

Figure 3.1 ASAP Roadmap

The Solution Manager provides sophisticated details about the ASAP roadmap so that it can be used as a tool deployed from project management down to the lowest level (see Figure 3.2).

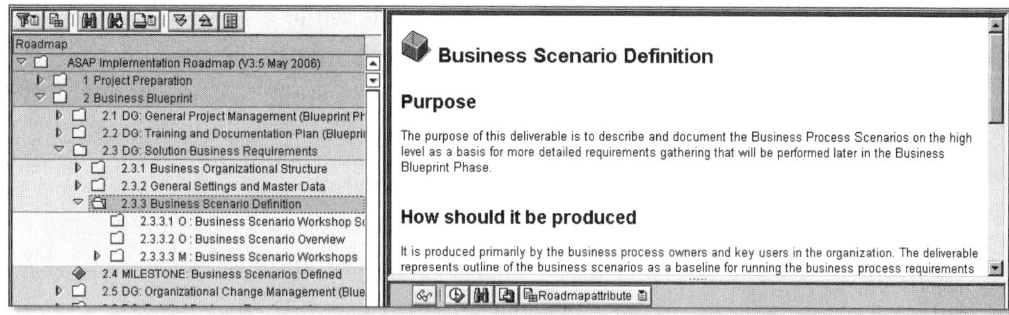

Figure 3.2 ASAP Roadmap in Solution Manager

Phase 1: Project Preparation

The project preparation phase is actually self-evident and quite simple in terms of content. However, failure occurs so frequently in practice that we think it will be important to describe it in some detail. Basically, the prerequisites for the actual project should be created in this phase. These include:

- Defining the project team
- Training the project team and decision makers
- Providing project rooms
- Providing the technical infrastructure
- Defining project standards (forms, templates, document conventions, etc.)

This all may sound simple, but in fact a lot of time is lost in projects because these issues were not dealt with up front. These prerequisites should be clarified throughout the project, in particular for projects whose scope exceeds that of SAP ERP HCM.

Phase 2: Business Blueprint

Before you start the implementation, you should know exactly what is to be implemented. In addition, the project requirements must be defined, and the project scope must be documented in a form that is understandable to all those involved. Because changes during the course of the project aren't provided for by pure theory, but correspond more to actual practice, an essential factor is that the documentation on requirements is always kept up-to-date as a part of the change management.

It is no longer feasible to establish requirements without any system reference once you leave the general levels and go into further detail. Responding to extensive, detailed question lists, without knowing the background to the questions, causes those involved in the project to be wary and threatens acceptance of the implemented system. In addition, there are frequent misunderstandings at this level.

Therefore, when you establish the detailed requirements you should use two means of support:

- Create a prototype that will be used again in the next phase for implementation
- Visualize the processes using modeling tools

Both means provide the project participants with alternatives and their advantages and disadvantages. The detailed requirements can thus really be established by the entire team. Both the prototype and the process models are used for further training of the project team.

Note: Use of Prototypes

It is frequently supposed that the target processes can be defined as far as the details level without any concrete mapping of a prototype in the system "on paper" (or in some documentation tools). The hope is that afterward only the system tables must be set according to the documentation, and that an ideally configured system exists. In practice, a process definition is not possible at the detailed level without the ability to run the processes through ever more refined development systems (prototypes). This is to be supported by a rough process definition before the start of the system configuration and a continuous refinement during the project.

An alternative to the prototype can also be a "neutral" training system such as SAP's IDES system. In this case, however, an efficient, basic configuration must be carried out at the beginning of the implementation phase. No reusable project work can be carried out based on the IDES system. The IDES is preconfigured in such a way that it rules out later release changes.

Phase 3: Implementation

Based on the prototype, this phase of the implementation (also called Realization) incorporates the gradual refinement of the mapped processes in system configuration and programming. Here, in particular, intensive transfer of know-how from the consultants to the internal team members takes place. In general, this transfer happens "on the job." Additional training can, however, be carried out for specific issues. This also depends on the size of the project team.

You should not lose sight of the results processed in phase 2. Deviations should be agreed upon with those affected and with those responsible, and the documentation must be adapted.

Phase 4: Final Preparation

In this phase, the immediate preparations for taking the system live are carried out on the basis of the almost entirely configured system. Changes to the system configuration in this phase must be coordinated and approved even on the details level because they can affect such tasks as the integration of legacy data or end-user training.

Essential elements of this phase are:

- Integration tests and final tuning
- Interface tests
- Role-specific end-user training
- Going live check

Phase 5: Go-live and Support

The final data transfer and launch of the productive operation with the new system take place here.

A hotline must now be available for the end users. The project team gets support from the consultants' side. Especially with technical problems such as poor system performance, SAP can provide the relevant services.

A lot of time is frequently required to transfer legacy data. This is generally not the case for personnel master data, as its data structures are quite simple. Other data in SAP ERP HCM, such as organizational structures, are more complex and require a higher level of effort during the interface programming, but the transfer itself is generally less time-critical than it is, for instance, in logistics, due to the difference in the quantity of data. However, an early test with real data from the legacy system is important. Such a test not only enables you to make statements on the runtime but also on the quality of the legacy data. In SAP ERP HCM, very detailed plausibility checks are usually carried out with regard to the data entry. If this was not the case in the legacy system, the data transfer can require a large amount of subsequent work and can compromise the production start if this additional work hasn't been allowed for.

Continuous Change

In the phase of continuous change, the importance of phase 2 becomes obvious. In an implementation project carried out in a short time frame with an unchanged team, you may be able to manage with less documentation. However, if changes are necessary after a long period of time, new components are introduced, or an upgrade is implemented, documenting the processes and system settings based on these processes is extremely helpful. Here you must ensure that the continuous change also applies to the documentation!

3.1.3 General Project Management

In a project with a primarily technically orientation and a technically oriented standard procedure as described earlier, the principles of holistic project and change management are frequently forgotten. Because these include some of the most important reasons for the failure of many projects, it is advisable to not implement project management on a mere technical basis and to not use one single tool only.

3.2 Tools

There are many different project management tools, all of which cannot be listed within the scope of this book. The following section provides some examples that are particularly suited in the context of an SAP ERP HCM project.

3.2.1 SAP Solution Manager

A large number of project management tools are available these days. The Solution Manager, in replacing the former ASAP method, provides an extensive collection of tools specifically for SAP projects.[1] The Solution Manager can be used for

---

1 You can find detailed information on ASAP on the Internet at *http://service.sap.com/asap* (registration required).

project management, but also for managing system landscapes and for supporting maintenance work. We only discuss the project management aspect here.

Solution Manager is divided into an area for the system operation and one for project support. The latter basically contains the following components:

- Project management helps (roadmaps), also for special project types, such as rollout projects
- Accelerators: checklists, instructions, or templates for certain subjects; links in the SAP Service Marketplace
- Predefined scenarios (structured up to the process step level); in the HCM system, however, there was almost no content available at the time of printing.
- Integration in the implementation guide (IMG) of several systems
- Definition of the system landscape
- Automatic customizing distribution
- Test organization
- Internal message management with the option to forward messages to SAP AG

To what extent the Solution Manager can be specifically used in a concrete SAP ERP HCM project depends, among other things, on the following factors:

- Quality and scope of the predefined HCM scenarios available at the project start
- Scope of the project (additional processes in addition to HCM, the number of systems involved, the number of project team members)
- Integration in the documentation and project management tools existing in the company
- Level of experience of the project participants; in particular, use is recommended for teams with little HCM and project experience.

In most cases it is useful to use some of the existing checklists and forms. The same applies to the basic philosophy expressed by the roadmap, which can be used in most cases. To what extent a complete use of the Solution Manager is useful must be considered in each individual case.

For rollout projects, there is special functionality available to define templates. In such projects the use of the Solution Manager is definitely worthwhile.

3.2.2 Process Modeling

It has been generally accepted that the processes to be mapped must be clearly defined prior to the system's implementation. Frequently, it is assumed that this is no problem at all because these processes are generally known. In real life, however, this assumption is wrong and the graphic modeling of processes is usually the best method to agree on and define the processes. Both suitable tools and reference models can make modeling more efficient.

Tools

A broad range of tools is available to model and optimize business processes. For the processes described in this book, the *ARIS Design Platform* from IDS Scheer AG was used (although the normal modeling conventions were not adhered to for reasons of space). The ARIS product family is specifically suited for use in the SAP ERP HCM environment, because coupling with SAP ERP and Solution Manager in general and the HCM system in particular is possible.

A few other products also fulfill these criteria. The following factors are particularly relevant for selection:

- Usability
- Price (huge differences!)
- Reusability of the models (e.g., for International Standards Organization (ISO) certification)
- Web-enabledness of the models
- The option of distributed modeling
- Database-based tool versus graphic tool
- Coupling with SAP ERP
- Integration with SAP Solution Manager
- Coupling with SAP HCM, in particular, with the organizational management
- Variety of model types offered
- Market share
- Interfaces

Whatever product you decide on, the process-oriented documentation is particularly useful in larger projects. Rollout projects rarely function without visualized and fine-tuned business processes. However, it is rarely of any use to describe extensive internal processing of the system (e.g., net payroll) in a process model. The interaction between the users and the system is much more important. In other words, which data is entered and which data is output by the system.

Reference Models

In addition to the models provided in the SAP Solution Manager, other reference models can also act as suggestions or templates, and tools for the project work. For example, SAP provides Solution Maps (see Figure 3.3), Solution Composer, and Business Case Builder.

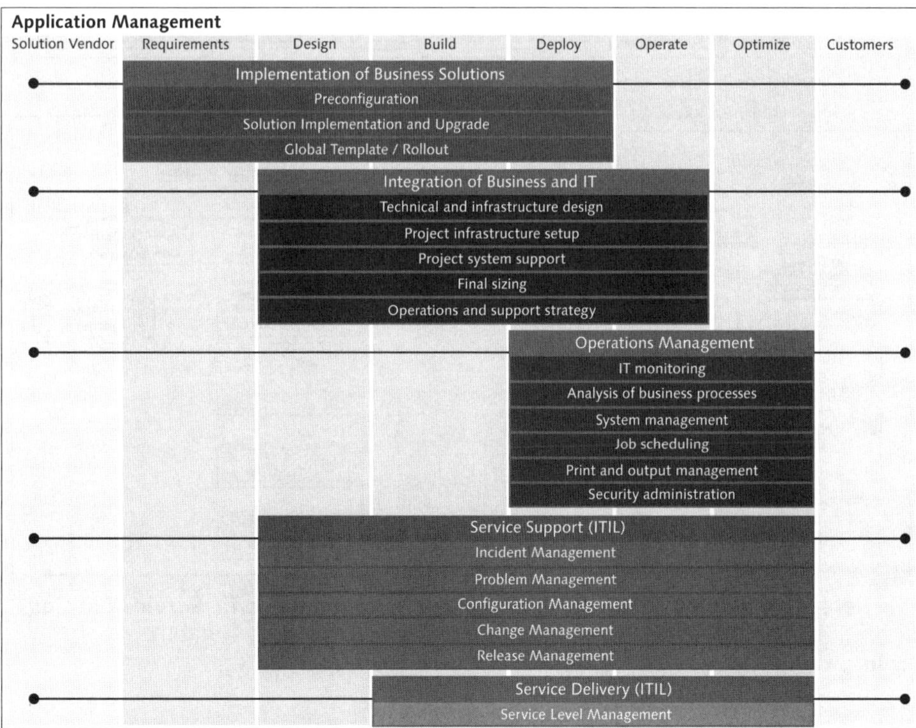

Figure 3.3 Section of the SAP Solution Map for an IT-Support Organization

For the implementation, optimization, or outsourcing of HCM processes, for instance, we like to use a standardized HCM services catalog. Such a catalog does not yet contain any detailed description of process flows, but rather a structured display of the services in personnel management (in general these are between 100 and 1,000 services).

This means it can be easily adapted to the specific conditions of a company and can then be used to define the project scope in a structured procedure (see Figure 3.4).

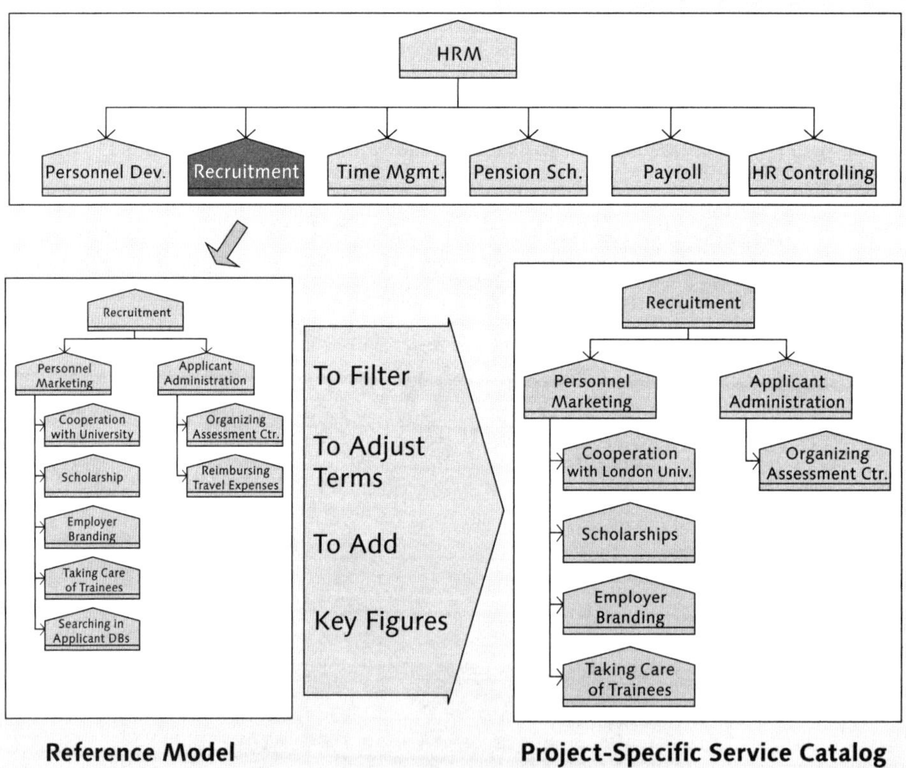

Figure 3.4 HR Services: From the Reference Model to the Project Focus

3.2.3 Implementation Guide (IMG)

You can find a brief description of the IMG in Appendix A, "Cross-Process Customizing Tools." In addition to the structured access to customizing activities, it offers functionalities for project management such as status management, degree of completion, scheduling and resource assignment, and the option to place the documentation in a useful manner.

In many cases the functions are used in a limited manner during and after implementation, although managing the guide is very easy to handle. In addition, it is also integrated in ASAP. Overall, it is a recommended tool.

3.3 Critical Success Factors

- Timely definition and training of the project team
- Comprising the project team of IT and personnel management experts
- Awareness of the high complexity of customizing, in particular in Payroll and Time Management modules
- Providing sufficient know-how for the technologies required for the project (e.g., ABAP, Portal, Workflow, Business Server Pages (BSP), Web Dynpro); here you can often reduce complexity and the risk by restricting the number of technologies used and using existing know-how (e.g., by restricting to Web Dynpro for ABAP and omitting Java.
- Ensuring a stable technical infrastructure, in particular for the development and customizing systems (data backups must be carried out way before the productive operation starts)
- Early integration of employee representatives
- Clarification of the structures in SAP ERP HCM and in particular clarification of the use of organizational management (thereby integrating the remaining processes, especially accounting)
- Timely checking of the data quality in the legacy system
- Establishment of an extensive test environment, especially for payroll and time evaluation
- Modeling of the business processes for decentralized use
- Experienced project management (HCM is one of the more complex solutions of SAP Business Suite)
- Creation and, in particular, maintenance of the documentation

In SAP, Personnel Administration forms the core of HR management. It is where HR master data and organizational structures are managed and made available via reports, and it forms the basis for all other areas. This chapter introduces the basic principles of personnel administration and the relevant infotypes.

4 Personnel Administration

This chapter mainly deals with the concept of the infotype, which is used in the SAP system to store master data. We will introduce the most important infotypes in personnel administration using a variety of examples. This chapter also establishes the basis for the other areas covered in the book.

4.1 Business Principles

In addition to legal principles and structuring of work processes in personnel administration, we will stress the principles of organizational theory. We will explore the significance of personnel administration as a basis for other processes of personnel management and principles of personnel reporting. We will also describe the importance of a personnel database integrated across the entire enterprise. The remaining topics in this chapter will cover approaches to decentralized personnel work.

4.1.1 Organizational Structures in the Personnel Area

Organizational theory differentiates between *organizational structure* and *process structure* (see Figure 4.1).

The SAP system uses both areas of organizational theory. To structure the personnel dataset, the organizational structure discussed here is the more relevant area. The process structure will always be part of the subject matter in each chapter because of the process-oriented nature of the book, and will not be considered part of the specific content here.

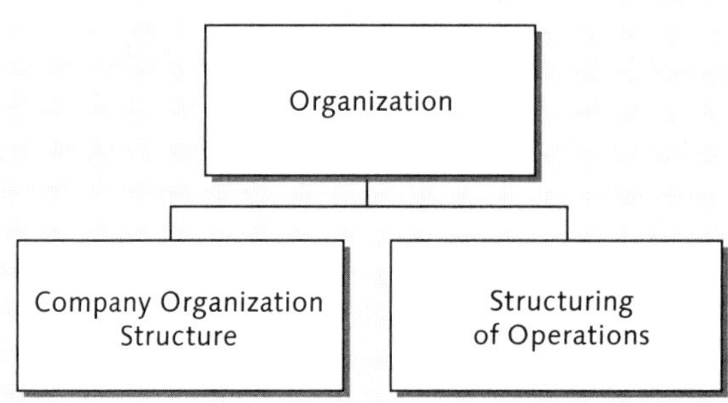

Figure 4.1 Organizational Concepts

Structuring the workforce can be considered from different perspectives. First, structuring is carried out according to the "normal" organizational structure, as described in the organizational chart of a company. This structure can be seen from different viewpoints (functional, product-oriented, market-oriented, etc.), and in the case of the matrix organization two or more of these views can be taken at the same time. There are other criteria that structure the workforce. For example, groups of employees are formed according to their group type (salaried workers, industrial workers, executives), their contract type (pay-scale, non-pay-scale), or employment level (part-time, full-time). Further structures are supplied by legal rules (pay-scale laws, insurance laws) and by the location of the employee, which more and more frequently cannot be determined from an organizational chart.

Also, a further structural attribute — the *project structure* — is increasingly gaining importance. In companies where work is frequently carried out on a project basis, membership in one or more project teams is often a more important criterion than the line of command or the location.

For personnel work carried out on a daily basis, the following decisions can be derived from the structures:

- Validity of business regulations (payroll, time management, travel costs reimbursement, etc.)
- Validity of regulations according to collective agreement
- Validity of legal regulations
- Responsibility of HR administrators
- Responsibility of authorities (e.g., tax office)

- Supervisors
- Treatment in legal statistics
- Treatment in statistics of the internal HR reporting
- Assigning personnel costs in the context of financial accounting (FI) and management accounting

This list, which is by no means complete, clearly shows the importance of the project step "clarifying the structures" regardless of the software selected. A yardstick for the quality of the structure is always the question: Can the administrator reach all decisions mentioned and assign the appropriate statistics based on the classification of an employee in the selected structure?

4.1.2 HR Master Data and Work Processes

The core of personnel administration is the personnel data itself. It provides the basis for reporting and the subsequent processes. To this end, completeness, quality, and timeliness are crucial.

Optimal definition of the processes for maintenance and quality assurance (QA) of the HR master data pays off in two ways:

- It provides an ideal information basis for the entire personnel work and therefore increases its efficiency and effectiveness. Lack of quality in this regard, however, accumulates negative impact as it moves down the process stream.
- Many maintenance processes run on a daily basis, so that optimal structuring provides continuous benefits.

Selecting Data

The decision as to which personnel data should be maintained is a fundamental one. The important consideration is that master data is not an end in and of itself. The selection of data should generally be determined by the following factors:

- Legal regulations (see Section 4.1.3)
- Requirements of evaluations and statistics (see Chapter 11, "HR Reporting")
- Requirements of downstream processes (see Sections 4.1.4 and 4.1.5)
- Requirements of the organization of the personnel administration itself (e.g., location of the file or responsible HR administrator)

An expansion of the database is always useless if the extra data can only be partly entered or is of a poor quality. Evaluations of the data then appear to be precise, but using the data often leads to incorrect conclusions. In this context, less is often more — only refer to data for which you can guarantee a sufficient quality.

When selecting data, however, you should not limit yourself to data controlled in the HR department. In most companies, great potential can be yielded from the step that leads from an HR *department* information system to an overall HR information system (see Section 4.1.5).

Maintenance Processes

The quality of the data is defined insofar as it can be interpreted in a standardized and correct manner. For everyone who must maintain specific data, a standardized process must be defined. If administrator A enters the business number in the field Phone number, but administrator B enters a private number, the data is practically worthless.

For reasons of timeliness, understanding the entire personnel management process is essential. An administrator in payroll will always ensure that the data he is responsible for is always up-to-date in time for the payroll run. He may be completely unaware that a colleague has just a week before carried out evaluations that form the basis for important decisions. These interdependencies must be realized and communicated.

Along with timeliness, they are the essential criteria for organizing data maintenance.

Organization and Work Distribution

Several helpful principles can be established for personnel administration:

- Data entry should take place as closely as possible to when and where the information is known
- Information output should meet information requirements as closely as possible
- Minimize the number of agents per process

- Minimize the number of information carriers per process (paper, email, phone, Information Technology (IT) system, etc.)
- Minimize the number of interruptions to a process

In the ideal situation, the employee enters all data by himself, the management and controllers evaluate all data themselves in the personnel system, and in the personnel department there is only one administrator for every employee for all areas.

The reality is often very different. The level of needed data protection and the qualifications for each role severely limit flexibility. The conflict between the required timeliness and availability of different data groups frequently blocks complete processing that is free from interruptions. However, the principles referred to should still be followed conscientiously. In cases where processing cannot be done by one person, teams can be formed.

The advantages of modern data-processing (DP) systems can only be fully exploited if decentralized concepts are used and a clearly defined work distribution is implemented in a seamless manner.

4.1.3 Legal Principles

Personnel administration is regulated through a variety of legal requirements, which differ from country to country and from state to state. The most important areas these regulations deal with are:

- **Data protection**
- **Employment law**
  (especially the equal-employment-opportunity regulations, which are very important in North America but become more and more important in Europe as well)
- **Tax regulations**
- **Collective agreements**
  (especially in the more unionized European countries)
- **Social security**

In general, these and other laws provide no detailed rules to implement HR processes in a DP system. Legal limits generally provide little scope within which to exploit ideal processes.

These restrictions apply to the U.S. and most other countries, although to very different extents. Make sure that you know about the specific regulations when doing a rollout project to another country. There may even be differences between different states.

4.1.4 A Basis for Other Personnel Management Processes

The quality of other personnel processes — above all personnel controlling — depends on the quality of the personnel administration. This dependency is particularly clear if you are working with an integrated DP system such as SAP ERP, which should always be the essential goal. Lack of timeliness and poor quality of data maintenance have an immediate impact on the results of the other management areas. This problem is, however, basically independent of the system. Even if work is being carried out in isolated systems or exclusively on paper, specific information is indispensable as a basis for the processes that are described in more detail in the following sections.

Time Management

When you do time recording via time-recording terminals (time clocks), time management depends most heavily on the timeliness of data. The employees generally expect their time accounts to be updated daily at the time-recording terminal. If a lack of quality in the basic data leads to errors, this leads to more time and effort on the part of staff, due to enquiries, and a basic mistrust of employees toward the system. Where access-control systems are linked, errors can even completely lock out employees.

Essential master data for time management includes:

- Organizational data that determines the assignment of employees to certain business regulations
- Assignment of the employee to a relevant time administrator
- Time model/shift plan
- Leave entitlement
- Assignment of the employee to the respective time-recording terminal

Payroll

The payroll processes a particularly large quantity of personnel data. This data may not need to be updated on a daily basis but rather on a periodic basis, and it must be up-to-date at the day of payroll run. Erroneous results are problematic in their own way because, in contrast to time management, corrections cannot be made daily but only in the subsequent payroll period, as otherwise it would require too much effort. The transfer of results to public institutions such as tax agencies underlines the importance of high data quality.

A basic problem is the need to remunerate employees before the end of the pay period for which payment is to be made. Because it is inevitable that not all data pertaining to the period can be known, the salary calculated is more or less an estimated value. When setting the due date for payment, the increased process costs of an earlier point in time should also be taken into consideration. Payroll systems available on the market can indeed process subsequent changes, but the effort involved in inputting these changes rises, and at the same time the employee's understanding of the remuneration payroll suffers. In the case of assumed fixed monthly salaries, it is surprising how many unexpected changes arise in the second half of the month due to overtime, unpaid absence, changes to the tax data, etc.

The following essential basic data is relevant to remuneration by the date of payroll:

- Organizational data that determines the classification by company, pay scale, and legal regulations
- Gross remuneration, including one-off payments
- Tax and social-insurance data
- Other services such as direct insurance, company car, etc.
- Address data to dispatch remuneration statements
- Data for the company pension plan
- Bank details

Personnel Planning and Development

Personnel planning and development processes also depend on data that must be updated on a daily basis. However, this dependency is all too often forgotten due to frequent structural separation of the processes of personnel administration, time management, and payroll. In extreme cases, personnel development managers have to face the fact that only at the time of the remuneration payment can they safely rely on the basic administration data.

Even if the organization places great value on the importance of personnel planning and development, the processes of data retrieval and recording frequently focus only on the goal of transferring the correct amount to the correct account on payday.

Therefore, care must be taken to ensure that the planning departments are provided with administrative information for their daily work. For example, this information can include:

- Pay-scale grouping
- Agreed gross salary
- Organizational assignment with history
- Marital status
- Native language
- Working time
- Scheduled absence times

It often happens that an employee has not even been entered in the system when the personnel development administrator wants to maintain a training schedule for this employee.

4.1.5 Companywide Integration of HR Data

In practice, many HR information systems are in fact HR *department* information systems. Beyond the HR department, data from the central system is used most frequently in the form of paper lists provided by the HR department. On the other hand, various types of HR data are maintained on a companywide basis. For example:

- Absence lists (whether on the basis of Microsoft Excel or a large chart) in all departments
- Birthday lists and anniversary lists in all departments
- Lists with salaries, paid bonuses, and objectives, which the management uses for budgeting and annual appraisals

- Remaining leave lists, which often show numbers different from those maintained by the HR department (in the worst case, the paper lists of the department office are more up-to-date than the central HR information system)
- Lists of assets such as laptops and company cars, for which, in the context of asset accounting, the employee who uses the items is also entered
- Data from the loan department of a bank concerning employee loans
- Service phone numbers maintained by the technical service, and room numbers and their publication in an internal phone book
- Assignment of keys and access cards for employees maintained by the security service in a file
- Organizational charts created by the organizational department that go down to employee levels in separate org-chart software
- Lists in Microsoft Excel format maintained by the security manager to check the timeliness of first-aid courses and hazardous-material training

Such structures have often grown historically and may have been useful at the time of their implementation. However, the availability of a modern system with a central database and potential for decentralized access provides much more useful options. The decentralized use of a companywide HR information system provides many advantages:

- Lower costs through elimination of duplicate entries
- Savings on system costs in the decentralized area and a decrease in the proportion of the Total Costs of Ownership (TCO) allocated to the HR department in the personnel system
- Improved data quality due to an improved communication between decentralized users and the HR department
- Elimination of contradictory datasets
- Increased data security through integration of previously decentralized data in the central security concept
- Improved transparency of existing datasets
- The possibility of aggregating previously separate datasets (e.g., on the department level)

- Having all of the data in one system makes it possible to provide people with necessary information about changes, e.g., new hires, or transfers. This can be managed by an interface with the company's email system (e.g., MS Outlook) so that messages are generated automatically whenever a predefined event occurs.
- Considerably improved data protection due to access control for the central system and transparency

In this context, the last item is definitely one of the most important. However, it can also become a problem, as the transparency which is suddenly available uncovers past failures. The existence of decentralized HR data is not always agreed upon by the employee representatives or data-protection officers. Often, the potential we described earlier is not fully used to avoid such problems. At this point, the only solution is an open dialogue and the awareness of the opportunity to solve a widespread problem.

Other obstacles that must be overcome on the way to companywide, integrated HR information systems can be:

- A blockade by decentralized users who regard the integration of "their" datasets into the entire system as an encroachment upon their "sovereign territory"
- The difficulty of identifying decentralized datasets, especially if they were not recorded in digital format
- The problem of converting decentralized datasets, which are mostly maintained without conventions or with very different conventions
- Complicated assignment-to-data of the central system because only names have been maintained instead of personnel numbers
- A lack of acceptance of standards by the decentralized users
- A shift of costs that increase the workload in certain places despite the reduction of the overall cost structure

The procedure to establish a companywide integrated HR information system is illustrated in Figure 4.2. The detailed image suggests that the planning appears more complex than it actually is. In less extensive actions of this type, the project phases are not always as detailed as illustrated in the diagram. However, all of the steps shown in this process are essential for successful integration.

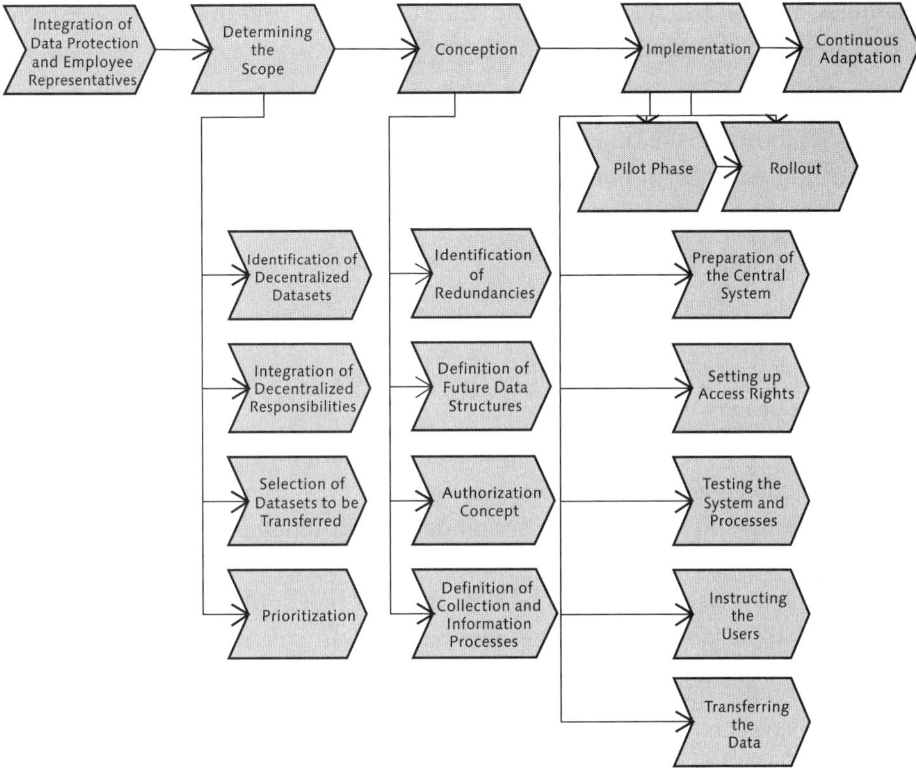

Figure 4.2 Process for Companywide Integration of HR Data

4.2 The SAP ERP HCM Concept

The SAP ERP HCM system inevitably follows the aforementioned principles. In doing so, it effectively fulfills business requirements in the area of personnel administration, although there are both strengths and weaknesses in the system, depending on the customer-specific requirements. In the following sections we will describe the basic concepts, the essential application components, and the fundamental and critical customizing activities. We will specifically focus on those aspects of implementation or optimization projects where important decisions are made — for example, in the company and employee structures. The data maintenance of infotypes and the data-maintenance processes are other essential aspects treated here. National specifics, especially with infotypes, are only touched on in examples. We will also discuss specific items that may appear to be weak areas and how they can be handled.

As an introduction to the system-relevant subjects, this section is more detailed than the sections on the other processes. Experienced users will skim over some passages, but will still find many interesting tips.

4.2.1 Personnel Numbers

The following sections deal with the main aspects of personal numbers.

Importance of Personnel Numbers

The personnel number is the system's central classification criterion for all personnel data. Each individual data record is assigned to the correct employee using the personnel number. This is true for master data organized in infotypes (see Section 4.2.2) and for the results of payroll, time management, company pension plans, and travel expense reports. It will be clear that it is practically impossible to make a subsequent change in a personnel number without creating inconsistencies in the database or losing the entire history of an employee.

In the HCM system, the personnel number can be a maximum of eight characters and is composed only of digits.

Assignment of Numbers

Assigning meaningful personnel numbers (e.g., personnel numbers of managers start with a 9) is absolutely not recommended. Because the smallest amounts of information occasionally read from the personnel numbers are absolutely static, meaningful personnel numbers always lead to unsolvable problems if the coded information is changed. Examples of this are the change of cost center, change of position, or moving from one employment grouping type to another (intern to regular employee, for example).

Also, it is not usually necessary to hide additional information in the personnel numbers in SAP ERP. All employee characteristics are documented through the structuring and data-entry options that we will describe in the following sections. Essential information that the administrator always wants to have access to when processing the data for an employee can be displayed in a suitable form. For example, it can be shown in the remuneration statement or as header information in all screens of HR data processing. Figure 4.3 shows an example of header details. The content of the headers can be flexibly adjusted through customer configuration.

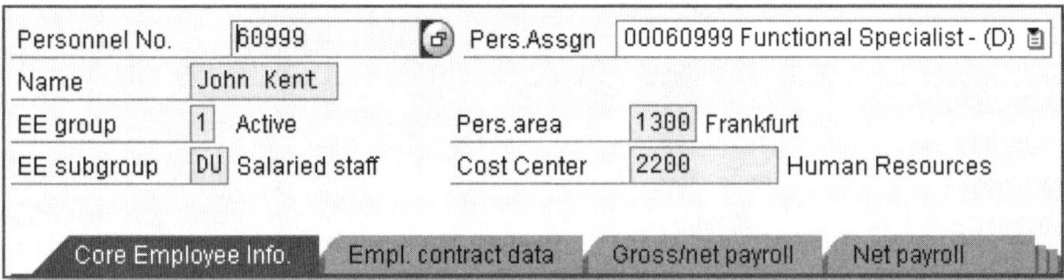

Figure 4.3 Header Entries in the HR Data Maintenance

There are two different options for personnel number assignment:

- In external number assignment the administrator manually enters a personnel number for each new employee. The assignment can then be carried out in any sequence.
- For internal number assignments the system automatically determines the next free number. In this case the administrator cannot make any changes.

In both cases, the available numbers can be limited by using the *number range*. Number ranges can, for example, be assigned separately for each subsidiary. However, you must remember that the information gained gets lost or becomes incorrect when an employee moves to another subsidiary.

Setting the number range and assigning it to parts of the enterprise structure is done through the implementation guide (IMG) menu path PERSONNEL MANAGEMENT • PERSONNEL ADMINISTRATION • BASIC SETTINGS • MAINTAIN NUMBER RANGE INTERVALS FOR PERSONNEL NUMBERS or DETERMINE DEFAULTS FOR NUMBER RANGES.

The current number, in particular, can be read or changed there (only to a higher number), and decisions can be made as to whether internal or external assignments will be done. In the example in Figure 4.4, the number of the interval 02 is to be assigned internally, while for intervals 01, 03, and 04 the personnel numbers must be assigned by the user. Which of the four intervals is relevant for a specific hiring action is determined in the IMG item Determine defaults for number ranges.

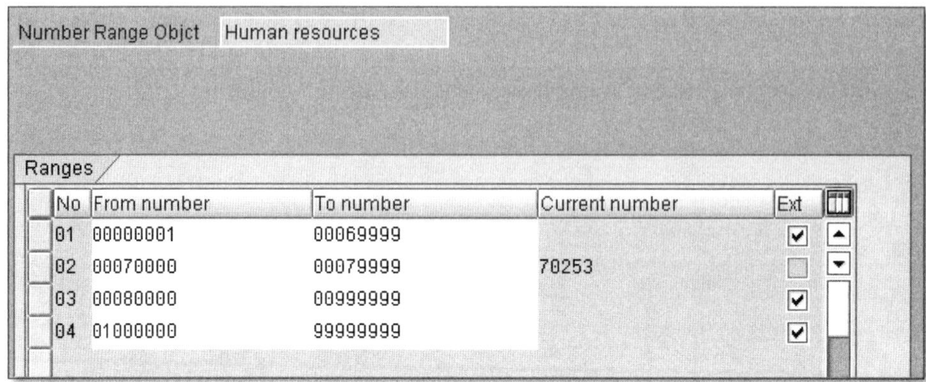

Number Range Objct Human resources

Ranges

No	From number	To number	Current number	Ext
01	00000001	00069999		☑
02	00070000	00079999	70253	☐
03	00080000	00999999		☑
04	01000000	99999999		☑

Figure 4.4 Number Ranges for Personnel Numbers

It is generally advisable to have an internal number assignment. Having a single number range for the entire company simplifies changes between individual subsidiaries.

Concept of the Reference Personnel Number

One of the previous weaknesses in the SAP ERP HCM structure lies at the personnel-number level. The personnel number is the ultimate key criterion for all data; it is not possible to enter several employment contracts for one person unless Concurrent Employment or Management of Global Employees is utilized (these components are discussed later in this chapter). The solution is to create a new HR master record for each employment relationship. This, however, leads to a redundant entry of a large part of the personnel data because the address or, for example, the name of the employee don't change through the additional employment contract.

The challenge is partly addressed through the concept of the reference personnel number. As the second employment contract is entered, it is connected to the first one by the Reference personnel number field. Certain data is then copied from the original personnel number and, during the course of time, additional changes such as a new address of one of the two personnel numbers always affects the other one as well. In contrast, other data points, such as the salaries for each contract, remain independent from one another.

The data (i.e., *infotypes*) that is or is not mirrored here is defined via the IMG path PERSONNEL MANAGEMENT • PERSONNEL ADMINISTRATION • CUSTOMIZING PROCEDURES • INFOTYPES • INFOTYPES • INFOTYPE • SELECTION BOX COPY INFOTYPE. There, for example, Infotype 0002 (Personal Data) is keyed to be mirrored. The corresponding field of the Customizing screen (Copy infotype) is selected in Figure 4.5.

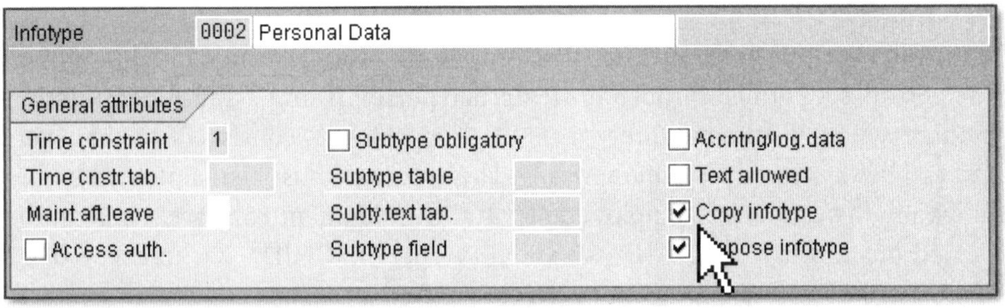

Figure 4.5 Setting the Relevance of the Infotype for Reference Personnel Numbers

Examples of the use of reference personnel numbers include the following:

- There are several contracts each with a low working time, as is often the case at universities offering several jobs to students.
- The work time for an employee is divided between two connected companies (e.g., a caretaker is employed by two affiliated companies located in the same building). However, if possible, this should be stipulated in one contract, and the costs should be split between the two companies.
- There are so-called *one-dollar contracts* for employees that are supposed to perform management tasks in affiliated companies.

Concept of Concurrent Employment

Since release R/3 Enterprise code 4.7, the function of *Concurrent Employment* is available. This function provides the means to track multiple concurrent employment relationships for one person within an integrated data record in SAP HCM. Concurrent Employment can also be adequately covered in other areas, such as payroll or time management.

This function contains personnel administration, benefits, time management, international payroll, and localizations for the U.S. and Canada. OSS Note 517071 provides precise information on the release of the functionality.

To use concurrent employment, it must first be released in Customizing. This can be done via IMG path PERSONNEL MANAGEMENT • PERSONNEL ADMINISTRATION • BASIC SETTINGS • BASIC SETTINGS FOR CONCURRENT EMPLOYMENT • ACTIVATE CONCURRENT EMPLOYMENT.

After this, the old personnel number represents a single employment contract. The person is identified through the (external) person ID or personal identification number, which is stored in Infotype 0709. The person ID consists of 18 characters and can be structured alphanumerically. This infotype must be maintained before activating the concurrent employment for all employment contracts. This can be carried out through report HR_CE_GENERATE_PERSONID_EXT. Infotype 0712 identifies the main employment contract.

Thus, an employee who has several employment contracts has a single unique person ID and several personnel numbers, which now represent personnel assignments within an enterprise (see Figure 4.6). In the application (e.g., in the master data maintenance), the user can select a person by his person ID and determine which personnel assignment to process. Through the user parameter HR_CCURE_PIDSL you can deactivate the person ID for each individual user. This is particularly useful in environments where a personnel administrator does not possess access rights for more than one personnel assignment (for example, if the employment contracts are located in different companies, which also have different personnel administrators).

Concept of Management of Global Employees

The Management of Global Employees (MGE) component provided since Extension 1.10 of R/3 Enterprise represents a comprehensive tool to map international employee assignments. The component is based on some concepts similar to concurrent employment. Here, too, every employee is given a clear person ID while the old personnel numbers identify the individual employment contracts. However, these work relationships must exist in different countries, that is, they must be assigned to different groupings for wage and salary payroll (MOLGA). This component will be discussed later in this chapter.

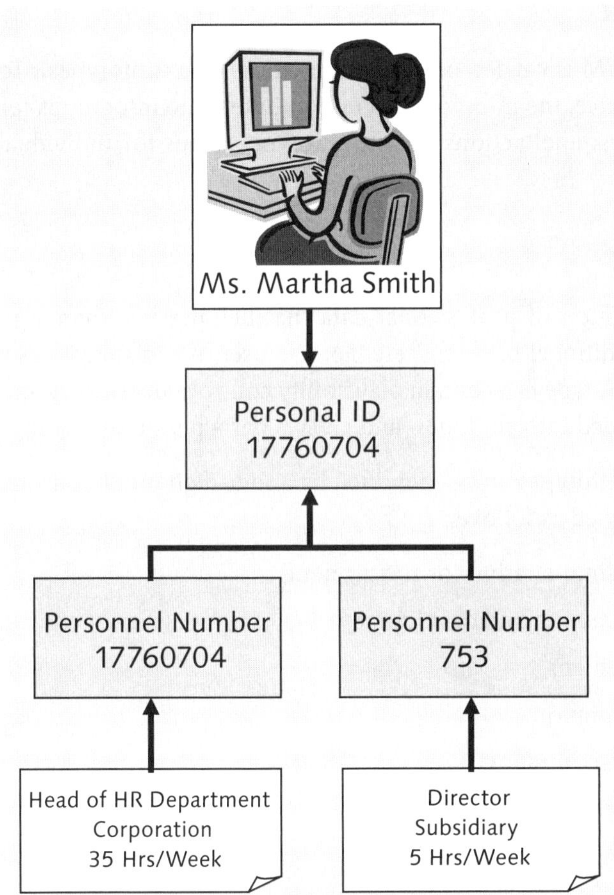

Figure 4.6 Relationship between the Personal ID and the Personnel Number

Searching for Employees

Even if the personnel number is the essential criterion for the DP system, it is unacceptable to mandate that a user always know the personnel number to maintain an HR master record. SAP ERP HCM offers extensive options for selecting the personnel numbers to be processed according to various criteria. These should be sufficiently dealt with in user training, because daily work becomes considerably more efficient with their use. Person selection is described in detail in the sections "Selecting the Personnel Number" and "Object Manager" (see Section 4.2.3).

4.2.2 Infotype Concept

Entering master data in HCM is carried out via information types (infotypes). To facilitate the data maintenance, the infotypes can be combined into infogroups for the implementation of personnel actions or into infotype menus for individual maintenance.

Infotypes

An *infotype* is the combination of professional data that belongs together, e.g., addresses, bank details, additional payment, etc. For the user, it is displayed as a screen for data entry. An infotype can contain plausibility controls, mandatory and optional fields, can be divided into subtypes, and always has a period of validity.

In addition to its name an infotype can be identified by a four-digit number. Here, the number ranges are defined as follows:

- 0000–0999 personnel administration (or recruitment)
- 1000–1999 personnel planning and development
- 2000–2999 time management
- 3000–3999 logistics integration
- 4000–4999 exclusively recruitment
- 9000–9999 customer-specific infotypes

Note to Programmers

For those interested in programming: In the database in administration and time management, the data for Infotype nnnn is always stored in the database table PAnnnn (recruitment: PBnnnn), with the exception of Infotype 2011, which represents table TEVEN.

The interface of the infotype screen can vary according to the status of the Customizing settings, depending on the data currently entered or other data of the same employee. For example, in Infotype 0016 (Contract Elements) for temporary employment relationships there is a field for the limit date.

Customizing the views of the infotypes can also be carried out independent of the data of the processed employees via Customizing (see "Customizing Infotypes" in Section 4.2.4). For this reason, the examples shown here will deviate partially from the interfaces of your systems.

Subtypes

Subtypes partition an infotype into screens of similar content. An example of this is Infotype 0009 (Bank Details) with the subtypes Main bank, Other bank, and Travel expenses (see Figure 4.7).

The views of an infotype can differ in appearance according to the subtype or can carry out other plausibility checks. For example, Infotype 0021 (Family/Dependents) has different screens for spouses and children.

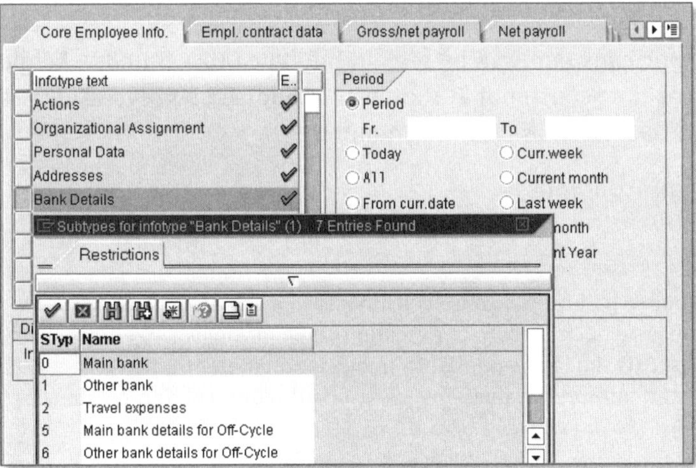

Figure 4.7 Subtypes in the Example of the Bank Details

Time Constraint

Time constraint is one of the essential attributes of the infotype concept in the SAP ERP system. It allows HR administration to build a history of data that changes with time. Time constraint describes to what extent an infotype or subtype can exist on a multiple basis and whether there can be gaps in the timeframe of an infotype's existence. A time constraint can be defined for a complete infotype or per subtype.

Personnel administration primarily uses the following three time constraint types:

- **Time constraint 1**
  For one point in time, there must be exactly one valid record and overlaps are not possible.

(Example: Infotype 0002 (Personal Data), in particular, the name of the employee)

- **Time constraint 2**
  For each point in time, there can be a maximum of one valid record. Gaps are allowed, overlaps are not possible.
  (Example: Infotype 0004 (Disability))
- **Time constraint 3**
  For each point in time, there can be any number of valid records.
  (Example: Infotype 0030 (Powers of Attorney))

The meaning of the time constraint can be seen in Infotype 0021 (Family). While subtype 1 (Spouse), has time constraint 2, subtype 2 (Child) allows several entries at the same time, and therefore has time constraint 3.

Figure 4.8 illustrates this concept.

Note: Importance of Time Constraints for End Users and Programmers

You should prepare your users for time constraints, because many errors and problems in the HCM application arise due to incorrect execution when making changes, copying, and inserting infotypes. It is similarly essential to understand different time constraints to successfully create and interpret evaluations for standard reports and to create specific queries or reports.

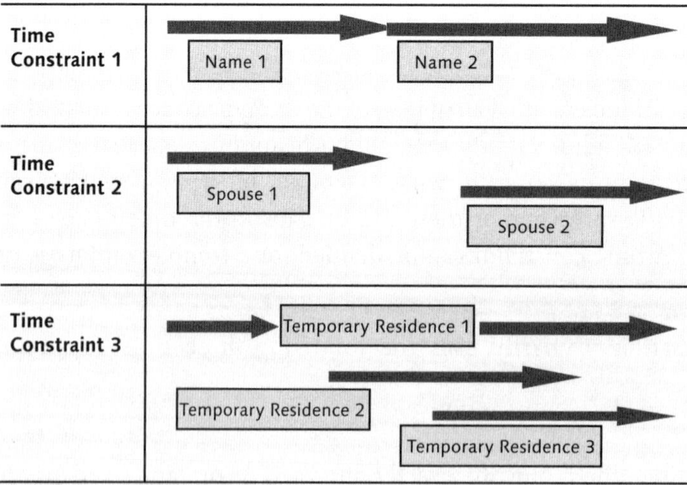

Figure 4.8 The Time Constraints in the HR Master Data

4.2.3 Data Maintenance in Infotypes

HR data is maintained by an end user through the use of infotypes. This section describes the work with personnel administration infotypes and in particular the most popular stumbling blocks when performing maintenance. In doing so, we will limit ourselves to maintaining individual infotypes, because this is the best way of clearly showing the underlying concept.

Specific data views sometimes combine several infotypes or segments from several infotypes to a screen. This is a trend that in the course of further development of SAP ERP HCM will definitely be promoted to offer users tailored interfaces for specific situations (for example, Adobe forms as a user interface technology). Although this undoubtedly means an improvement for end users, it makes customizing and programming more difficult. When working in the system configuration, it is often important to know the individual infotypes and their numbering.

The spin-off of the data entry screens from the individual infotypes becomes particularly obvious in Web-based applications (mainly within SAP NetWeaver Portal), because they often use individual fields from infotypes or combine fields of various infotypes in one form. The following sections first discuss the work with the infotypes in the core system, because this is also essential for the basic understanding of the infotype concept.

The Web-based maintenance or display in the portal is basically performed in three ways:

- Maintenance by the employees in Employee Self-Services (ESS)
- Maintenance by HR administrators that use the specific portal role (usually, HR administrators maintain the data in the core system as described later)
- Maintenance by managers through Manager Self-Services (MSS)

In all three cases, you can use both standard applications and customer-specific interfaces to maintain the data.

Master Data Maintenance — Initial Screen

Maintaining HR master data is carried out through the menu path Human Resources • Personnel Management • Administration • HR Master Data • Maintain. The basic screen for master data maintenance (see Figure 4.9) is divided into the object manager (left) and the actual maintenance screen (right).

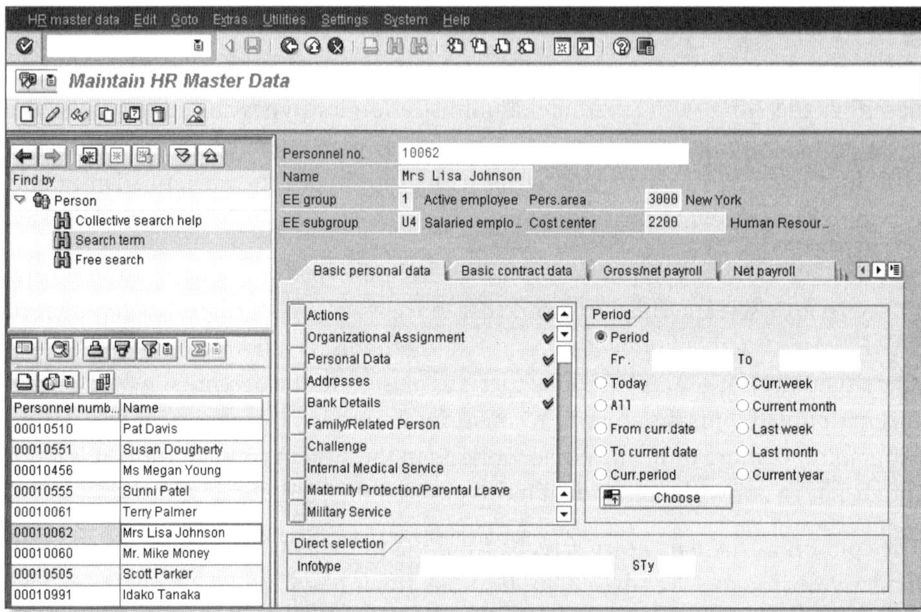

Figure 4.9 Master Data Maintenance — Initial Screen

Because this screen represents a large part of the daily work of an administrator in the backend Enterprise Core, like the maintenance screens for frequently used infotypes, much emphasis must be placed on optimal system configuration and user training. In comparison to payroll or time management, master data maintenance can at first seem to be relatively simple. It is exactly this perception that leads to frequent errors in data entry and maintenance.

It is indeed quite possible to implement a functioning master data maintenance with very little difficulty — and it can be used without much training — but in most cases neglecting this area leads to inefficiency and poor data quality. The current release of SAP ERP HCM now provides options to increase efficiency and the quality of the processes in this seemingly simple component. These are discussed as the chapter progresses, because their thorough use is recommended. Master data maintenance is sometimes perfectly suitable for system and process optimization six months after the start of production. Then, the first experiences of the users can be integrated in the optimization process. Due to the absence of deadline pressure and the knowledge that already had been gathered internally, optimization can be implemented with very little external support.

Using the basic screen for infotype maintenance is intuitive. Basically, you must fill out the selection fields for personnel numbers, information types and subtype (type), and for the period. Then you can use the menu or the push-button bar to select the required action.

Selecting the Infotype

There are several ways to select the required infotype:

- You can enter the infotype number
- You can enter the infotype name
- You can select the infotype field via the input help (F4 help)
- You can select a tab

The tab selection is particularly user-friendly and can be used to structure a task-specific interface (see "Infotype Menu" in Section 4.2.4).

Selecting the Personnel Number

The selection of the personnel number is supported in various ways. The users should also be aware of this support, otherwise a lot of time can be lost. When calling the input help, several search helps are provided by *matchcodes* and through free search (see Figure 4.10).

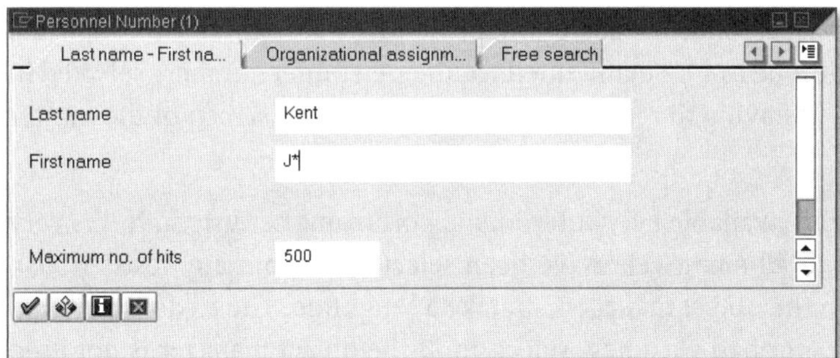

Figure 4.10 Search Help for Personnel Numbers

Most frequently, a name search is carried out here. This can also be used without F4 help by entering `=n.lastname.firstname` or only the beginning of the name in the personnel number field. In particular, for large organizations, searching through organizational assignment is very helpful. For example, this allows you to combine the search for last names and personnel subareas. The free search provides even more options, but a free search is more laborious due to the numerous possible search criteria. Search criteria grouped according to infotypes and freely selectable are used in the same way as they are in the Ad-hoc Query (see Chapter 11).

Users who are provided with free search as a first input help are often confused and cannot find their way back to the desired search help. In this case, you can use the Other search help button displayed in Figure 4.11.

Figure 4.11 Changing the Search Help

The search helps are generally usable in all screens that permit the entry of personnel numbers, and also in the selection screens for reports. Customer-specific search helps can be set up via the IMG (PERSONNEL MANAGEMENT • PERSONNEL ADMINISTRATION • BASIC SETTINGS • MAINTAIN SEARCH HELPS).

Object Manager

The object manager permits users to select personnel numbers and to maintain them in a personal to-do list. Selection is done through the matchcode options already referred to (see collective search help), the free search, and through the search term. An infotype can be maintained for the personnel numbers selected in the to-do list without having to return each time to the initial screen of the master data maintenance.

The to-do list remains available even after logging off from the system. If it is very large (for example, if all employees have been selected without any restrictions), calling screens with the object manager can take a long time. The to-do list should then be reduced or emptied via a new selection. If the object manager is not used or is not practical for the user due to its configuration (screen size, PC capacity), it can be switched off by an SAP Graphic user Interface (GUI) user at any time using the SAP Easy Access Menu path SETTINGS • HIDE OBJECT MANAGER.

Customer-specific adjustments to the object manager are possible in the IMG. If necessary, use the path PERSONNEL MANAGEMENT • GLOBAL SETTINGS IN PERSONNEL

MANAGEMENT • SETTINGS FOR OBJECT MANAGER. The settings to be implemented there are not limited to the object manager in the HR master data maintenance. Further variants are also used in other HCM transactions.

Basic Functions for Working with Infotypes

The actual work with infotypes involves the following activities:

- **Creation**
  Creating a new record with a beginning and end date. Other records are deleted or limited according to the time constraint. Examples: The birth of a child necessitates the creation of a corresponding record of Infotype 0021. After an employee moves to a new address, a new record is created in Infotype 0006 (Addresses), from 03/04/2007. In addition, the old address record is limited with the end date of 03/03/2007.
- **Change**
  An existing record of an infotype is changed for its entire period of validity. An example of this would be error corrections (e.g., an incorrectly written family name).
- **Copying**
  Similar to creation, with the difference that an old record is used as a template. Example: Changing the family name as of 3/10/2007 because of marriage. Note: Changing instead of copying frequently causes errors and destroys the history!
- **Delimiting**
  Upon entering a delimitation date, all records valid for this date are provided. After selecting the required records and clicking the Delimit button, the respective selected end date is set to the day *before* the delimitation date. Delimiting as such is only permitted for infotypes with time constraints 2 and 3. For infotypes with time constraints 1 and 2, creating and copying records can possibly automatically trigger delimitation, as no parallel records are permitted. The system notifies you about this by issuing a warning.
- **Displaying**
  In the display mode the user can see data but cannot change them. In many cases displaying something is the only function a user is authorized to use. But even if you have change authorization you should always use the display mode if you do not intend to maintain data. This protects against accidental changes and, in addition, other users cannot process HR master data as long as you are in the maintenance mode for this HR master data (locking mechanism).

- **Locking/unlocking**
  Locked records of an infotype are overlooked in further processing, in particular for payroll. Thus, this functionality is helpful if you are not sure of a specific data entry and there is still need for clarification, or if the effect of a deletion should be tested up front. In particular, the locked data entry and subsequent unlocking by another user is done to implement the dual-control principle. This is also supported by the authorization concept of R/3.
- **Deletion**
  Infotypes with time constraint 1 must be continuously available. Thus it is not possible to delete all data records of such an infotype. When deleting a data record, the system extends the predecessor to such an extent that in turn there are no gaps. This is signaled by a warning message.
- **Overview**
  An overview shows all entries of an infotype in the selection period in form of a list. Some of the functions for individual records described here can be executed directly from the list (see Figure 4.12).

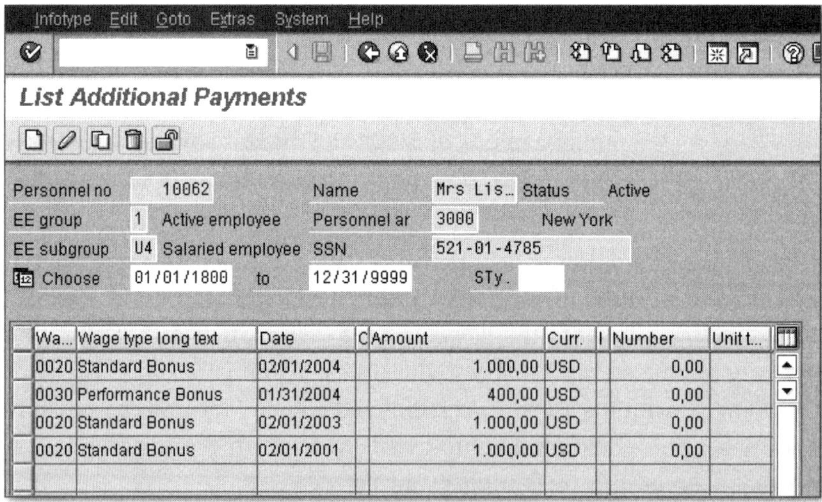

Figure 4.12 Overview of the Records of an Infotype

General Information on Maintenance in the Infotype Screens

Maintenance of the data fields in the screens occurs individually per infotype. This is described for selected infotypes in the following sections. Let's first make some general remarks concerning the maintenance of infotypes.

Fixed entry options exist for many data fields. These options are generally controlled by Customizing tables through which the selection can then be defined according to the specific company. However, you should be aware that some of these tables should not be, or only partially, changed via Customizing. These scenarios are described in further detail in the IMG documentation and are signaled by a warning when an entry is changed that should only be changed by SAP itself. Although you can change these tables if necessary for your company, an upgrade to a new release, however, might set back the changes. In addition, you must check whether legal requirements prohibit the change.

To improve user-friendliness, the interfaces in HCM are becoming more and more key-free — the user works solely with the complete texts (e.g., Angola) instead of the system-internal key (e.g., AO). For the system configuration or evaluation, it is still often helpful to know the system-internal key or to know how to reach the Customizing table that determines the selection.

By using the Customizing of Local Layout button or pressing Alt + F12 and then choosing Options, you can reach the options menu of the SAP GUI.

In the Expert tab you can click on the Show keys in all dropdown lists option to see the keys in the respective fields. Figure 4.13 shows the Language and Nationality keys in Infotype 0002 without keys and with keys.

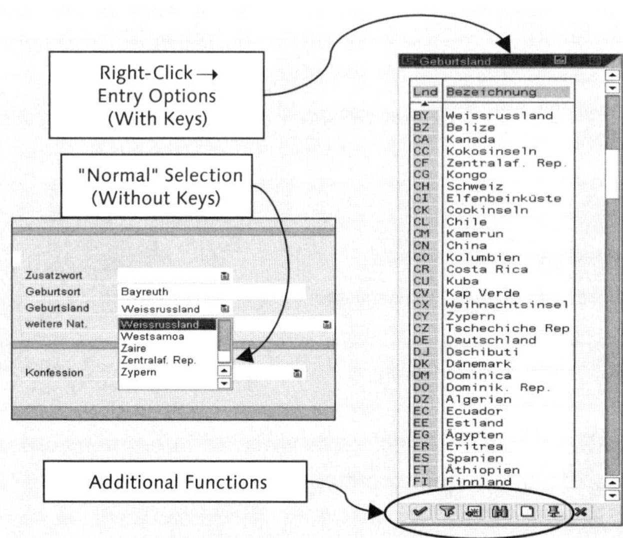

Figure 4.13 Input Help With and Without Key

If key-free help is always deactivated, you can adjust this via the GUI settings according to the respective PC installations (see Figure 4.14).

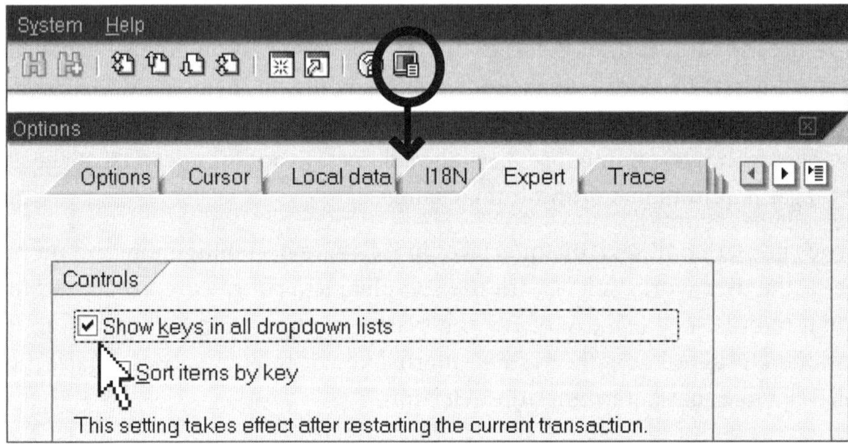

Figure 4.14 Deactivating Key-Free Input Helps

For many infotypes, it is possible to enter additional text comments. Additional text does not usually appear directly on the screen of the infotype but rather in a background editor, which you can reach through the menu path EDIT • MAINTAIN TEXT (see Figure 4.15).

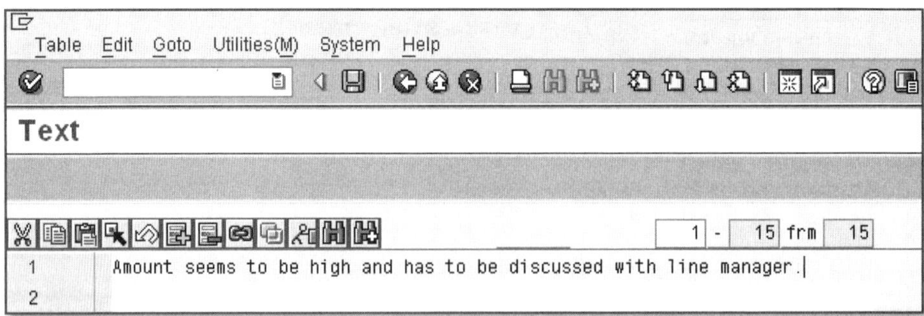

Figure 4.15 Maintaining an Additional Text for the Infotype

It is a useful convention to always maintain such texts when an infotype record is locked due to an existing clarification requirement.

You can recognize the existing background text and the lock identifier in the screen by the two symbols displayed in Figure 4.16.

Be aware that the background texts are difficult to report on. Even SAP Query doesn't provide these texts for reporting, because they are not stored in transparent database tables. Therefore, a somewhat more complex additional programming effort is necessary for evaluation and reporting purposes. In general, data that is required in reports should not be entered this way. Even entering data in the wrong row can lead to incorrect lists, even in the case of self-programmed evaluations. Instead, the infotype should be enhanced with customer-specific fields. These fields can then be evaluated via SAP Query and can be very easily implemented (see "Enhancing Infotypes" in Section 4.2.4).

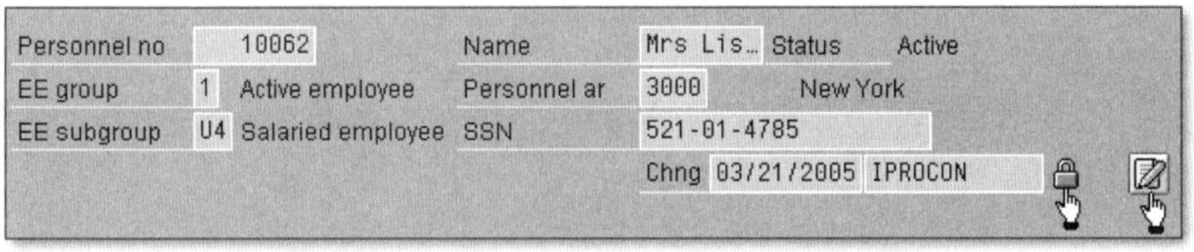

Figure 4.16 Symbols for Locks and Background Text

Some infotypes show a part of the background text in the basic screen. However, the same limitations also exist there with regard to their scope for evaluation. Figure 4.17 illustrates this in the example of Infotype 0030 (Powers of Attorney). The comments field in this infotype is an extract of the background text and is thus hardly suitable for evaluations.

Other special functions that you can access through the menu include the following:

- Assigning and displaying documents of an optical archive via menu path Extras • Display all Facsimiles
- Navigation to the overview of all records of the infotype
- Display and maintenance of data for cost assignments via menu path Edit • Maintain Cost Assignment

Another essential piece of information is the display of the date and the user name for the last change of the entry. You can find this information in the bottom line of the header data (see Figure 4.38 for an example). However, it is not logged here when the change to the validity ending occurs, because of a delimitation that was initiated by the creation of a new record. This situation can sometimes lead to confusion. Clearly, deletions aren't entered either, because then the modified record wouldn't exist. To get a complete change history for reasons of revision or to understand errors, you can capture/log the infotype changes using the standard tool provided for this purpose.

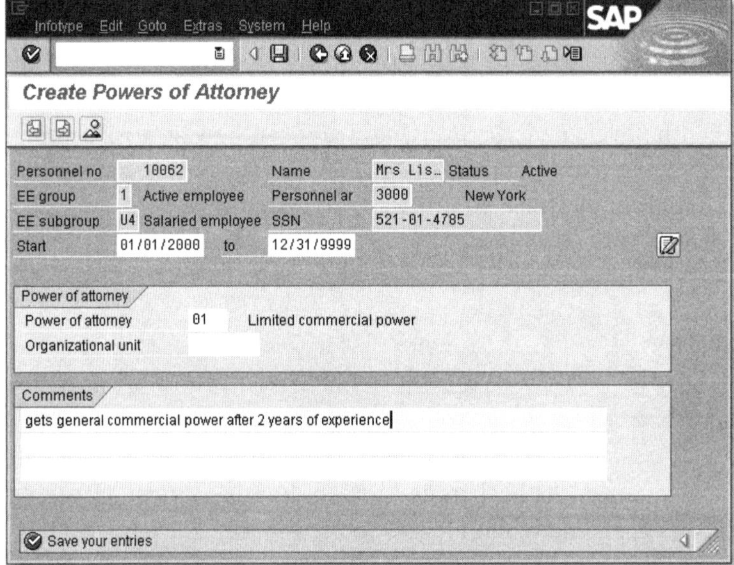

Figure 4.17 Background Text Partially Displayed

Logging infotype changes can be implemented via the following IMG path PERSONNEL MANAGEMENT • PERSONNEL ADMINISTRATION • TOOLS • REVISION • SET UP CHANGE DOCUMENT. There you can define which changes are logged on both the infotype and field levels.

Within the application, the evaluation of the change documents occurs via menu path HUMAN RESOURCES • PERSONNEL MANAGEMENT • ADMINISTRATION • INFO SYSTEM • DOCUMENTS • INFOTYPE CHANGE.

4.2.4 System Adjustments in Master Data Maintenance

You can improve the user-friendliness and thus the efficiency of the application considerably by using various simple Customizing settings. The following sections deal with the essential options.

Infotype Menu

You can enter the master-data maintenance by selecting different tabs. The structure of the individual tabs and the selection of available tabs can be defined as user-dependent via Customizing.

The settings can be done via IMG path PERSONNEL MANAGEMENT • PERSONNEL ADMINISTRATION • CUSTOMIZING PROCEDURES • INFOTYPE MENUS. The connection between the individual IMG activities is described here in more detail for three reasons:

- The documentation is quite unclear and old fashioned at this point. The user parameter PMN, which is referred to in the documentation, is no longer supported.
- In addition to the HR master-data maintenance, other menus are also controlled at this point. Furthermore, very similar user group–dependent customizing once again takes place regarding personnel actions (see Section 4.4.1).
- This is the first extensive Customizing activity described in this book.

SAP uses the *infotype menu* concept here for an individual tab, while the concept *infotype menu selection* is used for the summary of the described tabs.

Customizing is carried out in five steps:

To control user-dependent customizing — which is desirable in the context of the role-based application — you must maintain the user parameter UGR (user group) in all user master records. User parameters are maintained in the user administration or — provided they have the necessary authorization — by the user themselves via menu path SYSTEM • USER PROFILES • OWN DATA • TAB PARAMETERS (see Figure 4.18).

1. First, define the individual tabs in the IMG activity INFOTYPE MENU • USER GROUP DEPENDENCY ON MENUS AND INFO GROUPS (see Figure 4.19). This step can be left out if infotypes are only inserted or deleted in an existing tab. In this Customizing view, you can define whether the display is user-dependent, which default value (reference user group) should be set for parameter UGR, or whether a warning or an error is to be raised if parameter UGR is not maintained.

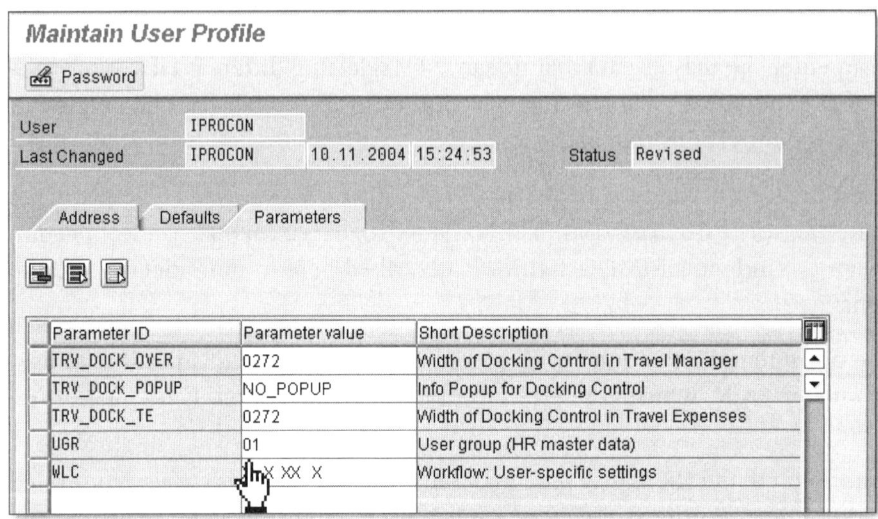

Parameter ID	Parameter value	Short Description
TRV_DOCK_OVER	0272	Width of Docking Control in Travel Manager
TRV_DOCK_POPUP	NO_POPUP	Info Popup for Docking Control
TRV_DOCK_TE	0272	Width of Docking Control in Travel Expenses
UGR	01	User group (HR master data)
WLC	X XX X	Workflow: User-specific settings

Figure 4.18 Maintaining the User Parameter UGR

Change View "User Group Dependency on Menus and Info Groups"

New Entries

Menu ty. I

Menu	Text	User-dep.	Reaction	Ref.
01	Core Employee Info.	☑		01
02	Empl. contract data	☑		
03	Gross/net payroll	☑		
04	Net payroll	☑		01
05	Payroll supplements	☑		01
06	Planning data	☐		00
07	Fast entry - master	☑		01
09	Fast entry - time	☐		00
16	Time data	☐		00

Figure 4.19 Defining an Infotype Menu with Reference User Group

2. Finally, the IMG activity INFOTYPE MENU • INFOTYPE MENU defines the infotypes that appear on the tab, depending on the parameter UGR (see Figure 4.20). If a reference user group was entered in the previous step, this group must at least exist for one entry.

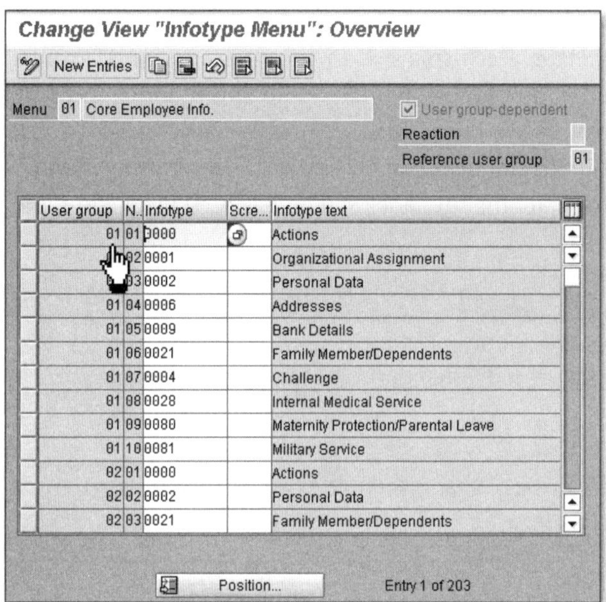

User group	N..	Infotype	Scre...	Infotype text
01	01	0000		Actions
	02	0001		Organizational Assignment
	03	0002		Personal Data
01	04	0006		Addresses
01	05	0009		Bank Details
01	06	0021		Family Member/Dependents
01	07	0004		Challenge
01	08	0028		Internal Medical Service
01	09	0080		Maternity Protection/Parental Leave
01	10	0081		Military Service
02	01	0000		Actions
02	02	0002		Personal Data
02	03	0021		Family Member/Dependents

Figure 4.20 Assigning Infotypes to an Infotype Menu (User Group–Dependent)

3. After the individual tabs (infotype menus) have been defined, you must define the infotype menu selection via IMG activity DETERMINE CHOICE OF INFOTYPE MENUS • USER GROUP DEPENDENCY ON MENUS AND INFO GROUPS. For master-data maintenance, this is carried out through the Menu 01 key. As was the case in the second step, the question of user group dependency is also handled here (see Figure 4.21).

Change View "User Group Dependency on Menus and Info Groups"

New Entries

Menu ty. S

Menu	Text	User-dep.	Reaction	Ref.
01	HR master data	☑		01
32	Payroll Information	☑		
BP	Benefits profile	☑		
EP	Employee profile	☑		94
HP	HR manager profile	☑		95
LP	Line manager profile	☑		96
PP	Payroll profile	☑		91
SP	Security profile	☑		92
TC	Trainer profile	☑		90
TP	Travel planning	☐		00

Figure 4.21 Maintaining the Menu Selection with Reference User Group

4. In the last step (IMG activity DETERMINE CHOICE OF INFOTYPE MENUS • INFOTYPE MENUS), you define which tabs are displayed. In the pre-selection you must again select Menu 01. Then you define which tabs are displayed in connection with the individual user groups (i.e., the characteristics of parameter UGR, see Figure 4.22). As the structure of the tabs has already been set in steps 2 and 3, the appearance of the master data maintenance screen has now been completely defined.

Note: Limited Number of Tabs

In contrast to what is specified in the documentation, you can only integrate 10 tabs into a menu. You should keep this in mind from the very beginning of your concept!

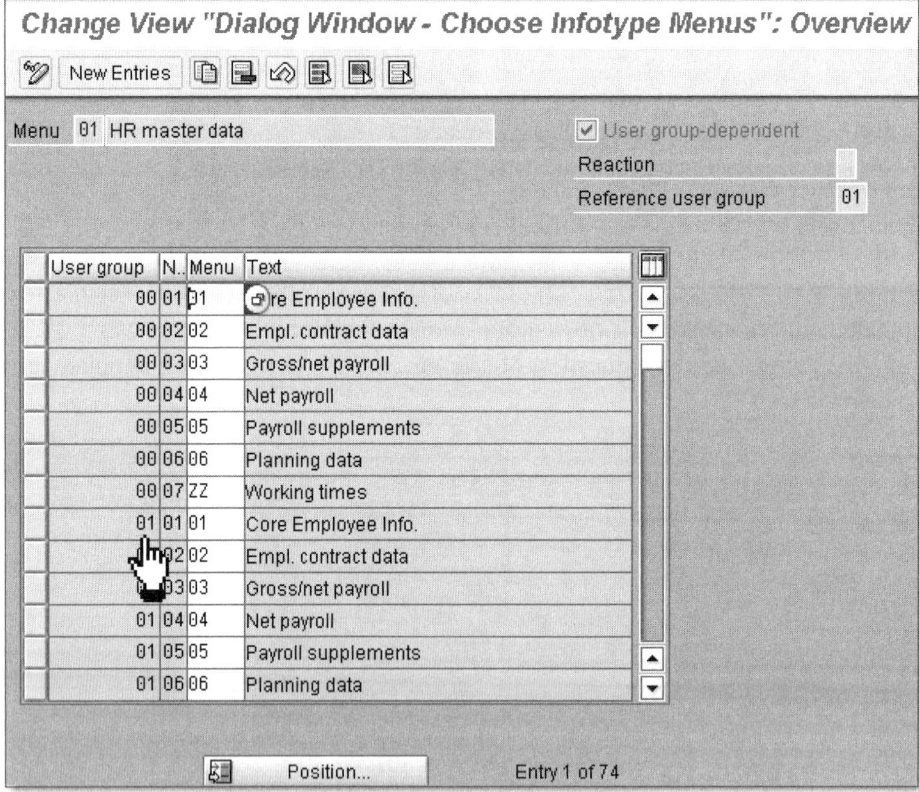

Figure 4.22 Defining the Infotype Menu to be Displayed (User Group–Dependent)

Excessive detailing of the user-dependent setting of this and other interfaces frequently leads to increased maintenance and required customizing changes.

Adjusting Infotypes

For many infotypes, there are individual options to customize screens, default values, input helps, and plausibility checks. These options are distributed in several substeps in IMG path Personnel Management • Personnel Administration (see Figure 4.23) and some of them are dealt with in connection with the respective infotypes in the following sections of this chapter. First, we will describe the adjustment options generally provided for all infotypes.

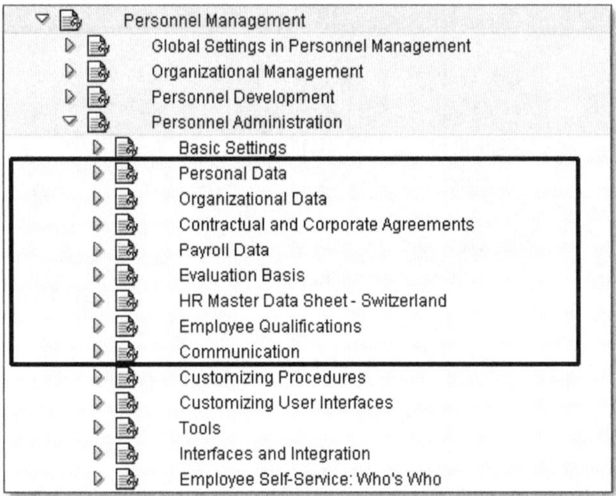

Figure 4.23 Infotype-Specific Settings in Personnel Administration

The adjustment options essentially amount to three processes whose IMG paths are as follows:

- Screen control Personnel Management • Personnel Administration • Customizing User Interfaces • Change Screen Modifications
- General infotype properties Personnel Management • Personnel Administration • Customizing Procedures • Infotypes • Define Fields Relevant for Retroactive Accounting
- Dynpro header Personnel Management • Personnel Administration • Customizing User Interfaces • Change Screen Header

Screen control permits you to hide individual fields of an infotype, or to declare them as output-only or as a mandatory field.

To use the table in the IMG, you must first know exactly which *Dynpro* (screen) you actually want to adjust. To do so you must call the system status from the entry screen of the infotype (menu path SYSTEM • STATUS). The two fields, Program (screen) and Screen number (see Figure 4.24) indicate the entry to be processed for adjustment (see Figure 4.25).

In general, the name of the module pool is MP<infotype number>00, while 2000 is the Dynpro number for the full screen.

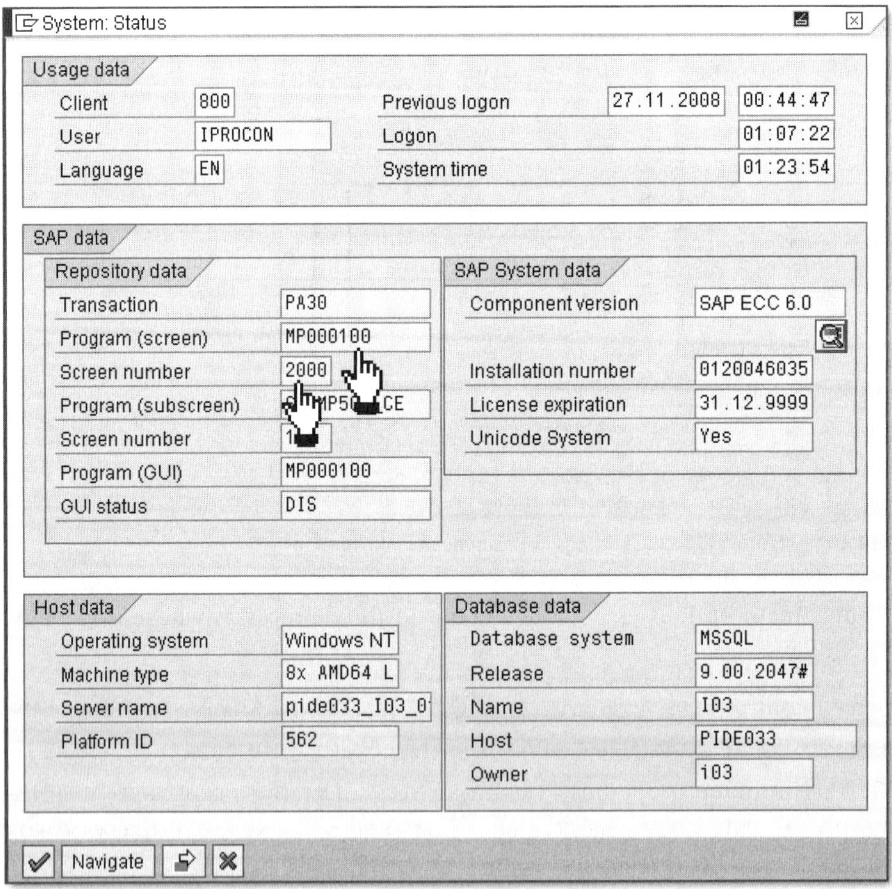

Figure 4.24 Determining the Current Dynpro from the System Status

	Screen	Feature	Variable key	Alternative screen	Next screen
	2000	P0001		2000	0

Figure 4.25 Basic Entry in the Screen Control

As the maintenance views can differ according to various criteria, there are usually a few additional entries for each basic entry. For this reason, there is a feature available with the basic entry, which supplies a variable key as a result. The maintenance of features is described in further detail in Appendix C, "Explanation of Process Models." Criteria considered in the respective feature are organizational attributes but can also be infotype-specific attributes, such as the subtype. Very often, the variable key provided by the feature depends on the respective country.

The actual relevant entry is identified depending on the value in the screen controls table. Thus, for example, the standard setting for Infotype 0001 for Sweden goes to a separate row with variable Key 23, and from there calls Dynpro 2023 instead of Dynpro 2000. Even though for Japan variable Key 22 calls Dynpro number 2000, the individual entry enables you to show additional fields or to declare them as mandatory fields. As the infotypes for recruitment are also controlled by this table, a differentiation by transaction classes is predominantly carried out (A = Administration, B = Recruitment). In the example of Infotype 0001, variable Key B leads to Dynpro 2100 for recruitment.

Further details are provided and described in the documentation. It is worthwhile to review the example of Infotype 0001 with the feature P0001 to understand the concept.

A few important tips on this subject:

- Converting mandatory fields to optional fields should be performed with caution. In general, the fields keyed as mandatory by default are actually required for successful data processing and also for legal reporting purposes.
- You can also control custom Dynpros using this table (good knowledge of Dynpro programming is a prerequisite). For full screens, it is important that you use the numbers in the range between 2000 and 2999, whereas for list screens you should use the range between 3000 and 3999. As this is not a customer namespace, it technically represents a modification. If possible, you should therefore not work with custom Dynpros but rather with enhanced standard Dynpros.

- You should refer to the documentation for the Subsequent Dynpro field if this field is not set to zero.
- Some fields can only be shown or hidden together as a group. This is because they have a joint grouping (see Figure 4.26). Developers who enhance infotypes or who define their own infotypes should be aware that this grouping is the third grouping in the attributes of the Dynpro field. If there is no grouping entered there, the field cannot be controlled by the screen control.

Screen Control

Grp	Field Name	Field text	Std	RF	Opt.	Outp	Hide	Init
001	P0001-BUKRS	Company Code	●	○	○	○	○	○
[illegible]	P0001-WERKS	Personnel Area	●	○	○	○	○	○
[illegible]	P0001-KOSTL	Cost Center	○	○	●	○	○	○
004	P0001-PERSG	Employee Group	●	○	○	○	○	○

Figure 4.26 Grouping in the Screen Control

It can also be very helpful to adjust the *general infotype properties*. The settings are individually documented. Therefore, we only list the essential options of these Customizing activities:

- Defining whether the subtype must be entered before calling the infotype (This should be the case if Dynpro modifications or different checks and default values are controlled with regard to the subtype.)
- Choosing whether to enter the assignments to objects of cost accounting (CO) and logistics (e.g., nonrecurring payments)
- Behavior of the infotype in connection with the reference personnel numbers
- Choosing whether to maintain a background text
- Taking action for entering employees who have left
- Time dependency of authorization checks
- Interpreting beginning and end dates when making selections through master data maintenance
- Taking action regarding retroactive calculations in time management and payroll (This is one of the most important properties and will be dealt with especially in the respective chapters.)
- Dynpro numbers (before any modifications are carried out via screen control)
- The number of the Dynpro header

- The text of the infotype
- Possible reasons for changes (The reasons specified here can be entered for information purposes when changing an infotype. For some infotypes the field must first be shown by using the screen control. For other infotypes it is not available at all.)

The last general customization option refers to the Dynpro header. The header contains certain pieces of information on an employee that should always be displayed when working with master data (e.g., name and cost center). The data displayed in each case can be defined according to the specific infotype here. The settings are country dependent.

We will now describe the individual steps to perform (see Figure 4.27). Via the infotype properties, each infotype is assigned a Dynpro header number. Each Dynpro header number, in turn, is then assigned a header modification in the form of a two-digit key. In the next step, all fields that are displayed in the header are assigned to the Dynpro modification. The most important action is to carry out a generation afterward using the button beneath the control table. If necessary, this generation must also be performed after a completely new installation of a standard system. As the field names automatically taken from the data dictionary can sometimes be confusing, you can replace them with your own texts. It is also possible to display a photo. To do this, however, the photos must first be stored in the system.

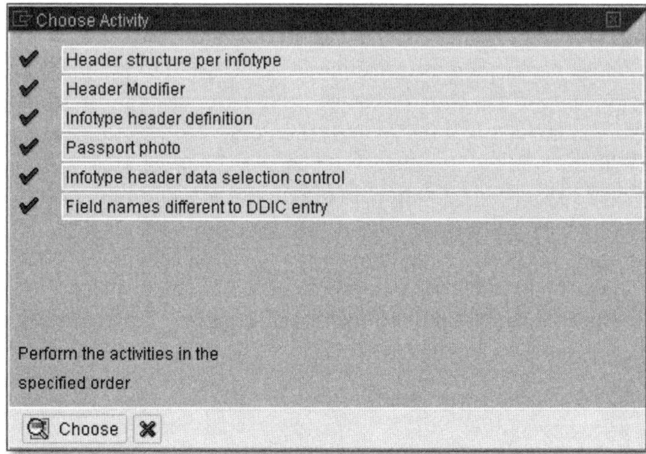

Figure 4.27 Steps for Customizing the Infotype Header

Discussions often arise concerning the displayed data, as each user assumes a different key date. As a rule, you can display the data as valid on the current date or the start date of the current infotype. Either method can be useful. The most important thing is that the users are aware of this.

Enhancing Infotypes

Enhancing infotypes is actually a part of user interface programming and we will therefore only deal with it briefly. It is important to know that enhancement of an infotype by additional fields is rather simple and can be done without any modifications. If no special processing or check logic is required for the new fields, then enhancement can essentially be done without programming knowledge. However, a basic understanding of the data dictionary and the table structure in the system is required.

The enhancement is carried out via Transaction PM01 using the Enhance Infotype and Enhance List Screen tabs. The online documentation describes the process very well and in detail. We recommend you use the Create All button, which should guide you through the entire process. There is, however, one restriction: The additional fields appear at the bottom edge of the screen.

Tip: Including Customer-Specific Display Fields

Programmers who want to deal with the subject in more detail should know that if additional fields are displayed in the Dynpro without additional fields being required in the database, automatic generation does not function at first. You need to make an entry in the customer include of the database structure. However, to still work with the enhancement that is convenient and does not require modification, it is advisable to integrate a dummy field in the customer include of the structure, which is then removed again from the user interface. If the customer include of the Dynpro is then available after the automatic generation, existing fields or fields to be calculated can then be integrated there. A frequently used example is the display of additional communication numbers in the U.S. version of Infotype 0006 (Address Data). Infotype 0006 provides additional fields for phone, fax, pagers, mobile phones, etc. In some country-specific versions, such as the German one, these fields are not available in the Dynpro and cannot be displayed via screen control. As the use of the Dynpro for another country would turn off the specific entry checks, it is a good idea to enhance the specified country Dynpro.

Creating New Infotypes

Basically, the creation of new infotypes is as simple as enhancing the existing ones. You are also supported by Transaction PM01, whose online documentation is very helpful.

You can implement infotypes with simple interfaces very easily without calculations and checks. A typical application is an infotype that is only used to store historical data from legacy systems and will no longer require maintenance in the future. You can, however, implement much more complex applications that result in a correspondingly high level of effort in programming.

In general, you can store in new infotypes all personnel data for which there are no entry options in the standard version. This enables you to make complete use of cross-infotype standard processing. Custom infotypes are completely integrated in normal master-data maintenance, cross-infotype customizing, and the evaluation via queries.

When you create your own infotypes, it is essential that you keep the customer namespace between 9000 and 9999. In addition, you must be able to manage the data dictionary and the table structure and have basic knowledge of the screen painter.

Plausibility Checks and Default Values

For each infotype, you can store default values or plausibility checks that go beyond the customizing options. You can do this through programming in two function exits in SAP enhancement PBAS0001:

- EXIT_SAPFP50M_001 is called when an infotype is created or copied. Here you can program default values in particular.
- EXIT_SAPFP50M_002 is called after entries have been made in the screen and fields have been verified. You can store entry checks here and also change field content depending on entries made.

To do this, you need to have programming knowledge and project-management knowledge concerning SAP enhancements. As the documentation contains examples in the system, implementation is then quite simple. The function exits do not represent a modification to standard SAP code, but they do require ABAP development.

For the project manager or key user, it is important to know that this option exists. The actual implementation is then easy for a programmer if he knows the data structures of SAP ERP HCM and observes the documentation of the function exits.

From release 4.6C on, there is another option available to access the infotype processing through additional checks — Business Add-In (BAdI) HRPAD00INFTY enables you to store customer-specific programming codes in three different places (processing times):

- **Process Before Output (PBO)**
  Here, you can interfere immediately before the data is output on the screen.
- **Process After Input (PAI)**
  This point in time is particularly suitable for entry checks.
- **IN_UPDATE**
  At this point you can call processing at the time of saving.

A prerequisite for using this method is knowledge of HCM data structures and the technical infotype concept. In addition, the programmer must be familiar with ABAP Objects and BAdI technology.

4.2.5 Structures in Personnel Administration

As described in Section 4.1.1, clearly defined structures are an essential factor in structuring a DP-supported personnel administration system. We will now present the different views of the structure in HCM. We will specifically explore the controlling effect of the individual structuring attributes and the evaluation aspect. Both aspects are crucial for defining the structure at the beginning of a project. Even if these definitions are changed as the project progresses, a precise description is necessary at the beginning as Customizing also relies on these results to a large extent.

Enterprise Structure

The structural outline in the SAP ERP HCM system is primarily carried out through the concepts of the personnel area and the personnel subarea. They frequently represent the company and location views but can be defined for other evaluation requirements on a lower level of the hierarchy.

The two concepts are integrated in the accounting structures. Here, you must ensure that a company code (independent accounting unit) is on a higher (or equal) hierarchy level than the personnel area. Hence, a personnel area is assigned to exactly one company code. The cost center and the business area can also divide the head count as further structural elements of accounting. They are not integrated into the hierarchy of the personnel area and the subarea; that is, employees of different personnel areas can theoretically be assigned to the same cost center. The meaning of this and other structural concepts will be closely considered in the context of Infotype 0001 (Organizational Assignment) in Section 4.3.2.

As a result, the integration concept looks like the one illustrated in the simplified graphic in Figure 4.28. There, abstractions made from special cases and the connections between the HCM enterprise structure, HCM organizational management, and accounting are illustrated. Organizational management is described in Chapter 5, "Organizational Management in SAP ERP HCM."

The client is the major organization criterion above all other components in the system. It represents a self-enclosed world of its own (at this point we will ignore the coupling of different systems via Application Linking and Enabling (ALE) as a special case that creates an artificially enlarged client).

The essential decision criteria for forming personnel areas are:

- Company code
- Country version for payroll

For the personnel subarea, the main criteria generally are:

- Location
- Company number/tax office

The personnel area/subarea combination mainly controls the following functionalities:

- Public holiday calendar
- Bonus calculation
- Permissibility of wage types
- Eligibility and quota deduction of leave types
- Eligibility and removal of time quotas

- Eligibility and design of work schedules
- Eligibility, counting, and validation of absence and attendance types
- Time evaluation and error messages in time evaluation
- Wage-type generation
- Wage-type evaluation
- Plausibility checks in infotypes
- Eligibility and evaluation of substitutes
- Assignment of pay-scale type and pay-scale area
- Assignment to a legal entity
- Exception handling in statistics
- Reporting to authorities for social security
- Assignment of tax office number and municipality number
- Eligibility check and calculation in travel expenses

This list, which does not contain all possible system impacts of the grouping, makes it immediately clear that the division of personnel areas and personnel subareas is subject to numerous external factors. In addition, two hierarchy levels are insufficient to structure a medium-sized or larger organization. Additional structuring through company code and cost center can be helpful but are also subject to constraints on the accounting side that may counteract the requirements of personnel management. We recommend that you implement organizational management to map the organizational structure (see Chapter 5) and to regard the enterprise structure described here as a control element for the administrative processes.

You can maintain personnel areas and subareas via the following IMG path ENTERPRISE STRUCTURE • DEFINITION • HUMAN RESOURCES MANAGEMENT. We strongly recommend here that you create new elements by using the copy function only. When copying from the personnel subareas, you will have to get used to the copy tool asking from which area you want to copy a specific subarea. But if you always stick closely to the documentation and user guide, you won't get confused. As a matter of fact, the copy function works quite well! The assignment of personnel areas to company codes and of personnel sub-areas to personnel areas is done via the path ENTERPRISE STRUCTURE • ASSIGNMENT • HUMAN RESOURCES MANAGEMENT.

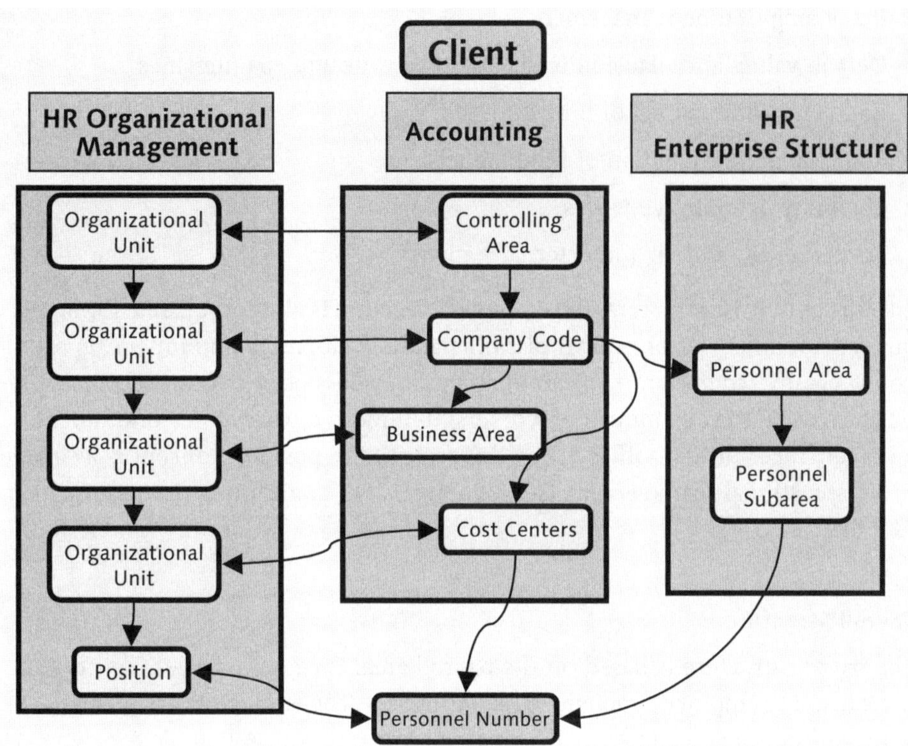

Figure 4.28 Integration Concept of the HR Structures

Employee Structure

Regardless of their enterprise or organizational assignment, employees can be divided into employee groups and subgroups. The employee group is the more general criterion (e.g., regular, retiree, external). The employee subgroup, on the other hand, is generally a more precise criterion (e.g., hourly full-time workers, salaried full-time workers) and is subordinate to the group. An employee subgroup can be permissible in all employee groups or can be limited to just one group. In addition, a specific employee structure can be defined for each country.

The employee structure controls the following aspects:

- Pay scale structure
- Permissibility of wage types
- Processing in payroll

- Processing in time management
- Default values and plausibility checks in the infotype maintenance
- Eligibility and removal of time quotas
- Eligibility and evaluation of time models
- Eligibility of incentive wages
- Treatment in internal and external statistics

Like the enterprise structure, the employee structure is also responsible for numerous control tasks. For personnel planning and development and for HR reporting you generally require more differentiation that is less geared toward formal criteria (such as salaried or industrial workers), but more towards the work duties and tasks (engineer or loan officer). For this reason, the position concept is available in organizational management (see Chapter 5, "Organizational Management in SAP ERP HCM").

Payroll Structure

The payroll structure is based on the payroll area. It contains fewer control functions than the employee and enterprise structures. The employees are merely summarized from the perspective of the payroll organization. All employees who are accounted for on the same day in the same payroll run are assigned to the same payroll area.

In addition to the payroll date, this assignment also controls the following aspects:

- The earliest date possible for retroactive calculation (which can be further limited on the levels of individual employees)
- The release of payroll-relevant data for maintenance

Assignment to a payroll area is done via the corresponding field in Infotype 0001. Default values can be generated for this through various indicators, such as employee personnel area, etc., so that basically, when you hire a new employee the payroll area doesn't need to be entered manually.

As the payroll area exclusively controls the payroll organization it will be described in more detail in Chapter 9, "Payroll."

Further Structures

You can also structure the staff according to many different data elements and, as a matter of fact, you should do so. Most of these data options only affect individual aspects (e.g., an individual infotype and some evaluations).

Examples of additional data (with the relevant infotype indicated):

- Pay scale structure (Infotype 0008)
- Assignment to administrator (Infotype 0001)
- Assignment to a supervisor (Infotype 0001)
- Nationalities (Infotype 0002)
- Gender (Infotype 0002)
- Contract type (Infotype 0016)
- Assignment to travel cost regulations (Infotype 0017)
- Education (Infotype 0022)

Like the personnel area/subarea and employee group/subgroup, the data items in this list always have two functions:

- Control of system behavior, although most of the times in narrowly defined areas
- Selection within evaluation/reporting

The latter is, to some degree, limited in the standard reporting, as not all of the criteria referred to here can be used for selection. For this, however, the system provides a solution through an enhanced selection and a selection via ad hoc queries (see Chapter 11, "Reporting").

Many of these structures can be derived from the main structures. For example, the travel-cost regulation for the employee subgroup Sales representative regarding the use of private cars may be different from the regulation that is valid for the rest of the staff. Therefore, by default, the main structures can be combined under different viewpoints to new structures.

Combining Structural Elements

In the HCM system, deriving a new structure from existing main structures is generally referred to as *grouping*. The term *modifier*, which comes from the days of release 2.2, is also still used. Suitable definition of the basic structures and subsequent grouping is an important customizing activity for personnel administration. This should be carried out in collaboration with an experienced consultant, but should not be put completely in the hands of people outside the enterprise, because an understanding of the structures created is a prerequisite for subsequent maintenance of the system.

A simple example involves the grouping of employee groups and subgroups for the eligibility of primary wage types (wage types entered in infotypes). This enables in-depth control of eligibility and, consequently, of plausibility checks in data entry, without having to enter the wage types that are eligible for each individual employee subgroup.

In Customizing, grouping is basically performed in three ways:

1. **Maintenance views for customizing tables map the given structure in a specified manner to the defined structure (e.g., the assignment of a public holiday calendar to a personnel subarea).**
   In the IMG, these groupings are usually assigned to the relevant aspects at a suitable point. You can access the example of the public holiday calendar via IMG path TIME MANAGEMENT • WORK SCHEDULES • WORK SCHEDULE RULES AND WORK SCHEDULES • DEFINE GROUPINGS FOR THE PUBLIC HOLIDAY CALENDAR, and this is illustrated in Figure 4.29. For the most important groupings, maintenance views V_001P_ALL (personnel areas and subareas) and V_503_ALL (employee groups and subgroups) — which you can reach via Transaction SM31 — provide a very good overview. This type of combination is very easy to maintain. Copying personnel areas, personnel subareas, employee groups, and employee subgroups using the IMG copy tool also copies these groupings.
2. **Features integrate an employee through a decision tree into the new structure.**
   The maintenance of features is described in further detail in Appendix A, "Cross-Process Customizing Tools." For example, let's take a look at feature CONTR, which sets default values for some of the fields of Infotype 0016 and thus performs a structuring with regard to the form of contracts (duration of sick pay, probationary period, notice period). Figure 4.30 shows a simple form of the CONTR feature. Here, all contract elements are set for Australia, Italy, Portugal, and Norway. For Hong Kong and Argentina, only some of the fields are set. Figure 4.31, for example, shows how a certain employee (of a German

personnel area) is assigned to a group of contract elements. As in this example, the return values of a feature can provide default values for specific infotype fields.

Personnel area	Personnel Area Text	Personnel subar...	Pers. subarea text	Holi...
300	Corporate - United States	0001	Philadelphia	US
300	Corporate - United States	0002	Chesterbrook	US
300	Corporate - United States	0003	Los Angeles	US
3000	New York	0001	Manhattan	US
3100	Chicago	0001	Chicago	US
3100	Chicago	0002	St. Louis	US
3100	Chicago	0003	Ohio district	US
3100	Chicago	0004	Minneapolis	US
3200	Atlanta	0001	Atlanta	US
3300	Los Angeles	0001	Foster City	US
3400	Boston	0001	Boston	US
3500	Philadelphia	0001	Philadelphia	US
3600	Corporate - SAPCOE II	0001	Corporate	US
3600	Corporate - SAPCOE II	0002	Electric	US
3600	Corporate - SAPCOE II	0003	Gas	US
S300	Atlanta (Services USA)	0001	Atlanta	US

Figure 4.29 Grouping for the Public Holiday Calendar

Status G

	Variables Argument	F	D	Operationen
000010			D	MOLGA
000020	**			&CONTR= / - / - / -13-13- ,
000030	01		D	PERSG
000040	01 *		D	PERSK
000050	01 * **			&CONTR=42/010-6/012-3/012-13-13-01, "GERMANY
000060	01 1		D	PERSK
000070	01 1 **			&CONTR=42/010-6/012-3/012-13-13-01,
000080	01 1 DU			&CONTR=42/010-1/013-6/012-13-13-01,
000090	27			&CONTR= / - / -3/012-13-10- , " HONG KONG

Figure 4.30 Example of the CONTR Feature

3. **The detail flow of payroll and time evaluation is controlled by calculation rules (see Chapter 8, "Time Management," and Chapter 9).**
   These rules contain similar decision trees in the same way features do, and they can control processing through the main structures.

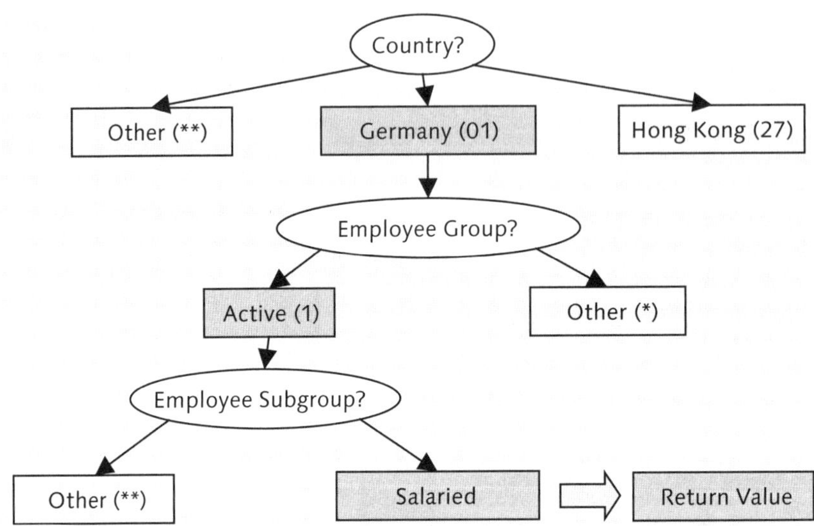

Figure 4.31 Grouping a Specific Employee via the CONTR Feature

When copying structural elements, the features and calculation rules are not automatically updated or appended with the new structural elements. Although the copy tool does provide a list of all potentially affected features, this list contains many standard examples provided by SAP that are not relevant for your specific installation. We therefore recommend that you document in a simple form the use of personnel areas, personnel subareas, employee groups, and employee subgroups in calculation rules and features. By doing so, you can quickly establish which additions are necessary when creating new structural elements.

To simplify the maintenance of calculation rules in the case of structural changes, it is advisable to use the Employee subgroup grouping for personnel calculation rule (see view V_503_ALL). In addition, the decisions derived from the structures should be based on the initializing calculation rules MODT and TMOD (and their customer-specific copies) as much as possible.

Organizational Management

Organizational management is a varied and flexible option to structure the enterprise from an HR perspective, and providing the foundation for position control, structural authorizations, and MSS functions. Organizational management is further described in Chapter 5.

4.3 Selected Infotypes for Personnel Administration

This section describes some important and representative infotypes used in personnel administration. We limited our description to internationally applicable infotypes and tried to avoid national specifics.

4.3.1 Infotype 0000 (Actions)

The action concept is described in further detail in Section 4.4.1.

4.3.2 Infotype 0001 (Organizational Assignment)

Organizational Assignment is one of the most important infotypes and must exist for each employee from the time they are first entered in the system. It is retained even after the employee has left. Most other infotypes can only be entered in the validity period of Infotype 0001. Only infotypes that solely contain personal information and bear no relation to the relationship between the person and the company can start before the beginning of the first organizational assignment. An example of this is Infotype 0002 (Personal Data).

Customizing of the some of the Infotype 0001 data can be reached via IMG path Personnel Management • Personnel Administration • Organizational Data • Organizational Assignment.

Infotype 0001 basically fulfills four functions:

- Classification of the employee in the enterprise structure
- Classification of the employee in the personnel structure
- Classification of the employee in the organizational structure
- Assignment of the employee to support the process structure

First of all, in Infotype 0001, assignment of an employee to a *personnel area* and a *personnel subarea* is entered. Personnel area and subarea are already assigned to a legal entity and a company code (and indirectly a controlling area) is derived as per Customizing, so the employee is also linked to these elements via his Infotype 0001 record. The cost center is also stored and can be maintained in Infotype 0001. However, if the integration into the organizational management is active, the cost center is derived from this and can no longer be changed in Infotype 0001. This situation is also illustrated in Figure 4.32.

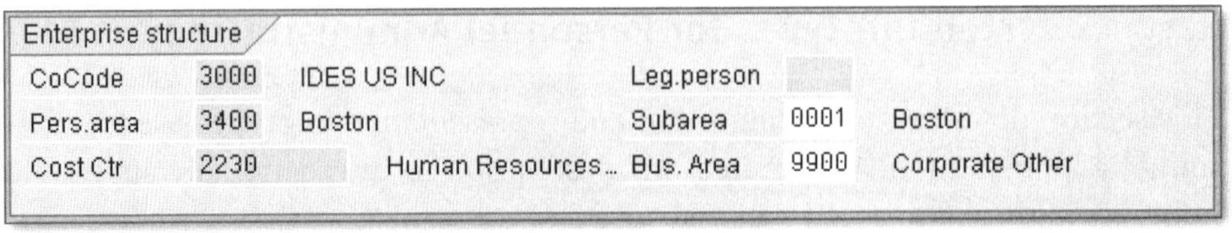

Enterprise structure					
CoCode	3000	IDES US INC	Leg.person		
Pers.area	3400	Boston	Subarea	0001	Boston
Cost Ctr	2230	Human Resources...	Bus. Area	9900	Corporate Other

Figure 4.32 Enterprise Structure in Infotype 0001

Also, the personnel area cannot be changed through simple maintenance in the infotype. To make this change, you must carry out an action (e.g., organizational change), which enables you to change the personnel area (see Section 4.4.1). The reason for this is the importance of control within the personnel area. Making a change without an action and without including other data (e.g., the basic amounts to change the pay scale area) can lead to data inconsistencies. As this danger also exists for other data of Infotype 0001, the company-specific conditions should be checked. From this check, conventions can be derived for which an action is needed via Infotypes 0000/0302 for organizational changes, for reasons of data quality or evaluation. Generally, when integration with organizational management is active, most of the data in Infotype 0001 defaults based on the organizational management integration points.

The business area can be freely maintained. Its use must comply with accounting, as it will also be transferred into accounting through the posting interface of the payroll.

With regard to direct maintenance for *employee group* and *subgroup*, the same conditions apply as those of the personnel area. The payroll area can basically be freely accessed. In general, though, it is derived from other fields of Infotype 0001. Therefore, you can use the feature ABKRS to implement a system default of the payroll area value, e.g., depending on the employee group. In the example in Figure 4.33 the payroll area U.S. is suggested based on the employee subgroup.

The work contract field is maintained in specific circumstances, such as in Germany for different statistics based on legal limits; it can normally be derived through the employee subgroup. For other countries, this field should be used for individual analyses, if necessary. You can store the possible adjustments in Customizing for Infotype 0001.

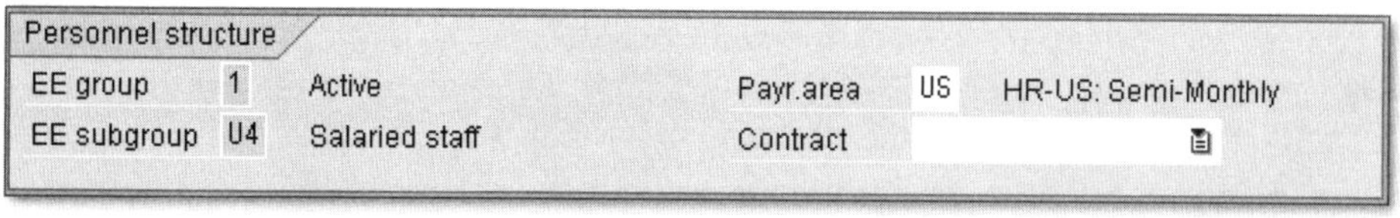

Personnel structure					
EE group	1	Active	Payr.area	US	HR-US: Semi-Monthly
EE subgroup	U4	Salaried staff	Contract		

Figure 4.33 Personnel Structure in Infotype 0001

Infotype 0001 enables the assignment of employees to *organizational units*, *positions*, and *jobs*. This can also be done without using the Organizational Management module, but this is not a practical approach in today's enterprise environment and should be considered only in very rare and exceptional company situations. You can create the corresponding organizational objects by customizing the infotype in simple tables, but this does not allow you to map any real structure. For this reason, and because of the additional functionalities, the use of organizational management is strongly advised.

Integration of organizational management is effected in two steps:

1. In IMG path PERSONNEL MANAGEMENT • ORGANIZATIONAL MANAGEMENT • INTEGRATION • INTEGRATION WITH PERSONNEL ADMINISTRATION • SET UP INTEGRATION WITH PERSONNEL ADMINISTRATION the entry PLOGI-ORGA in the Basic settings must be set to X (see Figure 4.34). There are more control options in the same table, and these are well-documented. You cannot access the documentation intuitively, instead, position the cursor on the entry in the column Sem. Abbr. (semantic code) and click on the Documentation button (see Figure 4.34). Do not become confused by the seemingly technical appearance of the table. It is only a collection of individual control indicators that are each individually documented. Different views of this table will be presented frequently throughout Customizing in SAP HCM.
2. Now that the integration is basically activated, in the second step you must establish which employees participate in the integration. In some companies these are all employees; in others contractors or temporary workers are excluded. This control can be carried out through the feature PLOGI, which you can reach through the same IMG path. In the simple example in Figure 4.35 the integration is activated for all employees.

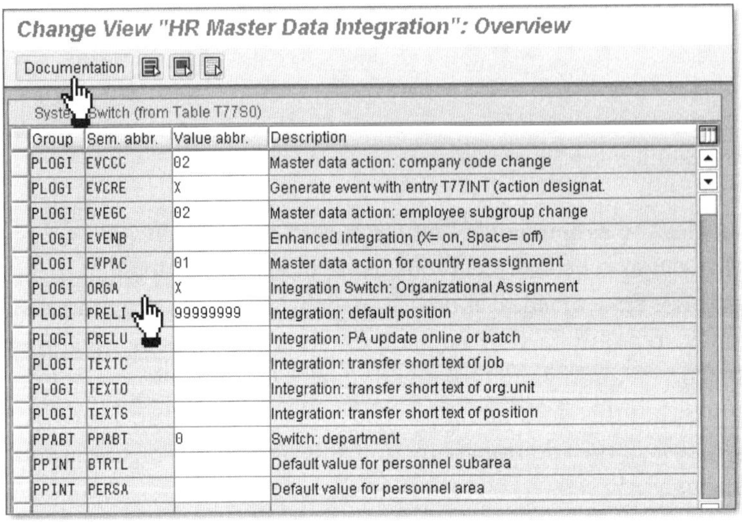

Change View "HR Master Data Integration": Overview

Documentation

System Switch (from Table T77S0)

Group	Sem. abbr.	Value abbr.	Description
PLOGI	EVCCC	02	Master data action: company code change
PLOGI	EVCRE	X	Generate event with entry T77INT (action designat.
PLOGI	EVEGC	02	Master data action: employee subgroup change
PLOGI	EVENB		Enhanced integration (X= on, Space= off)
PLOGI	EVPAC	01	Master data action for country reassignment
PLOGI	ORGA	X	Integration Switch: Organizational Assignment
PLOGI	PRELI	99999999	Integration: default position
PLOGI	PRELU		Integration: PA update online or batch
PLOGI	TEXTC		Integration: transfer short text of job
PLOGI	TEXTO		Integration: transfer short text of org.unit
PLOGI	TEXTS		Integration: transfer short text of position
PPABT	PPABT	0	Switch: department
PPINT	BTRTL		Default value for personnel subarea
PPINT	PERSA		Default value for personnel area

Figure 4.34 Control Options for the Integration into Organizational Management

For active integration you only have to maintain the position in Infotype 0001. Job and organizational unit (and cost center) are then automatically derived from the position assignment. The organization of this structure is described in more detail in Chapter 5.

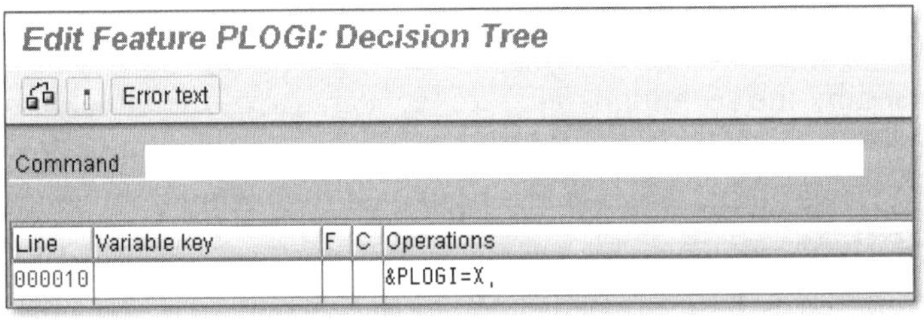

Edit Feature PLOGI: Decision Tree

Error text

Command

Line	Variable key	F	C	Operations
000010				&PLOGI=X,

Figure 4.35 Integration through the Feature PLOGI is Usually Active

The organizational key is, in many cases, a very helpful field. It can be populated manually or according to fixed rules from further fields of Infotype 0001 (also through nondisplayed fields such as the employee name). It is also possible to provide a table with permitted entry values. In the example in Figure 4.36, the organizational key includes the personnel area and cost center (with leading zeros). How it is composed and whether the value determined can be manually overwritten are defined by Customizing for Infotype 0001 (Set up Organizational Key).

The organizational key is not only available as a selection criterion for most of the reports but is also available in the authorization check. For example, you can use it to carry out an authorization check indirectly through cost centers (which is not possible directly) or through combining the personnel area and the employee group (if your processing is organized in this manner).

Note: Evaluation of Defaulted Fields

The following information is important for programming and also for creating queries: The data derived from the organizational management (cost center, organizational unit, and job) and the company code derived from customizing that populate Infotype 0001 are redundantly saved in the database in the relevant infotype record. They are not dynamically derived when the infotype is called. This simplifies programming.

Assigning an employee to *administrators* as the last function of the Infotype 0001 (see Figure 4.37) can be regarded as an aspect of organizational structure. However, this assignment mainly serves to control the process structure within the personnel department. In the HCM system, the assignment particularly affects:

- Dynamically generated emails that are directed to the responsible administrator (see Section 4.4.2)
- Authorization for the HR master record maintenance
- Employee information regarding his responsible administrator (e.g., on the remuneration statement)
- Selection criteria for reporting
- Task monitoring per administrator (see Section 4.3.6)

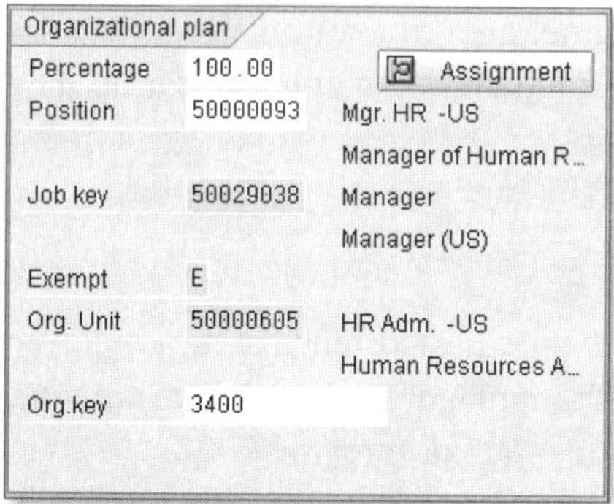

Figure 4.36 Organizational Structure in Infotype 0001

SAP ERP HCM provides three administrator fields. The supervisor field can be used as a further assignment, though that does not deliver the same functionality.

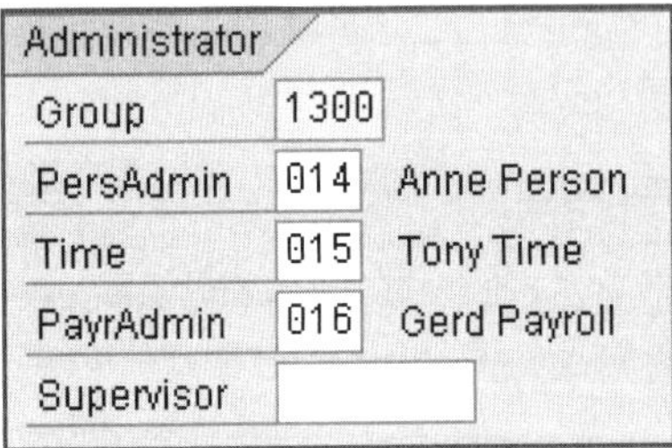

Figure 4.37 Infotype 0001 Also Supports the Process Structure

First, the employee is assigned to an administrator group. All administrators of this group can then be assigned in Infotype 0001.

The administrators must be defined in the Customizing for Infotype 0001. During this process, they are divided by administrator group but not by administrator type, that is, all transactional users can be assigned to the relevant group respectively as time, payroll, or HR administrators. To structure this cleanly, it is advisable that you create number conventions. Names, phone numbers, and SAP user names in particular are maintained per administrator. The user names are required to guarantee the functionality of dynamic emails (see Section 4.4.2).

Assigning an employee to the administrator group is done through the feature PINCH (similarly in Customizing for Infotype 0001). It allows for a separation by employees and applicants (for recruitment, the same administrator table is used) and the automatic transfer of the personnel area code as the administrator group. If the administrators are assigned per personnel area, the automatic transfer is quite useful because the feature then also remains unchanged if you set up new personnel areas.

4.3.3 Infotype 0002 (Personal Data)

Infotype 0002 is a critical infotype because it defines the existence of the employee as a person by storing names and date of birth (see Figure 4.38). Other infotypes for the person cannot exist before the beginning date of Infotype 0002.

The data saved in Infotype 0002 is also strongly dependent on the country. In the U.S., for example, a social security number is saved. In other countries, various numbers for legally required notifications must be maintained. Insofar as other countries are not supported by the system as delivered, an enhancement of the infotype is required.

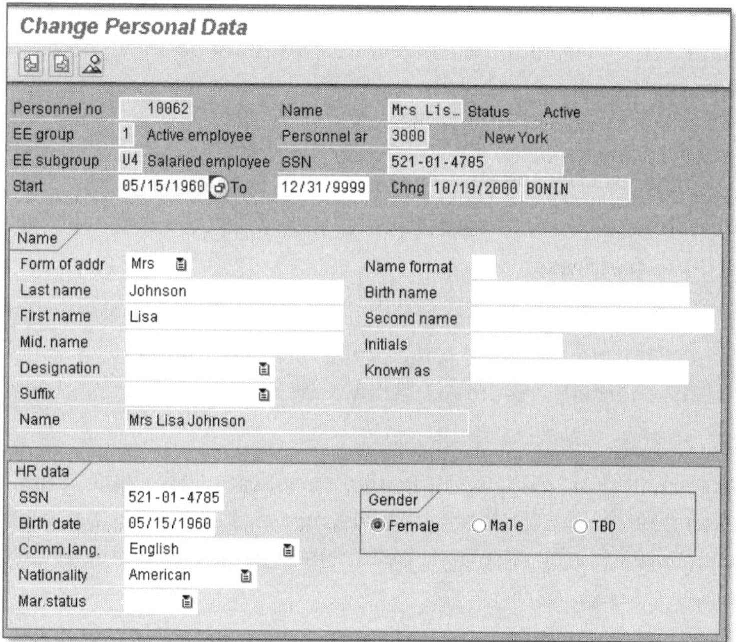

Figure 4.38 Infotype 0002 (Personal Data)

One important field in Infotype 0002 is Language. This serves not only as additional information but is also used at certain points of the system if documents or emails are output for the employee.

For example, when outputting the time statement you can determine that it is to be created in the employee's language. In this case, the language field of Infotype 0002 is relevant. Therefore, if you create the documents for the employees in a selection of languages (e.g., English, German, Spanish, and French), but not necessarily in the mother tongue of the employee (e.g., Croatian), this field should be populated with the chosen language of communication. The mother tongue can then be maintained for information purposes in another place (e.g., in a customer-specific field or as a qualification in the component for personnel development or in Infotype 0024 (Qualifications)).

Customizing for Infotype 0002 can be found via IMG path PERSONNEL MANAGEMENT • PERSONNEL ADMINISTRATION • PERSONAL DATA • PERSONAL DATA. Pay particular attention to the name formatting Customizing. In the standard version it has a country-specific design. As a result, the formatted name (as stored in Infotype 0001 (Table PA0001)) is displayed in different ways in evaluations for the employees, depending on the respective country. However, if this is not desired, you need to configure it via Customizing.

For the U.S., there is also Infotype 0077 (Additional Personal Data), in which data on military status, veteran status, and disability are maintained.

4.3.4 Infotype 0006 (Address)

Addresses contain probably the most country-specific information besides the data on net payroll (tax, social insurance, etc.). One of the most obvious reasons is the difference in postal code formats. Figure 4.39 shows the standard delivery screen for the U.S.

Beside the address format, there can also be further specifications for other countries. In the German payroll version, the field Distance in kilometers (between place of residence and workplace) calculates the imputed income of company cars (together with Infotype 0032).

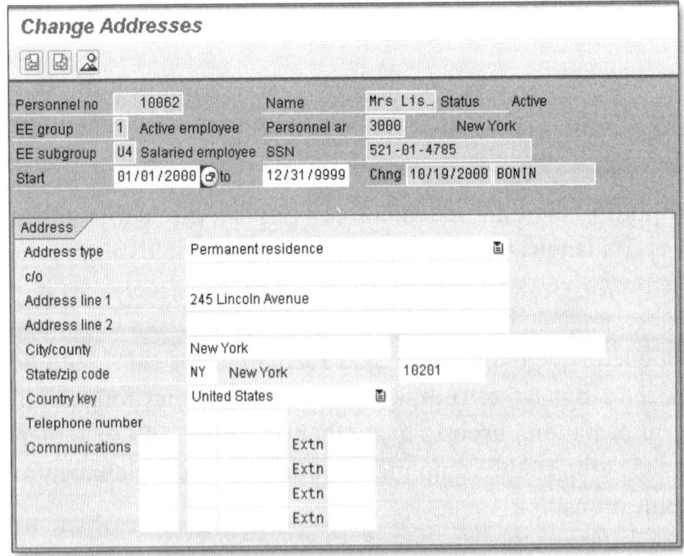

Figure 4.39 U.S. Address Data

When creating a new address record you can use the Foreign address button to select another country. This allows you to enter an address in the Mexico country format, for example (see Figure 4.40.) In addition, Infotype 0006 offers several subtypes. Here, you can enter temporary residences, for example. The subtype Permanent residence is generally used when outputting correspondence. In some cases this can be controlled by customizing or directly by the application.

Customizing for Infotype 0006 can be found via IMG path PERSONNEL MANAGEMENT • PERSONNEL ADMINISTRATION • PERSONAL DATA • ADDRESSES.

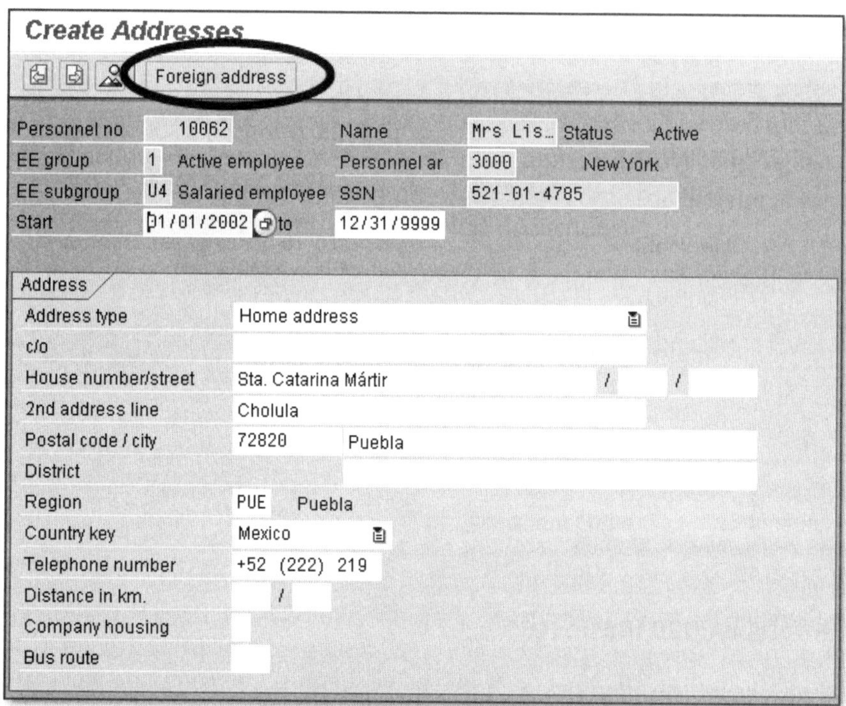

Figure 4.40 Foreign Address in Mexico

There is a standard application in ESS for changing an address (see Figure 4.41). However, in the German payroll version, Infotype 0006 also includes the distance in kilometers that is used, for example, to calculate the imputed income of company cars and therefore has an influence on payroll. Thus, you shouldn't change Infotype 0006 without further checks. You can handle this problem efficiently by means of dynamic actions (see Section 4.4.2) that inform the responsible administrator when Infotype 0006 is changed and a company car is used.

Figure 4.41 Maintaining the Address

4.3.5 Infotype 0008 (Basic Pay)

Customizing for Infotype 0008 is quite extensive, because the complete pay scale structure is integrated. Figure 4.42 shows an example of a salaried employee with a single indirectly valuated wage type in Infotype 0008, representing a semimonthly salary. Indirect evaluation is treated in detail in Chapter 9. This basically means that the amount of the wage type is not manually but indirectly maintained (e.g., through a pay-scale table or derived from other wage types). This is indicated by the I next to the currency column. To decrease the maintenance effort and to increase the data quality, indirect evaluation should be used as frequently as possible.

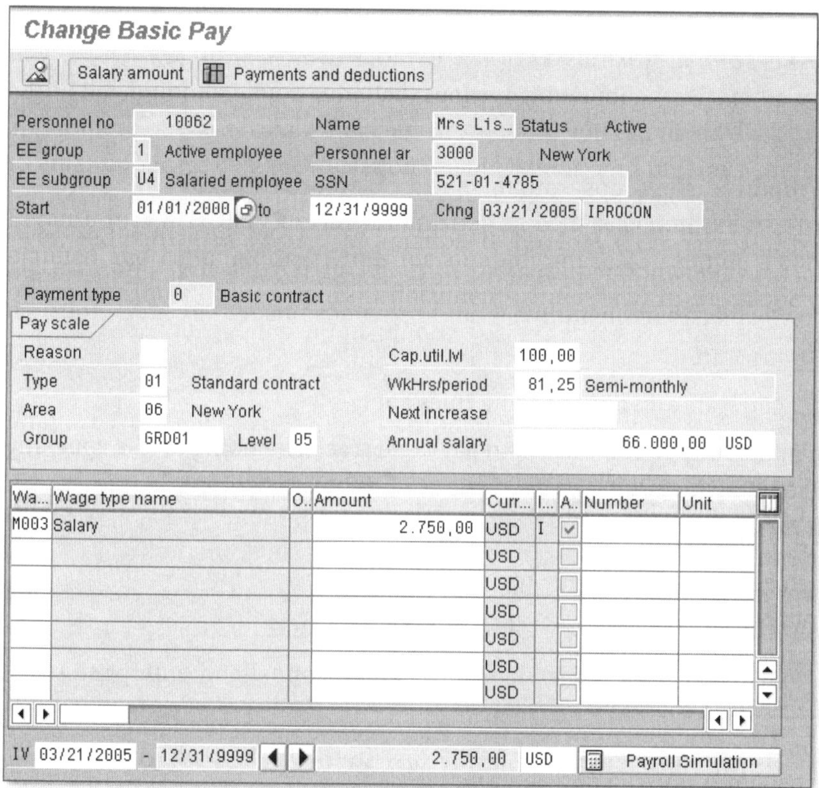

Figure 4.42 Basic Pay with Indirect Evaluation through Pay Scale

Note: Avoid Manual Maintenance of Indirectly Evaluated Wage Types!

A frequent application error is that a wage type to be indirectly evaluated is changed manually because, for example, the pay-scale table has not yet been updated. From this time on, however, the wage type of this employee is directly evaluated (the "I" is omitted), and the next update of the pay-scale table does not have any impact. Where possible, you should customize indirectly evaluated wage types so that the amounts cannot be manually overwritten.

In one record of Infotype 0008, you can enter 40 wage types (up to release 4.6C you can only enter 20). This is usually not required, though, if you really limit yourself to the basic pay and use Infotypes 0014 (Recurring Payments and Deductions) and 0015 (Additional Payments and Deductions).

Customizing of Infotype 0008 can be performed via IMG path PERSONNEL MANAGEMENT • PERSONNEL ADMINISTRATION • PAYROLL DATA • BASIC PAY. There, you must essentially make the following settings that are documented in detail in the IMG:

- Group employee subgroups from the pay-scale point of view

  Do not differentiate more than is necessary, as each grouping created results in additional maintenance requirements throughout payroll and time management customizing tables!
- Pay-scale structure

  Combine pay-scale areas, if the same rules apply.
- Default values for pay-scale type and pay-scale area, depending on the company and personnel structure
- Pay-scale tables
- Working time according to pay scale
- Establish which wage types are allowed for basic pay
- Default values for wage types, depending on personnel and enterprise structure

  This item is particularly helpful. In the first step (via the path WAGE TYPES • ENTERPRISE STRUCTURE FOR WAGE TYPE MODEL) you determine codes for the wage-type models, depending on your specific structures, via the feature LGMST. These codes are populated in the next step (via the path WAGE TYPES • REVISE DEFAULT WAGE TYPES). This eventually determines which wage types are actually suggested and if they can be manually changed. The time that you invest here pays off in the form of more efficient processes.
- Display a button through which you can reference the simulation of the employee's payroll

  This functionality is very useful for payroll administrators.

4.3.6 Infotype 0019 (Monitoring of Tasks)

Infotype 0019 enables you to create tracking deadlines for different subjects (date types). These, however, do not trigger pop-ups to appear when you log onto a system, similar to the way some email and calendar systems do. This would not be an appropriate function due to the number of deadlines an HR administrator generally has to observe. For example, there can be a flood of deadlines at the end of the quarter (end of the probationary period, phasing out of part-time agreements, etc.). In general, it is more useful for the administrator to determine his own work rhythm and check the deadlines at a suitable time, for example, when probationary periods are due to expire during the coming four weeks. A convenient report is provided via the menu path HUMAN RESOURCES • PERSONNEL MANAGEMENT • ADMINISTRATION • INFOSYSTEM • REPORTS • EMPLOYEE • DATE MONITORING.

You enter the tasks to be monitored in Infotype 0019 (see Figure 4.43). In most cases (e.g., missing social insurance number, the end of a temporary work contract, etc.) you can create default settings for task monitoring via a dynamic action so that the administrator only has to save it. At this point it is worthwhile to exploit the benefits of dynamic processes (see Section 4.4.2).

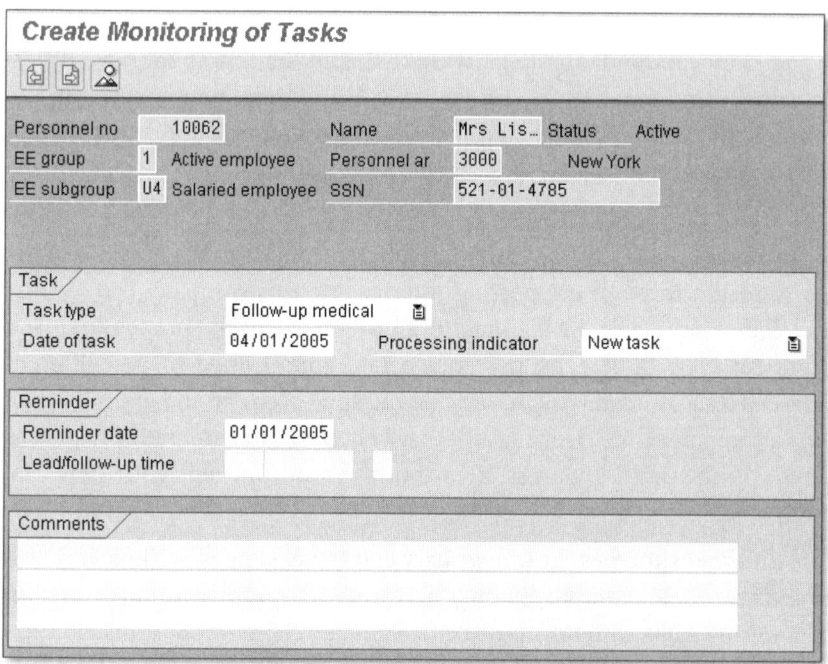

Figure 4.43 Task Monitoring in the Follow-up Medical Example

Customizing of task monitoring can be performed through the IMG path PERSONNEL MANAGEMENT • PERSONNEL ADMINISTRATION • EVALUATION BASIS • MONITORING OF TASKS. There, you only have to create the different task types and characterize them with regard to the lead time. Please note that while doing this the administrator who monitors the deadlines, and the employees or management to be involved, often require some lead time. Always create a task type other deadlines that can be further characterized via user-defined text depending on the situation.

4.3.7 Infotype 0027 (Cost Distribution)

In many cases, employee costs are distributed across several cost centers over long periods of time. This can be very easily done via Infotype 0027 (see Figure 4.44). However, you should note the following:

- For evaluations in SAP ERP HCM the employee is always selected under his master cost center from Infotype 0001.
- Enter only the portions that differ from the master cost center in Infotype 0027; the rest will be automatically posted to the master cost center. If you enter the master cost center redundantly (e.g., with 75%) and the rest at 25% to a different cost center, the new master cost center will be completely ignored in the case of an organizational change and the old cost center will still be debited at 75%. In certain circumstances, it is useful to integrate Infotype 0027 in the organizational change action.
- Even if a different company code is entered here — if, for example, 25% of the expense is posted through the posting interface on this company code — the company code that makes the payment is always 100% of the master company code from Infotype 0001. The percentage rate apportioned to the different company code accumulates to the document split account and must be balanced via a company code clearing. Alternatively, you can automatically post to company-code-clearing accounts. This must be reconciled with financial accounting.
- There are different subtypes for wage/salary and travel expenses. Thus, it is possible to indicate that an employee only performs 10% of his working time but 50% of his trips for a different cost center. Since release 4.6B, a distribution from the wage/salary subtype is completely ignored by the Travel Expense module. In previous releases or old patch levels, the distribution of wage/salary is considered for travel expenses as well — if no travel expenses subtype is maintained.
- Besides cost centers, you can distribute the costs to orders or projects (WBS elements). In the public sector there are also funds available.

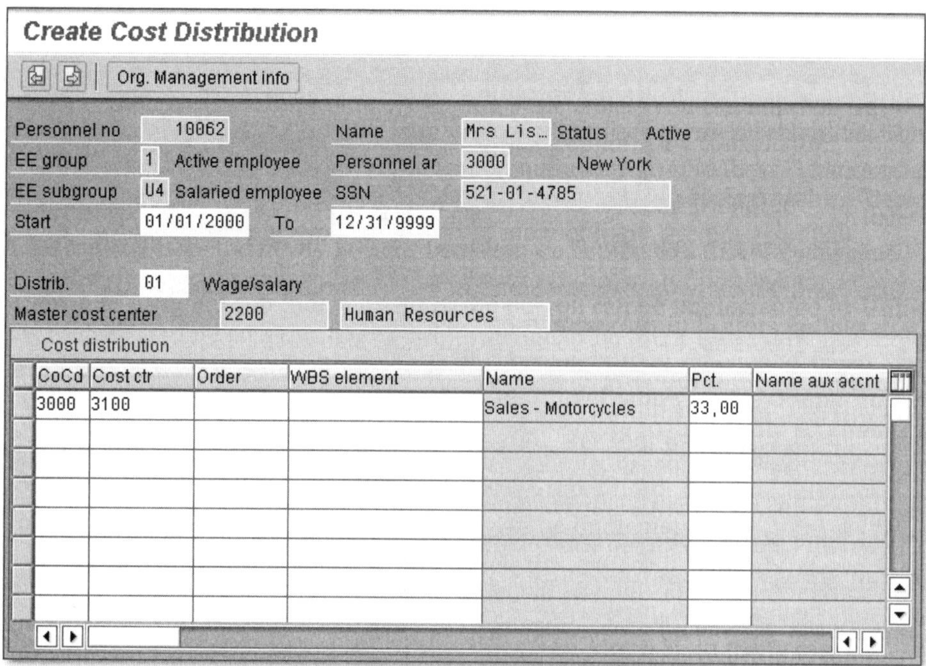

Figure 4.44 Cost Distribution to the Cost Center

4.3.8 Infotype 0011 (External Transfers)

External Transfers can trigger any number of employee-related payment transfers to a third party, which are generally retained from the net amount paid to the employee. Examples include rent payments or loan repayments, which in some countries (e.g., Slovenia) are frequently directly transferred by the employer.

The infotype can also be used to make up for missing country-specific requirements such as garnishments in country versions which do not support specific garnishment processes. In these cases, the specific checks and calculations are not supported but at least the process can be reflected in an integrated manner.

In addition to the transfer to predefined recipients, which are created in Customizing for Infotype 0011, recipient data can also be entered directly (see Figure 4.45).

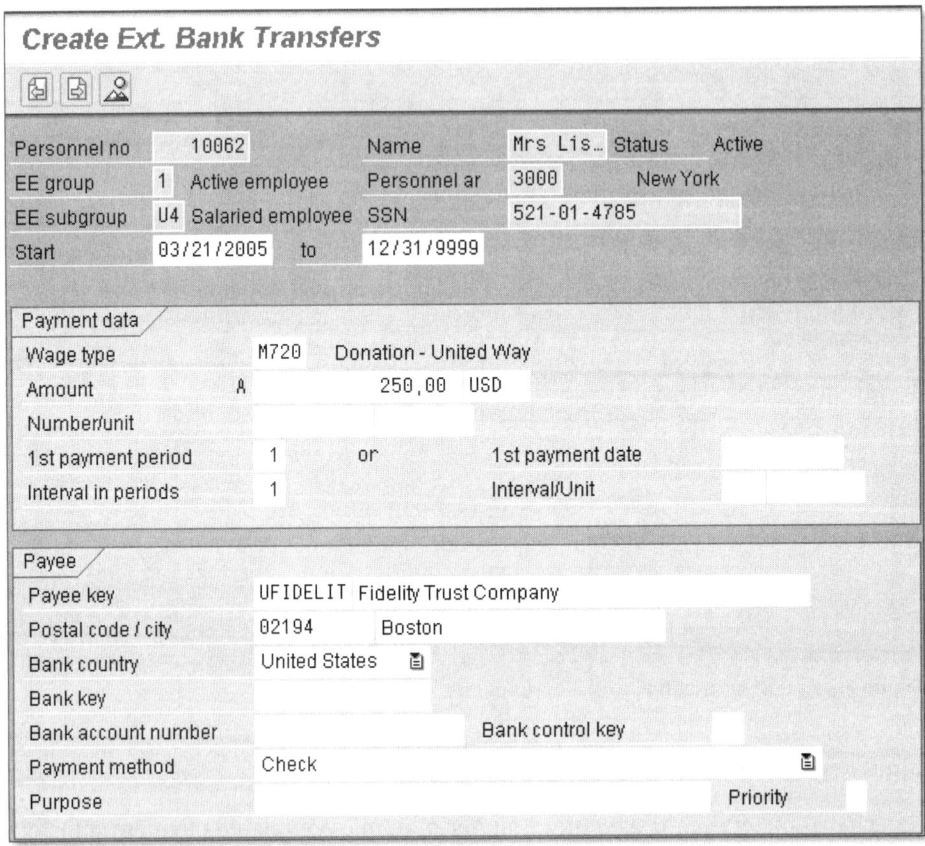

Figure 4.45 External Bank Transfer

4.3.9 Infotype 0022 (Education)

In Infotype 0022, the education of an employee is documented. This can include school and high school attendance but also individual training courses. The latter can be documented in Infotype 0022 if training and event management is not implemented, or if you choose not to define education in the qualification catalogue in Personnel Development. Figure 4.46 shows the documentation of education.

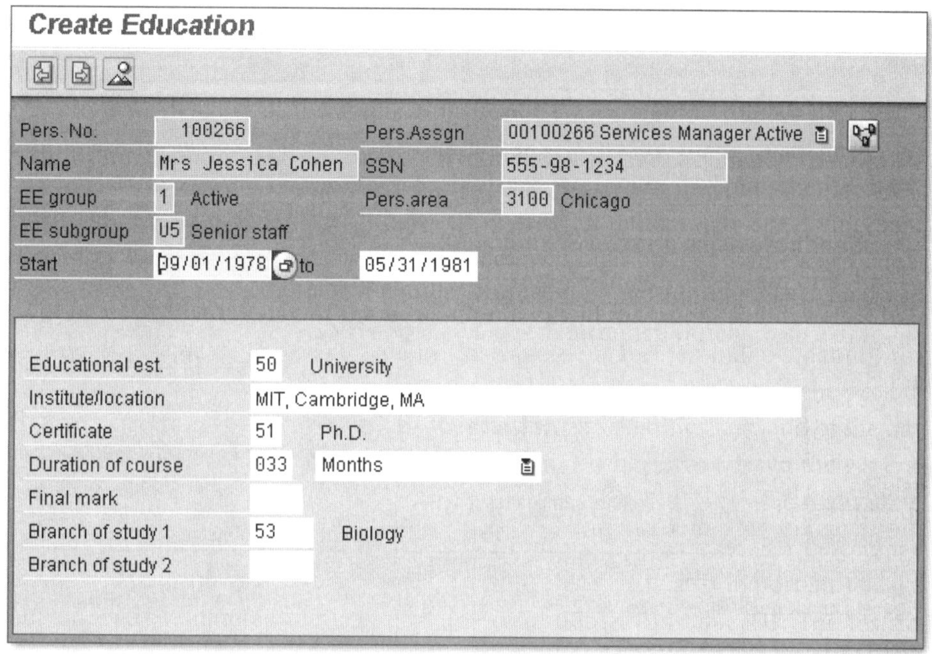

Figure 4.46 Education in Infotype 0022

For each phase of school and professional training (elementary school, high school, etc.) an individual record for the infotype is created. The central concept in Infotype 0022 is the educational establishment type (high school, business school, etc.). It defines the following:

- Which certificates are available for the entry?
- Which branches of study are permissible?
- Is it a course? (There are additional input fields for a course, see Figure 4.47.)

Tip: Handling of Repayment Obligations

If the validity period of an Infotype 0022 record with a repayment obligation is still relevant when an employee leaves the company, you can include a display of this infotype in the leaving action, and the transactional user will be automatically notified of the due repayment at the time the employee leaves the company.

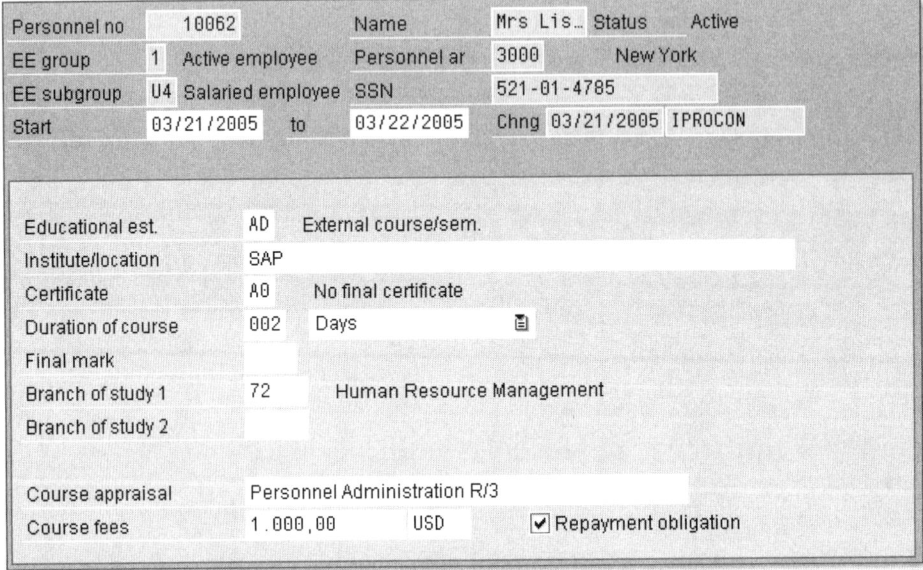

Figure 4.47 Course in Infotype 0022

Customizing is carried out via the IMG path PERSONNEL MANAGEMENT • PERSONNEL ADMINISTRATION • EMPLOYEE QUALIFICATIONS • EDUCATION AND TRAINING. Here, you must carry out the following steps:

- Create the permissible school types and flag as "course," if necessary
- Create the permissible certificates and branches of study
- Assign the certificates and branches of study to the corresponding school types

Through this structure it is possible to assign a certificate or a branch of study to several school types. For example, a high school degree can be earned at a public or a private school.

The field Education/training (hidden in SAP standard delivery and in Figure 4.48) is completely separate from the school type in Customizing. This means that every school type can be combined in the entry with every type of education/training. In general, the field is used to enter a professional training or a study goal. Permissible educations are similarly defined through the aforementioned IMG path and combined into categories (e.g., degrees in business or degrees in language). The education and training category can then be used for evaluation purposes.

The education data of employees is indeed frequently required, but in many companies it is not entered because the data entry is quite complex.

A solution to this problem could be to delegate the entry to the employee himself.

4.3.10 Infotype 0077 (Additional Personal Data)

Apart from standard personal data stored in Infotype 0002, other personal data is stored in Infotype 0077. Information in this infotype is used mainly for statistical and legal reporting purpose.

For some employers in the U.S., it is a legal requirement to submit periodic reports containing the following information:

- **Ethnic origin**
  This is the only required field for this infotype. The standard values are delivered by SAP. You can define your own values via IMG path Personnel Administration • Personal Data • Additional Personal Data • Enter Ethnic Origin.

  Note that as of version 4.6C new changes were delivered in accordance to U.S. Federal standards that allow the selection of multiple race entries and an increased number of ethnicities.
- **Race data**
  Check the race(s) applicable to the employee.
- **Military status**
  Stores the military information of the employee. The possible values can be maintained via IMG path Personnel Administration • Personal Data • Additional Personal Data • Enter Military Status.
- **Veteran status**
- **Disability**
  If this infotype is used, we recommend that you have this information record included in the New Hire Action. Authorizations to access this infotype should be strictly controlled because it contains confidential personal information.

Note

SAP now offers a support package for release 4.6C and above.

4.3.11 Infotype 0094 (Residence Status)

According to the U.S. *Immigration Reform and Control Act (IRCA)*, an employer must verify if an employee is legally allowed to work in the U.S. The employee needs to provide proper identification and other legal documents. Infotype 0094 can be used to store residency status and other information collected during the verification process and later used for statistics and reporting. The information is divided into two parts:

Personal identification

Residency status indicates the legal status of the employee. Standard settings include:

A Nonresident alien

C Citizen

N Noncitizen resident

ID types, ID number, and ID expiration date are used to record the ID used for the employee's identification.

Employment Verification

Work permit type, number, and expiry of work permit are used to store information on work permits issued by authorities. Those fields are only for non-U.S. citizens.

If the Expiry of Work Perm field is filled and the residence status is set to A (nonresident alien) in the Personal Identification section, upon saving, the system can prompt the user to create an Infotype 0019 (Monitoring of Tasks) subtype 71 (work permit expires).

You can change the customizing by the IMG path PERSONNEL ADMINISTRATION • PERSONAL DATA • RESIDENCE STATUS • RESIDENCE STATUS. By selecting different options in the Choose Activity window, you can define residence status, ID types, and work permit types.

4.3.12 Infotypes for U.S. Employee Tax Information

There are several infotypes used to store tax information for U.S. payroll. Those infotypes serve the legal requirements and are therefore of great importance. The data accuracy must be ensured to allow correct net payroll calculations.

Infotype 0207 (Residence Tax Area) is the U.S.-specific infotype that stores the residence tax area of the employee. An employee's taxation largely depends on the residence tax area. The net payroll calculation reads this infotype for taxation purpose. The U.S. tax calculation is partly done by a third-party tool, *BSI TaxFactory*, which is described in Chapter 9.

Infotype 0208 (Employee's Work Tax Area) is needed when the employee works in more than one locality within one tax year and is required to pay tax to a work location other than the resident tax area. The tax-area information in Infotype 0208 overrides information in Infotype 0207 to a certain percentage. Thus, the tax can be distributed to different work areas and residence areas proportionally. The IMG path for setting up a tax area in the U.S. would be PAYROLL • TAX • TAX DATA MAINTENANCE • TAX AREAS.

Infotype 0209 (Unemployment State) is another infotype related to U.S. tax. It is used to assign an unemployment state for an employee's payment of unemployment insurance.

Most of the customizing for those infotypes is delivered by SAP as a standard setting for U.S. taxation. Although the user can make changes to the settings in IMG, it is recommended that you update the tax area only through the HR Hot Packages (formerly known as LCP).

4.4 Actions in Personnel Administration

To support actions in personnel administration, three concepts are available that vary in their implementation with regard to their flexibility and complexity. Figure 4.48 provides a brief overview of these alternative concepts.

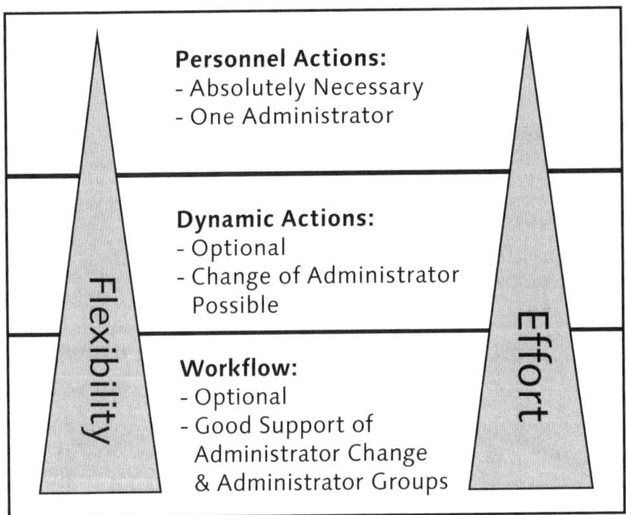

Figure 4.48 Alternatives to Support Process Flows

4.4.1 Personnel Actions

A personnel action essentially fulfills two tasks:

First, it allows you to maintain a previously defined sequence of infotypes, without each infotype having to be called individually. This saves time and also ensures quality as it supports the observance of standard procedures. It represents a sort of mini-workflow in which the transactional user doesn't change.

Second, it documents essential events in the history of an employee. In particular, the change of different attributes of an employee can only be effected via an action (e.g., employee group and subgroup, personnel area, and employment status). This further enables quality assurance — the attributes referred to have an extensive control function in the master data area. For example, if the employee subgroup is changed without checking the infotypes controlled by it, there will more than likely be inconsistencies. An example would be changing the employee subgroups to non-pay-scale employees while there is still pay-scale pay stored in the basic pay infotype. When making a change via an action, all of the critical infotypes can be integrated in the process so that no essential adjustment is overlooked.

Examples of personnel actions are:

- Hire
- Leave
- Retirement
- Organizational change
- Promotion
- Increase of basic pay
- Beginning of semi-retirement
- Beginning of a part-time employment during parental leave

Personnel actions are basically saved in Infotype 0000 (Actions). The list screen of this infotype gives an overview of the history of the employee (see Figure 4.49).

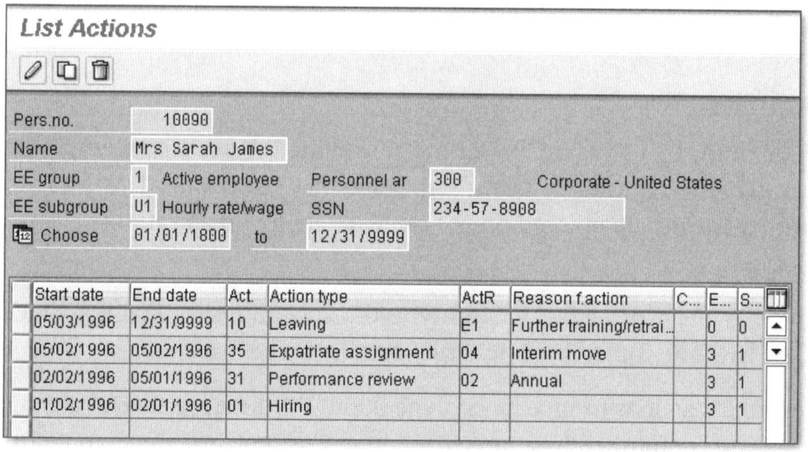

List Actions

Pers.no. 10090
Name Mrs Sarah James
EE group 1 Active employee Personnel ar 300 Corporate - United States
EE subgroup U1 Hourly rate/wage SSN 234-57-8908
Choose 01/01/1800 to 12/31/9999

Start date	End date	Act.	Action type	ActR	Reason f.action	C...	E...	S...
05/03/1996	12/31/9999	10	Leaving	E1	Further training/retrai...		0	0
05/02/1996	05/02/1996	35	Expatriate assignment	04	Interim move		3	1
02/02/1996	05/01/1996	31	Performance review	02	Annual		3	1
01/02/1996	02/01/1996	01	Hiring				3	1

Figure 4.49 List Screen of the Actions

Infotype 0000 saves the type and reason for the processes, and also the status of the employee regarding employment and special payments, and a customer-specific status. In general, every status is available in reporting as a selection criterion. The type of action controls the infotype sequence to be maintained, and, like the action reason, also serves informational purposes.

In addition, action type and reason have different country- and industry-specific control functionalities, for example:

- Germany: Reasons for notification (public social security)
- Austria: Damaging actions/action reasons to determine tax days
- Switzerland: Exceptional actions concerning reduced working hours
- Spain: Seniority calculation

Employment Status

Employment status is quite significant. It determines whether an employee is active in the company. Non-active statuses determine whether workers are withdrawn, inactive, or retired.

Employment status is considered in reports and processes such as payroll, time management, travel management, company pension plans, training and event management, compensation management, and organizational management. For example, after they leave, employees cannot be posted to training sessions and receive no basic pay.

Additional Actions

Infotype 0000 must, by its nature, have time constraint 1. After all, an employee cannot have two different employment statuses at the same time. This leads to problems if two actions are entered on the same day (e.g., organizational change and promotion).

The solution has been provided by Infotype 0302 (Additional Actions) since Release 4.0. It has time constraint 3 and can basically save all actions.

Determining which actions to save in Infotype 0000 —if there are several actions on one day — is accomplished by a prioritization in Customizing. Here, you must ensure that actions that change the status must always save a record in Infotype 0000 and therefore must not conflict with one another.

As Infotype 0000 is generally incomplete due to the actions carried out on the same day, Infotype 0302 should always be evaluated for self-created queries or reports. Customizing should always be controlled so that all processes are stored in Infotype 0302 — even those that are already saved in Infotype 0000. This leads to the following division for evaluations through query and custom developments:

- Evaluation via actions and action reasons (related to key dates): Infotype 0302
- Evaluations via the status of an employee (related to the period): Infotype 0000

Infotype 0000 is suitable for display in the master data. The additional actions that occur in the period of the record displayed are shown in the display (see Figure 4.50). A direct maintenance or display of Infotype 0302 in the HR master data is not possible.

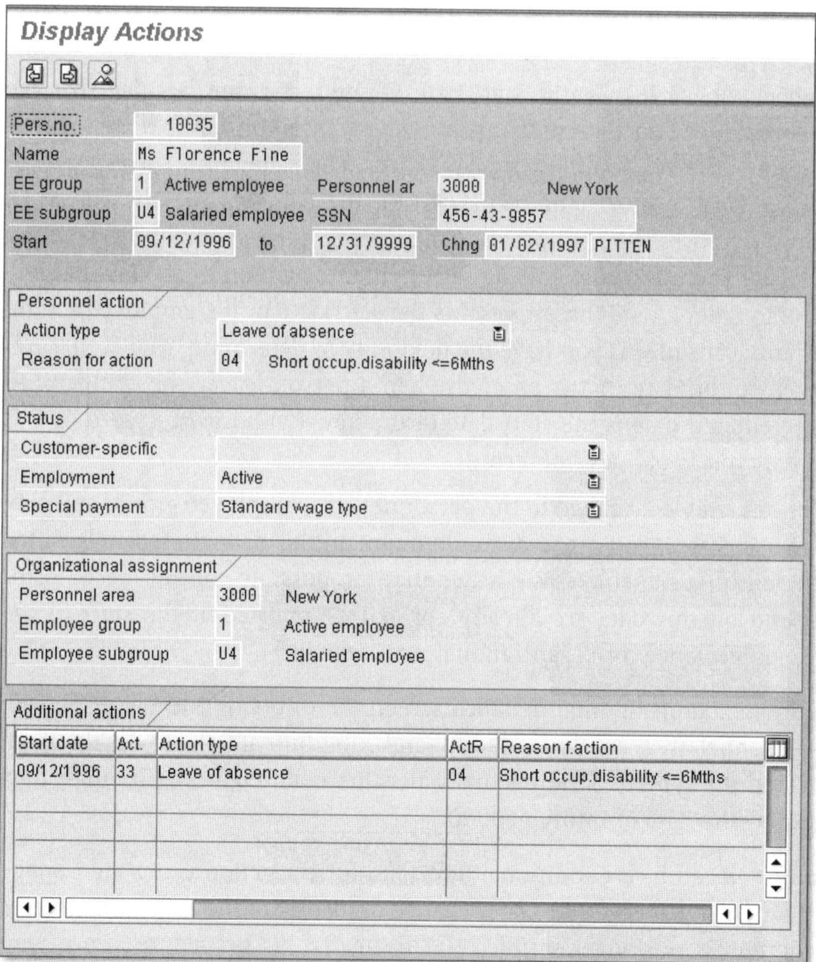

Figure 4.50 Single Screen Actions with Integrated View of the Actions to be Added

Data Maintenance in Actions

Actions are called through the *action menu* via the SAP Easy Access menu path Human Resources • Personnel Management • Administration • HR Master Data • Personnel Actions.

After selecting a personnel number, a start date, and the desired action, the action is launched via the Execute button. Please note the following special characteristics:

- No personnel number is entered for a setting as long as no external personnel number allocation is activated.
- When an employee leaves, the start date is entered as the last day that the employee belonged to the company. However, Infotype 0000 is then saved with the start date of the following day. Thus, while the entry corresponds to common language use (left on 12/31/2006), the data is correctly stored for evaluation purposes (the employee still counts as a member of staff on 12/31/2006). There is a customizing setting in the creation of actions that will allow you to enter a date that represents the start date of the employee's withdrawn status. This means you have the flexibility to determine what scenario is best suited to the date that is entered when a person leaves the company — either the entered date is the start date of the new (withdrawn) record or it is the end date of the old (active) record.
- Some actions enable a change to the personnel area, employee group, and subgroup. In such cases, you can and should maintain this data immediately in the action menu (first screen). This ensures that the possible control mechanisms that depend on this data are already correctly supported at the start of the action (e.g., relevance for organizational management).

After calling an action, the maintenance screen for Infotype 0000 is displayed. Position, personnel area, employee group, and subgroup are already maintained here (provided the type of action actually permits maintenance), although they actually display the data of Infotype 0000.

At this point you can insert additional infotypes for the action using the Change info group function. However, in a later change or display of the action, the change to the infogroup is no longer visible, which means this procedure is not very advantageous. The concept of the infogroup is explained in more detail in the next section.

Saving the action infotype then triggers additional infotypes of the action. During this process, infotypes for creation, copying, changing, or display can be suggested. The latter is scarcely used but is definitely quite useful if certain subjects are to be checked in connection with an action. For example, in a change of department, displaying the objects on loan can be helpful to reclaim an item, such as a key.

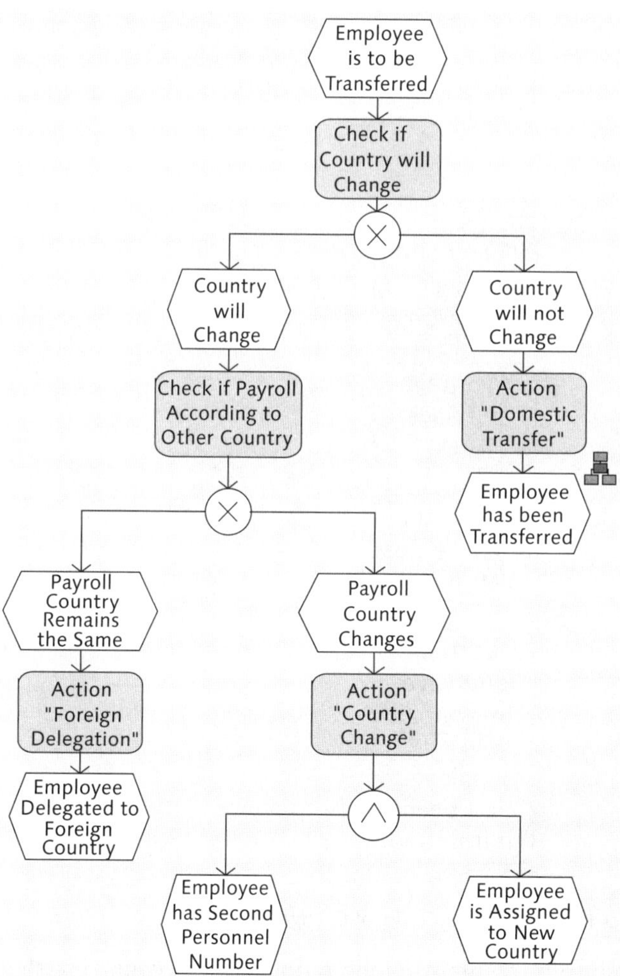

Figure 4.51 High Level Process for Organizational Change

Subsequent correction of actions is often quite complicated. Through the maintenance of Infotype 0000, all infotypes of the action can be maintained in sequence via the Execute info group function. Changing the date can create data inconsistencies throughout the employee record. For this reason, the date entries of the individual infotypes must be changed and Infotype 0000 must then be deleted and recreated. Only for changing entry and leaving dates is there a special function provided through the menu path HUMAN RESOURCES • PERSONNEL MANAGEMENT • ADMINISTRATION • HR MASTER DATA • MAINTAIN • UTILITIES • CHANGE ENTRY/ LEAVING DATE. Before you use this, you should refer to the detailed notes in the online documentation.

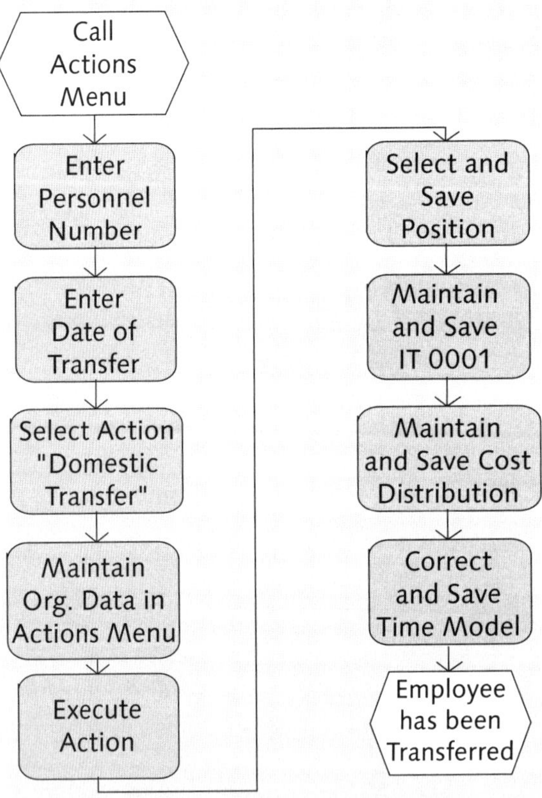

Figure 4.52 National Transfer as Part of the Organizational Change Process

Changing to a different country presents a unique problem if the country assignment for payroll is changed at the same time. In this case, you must assign a new personnel number, which is supported by the system if the action used is customized correspondingly. This is not necessary if it is a temporary assignment and the employee will continue to be accounted for according to the law of the previous country, or if payroll for this employee is not activated. Companies with a considerable number of expatriates should consider the "Management of Global Employees" solution (see 4.5.3)

Fast Entry for Actions

For some actions, maintaining only a few fields in several different infotypes is inefficient. It is then clearer and faster to maintain all of these fields on one screen. Fast entry can be used for this, as only selected fields of the infotypes are shown. The organizational change or the mini-master entry of external employees for settlement of travel expenses is often a useful application of this method.

You can reach fast entry via the menu path Human Resources • Personnel Management • Administration • HR Master Data • Fast Entry: Actions. Then the previous data of the HR master data will be applied. Figure 4.53 shows an example of this.

If additional fields are also maintained for individual infotypes, the fast-entry screen offers the option of selecting these infotypes. Maintenance for these infotypes is then provided once the fast-entry screen is saved. The example in Figure 4.53 shows this selection for Infotype 0008 (Basic Pay).

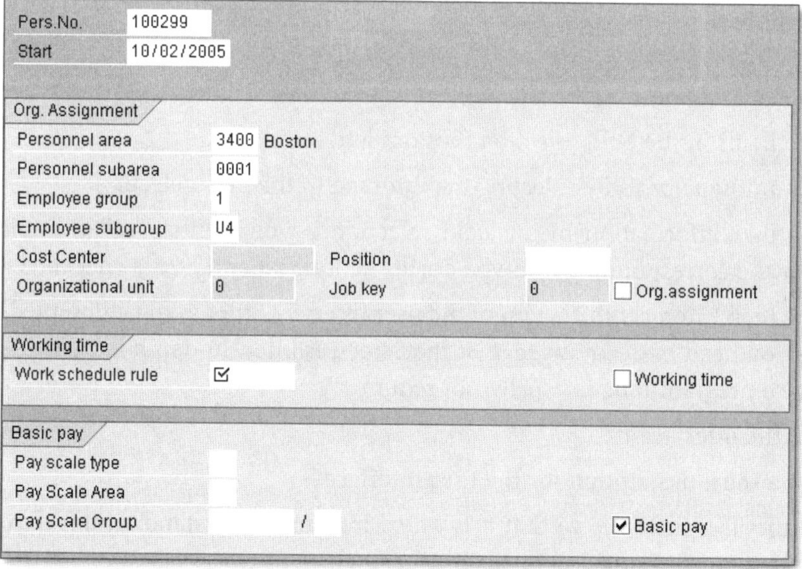

Figure 4.53 Fast Entry for the Action Organizational Change

The screens for fast entry for actions can also have a field-by-field enterprise-specific configuration. IMG path Personnel Management • Personnel Administration • Customizing User Interfaces • Fast Entry for Actions provides the Customizing tool for the fast entry for actions (see Figure 4.54).

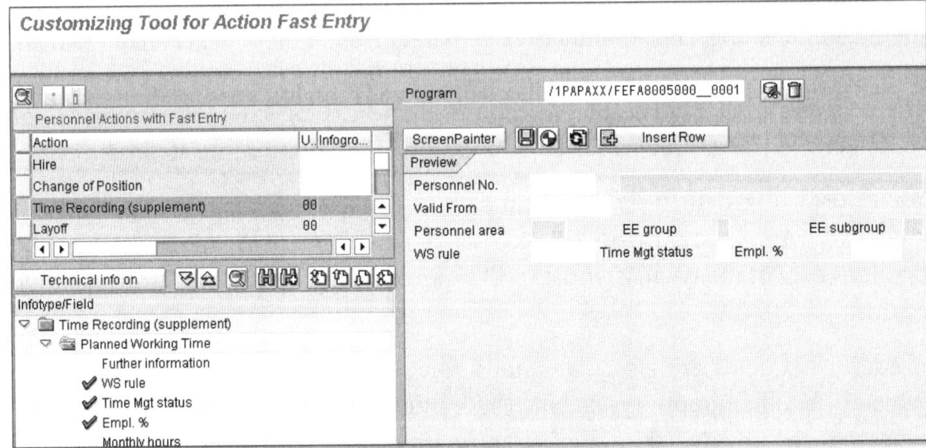

Figure 4.54 Customizing Tool for Action Fast Entry

The following steps are required to define a new user interface for fast entry for actions:

1. Select the action type
2. Select the fields in the field selection (bottom left)
3. Define an infotype basis by selecting the infotype in the field selection
4. Select Further information in the field selection if you want to call the full screen for the corresponding infotype during action fast entry via a checkbox
5. Call the Screen Painter if the layout of the user interface still has to be designed. (For this you need basic knowledge of the Screen Painter. In-depth knowledge of interface programming is usually not required.)
6. Generate the interface
7. Maintain a short description for the user interface
8. Activate the user interface so that it is called instead of the standard interface when calling the fast entry

In this process you must ensure that it is impossible to maintain inconsistent datasets (you must take particular care of mandatory fields). Plausibility checks and default values can be individually programmed through BAdI HR_FAST_ACTION_CHECK.

Customizing Actions

Enterprise-specific adjustments in customizing essentially define:

- Available personnel actions in the action menu
- Infotypes called in an action (summarized in an *infogroup*)
- Miscellaneous additional properties of the actions themselves

Similar to the infotype menus (see Section 4.2.4), the first two items can be controlled, dependent on the user group. Figure 4.55 provides an overview of the context.

Customizing for personnel actions can be found via the IMG path PERSONNEL MANAGEMENT • PERSONNEL ADMINISTRATION • CUSTOMIZING PROCEDURES • ACTIONS.

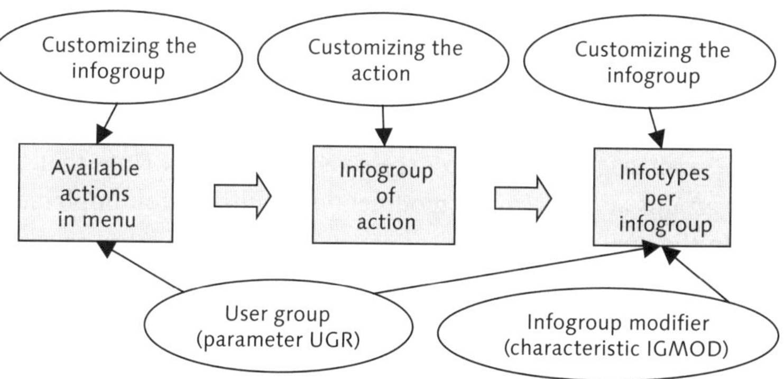

Figure 4.55 Context of the Customizing of Actions

Here, as is so often the case, the IMG items are arranged in the sequence in which they are to be processed (an infogroup must first be created before it can be assigned to the action). To understand the design, however, you must proceed the other way around; that is, you must first consider which actions you require before you determine which infotypes have to be assigned to them via infogroups.

The process consists of the following steps (for more information, please refer to the standard documentation):

1. Create the required action types through the item Set up personnel actions. If possible, copy these from default templates and do not concern yourself with further properties and priorities in the first step.
2. Define the action menu (depending on the user group).
3. Check which actions should depend on the user group or on organizational attributes of the employees. (For example, for employee subgroup Temporary personnel, Infotype 0022 (Education) should not appear in the hiring action.)
4. For default variants of the respective actions, maintain the infogroups (depending on the user group). Use the standard templates from SAP as examples, with regard to leaving operations. If possible, never use the operation MOD (change).
5. In the feature IGMOD (via the path DEFINE INFOGROUPS • INFOGROUP MODIFIER), create a decision tree that differentiates treatment for employees in actions (e.g., according to country grouping and employee subgroup). The return value of the feature (infogroup modifier) is then the key in the infogroup definition. Leave the return value empty for the standard variant already created. Here, you should not make too detailed a differentiation. It is better to accept a non-required infotype in an action than to put up with a system that has become unmanageable due to excessive customizing. Note that the number of user groups and infogroup modifiers multiplies if you implement the infogroups in the next step.
6. For each combination of user group and infogroup modifiers, define which infotypes should be contained in the action.
7. Assign the correct infogroups to the actions via the path SET UP PERSONNEL ACTIONS • PERSONNEL ACTION TYPES.
8. Then, define further properties for the actions and, if necessary, the prioritization regarding Infotypes 0000 and 0302. In the maintenance view path SET UP PERSONNEL ACTIONS • PERSONNEL ACTION TYPES, refer to the field help [F1] of the respective fields and follow the default examples.
9. For each action type create at least one reason. This can be empty — and indeed should be, if the action concerned has only one reason —to reduce maintenance effort. You can also create further reasons for evaluation and

information purposes. Depending on the country, certain actions (especially leaving the company) require differentiation according to different reasons (e.g., termination by employee, termination by employer, death).

10. Observe as necessary other country-specific customizing of actions and reasons. Otherwise, creating new action reasons or actions can lead to errors in payroll or its postprocessing.

After this, you can execute the actions. The infotypes to maintain and the available actions and reasons are defined.

Item eight defines the following essential properties of the actions:

- Is it an initial hiring or a hiring action through the Recruitment module (see Chapter 6, "E-Recruiting," and Chapter 7, "Traditional Recruitment")?
- Which status is set, and how? Note that not all actions can change the status!
- Which specific check routines are run for the sequence of actions (e.g., reentry only after previous leave)? These checks are also based on the employment status.
- Which organizational attributes are maintained in the action?
- Does the action record start at the action date entered (e.g., entry) or on the following day (e.g., termination)?
- Is a record saved in Infotype 0000 or in Infotype 0302?
- Is it a change of country regarding payroll?

This shows that an action is far more than the progression of certain infotypes. Dealing incorrectly with actions or avoiding them through direct maintenance of infotypes usually leads to errors in further processes built on administration.

The special case of country change will not be discussed further. The only important thing to remember here is that using a workflow is necessary for an extensively automated treatment (see Section 4.4.3).

Customer-specific status is an important last point. You can use this to obtain additional selection options in evaluations or control options in time management and payroll. You can maintain your own entry options through Create customer-specific status. For example, if you have three fundamentally different business regulations due to mergers or takeovers, but the employees involved are thoroughly mixed at an organizational level, this attribute can be used as a means of differentiation.

4.4.2 Dynamic Actions

By using dynamic actions, you can often avoid the much more complicated use of SAP Business Workflow.

Concept of Dynamic Actions

Dynamic actions can be started automatically from the processing of personnel administration infotypes (including time management) or from applicant data administration. When specific events occur, you can execute predefined actions.

You can consider the following triggering events:

- Creating an infotype record
- Changing an infotype record
- Deleting an infotype record

These three events can trigger the following actions:

- Checking additional conditions before the actual action is triggered (e.g., checking if the field Social security number is maintained). You cannot carry out any plausibility checks on data maintenance with this action. The check only controls if the actions of the dynamic action defined in the following section are executed.
- Calling another infotype and setting specific values (e.g., creating Infotype 0019, task monitoring with task type Social Security Number (SSN) if the corresponding field is empty).
- Sending an email to a defined recipient (or distribution list) or to a transactional user responsible for the employee (according to Infotype 0001 (Organizational Assignment)). This makes it possible to integrate other agents or to inform third parties in a workflow. If you completely exploit the options of Business Workplace for this (substitution, forwarding, distribution lists), you can often avoid the much more complicated use of SAP Business Workflow.
- Calling a custom program routine. This variant provides considerable flexibility. Any form can be called in an ABAP/4 program that is named. Restrictions arise

only because of the limited option of value transfer between the program that performs the call and the infotype to be called.

The standard releases deliver some specific dynamic actions. In personnel administration, these are generally useful but not always necessary depending on company-specific needs. In recruitment, however, the entire process cannot function properly without the supplied dynamic actions.

Figure 4.56 shows the process of a dynamic action as it is supplied by default: Depending on the time-management status for the employee to be processed, after maintaining Infotype 0007 (Planned Working Time) Infotype 0050 (Time Recording Information) is called. This happens because maintenance of a time-recording ID is required only in the case of a positive entry for the time-management status.

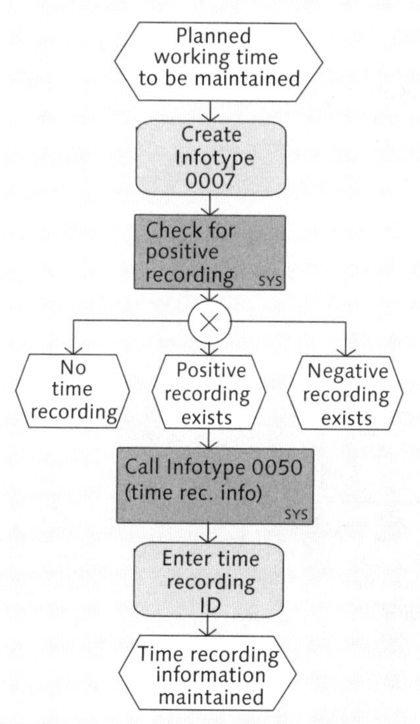

Figure 4.56 Process for a Dynamic Call of Time-recording Information

In Figure 4.57, the same example is slightly modified. Depending on the organization of the work, it can be useful to have the time-recording ID maintained in a different department. In this example, the department responsible for IDs automatically receives information that a new ID is required. To avoid further dividing the process, the number of the newly created ID is also entered in the HR master data by this department.

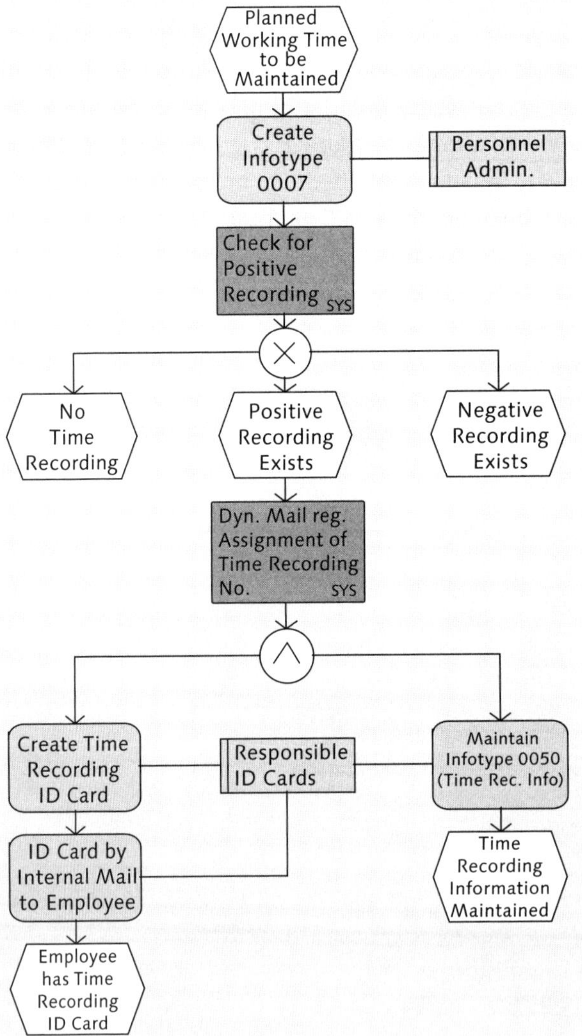

Figure 4.57 Dynamically Calling the Time-recording Information with a Change of the Agent

Customizing Dynamic Actions

You can set dynamic actions via IMG path Personnel Management • Personnel Administration • Customizing Procedures • Dynamic Actions. Dynamic emails that represent a special form of dynamic actions are described in the following section.

Dynamic Email

Dynamic emails are set via IMG path Personnel Management • Personnel Administration • Customizing Procedures • Setting Up Mail Connection for Infotype Changes.

The customizing corresponds to the other dynamic actions and is carried out through the same customizing view. This also means that a dynamic email can be triggered along with other actions and that the same additional checks (action P) can be integrated up front. Triggering an email is carried out via action M. In the variable function part, a feature is then addressed that determines the properties of the email.

In the feature, the following settings are done:

- **Text of the email**
  Here, in particular, variables from the addressed HR master data can be included. If the email is generated because of a change to the infotype record, you must know whether you want to integrate the content with the status before or after the change.
- **Recipient**
- **Send attributes**
  Storage in the sent items folder, etc.
- **Processing of infotypes from the email**
  Example: By clicking within the email Infotype 0050 is called to be maintained for the affected employee.

The feature M0001, delivered in the standard package, provides a suitable copy template. Both the documentation of this feature and that available in the IMG provide a very good description of customizing at the details level. Figure 4.58 gives you an overview of the control of dynamic emails. The processed infotype, the type of processing, and optional additional checks on the content of infotype fields determine whether an email is triggered and which feature is processed. The feature then determines the email more precisely. If the feature determines one or more of the transactional users assigned in Infotype 0001 as a recipient, then this infotype is also essential for sending the email. The title of a standard text determined in the feature must also be filled with content via the standard text maintenance.

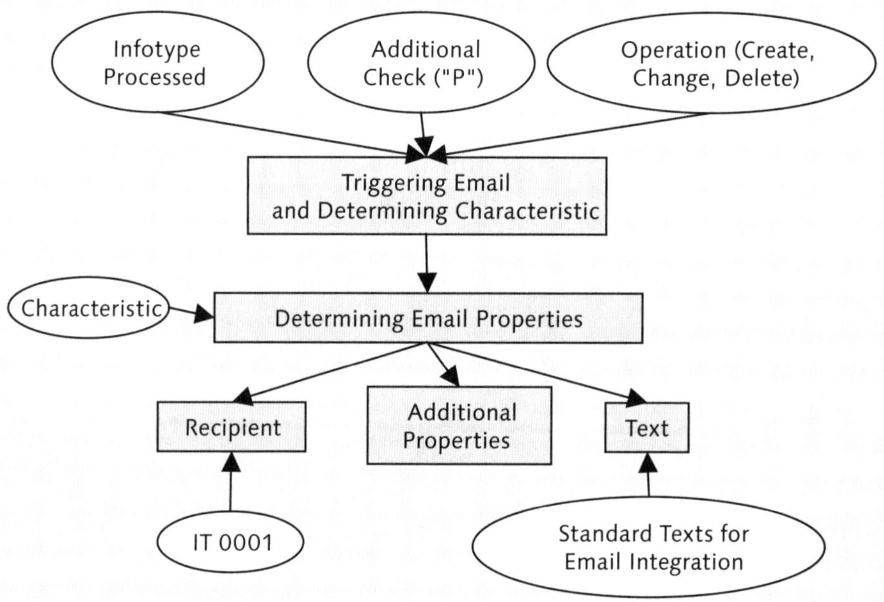

Figure 4.58 Customizing Dynamic Emails: an Overview

If dynamic emails are used to a large extent or the decision trees in the feature are deep, it is advisable to distribute the logic across several features. It is, for example, useful to use one feature per infotype. This means you can also avoid the infotype number as a criterion at the root of the feature.

It is also advisable to use the transactional class as a decision criterion (A for personnel administration and B for applicant data) from the beginning, even if the Recruitment module is not used at the start. Otherwise, there must be a complete revision of the dynamic actions during a later implementation of recruitment as in most cases their behavior should not be the same for applicants and employees.

Dynamic emails are extremely suitable for informing different people about new employees, transfers, etc. Their potential is rarely fully utilized. This is often because the use of the concept is limited to emails within Business Workplace. External mail systems such as MS Exchange can generally be integrated with the SAP environment with some development effort. This means that even employees who do not usually work with the system (e.g., those responsible for access control or the distribution of mobile phones and laptop computers) can be informed.

If you are building an extensive communication concept on the basis of the dynamic emails in the HCM system, two recommendations must definitely be considered:

- Always use distribution lists as recipients, and never use individual email addresses. This makes maintenance considerably easier even if the distribution lists sometimes only consist of one address.
- Document the different mails clearly in table form according to the triggering events, recipients, and texts.

4.4.3 Business Workflow in the HCM System

In contrast to dynamic actions, workflow is still somewhat more complex and therefore provides various possibilities for use. In this section we briefly deal with the essential differences between workflow and dynamic actions, as there are entire books available that deal with the subject of workflow.[1]

By using Business Workflow, you can map entire business processes in the system and can control their flow. Tasks can be sent, their fulfillment can be monitored, and their transactional users can be prompted to react. Workflow-management systems control processes according to a predefined model. The objective of such a system is to provide a comprehensive support of business processes. The area of workflow use is far more extensive than that of the dynamic actions.

1 For example, Rickayzen, Dart, Brennecke, Schneider: *Practial Workflow for SAP*, SAP PRESS 2002

Dynamic Emails vs. Work Items

One area in which workflow is used is the improvement of the information flow. If dynamic emails are sent to several responsible agents (distribution lists), for example, due to infotype changes, then there is no guarantee that the tasks are actually completed or that parallel work on the same task is avoided. Second, there is no notification as to whether the responsible agent has accepted the task sent with the email.

In contrast to dynamic actions, workflow does not send any emails but rather work items. These work items can be sent to several transactional users. The vital thing about workflow is that a work item disappears from the inbox of the other recipients as soon as the transactional user of this work item has accepted it for processing. This ensures that two or more users cannot attempt to process the same case.

By processing the work item, you can make sure that the Workflow can, for example, send a message to the sender of the work item if the work item was not accepted within a defined period. In addition, *dialog work items* can be sent that require addressees to make a certain decision and to document this in the dialog with the work item.

Dynamic Actions vs. Controlling Complex Approval Procedures

A workflow system can also be used to control complex processes, such as approval procedures. A classic example of this is the leave request, which a transactional user fills out in electronic format by starting a workflow that begins with a form. The user enters the request data into this form. The work item Leave request is sent to the superior. The superior decides on this request by clicking the mouse button. If the leave request is not approved in its current form, a workflow system can ensure, in contrast to the dynamic actions, that the request is returned to the original sender for revision. The process then continues until a final denial or approval of the request is reached. While the work item Leave request is still in circulation, the workflow system can remind either the transactional user of the work item or the sender of the outstanding processing request at predefined intervals. Figure 4.59 shows a classic leave request workflow.

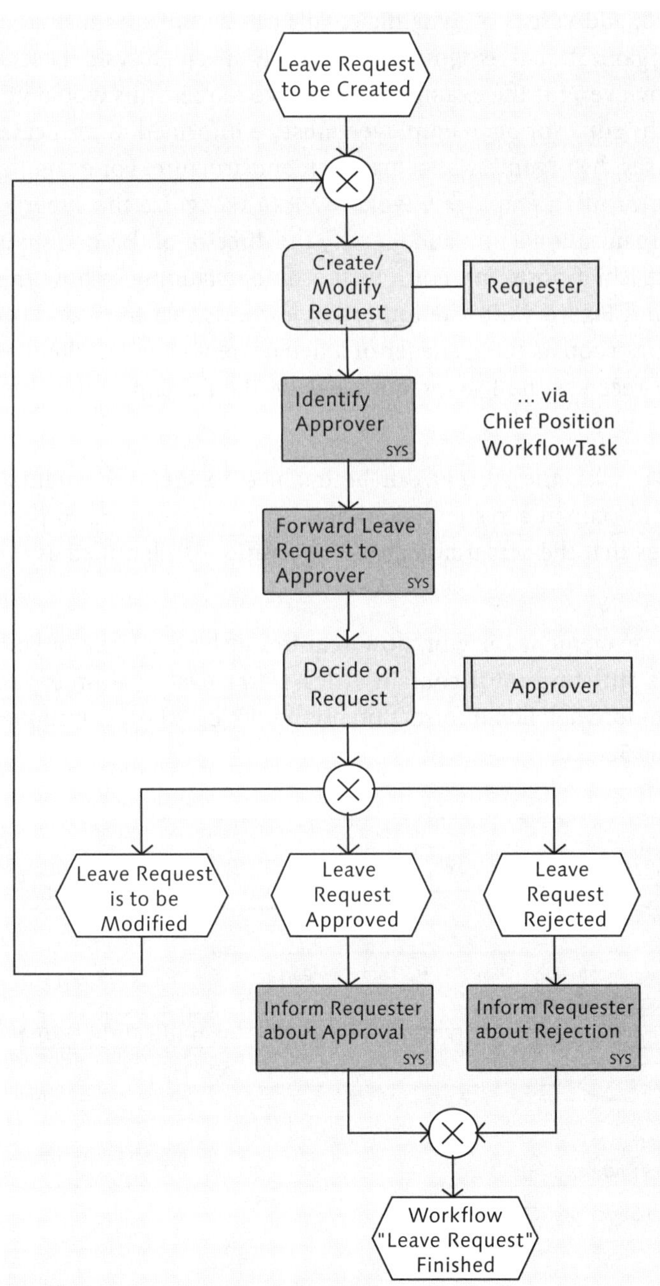

Figure 4.59 Leave Request Workflow

As previously described, addressees of dynamic emails can be the administrators from Infotype 0001 (Organizational Assignment), explicitly specified system users, or distribution lists. However, for the example of the leave request this would not be sufficient, because the superior of an employee must be informed. In this case, the workflow system uses the organizational management structure. For example, to determine the superior of an employee, workflow can recognize the superior through the assigned organizational unit and identify the director of this or a superior organizational unit (chief position). For a further understanding of how this works, see Chapter 5 and Figure 4.60. The important lesson is that the workflow system is very flexible; as soon as the manager of a department changes, the new manager automatically receives the leave requests as he then occupies the chief position.

By assigning workflow tasks, the system can be enabled to identify potential recipients for tasks that occur in a system. Workflow tasks are assigned to positions, a fact that ensures that the actual holder of the position is identified as the recipient.

Using organizational management for workflow requires at least a basic organizational structure. This structure must contain at least organizational units and positions. You will find more detailed information on the subject of organizational management in Chapter 5.

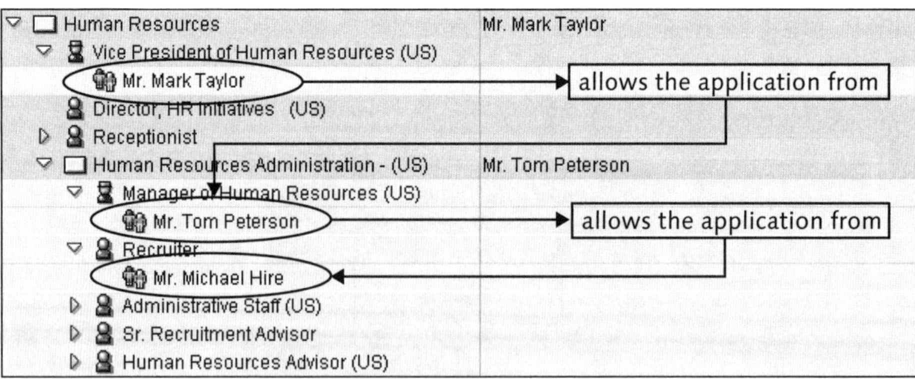

Figure 4.60 Identifying the Superiors (Chief Positions)

Dynamic Actions vs. Controlling Individual Processes

Unlike dynamic actions, a workflow system can control a process if you must react to an error within a process.

Using Workflow Templates

SAP provides more than 100 workflow templates that you should check for usability, and adjust if necessary. For personnel management alone, there are now about 46 template processes. At this point we'd like to refer you to the online documentation (via the path SAP NETWEAVER • SAP WEB APPLICATION SERVER • BUSINESS MANAGEMENT • SAP BUSINESS WORKFLOW • REFERENCE DOCUMENTATION • WORKFLOW SCENARIOS IN THE APPLICATIONS • PA PERSONNEL MANAGEMENT: WORKFLOW SCENARIOS). Before a workflow is implemented in the company, you must document the business processes (actual), analyze them, and, if necessary, size them down (planned/SAP planned). Then you should check the workflow templates for their usability.

Workflow Information System

You cannot monitor the runtime of dynamic actions. That's why it is difficult to draw a conclusion as to how the implementation of dynamic actions has actually affected the runtimes of processes. The evaluation options of workflow systems, for example, can be used to determine the lead times of individual processes.

4.4.4 Procedures in SAP NetWeaver Portal

The portal environment provides another specific support for flows tailored to the typical portal user — so-called roadmaps, which indicate the individual steps the user performs in the process. Such roadmaps are used in simple applications for master-data maintenance, but they can also guide users through complex processes related to the portal role HR Administrator (e.g., birth of a child, see Figure 4.61).

They are designed to help users navigate through the screens in the portal. The holistic process can be controlled in the background with workflows, actions, or the specific process control of the portal application for HR administrators (HR Administrative Services, see Section 4.5.6).

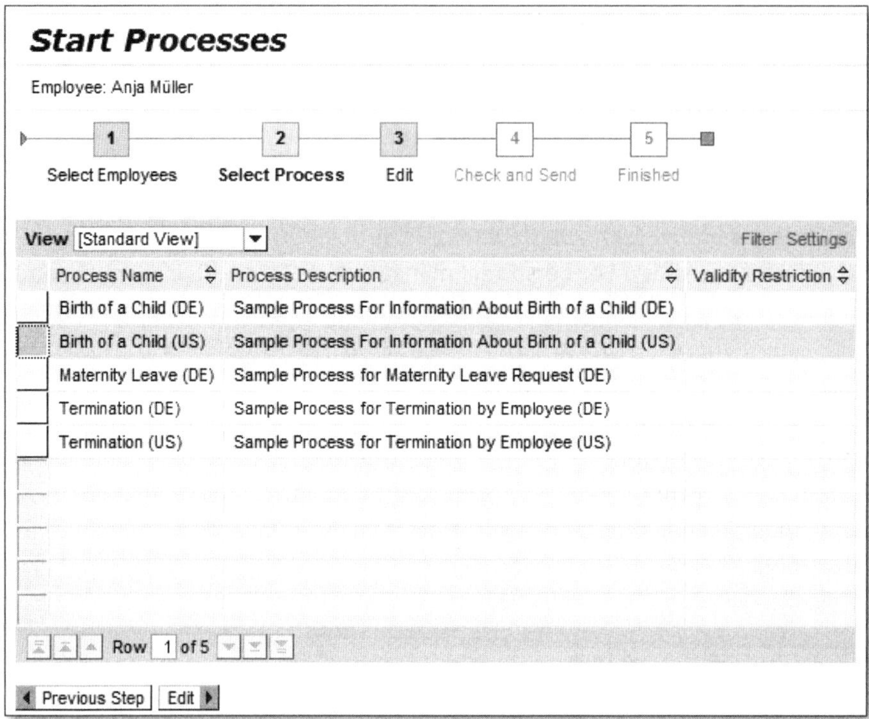

Figure 4.61 Roadmap for the Birth of a Child Process Examples

4.5 Process Examples

The examples in this section partly integrate organizational management, the conception of which is described in Chapter 5.

4.5.1 Hiring an Employee

The process is illustrated in Figures 4.61 and 4.62 and shows an overview of the outline process from emergence of workforce requirements through hiring the employee to his integration with the overall personnel management processes. It is important that the design of the procedures within the individual subprocesses always supports the overall process.

Figure 4.62 shows the importance of organizational management for the first process steps. Recruitment is based on vacant positions. To hire an employee, the position for maintaining the organizational assignment must be known.

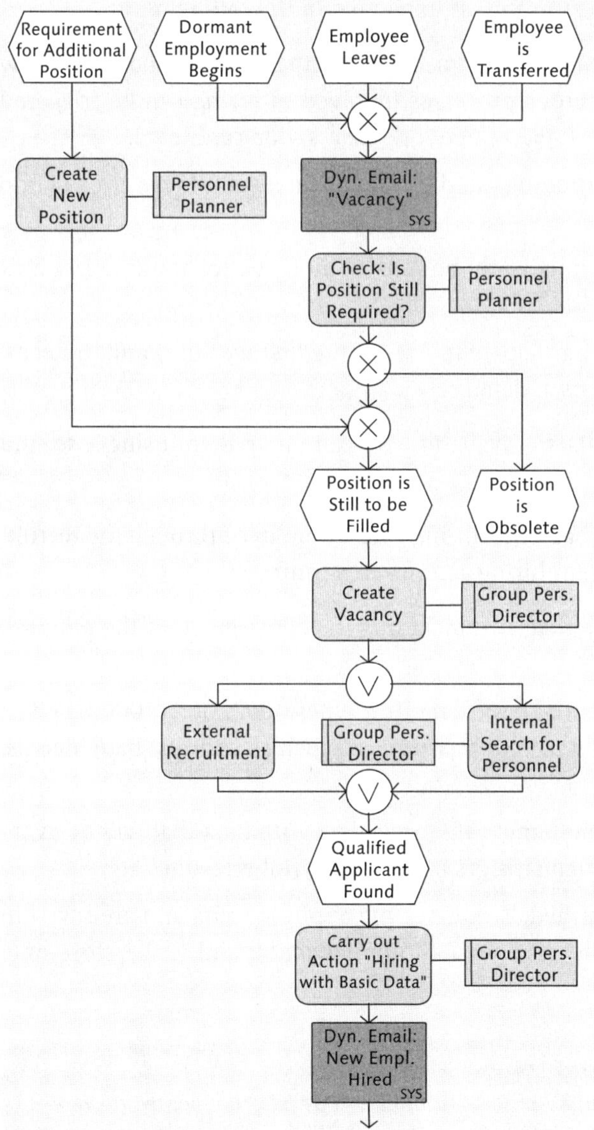

Figure 4.62 Workforce Requirements, Recruitment, and Hiring

To include the employee as quickly as possible in personnel administration after a successful search for staff, it is advisable to add the applicant data to the basic data already known. Even if some information is still missing, such as tax data, social security number, etc., which are required for payroll, the entry of basic data as early as possible is nevertheless useful, as explained in the following:

- You can use dynamic emails to inform other company areas about the new employee so that the numerous processes involved in hiring can be triggered (providing a phone, PC work place, network user, swipe card, etc.).
- Statistics for personnel controlling can then take the new employee already into account.
- The HR department can immediately book the employee for training in event management systems.
- The employee can already participate in ESS on the first workday and, if necessary, maintain some of his own data.

Once the complete documents are available you can enter them using a second action (see Figure 4.62).

For Customizing, this means that when hiring a new employee through the recruitment component three different hiring actions are required:

- An action for the ideal case that, in concluding the contract, all of the required data exists
- An action to enter the essential basic data (Infotypes 0000, 0001, 0002, and, if necessary, further data known from recruitment, such as address, bank details, etc.)
- An additional action to complement the basic data with data that will be available at a later stage, in particular, a great deal of payroll-relevant data

The first two actions are identified as transferring applicant data and are saved in Infotype 0000. The last one is merely an additional action and is therefore only stored in Infotype 0302.

Tip: Identifying the Significance of the Entire Process

Such a process, or a similar outline process, should be posted prominently in every HR department to remind the employees that the quality of the entire process depends on their participation. This is particularly helpful if team composition is not customer-oriented but function-oriented.

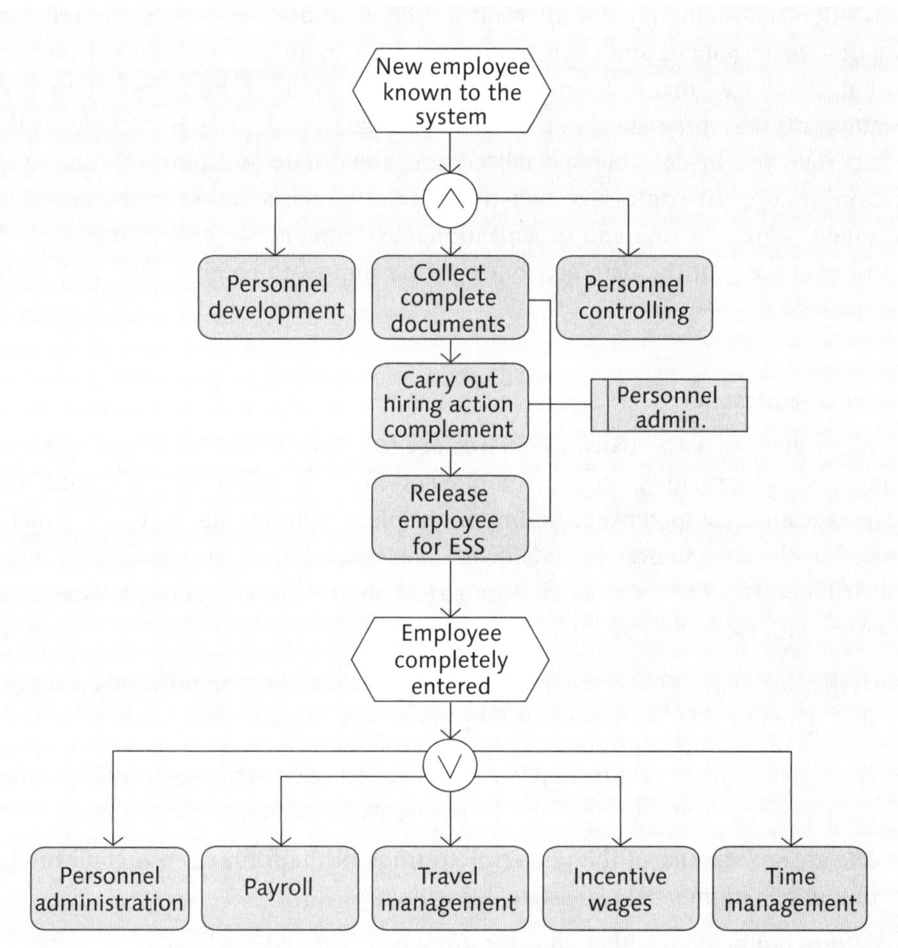

Figure 4.63 Integrating the Newly Hired Employee from the System Perspective

4.5.2 Decentralized Use of Personnel Data

As already described in Section 4.1.5, SAP ERP HCM should not be implemented only for the HR department. Only by expanding implementation beyond HR can you fully realize the high potential of the system. This expansion is often blocked due to fears that data protection could be violated. However, the authorization concept in SAP ERP HCM provides for detailed limitations, and the simple processes described in the following section can be simply and securely implemented with regard to authorizations.

It is often the seemingly unimportant infotypes, those not particularly relevant for time management and payroll, that are most useful if they are implemented in a decentralized manner. One common feature in all of the following process examples is that integration in the HR master data in SAP ERP HCM reduces the effort involved in entering specialized additional data and improves the evaluation options, in contrast to isolated solutions such as those based on office products. Finally, name and organizational assignment are always maintained, and the entirety of the data generates greatly improved combination options in reporting.

Loans Department

In many areas of a company, it is necessary to know the power of attorney and competencies formally granted to employees. In the loans business of a bank, the loan-allocation competence is an important piece of information. This is usually stored in the user master records of the corresponding IT systems of the loans department. However, a separate summary is often required that is partly supplemented with further personnel data.

Basically, Infotype 0030 (Powers of Attorney) is suitable for this. This infotype enables you to enter the following data (see Figure 4.64):

- The type of power of attorney (credit allocation competence, general commercial power of attorney, etc.), which represents the subtype of Infotype 0030
- The area of validity of the power of attorney in the form of an organizational unit (e.g., Commercial real estate department)
- A free commentary, although this cannot be evaluated easily

Because loan-allocation competencies often vary strongly with regard to the amounts that can be allocated, it is not always useful to create an individual subtype for every loan limit that is conceivable. Therefore, it is a good idea to enhance the infotype by a customer-specific amount field, and it makes even more sense to supplement it with a currency field.

In addition, the integration into the process of personnel administration must be ensured. In the case of displacement, leaving, or the beginning of dormant employment, the person responsible for the powers of attorney maintenance should be automatically informed. For this reason, you should use the concept of dynamic actions (see Section 4.4.2).

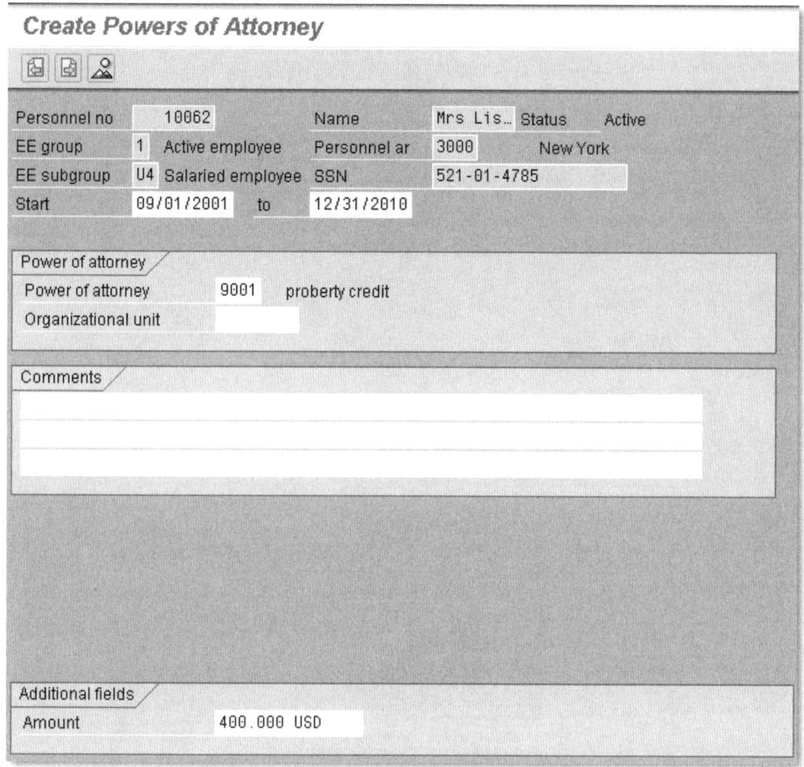

Figure 4.64 Infotype 0030 (Powers of Attorney) with Additional Field

Customizing the types of power of attorney is carried out via the IMG path PERSONNEL MANAGEMENT • PERSONNEL ADMINISTRATION • CONTRACTUAL AND CORPORATE AGREEMENTS • POWERS OF ATTORNEY.

As access authorization can also be limited on the subtype level, it can be ensured that loan allocation competences, for example, can be maintained in the loan department, whereas general commercial powers of attorney are maintained in the HR department.

You can round off this process if you connect an optical archive to SAP ERP HCM. It is even possible to assign scanned signatures to Infotype 0030. Figure 4.65 shows an overview of a sample process.

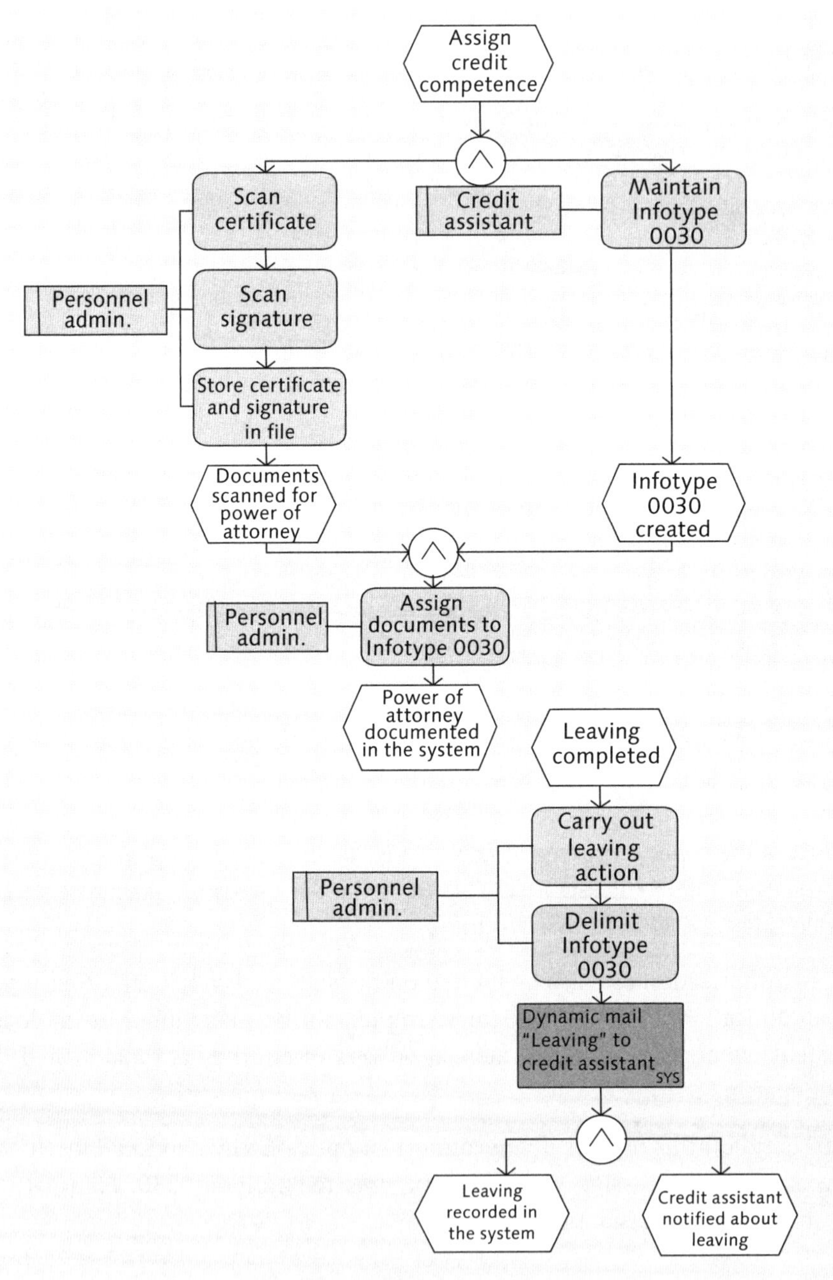

Figure 4.65 Decentralized Use of Infotype 0030 (Powers of Attorney)

Administering Objects on Loan

Lists are drawn up at many places in an organization to establish which employees are provided with which working materials by the company. These range from keys and access cards to books and mobile phones and laptops; often there are many different lists in many different formats at different places. If an employee leaves the company or is transferred to a different location, it is often uncertain whether the objects on loan are reclaimed. On the other hand, if the items are reclaimed, a process card is used that the employee must work through step by step on the last day or days of work. The entire process is more reminiscent of retirement day from the army in the nineteenth century than representative of management in a modern company.

Infotype 0040 (Objects on Loan) can be used here. The various types of objects on loan represent the subtypes. In addition, a free text field is available (see Figure 4.66). For actions for organizational change or leaving, the objects on loan can be integrated and messages for the responsible departments can be generated. Decentralized maintenance at various points is once again nonproblematic, as access can be limited to the subtype levels by the authorization concept.

The Asset number field enables integration into asset accounting. This way, you can immediately send a notification message, including the asset number, to asset accounting in the case of a loss or damage.

Customizing for the objects on loan can be reached via IMG path PERSONNEL MANAGEMENT • PERSONNEL ADMINISTRATION • CONTRACTUAL AND CORPORATE AGREEMENTS • OBJECTS ON LOAN. There you also can activate the integration into asset accounting in addition to defining the possible subtypes.

Verifying Instructions

It is often necessary to verify and document various instructions and briefings that must be repeated on a regular basis. For example, the security officer must check regularly if certain employees are instructed in the use of hazardous materials or fire prevention. Banks must provide evidence of compliance instructions for certain groups of employees.

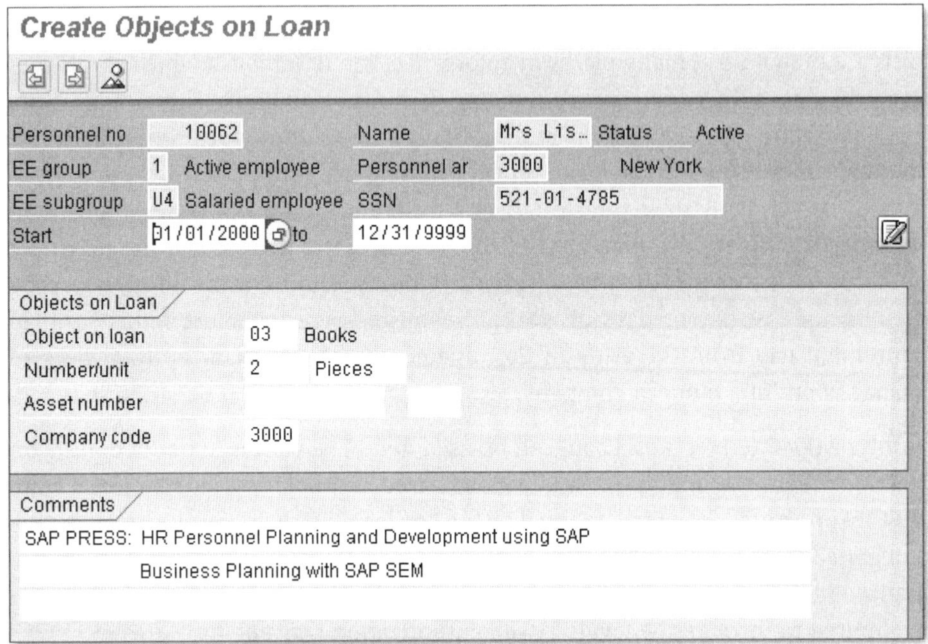

Figure 4.66 Infotype 0040 (Objects on Loan)

In SAP ERP HCM all this is mapped through Infotype 0035 (Company Instructions). For instructions that are periodically repeated it is advisable to set the end of the validity period correspondingly (see Figure 4.67) and to remind employees of repeat instructions by implementing task monitoring. Task monitoring can be created through a dynamic action when saving Infotype 0035; but it depends on the infotype's subtype.

Customizing instructions can be reached via IMG path PERSONNEL MANAGEMENT • PERSONNEL ADMINISTRATION • CONTRACTUAL AND CORPORATE AGREEMENTS • COMPANY INSTRUCTIONS. There you can only define the instruction types.

Create Company Instructions

Personnel no	10062	Name	Mrs Lis...	Status Active
EE group	1 Active employee	Personnel ar	3000	New York
EE subgroup	U4 Salaried employee	SSN	521-01-4785	
Start	10/01/2001	to	09/30/2003	

Instructions

Instruction type	01 Accident prevention
Received on	09/29/2001

Comments

Figure 4.67 Instructions in Infotype 0035

More than a Phone Directory: Who's Who in ESS

In many companies, a Web-based telephone directory is created with great effort. In most cases there are several telephone directories that indicate the room, the organizational assignment, and the function of an employee. Some of these directories contain employees who left the company a long time ago.

But particularly scary is the fact that such a phone directory is the most reliable organizational manual in many companies. The data there is more up-to-date than that contained in each org chart or personnel capacity planning document. The reason for this is clear — the first thing that every employee needs is a telephone. For this reason, the relevant department is best informed about new employees, their phone numbers and work places.

You should make use of this situation and have the corresponding service department directly maintain the phone number in SAP ERP HCM. Depending on the relevant convention, this can be done in Infotypes 0032 (Internal Data) or 0105

(Communication). When using Infotype 0032, the basic problem is that it also contains the value of the company car, which is used to calculate the imputed income, for payroll in some countries (see Figure 4.65). If you use this function, you cannot permit a decentralized maintenance of this infotype for data-security reasons.

Infotype 0105 uses an individual subtype for each number (phone, fax, company credit card, SAP user name, etc.). This allows for a fine structuring of the access authorization. Customizing for the different types of communication can be reached via the IMG path Personnel Management • Personnel Administration • Communication • Create Communication Types.

The third variant would be the maintenance of the objects Work center or Position in organizational management, which will not be discussed in more detail here.

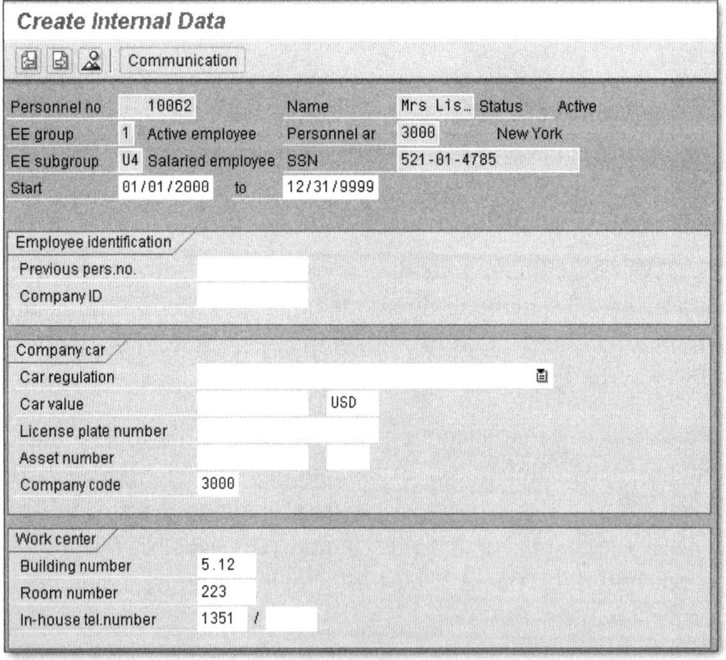

Figure 4.68 In Addition to Phone Numbers, Infotype 0032 Contains the Value of the Company Car

The Who's Who of SAP ERP HCM ESS is based on information from HR administration and enables each employee to access an employee directory, locating the relevant phone numbers and department names and even photos of the individual employees through their web browser.

Customizing for the Who's Who (previous installation and setting up of ESS is assumed) is done via the IMG path PERSONNEL MANAGEMENT • EMPLOYEE SELF SERVICE • EMPLOYEE SELF SERVICE (ITS-VERSION) • OFFICE. There the following items can be defined:

- The document type in which the photos of the employees are stored
- Limitations of the employees integrated in the directory
- Country-specific structure of the employee directory concerning selection fields and the data displayed. You can also do this to the infoset query (see Figure 4.69). In addition, the settings to be carried out depend on the selected ESS service for the employee directory.

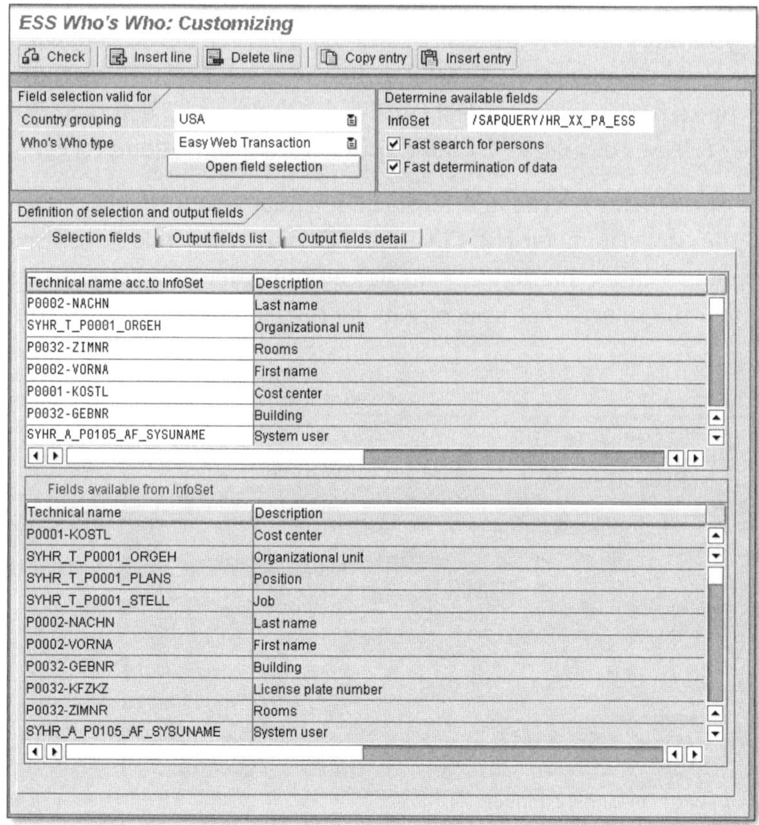

Figure 4.69 Customizing the ESS Employee Directory

4.5.3 Managing Expatriates

The Management of the global employee component provided since Extension 1.10 of R/3 Enterprise represents a comprehensive tool to map international employee assignments. The component is based on some concepts similar to concurrent employment (see Section 4.2.1). Here, too, every employee is given a clear person ID while the old personnel numbers identify the individual employment contracts. However, these work relationships must exist in different countries, that is, they must be assigned to different groupings for wage and salary payroll (MOLGA).

As a component of an extension, this function must also be activated for you to use it. The activation must not be undone, as is the case with other components of the extension. A modification will be necessary if you want to activate the function. You can perform this modification in the CHECK_RELEASED method of the CL_HRCE_MASTERSWITCHES class. There you must activate the line `ce_is_released = true.`; that is, you must remove the asterisk at the beginning of the line. Only after doing this can you maintain the CCURE switch in table T77S0. Please also refer to the most up-to-date version of OSS Note 540451 (release 4.7 before SP 20) or 662136 (higher releases or release 4.7 after SP 20) for the activation process.

In general, if the component is activated it can be separately controlled for each individual user. The user parameter HR_CCURE_PIDSL with the value "-" is used to hide the personal ID in the master data display and maintenance screens (see Figure 4.70), so that the selection can once again be carried out with the personnel number.

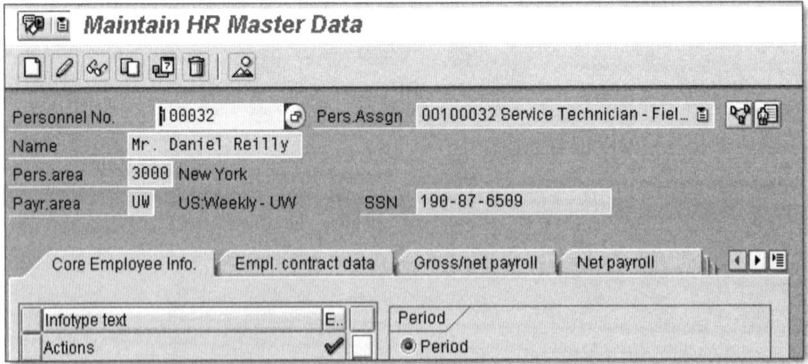

Figure 4.70 Selection with Personnel Number

The entire process from planning via assignment to return (or alternatively to changing to another global assignment) is supported by the system (see Figure 4.71). There are some additional infotypes, actions and Customizing tables involved in this process. We will not go into detail on customizing here, as it is quite extensive. The important aspect for the majority of users and decision makers is the basic scope of functions.

The individual phases (see Figure 4.71) are partly supported by actions. In the following sections we will discuss these phases briefly.

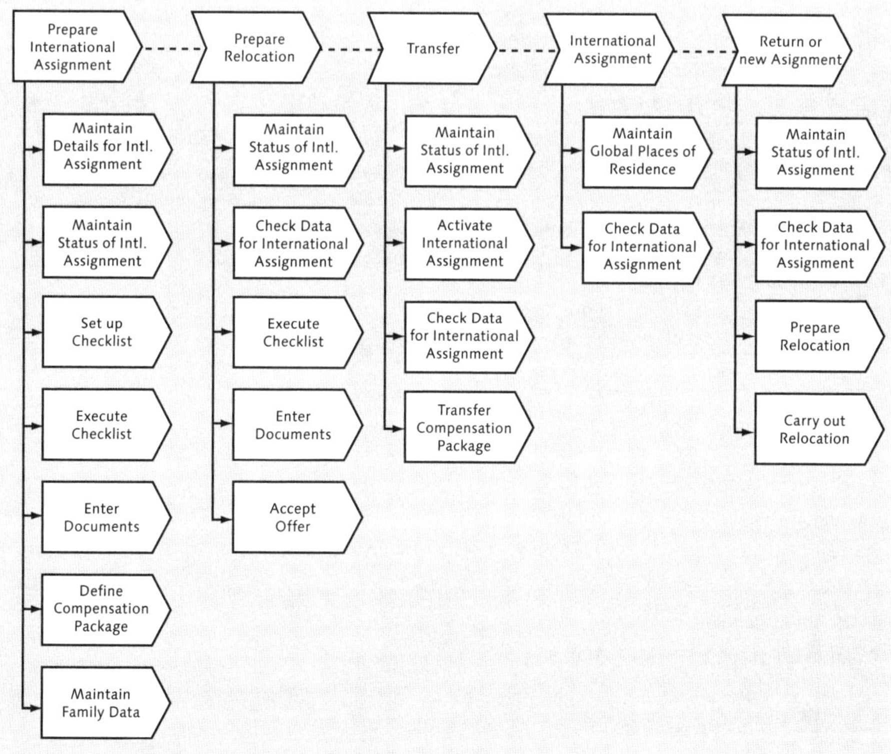

Figure 4.71 The Basic Process to Manage Global Employees

The preparation of the international assignment is triggered with the action Planning Global Assignment. For the time being the employee (along with his new contract) has the employment status Left company to indicate that the international assignment is planned. The general conditions for the international assignment are documented in the infotypes described next:

- **Infotype 0710 (Details on Global Assignment)**
  You must first maintain this infotype. It determines the essential attributes of the assignment — the duration and family accompaniment affect the compensation package in Infotype 0706. Furthermore, it is indicated whether the employee will be promoted due to the assignment and who is the responsible manager in the home country. Figure 4.72 provides an overview of the additional information provided by Infotype 0710.

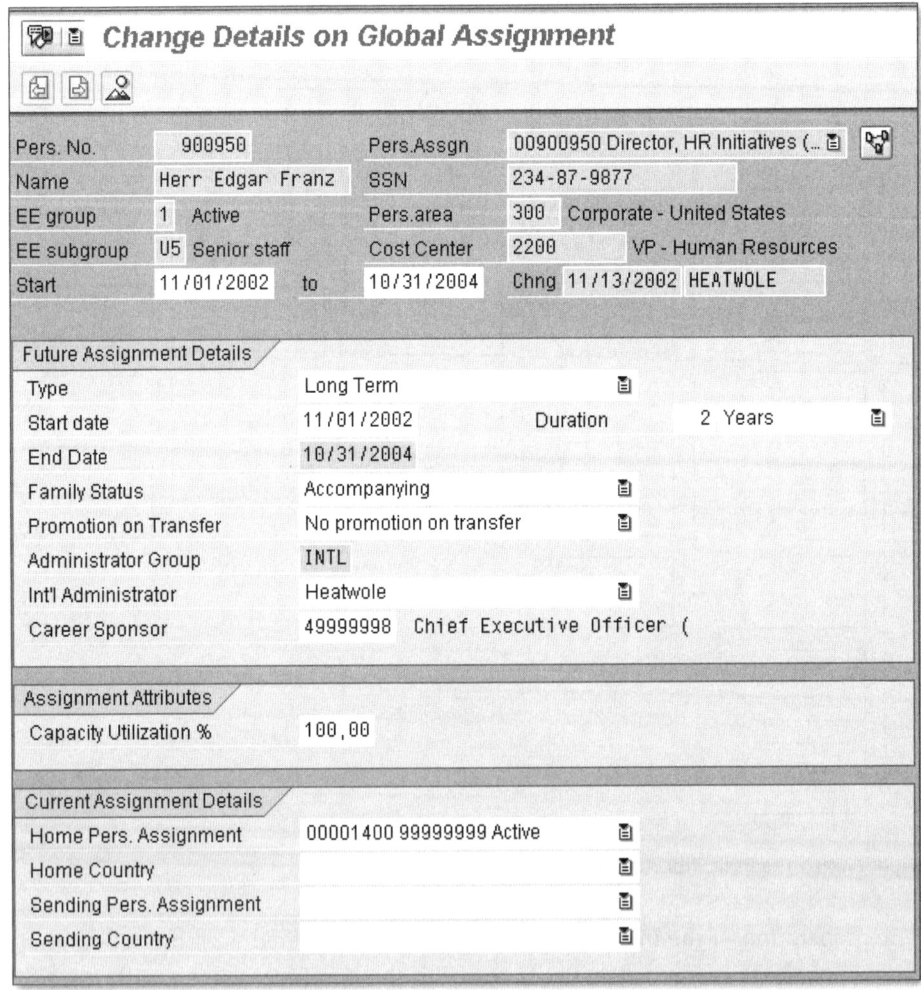

Figure 4.72 Infotype 710 with the Main Characteristics of a Global Assignment

- **Infotype 0715 (Status of Global Assignment)**
  This infotype is to be maintained next. This sequence is also defined in the default actions. It documents the status of the assignment from planning to end. The Refused by management or Refused by employee statuses are both possible here. In process means the employee is currently on an international assignment.
- **Infotypes 0702 and 0703 (Documents)**
  The most important information for necessary documents (passport, visas, etc.) is maintained in Infotype 0702. Infotype 0703 fulfills the same functions for family members.
- **Infotype 0704 (Information on Dependents)**
  The relevant information for family members is stored here (Who accompanies the employee? Which schools are required?)
- **Infotype 0705 (Information on Checklist)**
  A checklist is structured using this infotype. It enables you to control many tasks of the assignment process. There is a responsible person and a status stored for each checklist item. In addition, you can define which items must be completed before a transfer can take place.
- **Infotype 0706 (Compensation Package Offer)**
  In addition to general data, such as exchange rate and cost-of-living index, this infotype contains the different items of the compensation package for the home and host country. A possible integration into payroll and the required flexibility due to the many relevant countries makes customizing very extensive.
- **Infotype 0707 (Activation Information)**
  Here you can specify whether a particular percentage rate of salary should be paid out in another (more stable) currency. In addition, you can determine if taxes, health insurance, child benefits, and other similar components are to be paid in the home country or in the host country. The category types are processed depending on the country during activation.

Infotypes that were created in the first phase are partially maintained in the other phases. This is especially true for the status of the international assignment, which is continuously adjusted.

In the second phase, the checklist from Infotype 0705 is worked off and the required documents are provided.

If the required steps of the first phase have been completed (the mandatory items in the checklist) and the employee has accepted the offer, the new employment contract can be activated. To do this, report RPMGE_ACTIVATION is activated, which simultaneously launches the activation in the host country. A requirement for the activation is that Infotype 0715, subtype HOST, has the status Must be activated. Upon activation, the employee receives the employment status active while the activation date is entered in Infotype 0707. Infotypes 0008, 0014, and 0015, which are used to define salary, are derived from the compensation package offer. The personal data remains the same. Then the report is used to carry out the activation in the home country. The actual employee contract receives the employment status dormant.

During the international assignment, the normal processes of personnel administration and payroll continue as before. If necessary, the absence times during the assignment are documented in Infotype 0708 (Details of Global Commuting). This infotype is used to monitor tax regulations (e.g., the 183-day rule that applies in Germany). However, it is not taken into consideration by the time management, remuneration payroll, or travel-cost management components.

Upon return the relocation process starts again. As an alternative to moving back into the home country another assignment can follow immediately.

4.5.4 Data Maintenance in ESS

In ESS, employees can change or display their own data in the system. In most services of the SAP standard, HR master data assume an important role. In most cases, addresses (see Section 4.3.4) and bank details are changed (see Figure 4.73). Standard services also include:

- Entry of family members
- Infotype 0002 (Maintenance of Personal Data)
- Maintenance of communication data
- Registration as a customer of the Employee Interaction Center (EIC) (see Section 4.5.7)

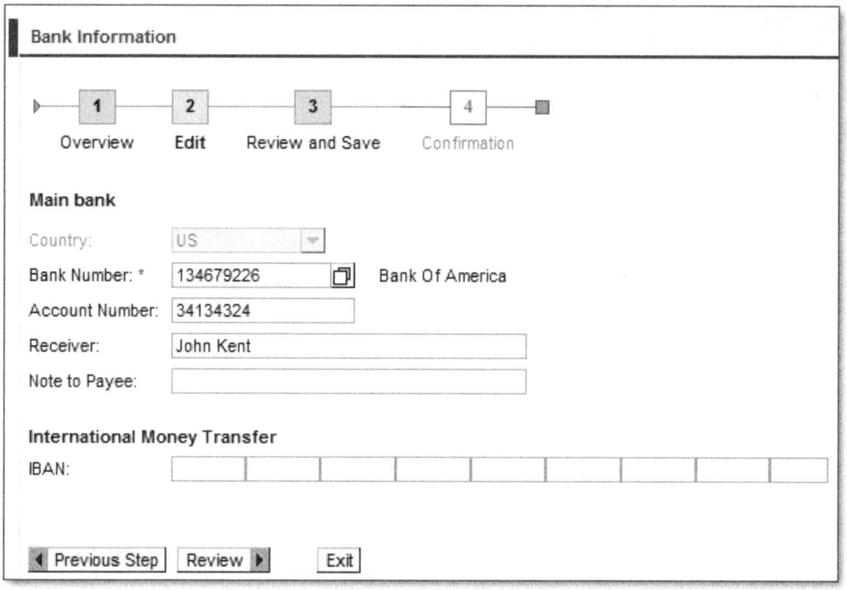

Figure 4.73 Maintaining the Bank Details in ESS

In addition to simple data changes, the system also supports more complex processes for certain events. These life and work events include, for example:

- Registration for benefits
- Marriage
- Birth/adoption
- Maternity leave
- Divorce
- New job
- Organizational changes
- Leave

You can use the same processes that are provided for the HR administrator role (see Section 4.5.6).

Besides the standard applications, customer-specific services are also commonly used today. They can often be implemented with little effort. That means implementing a customer-specific application for employees also makes sense for one-time jobs, such as event-related data queries. Customizing the ESS is carried out via the Homepage Framework (IMG path: CROSS-APPLICATION COMPONENTS • HOMEPAGE FRAMEWORK) and via service-specific settings in the IMG (PERSONNEL MANAGEMENT • EMPLOYEE SELF-SERVICE). In addition, the specific Customizing settings of the individual infotypes, which have been partly discussed in this chapter, usually apply, too.

4.5.5 Access to HR Master Data by Managers

MSS is an application supported with SAP NetWeaver Portal and enables managers to display master data and trigger changes.

Personnel Reports for Managers

Besides the profile overview, there are various reports available that use SAP NetWeaver Business Intelligence (BI) to display master data. Figure 4.74 shows a sample headcount report for the sales and distribution manager sorted by organizational units (chart) and drilled down to employee subgroups (table below the chart).

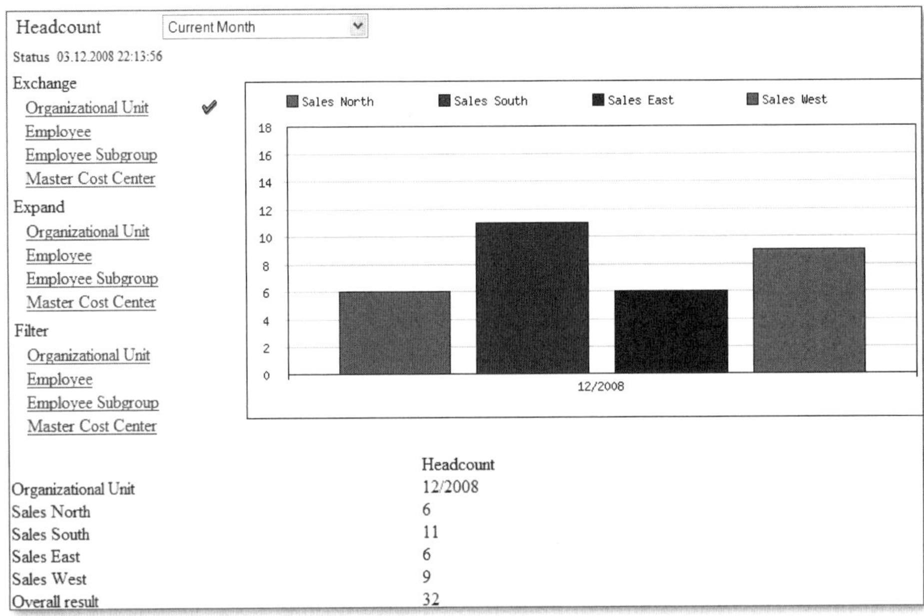

Organizational Unit	Headcount 12/2008
Sales North	6
Sales South	11
Sales East	6
Sales West	9
Overall result	32

Figure 4.74 Example of a Headcount Report

Employee Profile

Figure 4.75 shows an employee profile in MSS that contains HR master data and additional data, for example, from time management and personnel development.

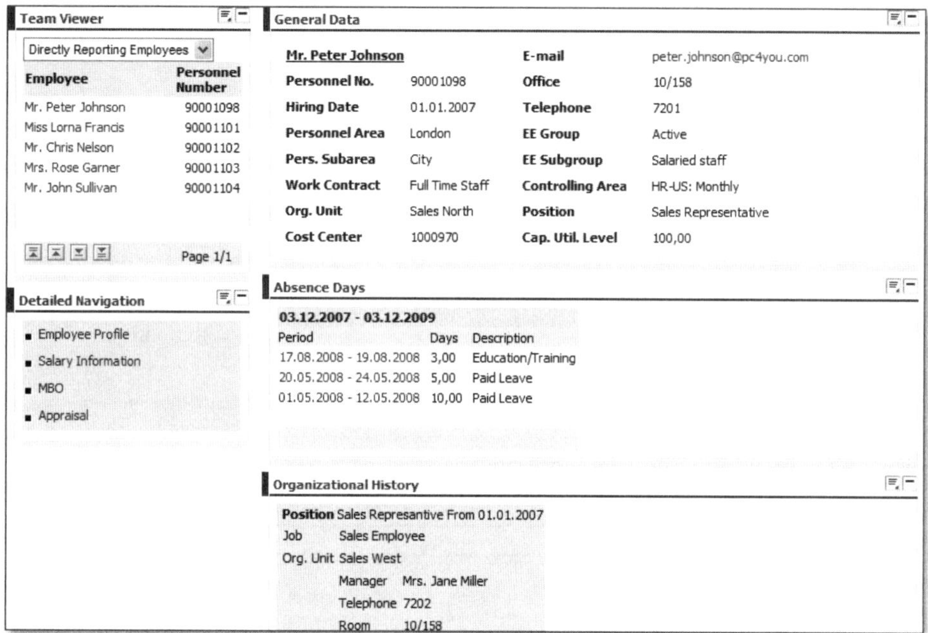

Figure 4.75 Employee Profile in MSS

Personnel Change Request

In addition to displaying data, the manager can also trigger master data changes, which will then be processed by the responsible HR administrator (if necessary, by means of the respective portal role, see Section 4.5.6). For this reason, the system provides specific forms for different data changes. These forms can be customized if required. The personnel change request involves five steps:

1. Selecting the employee from the list of employees that are assigned to the manager (see Figure 4.76)
2. Selecting the desired change in the form selection (see Figure 4.77)

3. Filling the form
4. Checking the data entered
5. Submitting and confirming the personnel change request

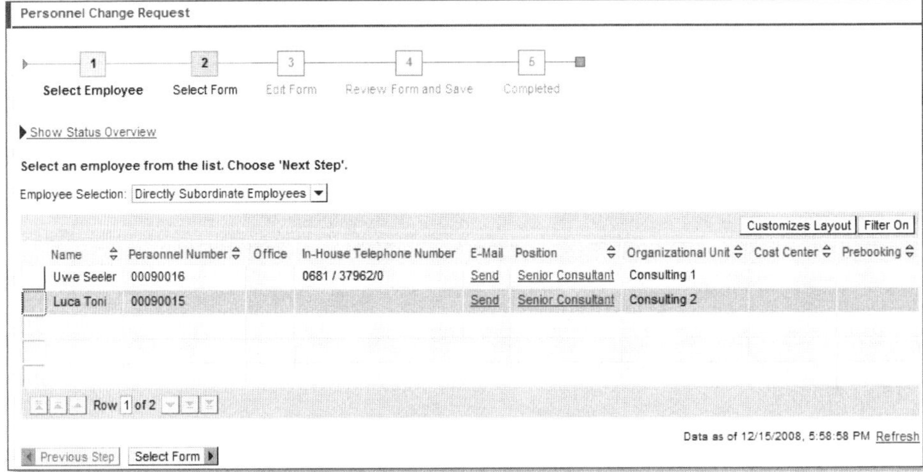

Personnel Change Request

1 Select Employee · 2 Select Form · 3 Edit Form · 4 Review Form and Save · 5 Completed

Show Status Overview

Select an employee from the list. Choose 'Next Step'.

Employee Selection: Directly Subordinate Employees

Customizes Layout | Filter On

Name	Personnel Number	Office	In-House Telephone Number	E-Mail	Position	Organizational Unit	Cost Center	Prebooking
Uwe Seeler	00090016		0681 / 37962/0	Send	Senior Consultant	Consulting 1		
Luca Toni	00090015			Send	Senior Consultant	Consulting 2		

Row 1 of 2

Data as of 12/15/2008, 5:58:58 PM Refresh

Previous Step | Select Form

Figure 4.76 Personnel Change Request: Employee Selection

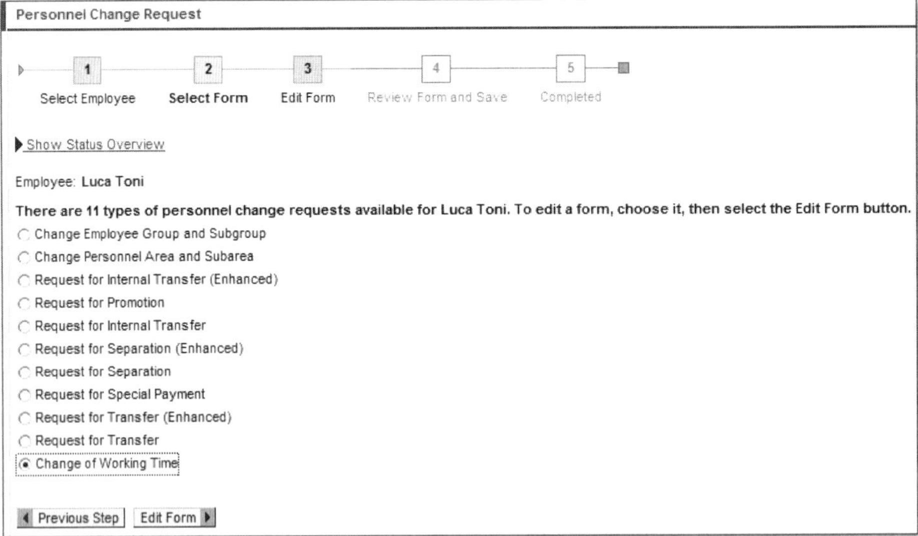

Personnel Change Request

1 Select Employee · 2 Select Form · 3 Edit Form · 4 Review Form and Save · 5 Completed

Show Status Overview

Employee: Luca Toni

There are 11 types of personnel change requests available for Luca Toni. To edit a form, choose it, then select the Edit Form button.

- Change Employee Group and Subgroup
- Change Personnel Area and Subarea
- Request for Internal Transfer (Enhanced)
- Request for Promotion
- Request for Internal Transfer
- Request for Separation (Enhanced)
- Request for Separation
- Request for Special Payment
- Request for Transfer (Enhanced)
- Request for Transfer
- Change of Working Time

Previous Step | Edit Form

Figure 4.77 Personnel Change Request: Form Selection

Aside from basic knowledge about Customizing in the HCM core system, as described in this chapter and subsequent chapters, this process also requires experience with portal technology and Adobe Interactive Forms. These forms provide a very user-friendly interface and can be adopted to support a custom process. However, doing your own interactive forms may require an additional license.

4.5.6 HR Business Partner: Support for the Decentralized Personnel Administration

In the context of the modern organization of personnel work, the HR Business Partner concept plays an increasingly important role. In addition to the central Shared Service Center and Center of Competence, the HR Business Partner represents the contact person for the HR function on site. In this role, the maintenance of the HR data in the system plays only a minor role, because the Shared Service Center is usually responsible for this. However, in certain individual cases the HR data is still maintained in the system.

For this person's subgroup and for other employees who occasionally maintain HR data, although it doesn't constitute their main task, SAP offers a user-friendly interface by providing the portal role HR administrator in *HR Administrative Services*. Employees whose main task is the maintenance of HR master data should use the core system as described in Sections 4.2 and 4.3.

After accessing the portal, there are two views available for the HR administrator:

- The work overview that displays pending or completed tasks (see Figure 4.78)
- The employee view that provides an overview of selected data of the employees (see Figure 4.79)

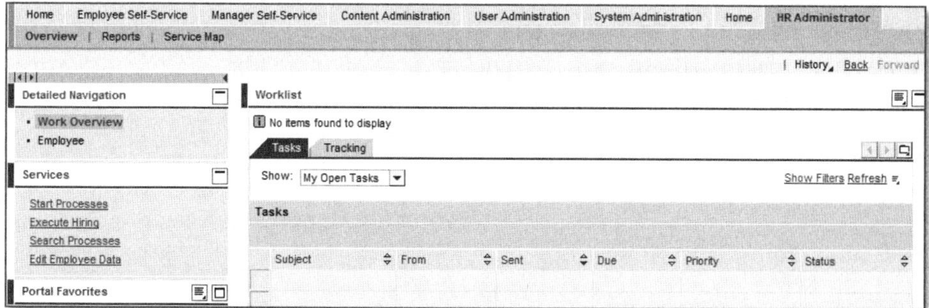

Figure 4.78 Work Overview for HR Administrators in the Portal

The basic services available for the administrator include:

- Processing employee data
- Starting reports
- Starting, tracking, and processing processes (whereas hiring is a special case)

IMG path Personnel Management • HR Administrative Services • HR Administrator • Employee Data Maintenance defines the infotypes available for the maintenance of employee data.

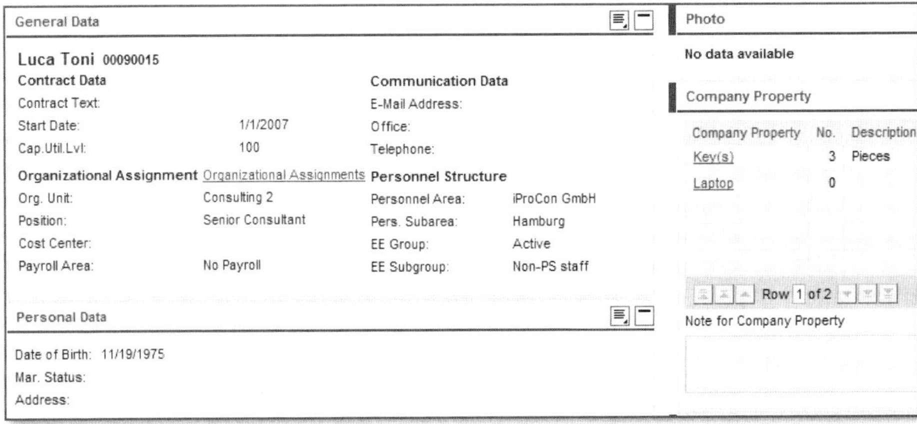

Figure 4.79 Employee Overview for HR Administrators in the Portal

The available evaluations are defined via IMG path Personnel Management • HR Administrative Services • HR Administrator • Set Reports.

The configuration of the specific processes is more complex, particularly because it requires various forms. For an initial test run, you should transfer the sample processes of SAP into your test system. This can be done via the IMG path Personnel Management • HR Administrative Services • Form/Process Configuration • Sample Processes for HCM Processes and Forms. Sample processes are:

- Hiring
- Birth of a child
- Termination

- Maternity protection
- Marriage

For business-specific processes and forms, IMG path Personnel Management • HR Administrative Services • Form/Process Configuration provides the sections Form Configuration and Process Configuration and further settings under the path Personnel Management • HR Administrative Services • HR Administrator. Note that this also requires technical knowledge about:

- Adobe Interactive Forms, Adobe LifeCycle Designer
- BAdI programming and ABAP Objects
- Workflow
- Portal

You must always clearly define which processes are permitted for which employee group and what has to be entered in the feature PASRG. This holds particularly true for country-specific processes. Performing a process not permitted for the country you are using it for leads to an error message.

4.5.7 HR Shared Service with the EIC

The EIC is a specific application that is tailored to the requirements of an HR Shared Service Center or a provider of HR outsourcing services. The EIC uses elements of Customer Relationship Management (SAP CRM) and can be basically described as a CRM system with call center solution for personnel services. A detailed technical description of this component would go beyond the scope of this book. Thus, we limit our description to a brief overview.

Requests by employees, managers, and externals can trigger requests via various channels. Requests that cannot be processed via self-services or that are directly addressed to experts outside the service center are accepted by service agents via the EIC (see Figure 4.80). Consequently, the optimal management of the various communication channels is critical and requires an efficient technical solution and the appropriate culture.

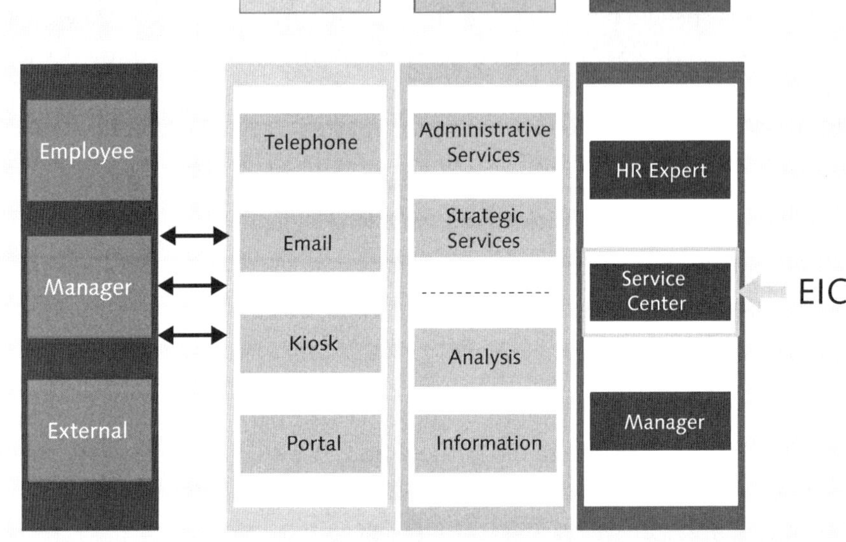

Figure 4.80 Communication Channels in the EIC

The core of the solution is the *Agent Desktop*, which directly accesses the SAP HCM core system and is designed to ensure that the service agents work efficiently. Among other things, it includes the following functions:

- Web-based design in the user interface
- Tools for decision-making support
- Support of the interaction with employees
- Telephone integration
- Management of various communication channels (telephone, email, online requests)

Figure 4.81 shows the process of an EIC request.

From Enhancement Package 1 for SAP ERP 6.0 on, the EIC solution contains additional features, such as:

- Monitoring of Service Level Agreements (SLA)
- Customer surveys

- Key Performance Indicator (KPI) reporting
- Integration of the management of global employees for expatriates (see Section 4.5.3)
- Automatic response of requests and substitution rules

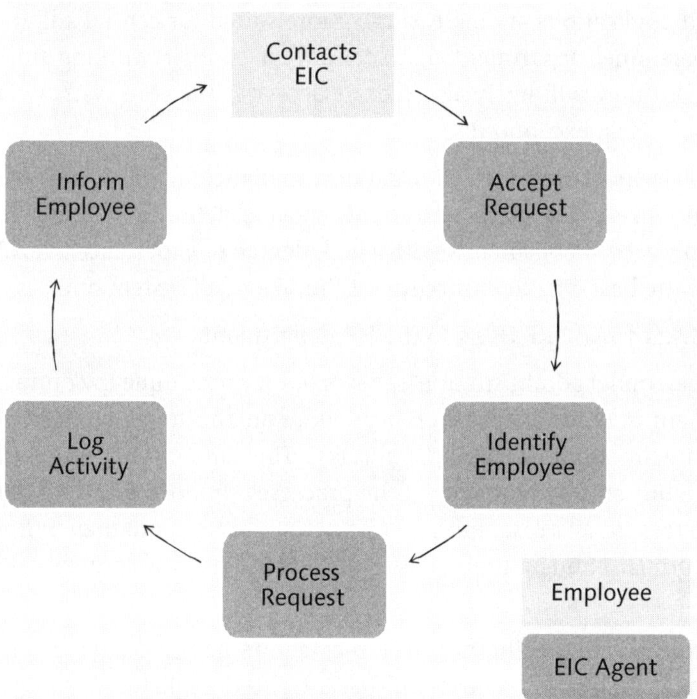

Figure 4.81 Process of an EIC Request

4.6 Critical Success Factors

- Organizational management is integrated in the personnel administration insofar as it is required as the basis for the processes described in this book.
- Free yourself from the terminology. In SAP ERP HCM many terms are used in an unusual manner or in another sense than you are used to in your daily business. This cannot be avoided when working with a standard software package. Try to apprehend expressions such as *employee subgroup*, *job*, and *position* in the

system environment as what they represent in SAP ERP HCM. There are more important things to discuss than names.

- Clarify the HCM structures by considering the structures of other processes as well.
- Integrate the portal function where it actually increases the efficiency of processes. Web-based applications are increasingly more suited for central administrators of the personnel department that spend a lot of their working time with the system, but they will likely also require access to the core system via an SAP GUI (the EIC is an exception).
- At an early stage, clarify the processes for data maintenance, in particular, the work distribution and decentralized entry. This process definition should be supported by employees or consultants with a high degree of experience in SAP ERP HCM. This is the best way to ensure full utilization of all system options.
- Do not limit the use of SAP ERP HCM to the HR department.
- In Customizing, personnel administration appears to be very simple in contrast to time management or payroll. However, it provides an enormous number of options that optimally support your daily tasks. The amount of resources invested here depends on the frequency of the processes supported and on the number of employees. In any case, for larger companies with more than 5,000 employees, an optimal configuration of the data entry process is definitely worthwhile.
- Consider right from the beginning not only the requirements of payroll and time management but also the central and decentralized evaluation requirements.
- Do not enter any data that you do not actually require, just because there happens to be a suitable infotype for it.
- The authorization concept for data entry and reporting is of great importance. It should be considered in connection with the role concept (see Section 2.3). Involve the data-protection officer as early as possible.
- Avoid processes where the work is divided between too many persons. The days of the separation between salary accountants and personnel attendants on one hand and workers responsible for data entry on the other are definitely over. The processes are only slowed down and made more expensive by this separation.

Organizational Management is a very powerful and flexible module. It not only describes the basis for the personnel planning and development processes, but is also required for an optimal implementation of personnel administration and personnel controlling. In addition, it offers extensive options for defining and evaluating structures.

5 Organizational Management in SAP ERP HCM

The following sections describe the classification and structure of Organizational Management in the overall system and in SAP ERP HCM. The main focus is on the support of processes in personnel administration through organizational management.

5.1 Classification in the Overall System and in SAP ERP HCM

To evaluate the capabilities and effects of changes in organizational management, we must first describe its meaning for personnel administration, personnel planning, and development.

5.1.1 Importance for Personnel Administration

Organizational management is actually assigned to the planning components of the SAP ERP HCM system, which are not the focus of this book. However, because it represents a utility for structuring even without the use of personnel planning and development, it should be mentioned here. Use of organizational management when using personnel administration is definitely advisable as a basis for structuring and evaluation. In addition, the component serves as an essential basis for evaluations in all other processes and is of particular importance for Manager Self-Services (MSS), Enterprise Compensation Management (ECM), performance management, and recruitment. In this context, the complete functional scope is not required. It is enough to discuss a pragmatic implementation using the following objects, which are described in more detail throughout the course of the book.

- *Organizational units* and their integration in the organizational structure
- *Positions* and their integration in the organizational structure and the assignment of owners
- *Jobs* as a means to describe and classify positions

More recent developments of the SAP system, such as E-Recruiting, are based on the objects of organizational management with regard to their integration with ERP Central Component (ECC). For example, organizational units, positions, and jobs can be used as integrative parts of E-Recruiting to create requisitions.

Organizational management is of particular importance in the SAP ERP HCM authorization check. By activating the structural authorization check, it is possible to assign authorizations based on the organizational structure. We will only introduce organizational management in general terms in this chapter. You will find a detailed description in the book *Mastering SAP ERP HCM Organizational Management,* also from SAP PRESS (for further information and reading recommendations refer to Appendix D, "Recommended Reading").

5.1.2 Importance of Personnel Planning and Development

The object types mentioned earlier are an indispensable basis for the personnel planning and development processes.

For the remaining processes of personnel planning and development, the basic objects of positions, jobs, and — frequently — organizational units are further characterized with regard to the following attributes:

- Requirement profiles
- Career paths
- Development plans
- Employee goals
- Appraisal models
- Planned costs
- Requirements

- Budgets
- Compensation

5.1.3 Importance of the Decentralized Use of HCM

Specific interfaces for decentralized use also require the clean maintenance of the organizational structure in many cases.

The Manager's Desktop (MDT) or the MSS cannot be used without organizational management.

In the Time Manager's Workplace (TMW), organizational management can also be used for selecting employees to process. But you are also provided with other options (e.g., time administrators, according to Infotype 0001 (Organizational Assignment)).

5.1.4 Importance of ECC in General

Organizational management is a basis for the following cross-process functionalities:

- SAP Business Workflow
- Assigning roles to users
- Evaluations for SAP NetWeaver Business Intelligence (BI)
- Cross-module company organization along with controlling

5.2 Structure of Organizational Management

The following sections describe the individual components of organizational management and their interaction within the system.

5.2.1 The Plan Version

A plan version describes a specific data set from the personnel planning and development view. Different plan versions are specifically used to run through alternative planning scenarios. Therefore, it is possible to copy plan versions.

The active *plan version* or *integration plan version* has a special status. It is only set once during the initial implementation (usually to 01) and must not be changed after that. The integration plan version is the only plan version whose changes impact the active integration of personnel administration.

To change the plan version currently displayed or processed, you can use the menu path PERSONNEL • ORGANIZATIONAL MANAGEMENT • SETTINGS • SET PLAN VERSION (see Figure 5.1).

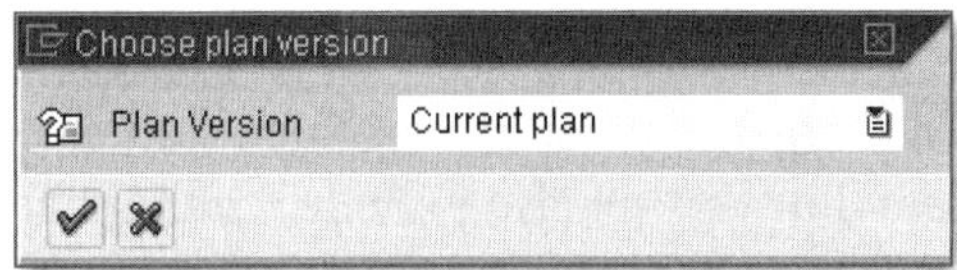

Figure 5.1 Selecting the Plan Version

5.2.2 Objects, Relationships, and Infotypes

While in personnel administration the "person" merely represents a type of information object — in organizational management different object types are processed. These are, for example:

- Organizational unit
- Position
- Job
- Task

In addition, *external object types* are also addressed. These represent objects that do not belong to organizational management and are not saved in its object structure, but are quite important for organizational management. These are, in particular:

- Person from personnel administration
- Cost center from cost accounting

To create relationships between these objects, relationship types are used. Each relationship possesses specific semantics, such as:

- Belongs to/incorporates (between organizational unit and position)
- Holder (between position and person)
- Manages/is managed by (between position and organizational unit)

This means different structures can be based on objects and relationships.

Infotypes are used to further describe objects beyond their structure relationship in the same way as in personnel administration. The infotype concept is very similar to that used in personnel administration, even though the technical implementation deviates in some respects. In particular, not all infotypes are permitted for all object types here. Thus, for example, the Infotype 1007 (Vacancy) exists for a position, but not for an organizational unit.

The concept of objects, relationships, and infotypes described here also applies to the other processes of personnel planning and development. Here, in particular, object types of different processes (e.g., organizational units and events) can be related to each other. The same infotype can also be used for objects of different processes. The number range for infotypes in personnel planning and development ranges between 1000 and 1999. More recent applications, such as E-Recruiting or SAP Learning Solution, are based on object types, relationships, and infotypes, where the number ranges of these infotypes range between 5000 and 5199.

Customizing for objects, infotypes, and relationships is carried out via the implementation guide (IMG) path PERSONNEL MANAGEMENT • ORGANIZATIONAL MANAGEMENT • BASIC SETTINGS ENHANCEMENT • DATA MODELING. For our present purpose, i.e., to use organizational management in a simple form as a basis for personnel administration and personnel controlling, no settings are required.

5.2.3 Selected Object Types

Basically, an *organizational unit* is an object of the organizational structure that has not been further specified. It can represent a business area, a team, an authority, a plant, or a department, among other things. This very general definition enables you to map as far into the depth of an organizational hierarchy as you want by using superordinate and subordinate organizational units.

In simple terms, a position is an element that a specific employee can occupy. A position can also be vacant, which means for recruitment that personnel are required and an employee should be searched for. Positions are assigned to an organizational unit by the relationship type "belongs to."

The *chief position* has specific characteristics. The owner of this position manages an organizational unit. From a technical point of view, a chief position emerges when a link of the type "manages" is created between a position and an organizational unit. The chief position is important in many areas. For example, it can be used to assign specific tasks in SAP Workflow (e.g., for determining who is allowed to approve leave requests), to identify the manager for the MSS, or to grant access rights to subordinate employees via the structural authorization check.

A *job* can be regarded as a prototype or template for a position. For example, "loan officers" usually describes a job, "loan officer no. 3 in the commercial real estate department" is a position. Jobs and positions are linked via the relationship types describes or is described by. Thus, the job concept provides a structure for the positions that can also be used for reporting purposes. The attributes are transferred to the positions derived from the inheritance (for example, workflow tasks). These attributes can be supplemented to the position.

5.2.4 Selected Infotypes

In many maintenance interfaces, the individual infotypes rarely appear. Instead, they are integrated in cross-application interfaces to align the process of the daily maintenance work with the tasks of a user role. You can reach the maintenance for individual infotypes through the menu path PERSONNEL • ORGANIZATIONAL MANAGEMENT • EXPERT MODE. Maintenance screens are provided there for organizational units, jobs, and positions for infotypes (see Figure 5.2). Under the menu item GENERAL, you can maintain infotypes for any object.

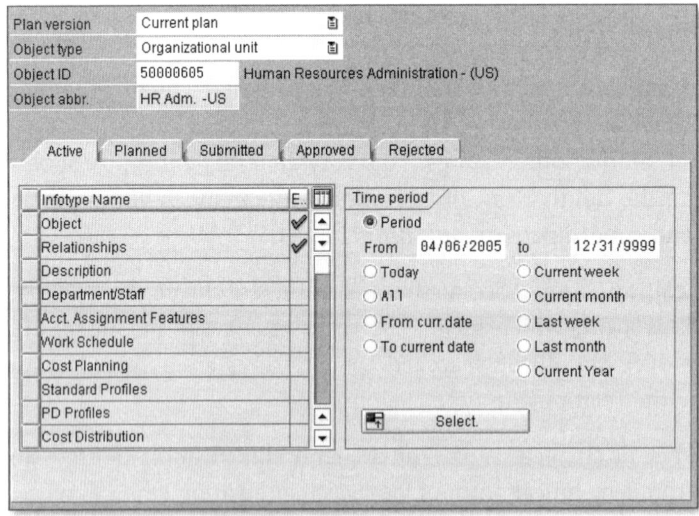

Figure 5.2 Expert Mode Independent of Object Types

The Infotype 1000 (Object) represents the object itself. It contains a name and an abbreviation, which may change over time. An object can be clearly identified using an eight-digit object ID. Infotype 1000 is thus comparable to Infotype 0002 in personnel administration. The name and abbreviation correspond to the name of an employee and the object ID of the personnel number. Figure 5.3 shows Infotype 1000.

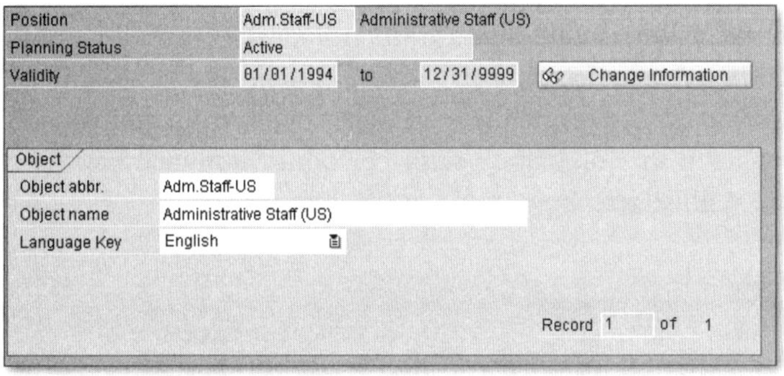

Figure 5.3 Infotype 1000 (Object)

Relationships are also stored in an infotype, namely Infotype 1001, where the relationship type represents the subtype. Direct maintenance of Infotype 1001, however, is an exception. The integrated maintenance interfaces enable reassignments (for example, via Drag & Drop), relationships, and simultaneous regeneration with relationships, without direct maintenance of Infotype 1001. The infotype contains the relationship type and the related object (see Figure 5.4).

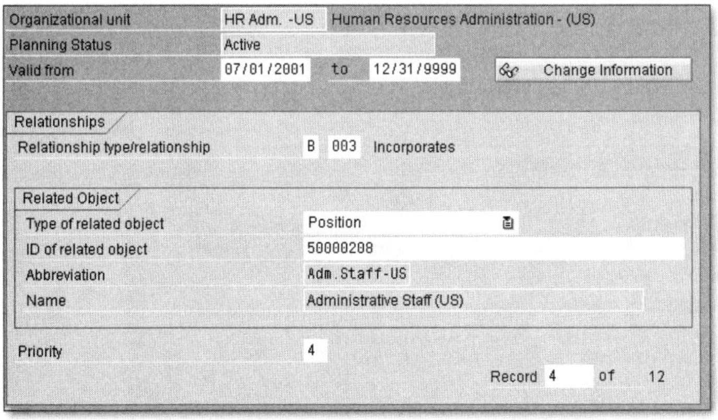

Figure 5.4 Relating the Organizational Unit to the Position

When a relationship is created, the corresponding relationship is also automatically created in the opposite direction. Thus, if the relationship Position belongs to organizational unit is created, the system automatically creates Organizational unit comprises position. Figure 5.5 shows the inverse relationship that corresponds to Figure 5.4. Therefore, relationships are always bidirectional and the relationship always consists of the direction (A: bottom up; B: top down) and the actual relationship.

Infotype 1003 (Department/staff) enables you to identify an organizational unit as a staff unit. This can be evaluated and displayed in a graphic. In addition, these department IDs can also be used to distinguish real departments from groups. This affects both evaluations and the integration with personnel administration (see Section 5.2.6). Figure 5.6 illustrates an example of Infotype 1003.

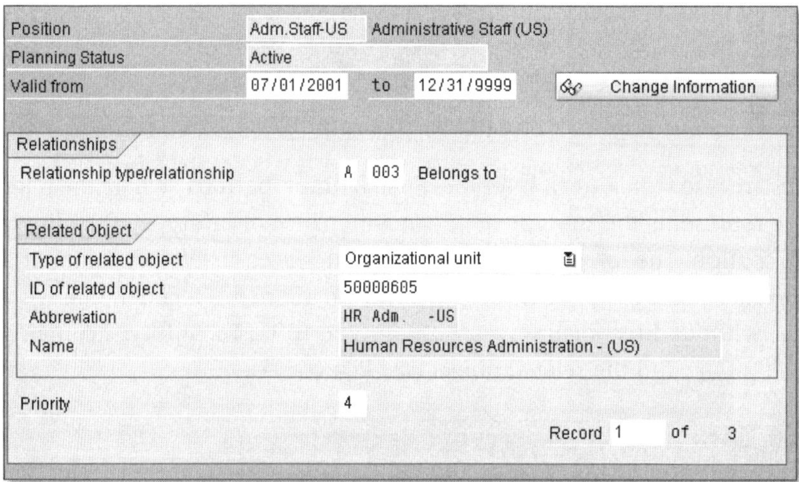

Figure 5.5 Relating the Position to the Organizational Unit

Organizational unit | HR Adm. -US | Human Resources Administration - (US)
Planning Status | Active
Valid from | 04/06/2005 | to | 12/31/9999 | Change Information

Department/Staff
☐ Staff
☑ Department

Figure 5.6 Department Identifier and Staff Identifier in Infotype 1003

Information on the vacancy is an essential element of manpower-requirement planning and recruitment. To really support requirement planning, the vacancy should be created as soon as the departure or transfer of an employee becomes known. This usually occurs automatically in the action Organizational change or Leaving.

The infotype itself contains a status indicator for the vacancy (see Figure 5.7). Open means that the search for personnel can begin immediately, while Vacancy filled requires no immediate action.

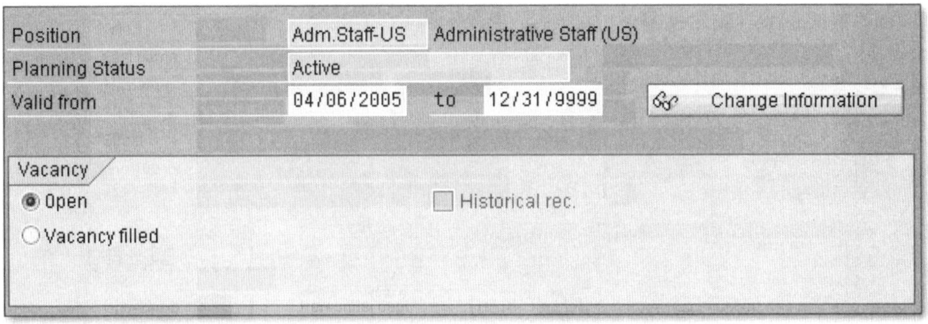

Figure 5.7 Infotype 1007 (Vacancy)

5.2.5 Designing the Organizational Structure

The organizational structure is initially created via the menu path PERSONNEL • ORGANIZATIONAL MANAGEMENT • ORGANIZATIONAL STRUCTURE • ORGANIZATION AND STAFF ASSIGNMENT • CREATE, to publish the root of the structure. You then can carry out further maintenance through the path PERSONNEL • ORGANIZATIONAL MANAGEMENT • ORGANIZATIONAL STRUCTURE • ORGANIZATION AND STAFF ASSIGNMENT • CHANGE.

To a large extent, the integrated maintenance interface abstracts from the infotypes, and is divided into four areas (see Figure 5.8). Due to split-screen technology, the four areas can be enlarged or reduced using a mouse, as is required for the current activity.

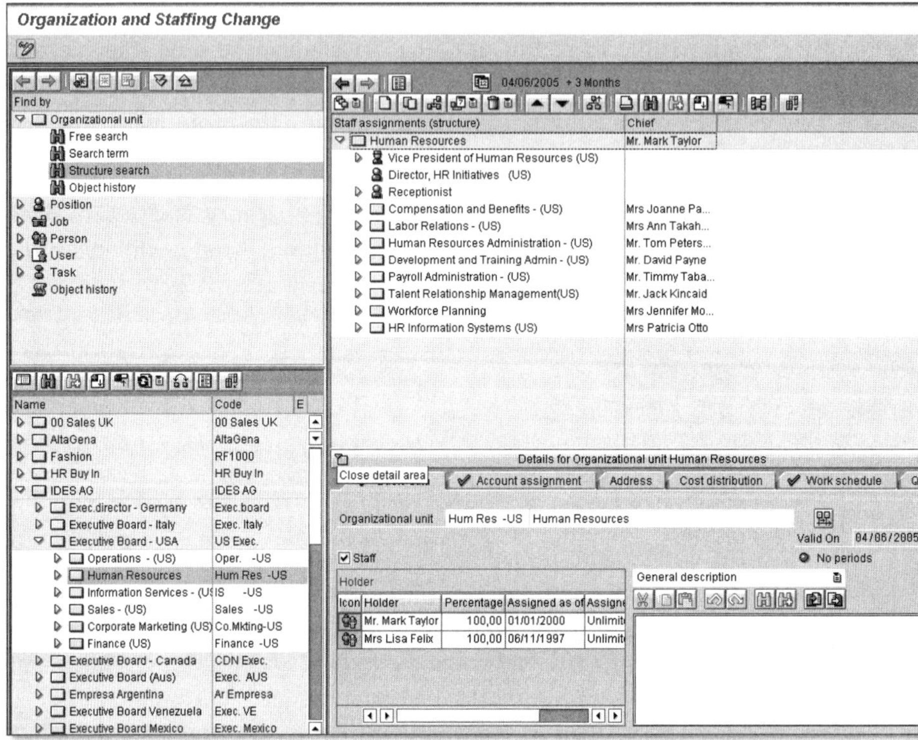

Figure 5.8 Maintenance Interface Divided into Four Parts

The upper left-hand pane is used to select objects and works like the Object Manager in personnel administration (see Figure 5.9).

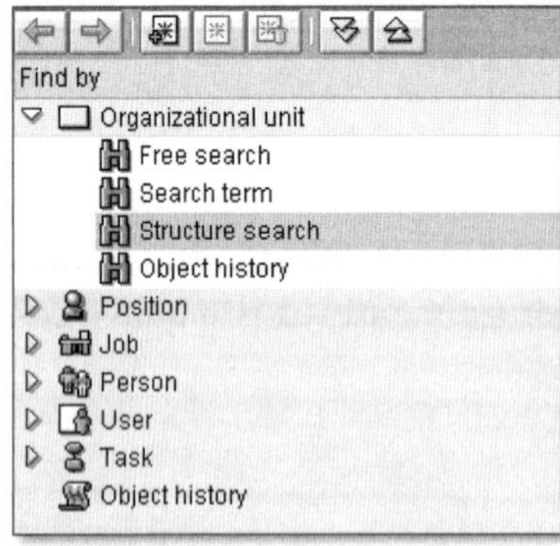

Figure 5.9 Selecting Objects

The lower left-hand pane manages the pool of objects already selected (see Figure 5.10). These can be selected as root objects for the work area or can be assigned to objects of the work area by Drag & Drop.

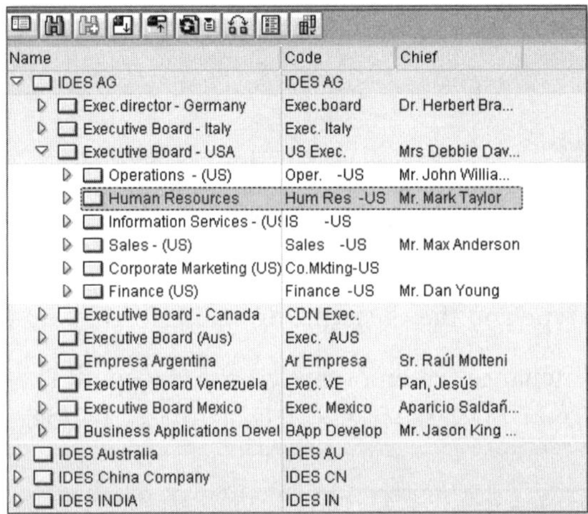

Figure 5.10 Object Pool

The actual work area is located in the upper right-hand pane. There you can use the Goto button to change between different views. In particular, you can change between the pure organizational structure and the staff assignments (see Figure 5.11).

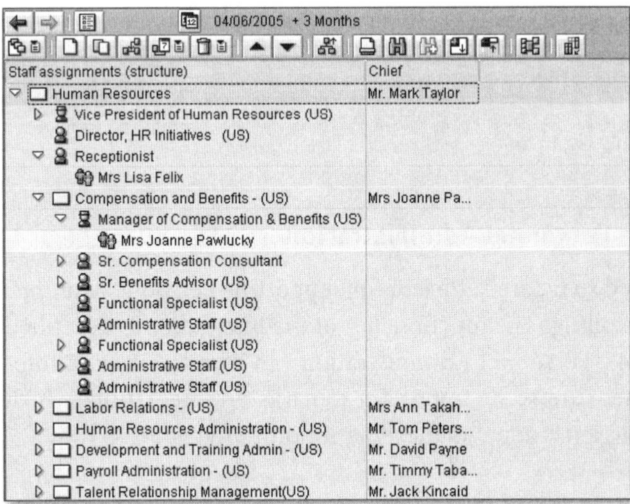

Figure 5.11 Staff Assignments in the Work Area

In Figure 5.11, the following functionalities are available:

- Creating, reassigning, delimiting, and deleting organizational units
- Creating, reassigning, delimiting, and deleting positions
- Changing the display sequence
- Assigning cost centers
- Assigning management functions
- Selecting objects for the details area

If you selected an object for the details area by double-clicking on it, different maintenance functions are available in several tabs (see Figure 5.12). Which tabs are available depends on the object type and the Customizing settings.

This configuration of the entire maintenance screen occurs via the IMG path Personnel Management • Organizational Management • Hierarchy Framework.

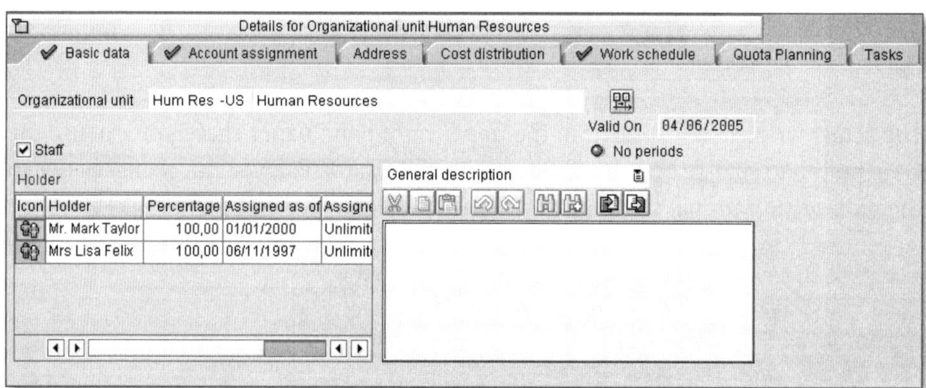

Figure 5.12 Maintenance via Tabs

5.2.6 Integration with Personnel Administration

The functionalities described so far are sufficient for supporting personnel administration and personnel controlling. The functionality of the integration is described in more detail in Chapter 4, "Personnel Administration," in correlation with Infotype 0001. Nevertheless here are some important remarks on integration, which you should read from an organizational management point of view:

- The teams that maintain the organizational management and personnel administration in the system must be completely aware of the integration aspects and their effects on the work of their colleagues.
- Note that retroactive organizational changes trigger recalculations in remuneration payroll that may lead to extensive adjustments in cost accounting (CO).
- You should also pay particular attention to the integration with recruitment or E-Recruiting and manpower requirement planning. These are based on the following prerequisites:
  - Vacancies must be maintained in a timely and correct manner.
  - Vacant positions must be delimited if they are definitely no longer required.
  - Positions for new employees must be created and correspondingly named.
- For a simple implementation of organizational management, which we hope to provide in this book, no customizing settings are required at first except for the definition of the integration itself via the characteristic PLOGI and the entries in system table T77S0 for the group PLOGI, which will be briefly discussed next.
  - The table entry PLOGI ORGA activates the integration between organizational management and personnel administration.
  - Using the PLOGI PRELU switch, you can then determine whether the data synchronization between organizational management and personnel administration is done via batch input (entry BTCI) or directly (entry "0" or ""). If the switch is set to direct update, changes to the data in the organizational management (for example, reassignment of an employee to another position) result in the direct change of Infotype 0001 (Organizational Assignment). If the update of Infotype 0001 is not completed successfully, the change is still updated in organizational management (for more details on problems with the integration of organizational management with the personnel administration, refer to Section 5.3).

5.3 Critical Success Factors

- In organizational management, many terms are used whose meaning in business life is different from the meaning in the system. For example, what is "Time Management" in SAP would more often be referred to as "Time & Attendance" in the business world. Unfortunately, this cannot be avoided in standard software that is used in many different areas and industries. So, within the environment of this system, terms like job or position should be perceived as intended with regard to SAP ERP HCM.

- Define the structures of the organizational management with regard to structures of other processes, for example, Workflow, Reporting, or Recruitment. It is particularly important in organizational management to have the actual structure of the enterprise available in any form. This information should be available before populating the structure in the system.
- If you use the structural authorization, you must check at an early stage whether the options of the standard are sufficient or whether you require new objects or relationships.
- The adaptation of the maintenance interface and the option to create your own objects and evaluation paths enable you to optimally support daily workflows. The amount of effort to invest in workflow optimization should depend on the frequency of the processes to be supported.
- Due to the many options available for storing data in positions or jobs, you run the risk of entering more data than is actually required. Therefore, you should always check whether the entered data can also be used in an economically reasonable way.
- The processes of data maintenance must be clarified at an early stage. These processes should be defined by employees or consultants with a high degree of experience in SAP ERP HCM.
- The maintenance of the organizational structure is a task that requires a very precise working method if organizational management is directly maintained in the live system. The meaning of correct maintenance becomes clear if you consider the fact that wrong reassignment of an occupied position can change the cost center assignment of an employee, which, in turn, can result in a recalculation and correction of the postings. So, changes to the organizational structure can only be implemented after coordination with the business areas that are concerned by the integration.
- Due to the close integration of organizational management with other processes you should not distribute the maintenance of the organizational management to various parts of the enterprise, but implement it as centrally as possible.

- In the integration with personnel administration, inconsistencies can occur between the organizational assignment according to PA Infotype 0001 and the assignment in organizational management to positions, organizational units, and cost centers due to various error sources. Some of the possible error sources during the integration with personnel administration are listed here:
- The retroactive definition of a mandatory field in Infotype 0001 (Organizational Assignment) results in an error message when Infotype 0001 is updated automatically. If this error message doesn't result in an action (filling in the mandatory field), and the action is cancelled by the user instead, Infotype 0001 is not updated; however, the data is already saved in organizational management. So the status of the organizational assignment in organizational management is different from the status in Infotype 0001.
- Transfer /leaving of obsolete positions. Here, the user is asked by the system to enter the delimitation date for an obsolete position. If a delimitation date is entered that is larger than the leaving or transfer date, this results in a gap for the assignment of the employee in organizational management.
- Customer-specific infotypes that write the relationship A/B 008 (holder) in organizational management during their maintenance and thus create relationships that are not consistent.
- Missing authorizations on the personnel administration or organizational management side that prevent an update of the respective side (for example, no authorizations for the maintenance of Infotype 0001 when reassigning a person from one position to another; in this case, an update would only occur on the organizational management side, but not on the personnel administration side).
- Use of User Exits/Business Add-ins (BAdIs) including plausibility checks in personnel administration that prevent Infotype 0001 from being saved.
- Occupied position was deleted (despite warning message).
- Dynamic measures on Infotype 0001 that may change the position data.
- Inconsistencies occur in the system if the following steps are implemented in the sequence described: Entering leaving action → Having position delimited → Extending position again → Deleting leaving.
- An interface program is implemented that writes relationships or organizational data.

E-Recruiting in SAP ERP HCM is a more recently developed component and varies considerably from the traditional recruitment solution described in the next chapter. E-Recruiting is built on a new technological basis that takes into account the new labor market for which you need to be proactive to capture the best talent.

6 E-Recruiting

Today, most job advertisements are published on the Internet and enterprises from specific industries less frequently accept conventional application processes in paper form, so we decided to discuss E-Recruiting before classic recruitment. However, the business basics described in this chapter will refer to both procurement paths, but for clarity, when talking about specific features of E-Recruiting or traditional recruitment we will indicate them as such.

6.1 Business Principles

Business principles provide the starting points for implementing the requirements in a personnel-management system. In addition to legal requirements, especially related to data protection, the different recruitment paths are of great importance when it comes to recruiting specialists and executives who are particularly scarce in the labor market. However, recruitment of junior employees and trainees in large numbers is also a central issue for applicant selection.

6.1.1 Goals of the Recruitment Process

For recruitment purposes, Human Resources (HR) should be made available through searches and provision so the workforce requirements can be met from quantitative and qualitative viewpoints. The goal of any recruitment process is to achieve the following targets in addition to providing qualified personnel:

- **Quantity target**
  HR should be recruited in sufficient quantities (number of jobs) and in sufficient duration (hours of work for each job).
- **Time target**
  HR should be employed promptly at the time scheduled for filling the job. In addition, the employee should be recruited for the desired staff assignment (fixed term or unlimited).

6.1.2 Recruitment Media

Before selecting the recruitment media, you should make a few key decisions. First, you must decide if you should recruit internally or externally. A preference for either internal or external recruitment will often be based on corporate HR strategy. For example, in a strongly unionized environment, you may have to focus on internal recruitment whenever possible. In the following sections we will briefly describe internal and external advertising and their characteristics.

Media for Internal Advertising

- **"Blackboard"**
  For internal job advertisements, standardized forms are frequently used. These forms provide a job description, important requirements, the length of the position (full time, part time, temporary, etc.), and the pay-scale category of the job to be filled. In addition to the classic "blackboard," which can often be found in cafeteria or canteen areas, internal advertisements are also being advertised more frequently on the company intranet or by sending an email.
- **Direct targeting and selection**
  While many jobs are advertising on the blackboard, there can also be targeted selection of a candidate for certain positions based on the specialization of the job or the level. A prerequisite for such a process is succession planning and personnel-development planning.
- **Advertising on the intranet**
  Companies are increasingly advertising certain jobs on the intranet and on the blackboard. Individuals in the commercial area are mainly approached here. Occasionally, there are also mailings to all employees stating that applications from employees' acquaintances are also welcome. With the new options of SAP ERP, E-Recruiting companies can actively search and address suitable internal employees.

Media for External Advertising

- **Job advertisements**
  Advertisements are still the most important instrument for external recruitment. The decision about which newspaper should be selected strongly depends on whom the advertisement is to address. In designing the advertisement, the proven AIDA (**A**ttention Interest Desire Action) principle should be observed. First of all, the applicant's attention should be drawn to the advertisement (Attention). For well-known companies, the company logo can achieve this effect. The required attention can also be raised by directly addressing the reader. Interest in the advertised job (Interest) can be generated by highlighting a few task areas or by mentioning the characteristics of the company culture. The desire to apply for the job (Desire) can be generated by emphasizing particular employee benefits of the company or the career opportunities related to the advertised job. Regarding the action element, printed adverts have a clear disadvantage against online adverts, where you can offer a button to click in order to apply or get in touch.
- **Job agencies (public or private)**
  Job agencies can also be used to find new staff at relatively low cost. This applies especially to public agencies. However, in some countries and regions these agencies may not have a good reputation among the most-wanted groups of candidates. And, public agencies tend to focus on candidates that are already unemployed. As a result, employers will not be able to reach potential employees who currently have jobs but are looking for new opportunities.
- **Headhunting**
  Headhunters are basically "researchers" seeking specific groups or people who currently hold positions corresponding to those the company desires to fill, and they ascertain those individuals' willingness to move. Due to the high costs, headhunters are usually only used for recruiting executives and specialists who are rarely found in the labor market. The advantage of this recruitment method is that applicants who are currently not looking for a position are also addressed. In addition, the competition can possibly be weakened by this, while at the same time the personnel department in your own company can be relieved of work.
- **Temporary or Contract Personnel**
  This method of recruitment is used to cover short-term requirements. In general, this doesn't involve any application process; instead, a few temp agencies are addressed directly. Many countries have legal restrictions regarding the duration for which temporary staff are allowed to be employed for.

- **Internet**
  As already mentioned at the beginning of this chapter, today, job advertisements on the Internet and the handling of recruitment via this medium has become common practice. Some enterprises have even decided to only accept online applications and reject paper applications from the outset. It seems like a long time ago that only computer scientists were advertised on the Internet. Due to the fast proliferation of the Internet in the past few years, you can now find job advertisements for almost all job categories on the Internet. Due to the multiple methods of recruitment through the Internet and the new options, the subject of Internet recruiting is dealt with separately in Section 6.1.6.
- **Other (university contacts, allocation of degree dissertations, workshops, etc.)**
  These recruitment methods are generally used to recruit junior staff or interns directly from universities and colleges.

Decision Criteria for External Recruitment Media

If external recruitment is decided on, you must consider what external recruitment medium to use or who carries out recruitment. There are several criteria here that should be taken into account when trying to make a decision (see Figure 6.1).

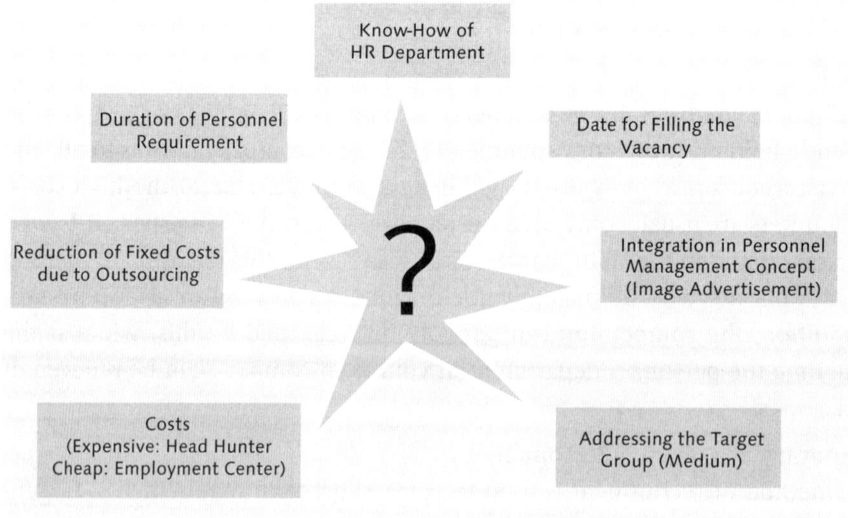

Figure 6.1 Decision Criteria for External Recruitment

6.1.3 Managing the Application Process

By managing the application process we mean all actions, from receipt of the application to the creation and delivery of the employment contract to the new employee.

In today's labor market situation, especially with regard to specialists and executives, and particularly in the Information Technology (IT) sector, it is increasingly important for a company to appear as an attractive employer. This can be achieved up front by the design and contents of the recruitment media; however, it should not stop there. Again and again, companies that look attractive from the outside can make serious mistakes when managing the application process (e.g., by replying late). Candidates expect an immediate confirmation, when they apply online, but as they know that this is usually automated, they'd also expect a personal reply pretty soon – particularly, if the employers sell themselves as dynamic organizations.

However, managing other applicants, such as junior staff and trainees, places great demands on the respective administrators and the software. Because applications for trainee positions are received in many ways, mastering the huge number of such applications is always a challenge for the HR department. An initial preselection takes place when the application files are reviewed by the HR department and applications that are obviously incomplete are filtered out.

Requirements for the Application Process from the Applicants' Point of View

If you placed yourself in the position of an applicant, you would find out quickly what is important in managing the application process. You would want for example:

- **Fast feedback upon receipt of the application**
  If a company has succeeded in attracting applicants, it is extremely important to respond as quickly as possible to interesting applicants. This begins with informing the applicant as soon as possible that their application has arrived and is already being processed. In the context of quality assurance, many companies have determined specific response times, which should not exceed a maximum of two weeks. When supporting such a goal, it is important to use the correct instrument to enable you to enter and evaluate applicant data in as efficient and uncomplicated a manner as possible, and also to enable fast correspondence.

- **Fast availability of the status of the application**
  It should be possible to provide a statement on the status of an application upon an applicant's request immediately. A status statement might include such information as the person currently in charge, departmental flow, or correspondence. This point is also of great importance internally, because everyone with access rights constantly has information on the whereabouts of applicant files and the status of the application.

Requirements for the Application Process from the Point of View of the User Departments

- **Simple entry of applicant data**
  Entering the applicant data — especially when dealing with large quantities — must be manageable in an uncomplicated and simple way.
- **Identification of duplicate applications**
  You must be able to detect duplicate applications automatically. Here, you must make a distinction between indentifying multiple applicants and previous employees.
- **Ensuring comparability**
  The data basis for the selection process should be as equal as possible — i.e., the same information content should be available for all applicants. In addition, it is usually necessary to enter additional data for an applicant in a later step. For example, bank details must be entered if there is an interview or assessment center to settle the travel expenses of an applicant.
- **Maintaining and monitoring the status of the application**
  To manage the selection process, you need to enter all of the planned and completed activities for an applicant within a selection process (e.g., sending confirmation of receipt, transferring applicant files, interview). In addition, the status of an application must be available quickly and across different departments so that information can be received on it at any time. This information requirement is internal from the user department point of view and also external from an applicant point of view.

Equal Employment Opportunities (EEO)

EEO delivers some very important criteria for a proper recruitment process. There are several laws in the U.S. to enforce EEO regulations. These include:

- Title VII of the Civil Rights Act of 1964, which prohibits employment discrimination based on race, color, religion, sex, or national origin.
- Age Discrimination in Employment Act of 1967, which protects individuals who are 40 years of age or older.
- Title I and Title V of the Americans with Disabilities Act of 1990, which prohibit employment discrimination against qualified individuals with disabilities.

Different regulations may apply in other countries, so you have to check the legal requirements in every country in which you want to implement a recruitment process. The HCM system should provide the necessary information to answer inquiries from the U.S. EEO Commission and do the mandatory reporting.

6.1.4 Applicant Selection

In this section, we will explain the process of preselection of applicants and then describe the actual selection process and the different selection procedures in further detail.

Preselection

In the applicant preselection stage, the incoming applications are divided into three categories:

- **A applicants**
  These are applicants who seem to be suitable based on the documents provided. These are the candidates you want to consider in more detail in an interview. The A criteria can be derived from
  - Request for personnel from the user department
  - Requirements profile
  - Job description
  - Company principles (e.g., to employ university graduates only)
  - Application principles

  Criteria typically include:
  - Completeness of the application documents
  - Age

  - Industry experience
  - Years of work experience
  - Final qualification
- **B applicants**
  These are interesting applicants who are not assigned to group A due to small irregularities in their CV or similar reasons. These applicants provide a reserve in case some applicants from group A were not suitable or canceled their application.
- **C applicants**
  Applicants who, based on their qualifications, do not suit the advertised job or whose application documents are incomplete. These applicants are generally refused immediately.

Selection process

The applicant selection can be carried out in different ways. This depends on several factors:

- **Applicant group**
  If this involves, for example, trainees, then proficiency tests, group exercises, and subsequent interviews or preliminary interviews are often carried out. The selection of specialists, on the other hand, is generally done through first and, if necessary, second interviews.
- **Type of job to be occupied**
  If specialists and executives must be selected, assessment centers are usually carried out in which the applicants go through different test scenarios or various levels of interviewing for at least one day.

6.1.5 Recruitment Controlling

Recruiting incurs costs for the external/internal recruitment media, and uses internal HR. The task of recruitment controlling is to find out the level of success related to the resources used. The efficiency of recruitment actions is determined to make decisions for or against specific actions. Recruitment controlling controls personnel management work and must be considered as operational controlling.

A prerequisite for an effective recruitment controlling is high transparency of the costs related to HR processes. To determine these costs, the following questions must be answered:

- **Which parts of the company can be involved?**
  - **Personnel marketing**: Publish information on the Internet, recruiting days, participate in applicant forums, etc.
  - **Psychological service**: Creating a selection process and its constant revision (e.g., AC, tests, interview guidelines)
  - **Recruitment**: Implementing the selection process, concluding the contract, etc.
- **How can you identify the costs?**
  - Defining a cost unit to Specialist recruitment
  - Post individual cost-unit costs (personnel costs, media costs, etc.) directly to the cost unit
  - Post overhead cost-unit costs to the cost unit (first option: apportionment of current costs; from the costs of the psychological service X% is assigned to the creation of an AC (Assessment Center) for specialists; second option: working with a planned allocation rate)

The second block of information is the use of recruitment media, for example. This can then be quantitatively determined if the incoming applications are assigned to a recruitment medium. This means evaluations can be made throughout the recruitment flow, which enables a statement on how many applications are related to a specific medium. Qualitative success can be determined on the basis of the number of applications that refer to a specific medium and have led to the conclusion of a contract.

What is still problematic in this context is the monetary evaluation of this success. For sales employees, for example, it is fairly easy to evaluate the success of their activities in monetary terms (number and volume of contracts concluded), whereas for HR administrators this is much more difficult. The dilemma is that while the costs can be identified on a quantitative basis, success can only be expressed in terms of quality. There are different examples of how you can work around or solve this problem. One option is to define the desired benefit. With regard to executives, this might translate to low fluctuation in the respective department.

This benefit can then be evaluated on a monetary basis, if you take into account the costs saved by avoiding the recruitment of new employees.

6.1.6 Internet Recruiting

There are several ways for companies to recruit personnel on the Internet:

- **Recruitment through their own website**
  The option of creating online applications directly for job advertisements and transferring the data directly to an existing ERP system relieves the HR department considerably from administrative tasks such as entering applicant master data. The latest developments in this area, such as SAP ERP E-Recruiting described in this chapter, support not only the administrative processes, but also enable a comprehensive talent management. To "lure" applicants to a specific website, there are traffic generators, such as entering the website into search engines (MSN, Google) and directories, such as Yahoo. Entries in meta-job exchanges in which only career-relevant websites are entered (e.g., *www.monster.com*, *www.careerbuilder.com*, *http://hotjobs.yahoo.com*) are possible. The talent management provides even more service and supports enterprises in establishing long-term relationships to the applicants (talent relationship management). This means that even if no suitable job is available for an applicant, he can still be interesting for the enterprise sometime in the future.
- **Using commercial job exchanges**
  Today there is a large offering in this area, ranging from the job exchange that provides the entire range of jobs, through specific job exchanges for specialists and executives, to regional job exchanges. The range of activities of these exchanges includes the following:
  - Entering the company profile
  - Entering the job offers
  - Online applications
  - Job-search database
  - Link to the company website
  - Link to the company-specific E-Recruiting system
- **Job-search databases**
  The active search of companies for new employees is the focus here. In job-search databases, you must beware of nonactive individuals who have been listed there for a long time. It is crucial that the data be up-to-date.

The integration of online applications with SAP ERP HCM systems means that many steps of the advertising and application process can be automated:

- Automatic delivery of the applications to the correct contact
- Informing applicants by mouse-click or automatically on receipt of the application
- Making information on the status of the application available online in the recruitment process
- Applicant correspondence by email

6.2 Specific Features of E-Recruiting

Most of what is said about the general business basics described in the previous sections is also true for E-Recruiting, as we are talking primarily about a different technical approach — the talent management. However, new technology allows some major changes to the business processes, which have to be discussed here.

6.2.1 War for Talent

Even in countries with high unemployment it is more and more difficult for companies to attract specialized or high-potential candidates, as you can see even today in the U.S. Most organizations expect this problem to grow, given the aging population in many parts of the industrialized world and ever-increasing skill requirements for the top technical and managerial positions.

On the other hand, most organizations see a sharp increase of applications from candidates with only average or low skills. The challenge to the HR department will be to manage this workload efficiently while still finding the best candidates to ensure their companies' competitiveness.

6.2.2 Sourcing and Retention

Considering that the highly talented tend to behave as self-confident business partners in the labor market today, the traditional recruitment process is just not enough. What you need is a comprehensive talent-relationship management.

Research shows that the majority of employees are neither 100% loyal to their employers nor actively looking for a new job. More than 50% are interested in a good opportunity but may not even read the help-wanted section of the newspaper or scan Internet job sites. A company that attracts talent and builds relationships with talented people even before they are urgently looking for a new job has a considerable advantage, which is the idea behind the concept of the talent pool. Employees who are screening the job market without an immediate wish to change their employers are invited to an uncommitted registration. They can look around and get acquainted with the company. When a promising opening arises, they are available without the need for much advertising. The talent pool also allows for a reasonable segmentation of candidates so that you can concentrate on your target groups.

This also allows you to apply well-known principles of customer relationship management to your recruiting processes. It is obviously more efficient and more effective to build and maintain long-term relationships than to search for short-term contacts every time you need them and then lose them again.

What is true for external candidates is also true for internal talent. After all, your best employees are potential candidates for your competitors, and it would be naïve to assume that they do not watch the job market. So, because they are watching anyway, why not make sure that the internal job market of your company is at the top of their list? Allow your employees what you allow external candidates. When change is due, it is better they choose a new job in your company than leave for the competition.

6.2.3 Controlling Recruitment Processes

Measurement of the recruitment performance is becoming more and more important. There are well-known key figures such as:

- **Cost per hire**
  All internal (e.g., time spent by recruiters) and external (e.g., cost of a job advert) costs that are spent to fill a position
- **Time to fill**
  Time that passes from the opening of a position to the hiring of a new employee
- **Cost of staff turnover**
  All costs caused by an employee leaving (including hiring and training costs

and the costs caused by the vacancy, to name but the most important components)

With E-Recruiting, it can be more challenging to assign the costs to a specific hiring event, because the costs for the talent pool must be shared by all hiring activities in some way. Moreover, there are often requirements for more detailed information. One way of dividing the time to fill a vacancy is as follows:

- The time from the moment the vacancy is known to the moment when a job advertisement is published (online or in print)
- The time between the publishing of the advertisement and the invitations to first interviews
- The time between the interviews and the hiring decision

With a specialized e-recruitment system, the expectations in this area are particularly high, because there the recruitment process is implemented almost exclusively with system support and should therefore be efficient.

6.2.4 Processes and Organization

This new world of recruitment can be quite a challenge for the HR department. It differs from the traditional process in a number of ways.

- The candidates can contact the company in many different ways, and they can decide how to go about it.
- Working with a talent pool requires completely new processes, because, after the initial registration, the initiative often must come from the employer.
- Besides the processes surrounding applications and job openings, something must be done for the retention of talent in the pool.
- Line managers expect to be involved more actively in the selection process and get quicker results so they can respond to changing market requirements
- Cost per hire is an important key figure, and budgets for HR are often limited.
- Recruitment, staff retention, succession planning, and career development are interconnected. They can even be seen as parts of the same complex process.

All of this requires significant changes to the old organization and processes.

6.2.5 Recruitment Service Providing

In recent years, more and more companies have outsourced parts of their recruitment processes or built corporate service centers to act as service providers. The pressure to reduce costs, together with the increasing complexity of the processes, may be major reasons for this.

However, with this step, the processes often become more complex because of increased coordination requirements. So, it is even more important to have well-defined and sensible processes and a clear organization with appropriate IT support.

6.2.6 Technology

Most organizations seriously working with E-Recruiting have to face technological challenges, including:

- Candidates send information in many different forms. Not only must paper-based applications be processed but also electronic documents in a variety of formats such as Microsoft Word, PDF, TIF, and JPG. One possibility is to have all applicants fill in an online form with the most important information.
- Data security is always an issue, and it has two sides:
  - Candidates who register and enter confidential data want to be sure that no unauthorized access of this data is possible.
  - It makes sense that the recruiting system interacts with the operative SAP ERP HCM system. Because this interaction opens up a connection between the HCM system and the outside world via the Internet, technology must guarantee that data of the operative HCM system cannot be accessed from outside the organization.
- International recruitment is often a reason for changing from traditional recruitment processes to E-Recruiting; however, this means that the system has to:
  - Comply with legislation of different countries regarding data security, accessibility, etc.
  - Be multilingual
  - Deal with different formats for addresses, names, etc.
  - Take into account different education systems and grading systems

6.3 The Process in SAP ERP HCM

The following descriptions mainly focus on the aspects of personnel administration that deal with the application process in the E-Recruiting system and not on the processes in personnel development. However, you cannot always make a clear distinction here. If you're interested in planning processes, such as career and succession planning using SAP ERP E-Recruiting, refer to the latest edition of the SAP PRESS book Personnel Planning and Development with SAP ERP HCM (Richard Haßmann, Jill Hatton, Christian Krämer).

6.3.1 Overview

Figure 6.2 shows the main functional areas of the solution. In the center of the whole process stands the Talent pool, where candidates can maintain their data. How much data they enter can be decided by the candidates within the restrictions that the employer sets in the Customizing.

Registration is the first step. At this point, it is generally not required that the candidate enters all of the data. You can expect, rather, that many candidates will enter more and more data with time and only offer the full set of data when they find an attractive vacancy.

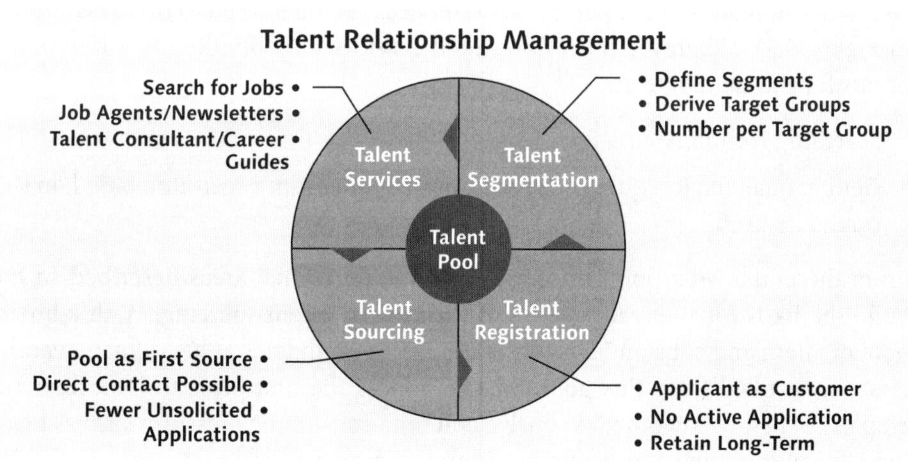

Figure 6.2 Functional Overview of SAP E-Recruiting

The data maintained in the talent pool usually includes:

- Personal data
- Communication data (address, email, phone, etc.)
- Employment preferences (such as functional area and salary expectations)
- Work experience
- Education
- Skills profile (qualifications)
- A range of attachments such as certificates and reference letters
- A cover letter

Although it is possible at this stage to see active applications for a particular vacancy, and although in most cases this is encouraged, the employer's main aim in registration is developing a long-term relationship.

How much effort is invested in this relationship and whether a candidate receives invitations to apply for specific jobs can be decided in the talent segmentation process. It allows the employer to assign candidates to a talent group (see Section 6.3.6) and to assess candidates in a detailed appraisal form (questionnaire) (see Section 6.3.5) that can be fully customized.

To retain candidates in the pool, several services can be offered to them (as shown in Figure 6.2). Whatever the value-added services may be, the most important points for the candidate are:

- Searching for interesting job postings
- Getting qualified job offers or invitations to apply from a recruiter, based on the candidate profile.

From the employer's point of view, the three functional areas described so far build the basis for the real purpose of the system: talent sourcing. With a broad pool of talent and substantial information about candidates at hand, many vacancies can be filled from this pool. So, the pool is the first place to look for new employees before any other expensive and time-consuming measures such as placing job advertisements or hiring head-hunters are necessary.

To do this, requisition management is a very important feature of the solution. Recruiters define the requisitions and related job postings that are requested by the managers who are looking for new employees. These requisitions (see Section

6.3.3) hold the data about the job requirements that will be matched with the candidates' data.

Note that the whole system works for internal and external candidates. With ERP version 6.0, succession planning is included as an explicit component represented by its own portal role, the Succession Planner. This shows an important development within SAP ERP HCM: Recruiting and personnel development get more and more integrated in the Talent Management solution, which is comprised of the components E-Recruiting, Learning Solution, and Performance Management. With this development, the software is ahead of many HR departments, where these two functions do not work closely together. As a matter of fact, recruitment and personnel development are often alternative or even hybrid solutions to the same problem. So, they should be dealt with together as SAP ERP HCM suggests.

6.3.2 Processes and Roles

The application is based on several roles, which are described in detail in Section 6.4. A role is not merely a set of authorizations, as it is sometimes understood. In the context of E-Recruiting, a role represents a set of functions together with the corresponding user interface tailored to the requirements of the role. The most important roles and their interactions are represented in Figure 6.3. This figure shows the main process, starting with a candidate's interest in the company and the creation of a vacancy, up to the application. However, this process as shown is rather simplified because it does not take into account the various outcomes each step could have. It merely concentrates on the most interesting outcomes that keep the process going.

The first part of the process shows two independent branches:

- The candidate registers in the talent pool and maintains some data.
- A manager needs a new employee and requests a requisition, which is created by the recruiter along with one or more postings.

The second part of the process shows how the candidate and the requisition — or rather a job posting contained in the requisition — can get together. There are two ways for this to happen:

- The candidate searches for interesting positions and finds a match.
- The recruiter searches for candidates matching his requisition and finds one. In this case, he would invite the candidate to apply for the position in question and provide all of the necessary data.

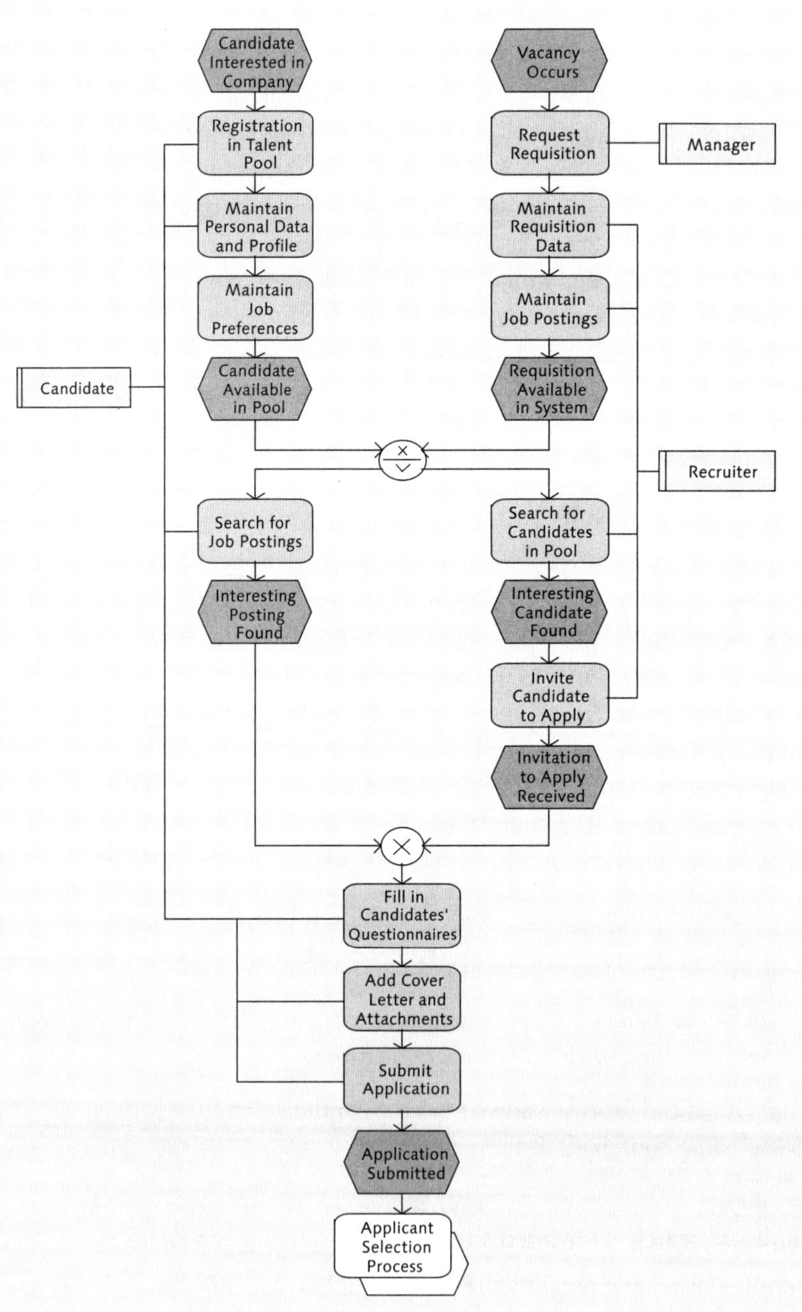

Figure 6.3 Process Overview: Candidate, Manager, and Recruiter

In both cases, the candidate will complete his data. Usually, he will upload a cover letter and other attachments and may have to fill out some additional information. With this done, he can submit the application.

But the process doesn't stop there, as the usual course of a selection process with correspondence, interviews, etc., and further roles are likely to be involved. The process flow is controlled by so-called process templates (see Section 6.3.4) together with SAP Workflow.

In the following sections, we will discuss the most important concepts of the solution and then look at the different roles.

6.3.3 Requisitions

Together with the candidates themselves, requisitions are the central objects of the whole solution. Requisitions provide the means to get vacancies for the processors of E-Recruiting and to all other persons involved (see Figure 6.4).

Each requisition contains one or more job postings that are dealt with together and have similar requirements. Each job posting can be published via one or more publications.

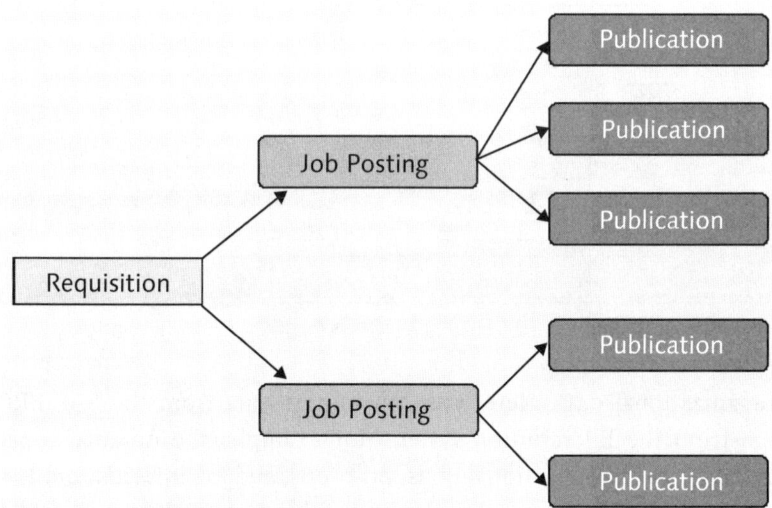

Figure 6.4 Structure of a Requisition

A requisition is maintained in nine steps, which do not all have to occur in every organization.

1. Maintain general job information, which contains administrative data about the requisition process and the basic job details such as description, function, and salary (see Figure 6.5). The more detailed the data entered, the better the search can be implemented.

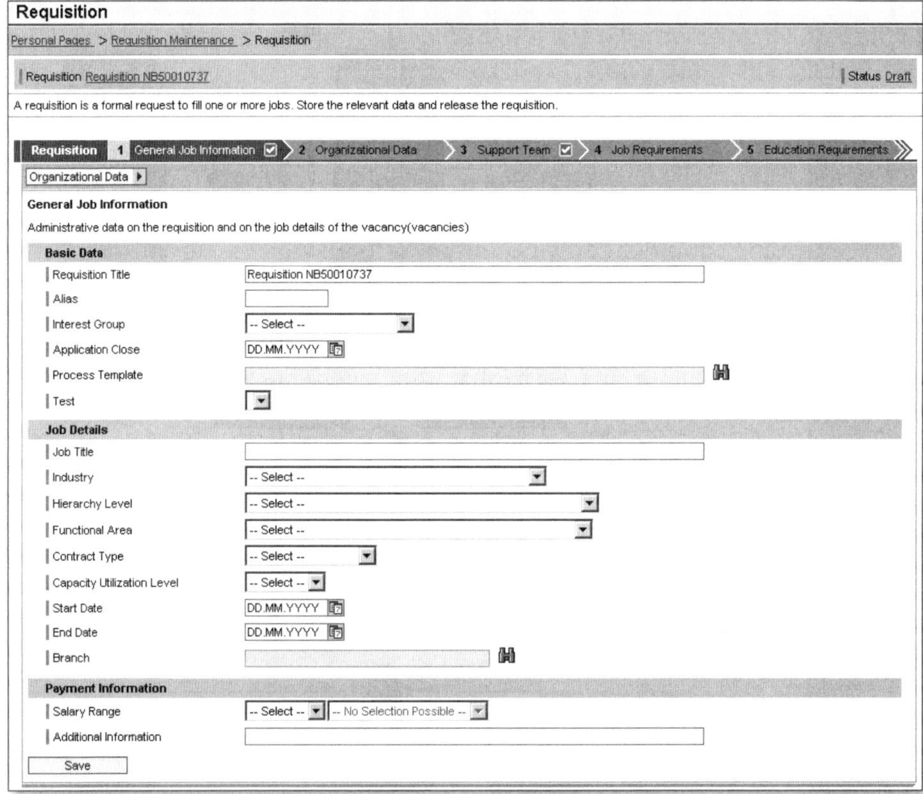

Figure 6.5 Creating a Requisition

2. Maintain organizational data. Here, you can import data from the SAP ERP HCM system from the E-Recruiting system, for example, the organizational structure including the organizational units, positions, and job information. For the organizational data you can also determine how many jobs are to be searched via the requisition.

Note

By default, Full Time Equivalent (FTE) cannot be entered here.

3. Define the support team. This is the team working with the requisition in several roles. You needn't define all possible roles for a requisition. The extent to which you define them depends on your process. Generally, at least a recruiter and a requesting manager are involved. Other roles that could be involved include a decision maker to approve the postings, an administrator, or a data-entry assistant (see Figure 6.6).

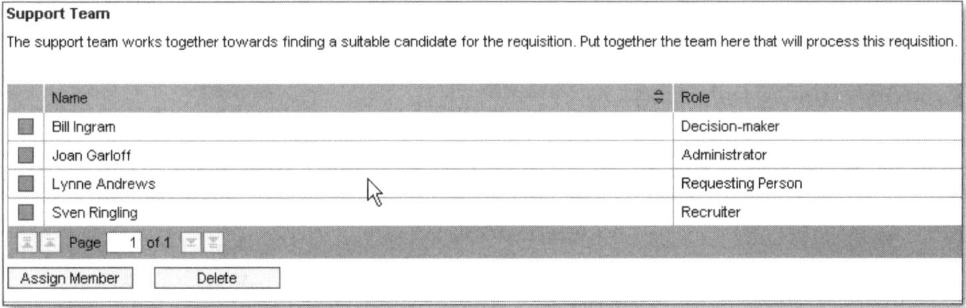

Figure 6.6 Defining the Support Team

4. Maintain job requirements relating to the employment experience of the future position holder.
5. Maintain education requirements.
6. Add attachments (such as a detailed job description in the form of a PDF file).
7. Set the status of the requisition; only if the requisition is released can the included postings be published for the talent pool.
8. The data overview shows the recruiter what data has been maintained so that he can easily identify any missing data.
9. In the last step, the job postings are included in the requisition (see Figure 6.7).

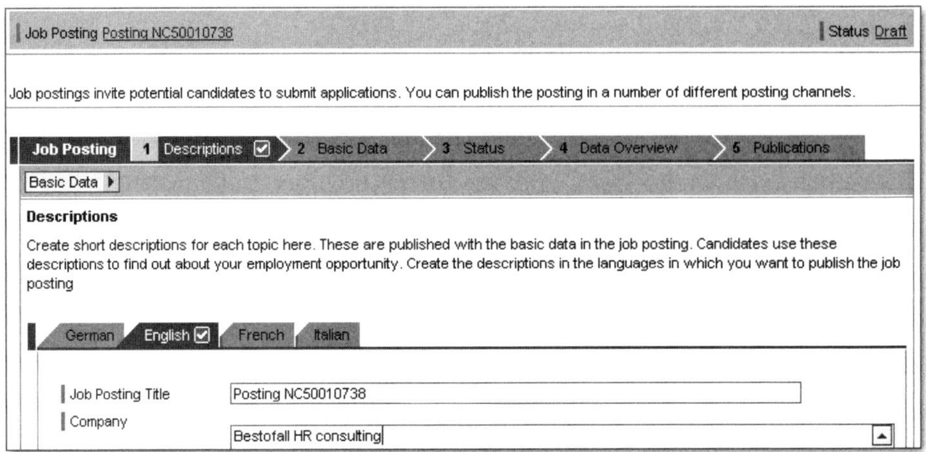

Figure 6.7 Creating a Job Posting

Figure 6.5 shows the design of a step-by-step procedure typical for the E-Recruiting solution. A step that is often included in such procedures is the data overview, though this is not shown in the figure. Step nine leads to another step-by-step procedure as shown in Figure 6.7. While the requisition is an object for internal use (though the data assigned, such as salary and requirements, has important external effects), the job posting is meant for the outside world. This is particularly clear when you note the multilingual descriptions that can be seen on the lower tabs in Figure 6.7. After all, it is not the requisition but the job (posting) a candidate is looking for.

Most of the data a job posting needs is already maintained on the level of the requisition, so there are only five steps involved in creating the posting:

1. The general description
2. Some basic administrative data
3. The status, which has a similar meaning as the status of the requisition
4. The data overview mentioned earlier
5. The publications of the posting (see Figure 6.8).

If you are familiar with the traditional solution in SAP ERP HCM, which will be described in Chapter 7, "Traditional Recruitment," you will be pleased to see that it is not necessary to create a new posting for each publication. Instead, it is possible to assign several publications to one posting. In this case, the data structure of the E-Recruiting solution does represent the real world much better than the traditional solution. The publication gets most of its data from the posting and the requisition, so that the most important information is the posting channel and the time period through which the publication is continued. As with requisitions and postings, the publication has a status. The status shown in Figure 6.8 is Draft, which means that it cannot be seen by candidates. A publication can only be Released, when both the posting and the requisition are released.

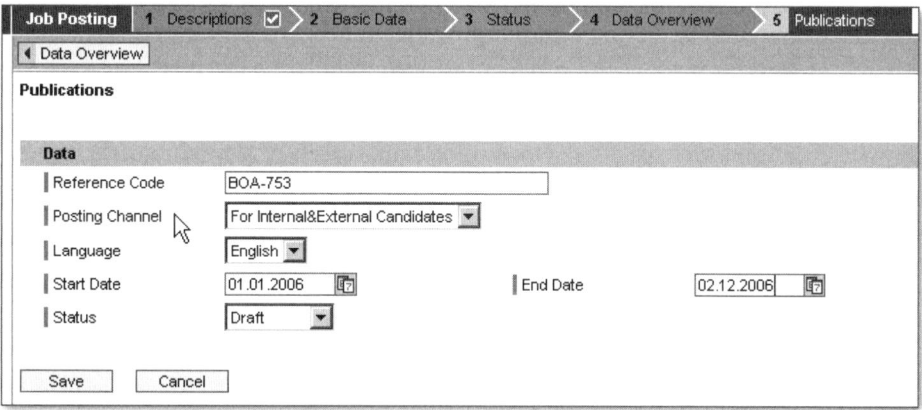

Figure 6.8 Maintaining a Publication

6.3.4 Process Templates

The tracking process of an application for a particular posting is defined by a so-called process template. It consists of an ordered set of process steps and activities and is assigned to a requisition (see Figure 6.9). Through the template, the recruiter is guided through the process, but he is not forced to perform all of the steps or to perform them in a predefined order.

Although the process template does more or less take the role of actions, activities, and feature PACTV of the traditional recruitment solution (see Section 7.1.5), there are some significant differences:

- A process template is defined by the end-user (e.g., the recruiter) in the normal application, while feature PACTV must be maintained in Customizing.
- The concept of the process template is more flexible. It is much easier to establish different processes for different target groups.

- To achieve the same level of support for the communication between process participants as in traditional applicant data administration, SAP Workflow must be included.

The concept of the process template has four levels:

1. The process template itself (e.g., High Potentials North America)
2. A set of process steps or subprocesses (e.g., Application-Entry or Prescreening) is assigned to the template. They are just called "process" in the system.
3. A set of activities (e.g., first interview or rejection after interview) is assigned to each process. Note that the types of activities and the available processes are defined in Customizing. Only the assignment can be done by the recruiter.
4. Special content such as letters or questionnaires can be assigned to each activity.

The recruiter can create a new process template via the path PROCESS TEMPLATES • CREATE PROCESS TEMPLATE. At first, some header data, as shown in Figure 6.9, must be entered. The most important data is the status. The template can only be assigned to a requisition when it has the status released. You should only release it when it is definitely ready, as later changes can be difficult when the template is already included in a requisition.

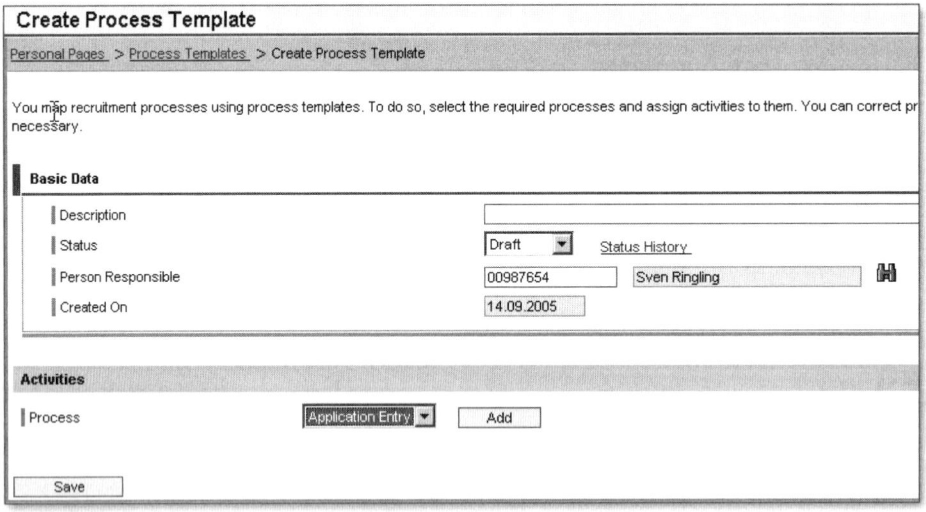

Figure 6.9 Header Data of a Process Template

Figure 6.10 shows a complete process template in which the processes Application Entry, Prequalification, Selection, Offer Phase, and Rejection are represented by five tabs. Eight activities are assigned to the process Offer Phase, and three of them have a letter form assigned.

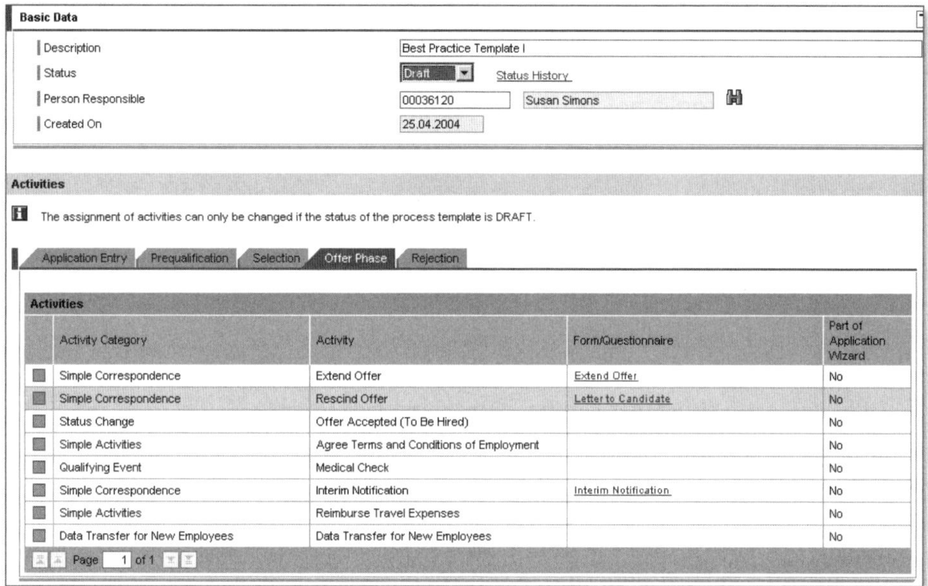

Figure 6.10 Process Template with Five Processes

6.3.5 Questionnaires

Questionnaires are a very flexible tool that allow gathering of any type of information from or about a candidate in a structured way. There are two types of questionnaires:

- General questionnaires that can be used to get additional information from the candidate or to enter the impression that the manager or decision-maker got from the candidate in an interview.
- EEO questionnaires are designed for the specific purpose of obtaining data necessary to comply with U.S. EEO regulations. EEO questionnaires are based on the same concept as general questionnaires but contain a special type of question.

Each questionnaire is composed of a set of questions from a pool of available questions. Each question can be assigned to several questionnaires. Both questions and questionnaires can be maintained by the end-user, usually the recruiter or an administrator.

As with process templates, the status field is important for questionnaires and questions. Both can only be used when the status is released. Keep the status set on draft as long as the question or questionnaire is not completed. The results of questionnaires could not be compared if changes were made to the already-released and used questionnaires.

There are five different types of questions for general questionnaires:

- **Single selection**
  A field where an answer from a given choice of predefined answers can be selected.
- **Input field**
  A field where a short text can be maintained freely.
- **Multiple selections**
  More than one answer can be selected from a given choice of answers.
- **Predefined scale**
  The answer can be chosen from a scale defined in Customizing.
- **Input area**
  An area to maintain a text; similar to the input field, but with more space.

Figure 6.11 shows one example for each of these types and Figure 6.12 shows them included in a questionnaire in the preview mode. This is exactly how a questionnaire would look to a candidate or anybody else asked to fill it in online.

	Have you ever bought a product from our company?	Single Selection
	Describe your experience in intercultural management	Input Field
	Which of these countries have you ever worked in?	Multiple Selection
	How would you rate your coffee brewing skills?	Predefined Scale
	Describe your problem solving approach!	Input Area

Figure 6.11 Questions of Five Different Types

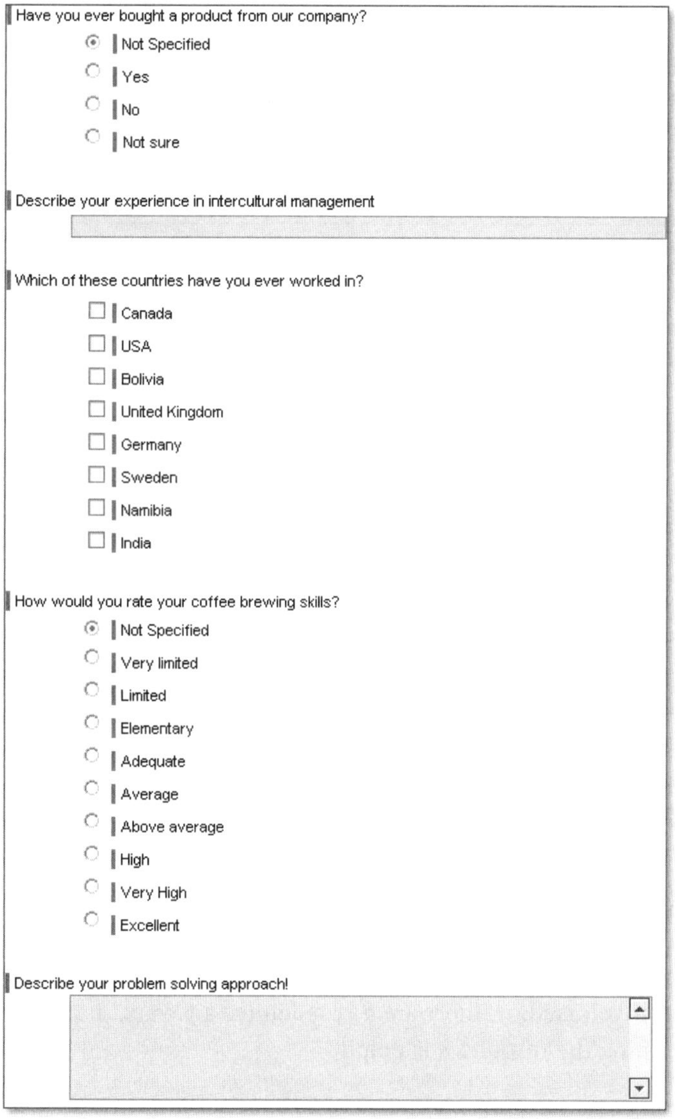

Have you ever bought a product from our company?

- Not Specified
- Yes
- No
- Not sure

Describe your experience in intercultural management

Which of these countries have you ever worked in?

- Canada
- USA
- Bolivia
- United Kingdom
- Germany
- Sweden
- Namibia
- India

How would you rate your coffee brewing skills?

- Not Specified
- Very limited
- Limited
- Elementary
- Adequate
- Average
- Above average
- High
- Very High
- Excellent

Describe your problem solving approach!

Figure 6.12 The Five Question Types in Preview

The maintenance of questions can be accessed by the recruiter via the activity Question Maintenance in the box Administration. Then he receives an overview, as shown in Figure 6.13, where he can display, change, or create new questions. The questions are assigned to one of four tabs for structuring purposes:

- Other
- Decision-maker related
- Candidate related
- Job related

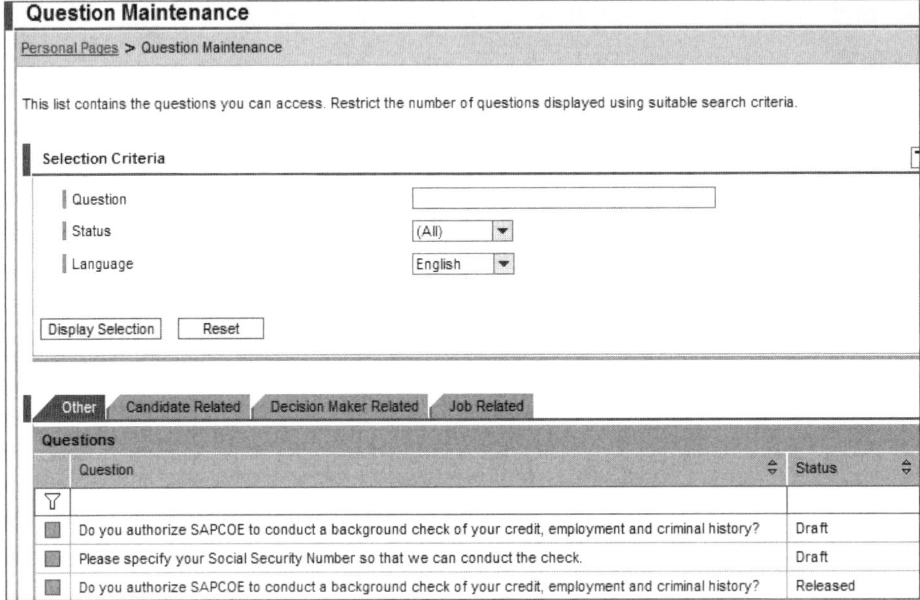

Figure 6.13 Question Maintenance — Overview

Figure 6.14 shows how an input field question is created. Just maintain the text of the question as it is supposed to be presented on the questionnaire and choose input field as the response type. When the question is ready for use in questionnaires, change the status to released. As there are no predefined answers, the lower part of the screen containing the responses is empty.

In Figure 6.15, a question with multiple choices is maintained. Here, you have to assign all of the possible responses. These are taken from a catalog of responses that can be maintained by the recruiter. Make sure that responses are reused whenever possible. Especially common answers like Yes or No will occur very often in the catalog when you do not check whether a response you need is already available before you create a new one.

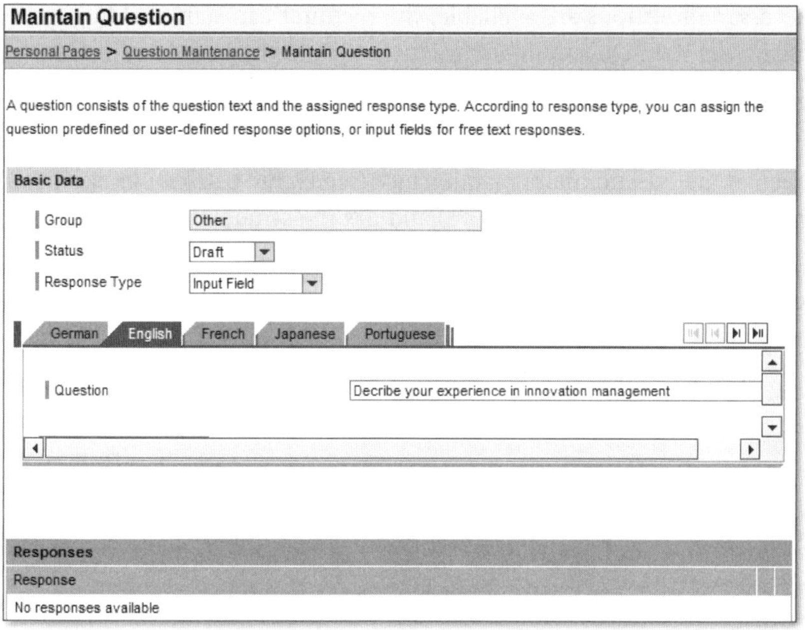

Maintain Question

Personal Pages > Question Maintenance > Maintain Question

A question consists of the question text and the assigned response type. According to response type, you can assign the question predefined or user-defined response options, or input fields for free text responses.

Basic Data

Group: Other
Status: Draft
Response Type: Input Field

German | English | French | Japanese | Portuguese

Question: Decribe your experience in innovation management

Responses

Response

No responses available

Figure 6.14 Maintain a Question with an Input Field

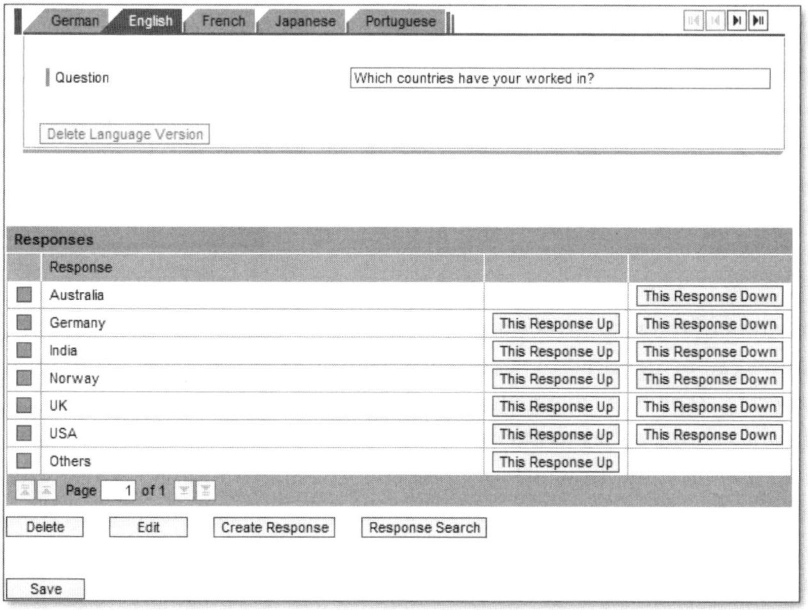

German | English | French | Japanese | Portuguese

Question: Which countries have your worked in?

Delete Language Version

Responses

Response		
Australia		This Response Down
Germany	This Response Up	This Response Down
India	This Response Up	This Response Down
Norway	This Response Up	This Response Down
UK	This Response Up	This Response Down
USA	This Response Up	This Response Down
Others	This Response Up	

Page 1 of 1

Delete | Edit | Create Response | Response Search

Save

Figure 6.15 Maintain a Question with Multiple Choices

Once the necessary questions are available, the recruiter can start building questionnaires using the item Questionnaire Maintenance in the box Administration. Because it is possible to create new questions right out of the questionnaire-maintenance screen, it is more convenient to stick to the sequence described here.

The first screen of the questionnaire maintenance (see Figure 6.16) looks exactly as for question maintenance (see Figure 6.13) and has the same purpose.

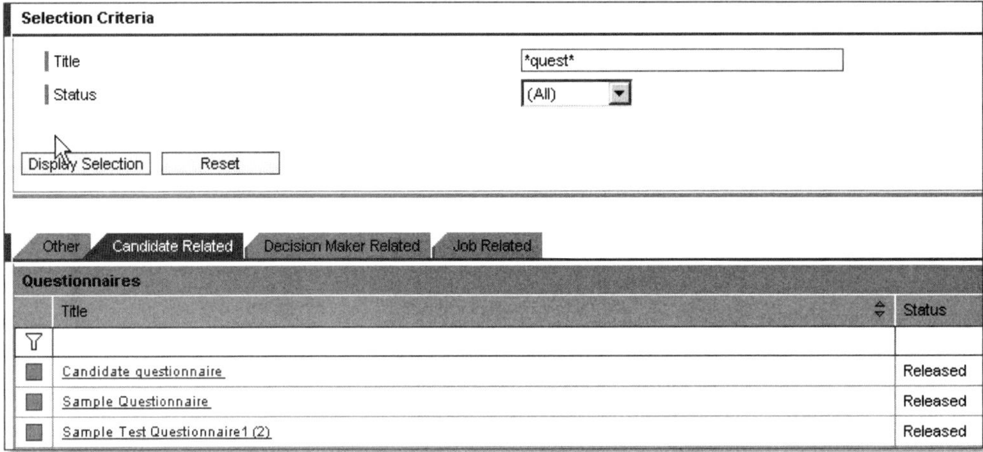

Figure 6.16 Questionnaire Maintenance — Overview

The maintenance of questionnaires involves three steps:

- Maintain a title
- Assign questions and define their sequence (see Figure 6.17)
- Rate responses

Besides the rating of the responses (that is, giving marks to each possible answer), some responses can be declared the expected response. A candidate who does not select an expected response is deemed unsuitable. For example, when a specific job requires that the candidate has worked in Sweden before, then your questionnaire could include the question, In which of these countries have you worked before? with the answer, Sweden, an expected response within the multiple choice. Note that the rating of the responses does not happen in question maintenance but always in the context of the questionnaire.

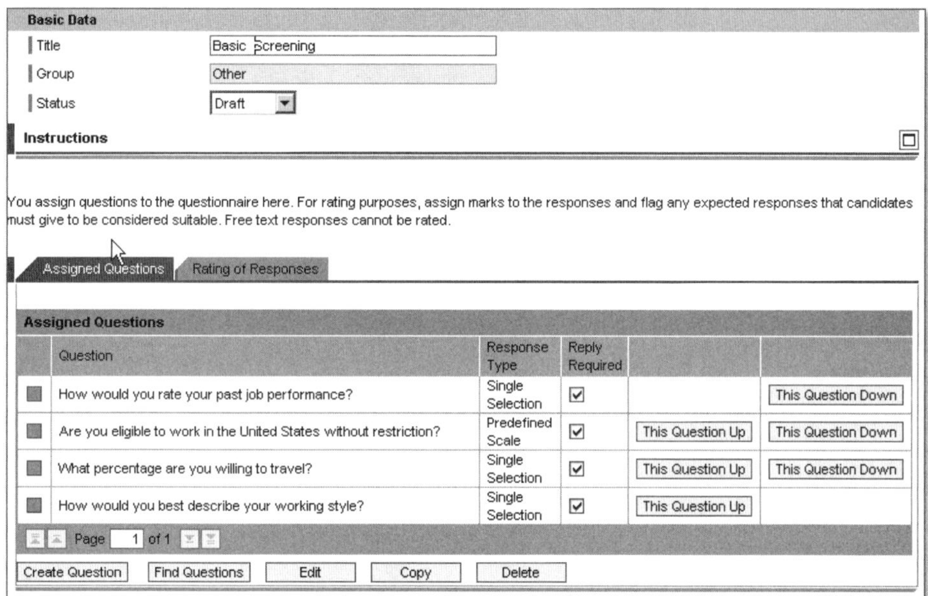

Figure 6.17 Assign Questions to a Questionnaire

While maintaining the questionnaire, you can get a preview with the attributes, showing the whole questionnaire with the rating of each answer and the expected-response flags (see Figure 6.18).

When the questionnaires are ready, they can be included in the process via the process template. An applicant can be asked to fill in a questionnaire, either as one step of the application wizard when applying for a job or via an email sent by the recruiter. This email contains a link to the questionnaire within the E-Recruiting platform and requires the candidate to log in before answering the questions online.

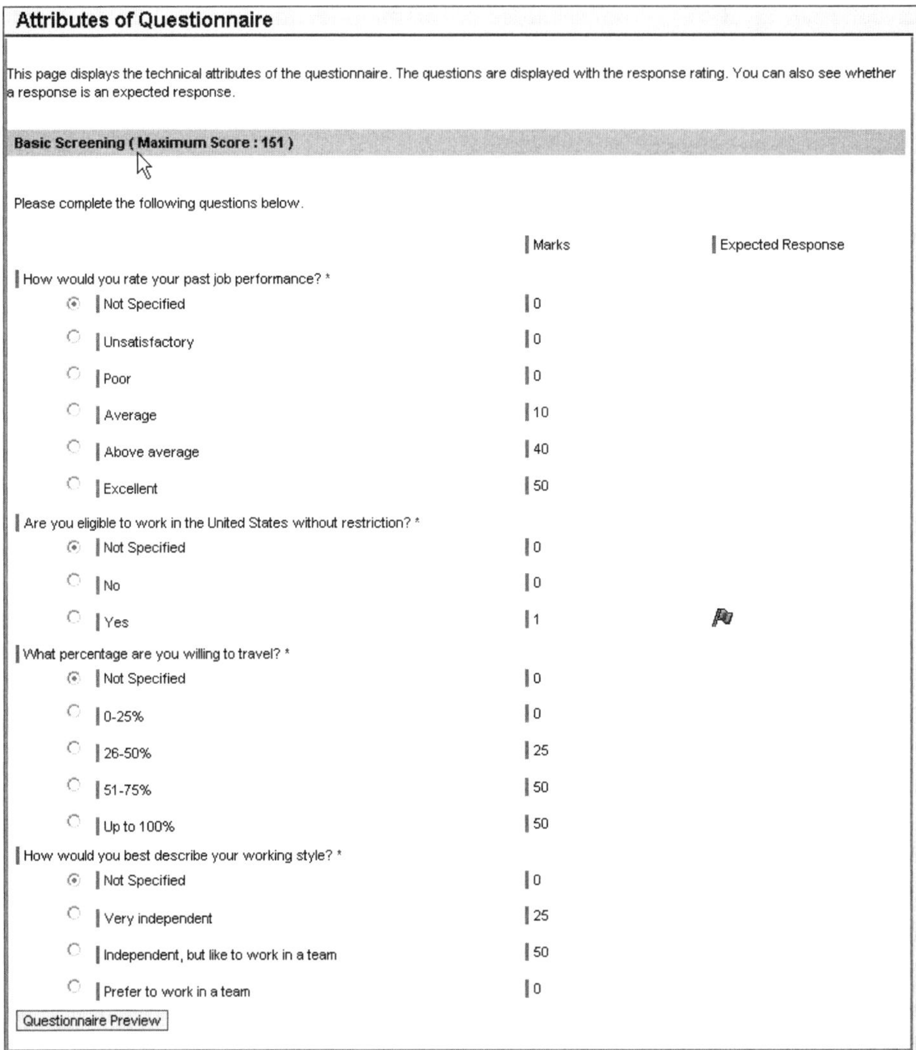

Figure 6.18 Preview of Questionnaire with Attributes

6.3.6 Further Important Terms

The following section describe some terms that you should be familiar with in the context of E-Recruiting.

Talent Pool

The talent pool comprises all candidates registered in the platform, including internal candidates.

Talent Groups

The recruiter can assign candidates to talent groups as a measure of talent segmentation.

Object Types

There are five types of objects used in the E-Recruitment solution:

- Candidate (NA)
- Requisition (NB)
- Posting (NC)
- Application (ND)
- Candidacy (NE) (A candidacy occurs only when a candidate is assigned to a job posting. When this has not (yet) happened, it is an application.)

Technically, these objects are used much like object types of organizational management, and the data is stored in Infotypes 5100 to 5199. However, this structure is hidden from the end-user. In Customizing, it is important to know the object types, as they are sometimes used to assign items, such as activities.

Statuses and Status Reasons

As in the traditional recruitment solution (see Section 7.1.4), statuses are used in E-Recruiting as well. However, different statuses are available per object type. The statuses for an application or a candidacy are:

- Draft
- In process
- Withdrawn
- Rejected
- To be hired

The statuses for a posting are:

- Draft
- Released
- Closed (meaning do not use anymore)
- To be deleted (but it can only be deleted when it is no longer used in active processes)

The same statuses can apply to requisitions, but for those there is a fifth status called on hold.

A candidate can have only two statuses:

- Locked (meaning that this user is not considered for vacancies)
- Released (meaning that this candidate can work on the platform and can be found by the recruiter for openings)

This is an important difference to the traditional recruitment solution — the status of a candidate does not correspond to the status of his application. This difference results from the completely different concept of E-Recruiting. The candidate is considered to be interesting not simply because one or more applications are pending. The long-term relationship E-Recruiting is aiming at can begin long before the first application and can go on afterward.

Status reasons can be maintained in Customizing and assigned when the status of an object is changed through an activity.

6.4 Roles in SAP E-Recruiting

As noted earlier, SAP's E-Recruiting solution is completely role-based. Each role is characterized by a set of functions. These are displayed on the start page, the so-called Personal Pages, in several boxes representing a kind of functional area as you will see later Figure 6.21.

All roles have one item in a box called Personal Settings as shown in Figure 6.19. These settings do not affect the process flow in any way but are merely used to adapt the user interface according to the user's preferences.

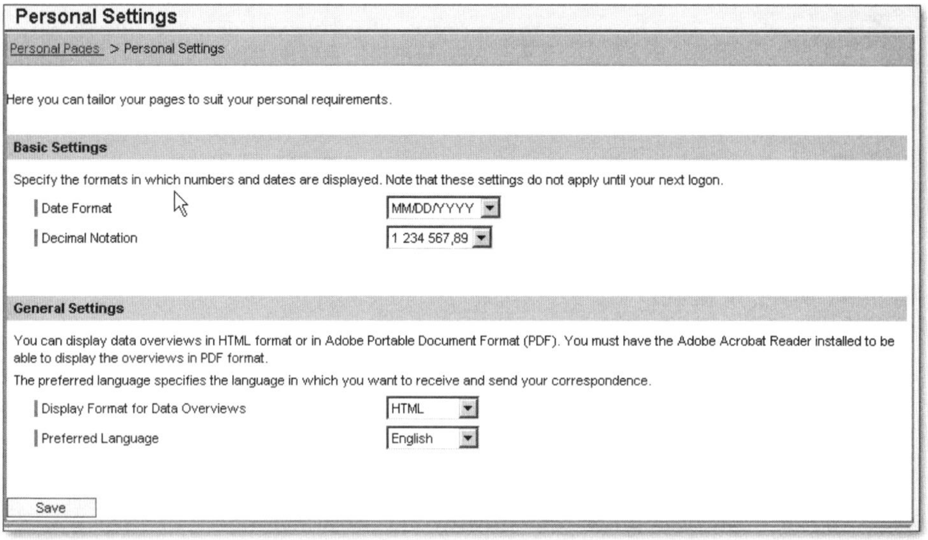

Figure 6.19 Personal Settings for All Users

6.4.1 The External Candidate

The external candidate is probably the most important role, because he is the one you want to attract to your company and who is most likely to be put off if the application is not well designed. As the visual appearance is more important for this role than for any other, there are plenty of screenshots for you to get an impression of the solution from the candidate's point of view. Note that most of the fields available for maintenance and the dropdown lists are subject to custom configuration and that the layout is usually adapted to the corporate design of the organization. These points apply not only for the candidate but for all roles.

The first step for an external candidate is registration (see Figure 6.20). This is a process very similar to other registration processes elsewhere on the Web, be it for an online shopping portal or a communication platform. An important issue here is the data privacy statement. According to the laws of many countries, you must make sure that the candidate accepts such a statement, and you may need different statements when working in different countries.

Registration

Do you want to find out more about your career options in our company?

We are constantly looking for talented and motivated new employees who can contribute to the success of our company. Take a look at our Job&Career pages and you will find valuable information about our company and current employment opportunities. If you are interested in a job, you can apply for it online directly. If you do not find any suitable vacancies but would still like to work for our company, you can register with us. We will contact you as soon as an employment opportunity arises that may interest you.

Name

First Name: Steven

Last Name *: Tether

User Data

User Name *: steven

Password *: ••••••••

Repeat Password *: ••••••••

E-Mail *: steven.tether@hotmail.com

Data Privacy Statement

We endeavour to ensure that the data you submit to us remains confidential and is used only for the purposes stated in the data privacy statement. Please confirm acceptance of our data privacy statement. Data Privacy Statement

☑ Yes, I have read the data privacy statement and I accept it

Register

Figure 6.20 Registration with Acceptance of Privacy Statement

After registration and with each further log in, the candidate gets his personal pages as shown in Figure 6.21. Besides the maintenance of personal data and communication data and the personal settings seen on the right side of the screen, there are two major functional areas in this role:

- The maintenance of the candidate profile
- The employment opportunities where the candidate can search for jobs and submit applications

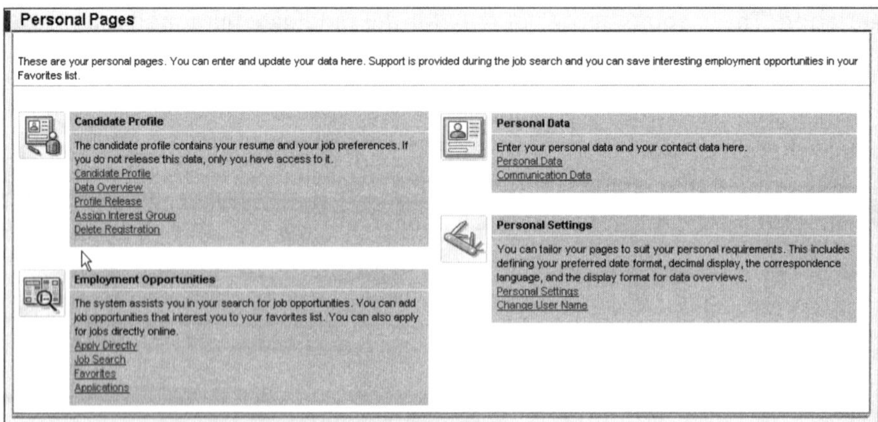

Figure 6.21 Personal Pages for an External Candidate

As one of the strong points of E-Recruiting is its global availability, a multilingual user interface can be very important. Figure 6.22 shows what a Spanish-speaking candidate would see on his personal pages.

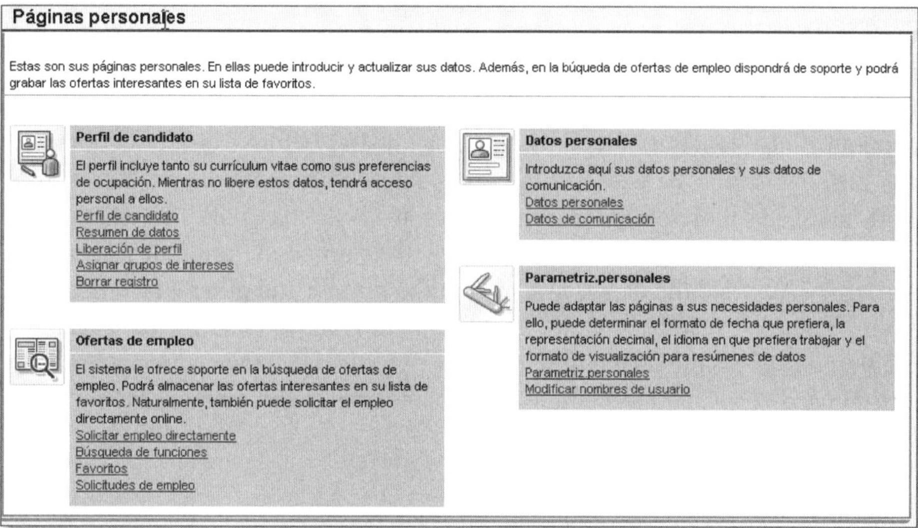

Figure 6.22 Personal Pages in Spanish: a Multilingual Platform

After registration, the candidate is not obliged to maintain any further data. It is his choice whether he maintains a comprehensive profile right at the beginning or just looks around a bit for interesting jobs. However, the employer may define some mandatory fields. There are four activities through which the candidate can maintain data about himself:

- The first step would be to maintain some personal data, such as gender and date of birth in the box Personal Data.
- In the same box via Communication Data, contact data such as email address, phone numbers, and postal address are maintained.

In the box Candidate Profile via the activity Assign Interest Group he can choose a group to be assigned to. This can include groups such as executives, lower management, technical staff, internships, etc. It is up to the employer whether or not to offer this option and how to use it. Considering that the profile data is extensive and not always maintained completely, the interest group can be handy for a first segmentation of the talent pool.

The most important activity is the maintenance of the Candidate Profile, which can also be found in the box Candidate Profile. This is what we want to focus on in the following paragraphs.

The candidate profile is maintained in eight steps, and the user is guided through these with the navigation bar shown in Figure 6.23. It is not necessary to complete each step before going to the next one. It is up to the candidate how much information he wants to reveal at which point in time. Although it is tempting to demand a huge amount of data from the candidates before considering them for any postings, it may be wise to allow candidates to concentrate on the essentials. With more and more online recruiting sites available that work in a similar way, candidates may not want to be bothered with maintaining too much data again and again. After all, the data is available in the resume and other attachments, so, from a candidate's point of view, it is redundant work to enter the data again for each employer. While demanding extensive profile data makes the process more efficient and reporting more interesting for the employer, some candidates might be put off.

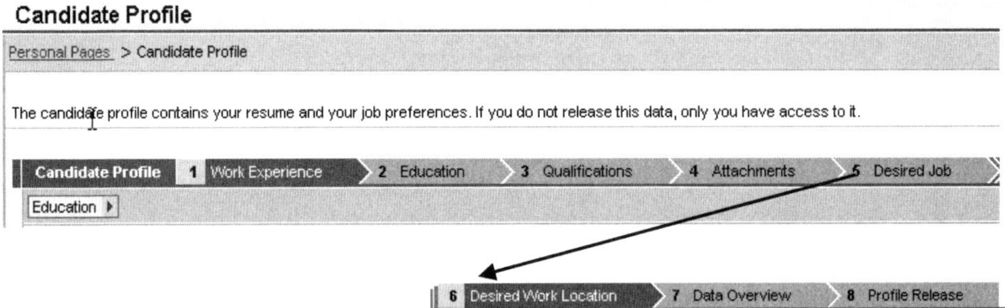

Figure 6.23 Candidate Profile: Eight Steps

Here are the eight steps of the profile maintenance as shown in Figure 6.23:

1. **Work Experience**
   In the work-experience step, data for all former jobs can be maintained. Figure 6.24 shows an example with data maintained for one position held by the candidate in the past. The data refers to the employer and to the position itself. While some fields can be freely filled with any text, others have predefined options in dropdown boxes. These options (here and for the following steps as well) are mostly defined via Customizing in a straightforward way.

What is your previous work experience?

List all work relationships to date individually.

Data

Employer	North Fork		
Not Under Notice	☐		
Start Date	09/01/1998	End Date	02/28/2003
Country	USA	Region	New York
City	New York		
Industry	Banking / Financial Services		
Functional Area	Information Technology		
Hierarchy Level	Professional I/Entry Level (more than 2 years work experience)		
Job Title	SAP developer		
Description			

Figure 6.24 Work Experience: One Former Employer in Detail

As there can be more than one former employer, the work experience view consists of a list with all former positions (see Figure 6.25), and each entry can be maintained in the detailed view as described earlier. This combination of overview list and detailed view is also used for other steps.

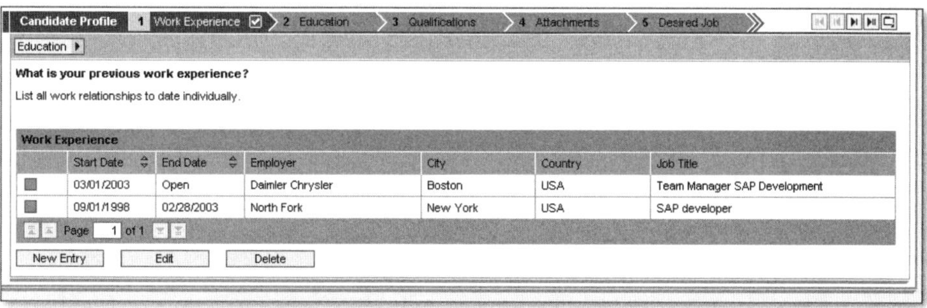
Candidate Profile | 1 Work Experience | 2 Education | 3 Qualifications | 4 Attachments | 5 Desired Job

Education

What is your previous work experience?

List all work relationships to date individually.

Work Experience

	Start Date	End Date	Employer	City	Country	Job Title
	03/01/2003	Open	Daimler Chrysler	Boston	USA	Team Manager SAP Development
	09/01/1998	02/28/2003	North Fork	New York	USA	SAP developer

Page 1 of 1

New Entry | Edit | Delete

Figure 6.25 Work Experience Overview

2. **Education**

   The Education view is designed exactly the same way. A list of educational institutes attended by the candidate is built via a detailed view, where data concerning the institute (e.g., school or university) and the type, content, and grades of the education (e.g., PhD in information science/cryptology rated summa cum laude).

What competencies and qualifications do you have to offer?

Rate your competencies and qualifications. You can use the text fields to provide additional information, if required.

Qualification Group: B-SAP Product Knowledge

Selected	Qualification	Proficiency
☐	Industry Solutions	Not rated
☐	R/2 Components	Not rated
☑	R/3 Components	Not rated
☑	mySAP Business Intelligence	Not rated
☐	mySAP Customer Relationship Mgmt.	Not rated
☐	mySAP E-Procurement	Not rated
☐	mySAP Financials	Not rated
☐	mySAP Hosted Solutions	Not rated
☑	mySAP Human Resources	Not rated
☐	mySAP Marketplace by SAPMarkets	Not rated
☑	mySAP Mobile Business	Not rated
☐	mySAP Product Lifecycle Mgmt.	Not rated
☐	mySAP Supply Chain Mgmt.	Not rated
☑	mySAP Technology	Not rated
☐	mySAP Workplace	Not rated

Other

EAI

Save Cancel

Figure 6.26 Qualifications per Group

3. **Qualifications**
   Under Qualifications, the candidate describes his skills profile. The skills the employer is particularly interested in are available in several qualification groups and the candidate can select the skills he has and rate them in a self-assessment (see Figure 6.26). The catalog behind these qualifications is based on the same technical framework as the qualifications catalog used in the personnel-development component of SAP ERP HCM. For information on its maintenance, refer to the SAP PRESS book *HR Personnel Planning and Develop-*

ment Using SAP ERP HCM. However, the same catalog is rarely used for E-Recruiting and for personnel development for several reasons:

- The internal skills catalog is probably much too large to bother the candidates with.
- The internal catalog may include skill descriptions that cannot be understood by an external person.
- Not all skills that are interesting from a development point of view are necessarily interesting for the recruiter and vice versa.
- You may not want the outside world to see your full skills catalog. This might not only allow insights into your HR processes but also betray your business strategy to your competitor (assuming that your personnel development is aligned to the overall strategy of your organization).

4. **Attachments**
   Attachments can be all kinds of documents such as Microsoft Word, PDF, or TIF. However, you should restrict the options for the candidate to those document types you can process easily with your IT infrastructure. We recommend accepting PDF files because it is a widely accept format. As most candidates will have access to an office product creating DOC files but not necessarily to a PDF converter, it will be difficult to exclude the DOC format. Figure 6.27 shows how an attachment is uploaded and included into the profile. The attachment type describes the content. The types allowed are maintained in Customizing and can include reference letters, resumes, certificates, etc.

Do you want to supplement your data by adding attachments?

You can attach electronically stored documents to supplement your data.

Data

Attachment Type	Reference
Language	English
File	C:\Documents and Settings\d001583 [Browse...]
Document Title	Reference Letter Mr. Bownes

[Save] [Cancel]

Figure 6.27 Upload Attachments

5. **Desired Job**

   For the recruiter, it is not only important to get data about the candidate, his experience, and his skills, but also to learn about his expectations regarding his future job. Moreover, it is important to show the candidate that the employer is not only interested in what he can get from the candidate but that he also listens to the candidate's expectations. Figure 6.28 shows how employment references concerning the industry, functional area, and hierarchy level are maintained as along with expectations toward the contract, such as salary and working time.

6. **Desired Work Location**

   The maintenance of the desired work location is very similar to the steps described before. This is particularly important for organizations with multiple locations.

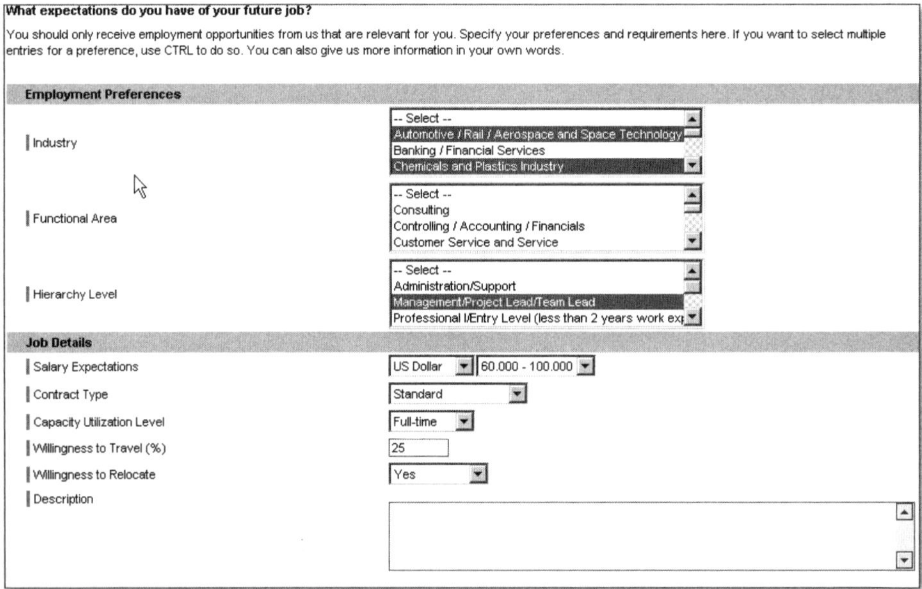

Figure 6.28 Expectations of the Desired Job

7. **Data Overview**

   Step seven gives the candidate an overview of the data maintained so that he can perform corrections or add missing data before releasing the profile.

8. **Profile Release**

   The profile release (see Figure 6.29) is the final step. With the release, the profile is available for the recruiter so that he can find the candidate and offer him appropriate jobs. As long as the data is not yet maintained as the candidate wants it to be or as long as he does not want to be contacted for job offers, he leaves the profile status "locked." Note that in this step the candidate is reminded of the data privacy statement he accepted upon registration. This acceptance cannot be withdrawn, because if it were, the candidate would have to leave the talent pool.

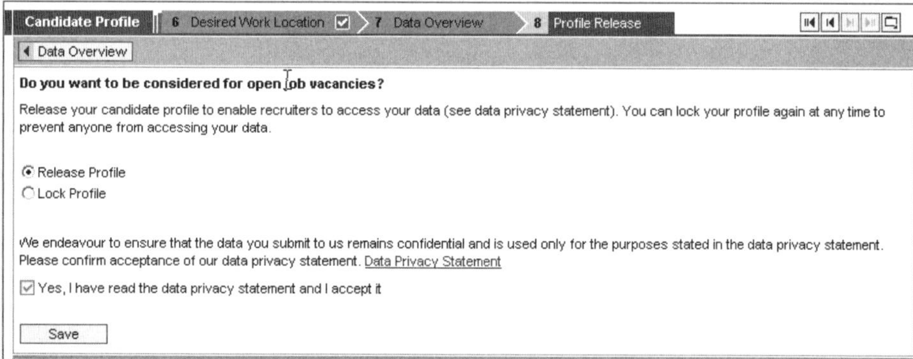

Figure 6.29 Release Candidates Profile

Now that the profile is released, the candidate can wait for the employer to contact him. However, he can also actively search for jobs and apply. To search for jobs, he can use the activity Job Search in the Employment Opportunities box. As Figure 6.30 shows, there are two options for searching, which can also be combined:

- Full-text search
- Search using the predefined criteria as they are maintained as information in the requisition data

Each search can be saved as a search query and thus be reused later.

Note that the match percentage is not an exact calculation. The calculation scheme used by the search engine is not really transparent and as a rule does not deliver exactly 100% when all search criteria are perfectly matched. However, the percentage is a good indicator for the matching. Just be sure you understand it not as a true percentage but as an open ranking, and — even if you are looking for perfect matches only — do not set the minimum matching percentage to 100%.

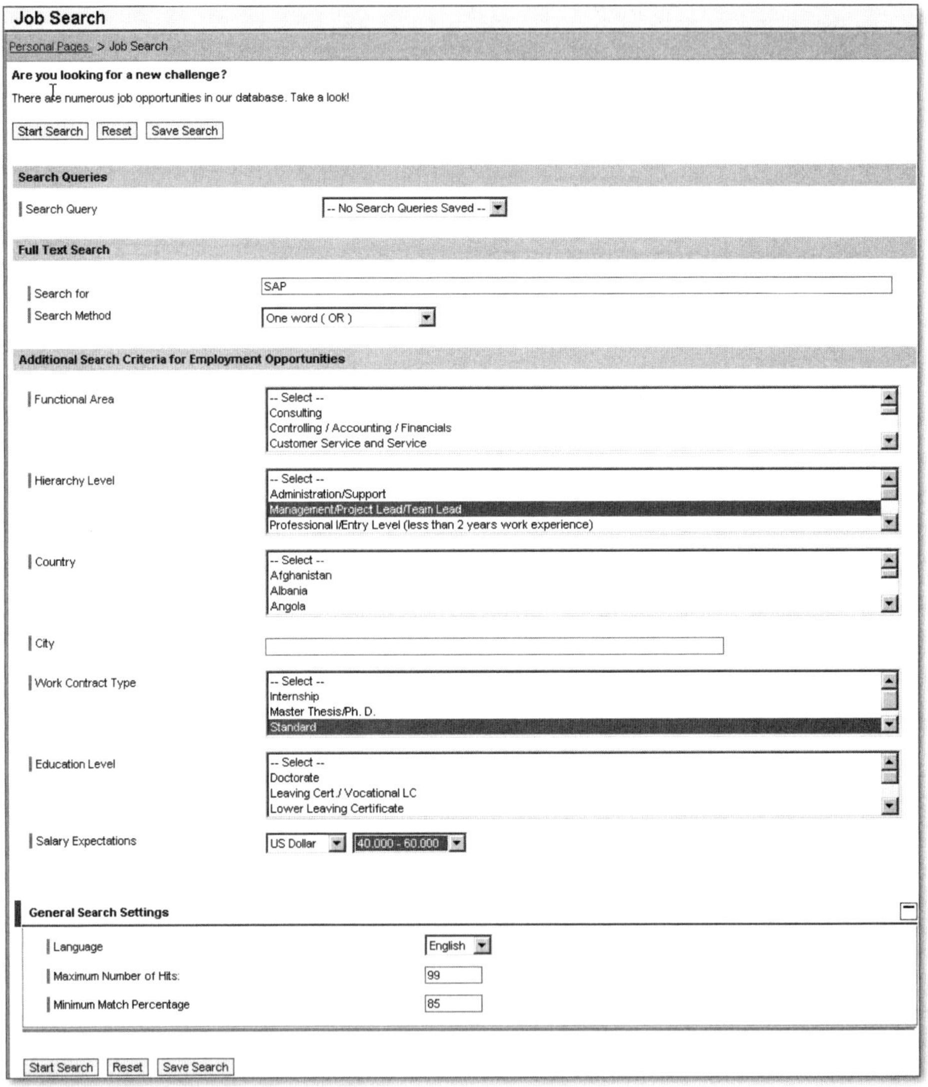

Figure 6.30 Searching for Job Postings

The candidate then gets a result list with jobs matching his search (see Figure 6.31) and has the following options for each posting:

- Display the data overview (as you will see later in Figure 6.33)
- Add to the favorites list
- Apply

When the jobs are already on the favorites list or an application has already been submitted, there are even more options as described in the following paragraph.

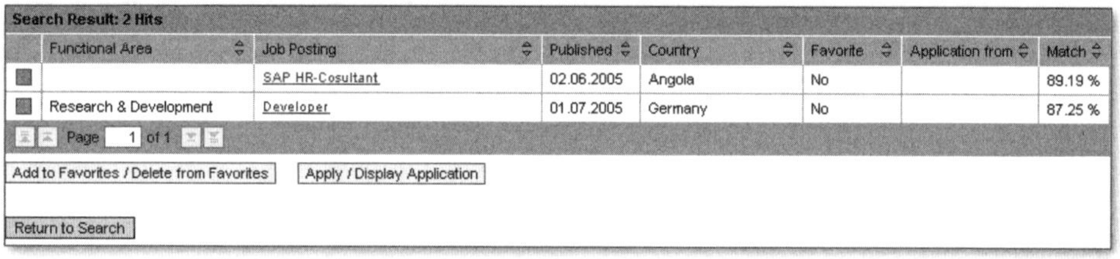

Search Result: 2 Hits

	Functional Area	Job Posting	Published	Country	Favorite	Application from	Match
■		SAP HR-Cosultant	02.06.2005	Angola	No		89.19 %
■	Research & Development	Developer	01.07.2005	Germany	No		87.25 %

Page 1 of 1

Add to Favorites / Delete from Favorites | Apply / Display Application

Return to Search

Figure 6.31 Results: Interesting Job Postings

Once a job has been added to the favorites list, it can be accessed through the activity Favorites in the Employment Opportunities box. Apart from displaying the data overview (see Figure 6.33) and applying for the job, the posting can also be removed from the favorites list (see Figure 6.32), and existing applications can be displayed.

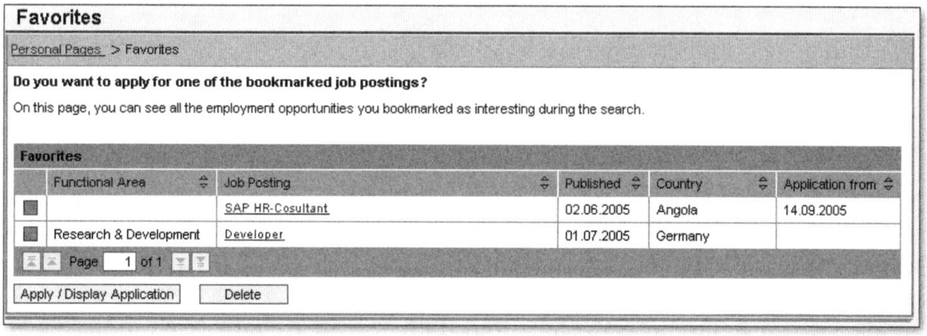

Favorites

Personal Pages > Favorites

Do you want to apply for one of the bookmarked job postings?

On this page, you can see all the employment opportunities you bookmarked as interesting during the search.

Favorites

	Functional Area	Job Posting	Published	Country	Application from
■		SAP HR-Cosultant	02.06.2005	Angola	14.09.2005
■	Research & Development	Developer	01.07.2005	Germany	

Page 1 of 1

Apply / Display Application | Delete

Figure 6.32 Favorite Job Postings with Applications

The data overview for the job posting (see Figure 6.33) can be displayed in PDF or HTML format, according to the personal settings (see Figure 6.19). In our example, PDF format has been chosen. In this case, the data overview is not used to check data for completeness and correctness but to get information about the posting.

The data overviews referred to on other occasions (e.g., requisition or candidate profile) look similar.

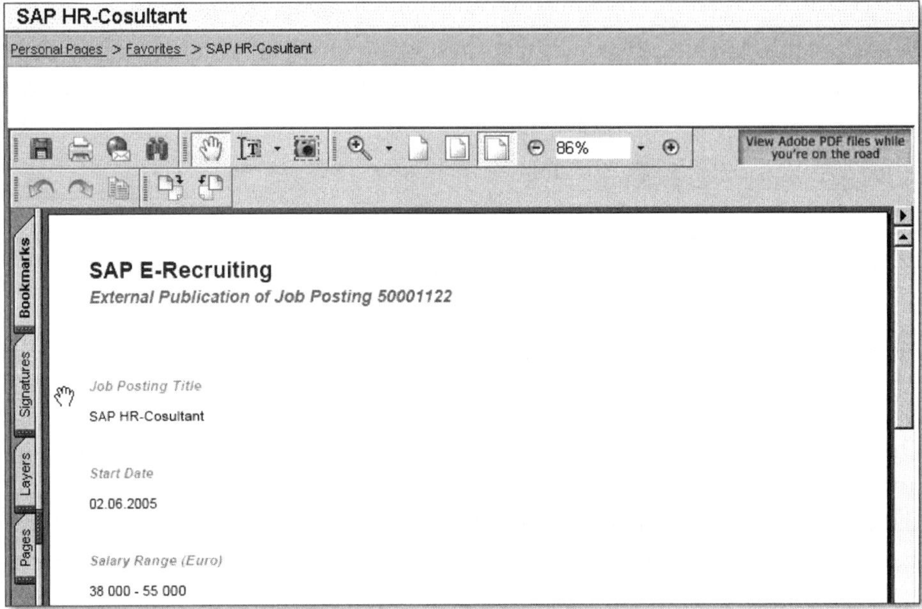

Figure 6.33 Overview of a Job Posting as a PDF File

The candidate has three ways to apply for a job:

- Applying for a job found on a search result list.
- Applying for a job on the favorites list.
- Applying directly for a job using the activity Apply Directly in the Employment Opportunities box. To do this, the candidate must know the reference code of the job posting (e.g., from a job advertisement in a newspaper).

In each of these three cases, the application wizard is started. As indicated in Figure 6.34 and Figure 6.35, this wizard guides the candidate through ten steps. However, steps one to seven contain activities already done when maintaining the candidate profile. So, if the candidate thinks that his profile is complete, he might as well start with the data overview in step eight to check the data and then proceed to the two final steps. Other steps could be included (especially questionnaires) depending on the custom configuration.

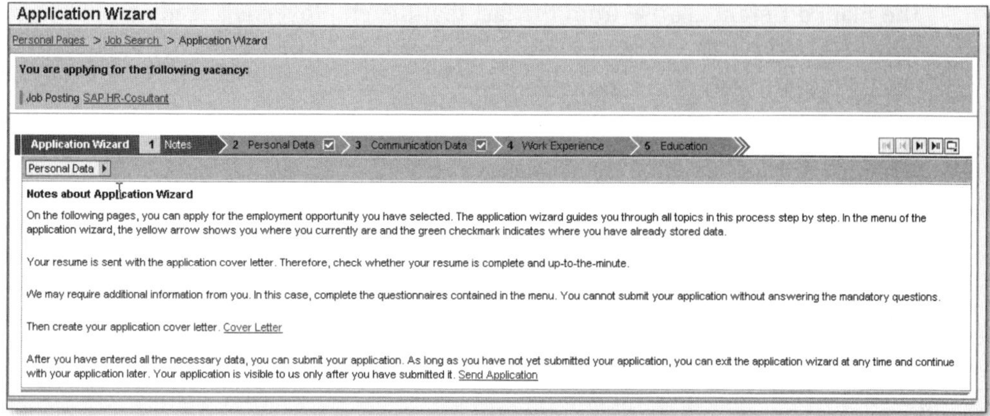

Figure 6.34 Application Wizard: Apply and Complete Profile Information

These final steps (see Figure 6.35) include:

- Uploading a cover letter (similar to uploading other attachments)
- Sending the application

Figure 6.35 Application Wizard: Send Application with Cover Letter

All applications can be accessed via the activity Applications in the box Employment Opportunities.

After the application is submitted, the process will not be completed. On the contrary, if the candidate is well suited for the job, there will be many more steps including correspondence, questionnaires, interviews, etc., where other roles are involved as well (especially the recruiter). These steps depend very much on custom configuration and on the process template assigned to the requisition. How this can be designed has already been discussed in Section 6.3.

6.4.2 The Internal Candidate

The role of the internal candidate is very similar to that of the external one, as can be seen from his personal pages in Figure 6.36.

The main differences arise from the fact that the employee is already represented in the SAP ERP HCM system with his master data, while some activities of the external candidate are not available here.

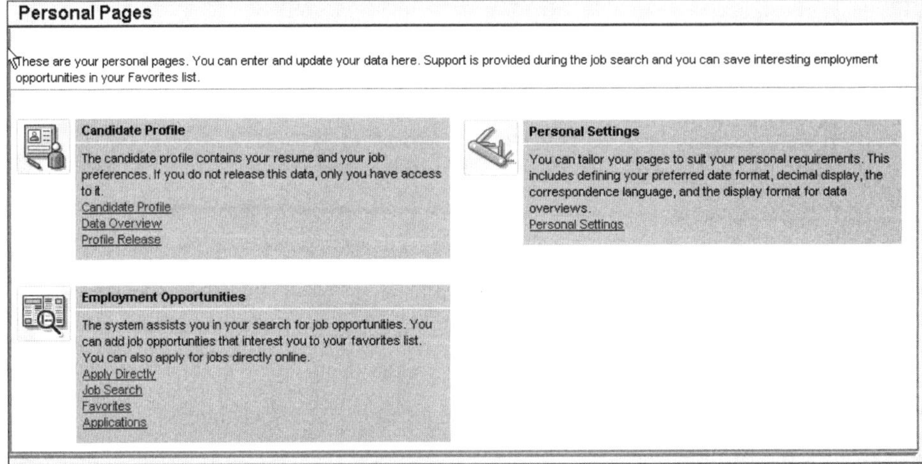

Figure 6.36 Personal Pages for Internal Candidate

An employee could register and apply like any external candidate. However, this would not make much sense because he would have to reveal his identity when he applies.

6.4.3 The Manager

The requesting manager plays a very important role in the whole process. Besides the candidate, he is one of the people who initiate the process as shown in Figure 6.3.

As the personal pages in Figure 6.37 indicate, the manager can be involved in defining the requisition and in the selection process. It is strongly recommended that each manager performs these activities himself on the system, as it is the most efficient process. This is especially true for the selection activities. However, it will often happen that the communication between the E-Recruitment system and the manager is paper-based and involves a recruiter in actually maintaining the data. It is a major task in any E-Recruitment implementation project to convince the managers of the added value they get from working directly with the system and using the possibilities of interactivity.

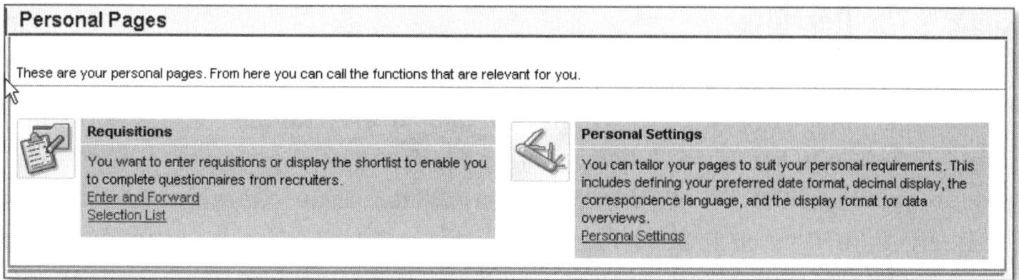

Figure 6.37 Personal Pages for Manager

If the managers do not feel able or claim not to have enough time to maintain the data of the requisition request online, you may have to make a concession to them by having this done by the recruiter. Because this is a lot of data to maintain (see Figure 6.38) and does not happen too often, you can get an efficient process in spite of this delegation. However, you should stick to a design where the manager is actively involved in the selection process online.

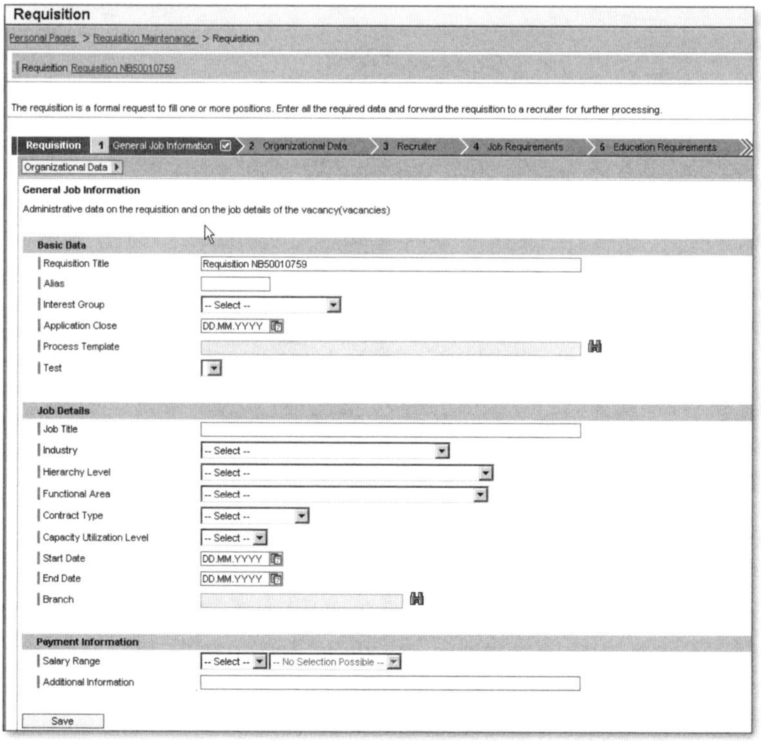

Requisition
Personal Pages > Requisition Maintenance > Requisition
Requisition Requisition NB50010759
The requisition is a formal request to fill one or more positions. Enter all the required data and forward the requisition to a recruiter for further processing.
Requisition | 1 General Job Information | 2 Organizational Data | 3 Recruiter | 4 Job Requirements | 5 Education Requirements
Organizational Data
General Job Information
Administrative data on the requisition and on the job details of the vacancy(vacancies)
Basic Data
Requisition Title: Requisition NB50010759
Alias
Interest Group: -- Select --
Application Close: DD.MM.YYYY
Process Template
Test
Job Details
Job Title
Industry: -- Select --
Hierarchy Level: -- Select --
Functional Area: -- Select --
Contract Type: -- Select --
Capacity Utilization Level: -- Select --
Start Date: DD.MM.YYYY
End Date: DD.MM.YYYY
Branch
Payment Information
Salary Range: -- Select -- | -- No Selection Possible --
Additional Information
Save

Figure 6.38 Creating a Requisition

6.4.4 The Recruiter

As can be seen from the personal pages in Figure 6.39, the role of the recruiter has the broadest range of functions. We have already dealt with the content of the box Administration in Section 6.3.4 and Section 6.3.5 and with personal settings at the beginning of Section 6.4. We will not go into detail regarding reporting. This can be freely defined via SAP Query based on three standard infosets, custom infosets (see Chapter 11, "HR Reporting"), or SAP NetWeaver Business Intelligence (BI). If you want to learn more about reporting in SAP ERP HCM, refer to the SAP PRESS book *HR Reporting with SAP*.

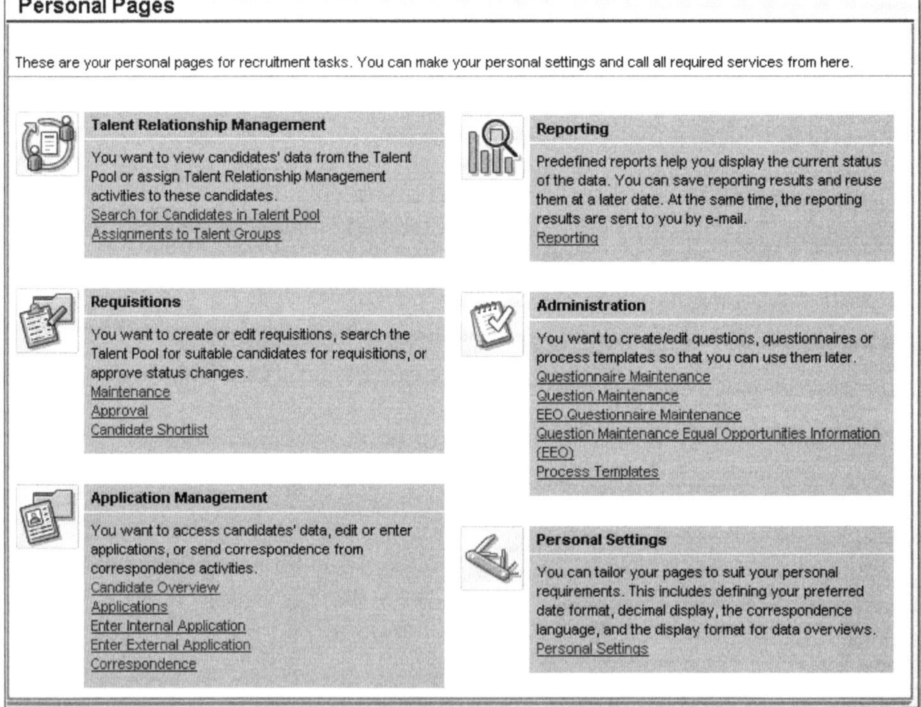

Figure 6.39 Personal Pages for the Recruiter

Next we'll discuss the three remaining boxes on the left-hand side. Assignments to Talent Groups is the simpler activity in the box Talent Relationship Management. It is a straightforward method of talent segmentation where each candidate can be assigned to a group from a predefined list.

The more unusual activity is the Search for Candidates in the Pool. The search functionality (see Figure 6.40) is similar to the search for jobs in the role of the external candidate, and everything explained there can be applied here as well.

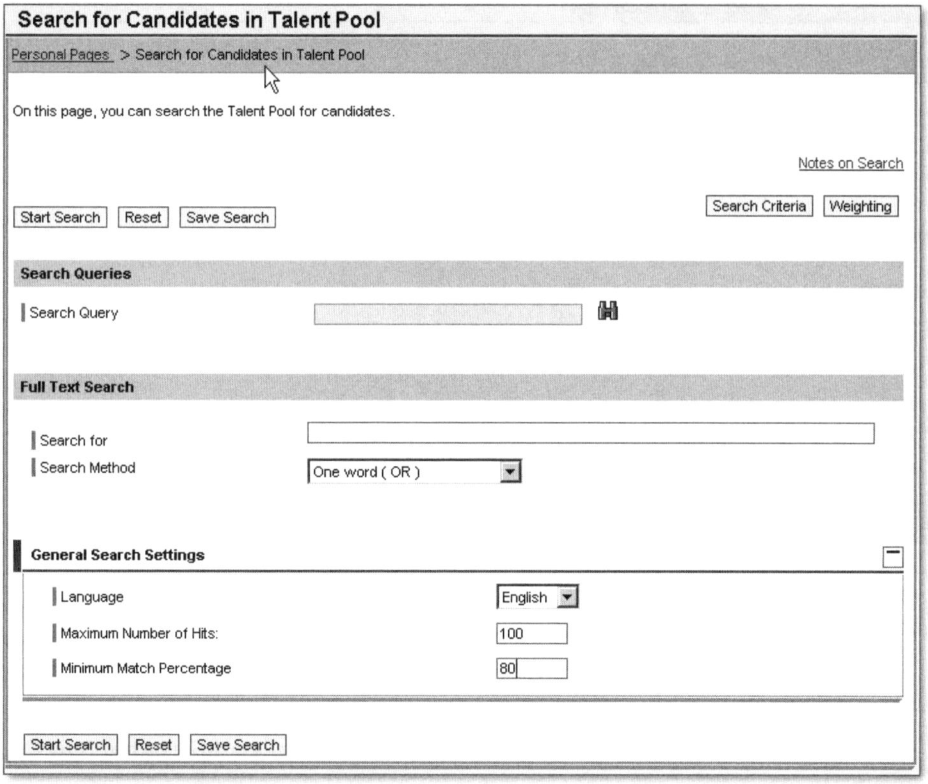

Figure 6.40 Recruiter Looks for Candidates in the Talent Pool

However, there are two major differences:

- The search criteria can be weighted.
- Besides the normal search template elements, qualifications and questionnaires can be used for the search. The search templates are defined in Customizing.

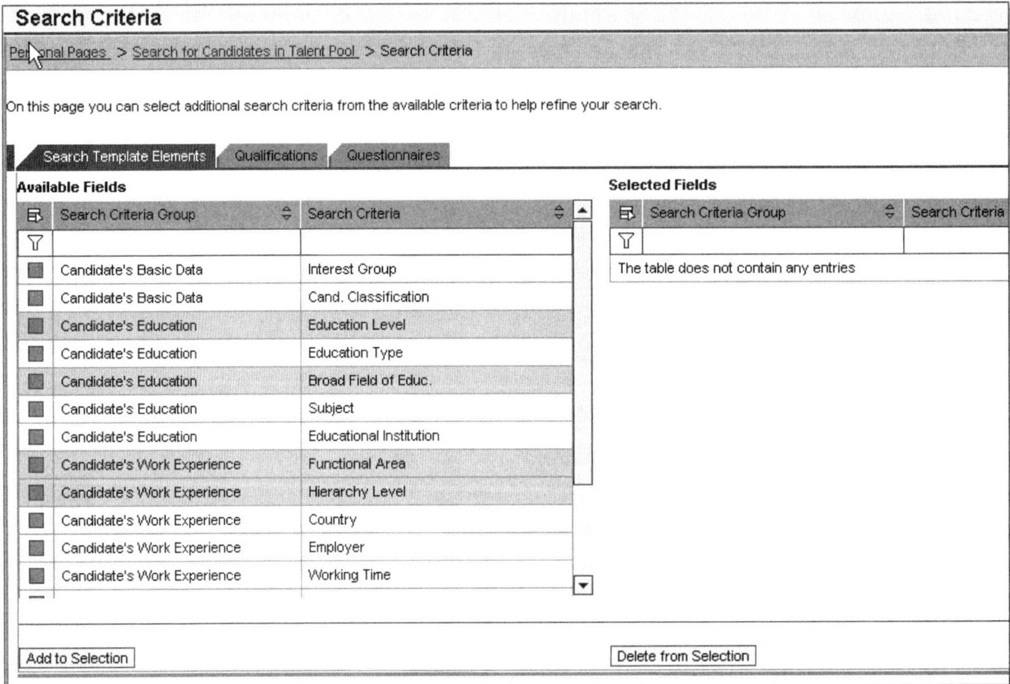

Figure 6.41 Selecting in the Search Criteria

It may seem awkward to have the recruiter maintain all of the search criteria. After all, the requirements for the job are maintained with the requisition data and in theory could be used as search criteria. It can be argued, though, that these criteria are often too restrictive or that other criteria are usually added. Although this may be true in many cases, it is one of the weak points of the system that at this point in the process no reference can be made to the data already entered. This is compensated to some extent by the feature that any search once conducted can be saved as a search query.

Figure 6.42 shows the precise search criteria and groups selected in Figure 6.41.

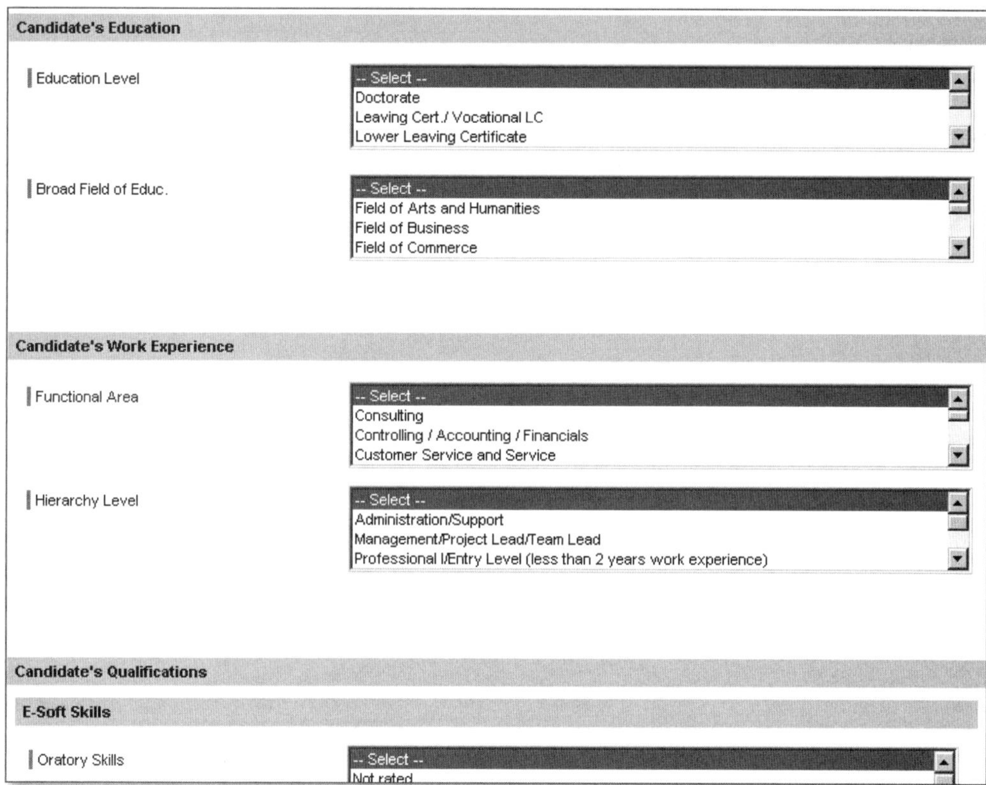

Figure 6.42 Filling in the Search Criteria

The maintenance and approval of requisitions have already been discussed. The remaining activity in the Requisitions box is the Candidate Shortlist. The recruiter can assign candidates to a short list for a posting, and based on this short list he can organize the management of the requisitions and candidacies. Figure 6.43 shows the selection of assigned candidates ordered by process (the processes are represented by tabs). You can also see that the candidates can be ranked by criteria entered via the Ranking Criteria tab. For each candidate, the profile, the data overview, and the activities assigned can be displayed.

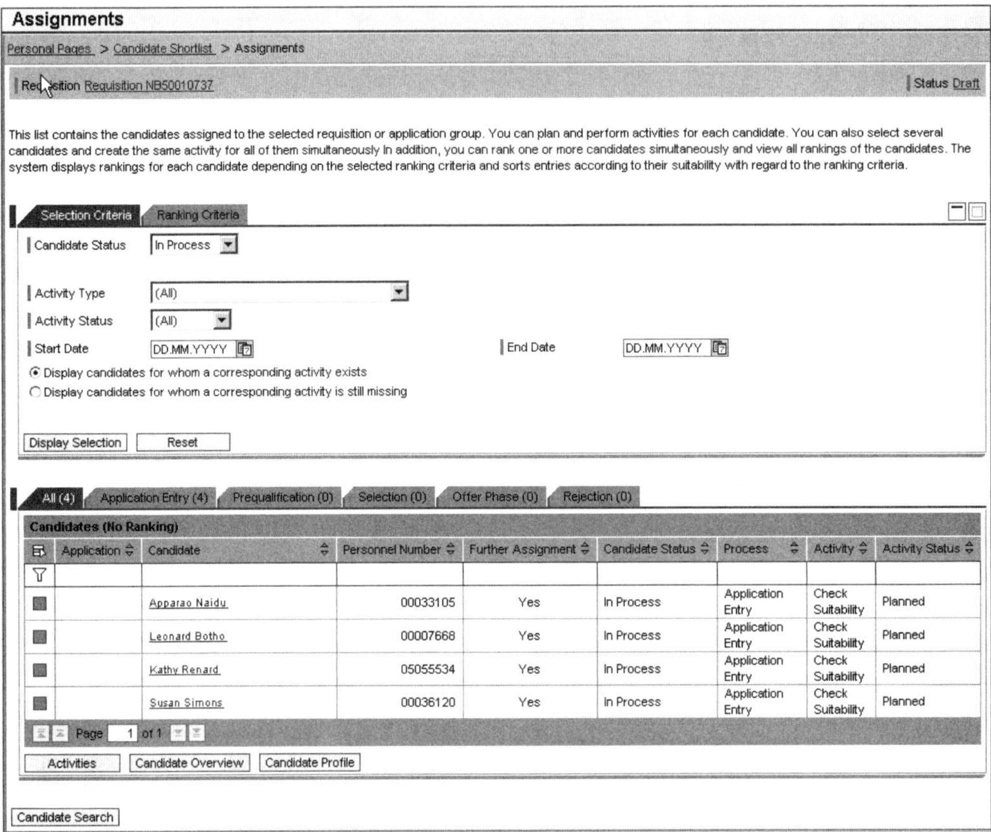

Figure 6.43 Working with Assigned Candidates

Most of the functions in the Application management box are controlled via the process templates discussed in Section 6.3.4. As we did with the role of the external candidate, we won't take a detailed look at the process of application management here. However, we want to mention that the recruiter has the option to maintain an internal or external application with all of the necessary data via the activities Enter Internal Application and Enter External Application. This is necessary if an application has not been submitted via the E-Recruiting system. Figure 6.44 shows how such a data entry screen could look.

Candidate and Application Data

Application Group	-- Select --
Reference Code *	
Form of Address	-- Select --
First Name *	
Last Name *	
Title	-- Select --
Gender	Unknown
Date of Birth	DD.MM.YYYY
Street	
Street (Continued)	
Country	-- Select --
Region	-- No Selection Possible --
City	
Postal Code	
Telephone	
E-Mail	
Preferred Language	-- Select --
Interest Group	-- Select --
Application Date	14.09.2005

Application Source

Application Source Type	-- Select --
Application Source	-- No Selection Possible --
Other Information	
Personnel Number	

Attachments

Document Title	Attachment Type	Language
No attachments currently exist.		

Add Attachment

Status

Status	In Process
Status Reason	-- Select --

Save | Save and Continue | Reset | Overview

Figure 6.44 Entering an Application Manually

6.4.5 The Administrator

The administrator is responsible for providing the prerequisites for the management of candidates and requisitions by:

- Maintaining the internal users
- Deleting the external candidates and their registration. Because the users for external candidates are created automatically with registration, no user maintenance is required. However, it may be necessary to deregister inactive users.
- Maintaining other current settings, such as branches and talent groups.

All of these functions are accessed via the administrator pages (see Figure 6.45).

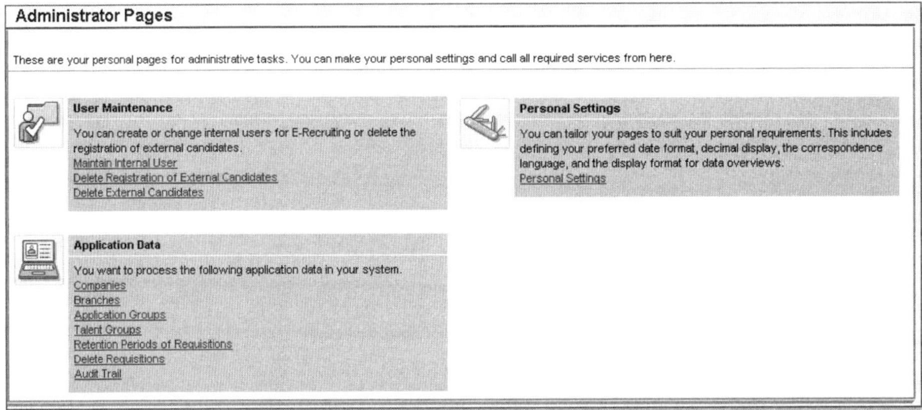

Figure 6.45 Administrator Pages

The administrator is often a key user or the person responsible for the customizing. His functions within the recruiting process itself are very limited.

6.4.6 Succession Planner

The succession planner is a new role with SAP ERP E-Recruiting 6.0; you should note that succession planning can be implemented for use on its own, without E-Recruiting. We will not discuss it further, because succession planning is not the subject of this book. For more information you may refer to the SAP PRESS book *HR Personnel Planning and Development using SAP*. You can see from the start screen of the succession planner in Figure 6.46 that this role is similar to the role of the recruiter but is missing some of those functions. In particular, there is no application management included, as succession planning doesn't require applications.

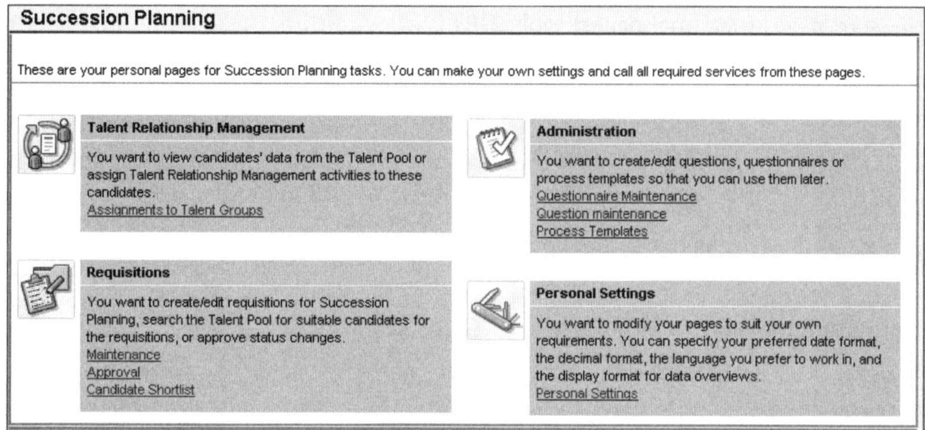

Figure 6.46 Personal Pages for Succession Planner

6.5 Customizing and Technology

The Customizing for E-Recruiting can be found in the IMG under SAP E-Recruiting and is divided into five major parts:

- Technical settings
- Basic settings
- Recruitment
- Succession planning
- Tools

It is neither possible nor necessary to describe all Customizing activities step by step. This is already done in the available documentation from SAP. We will discuss the first three points here and go into detail with several examples.

6.5.1 Technical Settings

Besides a variety of technical prerequisites (see Section 6.5.2), which should not be overlooked, and the configuration for reporting, we want to look at two points:

Start Pages

Via the IMG path SAP E-RECRUITING • TECHNICAL SETTINGS • USER INTERFACES • SETTINGS FOR USER INTERFACES WITH BSP/WEBDYNPRO FOR ABAP you can decide how the start pages (personal pages) look. This is done in three steps.

1. Define the links representing the activities. SAP delivers about 40 predefined functions.
2. Combine these links to form the groups representing the boxes on the start page.
3. Assign the groups to the start pages.

Field Configuration

Via the IMG path TECHNICAL SETTINGS • USER INTERFACES • SETTINGS FOR USER INTERFACES WITH BSP/WEBDYNPRO FOR ABAP in Interfaces, you can decide whether a field is displayed or hidden, input or output only, and optional or required. You also find directions on how to create new fields via BAdIs. However, this is not possible for every screen.

6.5.2 Basic Settings

Besides the available languages, there are three aspects that can all be maintained in a straightforward way:

- **Enterprise structure**
  Companies are defined in a simple table and branches are assigned to them. Note that the branches come from SAP Business Partner data.
- **Attachment types**
  You define attachment types in a simple table and you can implement the BAdI HRRCF00_DOC_UPLOAD to perform specific checks on the attachments, such as:
  - File Type
  - Size of the file
  - Number of files
  - Virus check

You can even perform a conversion from one type to another via this BAdI, but you need suitable third-party software to do this.

6.5.3 Talent Warehouse

The Customizing for the talent warehouse is pretty straightforward – once you know exactly what is needed. Most of the Customizing items here define the options for fields with dropdown boxes, such as:

- Industries (for work experience and desired employment)
- Education types
- Interest groups

As one example, Figure 6.47 shows the maintenance of salary ranges reached via the IMG path SAP E-RECRUITING • RECRUITMENT • TALENT WAREHOUSE • CANDIDATE • WORK EXPERIENCE/DESIRED EMPLOYMENT • SALARY RANGES • DEFINE SALARY RANGES. Note that this table (and some others) is not only used in the candidate profile but in the requisition, too.

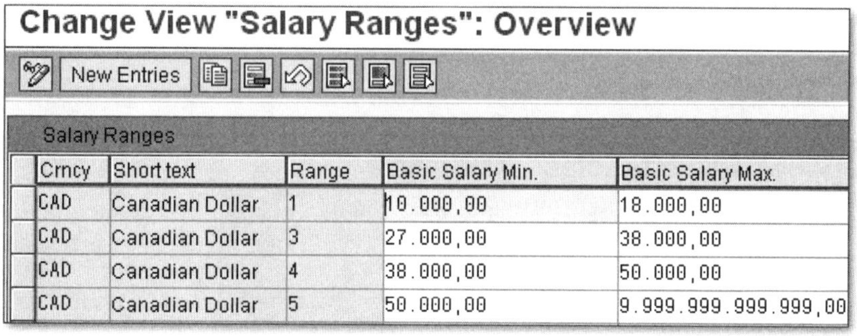

Change View "Salary Ranges": Overview

New Entries

Salary Ranges

Crncy	Short text	Range	Basic Salary Min.	Basic Salary Max.
CAD	Canadian Dollar	1	10.000,00	18.000,00
CAD	Canadian Dollar	3	27.000,00	38.000,00
CAD	Canadian Dollar	4	38.000,00	50.000,00
CAD	Canadian Dollar	5	50.000,00	9.999.999.999.999,00

Figure 6.47 Maintain Salary Ranges

Another very important point here is the Customizing for the search functions. The definition of Search Profiles and Search Templates requires a considerable effort, especially when done for the first time. However, it is worth the effort, as searching is a very important feature for candidates and for recruiters and it makes sense to adapt it as much as possible to meet your requirements. Each step is described in the SAP documentation within the IMG.

6.5.4 Applicant Tracking

This is probably the most intensive activity in Customizing, as the framework for process templates must be defined here.

We should examine the definition of scales for ranking and reporting. These scales are so-called quality scales, which means that they contain clearly defined countable (discrete) proficiencies. Via the path SAP E-RECRUITING • RECRUITMENT • APPLICANT TRACKING • DEFINE SCALES FOR RANKING AND REPORTING you get the table shown in Figure 6.48, where each scale is defined by a text. Then, the proficiencies are assigned (see Figure 6.49).

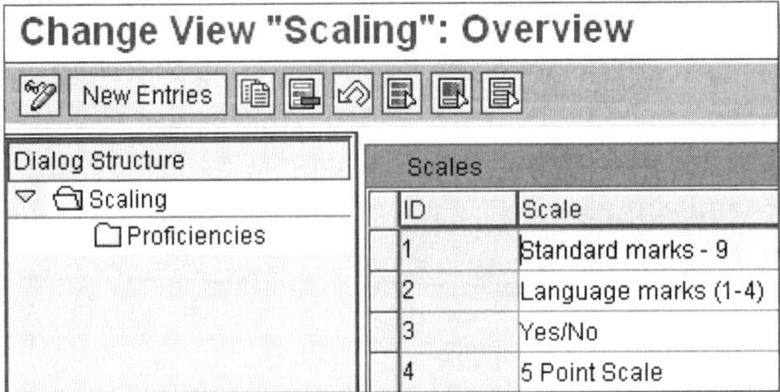

Figure 6.48 Maintain Scales

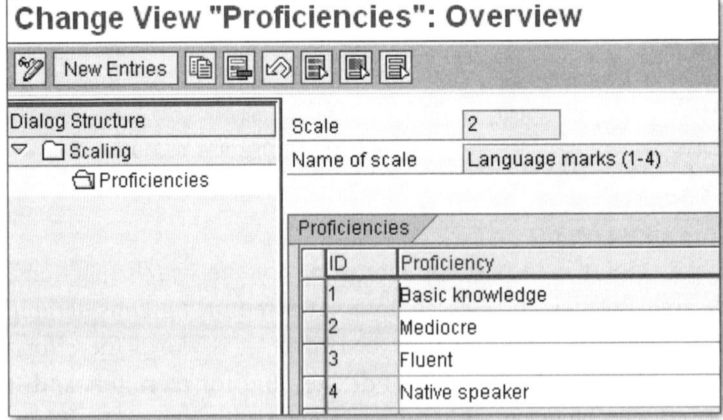

Figure 6.49 Define Proficiencies for a Scale

Each scale can be assigned to one or more scale types via the path APPLICANT TRACKING • ASSIGN SCALES TO SCALE TYPES. This determines where the scale can be used. There are four scale types available:

- Candidate ranking
- Ranking of candidates' assignments to requisitions
- Weighting of criteria for Search&Match
- Availability as successor

6.5.5 Activities

Although the Customizing for activities only provides the basis for the definition of process templates (outside Customizing) but does not control the process flow directly, you should know how your processes will look before doing this Customizing.

The first step would be to define the processes via the IMG path SAP E-RECRUITING • RECRUITMENT • APPLICANT TRACKING • ACTIVITIES • DEFINE PROCESSES. The group must always be recruiting as we are not dealing with succession planning here.

The second step requires some effort. You have to define the activity types and assign them to one of the following seven categories:

- **Simple activities**
  They just serve as a task list for the recruiter but have no specific behavior (call requesting manager after interview). They contain the data field's Status, Due Date, and Employee Responsible.
- **Qualifying events**
  They refer to an event, so that additional data such as time and address must be maintained (e.g., first interview).
- **Simple correspondence**
  Here, a letter form is assigned (e.g., interim notification).
- **Invitation**
  Activities of this category have a letter form assigned and refer to a qualifying event. This letter can include data for this qualifying event as well (e.g., invitation to assessment center).
- **Status change**
  Change the status of the process (e.g., rejection).

- **Questionnaires**
  Filling in of questionnaires can be requested via these activities.
- **Data transfer for new employees**
  When an applicant is hired, his data can be transferred to personnel administration. To do so, the connection between the E-Recruiting system and the ERP Central Component (ECC) system where the employee data is maintained must be configured accordingly.

When created, the activity types are assigned to the processes they occur in and to the objects they can be used for. Figure 6.50 shows some activities that can be used for candidacies and some that can be used for applications.

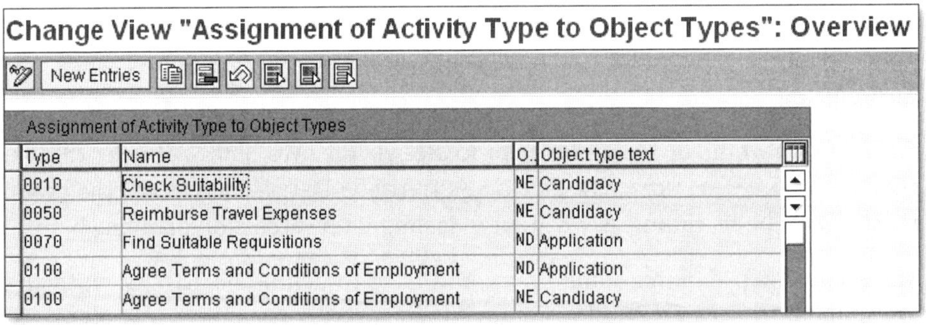

Change View "Assignment of Activity Type to Object Types": Overview

New Entries

Assignment of Activity Type to Object Types

Type	Name	O.	Object type text
0010	Check Suitability	NE	Candidacy
0050	Reimburse Travel Expenses	NE	Candidacy
0070	Find Suitable Requisitions	ND	Application
0100	Agree Terms and Conditions of Employment	ND	Application
0100	Agree Terms and Conditions of Employment	NE	Candidacy

Figure 6.50 Assign Activity Types to Object Types

The remaining items in this part of the IMG deal with settings for activity types of specific categories and with the workflow that can be started after an activity has been created.

Activities with correspondence must have a form assigned containing the letter via the IMG path SAP E-RECRUITING • RECRUITMENT •APPLICANT TRACKING • ACTIVITIES • CORRESPONDENCE • CREATE LETTER TEMPLATES • INDIVIDUALIZATION VIA LETTER SECTIONS •ASSIGN FORMS TO ACTIVITY TYPES. These forms must have been defined as smart forms (see Figure 6.51) before using the IMG path APPLICANT TRACKING • ACTIVITIES • CORRESPONDENCE • CREATE FORM (or Transaction SMARTFORMS). For further information on Smart forms, refer to the SAP PRESS book *SAP Smart Forms* by Werner Hertleif and Christoph Wachter.

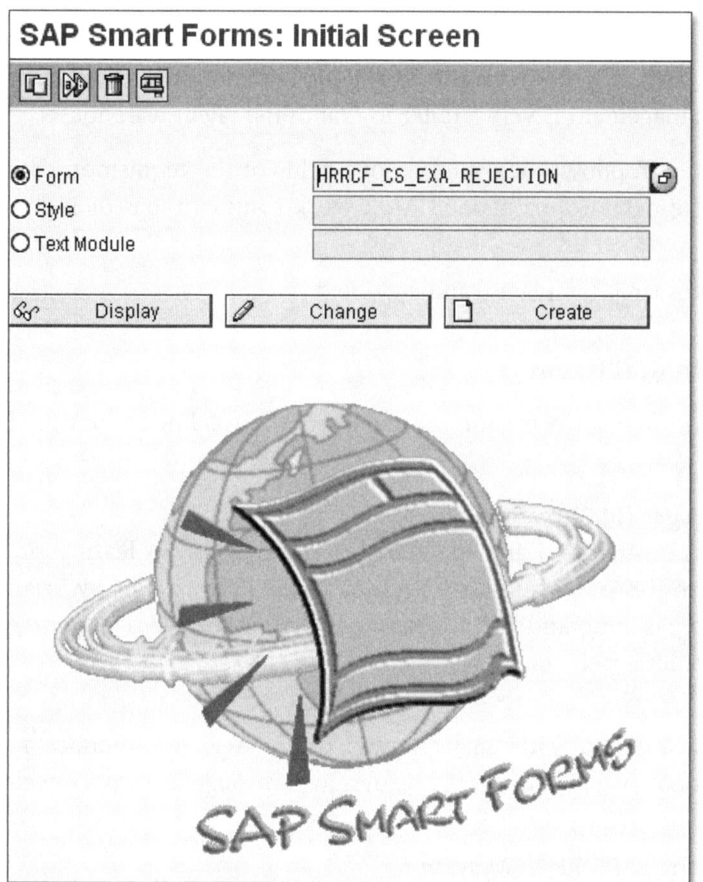

Figure 6.51 Maintain Forms for Letters with SAP Smart Forms

6.5.6 Questionnaires

The questionnaires are defined by the recruiter in the application as described in Section 6.3.5. There is not much Customizing to be done except for the scales, which are the same as shown in Figure 6.48. There are two questionnaire categories (job-related information and EEO), and they are created automatically in the customizing via the path APPLICANT TRACKING • QUESTIONNAIRES • UPDATE CATEGORIES. When assigning these categories to activity types, you also decide whether the questionnaires are integrated into the application wizard. If not, a link to the questionnaire must be sent via email.

6.5.7 Requisition Management

Besides the approval workflows for requisitions and job postings, the Customizing for the requisition management is very similar to that of the talent warehouse:

- The options for the dropdown boxes in various fields of the requisition data and the job posting data are maintained (e.g., work contract types or industries).
- Search profiles and search templates can be defined.

6.5.8 Further Technical Issues

Here is some additional information concerning the technical basis of E-Recruiting:

- **Business Server Pages (BSP) Technology**
  The Web-based user interfaces are implemented using BSPs. To learn more about BSPs, refer to the SAP PRESS books *Advanced BSP Programming* by Brian McKellar and Thomas Jung and *BSP Extensions: How to Master Web Reporting with HTMLB* by Frédéric Heinemann.
- **Smart Forms**
  Correspondence is realized with Smart Forms technology. An interface to Microsoft Word is not available but could be designed through a custom development.
- **Integration with the SAP ERP HCM system**
  Many issues arise when you require a connection to the ECC system where the SAP ERP HCM system is running (for example, organizational management or transfer of candidate to the employee master data). When SAP E-Recruiting, release 3.0 or higher, and SAP ECC 5.0, HCM Extension (EA-HR 500) or higher are used, both E-Recruiting and the ECC can be run on the same instance. However, this is usually avoided for security reasons (particularly if E-Recruiting is used for external candidates). To connect both systems, you need to configure Application Link Enabling (ALE) as described via the IMG path TECHNICAL SETTINGS • SAP ERP CENTRAL COMPONENT (ECC) INTEGRATION • SOFTWARE RUNS ON DIFFERENT INSTANCES.
- **Text Retrieval and Information Extraction (TREX)**
  The search functionality is provided by the search engine Text TREX. It works much like the search engines you know from the Web. This search engine is

also used in the SAP Enterprise Portal. However, for E-Recruiting purposes it must be installed in the configuration designed for a nonportal environment. You will find the installation guide *Installing Retrieval and Classification (TREX) in a Non-Portal Environment* on the SAP Service Marketplace (*service.sap.com*).

6.6 Critical Success Factors

In addition to the critical success factors we will cover in Chapter 7, "Traditional Recruitment," the following apply to E-Recruiting:

- When transitioning from a traditional recruitment solution, you should not consider the implementation of E-Recruiting as a mere change of the technical basis, where the processes aren't changed much except that email is used more extensively for communication. As we discuss in Section 6.3, the concept is completely different from the old solution and allows and requires completely different processes.
- Make sure you have the necessary skill set available for your project, including:
  - One person (probably a consultant) who has a very good knowledge of SAP ERP HCM as a whole (especially the data structure of personnel planning and development), customizing and processes in the SAP E-Recruiting solution (knowledge of the traditional SAP recruitment solution will also help to some extent), and recruitment processes in general.
  - Design and programming of BSPs. It depends on your requirements whether or not any changes to BSPs are necessary.
  - Design and programming of Smart forms
  - Workflow: It depends on your requirements how much workflow will be used.
  - Web Application Server/NetWeaver. It is necessary for the integration with the ECC system and the TREX search engine.
  - Architecture and security of Web-based applications.
  - SAP Query.
  - Possibly SAP NetWeaver BI.
  - Possibly ABAP Objects.

- Make sure that the managers are involved online in the whole process, especially in the selection. Because they may be on high hierarchy levels, it can be difficult for an E-Recruiting project manager to succeed in this without the help of a powerful project sponsor from the top management.
- When coming from the traditional recruitment solution, make sure that you have a solution for printed correspondence (Smart forms or Adobe PDF) that complies with your requirements, because the new solution lacks some of the flexibility you have when using Microsoft Word in the traditional solution.

This chapter deals with the characteristics of traditional recruitment in SAP ERP HCM, starting with the different recruitment methods and continuing through selecting applicants to hiring an employee. The individual steps in the HCM system are also described in the same way.

7 Traditional Recruitment

Despite the fact that E-Recruiting is being widely discussed and that the component is more current and more common, there are still customers that use traditional recruitment processes. However, new implementations of SAP's traditional recruitment component are not advisable, because this component is being replaced by E-Recruiting, as we discussed in Chapter 6, "E-Recruiting." The business principles are not included here intentionally, because we described them thoroughly in the previous chapter.

7.1 The SAP ERP HCM Concept

The following sections deal with the integration of traditional recruitment with the organizational structure and the individual components of the solution, including their interactions.

7.1.1 Integration in the Organizational Structure

Recruitment uses the SAP organizational structure to the extent that it uses *vacant* positions from organizational management. The vacancies are created using the Infotype Vacancy (1007) at a position in organizational management (via the path Personnel • Personnel Management • Recruitment • Advertising • Vacancy • Maintain). The positions to be filled are made accessible to application management by assigning this infotype (see Figure 7.1).

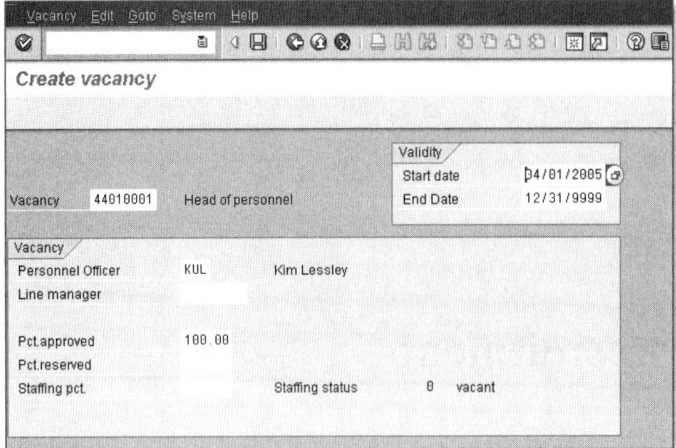

Figure 7.1 Setting Position as Vacant

Another way to use organizational management in recruiting is the creation of *requirement profiles* for the position. Together with their counterpart, the *qualifications profile* of the applicant, these enable a profile comparison to support the applicant selection. We will only deal with the options of organizational management for creating a requirement profile briefly, however, because this subject is part of personnel development, which will not be dealt with here (for more information refer to Appendix D, "Recommended Reading").

The prerequisite for both requirement and for qualifications profiles is the creation of a *qualifications catalog*. Our discussion has less to do with maintaining this catalog in SAP ERP HCM and more to do with the design activity in creating such a catalog. Determining the qualifications that already exist in a company and selecting the qualifications to be implemented in the system represent quite a challenge. The easiest way of doing this is to compile qualifications if there is a clear policy in a company regarding the requirements for a position. This is particularly true in public sector organizations, because there are straightforward job descriptions compiled from different activities which in turn result in grouping to a specific pay scale. The counterpart to this, the qualifications profile, and an example of a profile comparison are described in Section 7.1.3.

The final use of organizational management for applicant management is implemented by creating a job advertisement. In this step, the previously created vacancies are assigned to the job advertisements (see Figure 7.2). It is problematic if the job advertisement involves multiple positions, because you must create several similar vacancies to document how many positions are to be occupied. This occurs because — unlike in E-Recruiting (in requisitions) — there is no option in traditional recruitment to relate a quantity to a vacancy, which would document how many positions are to be occupied.

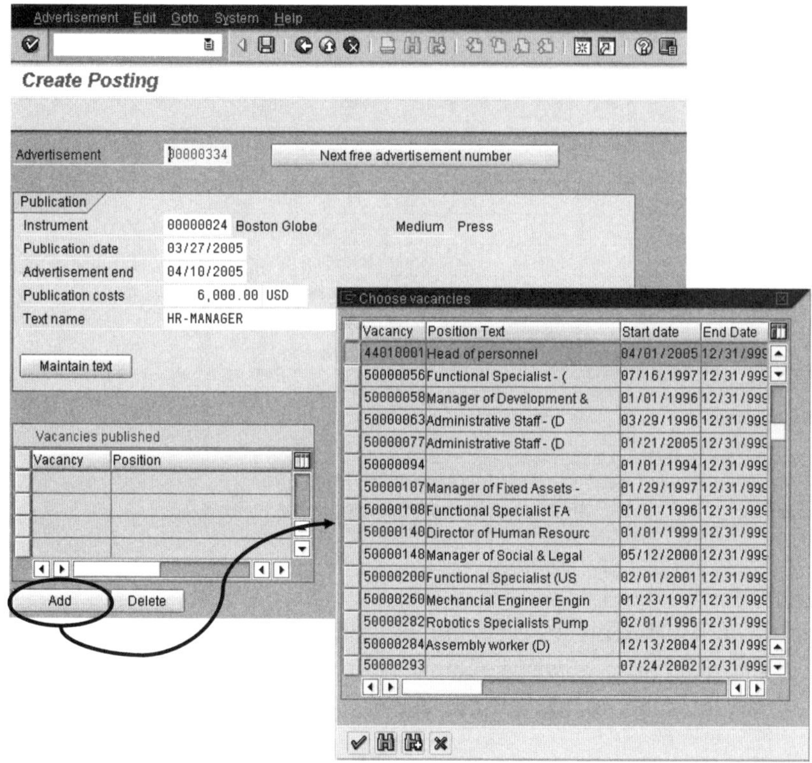

Figure 7.2 Linking a Job Advertisement with a Vacancy

7.1.2 Media and Instruments

It is first necessary to draw a distinction between the concepts of *media* and *instruments*.

A few examples, such as press or Internet/intranet, make it clear what is meant by the term media. This involves classifications and groupings that enable you to combine several instruments. In addition, you can assign a medium to unsolicited applicants through which they have contacted the company.

Media are created in the recruitment customizing via the implementation guide (IMG) path PERSONNEL MANAGEMENT • RECRUITMENT • WORKFORCE REQUIREMENTS

AND ADVERTISEMENTS • CREATE MEDIA. A characteristic of the medium is the applicant class assigned to it, which specifies if a medium is used to advertise internal or external applicants (see Figure 7.3).

Change View "Medium": Overview

New Entries

Medium	Name of medium	Applicant class	Applicant class text
01	Press	AP	External applicant
02	Employment office	AP	External applicant
03	Exec.search agency	AP	External applicant
04	Internal Job Posting	P	Internal applicant
05	Mail	P	Internal applicant
06	Internal press	P	Internal applicant
10	University	AP	External applicant
11	Trade fairs	AP	External applicant
12	Headhunter	AP	External applicant
13	Employee Referral	AP	External applicant
14	Walk In	AP	External applicant
15	Internet	AP	External applicant

Figure 7.3 Creating Media

In the recruitment instruments the type and methods of recruitment are mapped, for example, the placing of advertisements in the print media, personal contacts through headhunting, or referral by an employment center or recruitment agencies.

Recruitment instruments are further classified according to the medium used (e.g., press, employment center, recruitment agency).

Recruitment instruments are created in Customizing (IMG) for recruitment via PERSONNEL MANAGEMENT • RECRUITMENT • WORKFORCE REQUIREMENTS AND ADVERTISING • CREATE RECRUITMENT INSTRUMENTS (see Figure 7.4). A prerequisite for this is the creation of a recruitment medium, given that recruitment instruments are divided according to the medium used. For each recruitment instrument, you can store a contact person and an address key. You maintain the address of the contact person for the respective recruitment instrument through the work step Create addresses for recruitment instruments (via the path PERSONNEL MANAGEMENT • RECRUITMENT • WORKFORCE REQUIREMENTS AND ADVERTISING) (see Figure 7.4).

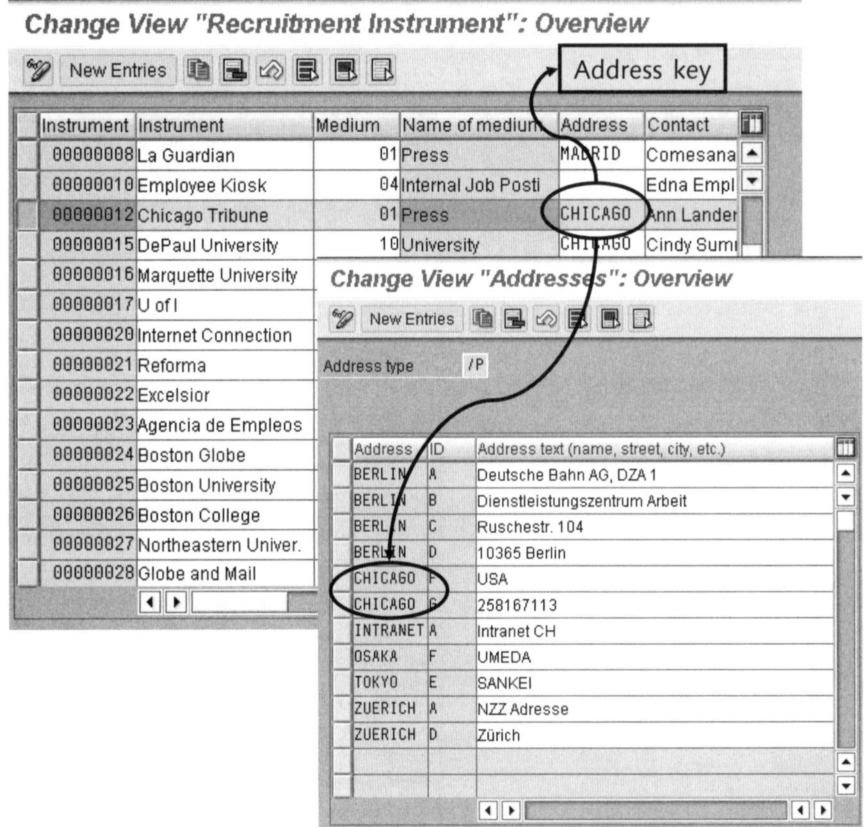

Figure 7.4 Creating Recruitment Instruments

The recruitment media and instruments are used when creating an advertisement (see Figure 7.5). In addition to the applicant, the central object in applicant management in SAP ERP HCM is the advertisement.

The purpose of assigning recruitment instruments to advertisements lies in recruitment reporting, in which we evaluate how successful a specific advertisement instrument was in comparison to the others. You can measure this, for example, by contrasting the number of applications and their quality (e.g., measurable by the number of people hired based on an advertisement) with the recruitment instrument. Additional criteria to define a successful advertisement instrument are described in Section 7.1.6. If several instruments are used for an advertisement, a separate advertisement must be created for each of these instruments. This could well seem cumbersome, but it enables you to evaluate the effectiveness of instruments, because the incoming applications are assigned to the advertisement to which they refer (e.g., advertisement in *The Economist*).

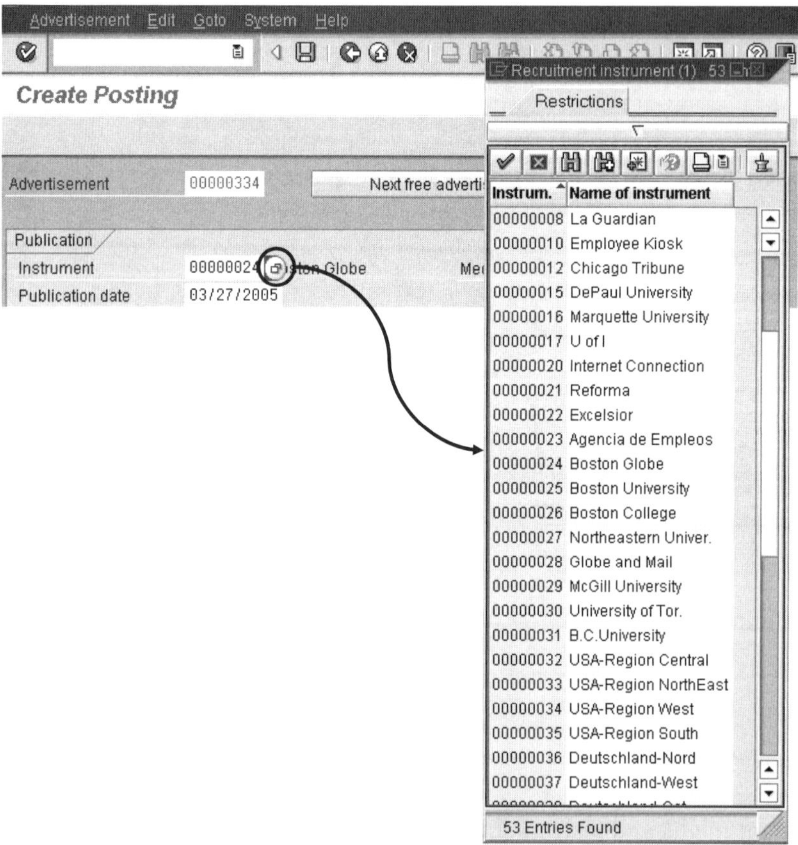

Figure 7.5 Assigning Recruitment Instruments to Advertisements

7.1.3 Applicant Master Data

The collection of applicant master data often represents a big challenge for the Human Resources (HR) department, in that a large quantity of applicant documents must be viewed in some fashion, and the interesting applications must be entered into a system. It is important to have an instrument at hand that enables you to enter the data as quickly and in as structured a way as possible. Figure 7.6 shows an example of an entry screen for the applicant master data. You can see that individual areas can be individually customized.

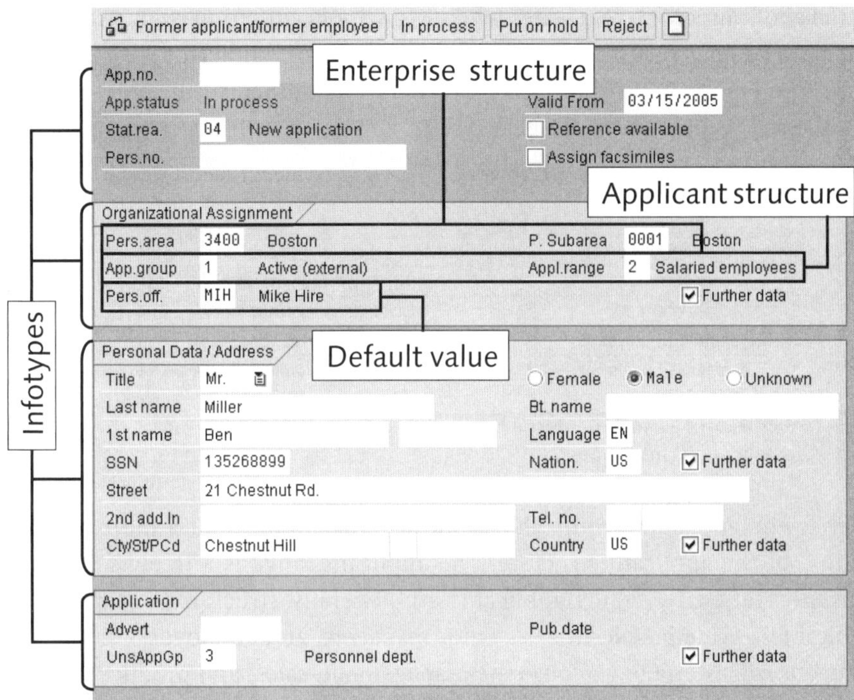

Figure 7.6 Entry Screen for Applicant Master Data

Applicant Structure

In comparison to the structures used in personnel administration (see Section 4.2.5), structures used in application management are also necessary for control and evaluation functions. Even if the definition of the applicant structure is subject to change throughout the course of the project, clarification should be as precise as possible from the beginning of the project, because customizing of applicant management is to some extent based on these early results. In addition to assigning applicants to the company structure displayed by the organizational structure of the HCM system, the applicants are assigned to *applicant groups* and *applicant ranges* (details on the definition and functions of the company structure with the personnel areas and subareas can also be found in Section 4.2.5).

Like the employee groups in personnel administration, the applicant groups are the result of a basic division of employees (e.g., employees with unlimited/fixed-term employment contracts, trainees, temps). Here, the decisive criterion is the type of employment relationship to be entered into. The applicant class is a property of the applicant group that states whether an applicant group comprises internal or external applicants (indicator P = internal applicant, indicator AP = external applicant, see Figure 7.7). Applicant groups are maintained in the IMG via the path PERSONNEL MANAGEMENT • RECRUITMENT • MANAGE APPLICANTS • APPLICANT STRUCTURE • CREATE APPLICANT GROUPS.

Applicant group	Applicant group text	Applicant class	Applicant class text
1	Active (external)	AP	External applicant
2	Active (internal)	P	Internal applicant
3	Student employee	AP	External applicant
4	Temporary worker	AP	External applicant
5	Retiree	P	Internal applicant

Figure 7.7 Creating Applicant Groups

Contrary to the applicant group, the applicant ranges represent a more refined breakdown of the applicant structure. The applicant range is a freely selectable structuring criterion by which applicants are generally structured according to hierarchical criteria (e.g., executives, senior managers, and employees) or according to functional criteria (e.g., corporate management, sales, and production).

For applications that are not directly related to an advertisement and thus to a vacancy, *unsolicited applicant groups* can be set up. The unsolicited applicant group is a freely selectable criterion to structure unsolicited applicants. For example, it is possible to summarize unsolicited applicants according to their desired position in the company (e.g., sales employee or personnel department employee). Each unsolicited applicant group must be assigned a group personnel director. This director acts as a suggested value in entering the master data when an applicant is assigned the corresponding unsolicited applicant group. A prerequisite for assigning a group personnel director is that these group personnel directors working in the company have been created in the system (IMG path PERSONNEL MANAGEMENT • RECRUITMENT • MANAGE APPLICANTS • CREATE GROUP PERSONNEL DIRECTORS).

To facilitate the decision of which applicant groups and subgroups are created, you must clarify what requirements the applicant structure should fulfill with regard to the following points:

- Different processing of different applicants with regard to
  - Applicant processes (see Section 7.1.4)

- Applicant correspondence (see Section 7.1.5)
- Applicant responsibility (Who processes whom?)
- Selection for the evaluation
- Authorization check

The more differentiated the controls are in this area, the more refined the applicant structure must be.

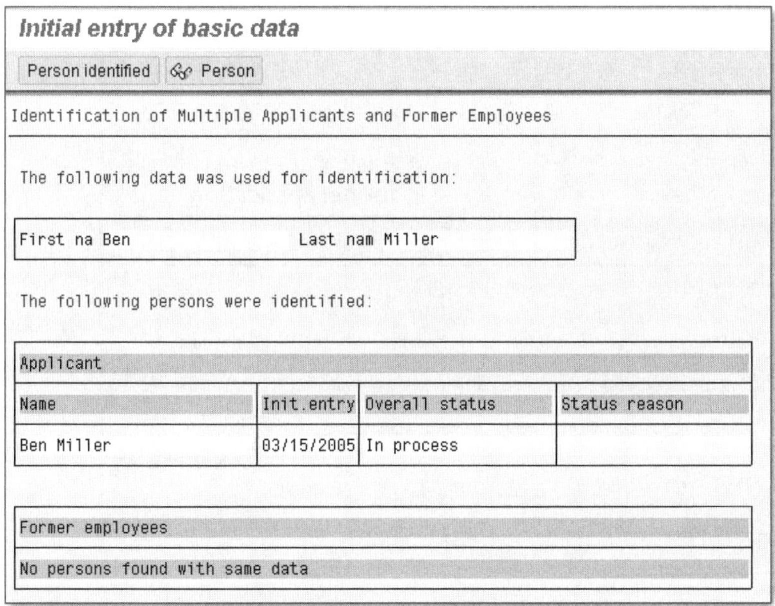

Figure 7.8 Recognizing Applicants

When the applicant data is initially entered, the system checks to see if the application is a duplicate application. Here, the last name in combination with the first name and the date of birth are used as a basis for comparison. When there is a hit, the system shows the result of the comparison. From here, you can navigate to the data of the person found (see Figure 7.8) to find out if it is the same person and what advertisement the application refers to. If you have recognized the person, you can confirm this in the system, and the applicant is set to the status Renewed application. In addition, the master data already entered is transferred (see Figure 7.9).

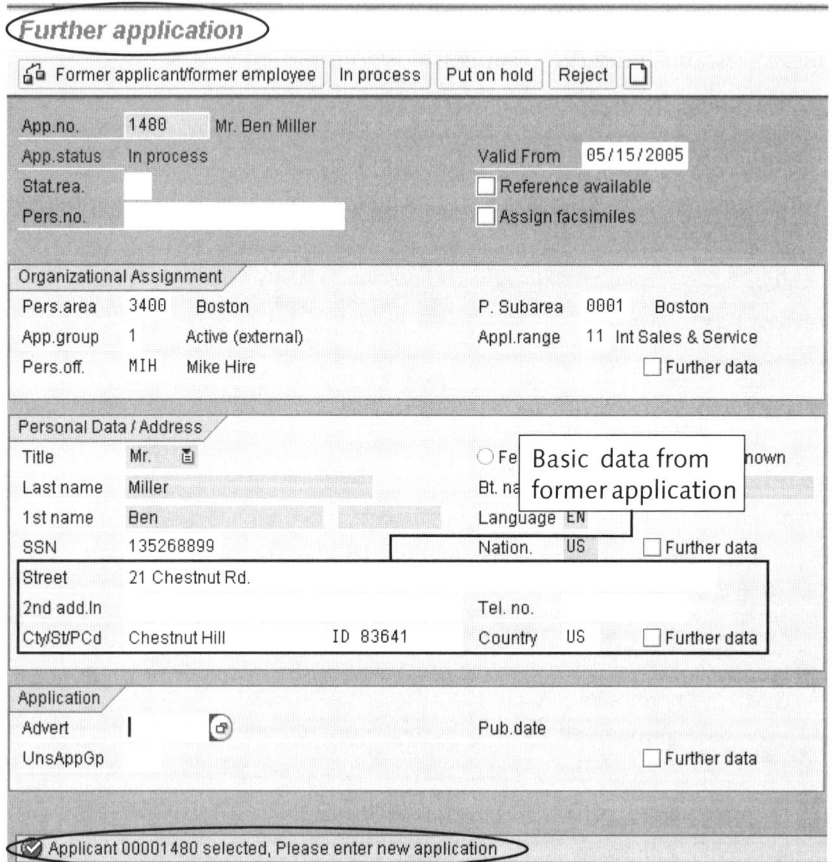

Figure 7.9 Master Data Transfer for New Application

Short Profile

By defining one or several short profiles of the applicants, evaluations can be defined individually by the customer. An example is the report to evaluate the applications received (see Section 7.1.4), for which a short profile can be called in each case for individual applicants. It is useful to create different short profiles that meet the different requirements of the company. For example, the short profile provided for a transactional user should meet certain administrative criteria. These might include displaying the applicant processes or the current status of the applicant in the application process. Line-manager applicants, on the other hand, would instead need short profiles that contain CVs and qualifications.

SAP provides two templates to create the short profile. These can be reached through the IMG path PERSONNEL MANAGEMENT • RECRUITMENT • MANAGE APPLICANTS • SHORT PROFILE. These templates can be copied and customized. For these documents the following information is available as text variables from the applicant master data (extract):

- Fields of the organizational assignment of the applicant: personnel (sub-) area, applicant group/range, etc.
- Fields of personal data of an applicant: first name, last name, gender, etc.
- Address fields: address
- Qualification fields: education, certificates, etc.
- Qualification fields: qualifications and their characteristics
- Overall status of the applicant
- Completed/planned processes

The data to be included in a short profile and if the data of the applicant should be included at all depends strongly on the information the data is supposed to provide. For a pure administration of the applicants without system support when selecting the suitable applicants, master data are sufficient, such as address, personal data, and the vacancy and advertisement assignment. However, if a company also needs support when selecting a suitable applicant, either for certain occupational groups or in general, further data is required. This is because both the requirements of the vacancy and the qualifications of the applicants are necessary if, for instance, profile comparisons are to be carried out.

Qualifications Profiles and Profile Comparisons

The use of profiles and profile comparisons is part of the personnel development components in SAP ERP HCM and can support the decision-making processes regarding the selection of suitable applicants or successors respectively. Because personnel development is not part of this book, we will only briefly describe the subject of profiles and profile comparisons here.

The *requirements profile* was already discussed briefly in Section 7.1.1. Creating a *qualifications profile* is the logical counterpart here if profile comparisons are referred to in selecting applicants. A predetermined qualifications catalog is required here too, which is used as a basis for both the requirements and the qualifications profiles. A qualifications profile consists of several components (see Figure 7.10):

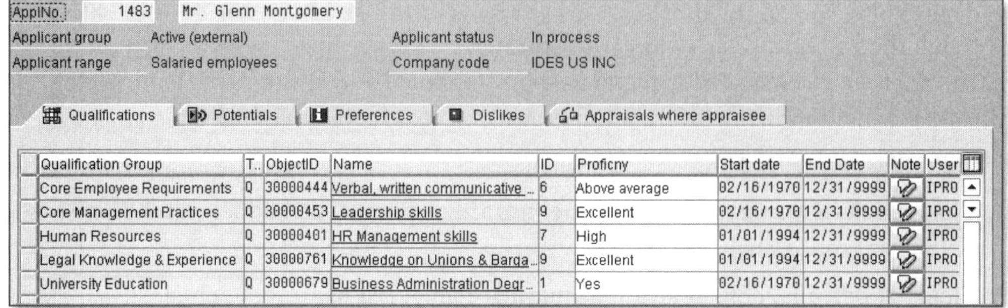

Figure 7.10 Qualifications Profile

- **Qualifications**
  The existing qualifications and their characteristics are entered here.
- **Potentials**
  You can enter whether a person has potential to occupy a specific position/job.
- **Preferences**
  If an employee is interested in a specific task or position, this can be entered here.
- **Dislikes**
  To avoid offering someone a specific position or task, this can be entered here as an exclusion criterion.
- **Appraisals received as appraisee**
  For an applicant these can be appraisals from an assessment center, and for an employee these can be appraisals by a superior.

To support the applicant selection, there is the option to contrast the qualifications profiles of the applicants with the requirements profiles of positions or jobs. A result of this comparison is shown in Figure 7.11.

7.1.4 Status, Actions, and Processes

To systematically log the process of an applicant from the first entry of his data in the applicant master data through the various selection processes to hiring or refusal, processes and actions are carried out in SAP ERP HCM that document the respective status of the applicant.

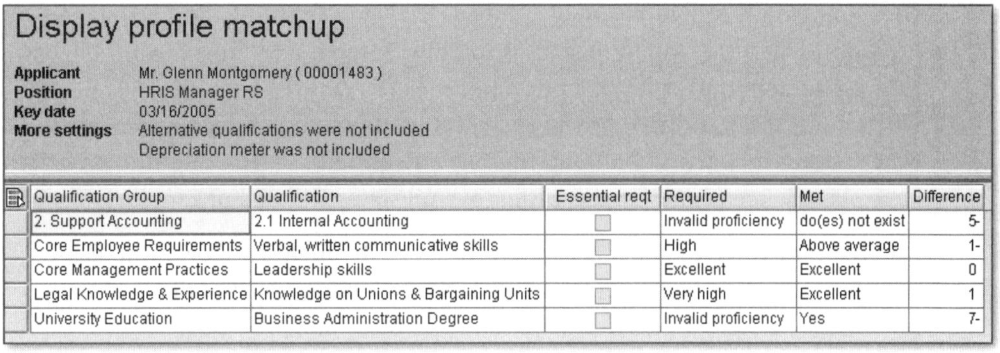

Display profile matchup

Applicant	Mr. Glenn Montgomery (00001483)
Position	HRIS Manager RS
Key date	03/16/2005
More settings	Alternative qualifications were not included Depreciation meter was not included

Qualification Group	Qualification	Essential reqt	Required	Met	Difference
2. Support Accounting	2.1 Internal Accounting	☐	Invalid proficiency	do(es) not exist	5-
Core Employee Requirements	Verbal, written communicative skills	☐	High	Above average	1-
Core Management Practices	Leadership skills	☐	Excellent	Excellent	0
Legal Knowledge & Experience	Knowledge on Unions & Bargaining Units	☐	Very high	Excellent	1
University Education	Business Administration Degree	☐	Invalid proficiency	Yes	7-

Figure 7.11 Profile Comparison between Applicants and Positions

You will find that SAP ERP HCM basically differentiates between two types of selection processes in recruitment:

- **Global selection process**
  Each applicant entered takes part in the global selection process of a company. This process decides if an applicant is of interest to the company. If an applicant is not refused, he can participate in one or several selection processes for a vacancy.
- **Selection process for each vacancy**
  Here, the applicant is assigned to the relevant vacancies.

Status

Both in the global selection process and in the selection processes for a vacancy, you can decide at any time whether there is still interest in an applicant. The respective status of an applicant in a selection process is mapped in the applicant status. There are two types of applicant status with regard to the selection processes:

- **Overall status**
  This status specifies the current status (e.g., in process, on hold, interview required) an applicant has in the global selection process of the company.
- **Status of the vacancy assignment**
  This defines which current status (e.g., in process, on hold, interview required) an applicant has in the selection process for a specific vacancy.

Depending on the system settings, the overall status is automatically assigned via an action when the applicant data is initially entered and must always be available for an applicant from this point in time. You can see from the overall status whether an applicant currently participates in at least one selection process (e.g., overall status In Process, On Hold, Interview Required), or if all selection processes have already been completed for him (overall status Refused or Employ).

An applicant receives a status-of-the-vacancy assignment as soon as he has been assigned to a vacancy. If an applicant has several vacancy assignments, a status of the vacancy assignment is available for all of these assignments. A selection process is completed if all applicants who are participating in the selection process have the status Rejected or the status To Be Employed.

The applicant statuses provided by SAP should be regarded as a default and not be supplemented. The following status categories for applicants are provided by SAP:

- In process
- To be employed
- On hold
- Rejected
- Contract offered
- Offer refused
- Invite

For some of the status categories, it may be necessary to specify reasons. For example, it is possible to connect the information on why someone has the status Rejected, with a reason for the refusal. In this case, reasons such as Insufficient Qualifications, Rejected After Conclusion of the Selection Process, and the like would be conceivable. The status reason can be purely informational, but it can also be used, for example, to establish which text templates are assigned to the relevant applicant process during automatic creation, and thus which letter the applicant will receive. The status reasons can be assigned to individual statuses (see Figure 7.12).

Change View "Admissible Combination of Status and Reason": Overview

New Entries

Status	Text for applicant status	Status reason	Text for status reason
1	In process	04	New application
3	On hold	03	Overqualified
3	On hold	05	No requirement
4	Rejected	01	Insufficient qualifications
4	Rejected	02	Formal error
4	Rejected	03	Overqualified
4	Rejected	05	No requirement
4	Rejected	06	

Figure 7.12 Admissibility of Status Reasons

In recruitment customizing, you establish which combinations between the overall status and the status of the vacancy assignment are admissible. It may not be permitted in a company, for example, to assign an invitation for interview to applicants who have the overall status Contract offered for another vacancy. This is controlled by assigning the admissible statuses of the vacancy assignment to the individual overall status. You can see an overview of the possible combinations in Figure 7.13.

The overall status of an applicant is set via the *applicant actions* in recruitment (e.g., the applicant action Initial core data sets the overall status In Process).

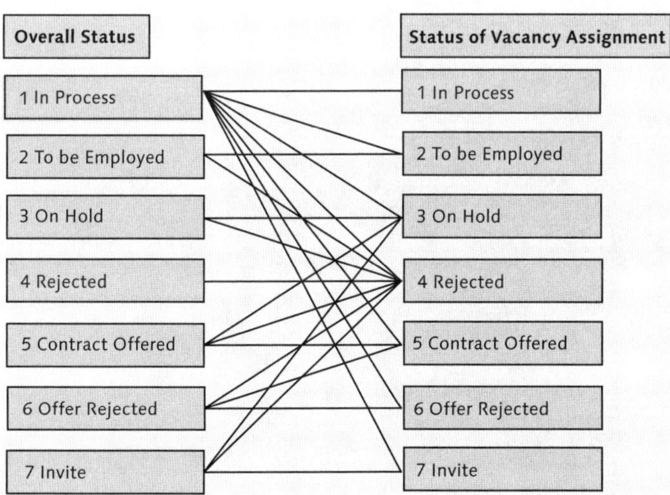

Figure 7.13 Combinations of the Overall Status with the Status of the Vacancy Assignment

Actions

In SAP ERP HCM, actions refer to a sequencing of infotypes, for example, organizational assignment and address, carried out in personnel management for an applicant or employee for a particular reason, such as initial entry of applicant data, hiring, change of cost center, leaving, etc. (see Figure 7.14). The infotype concept was described in more detail in Section 4.2.2.

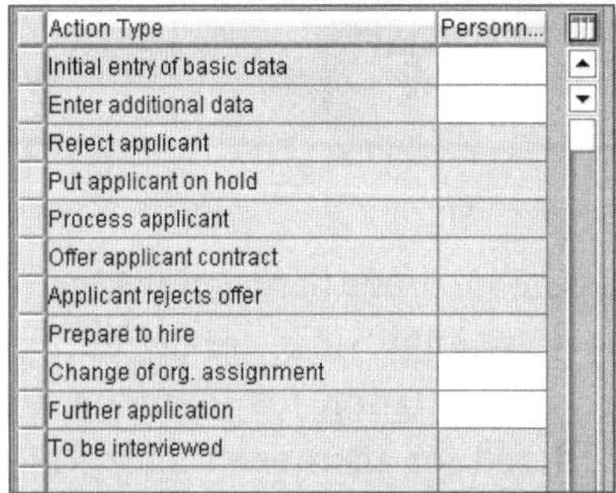

Action Type	Personn...
Initial entry of basic data	
Enter additional data	
Reject applicant	
Put applicant on hold	
Process applicant	
Offer applicant contract	
Applicant rejects offer	
Prepare to hire	
Change of org. assignment	
Further application	
To be interviewed	

Figure 7.14 Applicant Actions

The type and sequence of infotypes to be processed in recruitment by using actions is defined in recruitment customizing. Here, as in personnel administration, you can create *info groups* (sequences of infotypes, see Figure 7.15). SAP provides a range of applicant actions (see Figure 7.14). Customizing applicant actions is easy.

Change View "Info Group": Overview

New Entries

Info group 47 Init. core data

User group-dependent

Reaction

Reference user group 00

User group	Infogrmodi.	N..	Operation	Infotype	S..	Infotype text	Subty...
00		01	INS	0002		Personal Data	
00		02	INS	0001		Organizational Assignment	
00		03	INS	0006		Addresses	
00		04	INS	4001		Applications	
00		05	INS	4005		Applicant's Personnel Number	
00		06	INS	0105		Communication	0001

Figure 7.15 Info Groups of the Action Initial Core Data

You can navigate to the applicant actions via the IMG path PERSONNEL MANAGEMENT • RECRUITMENT • SELECTING APPLICANTS • CHANGE INFOGROUPS/APPLICANT ACTIONS. In recruitment, the following administration infotypes are available:

- Infotype 0001(Organizational assignment)
- Infotype 0002 (Personal Data)
- Infotype 0006 (Addresses)
- Infotype 0022 (Education)
- Infotype 0023 (Other/Previous Employers)
- Infotype over 0024 (Qualifications)
- Infotype 0009 (Bank Details)
- Infotype 0016 (Contract Elements)
- Infotype 0008 (Basic pay)
- Infotype 0014 (Recurring payments and deductions)
- Infotype 0015 (Additional Payments)
- Infotype 0007 (Planned Working Time)

If required, other recruitment infotypes can be made available. In addition to the personnel administration infotypes previously mentioned, there are specific infotypes for applicants. These are as follows:

- **Infotype 4000 (Applicant Actions)**
  Here, all actions are stored that have been carried out for an applicant. These can be processes for data entry (e.g., initial entry of applicant data, entry of additional data), but they can also be processes that change the overall status of the applicant (e.g., reject applicant, put applicant on hold). In addition to the action type carried out for an applicant, you can enter in the applicant actions infotype whether an applicant can produce a reference. If this is the case you can select the personnel number of the reference from the administration HR master data in a separate field.
- **Infotype 4001 (Application)**
  In this infotype you can enter if an application refers to an advertisement (vacancy) or arrived unsolicited (unsolicited applicant group).
- **Infotype 4002 (Vacancy Assignment)**
  Here you enter which vacancies an applicant is assigned to.

- **Infotype 4003 (Applicant Activities)**
  The entry, logging, and planning of activities for an applicant within the selection process is carried out via the applicant activities. Thus, applicant activities are administrative steps that an applicant runs through in the course of his application. In addition, the applicant correspondence is carried out through the applicant activities (more detailed information on the applicant activities follows).
- **Infotype 4005 (Applicant's Personnel Number)**
  The system automatically fills the infotype for all internal applicants. This means every internal applicant has a data record of this infotype.
- **Infotype 4004 (Applicant Activity Status)**
  There is exactly one data record of this infotype in the system for each applicant. The system automatically creates and updates this data record. The infotype displays the status of the processes carried out and supports the search for applicant data efficiently.
- **Infotype 0139 (Employee's Applicant Number)**
  This infotype is used in personnel administration in the following cases:
  - The external applicant joins the company as an employee.
  - The internal applicant, and thus an existing employee in the company, occupies the vacant job.

  You store the applicant number and the employee personnel number in this infotype. This means the infotype identifies the applicant with the employee.

When combining info groups and thus actions, you must note that Infotype 0001 (Organizational Assignment) must always be created as one of the first infotypes because it is used for authorization checks, screen layout, and plausibility checks within other infotypes.

Apart from the sequence of infotypes, you can also define which fields are shown during the initial entry of applicant data. In addition, the two-level process for the initial entry of data is defined here, establishing which data belongs to the core data and which belongs to the additional data.

This two-level process is especially useful for the initial entry of applicant data. First, you enter the core applicant data, and, in a second step, you can enter additional data. The basic data must be entered for each applicant, because it includes basic information for statistical purposes, such as the assignment of applicants to personnel (sub-)areas, applicant groups/ranges, names, and address. Additional data is only entered for those applicants who are of further interest to the company. Using the applicant action Enter additional data, you can, for example, assign an applicant to one or several vacancies. In addition, you can use this applicant action to enter applicant data on education, qualifications, and previous employers.

Because it is necessary in the administration of a selection process to enter all planned and completed activities for an applicant (e.g., sending a confirmation of receipt, transferring applicant documents, interview) in the scope of a selection process, the logging and planning of activities for an applicant is carried out through *applicant activities*.

Activities

Applicant activities are administrative steps that an applicant runs through in the course of his application. Applicant activities are created and processed for each action carried out with an applicant. The system creates some of the applicant activities automatically. For example, the applicant activity Confirmation of Receipt is automatically created after the action Initial Entry of Applicant Data. The applicant activities are partly created explicitly (e.g., transfer of applicant data to the user department). In deciding when and which applicant activities are created automatically, you are free to set the selection process yourself using your own customized actions and the automatic activities to be created.

The activities of an application have the following properties:

- **Activity type**
  You can use the activity type to determine the specific activity that is to be carried out for an applicant (e.g., sending out the confirmation of receipt, invitation for an interview, date of the interview).
- **Activity status**
  For each applicant activity, it is determined if the activity for an applicant is still to be carried out (activity status, planned) or if it has already been completed (activity status, completed).
- **Execution date**
  Regarding planned activities, the execution date specifies up to what day or on what day the activity should take place, and for completed activities it specifies when the activity took place.

- **Activity administrator**
  The administrator is responsible for ensuring that the relevant activity takes place on the specified date, or he assumes responsibility for carrying out the activity in the correct manner.

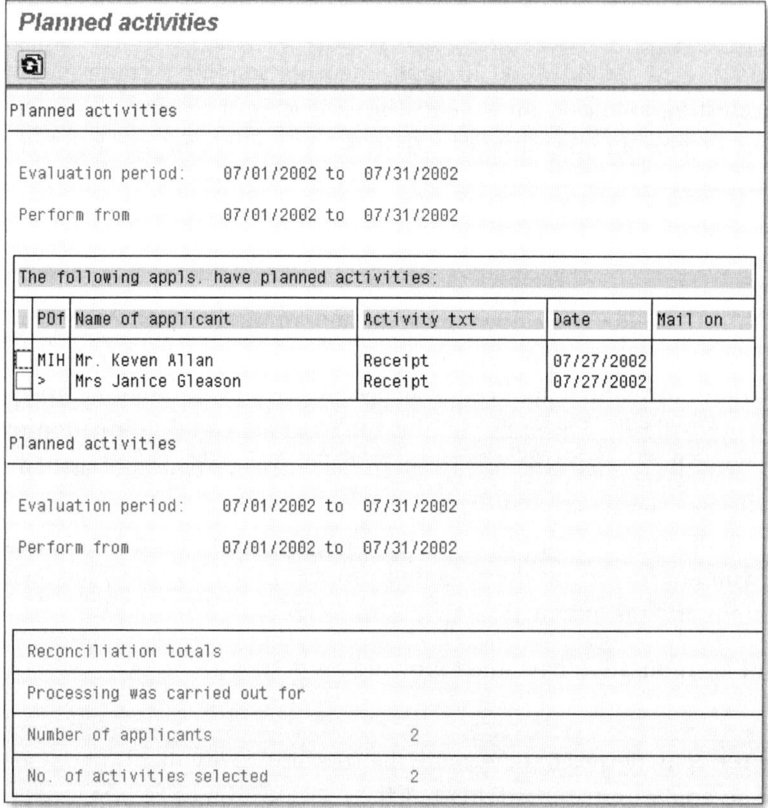

Figure 7.16 Planned Activities

The properties of the applicant processes enable you to carry out a control via the individual selection processes. The most important control instruments for the selection process are:

- **Planned activities**
  This evaluation monitors the planned activities according to the group personnel director. Thus, the recruiter can get an overview of the planned activities for each applicant (see Figure 7.16).

- **Applications**

  This report outputs a list of all applications (see Figure 7.17). The list contains the following information:

  - Applicant's name
  - Date of receipt of the application
  - Advertisement or unsolicited applicant group the application refers to

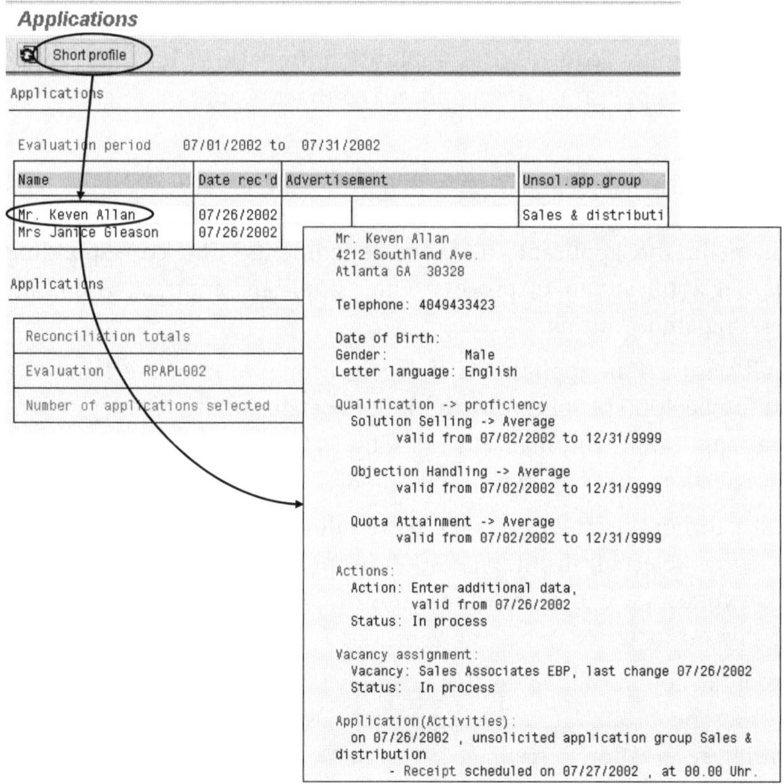

Figure 7.17 Evaluation of Applications and Short Profile

By entering selection criteria, the output quantity can be reduced. For example, when receiving applications you can determine that only the applicants who applied within the relevant time interval are selected. From the evaluation result, you can navigate to a *short profile* for individual applicants that can be adjusted according to your individual requirements (see Figure 7.17). You can find a description of the possible settings for the short profile in Section 7.1.3.

7.1.5 Controlling the Work Flow and Correspondence

The work flows in applicant administration are basically controlled via the personnel actions and the activities that arise from this. Here, *dynamic actions* (see Section 4.4.2) play a decisive role, because they control the triggering of actions during the maintenance of a recruitment infotype record. The standard settings provided by SAP can be described as follows:

1. If Infotype 4000 (Applicant Activities) is changed through one of the following actions, activities are automatically created in connection with the PACTV feature. The corresponding actions are: Reapplication, Initial core data, Put applicant on hold, Reject applicant, Offer applicant contract, Applicant rejects offer, Prepare for hiring.
2. If the overall status of an applicant is changed through one of the following actions in Infotype 4000 (Applicant Activities), a report is launched in which you can maintain the applicant's vacancy assignments. The corresponding actions are: Set applicant to in process, Offer applicant contract, Applicant rejects offer, Prepare for hiring.
3. If the overall status of an applicant is changed through one of the following actions in Infotype 4000 (Applicant Activities), the status of the vacancy assignments for the applicant is automatically set to the value of its overall status. The corresponding actions are: Put applicant on hold, Reject applicant.
4. If the overall status of the applicant is set to the value To be employed, Contract Offered, or Offer Rejected, in Infotype 4000 (Applicant Activities), a report is launched that you can use to change the status of those applicants that are also assigned to this vacancy.
5. If the status of the applicant is set to To be employed, Contract offered, or Offer rejected in Infotype 4002 (Vacancy Assignment), a screen is provided to maintain the staffing/reservation percentage.

As mentioned in item number one of the previous list, you control the automatic creation of activities through the feature PACTV (IMG path PERSONNEL MANAGEMENT • RECRUITMENT • APPLICANT SELECTION • APPLICANT ACTIVITIES • APPLICANT ACTIVITY TYPES • CHANGE AUTOMATIC CREATION OF APPLICANT ACTIVITIES). The following settings can be made for the activity to be created:

- **Process activity online or in background**
  Online means the activity is created in a dialog with the user, i.e., the user must enter data for the activity. In background means that the activity is created completely in the background and is provided with all of the necessary data. The activity Receipt confirmation is processed in the background, because it merely establishes that the applicant should receive a receipt confirmation.
- **Execution date**
  If an activity is processed in the background, it must be provided with an execution date and, if necessary, with an execution time.
- **Recurring work flag**
  If this flag is defined for an activity, Recurring work is automatically checked when the activity is created, and the activity can then be carried out through mass processing and set to Completed status.
- **Send mail flag**
  This flag specifies if an email is sent when the activity is created (reference to the MAIL feature).
- **Name of the text template**
  If an activity for the applicant correspondence is involved, the activity can be provided with the name of the text template.

Figure 7.18 shows an activity that was automatically created by the system on the basis of the initial entry of applicant data. The group personnel director can then create the correspondence for the applicant on the basis of this process. You can see an example of a confirmation of receipt in Figure 7.20.

In particular, the activities implemented for almost every applicant, such as the printing of the confirmation of receipt, are generally not called through the individual applicants and set to status Completed but are instead carried out via *recurring work*. In the SAP menu call Personnel Management • Recruitment • Applicant Activity • Print Letters (to create correspondence for several applicants at the same time) and Complete Activities (to change the status of the processes for several applicants at the same time).

The connection between applicant actions and the activities and letters that arise from this is once again clarified by an activity taken from practice (see Section 7.2.3).

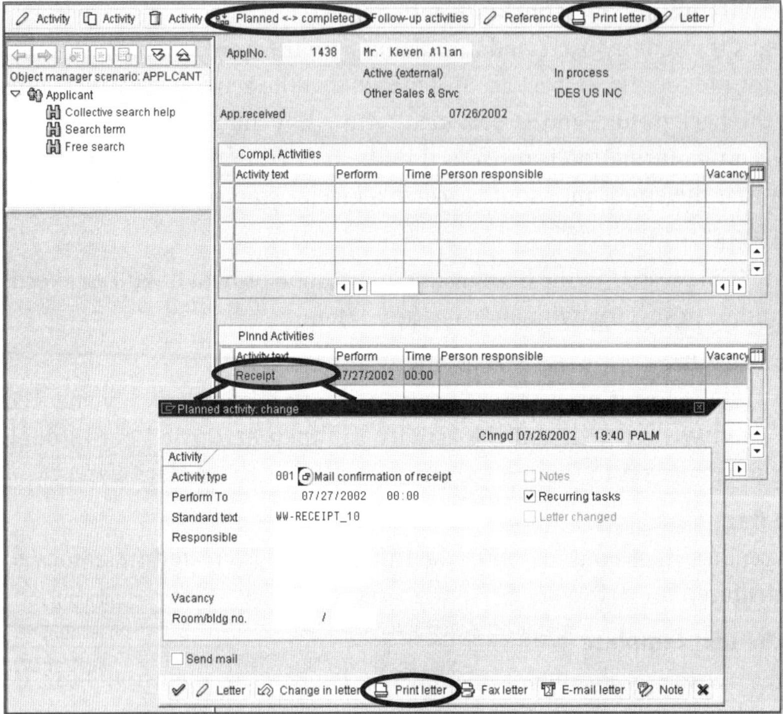

Figure 7.18 Planned Applicant Activity Confirmation of Receipt

For the applicant correspondence there are two possible word-processing systems available: *SAPscript* and *Microsoft Word*. When using Microsoft Word as a word processing system in recruitment you must note the following points:

- In the operating system of the presentation server you must maintain the environment variable `Path_to_codepage` (this usually occurs automatically during installation).
- You must fill the feature WPROC:
  By setting the return value RTF (see Figure 7.19) you can determine that Word is used for word processing.
  - You must also specify which Word versions you are using in the company. You can transfer this through a structured return. The system then checks the registry of the corresponding work station computer as to which version is being used and then automatically uses this version (for example, Word 8.0 and 9.0, see Figure 7.19).
  - A structured return is possible for versions from Word 8.0.

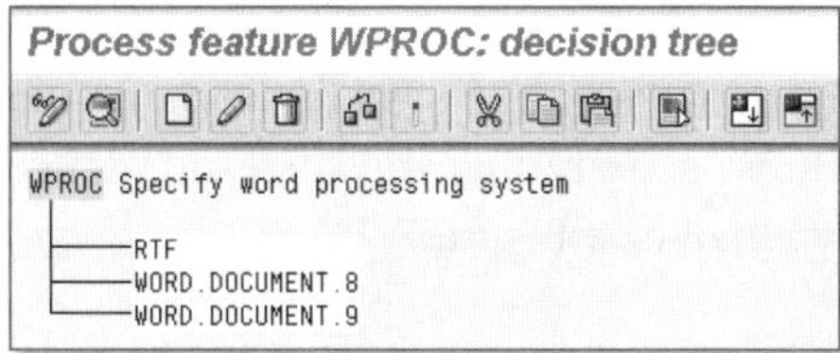

Figure 7.19 Feature WPROC

Due to the high degree of convenience, outputting letters through the Microsoft Word interface is highly recommended.

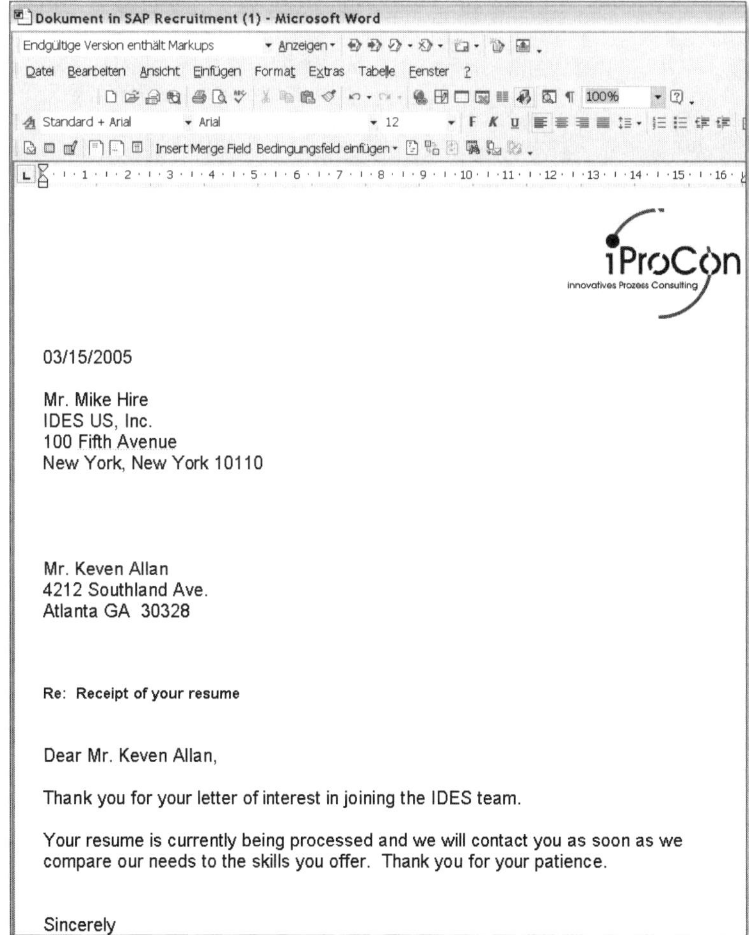
Dokument in SAP Recruitment (1) - Microsoft Word

iProCon
innovatives Prozess Consulting

03/15/2005

Mr. Mike Hire
IDES US, Inc.
100 Fifth Avenue
New York, New York 10110

Mr. Keven Allan
4212 Southland Ave.
Atlanta GA 30328

Re: Receipt of your resume

Dear Mr. Keven Allan,

Thank you for your letter of interest in joining the IDES team.

Your resume is currently being processed and we will contact you as soon as we compare our needs to the skills you offer. Thank you for your patience.

Sincerely

Figure 7.20 Correspondence Example: Confirmation of Receipt

To send emails to the applicants from an activity, it is necessary to connect email software such as MS Outlook or Lotus Notes to the SAP ERP system. By using the E-mail letter button you can determine from an activity that the correspondence with this applicant should be carried out by email (see Figure 7.21).

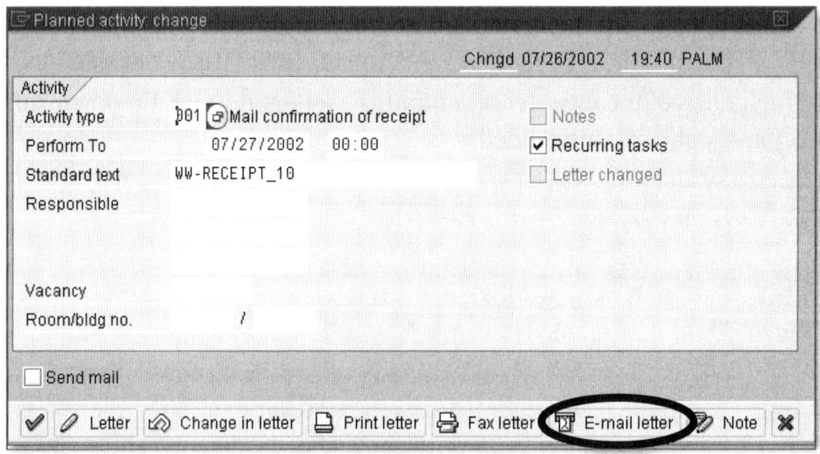

Figure 7.21 Sending an Activity Letter as an Email

By default, the document is then sent as a PDF attachment via email. The feature WPROC enables the user to decide via selection buttons whether the correspondence occurs by letter, email, or fax (see Figure 7.22). A prerequisite is that a blank character "" instead of RTF is returned (i.e., SAPscript instead of Word) in the feature WPROC. Then Transaction PBAT (Print letters) calls a program for SAPscript print.

Further data
Test
Performance date to 03/15/2005
Repeat
Activity type to
Activity last changed by to
Lang.for correspondence to
Communication type
Letter Fax Internet mail

Figure 7.22 Selecting the Sending Type for a Letter

When sending the letter by email and fax the data is retrieved from the following infotypes:

- Email address from Infotype 0105/subtype 0010
  - A list with email addresses is displayed so you can select the required email address from several email addresses (see Figure 7.23).

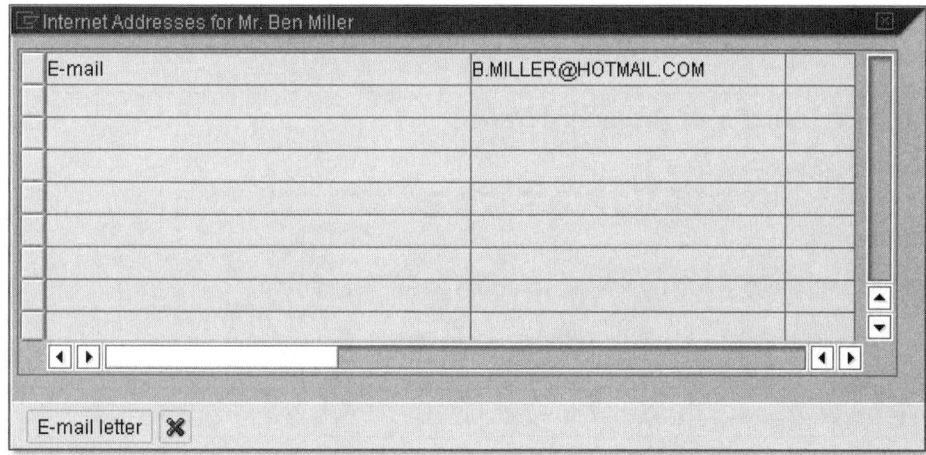

Figure 7.23 Selecting the Email Address

- Fax number from Infotype 0006 (Address) or Infotype 0105 (Communication)/ subtype 0005
  - For an individual printout, all numbers are provided for selection.
  - For a mass printout, all fax numbers from Infotype 0006 (Address) are used.

The decision for SAPscript as a word processor is a basic decision, because there is no option to switch between Word for letters and SAPscript for emails. It is also impossible to manipulate the subject line and mail text when sending emails.

An employee is hired at the end of a successful recruitment process. Due to integration with personnel administration SAP ERP HCM provides the option, based on integration with personnel administration, to transfer the application master data already entered through data transfer into the employee database (SAP menu path Personnel • Personnel Management • Recruitment • Applicant Activity

• Transfer Applicant Data • Execute). A prerequisite for an applicant to appear in this selection is the overall status To be employed. Once the hiring actions have been entered, the program for transferring the applicant data is started and then runs through the individual infotypes of the info group, similar to hiring without using recruitment. The applicant receives a personnel number and his master data from the applicant administration is complemented, if necessary. At the end of the action the administrator receives a statistic with information on the progression of the transfer (see Figure 7.24).

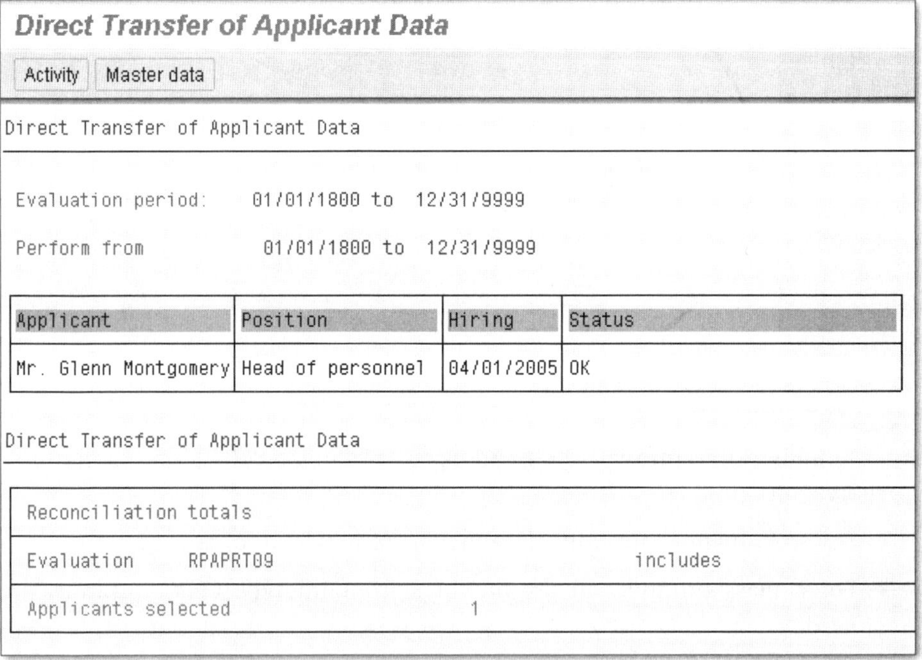

Figure 7.24 Result of the Data Transfer

7.1.6 Reporting

The aim of reporting in recruitment is to contrast the costs that have arisen from the recruitment process with the benefits. SAP ERP HCM supports this by providing an option to enter costs, e.g., of an advertisement, and also by providing the option to evaluate the recruitment instruments and media based on the following criteria:

- Costs of the recruitment instrument (see Figure 7.25)
- Status of the applicants (see Figure 7.26)
- The number of applicants per advertisement instrument (see Figure 7.27)

Evaluate Recruitment Instruments

Instrument | Evaluate advert | Applicant statistics | Applicant list

Evaluate Recruitment Instruments

Instrument	Number of adverts	Number of applications	Total cost	Cost per application
New York Times	3	102	2,253.50 USD	22.09 USD
Boston Globe	1	1	500.00 USD	500.00 USD

Figure 7.25 Costs of the Recruitment Instrument

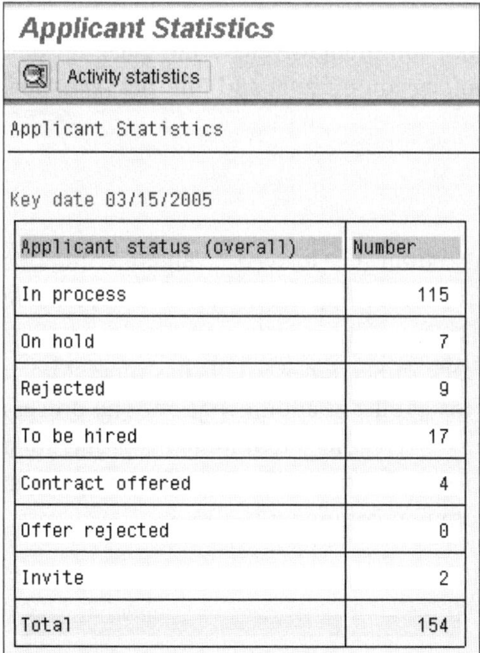

Applicant Statistics

Activity statistics

Applicant Statistics

Key date 03/15/2005

Applicant status (overall)	Number
In process	115
On hold	7
Rejected	9
To be hired	17
Contract offered	4
Offer rejected	0
Invite	2
Total	154

Figure 7.26 Applicant Statistics of the Recruitment Instrument

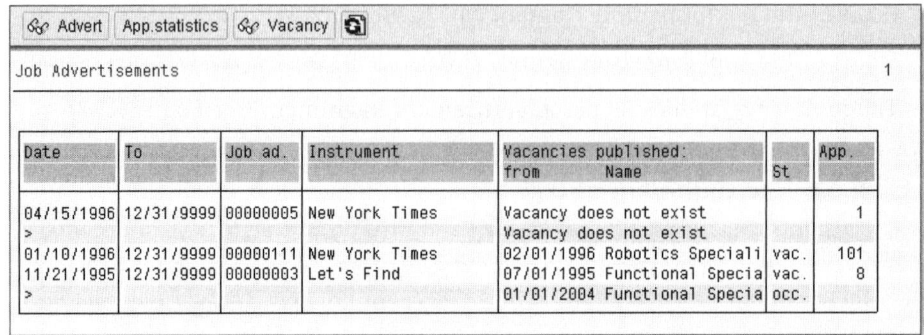

Advert | App.statistics | Vacancy

Job Advertisements 1

Date	To	Job ad.	Instrument	Vacancies published: from Name	St	App.
04/15/1996	12/31/9999	00000005	New York Times	Vacancy does not exist		1
>				Vacancy does not exist		
01/10/1996	12/31/9999	00000111	New York Times	02/01/1996 Robotics Speciali	vac.	101
11/21/1995	12/31/9999	00000003	Let's Find	07/01/1995 Functional Specia	vac.	8
>				01/01/2004 Functional Specia	occ.	

Figure 7.27 Number of Applicants per Advertisement

7.1.7 Integration with the Internet

With the increased use of the Internet for recruitment (see Chapter 6) there is also the option to integrate recruitment in SAP HCM with the Internet. There are no services for traditional recruitment that are available in the new technologies (Business Server Pages (BSP) or Web Dynpro for ABAP).

Chapter 6 provides an overview of a more comprehensive and far-reaching solution than traditional recruitment, with a focus on intranet and Internet scenarios.

7.2 Process Examples

The outline process of applicant administration is displayed in Figure 7.28. This contains, on a basic level, all of the steps that are implemented, from advertising to contract creation in the system. This process is already described in a similar form for personnel administration back in Section 4.5.1. It has merely been supplemented with a few components for applicant administration. The process represents an ideal situation, considering that creating a requirements profile for a job or position and a qualifications profile, and carrying out a profile comparison requires the use of the Personnel Development component.

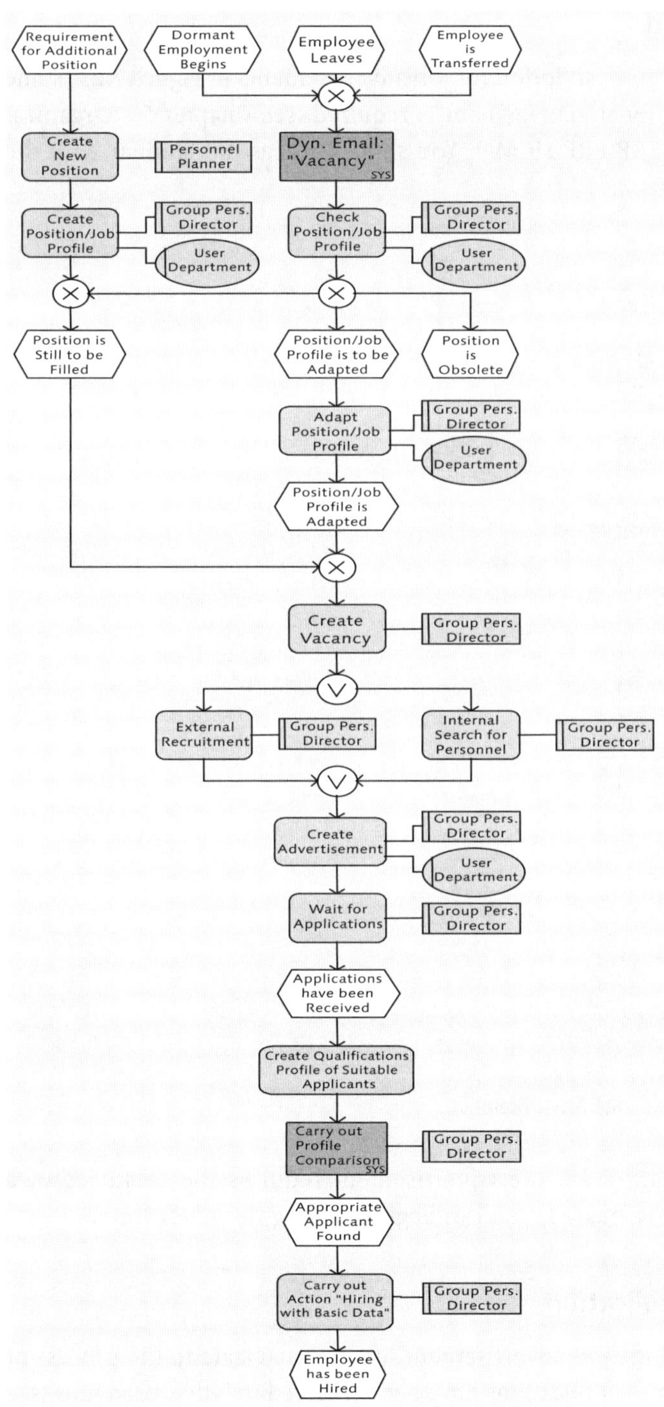

Figure 7.28 Outline Process of Recruitment

7.2.1 Advertisement

To understand the process description for job advertisements in Figure 7.29, some knowledge of organizational management is required (see Chapter 5, "Organizational Management in SAP ERP HCM"). You should at least be familiar with the concepts of *job* and *position*.

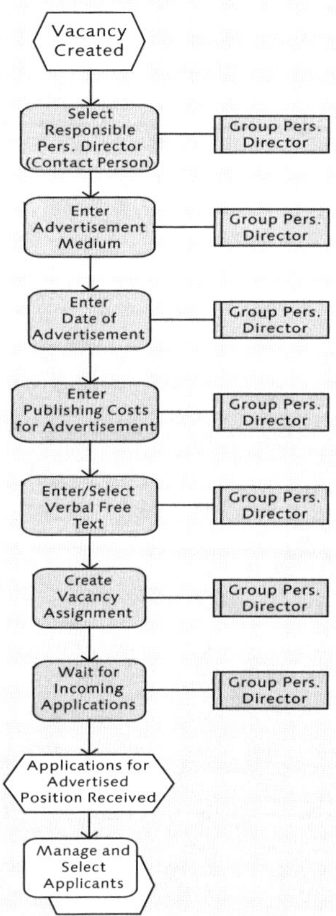

Figure 7.29 Sample Process Create Advertisement

As you can see in Figure 7.29, the advertisement requires the existence of a vacancy. If this vacancy is created, you can begin entering the advertisement.

7.2.2 Receipt of Application

Based on the process of the job advertisement, you can navigate to the process of receipt of application, once applications have been received for advertised jobs (see

Figure 7.30). The process of the receipt of applications once again clearly shows when the system carries out checks (duplicate application) and when it automatically creates an application process. The next step is the selection process.

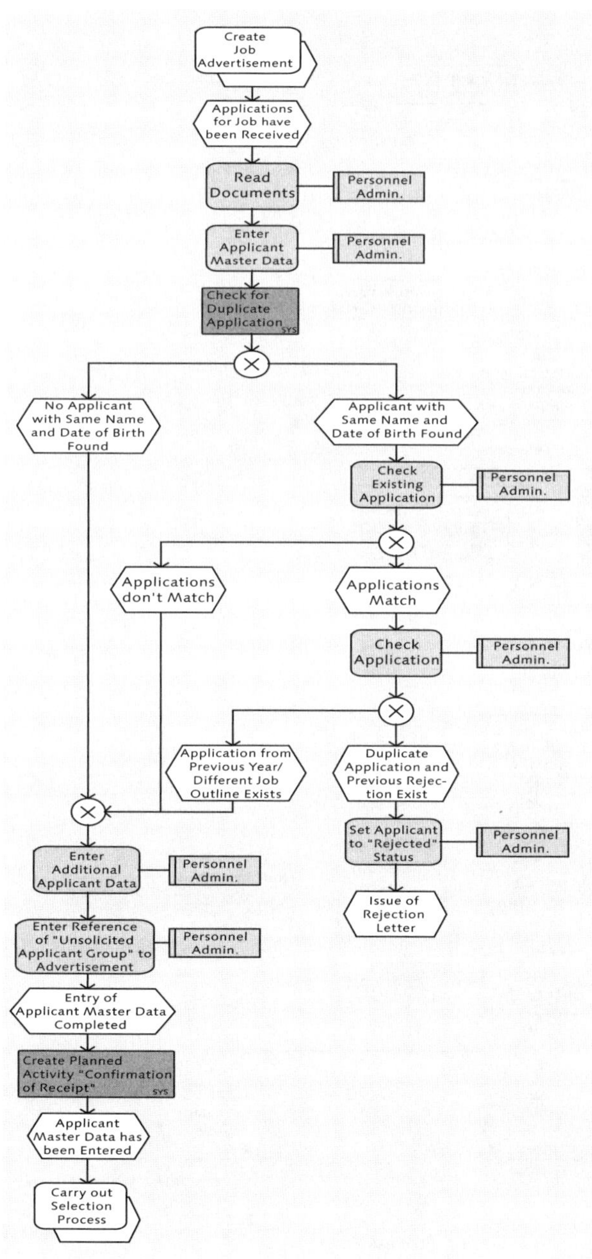

Figure 7.30 Sample Process Receipt of Application

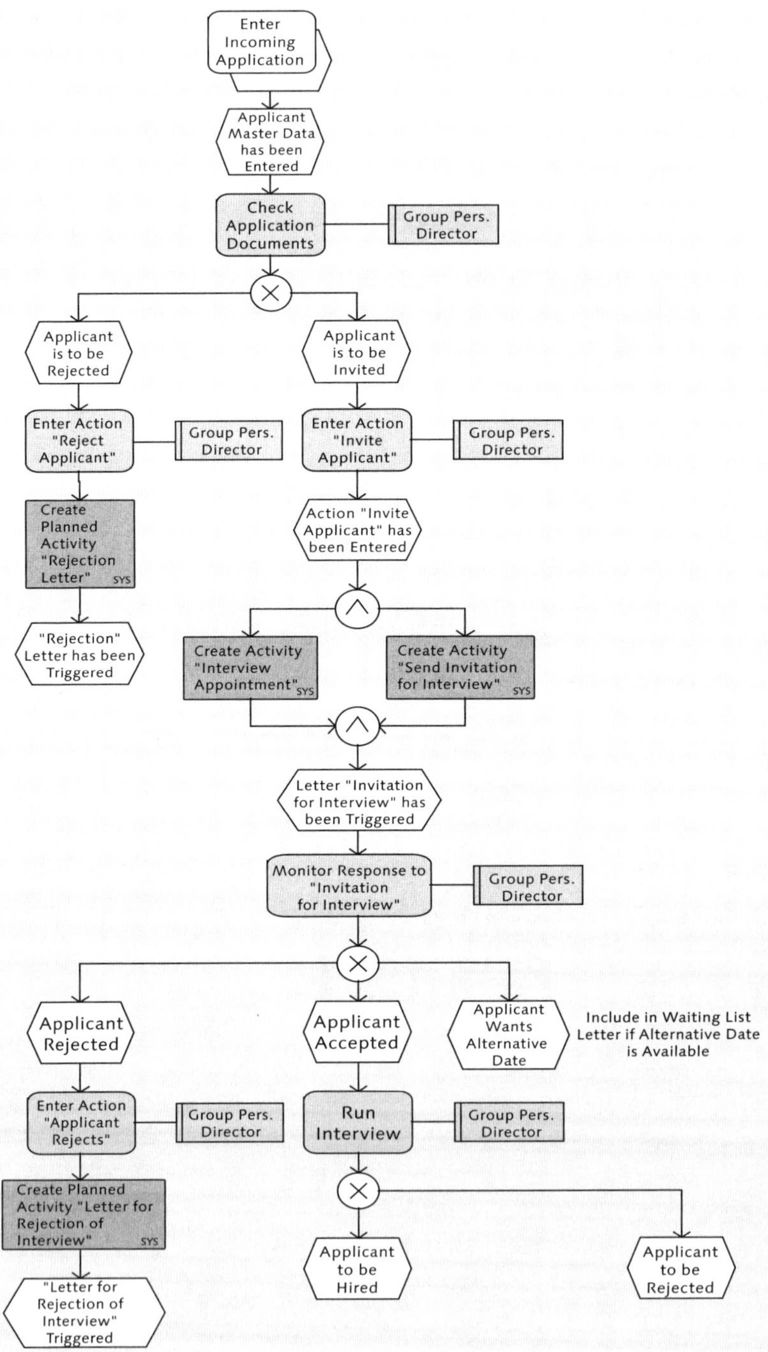

Figure 7.31 Example Process Single-level Selection Process Part 1

7.2.3 Single-Level Selection Procedure

This process once again clarifies in detail the relationship between actions and activities in applicant administration to control the application process. The first part of the process is concluded with the applicant rejecting the invitation for an interview and therefore receives a specific rejection letter (see Figures 7.31 and 7.32).

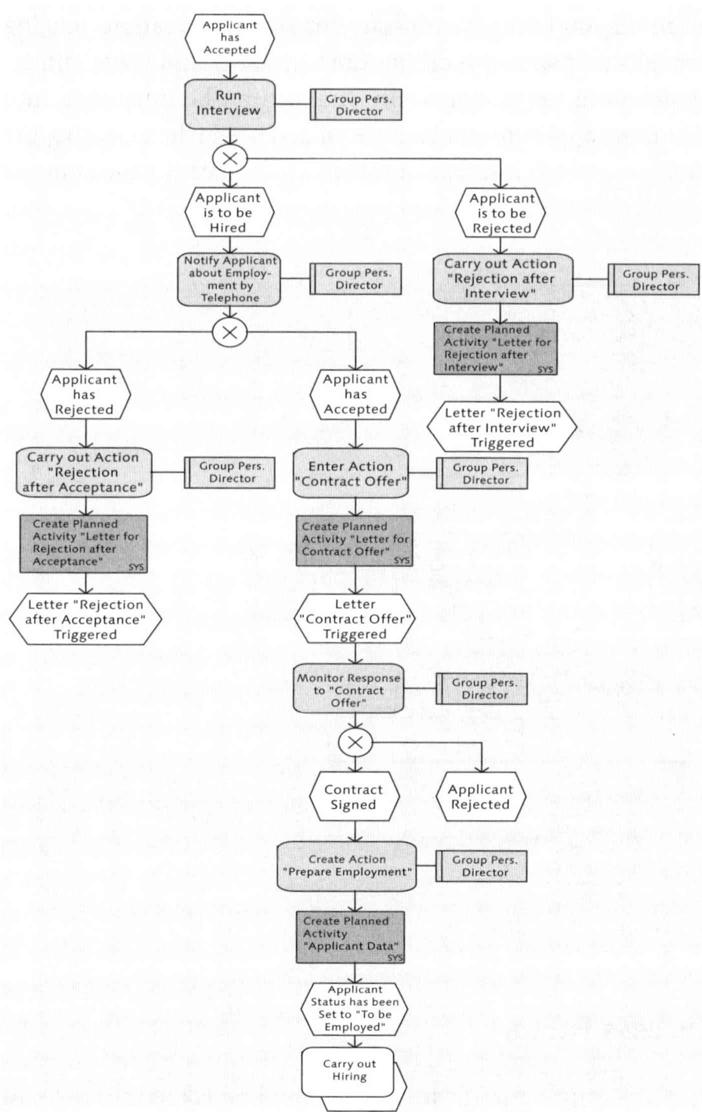

Figure 7.32 Example Process Single-level Selection Process Part 2

There is an alternate conclusion to the process: The applicant accepts the appointment for the interview and is to be hired after the interview (see Figure 7.31). Figure 7.32 displays the actions that are necessary for hiring. It also illustrates how the process continues if the applicant is rejected after the interview.

7.2.4 Contract Creation

A lot of information on the applicant is necessary for contract creation, ranging from the address through the planned working time to salary and leave entitlement. Because infotypes from personnel administration can be integrated into recruitment, this data on the applicant can be entered and used when creating the contract. Figure 7.33 shows which infotypes provide useful data for the contract creation.

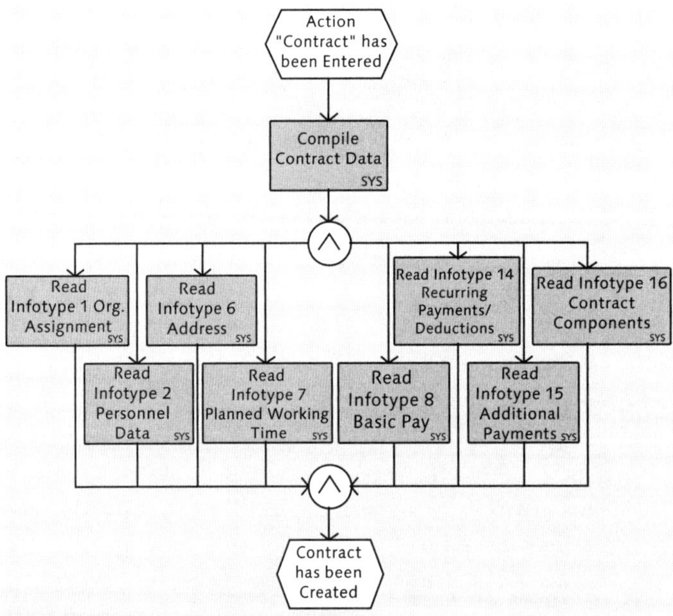

Figure 7.33 Sample Process Contract Creation

7.3 Critical Success Factors

This section points out and summarize factors that should be taken into account when implementing recruitment.

- **Applicant structure**
  As part of the conceptual considerations for structuring the applicants, you should ensure that the structure is conformed to the requirements of evaluations and controlling authorizations, and different processing of different applicants with regard to applicant activities, applicant correspondence, and the responsibility for the applicants. In addition, the selection options in evaluation are characterized by the selected applicant structure.
- **Processes**
  Based on the options for structuring the recruitment processes, the processes to be mapped must be known and documented as early as possible. This must be carried out before the beginning of the implementation, because basic changes to the processes shortly before production startup can lead to a complex customizing effort.
- **Correspondence**
  Due to electronic means of correspondence and the functions for automatically creating applicant correspondence, it is necessary to define standard letters. The conception of such standard letters entails a certain degree of effort that requires a huge amount of adaptation in most companies. This means you should deal with the creation of company-specific standard letters at an early stage.
- **Microsoft Word interface**
  Due to the integration of Microsoft Word with SAP ERP HCM recruitment, it is necessary to check at an early stage which versions of Word are installed at the relevant work centers. A standardized version structure is almost inevitable. In addition, extensive tests of the Word interface must be carried out both in the test environment and on the client's computers.

In this chapter we will discuss time management as the recording and processing of times for a normal working day, especially for purposes of managing time accounts and the monetary evaluation of that time. However, time management also involves the recording and processing of times for a company's activity output especially for the purposes of incentive wage calculation, so we will discuss that as well.

8 Time Management

Time management in SAP ERP HCM is characterized by a high degree of complexity and flexibility. Its Customizing doesn't provide as many configuration options as payroll but may involve the same effort, because you usually need to adapt the default settings a lot. The reason is that there are less legal regulations for time management than for payroll, although many legal implications still exist in some countries.

8.1 Business Principles

The previously mentioned fact that there are few legal regulations for time management means that most of the settings are internationally relevant. However, there are still a lot of laws and regulations that need to be considered. Apart from that, there are pay-scale and corporate regulations, which are often based on national de-facto standards. Consequently, there will be huge differences between the individual countries for international rollouts in time management. These differences are frequently underestimated because the SAP implementation guide (IMG) makes few distinctions in configuration steps for country-specific requirements. The following sections deal with internationally applicable aspects.

8.1.1 Objectives of Time Management

Time management documents the behavior of employees in regard to working time in general, including:

- Duration and position of attendance times
- Duration and position of break times
- Working times outside the company (e.g., business trips)
- Special absences (sickness, vacation, etc.)
- Types of activity during the times entered (productive hours, overtime, setup time, etc.)

In the area of incentive wages, this information is also combined with production data, such as:

- Number of pieces completed
- Standard times
- Scrap

Further information is then derived from this primary data. In addition, company regulations such as work schedules, flextime regulations, and rules for bonus calculation are applied. This time evaluation then supplies the following types of results:

- Status of the leave account
- Status of the flextime account and/or long-term account
- Overtime hours to be paid
- Bonuses for overtime, nightwork, work on Sundays, and public holidays.
- Bonuses to be paid for special activities
- Action required when the working-time law or the company's core-time regulations have been violated

In the incentive wage environment, piecework or premium regulations of the incentive wage components are used to calculate the remuneration.

Entering working times to calculate compensation in the form of money or time is not comprehensive enough as a primary goal of time management. This activity is, rather, a way to manage the "working-time" resource, and therefore is the basis for the output and performance of the employee.

Working time is the time that the company would like to implement most efficiently in the pursuit of its objectives. On the other hand, an employee who is working loses time that he otherwise could spend achieving personal goals. An interesting tension emerges where those involved pursue contradictory goals, such as:

- Provision of working times corresponding to the requirements for the activity output of the company
- Availability of free time corresponding to the private requirements of the employee
- Capability to plan free time for the employee
- Flexible availability of working time for the company

The primary goal of modern working-time management is to harmonize these goals as much as possible for the following reasons:

- Fulfilling company requirements, due to the pressure of the market, requires increasing flexibility of working time.
- Taking into account the requirements of the employees helps to bind them to the company and to use available working time optimally through the ability and willingness to perform at a high level.

Further goals are defined through legal or collective agreements, for which compliance must be monitored and documented, and also through personnel controlling.

To achieve the primary goals, the following are some of the approaches pursued in company regulations or collective agreements.

- Payment of bonuses for work performed during weekends or nights (In some countries the payment of such bonuses is taxed at a lower tax rate, and in come countries shift differentials are paid on this work time.)
- Flexible working-time models that are beneficial for both the private interests of the employee and the company
- Implementation of long-term time accounts that can be used for a sabbatical

- Delegation of responsibility for planning working times to the employees themselves (time-autonomous work groups)
- Possibility to donate leave entitlement to colleagues in special situations (such as severe illness of a child, spouse, or other relative)

Such and similar regulations are described in the following sections with regard to their implementation in SAP ERP HCM.

We can assume that in the area of time management great value is placed on correct maintenance of time data. Less emphasis, however, is placed on what is really done during this time. The question, "How long was the employee present in this month?" is generally answered with a time-management system. But the question, "What has the employee achieved in this month?" is often neglected. Time management as a method for efficient use of an important and expensive resource is actually a management task that all too often is delegated to a time-recording system.

This state of affairs is certainly due in part to the fact that it is far easier to measure time accurately than it is to measure performance. Thus, this chapter also deals with the recording and formal evaluation of attendance times. However, you should always be aware of the danger that this simplification involves. The emergence of a "seconds-counting culture" should definitely be avoided. Whether avoiding the recording of all work times (time management based on trust) represents the best solution, is questionable as well, however. For most employees, being able to prove their working times is reassuring, and should at least remain as an early-warning system for employees being overburdened or under-challenged (regardless of whether this is quantitative or qualitative).

Emerging developments in this area are certainly interesting, but in the medium term are not likely to completely replace the familiar forms of time recording and evaluation. Modern forms of work such as telecommuting speak against classic time recording, although Web-based time recording can now address this need. Developments such as life-working-time accounts further promote it.

8.1.2 Forms of Time Recording

You can basically differentiate between positive time recording and negative time recording (see Figure 8.1).

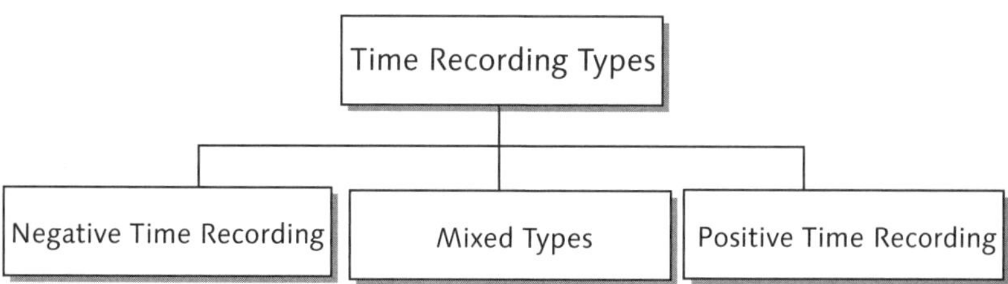

Figure 8.1 Forms of Time Recording

Negative time recording is based on a defined working time model, i.e., daily working time, weekly work schedule, etc. Only deviations to this are entered. This generally leads to consideration of overtime or shortfall of more than, say, 15 minutes and all-day absences or significant absences lasting less than one day, while smaller deviations are not considered. Only working duration is entered; the circumstances of working time are generally not relevant as long as they have no effects on payment (e.g., through night-work bonuses). The recording is mainly carried out manually by the employee, and the data is then entered and processed at central points, supported by the system. PC-supported recording (e.g., via Web-based interfaces) is used more frequently and extremely useful, as this clearly reduces administrative effort at central points.

Positive time recording is based on a working time model as well. However, it is not only deviations that are recorded here but also all clock-in and clock-out times. In conjunction with additional data, such as absences, the deviations from the work schedule can be calculated and evaluated automatically. Time-recording terminals are used for positive time recording in general (and Web-supported recording or even recording via WAP-capable mobile phones). Manual recording is also possible, but is rarely done.

In a mixed form both kinds of time recording are combined. This could mean that in the management area negative time recording is implemented, while in the production area positive recording is implemented. In practice, positive time recording is almost never implemented on a companywide basis, because many jobs are not compatible with this.

The basis of this book is essentially positive time recording, because it is more extensive and because the system design for negative time recording can be derived easily from this.

8.1.3 Legal Principles

A variety of regulations address working time. Some of them originate from legislation, others from collective agreements with unions or company-specific regulations. Most of them differ from country to country, and some even depend on the industry sector or the individual employee (e.g., restrictions for minors or pregnant women in some countries).

A very important issue is regulation of safety at work, which often requires clearly defined breaks, restrictions on the total working time of a person per day, or the time of exposure to certain conditions (e.g., to radiation).

In case of accidents or potential job-related illnesses, the employer should be able to prove with records from the Information Technology (IT) system that all regulations were observed. To allow managers to be proactive, it is a good idea to provide them with the necessary current data.

8.1.4 Concepts of Flexible Working Hours Policy

The scope of a policy for flexible working hours is, to a great extent, characterized by the form that activity output takes for the company in question. Factors which influence this are primarily:

- Adhering to fixed service times for the customers
- Adhering to specific reaction times to customer requests
- Attachment to fixed locations to guarantee these service times (call centers offer much more options than retail stores)
- Exchangeability of employees (coupling/decoupling of the person and function)
- The option of producing in the warehouse
- Necessity of replacement capacities for peak times and emergencies
- Ability to plan contracts
- Working in groups and on assembly lines, which makes it necessary for all those involved to carry out their work at the same time

Essentially, maneuverability is greater the further you diverge from working time as a measure of all things related to work results (with the familiar problems of measurability).

Despite the inherent necessities linking time to performance, concepts for decoupling working time from service and production times have already been implemented for several decades. Less-fixed methods are being used to provide the necessary capacity, while efforts are under way to better adapt the number of staff to the requirements. It is in the area of services that personnel bottlenecks can be cleared by the use of part-time staff.

The following concepts are being implemented to achieve the goals described in Section 8.1.1.

- **Classic flextime**
  The employee achieves his daily target time within a specified timeframe. If this is exceeded or fallen short of, the deviation is managed within a flextime account that generally shows an upper limit of 15 to 50 hours. Collected hours can be compensated for with free time or remunerated. Within a specified core time, the employee must be present.
- **Flextime without core time**
  Core times are generally stored in IT systems, and the core time deviations run to time administrators or the personnel department. There, they are either ignored or discussed with management to determine that this did not affect the regular operations. From experience, we see that core times only cause hassle. The scheduling of working time within the scope of flextime should be the responsibility of management.
- **Flextime with staffing guarantees**
  The staffing guarantee is the team-related further development of core time that is geared toward internal or external customers. Within a team, certain staff numbers are defined for certain time periods. Scheduling is the responsibility of management.
- **Flextime or choice of working time**
  Within an adequate notification period (e.g., six months) an employee can freely select his weekly working time within a defined corridor (e.g., 16 to 42 hours). This means long-term variations of the business workload can be reacted to, wherein special incentives are set for increasing or reducing working time.

- **Sabbaticals**
  They primarily serve the interests of the employee and are therefore an instrument of employee retention. By supporting sabbaticals in times of slow business, however, the objectives of the company can also be addressed.

  In some countries special effects on taxes and social security have to be observed.

- **Annual working time**
  The classic flextime account is not adequate when capacity requirements depend on the season and are subject to fluctuations. There are different methods of distributing working time sensibly throughout the year. The introduction of such a system is best scheduled for the beginning of a period of a high workload, as you can avoid the psychological problem of negative flextime balances.

- **Life working time**
  As the times in a life-working-time account are, to a large extent, outside the scope of scheduling, the account merely serves as a means of employee retention and long-term increases of capacity (see Section 8.5.4).

  However, this concept requires a strong controlling of the working time invested by the managers. It is all too easy for employees to earn a huge leave entitlement by lingering around in the company although no work is being done.

- **Home work/telecommuting**
  While home work was earlier the domain of manufacturing, where work was carried out for piecerate wages at home, telecommuting now offers more options. Modern time-recording systems even enable stamping via the Internet. The extent to which this is useful is questionable. Telecommuting demands mutual trust anyway and should be used to consider work results instead of working time. However, it frequently makes sense for the employee to perform PC-supported daily entries, even for reasons of self-control.

8.2 Design in the SAP System

In this section, we will describe the basic design in the system. The following sections of this chapter deal with the particularities that emerge due to specific interfaces for data entry, such as Time Manager's Workplace (TMW), Employee Self-Service (ESS), and Manager Self-Service (MSS).

8.2.1 Structures in Time Management

The structures of time management are based on the structures described in Chapter 4, "Personnel Administration." Essentially, the combinations of employee subgroup and group and of the personnel area and subarea are grouped under different aspects of time management. The requirements of time management definitely have to be considered when defining these structures. The grouping for the public holiday calendar is often an essential criterion for the definition of the structures. The country grouping (MOLGA) will also be relevant.

The following essential groupings of the personnel area and the personnel subarea (Customizing view V_001P_ALL) exist:

- Grouping for working schedule
- Grouping for time recording (used in many customizing steps, such as time types and time-evaluation messages)
- Grouping for additional time data such as absences and attendances, absence/attendance counting, leave types, time quota types, substitution, and stand-by duty
- Assignment to a public holiday calendar

The essential groupings of employee groups and subgroups (Customizing view V_503_ALL) are:

- Grouping for personnel calculation rules for control in the time-evaluation schema (also used in payroll)
- Grouping for time quota types
- Grouping for working schedule
- Indicator for participation in the incentive wage

Other structures that are important for time management are entered directly in the personnel master:

- Time administrator in Infotype 0001
- Separation of part-time and full-time staff via a part-time indicator in Infotype 0007
- Grouping to control the subsystem connection in Infotype 0050 (for time events, subsystems, employee expenses, access control)

- The grouping for the time-evaluation rules in Infotype 0050. This is not used by the standard time evaluation, but can be used in a custom evaluation scheme for structuring and as a decision criterion.

The multitudes of groupings that directly affect time management appear very confusing at first. They are very helpful, however, both in mapping different rules and in forming useful combinations, to keep the number of entries in the customizing tables as low as possible. It is therefore advisable to make distinctions only if it is really necessary. Otherwise, all employees should be controlled on the same grouping.

8.2.2 Public-Holiday Calendar

In the public-holiday calendar you can define which days are public holidays. When defining public holidays, you determine the rule under which the public holiday is created and which holiday class is assigned to it. The holiday class is used as a control criterion in time evaluation and the assignment of daily work schedules. The following holiday classes are possible: normal public holidays; half public holidays (e.g., New Year's Eve); and company-specific holidays, for which no bonuses are paid for working hours.

The SAP ERP 6.0 public-holiday calendar also maps guaranteed holidays, which are made up for when they fall on a day that is off anyway. This is, for example, practiced in Luxembourg and the UK.

Customizing is carried out via the IMG path SAP NetWeaver • General Settings • Maintain Calendar (in earlier versions you find it under Cross-Application Components). Note that the automatic transport connection is not active here — transport must be called manually. For transport, all public-holiday calendars are always overwritten in the target system. When changes are made to the public-holiday calendar you must regenerate the work schedule rules (see Section 8.2.4).

Note: Cross-Process Usage of the Public-Holiday Calendar

Note that the public holiday calendar is cross-client and is used in ERP Central Component (ECC) by several modules (e.g., production planning, Information Systems (IS) banking). You should only implement changes with the agreement of the system administration. You can also use your own calendars for HCM, though this causes redundant maintenance and disadvantages regarding integration.

You must check while setting up time management whether it is necessary to use several public holiday calendars. This is generally the case if the company is located in several states or regions. Do not use more public holiday calendars than necessary, as the number of calendars also determines the number of work schedule rules.

In addition to time management, event management and payroll also use the public-holiday calendar.

8.2.3 Concept Explanations for Time Management

For a better understanding of the following sections, some of the HCM concepts will first be explained.

Time Types

The concept of time type is similar to that of the wage type in payroll. The calculation for a time evaluation is implemented in the time evaluation and is partly saved and evaluated there. Time types can represent time balances or accounts (e.g., flextime balance), serve certain evaluation purposes (e.g., to the total of the work times over ten hours a day), or can be simply required for internal calculation of time evaluation (so-called utility time types). Time types are created using IMG path TIME MANAGEMENT • TIME EVALUATION • TIME EVALUATION SETTINGS • DEFINE TIME TYPES. There, you can set whether the values of the time type should be saved as per day or per month, whether they are reset to zero at the end of a month or year, and whether they represent a time account.

In addition to each time type saved as a balance, a time type can be entered to store the balance of the previous month or previous year. These time types can, for example, be used to print out previous monthly balances on the time statement of the current month. Figure 8.2 shows the definition of a time type. You should use a meaningful description for the time types. This description can be displayed on the time statement and may be useful for later changes to the time type (e.g., for utility time types).

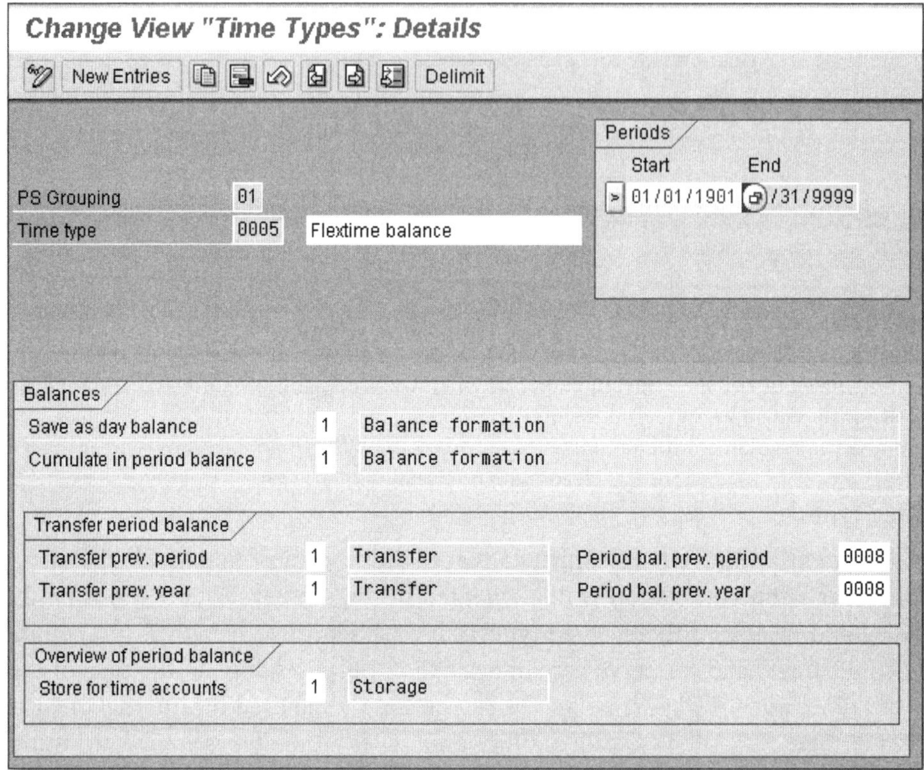

Figure 8.2 Time Type Settings for the Example of the Flextime Balance as in SAP Standard

Time Balance

This is a special case of the time type. Time balances are saved on a monthly or daily basis. Other time types are only used for internal calculations, are not saved, and can therefore not be evaluated. In general, however, you key all time types in such a way that they can at least be saved on a daily basis.

Time Account

A time account is also a special case of the time type. Time accounts are usually managed progressively (for example, flextime balance). In other words, a time account is not generally set to zero at the beginning of the month (however, this does not rule out a capping, e.g., at 25 hours). Time accounts receive a particular indicator in the time types table and are therefore prepared to display in the time recording terminal.

Time Quota

This generally means an absence quota. These are entered in Infotype 2006 (see Section 8.2.5). This concept represents an alternative to the time type for the mapping of time accounts and balances. In this case, there is little or no manual maintenance. The quota status in Infotype 2006 is automatically supplied from the time evaluation. The advantage of the absence quota is that the quota status, in contrast to a time type, can be read directly without a special report by displaying Infotype 2006. In addition, when entering absences that reduce the account, you can define in Customizing the online checking for the quota available. The concept of the time type, in contrast, allows for more flexible handling in the definition of the time-evaluation schema. In historically grown time-evaluation schemes (for releases lower than 4.5A), it is advisable to use the time type for the management of time accounts. As the effort involved in conversion tends to be very high, you would be likely to use this variant for later upgrades.

Time-Wage Types

Wage types populated with information in figures (hours, pieces, etc.) and transferred to payroll for monetary evaluation and, if necessary, to payment, are time-wage types. Time-wage types are the basis of the automatic interface between time management and payroll.

Time Evaluation, Time Accounting

Time evaluation is a program that runs at least daily or even more frequently and which calculates the essential results of time management (balance statuses, info time types, time-wage types, quotas) from the recorded employee data (including time stamps). You can call it via the following menu path HUMAN RESOURCES • TIME MANAGEMENT • ADMINISTRATION • TIME EVALUATION • TIME EVALUATION. It can also be called from the to-do list of the time administrator. In general, it also runs as a regular job. The time-evaluation flow is controlled by the customer-specific adapted schema (see Section 8.2.7).

Time Statement

The time statement is the form (online or as a printout), on which the essential results of time evaluation for the employee are displayed. Calling the time statement does not trigger a new calculation but rather merely displays the saved results of time evaluation. It is either called through the menu path Human Resources • Time Management • Administration • Time Evaluation • Time Statement or from the to-do list of the time administrator. It makes sense and is usually available in ESS (see Figure 8.3).

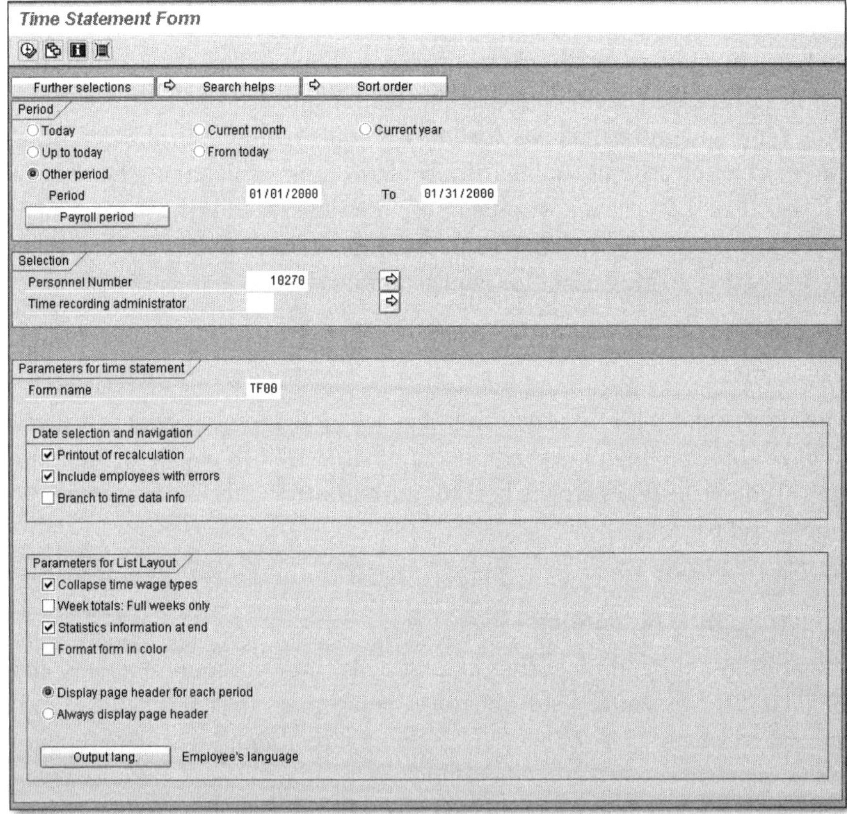

Figure 8.3 Calling the Time Statement Form

Figure 8.4 shows an example of a time statement and Figure 8.3 shows its selection screen (note the output language!). The form used here is of particular importance. You can call the form via IMG path Time Management • Time Evaluation • Evalu-

ATIONS AND THE TIME MANAGEMENT POOL • TIME STATEMENT FORM • SET UP TIME STATEMENT USING FORM EDITOR. The Form Editor since release 4.6C (as is the case with SAP ERP 6.0) is simple to handle and is sufficiently documented. The most important thing is that the time types to be displayed are saved with the balances required in each case (daily balance or monthly balance).

IDES US INC Time Statement List Page : 1

Philadelphia
Pers No. : 00010270 Name: Mr. Henry Miller EE Group: 1
Personnel area: 300 Cost ctr: 3200 EE subgrouU4

Payroll Period : 200001 From 01/01/2000 - 01/31/2000 WS Rule: FLEX

Individual Results

Day	Text	In	Out	From	To	Rec.	Skeleton	Flex	CViol	OT	DWS
03				07:50	17:05	9,25	8,09	0,09	0,00	0,00	FLEX
04				07:40	17:07	9,45	8,12	0,12	0,00	0,00	FLEX
05				07:55	17:13	9,31	8,23	0,23	0,00	0,00	FLEX
06				07:57	17:05	9,13	8,09	0,09	0,00	0,00	FLEX
07				07:53	17:02	9,16	9,04	1,04	0,00	0,00	FLEX
10				07:43	17:17	9,56	9,29	1,29	0,00	0,00	FLEX
11				07:55	17:05	9,16	9,09	1,09	0,00	0,00	FLEX
12				07:51	17:11	9,33	9,19	1,19	0,00	0,00	FLEX
13				07:42	17:12	9,50	9,21	1,21	0,00	0,00	FLEX
14				07:43	17:17	9,57	9,29	1,29	0,00	0,00	FLEX
17	M.L.K. Day from			07:56	17:13	9,28	8,00	0,00	0,00	0,00	FLEX
27				07:51	17:01	9,17	9,03	1,03	0,00	0,00	FLEX
28				07:47	17:08	9,35	9,14	1,14	0,00	0,00	FLEX
31				07:40	17:12	9,53	9,21	1,21	0,00	0,00	FLEX

Totals Overview

Type	Working Time	Overtime
Previous month's	15,00	0,00
Planned time	168,00	
Working time	187,36	
Revision	0,00	0,00
Balance	15,00	0,00
Excess/insuffici	19,36	
Remaining leave	0,00	

Figure 8.4 Example of a Time Statement Form

If forms were first processed through the maintenance for individual views, and are now to be maintained through the Form Editor after an upgrade, there can be problems. Frequently checking and resaving all form settings in the Form Editor is sufficient.

Time Events

Time events are actions related to points in time that supply the essential information for the calculation in the time evaluation. Examples include: Clock-in, Clock-out, Time ticket start, etc.

Time Pair

A time pair is the time span between two time-points, which may be formed through time events, attendance or absence entered, and corner times of the time model. The time pairs are the most important objects for processing the time-evaluation schema. In addition to the pure time span, they are identified through numerous attributes (e.g., overtime pair, break, origin). These attributes can then in turn determine the processing run in the schema.

Time Evaluation Messages

Time evaluation provides error or information messages for certain statuses that the time administrator can edit during error-handling of the to-do list. Errors can be keyed so that the time evaluation remains at the day where the error occurred, until the error is removed or further calculated. In the case of error messages, the employee receives out-of-date information about this day (through the terminal or the ESS); in the case of information messages, he can receive incorrect information in certain circumstances. The error messages are triggered in the time-evaluation schema and implemented via IMG path Time Management • Time Evaluation • Time Evaluation with Clock Times • Message Output • Create Message Descriptions.

As in the definition of the time types, take care that the personnel subarea grouping is used for time recording. You can also set whether the employee is shown a message at the terminal. For retroactive calculations, messages are always recreated if necessary. You can generally assume that the administrator or the employee took the hint and acted on the message. By using the Create once indicator, you can avoid multiple creations of the same message for the same reason.

8.2.4 Work Schedules

The concept of the work schedule enables you to determine the scheduled working time for an individual employee for each day in terms of position and duration. Moreover, additional information such as core times, flextime limits, general overtime approvals, etc., is assigned. The SAP concept can appear confusing at first glance. On closer inspection, however, you recognize that the multilevel concept makes it possible to extensively reuse parts that have been defined. This means the solution enables a swift mapping of rotating shift schedules. It appears to be quite cumbersome, on the other hand, for companies that have no rotating shifts. This means working schedules based on the public- holiday calendar are the basis for complete time evaluation and time recording.

Customizing the working schedules is done via IMG path Time Management • Work Schedules with several subdirectories.

Daily Work Schedule

The daily work schedule concept does not really refer to the content that it maps. Not only can you define working time within a calendar day, but also across several days, for example, a night shift. The single limitation is the scope of 24 hours. Each daily work schedule is thus assigned to the day on which it begins.

The daily work schedule also contains a work break schedule (see Figure 8.5). This is required before creating the daily work schedule.

Grpg	Break	N..	Start	End	P	Unpaid	Paid	After	RefTim	Type 1	Type 2
90	3SCH	01	01:00	01:15	☑	0,25					
90	3SCH	02	04:00	04:45	☑	0,75					
90	3SCH	03	09:00	09:15	☐	0,25					
90	3SCH	04	12:00	12:45	☐	0,75					
90	3SCH	05	17:00	17:15	☐	0,25					
90	3SCH	06	20:00	20:45	☐	0,75					

Figure 8.5 Work Break Schedule

You execute the following settings in the work break schedule:

- Situation of breaks with fixed time or in the context of a break
- The situation of breaks relative to the work start and planned working-time start
- Assigning the break to the previous day for cross-day models
- Identification as a paid or unpaid break

  Paid breaks frequently are not documented in the system. That can have the following disadvantages:

  - The break time cannot be evaluated.
  - Regulations that automatically assume and deduct a defined break time for the employee cannot take the paid breaks into consideration.
  - Adhering to regulations such as the working-time law in Germany and other countries cannot be monitored with the support of the system.

The work-break schedule has the same groupings as the daily work schedule.

The daily working time of the employee is stored in the daily work schedule itself. The system provides different options for mapping these.

- You define the working time as a fixed working time. In this case, enter a planned working time. The system calculates the planned working times from this by considering the work-break schedule. All times that fall outside the planned working time are not taken into consideration for the employee. However, if this is required, an adjustment in the schema or the entry of an attendance quota is required.
- You define the working time as flextime. In this case, you specify a working time frame, and within this frame establish the normal working time. The planned working hours are calculated from the normal working time. All times that lie within the planned working time are taken into consideration for the employee. In the standard version, the portion in excess of the planned working time is posted to the flextime account. Another form of processing is possible by adjustment of the schema.

In addition, the following information is stored in the daily work schedule:

- **Core times**
  In the standard version, violating the core time triggers a warning message for the time administrator.
- **Tolerances**
  Clock-in or clock-out entries are always set to the fixed time within the range of tolerance. For example, the normal work start is 8:00 a.m., and the begin tolerance is 7:45 to 8:00 a.m. In this case, each stamp that occurs in the period between 7:45 and 8:00 is automatically set to 8:00. The tolerance regulations can be mapped more flexibly in the schema (e.g., rounding all postings to the nearest five minutes).
- **Minimal, maximal working time and compensation time**
  You can enter these as fixed values and process them in the time evaluation. However, this information is not considered in the standard supply of the schema.
- **Daily work schedule class**
  This is an essential element of time evaluation and wage-types generation and acts as a control criterion. Thus, you can classify between, for example, night-shift models and other models and prevent a bonus being paid in the wage types generation if an employee arrives for the early shift before 6:00 a.m. In the time-evaluation schema, you can use this criterion for decisions in processing. The importance of each individual daily work-schedule class depends individually on its settings in wage-types generation and time evaluation. Therefore, significant documentation is extremely important. The daily work schedule class 0 is reserved for off work. In the current release of SAP ERP 6.0, models of other classes can also have a planned working time of zero hours. You must set the corresponding indicator here.

The daily work schedule (see Figure 8.6) provides a description of an individual working day with regard to the working time. In addition, it defines which daily work schedule is assigned to a certain day for a certain employee.

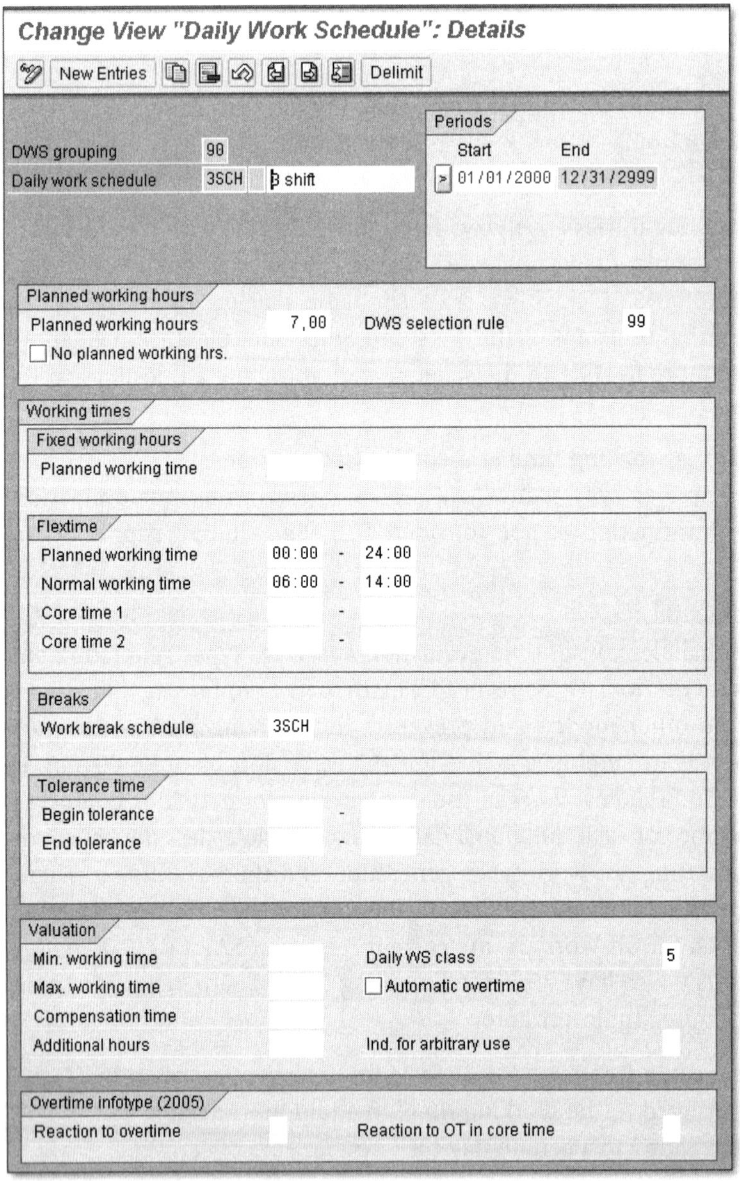

Change View "Daily Work Schedule": Details

New Entries | Delimit

DWS grouping 90
Daily work schedule 3SCH 3 shift

Periods
Start 01/01/2000 End 12/31/2999

Planned working hours
Planned working hours 7,00
DWS selection rule 99
☐ No planned working hrs.

Working times

Fixed working hours
Planned working time -

Flextime
Planned working time 00:00 - 24:00
Normal working time 06:00 - 14:00
Core time 1 -
Core time 2 -

Breaks
Work break schedule 3SCH

Tolerance time
Begin tolerance -
End tolerance -

Valuation
Min. working time
Max. working time
Compensation time
Additional hours
Daily WS class 5
☐ Automatic overtime
Ind. for arbitrary use

Overtime infotype (2005)
Reaction to overtime
Reaction to OT in core time

Figure 8.6 Customizing a Daily Work Schedule

Variants of the Daily Work Schedule

Frequently, an otherwise regular working time deviates from the normal value (e.g., on Fridays, before public holidays, and on half days). This means several variants can be defined for each daily work schedule.

The assignment of a variant to a certain day occurs through the daily work schedule selection rule. This is defined in Customizing and is assigned to each individual daily work schedule. Depending on the public holiday class for the current day, the subsequent day, and the weekday, a variant is selected. In the example shown in Figure 8.7, in rule 90, the variant B is assigned to all public holidays of public-holiday class 2 (in the standard variants, half-public holidays) and apart from that on every Friday (weekday number 5).

Rule	No	Holiday class	Hol.cl.next day	Weekday	Variant
		b123456789	b123456789	1234567	
90	01	..X.......	XXXXXXXXXX	XXXXXXX	B
90	02	XX.XXXXXXX	XXXXXXXXXX	....X..	B

Figure 8.7 Daily Work Schedule Selection Rule

In addition, you can also select variants depending on an absence (on days for which there is a half-day's leave, for example, a variant without a core time and without a break is selected). However, this occurs in the customizing of absence types.

Period Work Schedule

The period work schedule determines the sequence of the daily work schedules. It is the basis for the work schedule and sets the work rhythm. It can comprise one week and several weeks. It also can define periods that cannot be divided by seven. In this case you must conclude your period with "*." The example in Figure 8.8 shows a three-week schedule in which the free days change each week. However, model 3SCH is always assigned for the work days.

The period work schedule has the same groupings as the daily work schedule. Period work schedules are also classified. This supports both the counting of absences and enables evaluation within the time evaluation and wage-type generation. Therefore, precisely analyze the content that is connected to a period work schedule, such as overtime, shift bonus, etc. It's important to implement this concept early on to avoid a conceptual redesign during implementation and time evaluation. It is useful to classify shift-rotation schedules and classic part-time schedules separately, as these must be frequently handled with special care in bonus generation.

Grpg	PWS	Period WS text	Wee	01	02	03	04	05	06	07
90	3SCH	3 shift	001	3SCH	3SCH	3SCH	3SCH	3SCH	FREE	FREE
90	3SCH	3 shift	002	3SCH	3SCH	3SCH	FREE	FREE	FREE	3SCH
90	3SCH	3 shift	003	3SCH	3SCH	FREE	FREE	3SCH	3SCH	3SCH

Figure 8.8 Period Work Schedule

Work Schedule Rule

The work schedule rule establishes the time frame in which the employee works: daily, weekly, monthly, or annually. Further, it establishes the connection of the period work schedule to the real calendar. The reference date, for example, 01/07/2002, and the starting point, for example, 001, determine that the period work schedule starts on Monday 01/07/2002 and executes its rolling rhythm from then on. It is useful to select a Monday as a starting point, because the period work schedules also begin on Mondays and the assignment is then easier. It is not necessary to have a particular employee assigned to this work schedule at the starting point date. It is purely the abstract beginning of the rhythm of the period work schedule.

For reduced working hours, you can store an alternative work schedule and a percentage record for a shift bonus, which is not evaluated in the standard schema. In addition, a rule is assigned to determine the day type (e.g., this means weekend bonuses can be defined differently or completely disabled). Customizing the work-schedule rule is displayed in Figure 8.9.

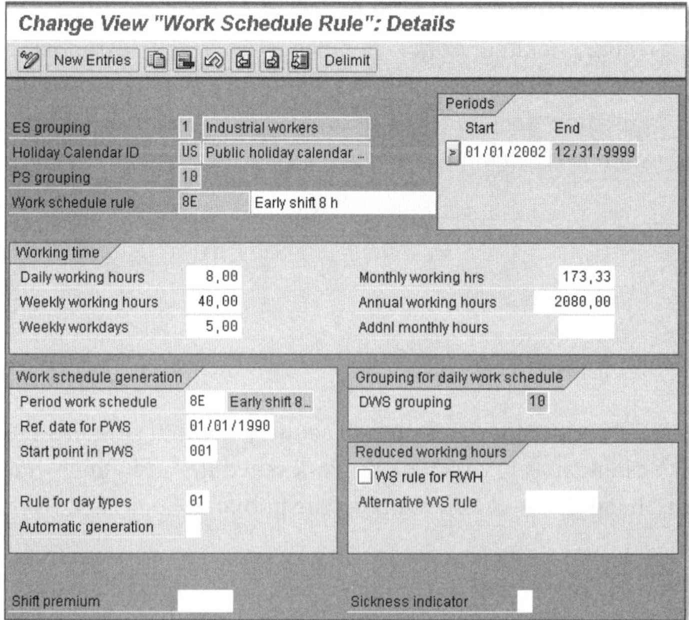

Figure 8.9 Customizing the Work Schedule Rule

Work Schedule

The work schedule contains the essential information for each individual work day. It is not manually maintained, but is instead generated on the basis of work schedule rules, period schedules, and public-holiday calendars. A work schedule is stored for each combination of work-schedule rules, groupings of the employee subgroups for work schedules, public-holiday calendars, and groupings for the personnel subareas for work schedules and daily work schedules. The resulting work schedule is then assigned to an employee based on the respective employee subgroup and personnel subarea. This plan can then be changed for the individual employee, but only after entering other time data (e.g., substitutions). The user does not directly assign the generated work schedule. The assignment rather takes place in Infotype 0007 (Planned Working Time) via the work schedule rule. Therefore, this can take into consideration a change of the public-holiday calendar that is due to an employee transfer, without having to maintain Infotype 0007.

Generating work schedules should occur approximately up to three years in advance to enable the recording of longer absences (e.g., parental leave). Although time evaluation functions correctly if no generation has occurred, it does generate temporary work schedules and therefore does not perform as well. The behavior of time management for nongenerated work schedules is set in the customizing of work schedule rules (see Figure 8.10). It is advisable to use the SAP standard configuration, so time evaluation does run free of errors, but a warning message regarding missing generation is created.

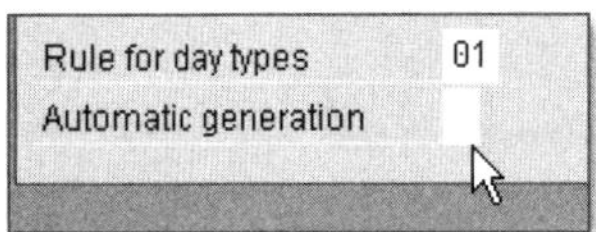

Figure 8.10 Indicator to Generate the Work Schedule Rule

Figure 8.11 shows a work schedule for the month of January 2000. It contains the information as to which calendar day, which day's work schedule, and which version is to be worked on. In addition, it also contains the public-holiday class from the holiday calendar.

The work schedule is assigned to the employee in Infotype 0007 (Planned Working Time) for the employee. You can assign standard values in this infotype via different features, which facilitate master data entry.

ES grouping 1 | DWS grouping 10 | Monthly hours 157,50
Holiday Calendar ID US | Period work schedule SW3W
PS grouping 10 | Work schedule rule SW3W1

Valid January 2000 | Chngd 04/06/2005 IPROCON

Work Schedule

D SU HC	D MO HC	D TU HC	D WE HC	D TH HC	D FR HC	D SA HC
						01
						1 FREE
02	03	04	05	06	07	08
FREE	GRV1	GRV1	GRV1	GRV1	GRV1	FREE
09	10	11	12	13	14	15
FREE	DAY1	DAY1	DAY1	DAY1	DAY1	FREE
16	17 1	18	19	20	21	22
FREE	1 EVE1	EVE1	EVE1	EVE1	EVE1	FREE
23	24	25	26	27	28	29
FREE	GRV1	GRV1	GRV1	GRV1	GRV1	FREE
30	31					
FREE	DAY1					

Figure 8.11 Generated Work Schedule

Figure 8.12 shows an overview of the context in which you customize the work schedule. The work schedule sets the basis for time recording and time evaluation. In the following section, the entry of time data on the application side is dealt with, along with the corresponding customizing.

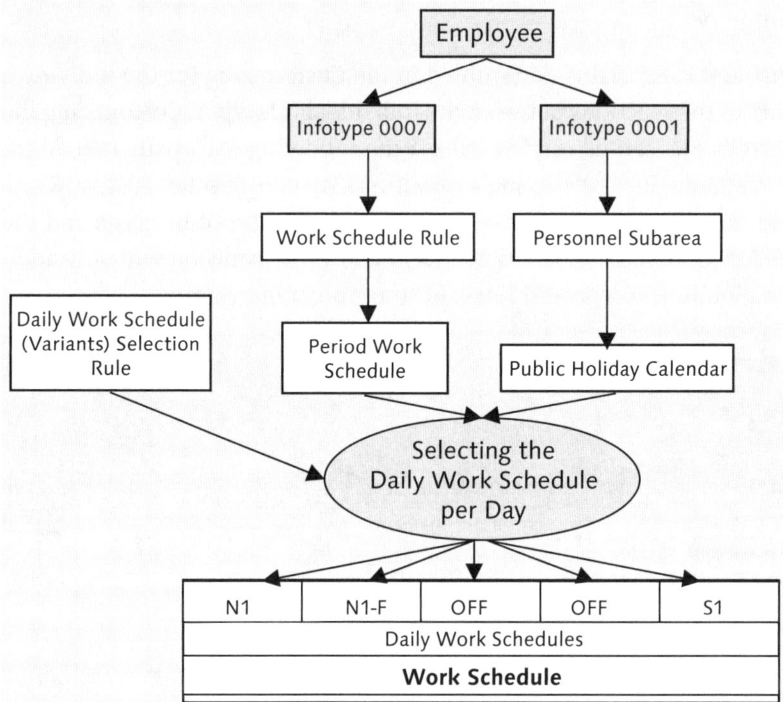

Figure 8.12 Customizing the Time Model and Connection to the Employee

8.2.5 Time Data Entry

Entering the time data is also done in infotypes. This practice corresponds to the infotype concept in personnel administration. The number area for time infotypes ranges from 2000 to 2999.

Maintaining these infotypes is carried out via the following menu path Human Resources • Time Management • Administration • Time Data • Maintain.

In this section, we will not only describe the pure entry of time data but also the way it displays its effect in time evaluation and the relevant customizing.

Collision Check in Time Data Maintenance

A peculiarity of time infotypes can be found in the collision check. For the infotypes described up to this point, only records of the same infotypes collide with one another, depending on the time constraint, and these records can delimit themselves from each other. In time management, this is also possible for records of different infotypes.

The time-constraint class that is determined in the Customizing for the individual infotypes controls the reactions between the individual infotypes. Customizing the reactions for collisions can be carried out via the following IMG path TIME MANAGEMENT • TIME DATA RECORDING AND ADMINISTRATION • SPECIFY SYSTEM REACTION TO OVERLAPPING TIME INFOTYPES. For each combination of infotype and the relevant time-constraint class, a reaction is defined for the collision with any additional combination of infotype and relevant time-constraint class.

Infotype 2001
Time con. class 01

Reaction when there is an overlap with existing infotype records

Infotype	Infotype text	Time cstr. class	Reaction indicator
2001	Absences	01	A
2001	Absences	02	E
2001	Absences	03	A
2001	Absences	04	A
2001	Absences	05	E
2001	Absences	06	A
2001	Absences	07	A
2002	Attendances	01	A
2002	Attendances	02	A
2002	Attendances	03	E
2002	Attendances	04	A
2003	Substitutions	01	W
2003	Substitutions	02	W

Figure 8.13 Reaction for Collisions of Time Management Infotypes

The example in Figure 8.13 is based on Infotype 2001 with time-constraint class 01 and shows the reactions of the infotypes depending on their time-constraint class. The reactions indicator can have the following characteristics:

- A – the old record is delimited, collisions are displayed
- E – the new record cannot be inserted, collisions are displayed
- W – the new record can be added, collisions are displayed
- N – like W, collisions are not displayed

If a corresponding collision occurs during the data maintenance, a warning message or error message occurs, and, if necessary, an existing record is delimited.

A realistic example is the collision of sickness and vacation (both are subtypes of Infotype 2001 with different time-constraint classes), as predefined in the standard version. If a sickness record is entered in an existing leave record, the former is delimited after a system warning. In the reverse case, the system does not allow the entry.

Infotype 2003 (Substitutions)

As substitutions in Infotype 2003 immediately change the work schedule of an employee, they are dealt with directly in the connection to Section 8.2.4. For a period or an individual day the employee can be assigned a deviating planned working time (see Figure 8.14). This means that the use of this infotype far exceeds the classic understanding of the concept substitution.

The deviating planned working time should occur, if possible, by assignment of a daily work schedule or a work schedule rule. The direct entry of times (also break times) or the assignment of a day type are also possible. If a real substitution exists, the deviating work schedule rule can be determined via the substituted personnel number.

It can also directly affect the payment. If the employee accepts a high-value activity, this is entered by assigning a position or a work place. A deviating payment can be determined from this.

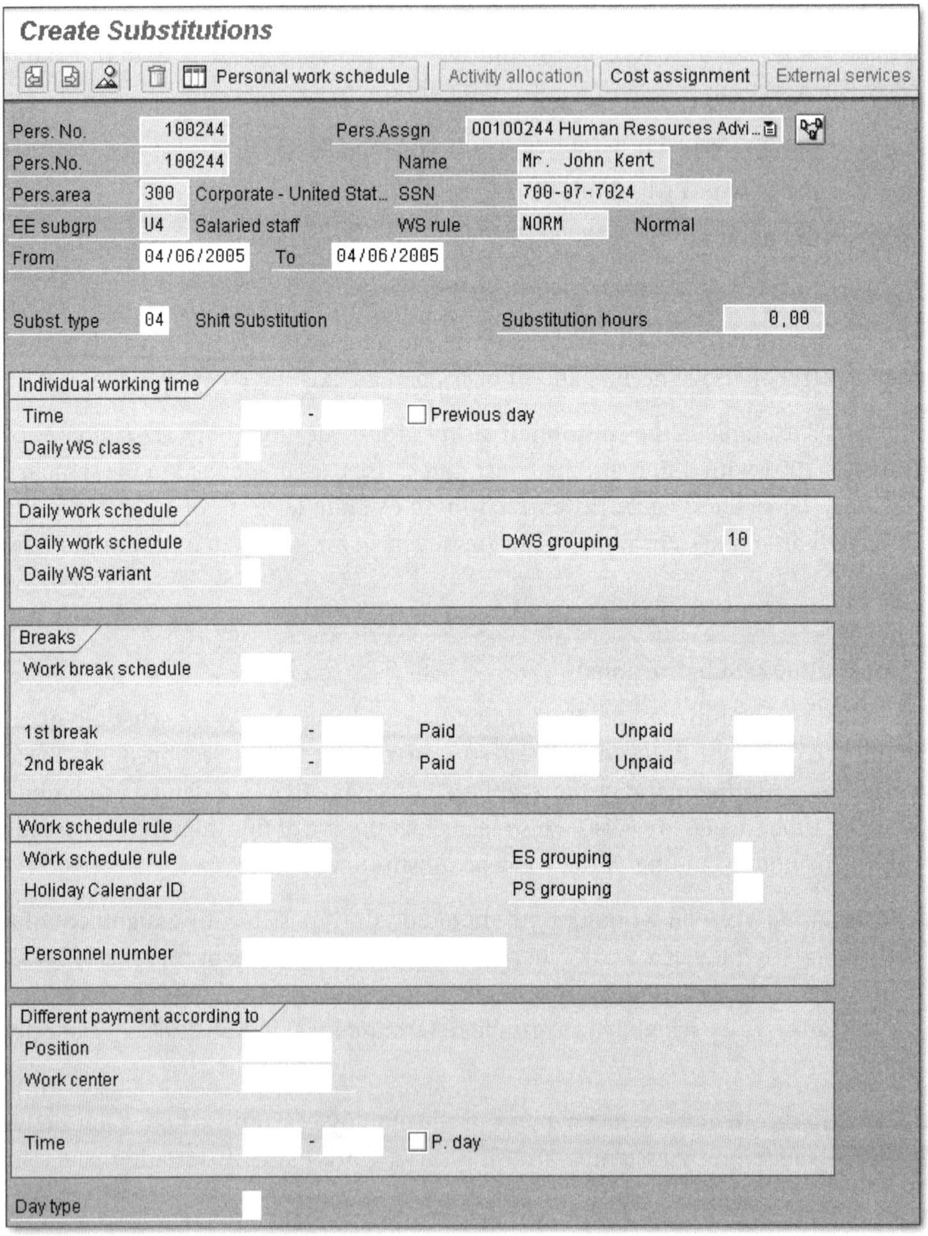

Create Substitutions

Personal work schedule | Activity allocation | Cost assignment | External services

Pers. No. 100244 Pers.Assgn 00100244 Human Resources Advi...
Pers.No. 100244 Name Mr. John Kent
Pers.area 300 Corporate - United Stat... SSN 700-07-7024
EE subgrp U4 Salaried staff WS rule NORM Normal
From 04/06/2005 To 04/06/2005

Subst. type 04 Shift Substitution Substitution hours 0,00

Individual working time
Time - Previous day
Daily WS class

Daily work schedule
Daily work schedule DWS grouping 10
Daily WS variant

Breaks
Work break schedule
1st break - Paid Unpaid
2nd break - Paid Unpaid

Work schedule rule
Work schedule rule ES grouping
Holiday Calendar ID PS grouping
Personnel number

Different payment according to
Position
Work center
Time - P. day

Day type

Figure 8.14 Infotype 2003 (Substitution)

Customizing the substitutions is carried out via IMG path TIME MANAGEMENT • TIME DATA RECORDING AND ADMINISTRATION • SUBSTITUTIONS. The substitution types are mainly defined there and are identified according to their relevance for shift-time compensation (payroll then ensures that the employee is not at a financial disadvantage due to the substitutions) and reduced working hours. The time-constraint class is also assigned according to substitution type here.

A suggestion value can also be defined for the Substitution type field through the feature VTART.

Infotype 2001 (Attendances) and Infotypes 2002 (Absences)

Attendances and absences are dealt with in a similar manner in Customizing and are also grouped according to the same grouping in the personnel area. For this reason, we will deal with them together, even though they are entered in different infotypes.

Originally, attendances and absences were part of time management. However, they have a strong influence on payroll. Absences can be paid and unpaid. Account information can be linked with attendance/absence for financial accounting (FI) and cost accounting (CO). In addition, paid absences can also affect payroll if the payment is made on the basis of averages.

Absences are entered in Infotype 2001. The individual absence types (mapped via the subtypes) differ strongly in some ways with regard to the data to be maintained. Sicknesses in many country versions require the entry of additional data that impacts the duration of the continued pay. Examples of absences are vacation, sickness, flexday, or military service.

Figure 8.15 shows the entry screen for vacation, which basically only contains the start and end dates (for records lasting less than one day, and start and end times), and the absence counts. Here you can differentiate between absence days and calendar days, as days that are off from work anyway are not counted as absent days. In addition, the field Quota Used shows how many days are deducted from the leave entitlement. The entry screen for vacation generally corresponds to those for most other absence types.

Figure 8.16 shows additional data used only for the substyle "sickness." This, along with other data, is used to calculate sick pay.

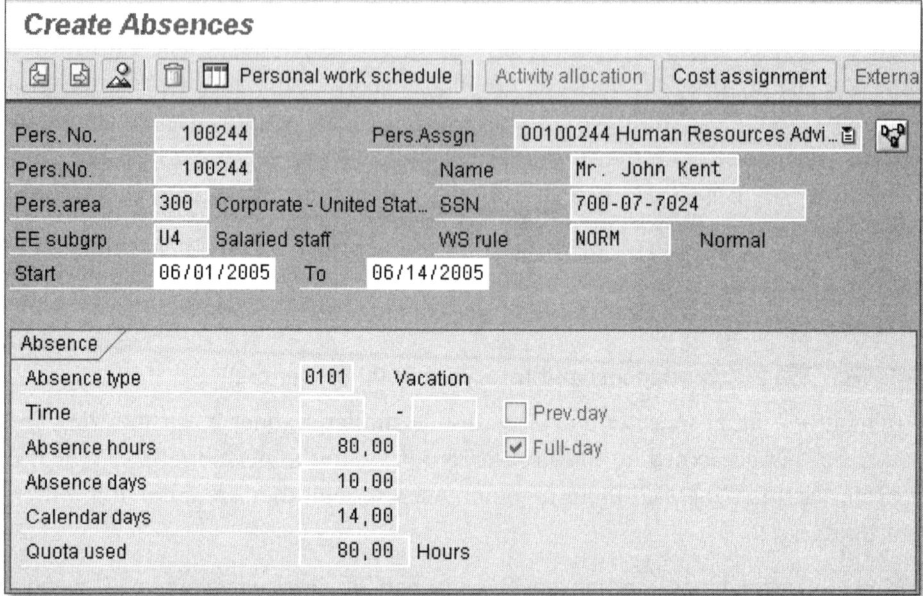

Figure 8.15 Absence: Vacation

Additional Information
Relationships /
Days credited
Reference number
Abs. due to accident
Work capacity pct.
Short-Term Disability Periods
STD period 1
STD period 2
STD period 3
Manual modif.

Figure 8.16 Absence with a Deadline for Continued Pay

Attendances are maintained in Infotype 2002. Their entry is more standardized than that of absences. Examples of attendances are business trips (see Figure 8.17), seminar visits, training school, etc. There is often confusion regarding the concept behind selection of attendances, as such events are also casually referred to as absences. In HCM terminology, they are constantly referred to as attendances if they are part of the working time.

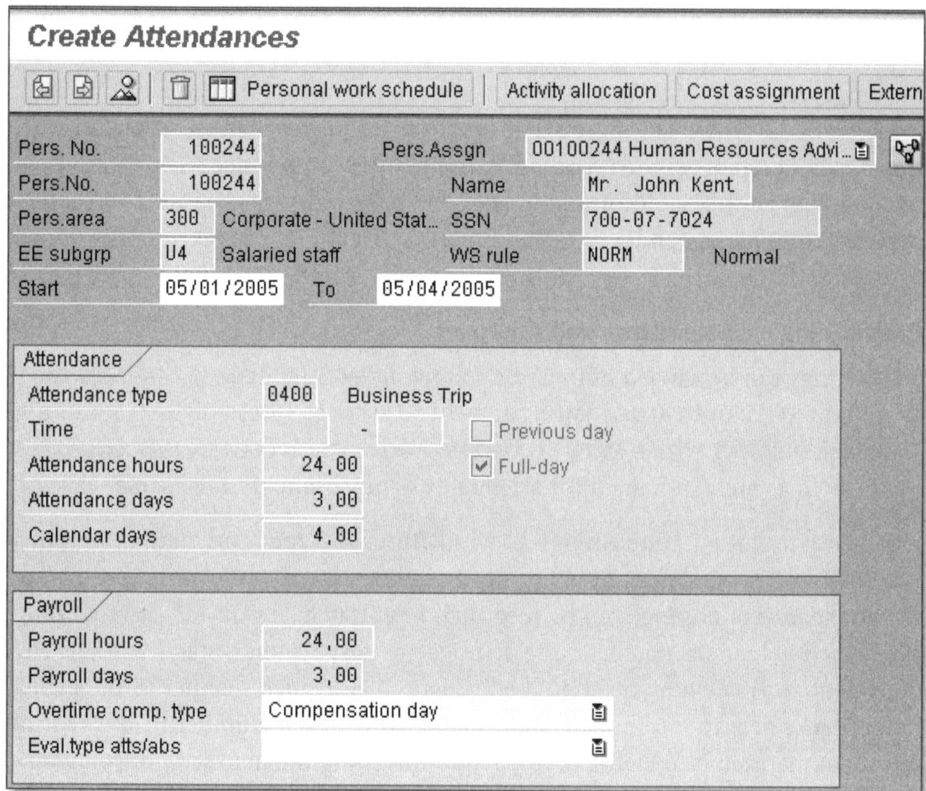

Figure 8.17 Attendance: Business Trip

In addition to information on the period and counting, similar to absences, attendances provide two additional entry options:

- The Overtime compensation type field specifies how overtime that occurs due to attendance is to be handled. In our example, it is remunerated. The entry of overtime in Infotype 2002 (or in special cases in Infotype 2001) may replace the entry in Infotype 2005 (see details in the section on Infotype 2005), which is mandatory in releases after SAP ERP 6.0.
- The Evaluation type field is not used in the standard version. It can, however, be used through the time-evaluation schema to generate wage types for specific activities (e.g., instructor activities). For correspondingly created interfaces, this field can also be used for absences. However, this is generally not a good idea.

In general, the attendance times for an employee are derived from the time stamps at the terminal and are only entered in exceptional cases (such as occasions when the employee cannot stamp because he is working outside the plant or office) via Infotype 2002. However, there are different recording scenarios, where all work times of the employees are recorded as attendances, and, if necessary, are supplemented with additional information (e.g., the assignment of times to cost centers, projects, or financial funds).

Customizing for Attendance and Absences

The settings can be carried out via the following IMG paths Time Management • Time Data Recording and Administration • Absences • Absence catalogue and Time Management • Time Data Recording and Administration • Attendances. Many settings are maintained for attendances and absences in the same way.

First, the activities Define Attendance and Absence Types and Determine Entry Screens and Time Constraint Classes are carried out. Here, you mainly specify how the attendance or absence can be recorded, how it behaves during the recording, and which values are enabled. The settings are easy to understand and are well documented. However, you should edit them in a detailed manner as the plausibility checks help to improve the data quality. The Screen Number field is worthy of special mention (see Figure 8.18). Without reading the help screen, you would never realize that this field determines whether the absence type deducts a quota (e.g., the leave quota). The documentation for this field must be closely considered in other respects.

Absence: General Settings

Att./absence ind.	A	Screen number	2001
Availability		Time cstr. class	1
Absence grpg	2	Att./absence class	1
☐ Check end date			

Figure 8.18 Screens and Time Constraint Classes

Even the activity Define Indicators for the Personal Calendar is easy to understand. Consider exactly what you want to see in the calendar view and enter it.

Counting (absences or attendances) is much more complex. You must define here how many hours or days of a certain attendance or absence are calculated, if it involves the deduction of quotas or payment. A detailed description would be beyond the scope of this book and would essentially repeat the already extensive documentation of the IMG. Therefore, at this point we will just make a few notes:

- First, consider the complete documentation on these customizing sections and the concepts of the attendance and absence quotas.
- If required, use the option of controlling the counting via the counting class of the period work schedule. This saves you having to create different absence types for the same content.
- In any case, you should use the new variant of the rules for absence counting. Note that in specific customizing views old and new control parameters are mixed. The old ones are then identified.
- Note the new field Deduction Over Interval End in the view Assign Counting Rules to Absence Types. This means you can map the widely used regulation that the remaining leave from the previous year expires at a certain date, but that a vacation that has begun before the end of the deduction period is valid and can be taken beyond the expiration date of the remaining leave.
- Depending on absences, you can also define which variant of the daily work schedule has to be used. This may be necessary if you are processing working times. Suppose, for example, that you have an average daily working time of seven-and-a-half hours for a five-day week. However, from Monday to Thursday you work eight hours, and only five-and-a-half hours on Friday. Absences are generally deemed to be seven-and-a-half hours. In this case, you can assign a corresponding daily work schedule in connection with the rules for variants, using the counting class. Note that the work-schedule selection rule must be assigned in the daily work schedule.
- You can define whether a quota can also be negative. From a business viewpoint it is useful if a vacation is taken in times of lower workload, even if the leave quota is depleted. This is especially true at the end of the year, when there is usually little work, and management would be pleased if fewer leave days were taken in the following summer when there is a higher workload expected.
- The core of the process is the Define Counting Rules activity. In the counting rules, you use a variety of criteria to specify how days and hours are counted. At first glance, the sheer number of criteria seems overwhelming, but usually

only a few are required. It rarely makes sense, for example, to count leave days on Mondays at 20%, Tuesdays at 40%, and other days at 77%. However, take note in each case that the daily schedule class 0 stands for days off and is generally not taken into consideration in absence counting. That saves you having to carry out the control via weekdays, which doesn't work in many shift models anyway. In the deduction rules, you can define the sequence in which quotas are deducted (for example, the number of leave days taken is to use up the quota special leave first, and only then the Annual Leave Entitlement). In the last category, rounding rules are defined that can be used in the counting rules.

The setting of attendance and absence types is usually concluded with the customizing of counting. All that is missing now are the activities for special absence data (maternity leave, parental leave, military service), which are pretty self-explanatory. It is some comfort that this complex customizing provides many options for company-specific adjustment — and that the settings for the other infotypes are much simpler.

Infotype 2004 (Availability)

Dealing with availability is a very company-specific process. Many default settings of the system refer to the German public sector, but can also be adjusted for other industries.

Using Infotype 2004 with automatic generation of free-time compensation or payment is very complex in Customizing, and is also complicated to some extent for data entry (according to the usage type). For lower volumes it is therefore worth thinking about the options for Infotype 2004 where it is not maintained at all or only for information purposes, and that payment or free-time compensation can only be entered directly via Infotypes 2010, 2012, and 2006.

There are two basic options for entering the infotypes: the direct entry of times or determination of the availability times using specific working time models (daily work schedules or work schedule rules). The former, because it is easier to customize, is more immediately flexible for unscheduled requirements. However, interpreting a start and end time through a longer period is problematic. According to the parameterization of function P2004in the schema, the complete period between the start time on the first day and the end time on the last day is calculated as availability time, and the same is true for each individual day for the period between the start and end times (see Figure 8.19).

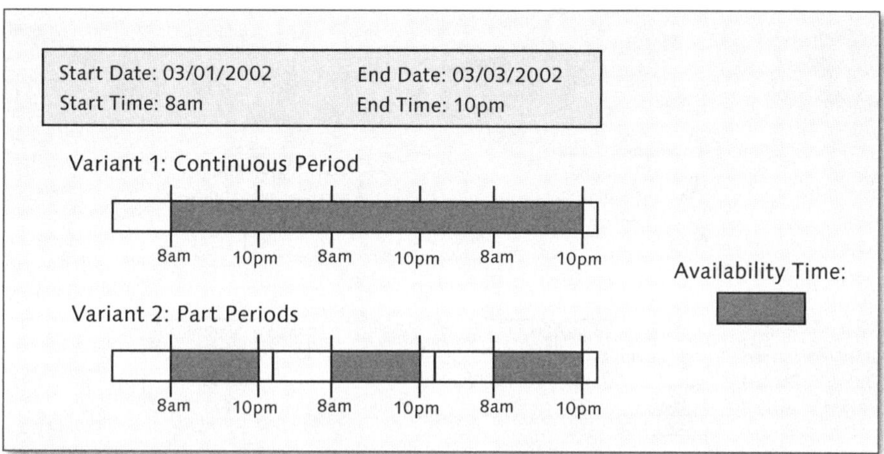

Figure 8.19 Interpretation of Availability Times

Figure 8.20 structures the options for availability recording and gives a basic description of the decision process regarding the mapping of availabilities in the system. In addition to the number of availability scenarios, there are other company-specific requirements that function as decision criteria. For reasons of simplicity, all are not detailed here.

If you are using the functionality of availabilities in Infotype 2004 to its full extent, you must adjust the customizing in the IMG and in the schema of the time evaluation correspondingly. You create the prerequisite that availabilities are to be taken into consideration by time evaluation, mainly by using function P2004, which is available in the standard version but not yet integrated in the schema. We will go into more detail on maintaining the schema in Section 8.2.7. You can navigate to further customizing via the IMG path TIME MANAGEMENT • TIME DATA RECORDING AND ADMINISTRATION • AVAILABILITY.

Essential properties are linked to the availability types that affect the time data: Maintenance, Time evaluation, and Capacity planning. However, the most decisive factor is how the availability process actually takes place: When is availability recorded, how is it credited, what happens if an employee has an off-site assignment, etc.

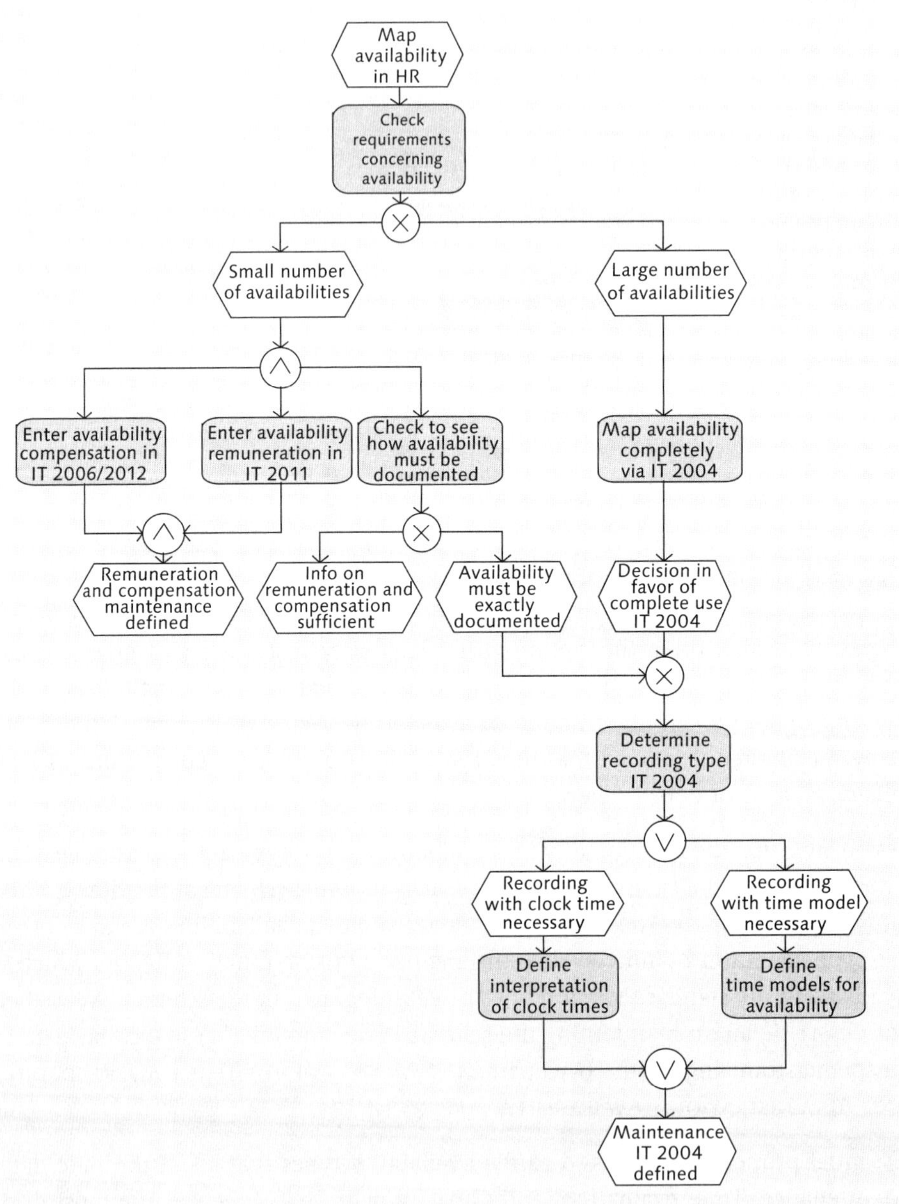

Figure 8.20 Decision on Mapping the Availability in SAP ERP HCM

Infotype 2005 (Overtime)

Overtime should be maintained for the most part in time management. If you enter the payroll amounts directly, information on exactly when the remuneration originated is lost. This means some options of the system – especially in reporting but also in some country-specific tax schemes – are not being used optimally.

Infotype 2005 should only be used for negative time recording, as overtime here is maintained in a fixed manner. In positive time recording, the attendance times for the employee are already known because of the stamps. Here it makes much more sense to maintain overtime through attendance quotas in Infotype 2007, or instead authorize them.

From release 4.6A, the relevant data fields for the entry of overtime are also available in Infotypes 2001 and 2002. Consequently, Infotype 2005 should be excluded for new implementations. According to SAP Note 952860, SAP ERP 6.0 is the last release where this infotype is available. To reduce the work, you should replace Infotype 2005 before you implement the next release.

In Infotype 2005, overtime is entered precisely to the second with break times, or as a pure hourly figure. Using the second option means losing the information about when exactly the overtime occurred.

Maintaining and customizing Infotype 2005 is quite easy. It is only processing the overtime in the time-evaluation schema that can be difficult. This is largely controlled by the overtime compensation type, which besides Infotype 2005 can also be used in Infotypes 2010, 2007, and 2002. It specifies which parts of the overtime are remunerated, or compensated for with free time. By default, the following overtime compensation types are provided, which can also be processed in the schema by default:

- Remuneration (basic pay and, if applicable, bonus)
- Free time for basic pay (and bonus remuneration)
- Free time compensation (basic pay and, if applicable, bonus)

You can create additional compensation types via IMG path Time Management • Time Data Recording and Administration • Overtime • Define Types of Overtime Compensation. However, you must then populate this with data in the time-evaluation schema.

Infotype 2006 (Absence Quotas)

Absence quotas can map different subjects, which allow for employees to have paid or unpaid absences. An essential characteristic is quota deduction. The combination of absences and absence quotas enables you to follow how often an employee is entitled to a certain absence.

Possible types of absence quotas are:

- Annual leave entitlement
- Educational leave
- Compensation time due to overtime
- Weekend compensation

Leave quotas in older release statuses were exclusively managed via Infotype 0005 (Leave Entitlement). Although this can still be used in SAP ERP 6.0, it is no longer maintained by SAP. A new implementation of time management should therefore use Infotype 2006 in each case. According to SAP Note 952860, SAP ERP 6.0 is the last release where Infotype 0005 is available. To reduce the work, you should replace it with Infotype 2006 before you implement the next release. Simultaneously, you must replace Infotype 0083 (Leave Compensation) with Infotype 0416 (Time Quota Compensation). SAP provides the corresponding migration tools.

Absence quotas (i.e., requirements) can be structured in the following ways:

- **Manual Entry in Infotype 2006**
  An essential piece of information besides the quota amount is the deduction period. This enables you to implement, for example, the company regulation that leave days must be used up by March 31 of the following year (see Figure 8.21).

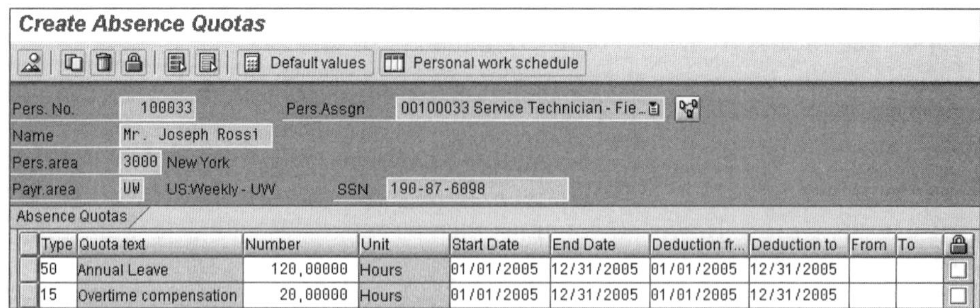

Figure 8.21 Entering Leave Entitlement as an Absence Quota

- **Entering a Quota Correction in Infotype 2013**
  This is used if the quota is not manually entered, but instead is automatically constructed in time evaluation (see Figure 8.22).

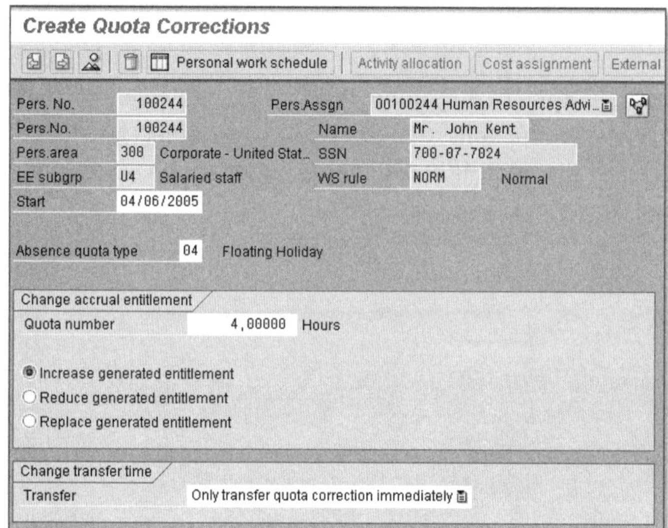

Figure 8.22 Increasing a Quota by Four Hours via Infotype 2013

- **Automatic Creation in Time Evaluation**
  Quotas thus structured cannot be changed manually in Infotype 2006 but by Infotype 2013. (For example, for each night shift, the quota Night shift bonus is increased by an hour. Or, at month's end, the flextime is capped at 20 hours and the figure in excess of this is transferred to the Annual working time account).
- **Mass generation**
  Absence quotas are generated via report RPTQTA00.

They can be deducted as follows:

- Manual maintenance in Infotypes 2006 or 2013
- Automatic deduction in time evaluation based on company-specific facts (For example, if the flextime account is negative at month's end it is canceled out by the quota Annual working time account.)
- Entering absences that are keyed for the respective quota with regard to the deduction

- Compensation via Infotype 0416

Customizing for the counting of absences and for deducting quotas has already been described. Through the IMG path Time Management • Time Data Recording and Administration • Managing Time Accounts Using Attendance/Absence Quotas the following settings can be performed:

- Definition of the attendance and absence quota types used with essential characteristics such as the type of deduction, rounding, time constraint class, deduction permission in excess of the existing entitlement, and restrictions regarding start and end times (see Figure 8.23)
- Calculating the entitlements

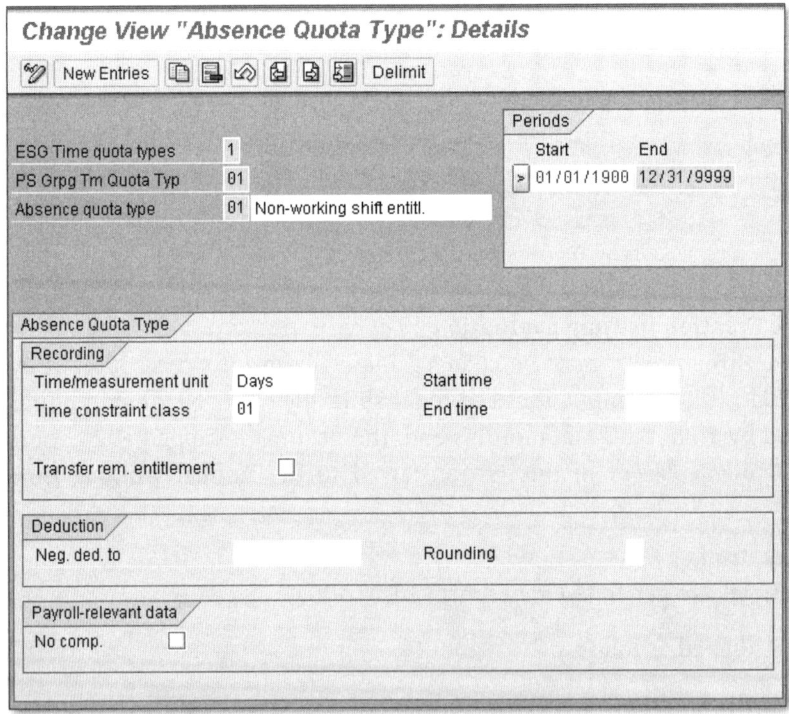

Figure 8.23 Customizing Absence Quota Types

- Rules to build up quotas (initializing, periodic, or current)
- Rules to deduct quotas

- Evaluating deducted quotas in the payroll (for example, if an absence record Vacation deducts the quota Annual leave entitlement, it is valuated on the basis of a three-month average. If it deducts the quota Additional leave, it is only valuated on the basis of the basic pay)
- Rules and valuation for payment
- Layout and content of the quota overview (you can reach this via the menu path HUMAN RESOURCES • TIME MANAGEMENT • ADMINISTRATION • TIME DATA • QUOTA OVERVIEW)

Absence Quotas vs. Time Accounts in Time Types

Previously, time accounts such as annual account, free time due to overtime, etc., were mostly executed in time evaluation as time types. The extensive functionality of Infotype 2006 and its integration in evaluations and maintenance interfaces makes it advisable to map time-off entitlement as far as possible. For a new implementation of time management you can use the following rules of thumb:

- Manage the flextime account via time type 0005 (using standard functionality).
- Manage other time accounts via Infotype 2006 and — if possible — automatically control its creation through the time-management schema.

Infotype 2007 (Attendance Quotas)

Attendance quotas strongly correspond with absence quotas. We will not go into further detail on the corresponding customizing. Their treatment in the time-evaluation schema follows in Section 8.2.7.

The important thing is to recognize the basic importance of attendance quotas. They have the following functions:

- Authorization of the attendance of employees at unusual times (days off, times outside working hours), which otherwise would not be considered in favor of the employee.
- Control of the valuation of attendance times (if possible, also within working hours) regarding compensation or remuneration (for this reason the overtime compensation type is also entered in an attendance quota in addition to the times)

The deduction of attendance quotas generally occurs as follows:

- Attendances from Infotype 2002
- Attendances that result from employee time stamps (Infotype 2011)

They are generally created by direct maintenance of Infotype 2007 (see Figure 8.24).

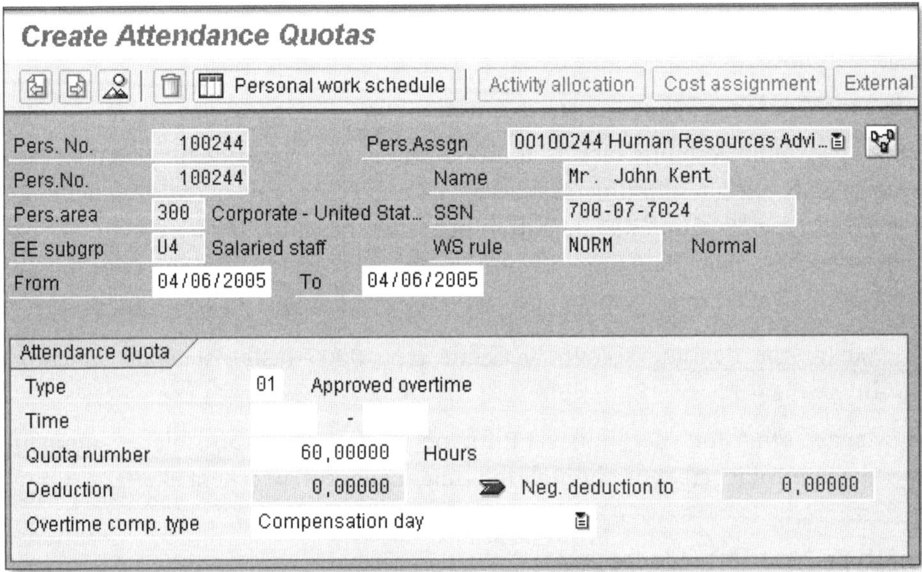

Figure 8.24 Authorization of 60 Overtime Hours for which Payment is to be Made

The advantage of using an attendance quota for overtime authorization, in contrast to a fixed entry of overtime (Infotype 2005), lies in the fact that the exact times don't need to be known at the time of entry. For example, it is possible to assign a quota of ten hours for a specific period or to allow overtime between 8:00 p.m. and 10:00 p.m. every day. The actual overtime is then determined automatically by the time evaluation, based on employee time stamps in the scope of the quota. This means it is sufficient to enter the overtime authorization (usually in advance). Every further step up to payment is done automatically, is documented, and can be evaluated. The part of the quota that has already been used (if, for example, 60 hours of overtime were authorized due to a software project for the period 12/01/2001 to 01/31/2002) can be directly read in Infotype 2007 (see Figure 8.24).

Infotype 2010 (Employee Remuneration Info)

Even if employee remuneration information is stored in a time-management infotype, it is processed by payroll. Data that emerges from specific working times of the employee and frequently accumulates in the area of the time administrator or the incentive wage administrator is maintained here.

All facts that are not automatically determined by time evaluation or the incentive wage are maintained via Infotype 2010, such as hazardous duty bonuses for certain periods or piecework rates for parts finished at home. Basically, this infotype allows you to enter hours, pieces, or amounts that are then transferred into payroll and valuated, if necessary. In addition, the valuation of hours or pieces entered by entering a deviating valuation basis can be influenced in different ways (see Figure 8.25).

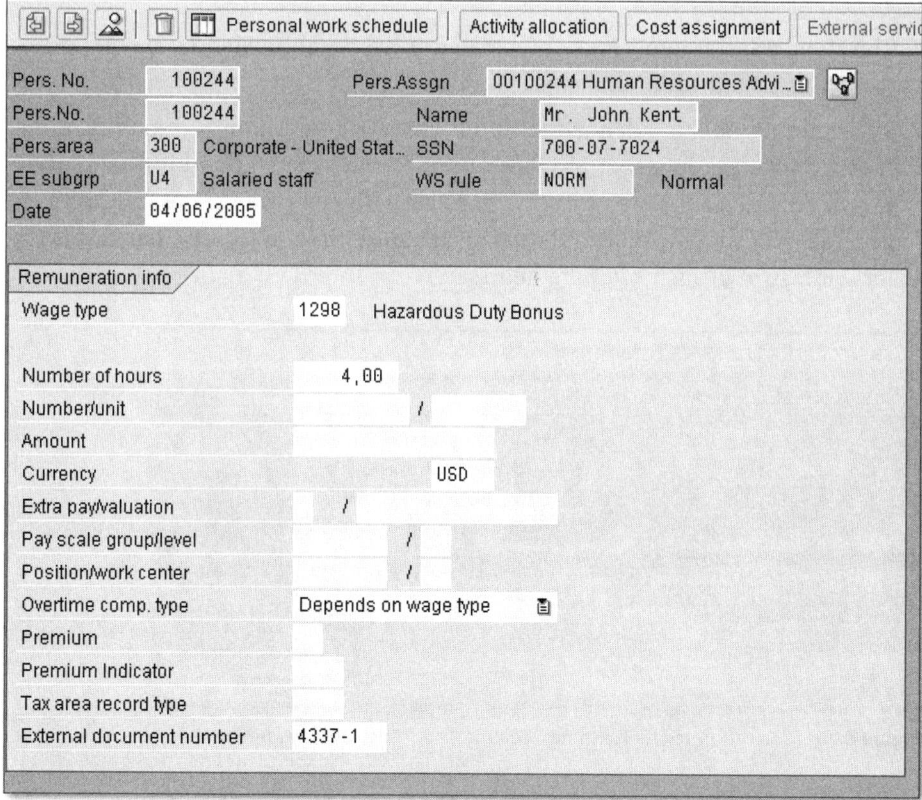

Figure 8.25 Hazardous Duty Bonus as Employee Remuneration Info with Reference to the Document Number of a Paper Document

Infotype 2012 (Time Transfer Specifications)

Time transfers are used to modify the values of time balances, time-wage types, or absence quotas. Here, the pure increase or decrease of an individual value is possible, and a transfer (e.g., transfer of x hours from the flextime balance to the annual working time account or posting the flextime balance into the time wage type basic wage overtime, which corresponds to a disbursement of the balance).

The enhanced functionality of Infotype 2006, together with Infotype 0416 (Time Quota Compensation) only partially replaces the functionality of Infotype 2012. A tool to directly change the values of certain time types is also required.

Maintaining the infotype is quite simple (see Figure 8.26). The corresponding customizing is carried out via IMG path Time Management • Time Evaluation • Time Evaluation with Clock Times • Processing Balances • Time Transfer. There are two essential steps to be carried out there:

1. The time transfer type must be created with an abbreviation and long text (sometimes with additional checks).
2. The transfers must be defined with the following questions: From which time types, time-wage types, or absence quotas is the value entered in the infotype drawn or added to? Here you can also work with percentage rates (e.g., 25%, to generate a flexday from four days of availability time saved up). For real transfers, at least two such rules are necessary.

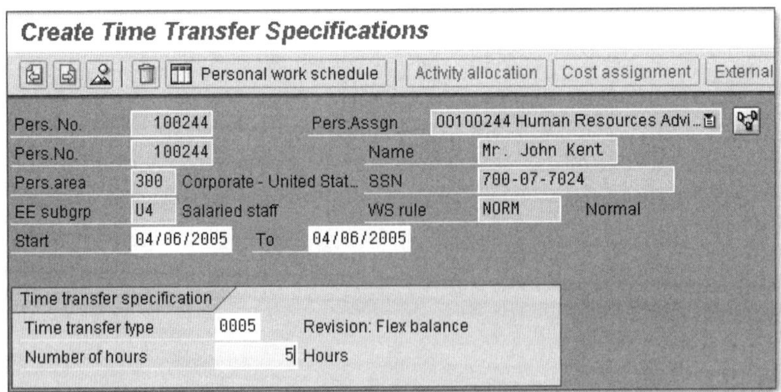

Figure 8.26 Correction to the Flextime Account (as a Time Type) via Infotype 2012

The actual transfer is performed by time evaluation, which analyzes the infotype entered and the relevant customizing. It is not necessary to change the schema and the standard supply for this reason.

Infotype 2013 (Quota Corrections)

Infotype 2013 changes absence quotas, particularly those that were generated by time evaluation and therefore cannot be directly manually maintained.

The hourly figure entered can increase, decrease, or completely overwrite the entitlement in Infotype 2006. You must also ensure here that maintenance in Infotype 2013 is not executed directly, but rather via time evaluation in Infotype 2006. As this is not necessarily updated daily, only at the month's end of the time evaluation can you accelerate this via the Transfer field in the quota correction.

Infotype 2011 (Time Events)

Time events are generally entered via time recording or Plant Data Collection (PDC) terminals (see Section 8.2.6). It is also possible to enter them manually and to change them via Infotype 2011 (see Figure 8.27). If you are familiar with the functionality of this infotype, the integration of a terminal only represents another technical path for maintenance.

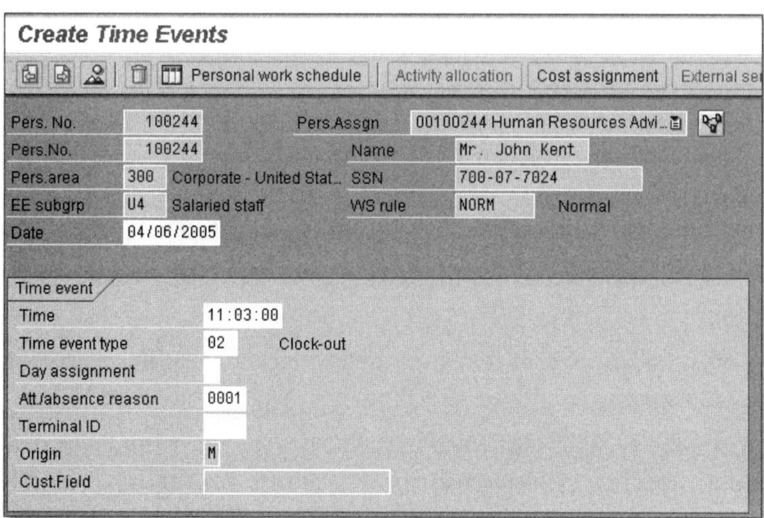

Figure 8.27 Clock-out Entry with Absence Reason Entered Manually

For reasons of revision, it is relevant that all time events be identified according to their origin (manual entry or terminal posting), and that the originals still exist in the database table TEVEN even after a manual change or deletion.

The essential information for a time event is the date, time, and type (clock-in, clock-out, etc.). In addition, the attendance and absence reason enables the triggering of the automatic generation of records of Infotype 2001 or 2002. A clock-out entry with the reason "flexday following day" then avoids the manual message and entry of a flexday via Infotype 2001. In standard Customizing, however, the time administrator then receives a message on such automatically generated absences and must release it.

In addition, extensive additional information can be entered that is not supported by all terminal manufacturers.

The recording of time events — whether this is done manually or through a terminal — requires the correct maintenance of Infotype 0050 (Time Recording Info). It contains the following information:

- The Time Recording ID Number enables the assignment of a time-recording ID card, and thus the postings at the time-recording terminal for the employee. Even if time events are exclusively maintained manually, this must always be maintained in the standard version and must be unique. Otherwise, you cannot save the infotype. This is even the case if the field is hidden via Customizing.

Tip: Preallocation of Fields

If you don't use ID cards, preallocate the field with the personnel number, because this is a unique figure. (To learn about preallocating field, refer to "Plausibility Checks and Default Values" toward the end of Section 4.2.4).

- The Time event type group determines the permitted time events.
- The Subsystem grouping determines the terminals at which the employee is allowed to stamp.
- The grouping of Attendance/absence reasons determines the reasons permitted (for example, only specific employees are allowed to post off-site work).
- The grouping Employee expenses determines which wage types can be posted through the subsystem (e.g., parking fees).
- The Access control group is then relevant, provided that the same subsystem is used for access control and determines when and how the employee has access.

Customizing for time events and Infotype 0050 are closely connected with each other and can be reached via IMG path Time Management • Personnel Time Events (for the PDC connection use Time Management • Plant Data Collection). In particular, the properties and effects of the grouping maintained in Infotype 0050 are set.

The customizing itself is easily executed by means of documentation. The important thing is to consider the groupings precisely in advance, and to leave scope for expansions of the three-digit abbreviations in naming conventions.

With regard to the time events enabled (by assigning the personnel time event type groups), we advise that you use Time Event Type 03 Clock-in/-out. It enables the HCM system to decide which posting should exist now (based on the previous posting and the time model), and considerably decreases the complexity involved in manual correction of missing postings. For the most part, only the time-event types set by default can be used.

Additional Information on Time Data

Additional data can be maintained according to the Customizing for most of the time data that can be entered. These comprise the following areas:

- **Cost assignment**
  Costs that are assigned to the data record via payroll can be assigned a different cost unit as primary costs (see Figure 8.28). This assignment occurs through the normal posting interface in payroll.

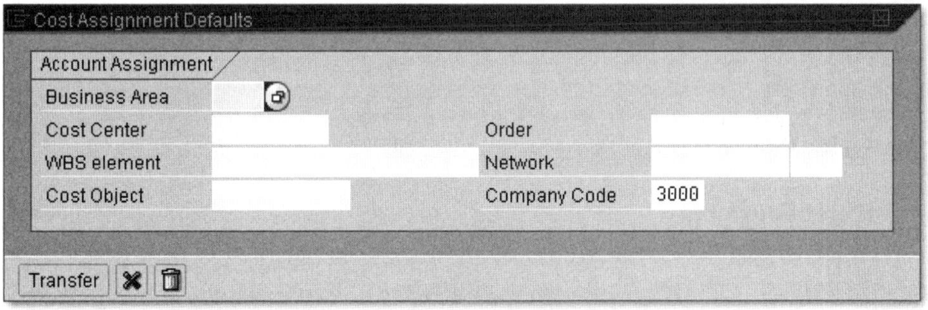

Figure 8.28 Entering a Different Primary Cost Assignment

- **Cost allocation**
  Using the RPTPDOC0 report (menu path Human Resources • Time Management • Administration • Environment • Activity Allocation), a secondary costs allocation can be carried out between the sender and the recipient. For this reason, the entry of a performance type for CO is of particular importance. An example is the compensation of a business trip that takes place to support another department or because of a project (see Figure 8.29). In addition, the costs can be assigned to the sender as primary costs via payroll. However, the sender is normally the master cost center for the employee.

- **External services**
  Integration to the R/3 component MM SRV is supported here. If the times of external service providers are entered in the HCM system, or also through the schema TM02, additional information can be stored here. These are provided to purchasing as purchasing documents, positions, and activity numbers for checking and settlement (see Figure 8.30).

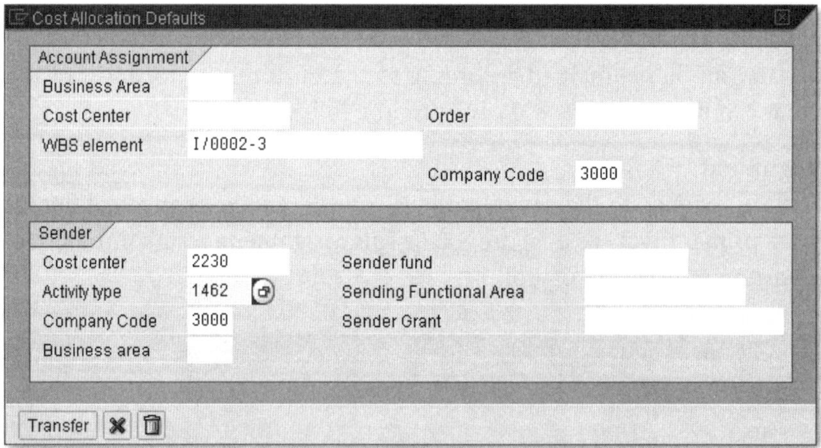

Figure 8.29 Debiting a Project (WBS Element) and Crediting the Master Cost Center (2230)

- **Different payment**
  This additional data enables you to assign a special payment to certain times. In the simplest case, this would be an hourly rate entered manually as a valuation basis (see Figure 8.31). Examples would be bonuses for instructor activities (entered as attendance in Infotype 2002) or noise bonuses for times that are spent in a particularly loud environment (entered through the time-recording terminal or directly in Infotype 2011).

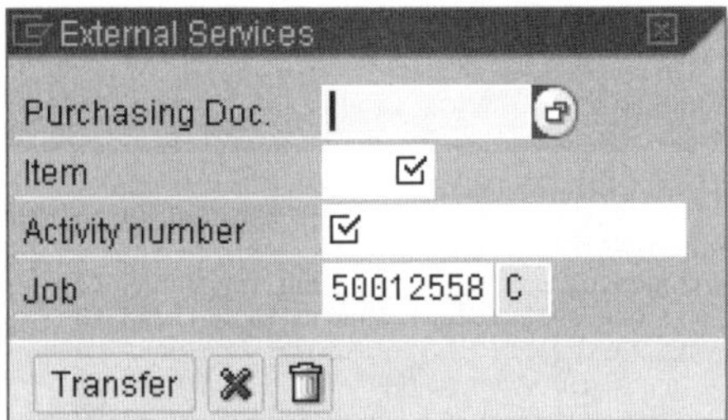

Figure 8.30 Entering Information on External Services

Different payment Attendances (Infotype 2002)
Premium number
Premium ID
Pay Scale Group
Pay scale level
Object type
Position
Extra pay ID
Valuation basis 27,50 USD
Tax Area

Figure 8.31 Valuation of an Attendance at a Fixed Hourly Rate

Weekly, Monthly, and Annual Entry

Previously, only the entry of individual facts was shown, and was supplemented by simple list entry screens as necessary. However, there are now further options for weekly, monthly, and annual entries, and for general list entry with additional data. These maintenance screens are primarily used for cost allocation, cost distribution, and external services, and can be found via the following menu path HUMAN RESOURCES • TIME MANAGEMENT • ADMINISTRATION • TIME DATA • MAINTAIN ADDITIONAL DATA.

The weekly entry (see Figure 8.32) is mainly used to maintain attendance records and their handling in cost allocation and cost distribution. Typical examples of the use of the weekly entry are project-time recording or compensation for times of service employees who maintain machines from different cost centers. In a similar way, the list entry records external services.

Maintain Weekly Entry w/Activity Allocation

Choose | New page

Pers. No.	10270		Pers.Assgn	00010270 Manager of Marketing A...
Pers.No.	10270		Name	Mr. Henry Miller
Pers.area	300	Corporate - United Stat...	SSN	145-99-9855
EE subgrp	U4	Salaried staff	WS rule	FLEX

	1 Sunday	2 Monday	3 Tuesd...	4 Wedn...	5 Thurs...	6 Friday	7 Saturd...	
	04/03/05	04/04/05	04/05/05	04/06/05	04/07/05	04/08/05	04/09/05	
	OFF	FLEX	FLEX	FLEX	FLEX	FLEX	OFF	
Standard	0,00	8,00	8,00	8,00	8,00	8,00	0,00	40,00
Abs. hrs	0,00	0,00	0,00	0,00	0,00	0,00	0,00	0,00
Att. hrs	0,00	8,00	8,00	8,00	8,00	8,00	0,00	40,00
Rec.hours	0,00	8,00	8,00	8,00	8,00	8,00	0,00	40,00
Rest	0,00	0,00	0,00	0,00	0,00	0,00	0,00	0,00

D	Start Date	End Date	Hrs	From	To	P	Type	Att./absence type	C	E..	Cost Ctr	Order	WBS Element	CostObje
2	04/04/2005	04/04/2005	8,00	08:00	16:00		0425	Instructor duty					X-IDES-TRAIN-STD-40B	
3	04/05/2005	04/05/2005	8,00	08:00	16:00		0425	Instructor duty					X-IDES-TRAIN-STD-40B	
4	04/06/2005	04/06/2005	8,00	08:00	16:00		0425	Instructor duty					X-IDES-TRAIN-STD-40B	
5	04/07/2005	04/07/2005	8,00	08:00	16:00		0425	Instructor duty			4100			
6	04/08/2005	04/08/2005	8,00	08:00	16:00		0425	Instructor duty					X-IDES-TRAIN-STD-40B	

Figure 8.32 Project Time Recording via Weekly Entry

Monthly entry maintains data for an individual employee from the overview of a calendar month. They should only rarely be used to support the optimal processes, because the form of the maintenance does not correspond to the usual data access. However, this can be frequently used if obsolete processes are mapped, in which monthly time recording cards are manually maintained in settlements and entered in the central personnel department. However, this is merely an interim solution until the implementation of decentralized entry concepts (e.g., via ESS).

The annual calendar provides a good overview of any 12-month period for an employee (see Figure 8.33). Depending on Customizing, it can show all attendances and absences. It is less suitable for maintenance, although there are exceptions to this. As a display tool, it is very suitable. You should ensure that records lasting one day are displayed in lowercase letters.

Via IMG path Time Management • Time Data Recording and Administration • Absences • Absence Catalog • Define Indicators for the Personal Calendar you can define which absences are represented by which letters (proceed in the same way for attendances).

As is the case for monthly entry, and to a limited extent for weekly entry, the annual calendar becomes obsolete in many areas due to the TMW, particularly the calendar view, as described in Section 8.4).

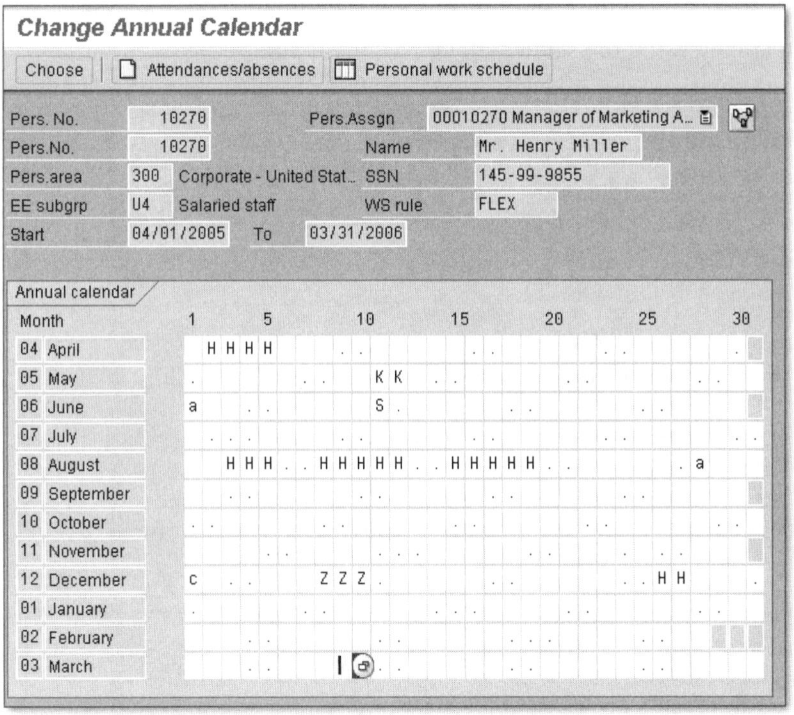

Figure 8.33 Annual Calendar with Attendances and Absences

Time Management Pool

The time management pool summarizes the essential tasks of the time administrator. This is not to be confused with the TMW (see Sections 8.3 and 8.4) that is implemented user-specifically and is strongly recommended for decentralized processing by the time administrator. You can replace the time management pool almost completely with the TMW or use it in parallel for central processing. The time management pool is, however, sufficient for pure central processing or for use by smaller companies. It can be used with a lot less configuration difficulty than can the TMW.

You can reach the time management pool via the following menu path HUMAN RESOURCES • TIME MANAGEMENT • ADMINISTRATION • TIME EVALUATION • TIME MANAGEMENT POOL. There are extensive options for selecting the employees to be considered. Selection through the time administrator enables each administrator to select his area of responsibility. You can reach the individual components of the to-do list directly by using the same path (see Figure 8.34).

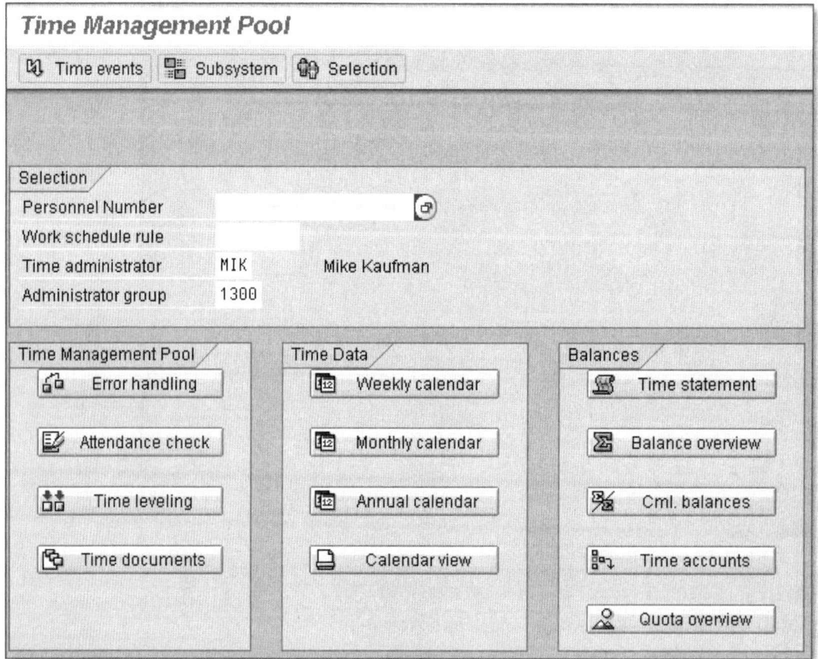

Figure 8.34 Time Management Pool

The following are the most important components of the time management pool that also display the daily business of the time administrator in the HCM system:

- **Error handling**
  All information and error messages for the selected employees can be overseen and processed here. Figure 8.35 shows the time management pool with several information messages and error messages.
- **Time leveling**
  In the incentive wage area, for example, you can identify which attendances for the employee are not covered by time tickets.

- **The calendar views – previously described** (weekly, monthly, and annual view)
- **Calling the time statement**
- **Balance overview**
  It provides an overview of the essential time balances for the employee (see Figure 8.36). The reason for a balance overview is the need for a form that can be implemented in the same Form Editor in Customizing, as can the time statement.

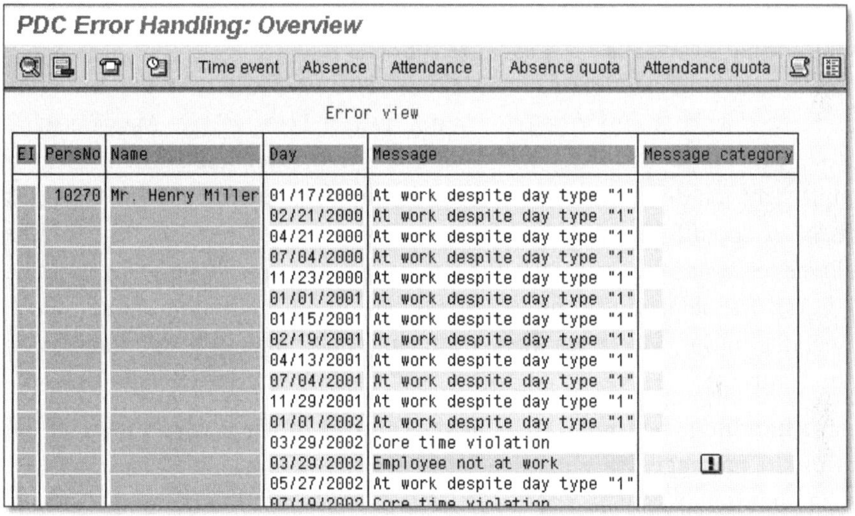

PDC Error Handling: Overview

Time event | Absence | Attendance | Absence quota | Attendance quota

Error view

EI	PersNo	Name	Day	Message	Message category
	10270	Mr. Henry Miller	01/17/2000	At work despite day type "1"	
			02/21/2000	At work despite day type "1"	
			04/21/2000	At work despite day type "1"	
			07/04/2000	At work despite day type "1"	
			11/23/2000	At work despite day type "1"	
			01/01/2001	At work despite day type "1"	
			01/15/2001	At work despite day type "1"	
			02/19/2001	At work despite day type "1"	
			04/13/2001	At work despite day type "1"	
			07/04/2001	At work despite day type "1"	
			11/29/2001	At work despite day type "1"	
			01/01/2002	At work despite day type "1"	
			03/29/2002	Core time violation	
			03/29/2002	Employee not at work	
			05/27/2002	At work despite day type "1"	
			07/19/2002	Core time violation	

Figure 8.35 Error-handling/Time-evaluation Messages

Pers No.	Name	CCtr	WrkTime	FlexTime	Ref. Date
00100036	Mr. David Johnson	4120	187,00	*51,00-	01/31/2002
00100036	Mr. David Johnson	4120	160,00	*51,00-	02/28/2002
00100036	Mr. David Johnson	4120	160,00	*59,00-	03/31/2002
00010270	Mr. Henry Miller	3200	187,49	15,00	01/31/2002
00010270	Mr. Henry Miller	3200	162,95	15,00	02/28/2002
00010270	Mr. Henry Miller	3200	163,47	10,47	03/28/2002

Figure 8.36 Balance Overview

- Report RPTBAL00 can be created using the Cumulated Balances button. This is an excellent way of evaluating time types on a daily and monthly basis, and time-wage types. It is also an instrument of quality control for the system settings and to control the resource work time. Its functionality is only limited insofar as the time evaluation provides the required info time types. For this reason, the settings for time evaluation should be derived from the evaluation requirements.

- Further displays provide an overview of the time accounts and quotas.
- Communication with the subsystem can be controlled, which normally takes place via background jobs. The Time events button enables you to check and, if required, subsequently post incorrect time events provided by the subsystem.

The time management pool can be adapted in Customizing to fit the specifics of your company in two ways:

- **The individual functions each execute reports.**
  In Customizing you can define, via IMG path TIME MANAGEMENT • TIME EVALUATION • EVALUATIONS AND THE TIME MANAGEMENT POOL • TIME MANAGEMENT POOL • SET UP POSTPROCESSING, which variant is to be executed in each case. For example, you can determine which form the time statement uses and in which language it should be called (while it is useful to use the language of the employee for a monthly print out, the language of the user logged on should be used here). The selection of the variants is carried out in feature LLREP, which is integrated in the IMG. Note the IMG documentation and the documentation for the feature.
- **In error handling the time data is always shown in the environment of the error or the message.**
  You can limit the display for specific groups of employees in a company-specific manner via the following IMG path TIME MANAGEMENT • TIME EVALUATION • EVALUATIONS AND THE TIME MANAGEMENT POOL • TIME MANAGEMENT POOL • LIMIT DISPLAY TO GENERAL DATA ONLY OR OF DATA TO ERRORS ONLY. This generally occurs via the feature REPTA. Depending on the time-recording indicator (Infotype 0007), this goes immediately to the subfeatures REPT1 (no time recording and negative time recording) and REPT2 (positive time recording of different forms). In an error-dependent case, you must simply maintain one table per message.

8.2.6 Connecting Time Clocks

Time recording comprises several areas. The categorization in Figure 8.37, for the sake of completeness, also contains the manual entry. Entry via the ESS is a good alternative, which can be used through a normal web browser. For smaller branches, for whom attaching terminals is not worthwhile, ESS entry is more useful than sending times by paper forms or by email to a central entry point. In this section, entry via terminals is described.

The person-time recording refers to pure people-related time events, e.g., clock-in, clock-out, start of break, etc. It is possible, since release 4.5, to carry out person-time recording in two ways: through the transceiver solution and through a Business Application Programming Interface (BAPI) with extensive options to transfer additional data.

Working-time recording refers to time events that originate from the employee's activities, e.g., setting up, tearing down, changing tools, etc.

In each case you must note the work distribution between the subsystem and HR. It is sufficient if the subsystem delivers the pure time events, or with extra information added. No further processing or interpretation is required; in fact, processing or interpretation would be disruptive. The interpretation of time events in conjunction with other time data is incumbent on SAP ERP HCM Time Management — beginning with the pair formation and ending with the transfer to payroll.

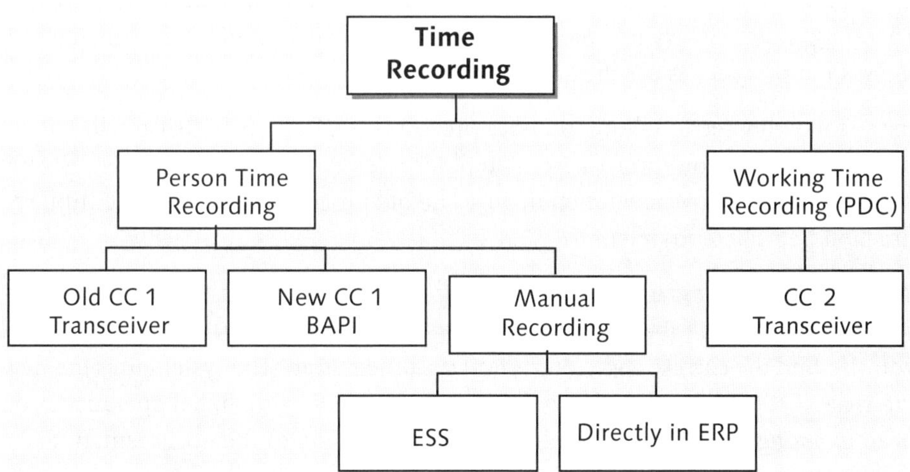

Figure 8.37 Variants for Time Recording

Some manufacturers of subsystems provide functionality similar to HCM time management. This is only useful if payroll occurs in a system other than SAP

ERP HCM that provides insufficient functionality in time management. The direct connection of a complete external time management system to HCM payroll is possible, but should be an exceptional activity (for example, if very special functionalities are required that the HCM system cannot map or can only do so with great difficulty). Unfortunately, many system providers are always trying to sell additional functionalities that are much better handled in HCM. This not only boosts license and maintenance costs, but also makes the processes unnecessarily complicated.

The following questions will now be dealt with:

- How do personnel-time and working-time recording interact with each other?
- How do the old and new communication channel 1 (CC1) function?
- What should you consider during analysis and conception?

Person Time Recording

SAP offers a certification procedure for the providers of time-recording systems. As certification does not encompass the entire process of subsystem connection, it is possible that a provider is only partly certified. This would mean they are not in a position to provide all functionalities that the connection basically provides. Therefore, check closely to what extent the interface of your potential time-recording system provider is certified by SAP.

In the following section, both interface processes (CC1 and HR PDC) are described. If you still use the old process from an older release, a conversion is usually only needed if you require new functionality. The old process will basically continue to function in a stable manner.

You define the process used in Customizing via IMG path Time Management • Personnel Time Events • Basic Settings • Define Communication Parameters. Here, you also find the corresponding technical documentation. The system uses the new interface (HR PDC) by default. To define the use of CC1 or parallel operation, you need to configure the corresponding settings according to the documentation.

The old integration is implemented using CC1. The communication between the SAP ERP system and the time-recording system (subsystem) is established via transceivers. The time-recording system provides a data record at the operation system level. Transceivers accept this data record and make it available to the ERP system. It is provided and posted there via Application Link Enabling (ALE) and Intermediate Documents (IDocs) for time management in HCM.

Apart from the technical integration, you must maintain the functionality of the entire connection. Define it in such a way as to answer the following:

- Are the participants to be classified in the time recording, i.e., grouped for the subsystem?
- Should attendance/absence reasons be entered in the terminal?
- Should information be displayed at the terminals?
- Should additional data such as canteen data be entered?

Infotype 0050 maps the connection between the personnel master data and the subsystem.

Like the old CC1, the new HR PDC interface is also based on IDocs. However, for communication it uses a BAPI. In addition, it provides extended functionality. It is then possible to enter, for example, a differing payment and cost assignment at the terminal. In addition, freely definable fields are available. Additional time-event types such as change or info postings are supported. For the design of the new CC1, the same limits apply as for the old CC1, supplemented with the additional functionality.

Working Time Recording

Working time recording, also referred to as PDC, is based on communication channel 2 (CC2). The following components can be tied to this interface:

- Production planning and control (PP)
- Production planning and control/Process industry (PP/PI)
- Maintenance or service management (PP/SM)
- Project system (PS)

Two processes are possible here:

- Confirmation occurs in relation to a certain point in time, i.e., work-time events (e.g., start of setup time) are transferred. Time tickets are generated in the time evaluation.

- Confirmation depends on the processing duration, i.e., the number of hours transferred. Data can be directly posted as time tickets without time evaluation.

Time-spot-related confirmation generally means less difficulty in making entries in production, but also more complex and finicky solutions in the ERP system and in the subsystem.

To reach a basic decision between both of these processes, an exact definition of the target process is necessary while considering technical determining factors. Here, the following areas are integrated in the conception:

- Data emergence in logistics
- Incentive wages
- Time management
- Payroll in general
- CO

Define the cross-area process at an early stage. This not only affects the customizing settings, but also the conception of the subsequent processes, the selection of hardware and software, and the cabling and elements that form the design in production.

For CC2, also check the certification of your time-recording system provider and all specific requirements that derive from your process, e.g., support for the operation use of multiple machines or machine cards.

Interaction of CC1/HR PDC and CC2 in the Incentive Wage

As each communication channel fulfills different tasks that span the entire working time for one employee, it is necessary for these to work in tandem. We will not name the exact tables involved here.

The starting point for the collaboration could be a clock-in entry for an employee at 6:00 a.m. In the database you can only see one record with this information (see Table 8.1).

Time	Pair Type	Time Event Info
06:00	At work	Person time event

Table 8.1 Database After Clock-In Entry

The employee reports at 6:15 a.m. setup start time, at 6:30 a.m. end of setup time, at 2:00 p.m. end of series of operations, and at 2:30 p.m. clock-out. You can now find the relevant information in the database (see Table 8.2).

Time	Communication Channel	Time Event Info
06:00	CC1	Clock-in
06:15	CC2	Beginning of setup time
06:30	CC2	End of setup time
14:00	CC2	End of series of operations
14:30	CC1	Clock-out

Table 8.2 Database with Postings After One Day

In the course of the time evaluation the time pairs displayed in Table 8.3 are mapped.

Current. No.	From ... To ...	Time Pair Info	Time Ticket Info
1	06:00–06:15	Personnel time	No time ticket
2	06:15–06:30	Setup time	Time ticket setup
3	06:30–09:00	Order time	Time ticket order
4	09:00–09:15	Break	
5	09:15–12:00	Order time	Time ticket order
6	12:00–12:45	Break	
7	12:45–14:00	Order time	Time ticket order
8	14:00–14:30	Personnel time	No time ticket

Table 8.3 Time Pairs After Pair Formation

As you can see, not only have the time events from CC1 been linked with the work time events of CC2, but the entire process has also been validated against the daily work timetable.

The generated time tickets are now provided for the incentive wages through integration. The settings necessary for this are available in the standard SAP version and can be adapted to specific company requirements without modifications.

Note: CC2 for Logistics Integration

Note that the executions for CC2 are only relevant for the HCM system, provided that time tickets must be generated in the time management from logistic time events. If they are generated from time-confirmation tickets in logistics (i.e., logistics supplies time-related information to the HCM system, with no time-spots), the CC2 has no impact in SAP ERP HCM.

8.2.7 Time Evaluation

Time evaluation occurs via report RPTIME00. To maintain optimal flexibility with regard to company-specific adaptations, the behavior of RPTIME00 is not only controlled via customizing tables, but also via a schema. The schema consists of functions, subschemas, and calculation rules. The latter are similar in their structure and characteristics, and consist of operations. Figure 8.38 shows the time-evaluation customizing context. The entire schema is also a component of Customizing and must be more or less radically adapted. Unfortunately, the processing is quite complex and the syntax of the available commands is not very intuitive. It is very similar to assembler programming. The schema should not be changed without experienced support.

The direction of development, however, shows that the importance of customizing in the schema is decreasing and in parts replaced by customizing tables. To this end, a customizing table was provided for release 4.6 to support the complex processing of time balance limits (capping, warning, updating, etc.).

The customizing in the schema is also supported via the IMG. Via IMG path Time Management • Time Evaluation • Time Evaluation With Clock Times (for negative recording: Time Evaluation Without Clock Times) the normal activities needed to adapt the behavior of the time evaluation are carried out. Normal customizing tables belong to this category, as do points in the schema and certain calculation rules for which sufficient instructions can be found in the documentation. Always work as close as possible to this guide.

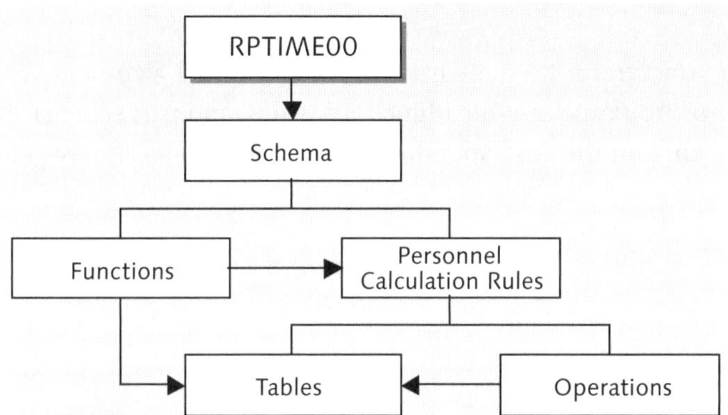

Figure 8.38 Overview: Customizing for Time Evaluation

In the following sections you should get a feel for the complexity and the options of customizing. In addition, you will receive basic tips on the process and will get to know the basics about the contexts and selected details.

It is not possible to handle the subject of schemas and calculation rules sufficiently within the scope of this book. However, the documentation provided by SAP is very extensive and helpful in many places. At the beginning, an experienced coach should always be available.

Schema

SAP provides different schemas in the standard version:

- TM00 – Personnel time events (positive recording)
- TM01 – Work schedule deviations (negative time recording)
- TM02 – External services management
- TM04 – Without clock times

In the following explanation, we will refer to schema TM00.

A schema consists of functions that on one hand process fixed parameters stored in tables, and on the other hand call part schemas or personnel calculation rules. Calling a personnel calculation rule can also be linked with parameters.

You can call the schema maintenance via Transaction PE01 or via menu path Human Resources • Time Management • Administration • Tools • Maintain Schemas. Transaction PE02 for the maintenance of calculation rules is adjacent in the menu.

Figure 8.39 shows an extract from the standard schema TM00 and gives an overview in the schema editor. You can see which functions, rules, and part schemas it contains. By double-clicking on the corresponding part schema, you can navigate to this schema.

000180	BLOCK	BEG					
000190	IF		NOT	SIMF			
000200	PERT	TD20					
000210	P2011						
000220	ACTIO	TD10					
000230	A2003						
000240	ACTIO	TD60	AB				
000250	P2001						
000260	P2002						
000270	PTIP	TD80	GEN				
000280	ACTIO	TD90					
000290	P2005					*	
000300	PTIP	TD40	GEN			*	
000310	ACTIO	TD30					
000320	DYNWS					*	

Figure 8.39 Extract from Schema TM00

The source code of the schema is listed. By clicking in the function fields Par1 to Par4 and calling the F1 help, you can go to the documentation for the corresponding function.

The basic structure of the schema corresponds to the sections of the IMG for Time Evaluation with Clock Times:

- **Initial Steps**
  In addition to specific checks, different groupings are set for the employees.
- **Providing Time Data**
  Time events, other time data such as absences, and work schedules are read in and mixed, so the time pairs are available at the end. These are provided in table TIP and are processed throughout the run of the schema.

- **Time Data Processing**
  On the basis of time pairs in Table TIP and different Customizing settings, the following processings are executed:
  - Processing beginning and end tolerances
  - Error checking and outputting messages such as Employee at work despite vacation
  - Characterizing time pairs via time types (attendance time, absence time, etc.)
  - Determining break times
  - Determining planned times
  - Processing absences (e.g., decreasing flextime balances in the case of absence —flexday)
- **Time Wage Type Selection**
  Attendance quotas are processed here and time-wage types for overtime and other times (e.g., night work) are generated.
- **Overtime Compensation**
  The wage types generated in the previous step are then further processed, in connection with the selected compensation. Here it is decided which parts are compensated by free time and which are transferred to payroll for payment. A monetary valuation does not occur here! The wage types are transferred with the number of hours, along with additional information if needed. Valuation with an hourly rate occurs in payroll.
- **Processing Balances and Message Output**
  The time accounts and time balances are processed according to company regulations (e.g., capping, or transferring to another account when exceeding an upper limit). Time transfers (Infotype 2012) are considered here. In addition to time types, attendance quotas are also generated. Furthermore, messages can be generated, depending on the status of the balances.
- **Month's-end Processing**
  Here, in turn, balance-processing is implemented on a monthly level. In addition, info time types can be mapped and messages can be output.
- **Storing Evaluation Results**
  This also belongs to month's-end processing and provides the results for evaluations and subsequent processes.

Calculation Rules

Calculation rules are essential components of the schema. They are called as parameters of some functions and control the processing in a detailed manner. The calculation rules provide the option of constructing a decision tree, and of using a large template of operations that shows the essential element of flexibility of time evaluation.

You can maintain the rules via Transaction PE02 (menu path Human Resources • Time Management • Administration • Tools • Tools Selection • Maintain Personnel Calculation Rules). In general, the standard rules should not be changed, but rather copied to custom rules and then adapted. We will not go into further detail on maintaining rules, as we would have to dedicate a whole book to this area. Remember that calculation rules provide high flexibility, but the often high once-off and maintenance complexity should not be underestimated. Figure 8.40 shows calculation rule TC40 as an example of overtime compensation which also calls rule TC41 as a subrule.

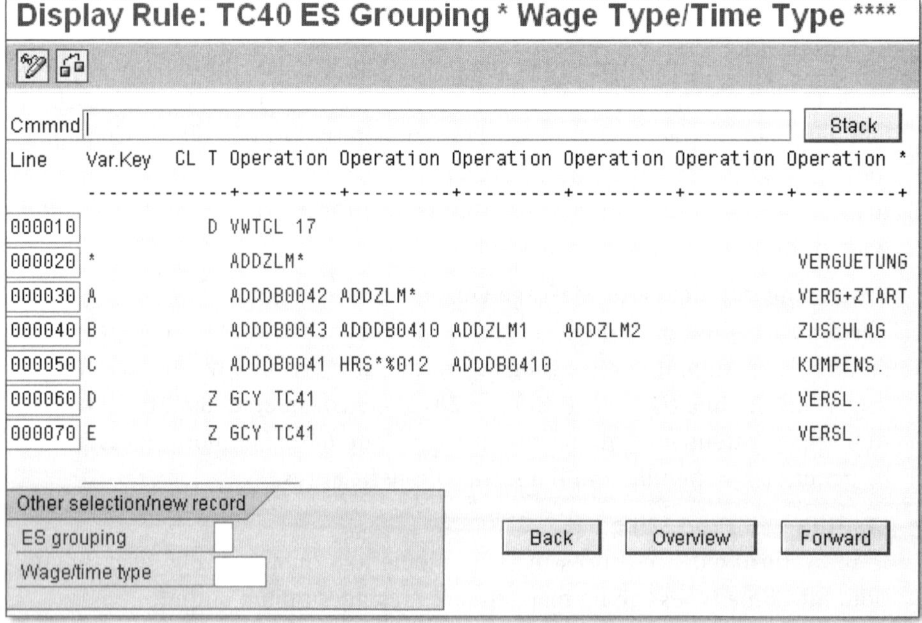

Figure 8.40 Example of a Calculation Rule

Basic Processing Logic

Even though we will not go into all of the details, we will summarize the logic in time evaluation. If you are familiar with the basic tables, you can build on this by doing some study yourself (if possible, with the support of a consultant).

Time evaluation works in daily processing primarily with six internal tables (there are still some others that, from the point of view of logic, are not essential):

- Table TIP contains all time pairs and is created every day in the first part of the processing. The time pairs are provided with numerous indicators in this table, which are essential for the creation of completely new processing steps. The documentation of these indicators and additional tables can be found in the SAP library via the following path PERSONNEL TIME MANAGEMENT • TIME EVALUATION • APPENDIX • INTERNAL TABLES IN TIME EVALUATION. This is an essential section of the documentation for those who are more involved with customizing the time evaluation.
- Daily balances of the time types are collected in table TES. At the end-of-the-day processing it contains the positive flextime balance for the day in time type 0005. The TES is generally populated when calculation rules process the table TIP and, if applicable, additional data, and thus derive the values for individual time types.
- In tables ZML (overtime) and DZL, the time-wage types, with the number of hours, and, if necessary, with start and end times are collected on a daily basis. The tables are generally populated when calculation rules process table TIP and possibly other data, and thus derive the values for individual time-wage types.
- In the end, processing daily balances of the time types and time wage types are accumulated in monthly tables. This occurs in tables SALDO and ZL.

Selected Processing

The settings for some of the relevant time-evaluation aspects were already described in previous sections. Here, two additional essential processing types are described in more detail: the time wage types generation, and the processing of balance limits.

A main aim of time management lies in preparing payroll-relevant facts in time management for subsequent processing in payroll. The wage type generation that generates wage types for payroll is the interface for this.

The functions DAYMO and GWT, along with the tables for the time wage types generation rules, provide you with powerful tools to carry out these tasks. The settings are carried out via the following IMG path Time Management • Time Evaluation • Time Evaluation With Clock Times • Time Wage Type Selection and Overtime Compensation • Define Generation Rules. Time wage type selection rules are primarily entered here, which describe the conditions for the emergence of a wage type (see Figure 8.41). At first glance, this table appears confusing. If you have clarified the conditions for the creation of wage types on a technical level, however, the maintenance of the table is not critical. Note that you do not necessarily require all of the criteria offered.

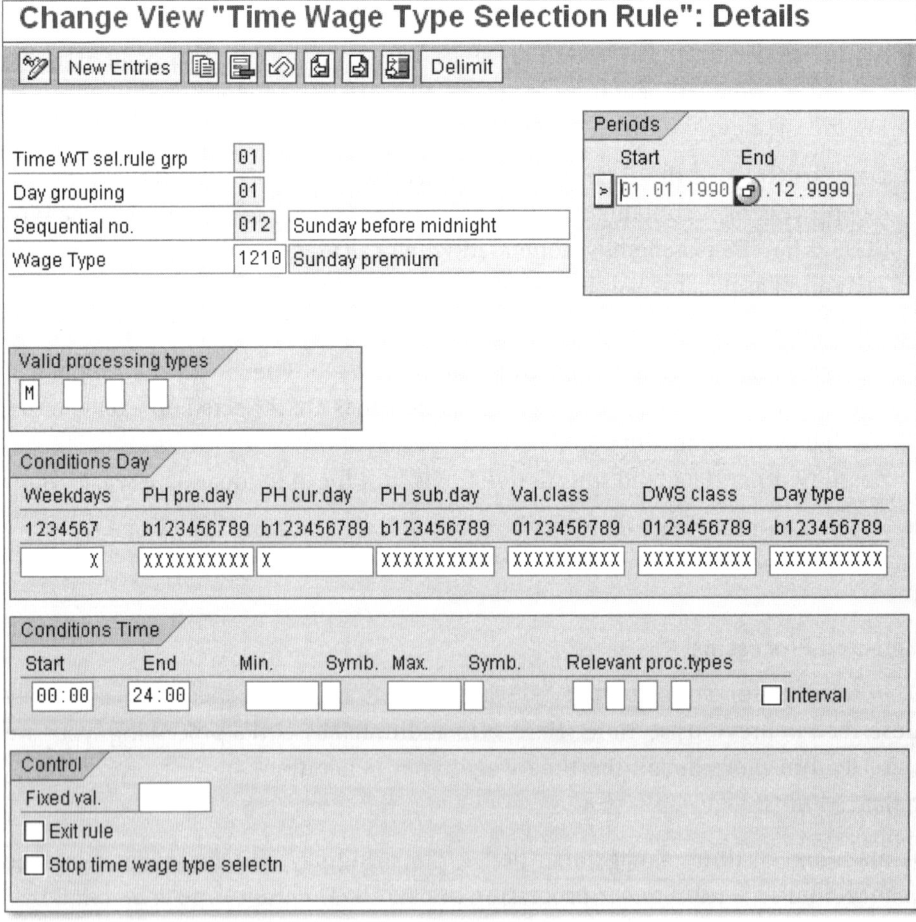

Figure 8.41 A Time Wage Type Selection Rule for Sunday Bonuses

The following criteria are available:

- The time wage types selection rule group and the day grouping are set in the calling schema via the function DAYMO and the calculation rule MODT.
- The valid processing type is assigned a time pair in time evaluation in table TIP (e.g., M for overtime, S for planned working time).
- The generation rule gets the conditions for the current day from the *personal shift plan (PSP)* for the employee. In the example shown, there are only limitations regarding the day of the week (Sunday) and the public holiday class (not a public holiday). The wage type in the example is formed independent of the public-holiday class of the previous day and the subsequent day, of the period-work-schedule evaluation class, of the daily work schedule class, and of the day type. All of these criteria could also be used to further break down the generation rules (e.g., in the case of daily working-time schedules for the night shift, if a rotating shift is worked on Sundays that follow a public holiday, then a wage type must be generated).
- The generation rule then gets the time conditions from table TIP. The restrictions to the times is of particular relevance for night bonuses (note that night work from 10:00 p.m. to 6:00 a.m. on the subsequent day must be entered with 22:00 to 30:00). You can generate a number of hours via the parameters Lower limit (Min.) and Upper limit (Max.), e.g., overtime up to two hours with a 25% bonus, after two hours at a 50% bonus.
- The Fixed value field enables you to generate entrance premiums, for example. This enables you to award an attendance that meets the conditions entered in the upper part of the screen, with the same number of hours of a defined wage type. This can be used for special actions such as an SAP going-live preparation over Christmas. For this reason, the rule is limited to the precise period of validity at the desired dates (for example, an employee who must be present at Christmas receives an additional eight hours on his flextime account regardless of the duration of attendance.) Such rules can be easily abused. Management is then responsible for ensuring that only the overtime actually required for the company is authorized.

The limits of time accounts, the processes for exceeding these limits, and the interaction between different accounts frequently conceal the large company-specific adjustment requirement. While older releases imposed considerable complexity on creating new calculation rules, the standard Customizing to some extent now provides extensive control tables. In the schema, the processing according to the Customizing settings is simply called via the LIMIT function, which is also contained in the standard schema.

You can reach the settings via the following IMG path TIME MANAGEMENT • TIME EVALUATION • TIME EVALUATION WITH CLOCK TIMES • PROCESSING BALANCES • BALANCE FORMATION • BALANCE LIMITS.

Basically, the following options of limit processing are available respectively for monthly balances and daily balances:

- First, always determine which threshold value (constant or variable from the time evaluation) is drawn on, and whether this is an upper or lower threshold. The time type (accumulated, or as minimum/maximum) is then entered and must be compared with the threshold value.
- The checks can be daily or monthly (the latter for monthly balances on a monthly basis). However, you can define the times for the checks yourself, for example, weekly.
- Then you enter how the system will react to a violation to the threshold value. The following options are available here:
  - Creating a time-evaluation message
  - Capping the balance
  - Switching excess to another time type
  - Transferring excess in a wage type
  - Transferring the old value of the processed balance in another time type so that it is still available for evaluation purposes
- It is even possible to output a message to provide a warning shortly before reaching the threshold value. To do this, you must specify a tolerance that enters at what interval for the threshold value the message is to be generated.
- By limiting the limit rule regarding the age of the employee, you can, for example, generate a message if a violation of the youth labor law occurs.

8.2.8 Incentive Wage

The component for the incentive wage in time management includes the entry or automatic generation of time tickets for individual and group premiums and their valuation with labor utilization rates.

Data Sources

The rules in the incentive wage are company specific. As a result, the remuneration also has to account for particular circumstances in production. This means there are frequently different incentive wage models within a company and even within a plant. In the following section, we will describe the standard solution and some strengths and weaknesses.

The HCM system requires basic data on the incentive wage in time tickets. These entry screens are similar to paper time tickets still used today for the initial entry of data that is relevant to wages. The time ticket data can be transferred to the HCM system via three different paths:

- Manual entry via the following menu path Human Resources • Time Management • Incentive Wages • Time Tickets
- Time evaluation that generates time tickets from work time events in logistics
- Transfer of time tickets from logistics via the following menu path Human Resources • Time Management • Incentive Wages • Environment • Subsystem Connection • Logistics Integration • Time Tickets • Create session

The last two variants are preferable because of data quality and entry effort. They must meet the following prerequisites:

- Logistics must be operational in the same system as HCM, or an ALE connection to the logistics system must be set up.
- The confirmations must be assigned to personnel numbers in logistics.
- Run-schedule headers are not used (the notification of goods receipt for run-schedule headers does not allow the entry of personnel numbers — a useful integration demands the modification of the system at several points).
- Only individual incentive wages; no group incentive wages are calculated. (Group numbers for SAP ERP HCM cannot be supplied in logistics. By assembling user exits, you can implement an integration with suitable conventions for group incentive wages without carrying out modifications.)

Systematics of Result Calculation

Further processing now occurs in the incentive-wage components. Figure 8.42 shows an overview of the process. The dates of the time tickets are processed for groups and employee levels according to the rules of a premium formula, and they then supply the result (e.g., performance efficiency rate).

The time-ticket values are first accumulated (actual times, standard times, time credits, etc.) via accumulation rules in collectors (result types). The result is finally calculated from these values, and additional parameters (e.g., a quality factor determined monthly) or a step function (can even lead to capping) can be integrated.

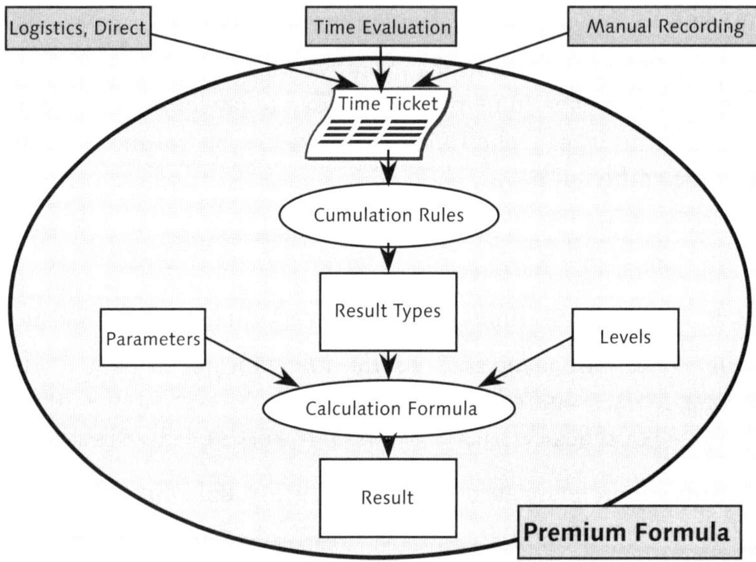

Figure 8.42 Results Calculation According to a Premium Formula

In general, at least one premium formula is required for each remuneration scenario in the incentive wage. The result determined via the premium formula on the time-ticket level or on the period level ultimately become the basis for the monetary valuation in the payroll.

There is a high flexibility in the calculation rule. It even enables the integration of customer-specific ABAP coding, so that almost every calculation rule can be implemented.

You can reach the Customizing settings for the premium formula via the following IMG path TIME MANAGEMENT • INCENTIVE WAGES • PREMIUM FORMULAS. A prerequisite is that the systematics displayed in Figure 8.42 were made from a company-specific viewpoint. Formulate the required formulas for the calculation rules, and clarify how the individual components of the formulas are to be determined (for example, what counts as secondary processing times, if these are required in the calculation). The differentiation between different types of actual times mainly occurs through the time-ticket types in which the times are entered.

Time-Ticket Types

Time tickets contain the information that is required to calculate the results. These are current and target values for working time, setup time, tear down time, and machine time, and quantities and scrap.

The HCM system uses the following time-ticket types in the standard version:

- **Premium time tickets**
  They contain times and quantities for individual employees (see Figure 8.43). A result can be formed here according to the time ticket (e.g., performance efficiency rate) and not just according to the period. The data for the premium time ticket is used exclusively to calculate individual premiums.

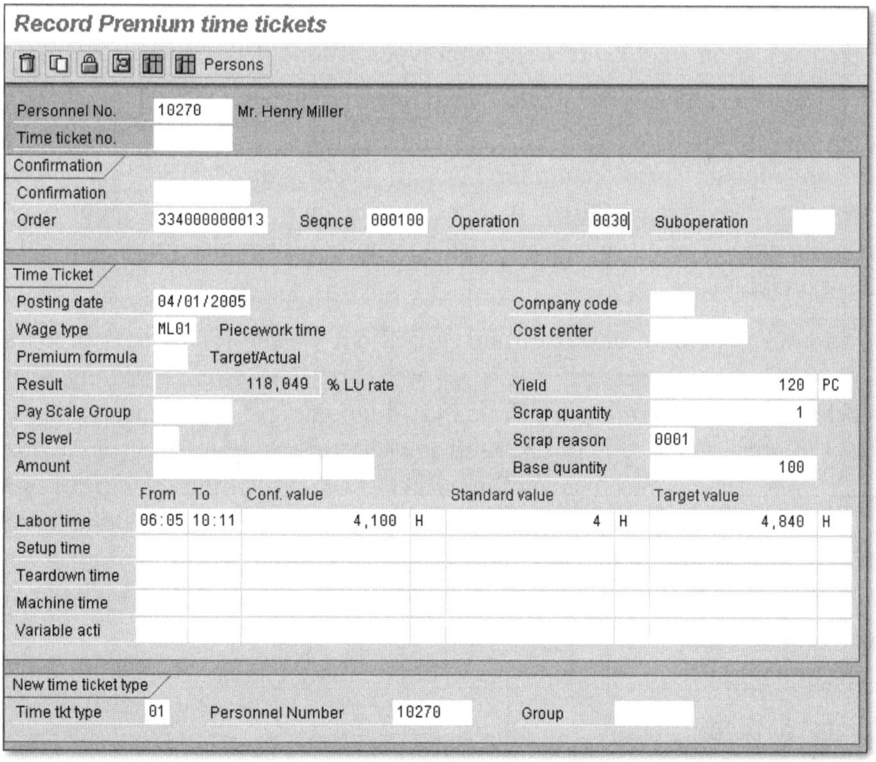

Figure 8.43 Example of a Premium Time Ticket (Individual Premium)

- **Quantity-based time tickets**
  They contain quantities for a work group. Because the times are not directly assigned here, a group result can only be calculated on the period level. The data for the quantity-based time ticket is used exclusively to calculate group premiums.
- **Person time tickets**
  These contain the attendance times for an employee in a group. In this case, an employee can be active in different groups on the same day in rotation. The data for the person time ticket is used exclusively to calculate group premiums.
- **Time-related time tickets**
  These contain the times for an employee that are not evaluated in the premium pay, but rather in the normal time wage. If necessary, however, the time is also valuated with a piece work average (e.g., the current month). In addition, the times of the time tickets can also influence the incentive wage results, for example, if they are input as malfunction periods or as secondary processing times in the calculation rule. There are several types of time tickets in one company, whose times are treated differently with regard to payment or evaluation.
- **Foreman time tickets**
  They are a mixture of premium time tickets, quantity time tickets, and person time tickets. They are used if a certain member of an incentive wage group (e.g., the foreman) not only contributes to the group result but also gathers an individual premium.

The customizing of time tickets can be carried out via the following IMG path TIME MANAGEMENT • INCENTIVE WAGES • TIME TICKET TYPES. To create your own time-ticket types, you should copy the standard time tickets. Note during conception that the time-ticket type can be used as a control criterion for accumulation in result types. The options to adapt time tickets, in particular the showing of free customer fields, have been described in sufficient detail. Interfaces can be adjusted more extensively, simply by copying and changing a Dynpro using the Screen Painter. However, as this falls into the area of interface programming, we will not go into the topic here.

Additional Settings

Additional Customizing settings are basically quite simple. However, a few settings are merely provided to activate user exits and Business Add-Ins (BAdIs), which then find their use if the corresponding programming is executed. You should therefore try to manage with as few user exits as possible. Although, in theory, user exits are "release durable," the user exits in the incentive wage have often required adjustments when changes have been made to standard structures.

Under the IMG path TIME MANAGEMENT • INCENTIVE WAGES • DEFAULT SETTINGS, the following settings are of particular importance:

- Definition of the employee subgroups that participate in the incentive wage model
- Settings for maximal retroactive calculation for the incentive wage
- Short open period for retroactive calculations (and retroactive entries) to avoid incorrect entries (e.g., incorrect annual figure).
- Using different parameters on the system, transaction, and user levels. The essential parameters are:
  - Flag indicating whether or not the breaks from the daily work schedule of the employees should be considered when calculating the actual time in the time ticket (do not set if the breaks are not precisely adhered to)
  - Indicators whether accumulations are formed not only on monthly levels but also on daily levels
  - Activating messages when creating, maintaining, and displaying time tickets; if required, they can be overridden on the user level
  - Initialization of fields when creating, maintaining, and displaying time tickets; if required, this can be overridden on the user level
  - Activation of user exits

Groups don't have to be created in advance in Customizing. Under the IMG path TIME MANAGEMENT • INCENTIVE WAGES • GROUPS only permissible group numbers are defined.

The integration to logistics is primarily a question of the subsystem settings (for the variants through PDC work time events) and the process definition in alignment with logistics. Via IMG path TIME MANAGEMENT • INCENTIVE WAGES • INTEGRATION WITH LOGISTICS, the subsequent changeability of time tickets from logistics is determined. In addition, you can set small integration here. This means that in manual entry of the time tickets, certain data is read from logistics (e.g., standard values) and set in the time ticket, based on the confirmation number that is entered or the order and sequence numbers.

Strengths and Challenges in Use of the HCM Incentive Wage

To decide if incentive wage processing is to be set in the HCM system, you must consider the following points. Alternatives include use of an external system or manual written entry where the completed remuneration data is provided manually or by machine via Infotype 2010 for the payroll.

The following are the strengths of incentive wage processing:

- The options for entering are quite comprehensive in the standard version.
- You can implement the confidentiality principle.
- The calculation process for the performance efficiency rate or additional results is extremely flexible.
- There is a high degree of flexibility in evaluating the payroll.
- An integration in the companywide data pool with personnel, logistics, and CO data is possible.
- The integrated process from logistics to HCM minimizes the complexity in making entries and maximizes the data quality.
- Time-leveling enables the checking of covered times for production employees.

On the other hand, you can identify the following challenges:

- You can only produce flexibility with a very high degree of complexity in Customizing and programming.
- Only a few reporting options are offered by default.
- The authorization concept and the locking concept for groups with frequent group changes can be disruptive depending on company processing steps.
- The ergonomics in the time ticket entry are far from ideal.
- The integration from logistics for serial orders and group premiums is problematic.
- The mapping of time tickets kept in reserve to improve the piece-rate during slack periods is quite unsatisfactory.

8.2.9 Reporting in Time Management

For the systematics of reporting and the use of queries, you can apply the same information that is detailed in Chapter 11, "HR Reporting."

The evaluations for time management are primarily based on the following points:

- Time types assigned as daily or period balances from time evaluation
- Time wage types that must be formed in time evaluation (if the monetary valuation is integrated in the evaluation, the evaluation must occur in payroll)
- Infotypes of time management
- Time ticket data, results, and accumulation of the incentive wage

The following section describes a few helpful reports by means of example. You can reach all of these evaluations via the following menu path Human Resources • Time Management • Administration • Information System • Report Selection:

- **Attendance and absence overview graphic**
  This evaluation should replace the Microsoft Excel–supported leave lists in the individual departments. It is an exceptional online tool that enables you to navigate from the overview screen to the details data. Figure 8.44 shows this overview by means of an example. It is possible to provide this evaluation to management decentrally via the Manager's Desktop (MDT) (see Section 2.5). However, for their vacation planning, managers also need the leave requests of their employees that are usually not yet entered in the system as absence records. At this point it is possible to introduce a new absence type that could be called Leave request. The employee can then enable the maintenance via the ESS (see Section 2.4). After completing the vacation planning the requests can be transformed into real leave records.
- **Evaluation attendance/absence data overview**
  It enables creation of different forms of absence statistics that, for example, aggregate the absence times in general or those restricted to certain types and connect them to the planned time. This also enables comparable statuses for employee sickness for individual departments.

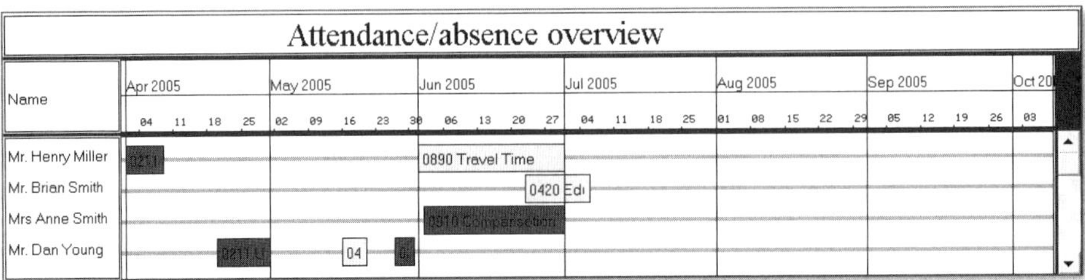

Figure 8.44 Attendances and Absences Overview Graphic

- **Evaluation of cumulated time-evaluation results**
  It enables almost any kind of meaningful evaluation that is based on daily balances, monthly balances, or time-wage types. Different summation levels are also possible here. The only limitation: It is not possible to display several time types in columns near each other. If several time types are being evaluated this only makes sense if they are to be added.
- **Time-balance overview**
  It provides an overview of several time types, but is less flexible in the output. The time-balance overview must first be set using the Form Editor of the time statement in Customizing. It is very useful in providing management with evaluations that can always be compared and which give an overview of the balance statuses of employees.
- **Quota overview**
  It provides a similar functionality for quotas from Infotype 2006 (Display Absence Quota Information).

8.2.10 Integration Aspects

The integration of time management in the SAP ERP system also contains module-internal components within HCM and module-external components in relation to accounting and logistics (see Figure 8.45).

Module-Internal Integration

Module-internal integration spans the collaboration with the part components PT Cross-Application Time Sheet (CATS) , PT Shift Planning (SP), Training and Event Management (PE)), and Payroll (PY).

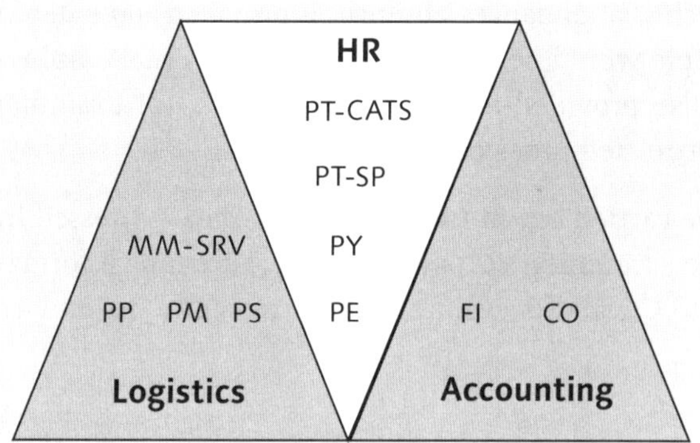

Figure 8.45 Integration Aspects of Time Management

The CATS enables you to enter time data across modules and to transfer data to other modules. Plausibility controls are available within the entry. This means, for example, that it is possible to check order numbers or cost centers. The transition is carried out via a defined interface.

You can plan the assignment of employees quantitatively and qualitatively and in relation to the present or the future with resource planning. Because this functionality is a component of time management, you can access the current status at any time, create a target plan on this basis, and, if necessary, transfer this as a new current status in time management.

Seminar participations or assignments as instructors in training and event management can automatically generate attendance records in Infotype 2002, in cases where the corresponding integration is activated in Customizing in event management.

Payroll accesses data records created in time management (time-wage types, absences, personal work schedules) and processes these in the payroll run.

Module-External Integration

Module-external integration concerns the processes of logistics and accounting. This is particularly relevant in logistics MM-SRV (External Services), PP (Product Planning), PM (Maintenance), and P (Project System). In accounting, Controlling (CO) and FI are affected. For the public sector, you must also consider funds management.

For the logistics module, data such as attendances/absences is provided and entered for capacity planning. An example would be working times for external employees by CATS. Logistics data is also provided for time management, for example, through confirmations for order-related times or incentive wages.

Integration in accounting can be carried out in two ways. Time data expressed in monetary values is transferred to accounting via payroll and FI. Pure time information, i.e., hours, is transferred to CO and is evaluated there according to activity types and used in cost allocation.

8.3 Time Manager's Workplace (TMW)

TMW has a similar purpose for time administrators as the MDT (see Section 2.5) for managers. However, while the MDT becomes obsolete when MSS is available via the portal (see Section 2.4.6), the TMW is still used, because the portal doesn't provide an equivalent tool for it.

8.3.1 Application and Functionalities

In most companies, time administration is carried out in a decentralized manner. Checking and error removal for postings via time clocks, the recording of attendance times (if no terminals are being used), and absences are being shifted more and more to decentralized units. This is supposed to facilitate the processes by recording the information where it occurs and making it easier to process queries. Administrative assistants or other employees take on the role of decentralized time administrators. For these employees time recording is only a "sideline job" that they accept along with their main job. This makes an easy-to-manage and easy-to-use interface especially important. Users who previously worked in decentralized island solutions, which weren't integrated with central evaluation systems and payroll, find the requirements of an integrated environment very complex anyway. Acceptance should therefore not be threatened further by unnecessarily complicated data entry, where the user has to navigate through many different screens.

TMW was specifically created by SAP AG for decentralized time administrators in departments, production islands, branches, or affiliates. The essential advantage here is that all administrative activities of time management are basically possible without a change of transaction. The TMW compiles all of the information on the different infotypes of time management into one interface that is attached to the existing data structures. It enables considerably easier maintenance than is possible through the individual infotypes of time management. The information entered through TMW is stored in the familiar infotypes of time management (e.g., absences in Infotype 2001).

Introduction in the TMW

When you first use the TMW, you must enter the profile and definition area for IDs. The profile determines the complete layout and the adjustable functionalities of the TMW. Instead of attendance or absence types and quota types, the TMW works with IDs that are compiled in the definition quantity and, if necessary, existing subsets of this definition area.

Figure 8.46 shows the initial screen for calling the TMW (Transaction PTMW, Easy Access Menu HUMAN RESOURCES • TIME MANAGEMENT • ADMINISTRATION • TIME MANAGER'S WORKPLACE).

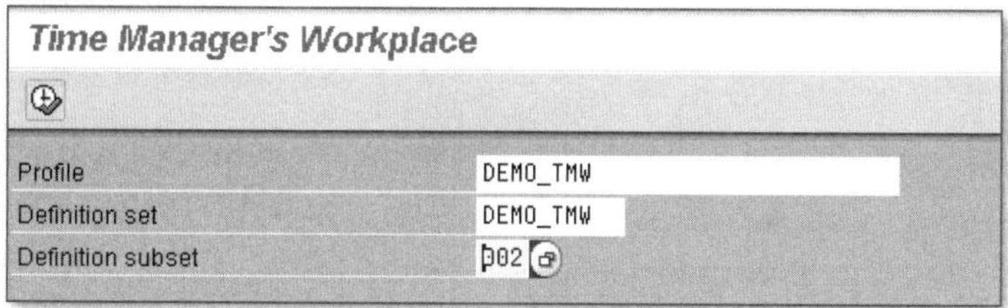

Figure 8.46 Initial Screen for the Initial Call of the TMW

The data is then stored in the user defaults as parameters PT_TMW_PROFILE (for the profile) and PT_TMW_TDLANGU (for the definition area and subset). If you want to avoid the initial screen, you can maintain this data upfront via the following menu SYSTEM • USER PROFILE • OWN DATA. In the Parameters tab, you can enter the corresponding values. Here the subset of the definition area is connected to the definitions area, separated by a slash (e.g., definitions area DEMO_TMW and subset 001, entry: TMW_DEMO/001). However, the simplest variant for the user is to specify the user parameter centrally through user administration.

Basic Structure

The TMW is divided into different screen areas. Figure 8.47 gives an initial overview of the graphical screen areas within the TMW. In the standard version, the

Dialog Messages area is located below the Editing time data in detail area. However, for reasons of clarity we recommend you place the dialog messages above the info area.

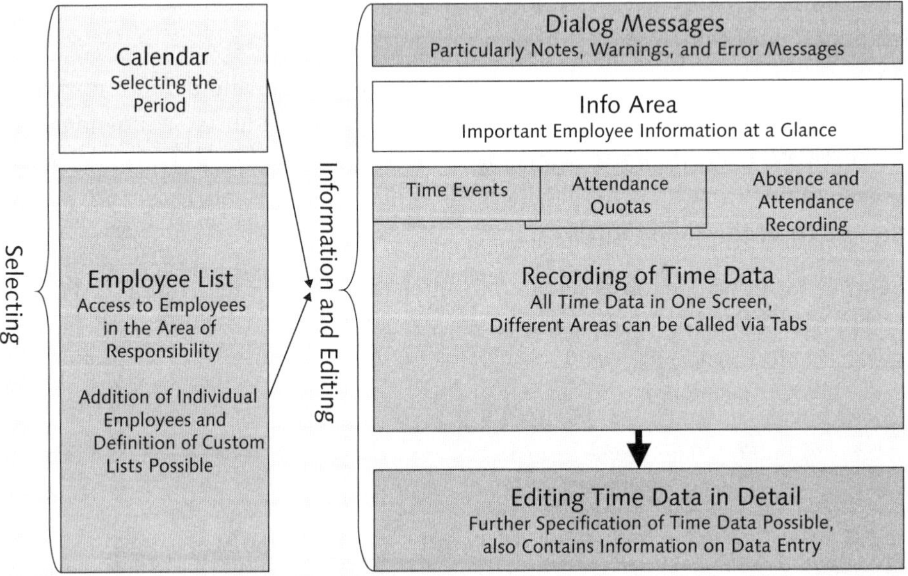

Figure 8.47 Layout and Screen Areas in TMW

The adjustment is executed via system table T77S0. Figure 8.48 shows the required settings.

Change View "System Table": Overview

New entries | Documentation

Group	Sem.abbr.	Value abbr	Description
PTMW	MLTOP	X	

Figure 8.48 Entry in System Table (T77S0) to Position the Message Line in the Upper Screen Area

The TMW provides the following views in the data-entry section that refer to the period and the employees:

- **One-day view**
  Places an employee into the data-entry section for maintenance on a specific day.
- **Multiday view**
  Enables you to maintain a period for an employee that is previously selected through the calendar.
- **Multiperson view**
  Permits the maintenance of time data for several employees at the same time for a selected day. You can transfer several employees into the data entry section by selecting the employee (hold down the [⇧] or [Ctrl] key and select) and then clicking the "Transfer Selected Records" button. In the multiperson view, you can maintain a one-day vacation absence for a team in one step.
- **Team view**
  The team view provides data for several employees for a selected period. This is particularly useful for planning vacations or shifts.

Figure 8.49 shows the use of the TMW.

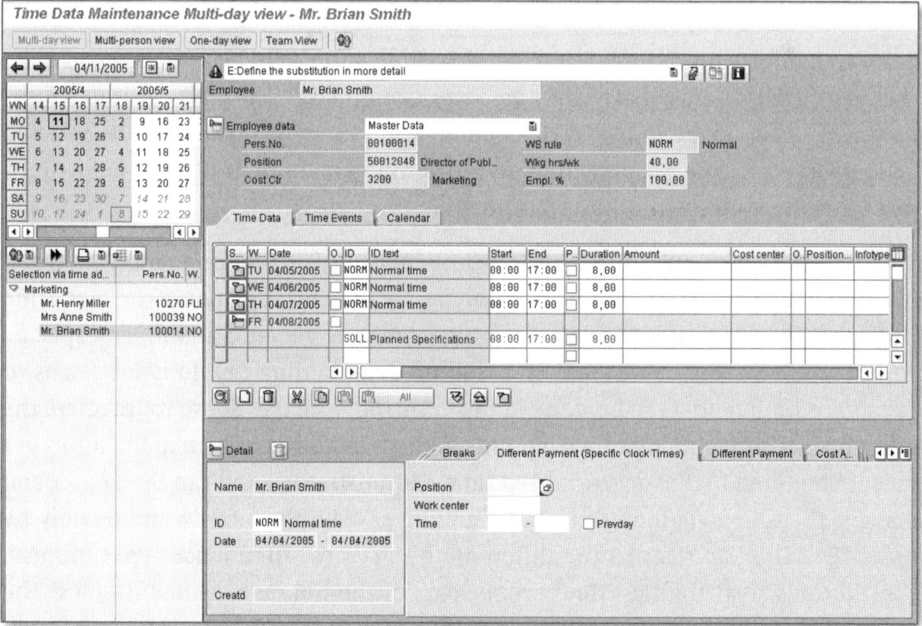

Figure 8.49 TMW in Use

The views can be called via the corresponding buttons in the upper part of the calendar. Via Customizing, you can define the available views, the tabs that are visible in each view, and the data to be displayed and maintained.

Working in the TMW

The period selection is very simple in the calendar. By clicking on the day, the week, the month, or by selecting a period, the days of the selected period are provided in the multiday view in the data entry section for making entries.

The employees assigned to the time administrators appear in the employee list. You can structure the selection of employees for the employee list very flexibly in Customizing. This way, you can make a selection via the time administrators from Infotype 0001 or via a predefined selection path. This also gives you the option to create your own employee lists in the application. This can be done by using the button EMPLOYEE LIST • MAINTAIN YOUR OWN EMPLOYEE LIST in a selection screen similar to the Ad-hoc Query. The temporary addition of individual employees in the employee list is possible through this button. The employee list can also be adjusted in the layout without a problem. The adjustment is carried out similarly to the layout formation in SAP List Viewer.

Employee information is not immediately visible upon calling the TMW, you must click on the Detail button or select an entry from the selection list for it to be displayed. The employee information is defined in Customizing and can be selected from a variety of master and time data. The implementation of new fields (e.g., from customer-specific infotypes) is possible through Customizing.

The data-entry section consists of tabs in which the data maintenance is carried out, and which actually contain the infotypes of time management. The tabs Time Data and Time Events are available in the standard version; a company-specific adjustment (showing additional tabs, hiding or renaming previous tabs, tabs to expand or limit fields) can be done in Customizing. It makes sense to integrate the infotypes according to logical viewpoints in the tabs and to only map the infotypes that are required by the decentralized time administrators. You can then enter and manage the time data for one or more employees simultaneously and flexibly by using IDs. The IDs refer to the different absence and attendance types, quotas, substitutions, availabilities, time events, etc., of the time-management types. The assignment takes place in Customizing. If you consider the data-entry section in more detail, you will notice that the entry of events for several days in the entry section no longer seems possible, because only one day can be edited at a time. It helps to open the details area, in which the data for events of several days can also be entered.

You can call the details area by selecting the tab and activating the Detail button under the period display in the data-entry section, or by double-clicking on the ID field. In this details area, you can carry out more detailed specifications to the time data entered in the data-entry section. You can see and store even more information in the details area, such as the information that must be added to an attendance quota (how many hours does it comprise, are the hours entered to be paid for or transferred to a time account, etc.) or additional information that can be entered as plain text. Establishing which information is displayed and maintained here is carried out in Customizing. You can make a selection here from a variety of data that is already available as standard. It is also possible to adjust both the tab itself and the tab content.

However, the TMW has a grave weakness when making entries: Field properties that were changed in table T588M (see Section 4.2.4, Figure 4.26) are ignored when making entries in the TMW. This leads to constant problems if certain field content is required for a smooth flow of time management, including time evaluation. The definition of a compulsory field in table T588M is sufficient for direct entry in time-management infotypes. When using TMWs, it is possible to forget the maintenance of fields. It is recommended to integrate programmed plausibility checks.

In the Dialog messages area, the user receives notes, warnings, and error messages as confirmations of their entries. In this area, you can also process error notifications (previously Time management pool, Transaction PT40). You can call the message processing in the menu via the path GOTO • PROCESS MESSAGES. The user can click on the line of the employee to be processed, after which the data for this employee appears in the entry section and, if necessary, in the details area. The error removal is then carried out there.

8.3.2 Customizing

Customizing the TMW is characterized less by complexity and more by a considerable scope. Nearly all screen areas can be flexibly adjusted to the company requirements. Customizing is carried out in the IMG via Time Management • Time Manager's Workplace.

Profile in the TMW

The central concept in customizing the TMW is the profile that is created for different user groups with the same requirements and activities. Therefore, depending on the specifics of the company, it makes sense to define several profiles. It would be conceivable here to have a profile for the administrative assistants who handle the employees in time management and a profile for those who are responsible for maintaining industrial workers. The TMW is called through the profile. This compiles nearly all settings, and this way looks after the layout, the information displayed, the data that can be maintained, and the available functionalities. The TMW establishes the following:

- Use of the initial period (the period selected in the calendar)
- Tasks that the users are allowed to execute (only managing time data or message processing)
- Permissible menu functions (navigating from the TMW to the display or the maintenance of master data, starting time evaluation, and displaying the time statement)
- Available employee information for the users
- Available views (one-day, multiday, and multiperson view) for the users
- Messages in the scope of message processing
- Available processing instructions (checkboxes that can be used to generate customer-specific records for Infotype 2012, which the time administrators no longer have to generate manually)
- Display of the names of the employees in the employee list and in the multiperson view
- Selection options for the users in the employee list and available fields in the list layout
- Appearance of the lines in the time-recording area when called

It is merely the IDs and the message-processing control that are not assigned to the profile.

Basic Systematics of TMW Customizing

The basic systematics for customizing appear quite simple. The difficulty — as is often the case — lies in the detail. Only an optimal well-thought-out customizing of the details level guarantees that the TMW actually reaches its aim: the efficient support of time administrators in their daily business. Figure 8.50 will clarify the basic process.

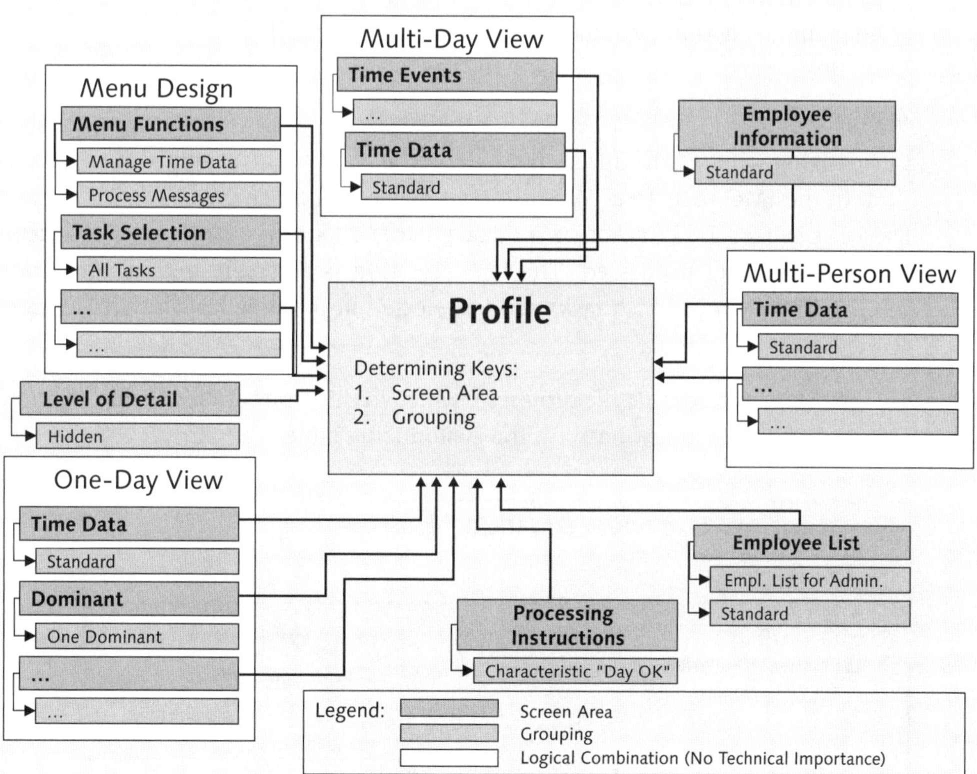

Figure 8.50 Systematics of TMW Customizing

For Figure 8.50 it is noteworthy that all of the screen areas display summarized information, data, and functionalities in TMW under a rubric (the screen area). No new screen areas can be defined.

Customizing is carried out — aside from the exceptions mentioned earlier — in a three-step process:

1. A Grouping is defined. The grouping, however, is not named as such. Concepts such as field selection, selection ID, or layout ID are used.
2. You establish which information, data, or functionalities the groupings span.
3. The grouping is assigned to the profile. You specifically establish here which information and data defined in the second step are visible to the user or can be maintained, and also that functionalities can be called.

Task Selection

Customizing will be introduced in detail on the basis of the example of task selection. In the IMG path TIME MANAGEMENT • TIME MANAGER'S WORKPLACE • MENU DESIGN • DEFINE TASK SELECTION • CREATE PROFILES AND ASSIGN FIELD SELECTIONS the two items are processed. The task selection is a screen area (abbreviation TSK) and it controls which tasks can be selected in the menu of the TMW under "Goto."

The first step is to now set the grouping, which in this case is called Field Selection. Figure 8.51 shows a new entry in the customizing table.

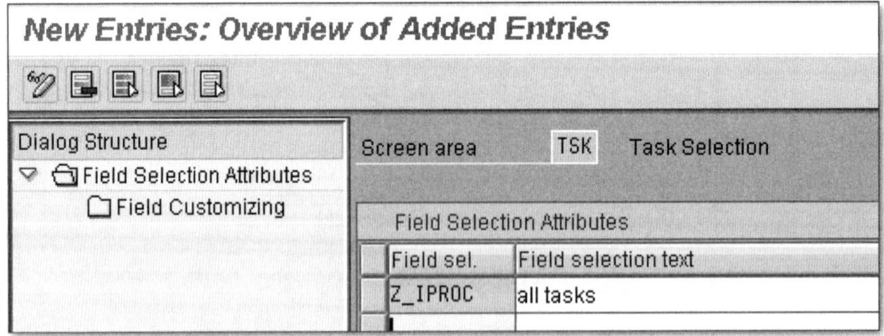

Figure 8.51 Forming a Grouping for the Task Selection

The second step is to establish the tasks that the grouping Z_IPROC spans (see Figure 8.52).

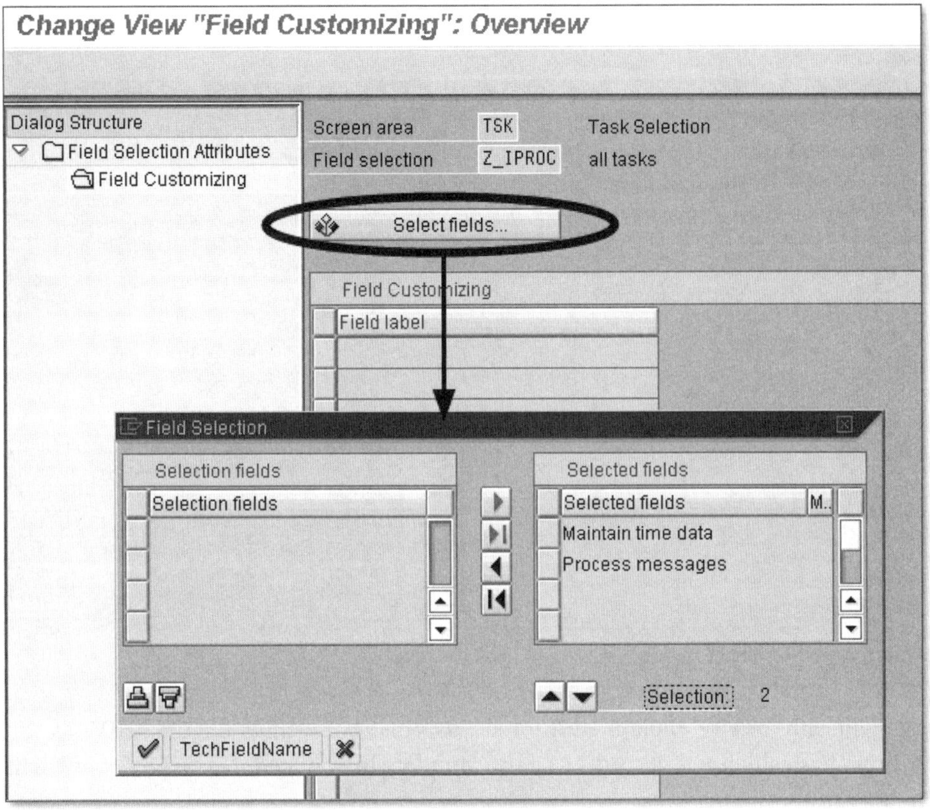

Change View "Field Customizing": Overview

Dialog Structure
Field Selection Attributes
Field Customizing

Screen area TSK Task Selection
Field selection Z_IPROC all tasks

Select fields...

Field Customizing
Field label

Field Selection
Selection fields
Selection fields
Selected fields
Selected fields M..
Maintain time data
Process messages
Selection: 2
TechFieldName

Figure 8.52 Establishing the Tasks that Can Be Executed

In the last step, you assign the field selection to the profile (see Figure 8.53).

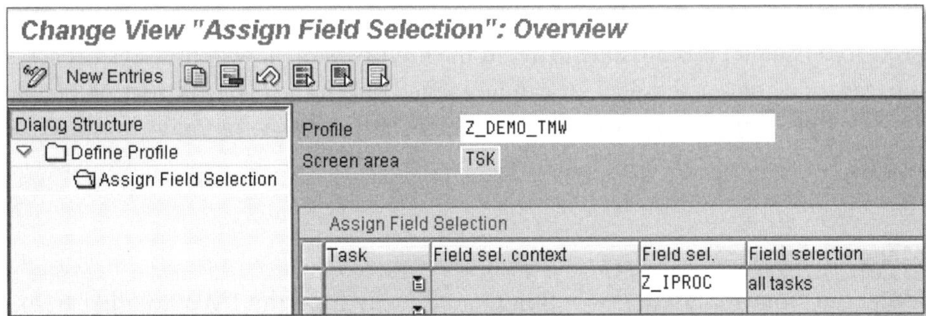

Figure 8.53 Assigning the Field Selection to the Profile

Figure 8.54 then shows the results of the Customizing settings in the application.

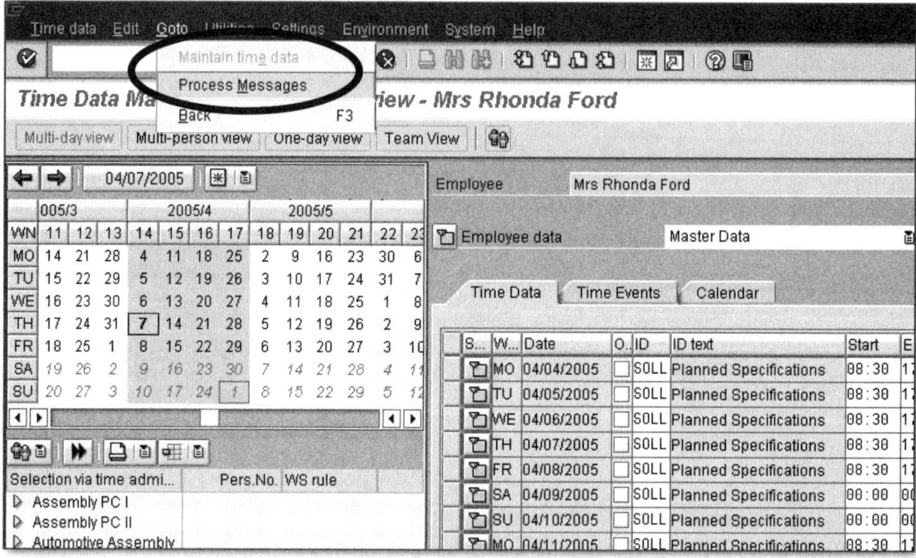

Figure 8.54 Results of the Customizing in the Task Selection

We will only briefly explain additional Customizing settings for the TMW as the process basically flows according to the template introduced. Nonetheless, we will name the special features.

Assigning Views

For both tasks (managing time data and processing messages) you can define which views are available (one-day, multiday, and multiperson) by calling the respective task. For example, it is possible to avoid the multiperson view in message processing. Customizing for these views can be carried out in the IMG via Time Management • Time Manager's Workplace • Menu Design • Define Views for Tasks • Create Profiles and Assign Field Selections.

Menu Functions

Menu functions represent the option to go directly from the TMW to other transactions. In the TMW, you can call these transactions via the menu items Utilities (start time evaluation, display time statement form, call employee) and Environment (maintain HR master data and display HR master data). The utilities Start time evaluation and Display time statement form represent time-management reports. If these menu functions are used, you must create the variants of the report and store them in the feature LLREP. The structure used for the feature allows for a very fine control up to the user level or a transaction. You will find more information on working with features in Appendix A, "Cross-Process Customizing Tools." You can define the settings in the IMG via TIME MANAGEMENT • TIME MANAGER'S WORKPLACE • MENU DESIGN • DEFINE MENU FUNCTIONS/CREATE PROFILES AND ASSIGN FIELD SELECTIONS.

Processing Instructions

In the TMW, processing instructions are represented by checkboxes from which a data record of Infotype 2012 (Time Transfer Specifications) is generated. This spares the time administrators the task of data maintenance for frequently recurring cases. An example of this would be the regular authorization of overtime hours. To implement this functionality, it is necessary to define previous time types, to create new personnel calculation rules in time management, and to adjust the schema of time management correspondingly. The settings will therefore not be dealt with in more detail here.

Employee List and Employee Info

The fields displayed in the Employee List are also implemented in Customizing according to the process introduced here (IMG path TIME MANAGEMENT • TIME MANAGER'S WORKPLACE • SCREEN AREAS • EMPLOYEE LIST • DEFINE EMPLOYEE LIST DISPLAY / ASSIGN FIELD SELECTIONS TO PROFILES). In addition, you have the option of displaying the employee list with a one- or two-level hierarchy.

The Employee information area involves the INF screen area. Here, the standard version contains predefined field selections that can be assigned to the profile. The definition of new field selections with fields is then only required if the standard is insufficient. For this reason, you must define the master data or time data upfront in the IMG via TIME MANAGEMENT • TIME MANAGER'S WORKPLACE • BASIC SETTINGS • SELECT HR MASTER DATA AND TIME DATA to define master data or time data, and to subsequently integrate it in a layout for employee information. The layouts are then accepted in the INF screen area and assigned to a profile.

Configuring the Data Entry

Customizing the data entry section is somewhat more difficult as the groupings are not immediately recognizable here and the definition of the column configurations occurs at an unexpected point.

The data-entry section can be set up separately for the one-day, multiday, and multiperson views (IMG path Time Management • Time Manager's Workplace • Screen Areas • Time Data Maintenance). The Time Data and Time Events tabs are available in the standard version. Both of these tabs can be set flexibly in terms of column configurations (i.e., which fields are displayed and which of those are prepared for entries for data maintenance). It is also possible to define additional tabs and to incorporate different views.

Additional tabs can be defined by copying existing sample entries provided by SAP. In each case a sample entry similar to the Time Data and Time Events tabs is available. You must copy sample entries because technical settings are attached to the sample entries that are required for the new tabs. You can integrate a new tab-strip in the data entry section in field-customizing of the IMG activity Add Tabs in Time Data Maintenance Screen Area and not — as you may have expected — when defining the field selection for the profile.

The column configuration for a new tab is carried out in the table of the tabs that the copy is based on. If a new tab was created on the basis of the tab Time Data, the column configuration is carried out in the IMG activity Define Table for Time Data. Here, you must create a new field selection with the corresponding field-customizing (answering the question: Which information should the columns displayed contain?). Finally, the assignment of the field selection to the profile for the screen area Time Events or Time Data is carried out (one-day, multiday, or multi-person view), not in the (one-day, multi-day, or multi-person view) tabs. Figure 8.55 clarifies the contexts.

You can only populate fields in the time-data table via user exits according to your rules, but not in the time-events table.

In the time-data entry area, you can also control whether certain lines in the TMW should be shown or hidden at start-up. If the decision is made in favor of hidden lines when entering the TMW, you can display these lines by clicking on the Detail button.

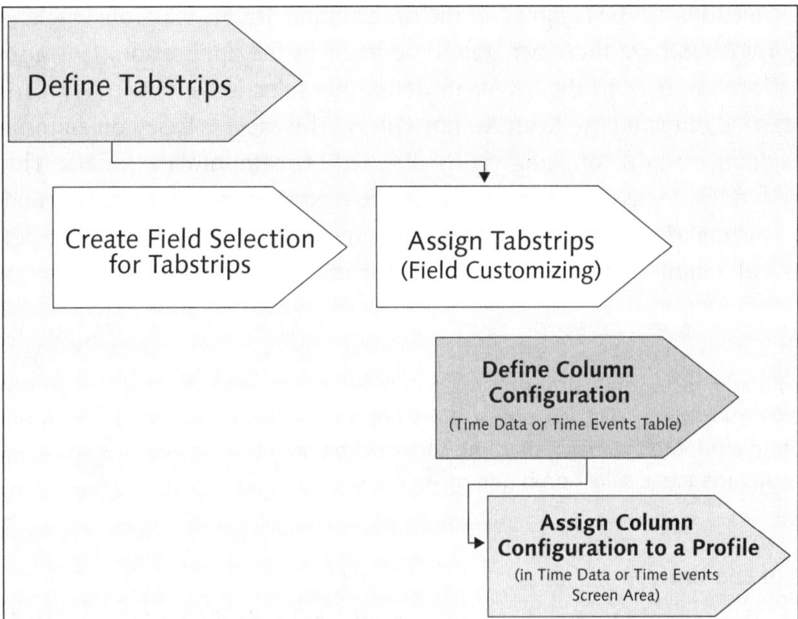

Figure 8.55 Customizing Context of Tabs

For the time data, you can define additional detail information according to infotype in the corresponding screen section. It is displayed as in the time-recording area in tabs. A fixed, defined quantity of tabs is available per infotype and for the individual work schedule. The existing tabs can be hidden according to company-specific requirements. The names of the tabs can also be adjusted.

Employee Selection

The selection of the employees assigned to the time administrators can be defined in the IMG via the path TIME MANAGEMENT • TIME MANAGER'S WORKPLACE • EMPLOYEE SELECTION. The definition of selection IDs specifies the actual selection of employees. The following options are available to establish the selection:

- Selection via a freely definable evaluation path
- Selection via the characteristics of different fields (e.g., via time administrators)
- Selection via a function module
- Selection by combining alternatives already mentioned

The defined selections can be assigned to the time administrators via profile assignment in the TMW and are then available by default in the application. It is also possible to allow the user in the TMW to define his selection interactively. The selection is carried out similarly to an Ad-hoc Query. This view is based on an infoset, which is defined in Customizing via IMG activity Create InfoSets for HR. The defined selection IDs are assigned to a group in the next step and are then assigned to a profile. This makes it possible to eliminate interactive employee selection, as the profile is not assigned any selection ID for the interactive search.

Tip: Consistency between Employee Selection and Authorizations

Align the time administrators' authorizations to the employee selection (e.g., by using the same evaluation path). This ensures against unpleasant surprises if the authorizations permitted are more extensive than the set selection, and the employee is permitted to make an interactive selection based on an infoset.

Entire View of the Profile

The profile of the central key for the TMW, on which nearly all settings depend, can be adjusted in the IMG activity Check and Complete Profiles. Here you can find all of the settings that were previously only partially available, in the form of a navigation tree. This is always helpful if the customizing knowledge is so good that the concepts used can be directly assigned to an area in the application. This means the changes can be carried out quickly and easily, provided the assignments of previous settings have already been completed.

Parameter Transactions

The implementation of parameter transactions is also relevant. Their use is recommended if several profiles are being used. A parameter transaction calls the TMW with the assigned profile, definition set, and, if necessary, the IDs and definition subset, as this transaction is assigned via the authorization of a specific role. The user can only call the TMW with parameters assigned to it in the role.

Message Processing

Finally, we will describe the areas without direct profile assignment. Message processing belongs to these areas, including the description of the messages. Messages can be summarized according to criteria such as the same processing procedures or similar message type (e.g., all types of violations against working time laws or flextime regulation). The functional area is the superordinate term for the messages that were summarized. In Customizing, the definition of the functional areas is carried out first and then the assignment of the messages to the functional areas. All messages that are assigned to a functional area are displayed in the message view under the nodes of a message functional area. The time administrators can then call the entire message functional area here.

A further help for time administrators is the processing methods for messages. Processing methods should support the time administrators in processing messages, by showing them a specific note text and defined contextual information. Customizing occurs in the IMG via TIME MANAGEMENT • TIME MANAGER'S WORKPLACE • BASIC SETTINGS • SET UP MESSAGE PROCESSING • DEFINE PROCESSING METHOD and the additional IMG activities underneath Define Processing Method. However, processing methods do not necessarily have to be used.

IDs for Time Data

IDs are another area without direct profile assignment. The IDs support simplified data maintenance by the time administrators. The events lie behind the IDs (absences, attendances, substitutions, etc.) of time management. Their importance should not be underestimated.

Tip: Naming Conventions for IDs

We recommend that you assign single-digit IDs for the time-management events that are most used (e.g., S for sickness with medical certificate or A for annual leave entitlement). In addition, you should select the ID so that alphanumeric sorting facts that belong together (e.g., all types of vacation) are executed immediately after one another. This represents a great relief to the time administrators responsible for data maintenance.

Customizing of the IDs is carried out in the IMG via TIME MANAGEMENT • TIME MANAGER'S WORKPLACE • IDS FOR TIME DATA. Several events, such as absences, can be stored per ID; one of them, however, must be specified as priority. The event defined as a priority is then created as standard under the ID, but can be overwritten by one of the other events defined under this ID. However, we advise against assigning an ID to several events as this regularly leads to misunderstandings and problems in the application.

In SAP ERP HCM, the concepts of the definition area and the definition subset are used to limit the IDs. The definition quantity is nothing other than the grouping of IDs. As the definition area is stored in the user parameters of the user, it means that the users do not have to reach a selection from the IDs that are available throughout the whole company. The subset represents another option for grouping within the definition area and can therefore further limit the selection of IDs. The use of the definitions area, and, if necessary, the definition subset, is always advisable if different employee groups are processed separately by different time administrators. You could, for example, determine a definitions area for administrative assistants and supervisors here. Administrative assistants provide the employees with rolling working time. Supervisors are responsible for industrial workers with shift service.

8.3.3 Amended Delivery as of R/3 Enterprise

From R/3 Enterprise on, TMW is not provided with the core but is available with Extension 1.1. This does not mean any initial changes to the functionality, but it does mean that after a release change to R/3 Enterprise you must activate the extension for HCM, as long as the TMW is being used. The calendar views of the TMW represent the major changes to the R/3 Enterprise, and these are described in the following section.

8.4 Calendar View in the TMW

The graphical calendar views provide quick processing and a quick overview of the employee time data. Information referring to less than one day is also in the foreground for the daily and weekly calendar. In the monthly and annual calendar, there is a quick overview of all-day information.

The calendar views are based on the "normal" TMW as it has already been described in the previous section. In this section we will describe the specific characteristics in the calendar views.

8.4.1 Calendar Types

Four views for the calendar maintenance are available in TMW:

- **Annual calendar**
  The annual calendar provides a complete overview of the situation and frequency of all-day and multiday time-data referring, such as shifts and absences of employees for a calendar year, or an individually selected period.
- **Monthly calendar**
  The monthly calendar enables a quick classification of employee multiday and all-day time information and information referring to less than one day that refers to a day of the week, through the period of a calendar month and an individually selected period of several weeks.
- **Weekly calendar**
  The weekly calendar, shown in Figure 8.56, provides a very good overview of the time situation of all-day time information and time information relating to less than one day, for the period of a week.
- **One-day calendar**
  The one-day calendar shows an overview of an employee's time data related to a time spot for one day.

8.4.2 Functional Span

Figure 8.56 illustrates the calendar elements using an example of a weekly calendar. We will briefly explain the most important elements in the following sections.

ZZMRE	i	Flextime negative red	01/01/2000	12/31/9999	60,00
ZZMYE	i	Flextime negative yellow	01/01/2000	12/31/9999	40,00
ZZPRE	i	Flextime positive red	01/01/2000	12/31/9999	50,00
ZZPYE	i	Flextime positive yellow	01/01/2000	12/31/9999	30,00

Figure 8.56 Displaying Time Data in the Weekly Calendar

The information for the day is processed in both of the following categories:

Dominant

The most important information for the day in each case is displayed in the dominant. A dominant always represents a full-day piece of information. You can display information from the following infotypes in the dominants line:

- Infotype 0007 (Planned Working Time)
- Infotype 2001 (Absences)
- Infotype 2002 (Attendances)
- Infotype 2003 (Substitutions)

The dominant is always at the foreground in all views. If the time data for a day is hidden in the multiday view and the multiperson view, only the dominant information is available.

Planned Working Time

This displays the personal work schedule for the employee. If there is no existing current change to the planned working time for the employee, the regular work schedule is displayed for the employee.

Time Data for the Day

Here, we avoid all-day time data or time data referring to less than one day, such as attendances and absences or remuneration documents for the day.

8.4.3 Processing Time Data

- The IDs identified in color are executed in a legend column beside the calendar view. You can accept the IDs with Drag & Drop and insert them in the calendar. You must select the ID. By re-clicking on it, you can drag this by holding down the mouse to the desired position in the calendar view.
- The dominant is overwritten, depending on the time recording, or an all-day record is generated by dragging the ID to the dominant's line.
- As an alternative to this process, you can select a day in the calendar and transfer this to an ID by double-clicking on it.
- By double-clicking on any line of any day — excluding the date line — you can enter multiday information, all-day information, or information referring to less than one day. The details view is automatically opened for this, in which you can specify time data, in a way similar to making entries in other views.
- To change planned specifications or time data that has already been entered, the details view will be highlighted as in other views.

- If time data was entered for the wrong day by mistake, you can remove this. For this reason the relevant time data can simply be dragged to the desired new position by Drag & Drop. The same is also true for multiday time data.
- All functions for the deletion, creation, etc., of time data are available in the list-oriented views. In the annual and monthly calendar in particular, for example, more frequently emerging time data can be quickly entered. You can also copy and delete multiday time data in the calendar views.
- By selecting a period in the Calendar screen, the system automatically selects the relevant view. If you click on an individual day in the calendar, you can call the daily schedule. You can switch between the different calendar views as follows:
  - By left-clicking on the mouse on the function Change view in the calendar view, which is one level lower
  - By clicking on the Day, Week, Month, and Year buttons in any calendar view
  - By double-clicking on the Current date, Calendar week, or Month in the view, which is further detailed by one degree in each case (depending on the calendar view in which you are currently located, you can reach the corresponding view)

8.4.4 Customizing

The calendar views are mainly provided in R/3 Enterprise and SAP ERP HCM. However, it is possible to request SAP to preinstall this in release 4.6C. In this case, customizing activities are not integrated in the IMG. For this reason, we will describe the customizing using the maintenance view. This can be used in all releases.

Including the Calendar in the Time Data Entry Screen Area

To include the tab for the calendar in the multiday view, you must carry out the following steps:

1. In the IMG you must carry out the activity Time Management • Time Manager's Workplace • Screen Areas • Time Data Maintenance • Multi-Day View • Add Tabs in Time Data Maintenance Screen Area.
2. Edit the action in the screen area Add Tabs in Time Data Maintenance Screen Area.

3. Select the field selection to add to the calendar.
4. In the dialog structure, select the customizing field by double-clicking on it.
5. Click on Select fields.
6. Complement the selection with the field Calendar.

Defining Data Sources of the Time Data
Here you define the data sources from which the information is displayed in the calendars.

1. Call Transaction SM34.
2. Enter VC_PT_FIELD_SELECTION_INF in the view cluster and select Maintain.
3. To process the time data, select the CAL screen area.
4. Select the field selection to be processed.
5. Select Field Customizing by double-clicking on it.
6. Select Select fields.
7. Select a maximum of two desired data sources and transfer them to the Selected fields area.
8. Then you must include the calendar type in the IMG for time management TIME MANAGEMENT • TIME MANAGER'S WORKPLACE • PROFILES • CHECK AND COMPLETE PROFILES.
9. Select the profile in which this new field selection is to appear.
10. Select Assign multi-day view in the dialog structure by double-clicking on it.
11. Enter the screen area CAL and hit [↵].
12. Enter the individual calendar types for the data sources required in each case.

Defining Information to be Displayed
In this activity you can determine the visual appearance of the calendar:

1. Select Transaction SM34.
2. Enter VC_PT_FIELD_SELECTION_INF in the view cluster and select the screen area CAL.
3. Select the field selection to be processed, and select Field Customizing by double-clicking on it.

4. Select Select fields.
5. Here you can select the information blocks to be displayed in the respective calendars. If required, you can enter a separating line between the individual blocks and change the sequence of the individual blocks.
6. Then you must include the calendar type in the IMG: TIME MANAGEMENT • TIME MANAGER'S WORKPLACE • PROFILES • CHECK AND COMPLETE PROFILES.
7. Select the profile in which this new field selection is to appear.
8. Assign the selection Assign multi-day view in the dialog structure by double-clicking on it.
9. Enter the screen area CAL and select [↵].
10. Here you can process the optical appearance by entering the individual calendar types for the desired field selection.

Defining the Layout of the Dominant Lines

In this activity you can define which information is to be output in the dominant lines of the daily schedule, weekly calendar, and monthly calendar.

In general, you can output fields from the following infotypes in the dominants line:

- Infotype 0007 (Planned Working Time)
- Infotype 2001 (Absences)
- Infotype 2002 (Attendances)
- Infotype 2003 (Substitutions)

Customer-specific fields can also be output in the dominant lines. There are three text fields and three hourly fields that can be populated with SAP expansion PTIMTMW.

In the annual calendar it generally makes sense to output dominants as the information displayed there is output once again either during the planned time or as time data. In the annual calendar it is advisable not to output any dominants.

The dominant for a day as it also appears in the list-oriented views, is always displayed. Depending on the width of the column, the ID of the dominant or the text of the dominant is output.

The following steps are necessary to maintain the dominant lines:

1. Select Transaction SM34.
2. Enter VC_PT_FIELD_SELECTION_INF in the view cluster and select the screen area CAL.
3. Select New Entries.
4. Create a field selection for the daily schedule, weekly calendar, and monthly calendar and specify a relevant name.
5. Select [↵] and select a field selection.
6. Select the Field Customizing by double-clicking on it.
7. Click on Select Fields.
8. Now you can select the fields that are to be output and determine the sequence.
9. Click on Next.
10. If necessary, you can specify in the Display Type field if the value or the text of a time recording is to be displayed. If nothing is entered here the system automatically transfers the value.
11. Save the entries and carry out the following IMG activity Time Management • Time Manager's Workplace • Profile • Check and Complete Profiles.
12. Select the profile that the list should read out when not using that set as default.
13. Select Assign Multi-Day View in the dialog structure by double-clicking on it.
14. Enter the screen area CAD and select [↵].
15. For the individual calendar types you must enter the desired field selection to display the dominant line in each case.

Defining Input Help for the IDs

With this activity you can form the list of IDs for the type of time recording at the left margin. These settings are also valid for the calendar types and the IDs.

There are the following options:

- For experienced users, it is possible to only output the IDs (field selection HIDE).

- For less experienced users you should output these with the texts of the IDs (field selection TEXT).
- The list can be completely hidden so that the users can enter new time data only via the details screen (field selection TDTYPE).

Implement the following steps in the IMG:

1. Select the path Time Management • Time Manager's Workplace.
2. Check the path Profile • Check and complete Profiles and complete it in the IMG.
3. Select the profile that the list should read out when not using that set as default.
4. Select Assign multi-day view in the dialog structure by double-clicking on it.
5. Enter the screen area TDT and select [↵].
6. Select New Entries and maintain the desired field selection.

8.5 Process Examples

The following examples illustrate the degree of flexibility for the time management design. These examples are internationally applicable.

8.5.1 Flextime Model with Traffic Lights

Flextime accounts in most companies have a fixed upper limit. When this limit is exceeded, the balance is often capped. The aim of not allowing flextime accounts to turn into self-service shops is definitely the right idea. However, the automatic capping shifts a management problem to the IT system. Balance statuses that are too high are caused by employees using their time irresponsibly or by a workload that is actually too high. The latter is more often than not a case of a lack of planning on the part of management.

Capping often serves to demoralize employees. The traffic light model, which is often used, is more useful. Once the yellow phase is reached, a conversation is triggered between the employee and the supervisor. As a result, the supervisor plans the working time of the employee restrictively and must therefore send him, home if he, is not absolutely needed. Once the red phase is reached, another conversation takes place, in which the personnel department and, if necessary, the employee representatives participate. Measures to improve the workload are then discussed with superiors. The planning of working time can be directly manipulated by the HR department.

The model may appear to be unrealistic. In practice, however, this often quickly leads to a responsible treatment of working time as a resource. This also provides as much, if not more, room to maneuver for lower threshold values as for upper threshold values. This lets the employee know that a positive balance status is not seen in a positive light.

Mapping in HCM is quite simple. In the standard version, the creation of a flextime balance is done via time type 0005. The threshold values must be stored in the system. This can be done via the table of constants T511k (see Figure 8.57). You can freely select the codes for the constants within the customer namespace.

ZZMRE	i	Flextime negative red	01/01/2000	12/31/9999	60,00
ZZMYE	i	Flextime negative yellow	01/01/2000	12/31/9999	40,00
ZZPRE	i	Flextime positive red	01/01/2000	12/31/9999	50,00
ZZPYE	i	Flextime positive yellow	01/01/2000	12/31/9999	30,00

Figure 8.57 Traffic Light Values in the Table of Constants

In the second step, you generate the messages to be created in case the values are exceeded (see Figure 8.58). You can reach the settings via the following IMG path TIME MANAGEMENT • TIME EVALUATION • TIME EVALUATION WITH CLOCK TIMES • PROCESSING BALANCES • BALANCE FORMATION • BALANCE LIMITS.

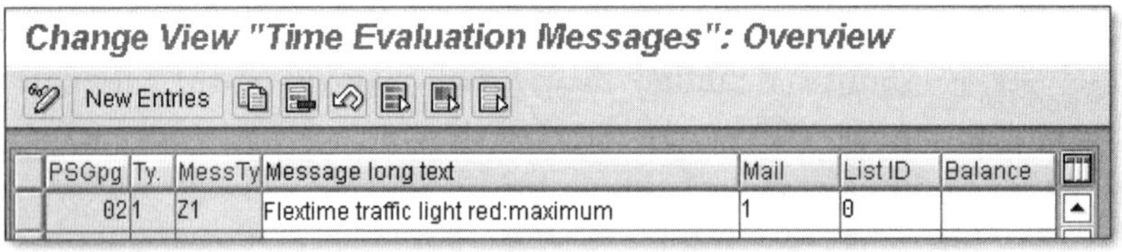

Change View "Time Evaluation Messages": Overview

New Entries

PSGpg	Ty.	MessTy	Message long text	Mail	List ID	Balance
02	1	Z1	Flextime traffic light red:maximum	1	0	

Figure 8.58 Time Evaluation Message for a Red Traffic Light

You can define the reaction when the threshold value is exceeded via the same path. You only need a part of the extensive customizing screens: definition of the comparison (time type 0005 with the table of payroll parameters T511k) and the message output. Figure 8.59 shows entries made for a red traffic light when the upper limits are exceeded.

Thus, the red and yellow traffic light stages are provided as notes in error handling. In addition, an email flag is transferred to the time-recording terminal that can be provided with corresponding text there.

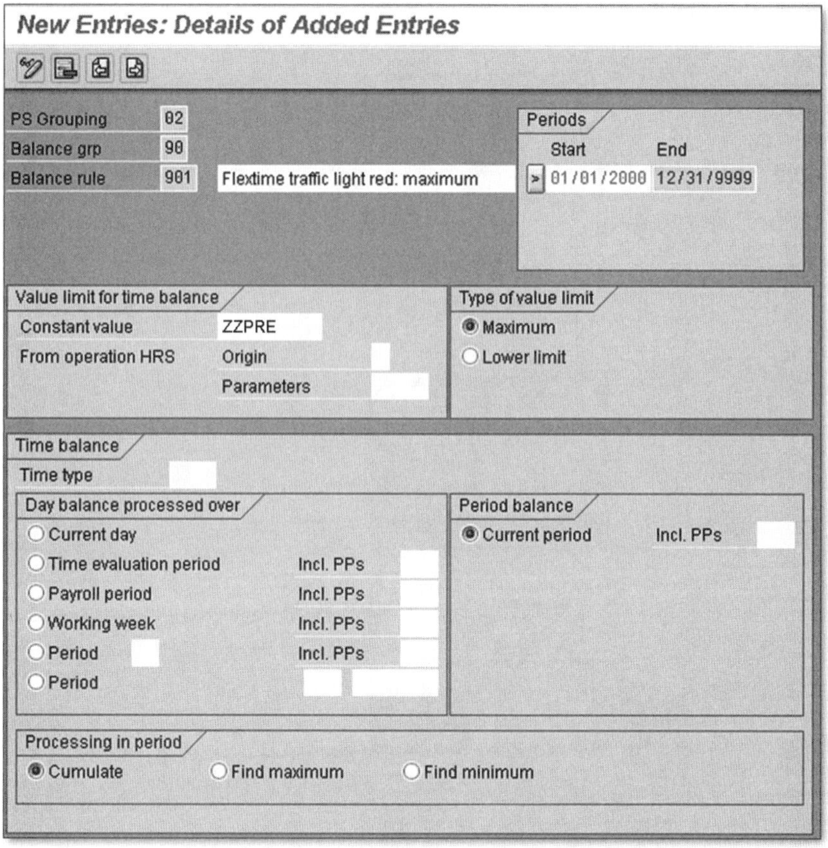

New Entries: Details of Added Entries

PS Grouping 02
Balance grp 90
Balance rule 901 Flextime traffic light red: maximum

Periods
Start 01/01/2000 End 12/31/9999

Value limit for time balance
Constant value ZZPRE
From operation HRS Origin
Parameters

Type of value limit
Maximum
Lower limit

Time balance
Time type

Day balance processed over
Current day
Time evaluation period Incl. PPs
Payroll period Incl. PPs
Working week Incl. PPs
Period Incl. PPs
Period

Period balance
Current period Incl. PPs

Processing in period
Cumulate Find maximum Find minimum

Figure 8.59 Activating a Message for a Red Traffic Light (Customizing)

If management is to monitor the traffic light status outside error handling, you can also use the evaluation RPTBAL00 (Cumulated Time Evaluation Results), which should be integrated in the MSS or MDT for this reason.

To identify when threshold values are exceeded in this evaluation, you can maintain the attributes LIMIE, LIMIS, and LIMIZ via the following IMG path TIME MANAGEMENT • TIME EVALUATION • EVALUATIONS AND THE TIME MANAGEMENT POOL • SET VALUE LIMITS FOR CUMULATED EVALUATION RESULTS. Figure 8.60 shows an overview of the process.

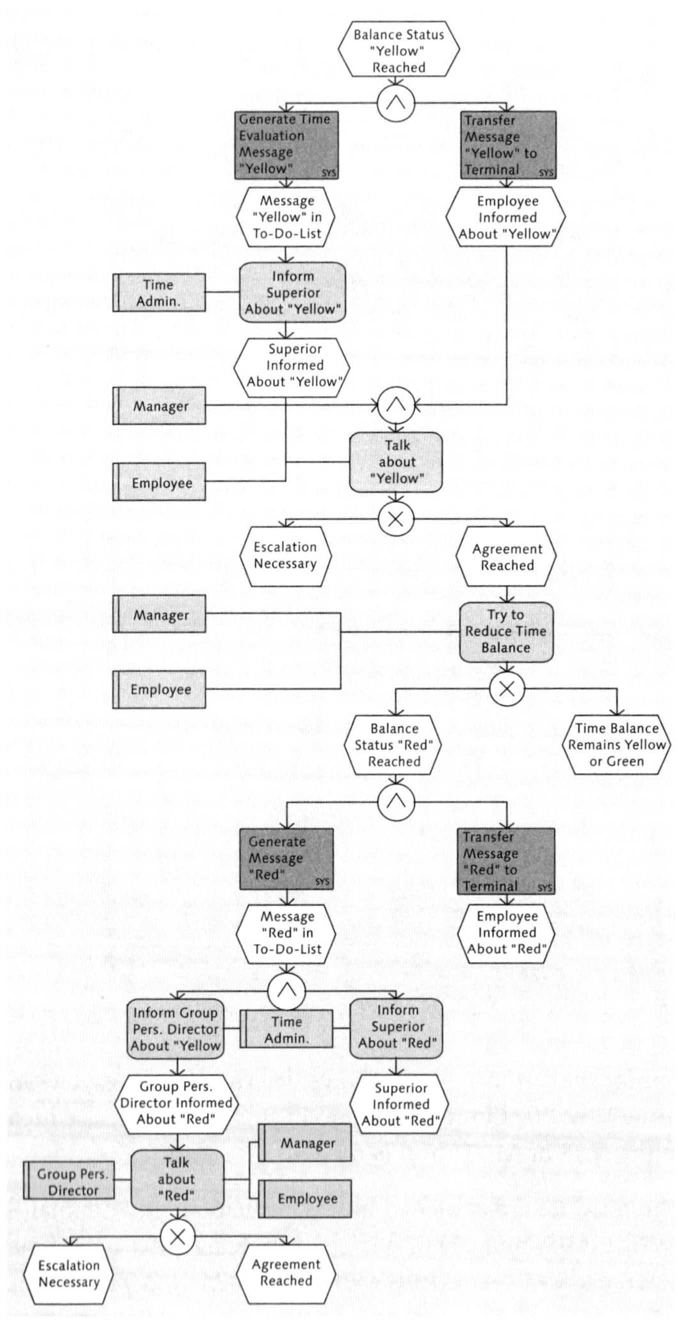

Figure 8.60 Approximate Process — Flextime with Traffic Light Regulation

8.5.2 Part-Time Model

Part-time models are widely available in some sectors today and are based on very different individual working time agreements. If there are 1,000 part-time staff in a company, there are often more than 500 different work schedule rules. This means the working time is ideally tailored toward the requirements of the employees on one hand and the company on the other. An advantage of part-time staff is mostly higher flexibility. Even if, for example, eight hours are agreed on Mondays and Wednesdays, short-term changes upon agreement can often be allowed for in the general rules (e.g., rush order in the department or a child's birthday).

However, it is not necessary that working time agreements should be precisely mapped to a time model in the HCM system. It is completely sufficient for flextime calculation to know the weekly working time and to distribute it equally, for example, to five days. An exact distribution of working time can be done within these conditions by written or oral agreement between employees and management.

For this reason, for a five-day week, you only need one time model in the system for constant flextime conditions. This is assigned to the employees via Infotype 0007 and supplemented there with the desired hourly figure or the part-time percentage rate (see Figure 8.61). Everything else is dynamically calculated by the system.

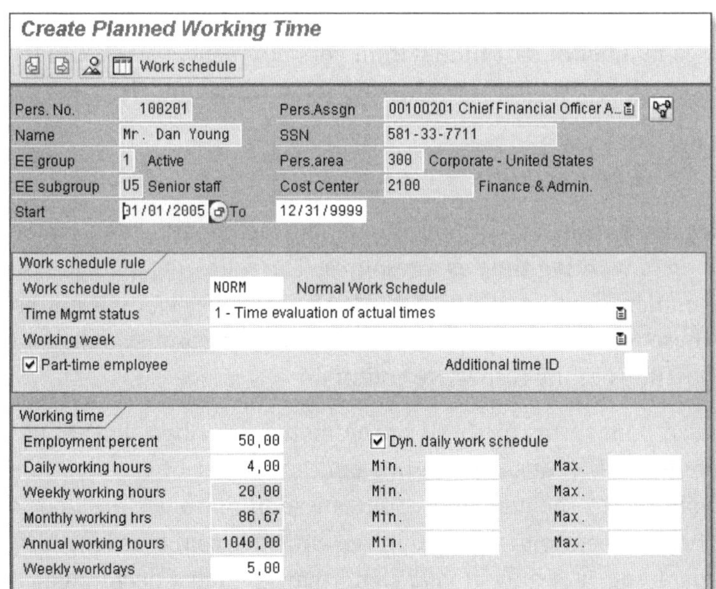

Figure 8.61 Part-Time with 50%

In this case, no additional maintenance activities are necessary as long as the weekly working time for the employee has not changed. The system accepts the same working time each day, and as long as the employee plans the attendance within the scope of flextime, no further interference is necessary.

In contrast to this, the detailed mapping of all time models in the system leads to considerable maintenance complexity, as the process in Figure 8.62 also shows:

- From the beginning of part-time work, a model must frequently be created. As creation occurs in Customizing, this cannot be carried out by decentralized time administrators. This merely assigns the newly created model.
- If the distribution of working time is changed over a longer period, the same complexity is necessary as at the beginning.
- Short-term changes to planning without information from the time administrators lead to error messages in time evaluation (e.g., Employee present on a day off). A telephone call is then made, and the change is then mapped by entering a substitution in Infotype 2003.
- The time administrator who is responsible for customizing the time model and the time administrator must always involved, which is not the case for a flexible part-time model. Only the time administrator must be involved there, when changes are made to the weekly working time.

If you deal with a large number of part-time staff in your company, you should try to avoid the detailed entry of working-time distribution in time models.

8.5.3 Life-Working-Time Accounts

Life-working-time accounts are a popular means of employee retention and can be used to optimally control working time as a resource. The following section will illustrate a possible implementation in SAP ERP HCM. However, we will not go into detail here, as these are often very specific to the company and also depend strongly on legal regulations in the respective country.

The normal flextime account forms the basis of the model described that should move within the predefined limits. At month's end, a section of the flextime account is then transferred to the annual account. In addition, overtime that is subject to bonuses, beyond flextime, is set up in the annual account, as long as it is not immediately paid out. It is only at year's end that you must decide which part of the accumulated times in the annual account is paid out, and which part is transferred to the life-working-time account.

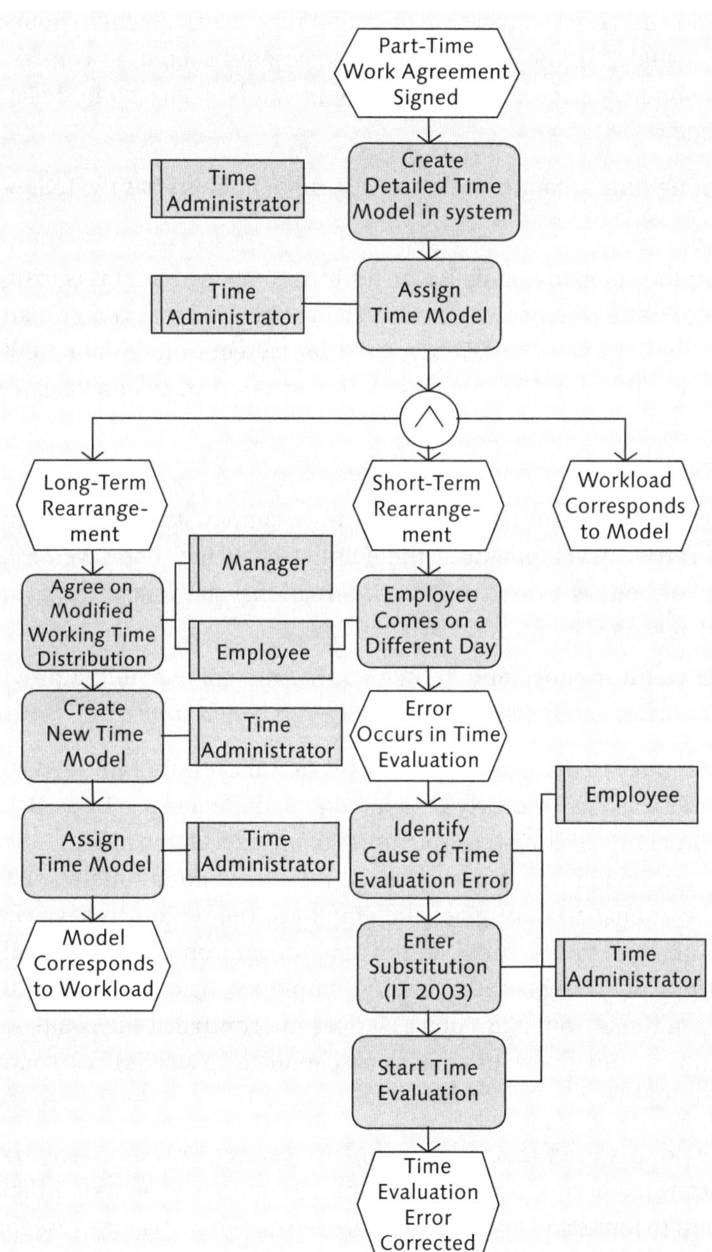

Figure 8.62 A Process with Detailed Work Schedules is Generally Inefficient

Flextime account and annual accounts are managed in time management in hours. The times that are included in the life-working-time account should, in contrast, be evaluated on a monetary basis so that this account can be managed in dollars or in another currency.

Managing life-working-time accounts in dollars instead of in hours has the following advantages:

- During change in the company (and also on an intracompany basis) it is easily transferable. Even in the case of a cost-center change, the old cost center manager would probably not want to take over any legacy with more than 1,000 hours of time-off entitlement. For this reason, it is easier to transfer a valuated account.
- A clearly defined interest calculation is possible.
- If the account is to be paid out after 30 years, for example, its value strongly depends on the carrier development of the employees. If the time saved as a sales assistant is paid out as a director of an international subsidiary, this is an interest return that cannot be justified by anything.
- The value of the credit is constantly known so that the corresponding provisions can be built up and an insolvency insurance can be put in place.

At first glance, the annual account can appear to be an unnecessary intermediate step. However, it is very useful to clearly separate the planning ranges. In particular, it should prevent short- or long-term planning being executed using the life-working-time account. In addition, payment from the life-working-time account is an exception. The annual account gives the employee the option to have the money paid out to them at year's end. The flextime account on the other hand, provides short-term scope for planning for the employee. The employee can extract any number of times from it, as long as it does not contradict the company requirements. For this reason, the values that can accumulate on an annual account are considerably too high.

The annual account adjusts itself to specific company requirements in exactly the same way as the transfer occurs between flextime accounts and working-time accounts, with regard to limits and authorization processes. This is also the case for the transfer into life-working-time accounts, where legal regulations come increasingly into play. The following methods are recommended for carrying out mappings in time management:

- Run the flextime account as in the standard version via time type 0005.
- Manage the annual account via a time type or an absence quota.

  The transfer into an annual account can be mapped via the following IMG path TIME MANAGEMENT • TIME EVALUATION • TIME EVALUATION WITH CLOCK TIMES • PROCESSING BALANCES • BALANCE FORMATION • BALANCE LIMITS.
- The life-working-time account can be built up by transferring the times of the annual account through a balance transfer or quota correction into a time-wage type called the life-working-time account. This is then provided to payroll for monetary valuation. Interest calculation should also be processed in payroll. As payroll is always aware of an employee's hourly rate, it can constantly display the value of the account in terms of hours or days (e.g., in the remuneration statement). The withdrawal in terms of time can then occur via a custom absence type called withdrawal of life working time, which is also transferred via the same time-wage type to payroll. The withdrawal in terms of money is even easier by entering a specific wage type in Infotype 0015.
- If it's possible for the employee to shorten his lifelong working time by about 4 years after 30 years of working 1 hour of overtime every day, it is the management's duty to treat the working time responsibly. This includes monitoring the development of balance statuses. If these statuses increase due to a high workload and don't decrease again at lower workloads, controlled intervention may be necessary. The provision of the corresponding evaluation options is well-supported technically by SAP ERP HCM. The aim should be to provide the relevant reports as online evaluations through the MDT.

The buildup process for a life-working-time account is illustrated in Figure 8.63.

- The model can also be supplemented by giving employees the option to extend their long-term account by waiving a part of their remuneration.
- In any case it makes sense (and is not too complicated) to regularly notify employees not just of their status but also on the development of their long-term accounts. The simplest way of doing this is to use a customer-specific ESS scenario.

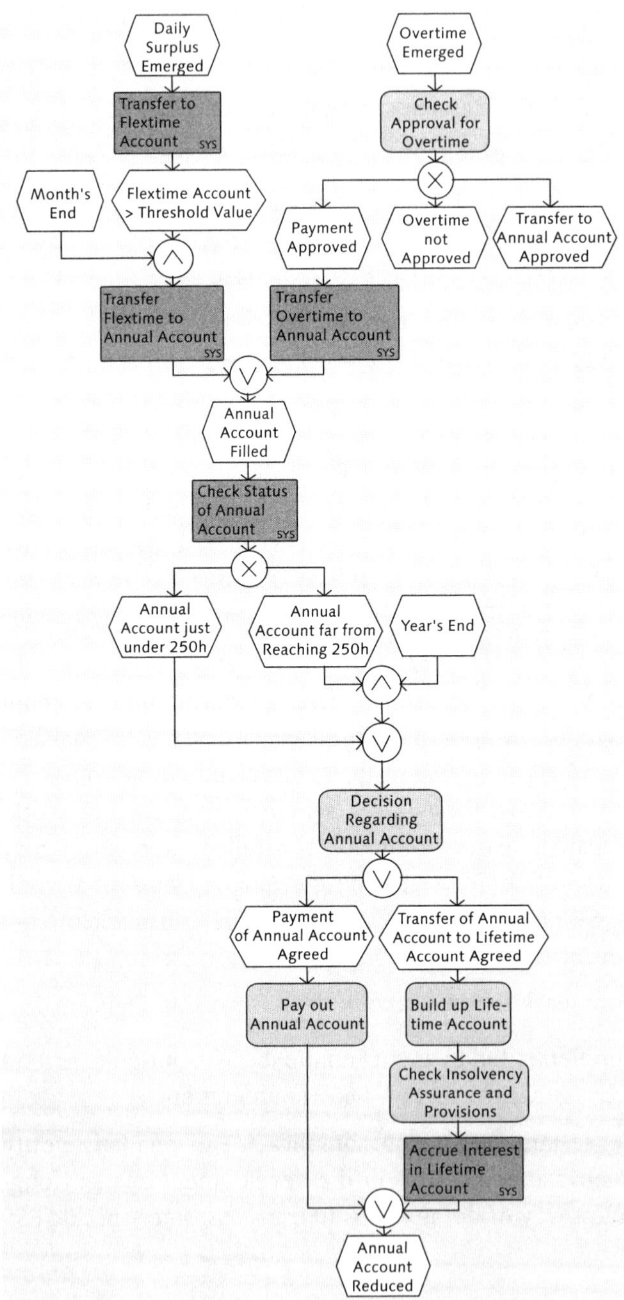

Figure 8.63 Building Up a Life-Working-Time Account

8.5.4 Self-Service Processes in Time Management

The processes in time management offer a substantial potential for increasing quality and efficiency when using ESS and MSS. The direct time-data entry in ESS by employees usually doesn't require much additional effort compared to conventional methods but significantly reduces the effort for the HR department. The immediately available additional information (for example, overview of the absence quotas for leave requests) and the traceability of the process and status also increase the quality.

The most important functions in ESS (see Figure 8.64) include:

- Entering attendance times — also for the amount allocation, e.g., for projects or external cost centers (see Figure 8.65)
- Entering or correcting time postings
- Displaying absence quotas
- Displaying time statements
- Requesting leaves

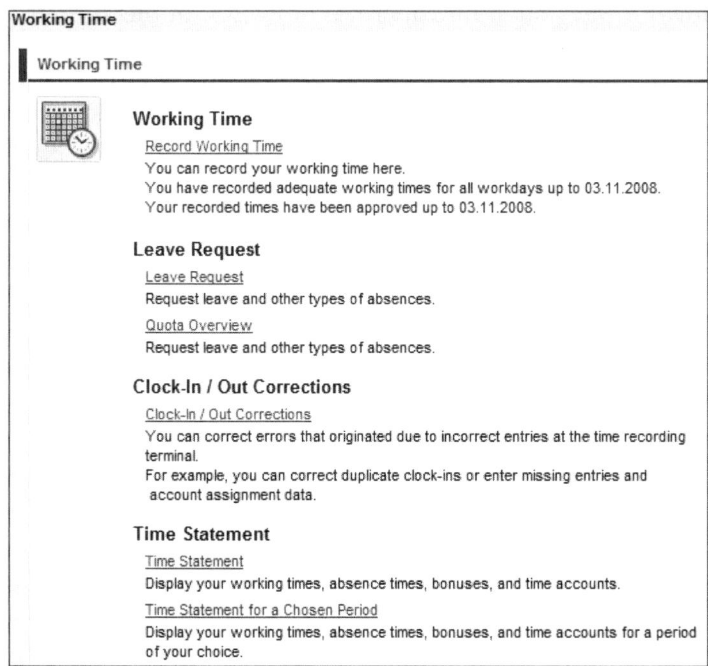

Figure 8.64 ESS Services in Time Management — Overview

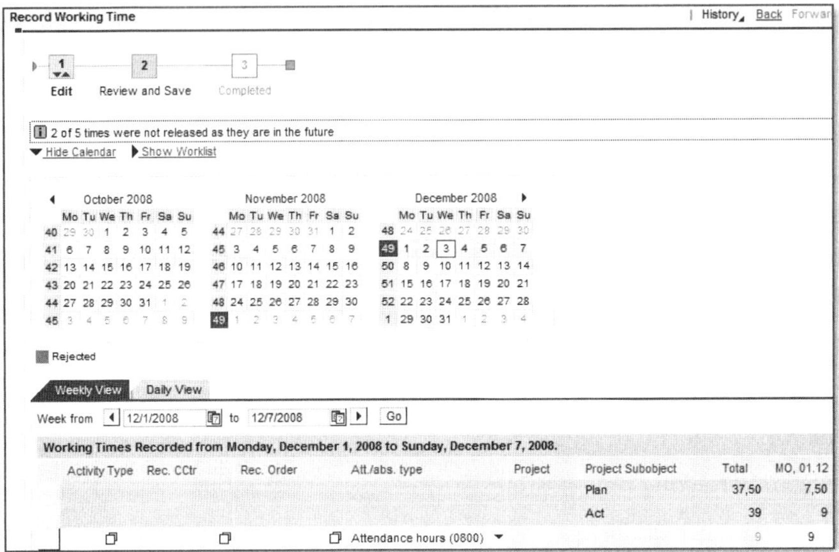

Figure 8.65 Entering Working Times for Allocation

The time posting or time posting correction options provided in the portal (see Figure 8.66) also allow for integration into approval processes. In this case, the manager views the request in the MSS to-do list and can release or reject the process here. Experience has shown that such approval processes quickly get out of control, so they are not processed very carefully anyway. In most cases it is useful to permit time-data changes by employees without approval processes but allow for an appropriate monitoring via evaluations.

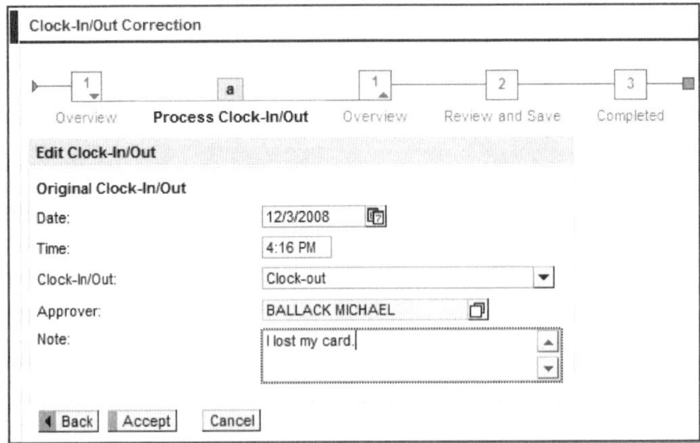

Figure 8.66 Time Posting in the Portal (Standard Service)

Figure 8.67 shows the screen for the entry of leave requests in ESS. The example displays a leave request that is integrated with an approval process.

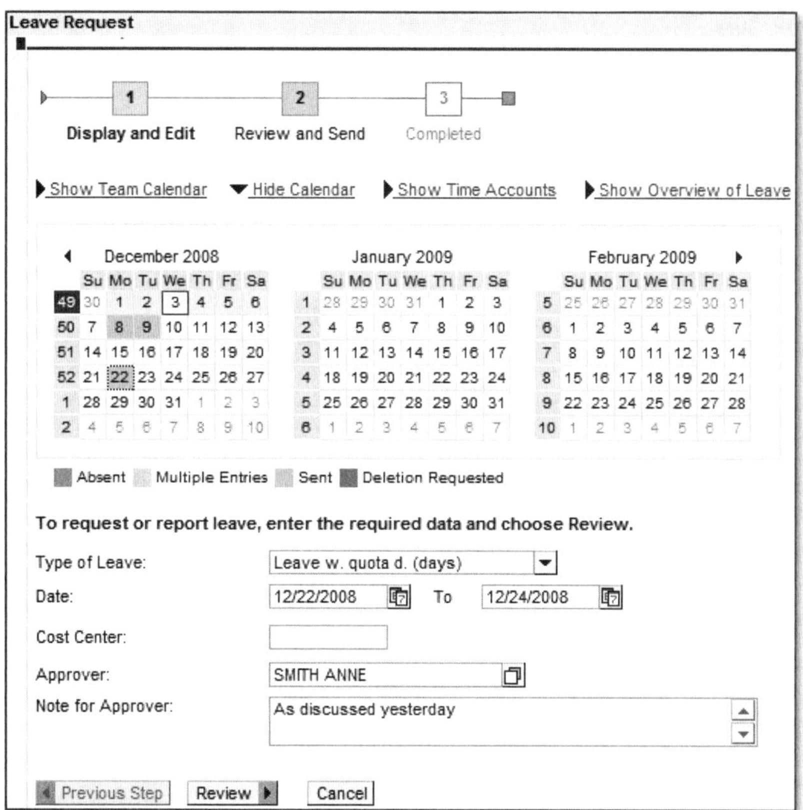

Figure 8.67 Entering a Leave Request in ESS

In addition to further parameters and depending on the absence type, you can define in the Customizing whether an approval is required and which fields are displayed in the screen. Figures 8.68 and 8.69 illustrate the various control options. You can reach them via the following IMG path Employee Self-Service • Service-Specific Settings • Working Time • Leave Request • Processes • Define Processes for Absence Types.

For example, if you select the Requester May Change Next Agent indicator, then the Approver field, as shown back in Figure 8.67, can be overwritten. This enables the requester to define a different approver, for example, if he knows that his superior is absent.

User Interface Elements

- [x] Display Field for Next Agent
  - [x] Requester May Change Next Agent
  - [ ] Not Necessary to Enter Next Agent
- [x] Use Notes

Field Selection for Additional Data: ZTEST

Explanation of Absence Type:

System Response

- [x] Requests Have To Be Approved
- [ ] EEs Not Permitted to Submit Requests
- [ ] No Changes to Leave Permitted
- [ ] No Deletion of Leave Permitted

Figure 8.68 Customizing the Absence Notification

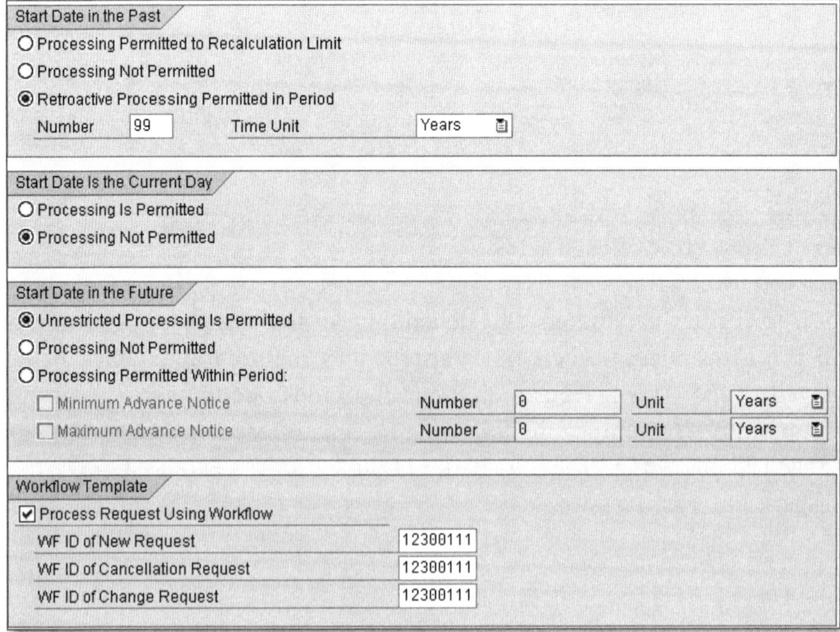

Start Date in the Past

- ( ) Processing Permitted to Recalculation Limit
- ( ) Processing Not Permitted
- (•) Retroactive Processing Permitted in Period

Number: 99 Time Unit: Years

Start Date Is the Current Day

- ( ) Processing Is Permitted
- (•) Processing Not Permitted

Start Date in the Future

- (•) Unrestricted Processing Is Permitted
- ( ) Processing Not Permitted
- ( ) Processing Permitted Within Period:
  - [ ] Minimum Advance Notice Number: 0 Unit: Years
  - [ ] Maximum Advance Notice Number: 0 Unit: Years

Workflow Template

- [x] Process Request Using Workflow

WF ID of New Request: 12300111

WF ID of Cancellation Request: 12300111

WF ID of Change Request: 12300111

Figure 8.69 Customizing the Absence Notification, Part 2

The leave request is one of the most used applications in ESS. Users highly appreciate the improved traceability compared to paper-supported processes where all participants blame each other when leave request forms get lost. Furthermore, the one-to-one reproduction of the paper-supported process also contributes to the popularity of this service. However, this means that the entire potential for increasing the efficiency isn't used. Because leaves are usually planned or reconciled within the departments in advance, the approval process is no longer required and can be replaced by an appropriate overview for the managers (see Figure 8.70).

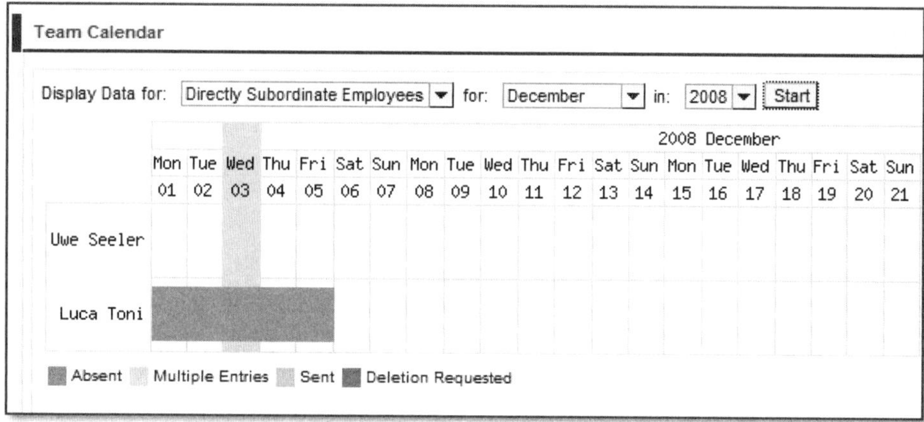

Figure 8.70 Absence Overview For a Team

The following evaluations are available for managers in MSS to enable them to better manage the "working time" resource:

- Attendances and absences (list and chart)
- Attendance and absence quotas
- Work schedules
- Time corrections

You can also easily integrate reports from SAP NetWeaver Business Intelligence (BI) into MSS as graphics. Figure 8.71, for example, illustrates the percentage of sicknesses and overtime per team.

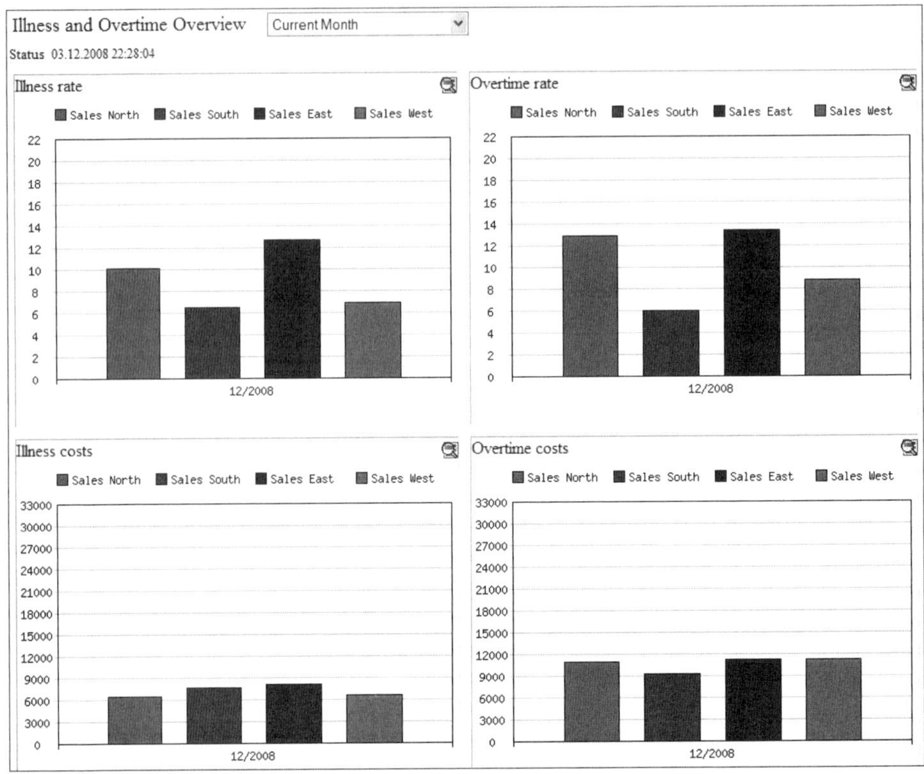

Figure 8.71 Graphical Overview of Sicknesses and Overtime from SAP NetWeaver BI

This concludes our review of SAP ERP HCM Time Management. For a very detailed look at this component, you can refer to the book, *Time Management with SAP ERP HCM* by Brian Schaer, also from SAP PRESS.

8.6 Critical Success Factors

- Exact knowledge of the actual processes (in particular, branch offices/branches). Knowledge of the collective agreements and official company regulations alone does not suffice.
- A clear definition of overtime processes. The approval processes should be sufficient and not require any exceptions. Following this principle, you must eliminate exceptions (you must avoid requirements such as, for overtime on Sundays, pay half the bonus and transfer the other half to the life account and place the basic salary in the flextime account).

- An end to reporting on paper. Information on working time must be current. That is only possible online. Use the environments provided for decentralized information and processing.
- Use of the environments provided for decentralized information and processing: ESS, TMW, and MDT.
- No detailed description of time models in the system.
- Early clarification of the extensive processes of logistics and accounting.
- Early clarification of data entry processes for master data in particular, which is relevant for time management, and for time data, which is relevant for payroll. Work distribution with other processes is important for efficient flows. The change of processors must therefore be kept to a minimum.
- Well-trained time administrators with extensive competencies so that work is carried out mainly on a decentralized basis. The central personnel department assumes the task of advisor and controller.
- Optimally structured user interfaces for time administrators (and those responsible for time ticket entries such as office supervisor writers). In most cases, the TMW is the optimal solution. Simple and efficient interface creation is especially important if the time administrators only spend a very small amount of their working time with data maintenance in the ERP system.
- Use of only the most necessary mobile solutions. Complicated entry processes on a mobile display or long maintenance times due to limited bandwidth both limit user acceptance.
- No delegation of management responsibility to the time-management system.
- Early integration test with the subsystems.
- Quality-assurance environment with a sufficient number of documented test cases. Changes in the customizing of the schema frequently have unexpected side effects, which are not picked up without a suitable quality-assurance environment.
- Abolition of regulations that were justified in older systems or in manual time management, but that just increases the workload in SAP ERP HCM. This mainly includes all types of rounding.

Payroll is based on the results of personnel administration, time management and — in some cases — the results of travel management and incentive wages. It is divided into the subprocesses of gross payroll, net payroll, and subsequent processing. The subsequent processing comprises legal and company-specific components.

9 Payroll

This chapter will convey the basic concepts and background of payroll. It is not a complete guide to setting up payroll, however, because of the complexity of the application and it would be beyond the scope of this book.

9.1 Business Principles

In our discussion we will try to avoid country and sector specifics, because legal restrictions do not leave much room for flexibility. These specifics are also frequently subject to legal amendments and are presumably only of interest to a small number of readers.

9.1.1 Basic Forms of Remuneration

In this section we will provide a description of the basic forms of remuneration, which include numerous possible hybrid forms based on the basic forms. These are supplemented by additional remuneration components, which we will cover in Section 9.1.3.

Incentive Wage

In the case of incentive wages, the employee is remunerated based on work results and not the time worked. It is generally assumed that this approach increases an employee's motivation.

The individual piecework is the value of the individual employee's piece performance. For each completed piece, he is credited a standard time that is measured against the actual time required. This relationship between standard and required time is referred to as the performance efficiency rate.

Performance efficiency rate [%] = Standard time x piece number / required time

If an employee exceeds a 100% performance efficiency rate, his hourly wage can be increased. On the other hand, a performance efficiency rate of less than 100% leads to a reduction, which, however, is limited in many pay scales. More complex, team-oriented production flows frequently do not allow any individual incentive wages. By introducing group incentive wages, an attempt is made to remunerate a team, such as a manufacturing center. In this case the performance efficiency rate is calculated similarly to the individual piecework, with the difference being that times and number of pieces of the entire group are included. The group performance efficiency rate is then applied to the individual hourly rate for the employees. While the piecework only remunerates target quantities, the premium wage incorporates other target figures, such as quality.

Hourly Wage

In the case of hourly wages, the employee is paid for the number of hours he is present at the workplace. He is remunerated a constant amount per hour. The hourly wage is particularly useful if the assignment of work results is difficult.

Monthly or Weekly (Periodic) Wage

Despite the fact that employees work the same number of hours per week, an employee who is paid an hourly wage each month receives a different pay amount, because some months have more days than others. So, the monthly (or any periodic) wage is an attempt to stabilize the basic wage of the employee by making sure that he receives a constant monthly amount. A semi-monthly or two-week calculation of the remuneration is also possible and is more common in the U.S.

In some remuneration models, absences of the employee (e.g., due to public holidays, vacation leave, sickness) are paid at the basic hourly wage plus an average value earned in the previous months. A performance variable is incorporated in this average (e.g., piecework) and a time variable as we will discuss next.

9.1.2 Influencing Variables of Gross Payroll

In addition to basic remuneration forms, other circumstances also affect the remuneration.

Overtime and Bonuses

If the work in question cannot be covered with the existing employee capacity, overtime is often utilized. Overtime is usually paid separately from regular salaries; in general, overtime bonuses accrue in addition to the basic hourly wage. However, employers frequently try to cushion short-term overtime through flexi-time regulations, because this means overtime bonuses can be saved. Overtime that accrues in one month is credited to a time account and can later be retrieved by the employee if there is less work to be done. Keep in mind, however, local labor laws will determine how overtime is paid and reconciled for bonus and additional pay purposes.

Times Subject to Bonuses

If the working time occurs during the night, the weekend (Sundays in the U.S.), or on a public holiday, additional bonuses (also known as shift premiums) may accrue and be paid to the employee, which obviously makes these shifts more expensive for the employer.

Expenses

When the employee is working for the employer, additional costs can occur (e.g., telephone, mileage, etc.) that may be reimbursed by the employer. Depending on the country of work, these expenses can be completely or partially exempt from taxation..

Nonrecurring Payments

Nonrecurring payments such as bonuses or vacation bonus are not part of monthly or periodic remuneration. Due to their lack of regularity, in many countries they are subject to special regulations with regard to taxation and such.

Absences

In terms of absences, there is a basic differentiation between paid and unpaid absences. Unpaid absences reduce the basic remuneration.

Performance-Dependent Remuneration Components

With the exception of incentive wages, basic forms of pay do not take employee work or performance results into account. For reasons of motivation and fair remuneration, these basic forms of pay in the U.S. for exempt or nonunion employees are frequently supplemented by a performance-dependent component of pay, which should preferably be oriented toward company goals.

Many companies derive the employee targets or goals that are relevant for remuneration from a company-wide balanced scorecard. This ensures alignment with company targets and goals.

9.1.3 Net Payroll

In net payroll, national legal regulations are taken into account, i.e., the taxes to be deducted and other government or legally mandated deductions.

However, U.S.Payroll in SAP EPR HCM does not include the full tax calculation scheme. You need an interface to an external BSI Tax Factory database. This sets the U.S. version apart from most other country-specific payroll solutions within SAP ERP HCM.

Special Processes

Within net payroll, a range of special processes is supported according to national laws. They considerably reduce the necessary process cycle times and therefore the effort involved in running a payroll cycle. In general, net payroll details depend on data stored in country-specific infotypes.

In the U.S., some commonly used and supported special processes include:

- Loans
- Garnishments
- Benefits (see Chapter 10, "Benefits Administration")
- FLSA

- Off-cycle payments
- Tip processing

9.2 Payroll Concepts in SAP ERP HCM

As with any software, making it as flexible as possible to meet a wide range of customer requirements means that the software has to have a sophisticated design. This is particularly true with payroll in SAP ERP HCM. Using the standard customizing option, extensive variation in payroll requirements can be accommodated. The payroll runs can utilize customer-specific schemas and rules, and even complex regulations from collective bargaining agreements and company agreements can be implemented. Standard processing can also be enhanced via numerous customer exits and Business Add-Ins (BAdIs). There are even tools to modify the coding in SAP, which can simplify maintenance and make modification a more attractive option. However, core code modifications should be considered carefully, because customer changes to standard SAP code will not be supported.

9.2.1 Structures for Remuneration Calculation

For the calculation of payroll, the selected settings of Infotype 0001 (Organizational Assignment) are of great importance.

The enterprise structure is mapped through the personnel area and the personnel subarea. In SAP ERP HCM, the personnel area is linked to the company code (which is generally a legally independent accounting unit) and therefore determines where wages and salaries are posted and where they are paid from. The personnel sub-area is a further breakdown of the personnel area, and can provide more detailed groupings of locations or functional areas.. Pay structure information and a variety of other data elements and national indicators (e.g., region and district, employer ID and industry code, tax company[1] and Equal Employment Opportunity (EEO) data) are derived from the enterprise structure.

The personnel structure consisting of employee group and employee subgroup also determines essential aspects of the payroll. On this basis it is decided whether an employee is a salaried employee or a wage worker, and if he is paid monthly,

1 The legal entity for tax reporting purposes. In SAP U.S. HR it should have a one-to-one relationship with the *Employer Identification Number (EIN)*.

semi-monthly, weekly, etc. The employee group and employee subgroup can identify employees for further groupings that are specific for payroll processing. Many payroll-related settings are defined based on the personnel structure and the enterprise structure.

All employees of an enterprise who are included in payroll on a specific key date are combined in a payroll area. The payroll area also controls the locking concept for the payroll, (i.e., if the employees of a payroll area are processed) the master data of these employees is locked for maintenance (excluding data that is relevant to the future). In addition, the payroll area is a component of the logical databases PNP and PNPCE and is therefore available as a selection criterion in almost all evaluations.

In this context, a payroll area can easily combine employees of different companies (personnel areas), as long as they are included in payroll on the same key date.

The cost center specifies the target account assignment for the personnel costs to be posted in SAP ERP Financial Controlling (CO). The cost center is also used for the travel-costs component for assigning travel costs as long as an override component is specified. If the Organizational Management component is not active with integration to personnel administration, the cost center is maintained for every employee in Infotype 0001. If PA-OM integration is active, the cost center information can be automatically defaulted from organizational master data to the employee master data.

Once these structures are in use, it is difficult to adjust them later on — especially because the personnel area/subarea and employee group/subgroup elements in Customizing are not provided with start and end dates, and therefore cannot be easily limited if they are no longer required. For this reason, it is advisable to check the enterprise, personnel, and organizational structures to be used precisely in terms of their suitability from all viewpoints (master data, authorization concept, time management, payroll, and reporting).

9.2.2 Payroll Principles

In this section we will discuss the various principles involved with payroll, beginning with the wage-type concept.

The Wage-Type Concept

Wage types are the central processing instruments of payroll. Entries are made using wage types in the provided payroll-relevant infotypes, e.g., as basic salary or overtime. The entire additional processing is carried out using wage types as well. Specific wage types are mapped in the net payroll, for example, for taxes and other deductions (such as benefit plan contributions) to be paid. The result of the payroll – the payroll account – contains the wage types used and calculated in the employee's payroll.

The wage types thus form the basis of payroll. They are dependent on the country, i.e., the same wage type can have a different meaning in a German payroll than in a payroll in the U.S. They also have a validity period within which they can be used. This also means that one wage type can exist at different times with different properties. This becomes necessary if the characteristics of a wage type change at a particular time, an example being an anniversary bonus that is subject to tax from January 1.

A wage type is identified by a four-digit key composed of figures, letters, and special characters. The related text is language dependent:

- Different texts can be displayed for the same wage type for a German and for an English transactional user who each log on in their native language.
- A German-speaking employee can have German texts printed on the remuneration statement, and an English-speaking employee can have them printed in English.

The following conventions exist when creating four-digit wage type keys in SAP ERP HCM:

- Wage types that begin with a slash (/) are called technical wage types. Most of the processing work is carried out using these technical wage types. They represent the rules for the payroll. For U.S. payroll there are about 900 of these wage types.[2]

2 The number of technical wage types can be a first indicator for the complexity of a payroll solution within SAP. German payroll has about twice as many technical wage types as U.S. payroll, while the UK solution has only about 500. A low number of technical wage types can indicate either that payroll in the respective country is quite simple or that the SAP-based solution does not cover the whole range of legal requirements.

- Wage types that begin with a number from 0 to 9 are freely available to the customer. This area is always empty in a newly supplied system.
- Wage types that begin with an M are SAP model wage types. To provide a guide to customer configuration work, these model wage types can be used as templates for each wage type that the customer requires for his company.

If the rules for payroll are controlled by wage types, it is useful to keep these up-to-date with SAP. This is the reason for the customer namespace for wage types. All other wage types can be and are overwritten by SAP when importing updates (support packages) and this way are constantly adjusted to the newest conditions. This is also the case with model wage types. For this reason, they should not be used in a production environment. A payroll with model wage types would be unstable, especially if these were customized.

The wage types used by customers always begin with a digit and are generally created by copying them from a model wage type.

Customizing Wage Types

The wage type copier was especially developed by SAP for this reason (Transaction PU30). It copies and deletes all properties of a wage type, regardless of whether it is a model wage type or another already-existing wage type that is to be copied (see Figure 9.1).

To process wage types more simply, they are summarized into wage-type groups. For example, for each infotype that contains wage types there is a specific wage-type group. This ensures that the maintenance interface for wage types remains manageable. Wage types can also be contained in several wage-type groups.

The characteristics of wage types are determined by an amount field, a quantity field, and an amount-per-unit field. This means wage types are capable of saving any values. Whether and how a wage type is processed depends on Customizing.

Each wage type contains the following control information:

- **Valuation**
  If a pay amount is not directly provided along with a wage type, payroll must carry out this task and determine the relevant pay amount. However, the amount can only be determined if the wage type contains a quantity. For example, for overtime accrued, overtime wage types are recorded in terms of hours.

These wage types must then contain the information that their evaluation basis is the personal hourly wage of the employee (if necessary, in connection with a percentage rate that reflects an overtime bonus).

- **Cumulation**
  Pools are formed using accumulation. These pools represent the interface for the net payroll, i.e., the accumulation must be completed at the end of the gross payroll. By accumulating a wage type in certain pools, specific characteristics are defined in the wage type. For example, a wage type that is subject to tax is accumulated in the "gross tax amount" pool. These pools are integrated in SAP ERP HCM as technical wage types. They begin with "/1."

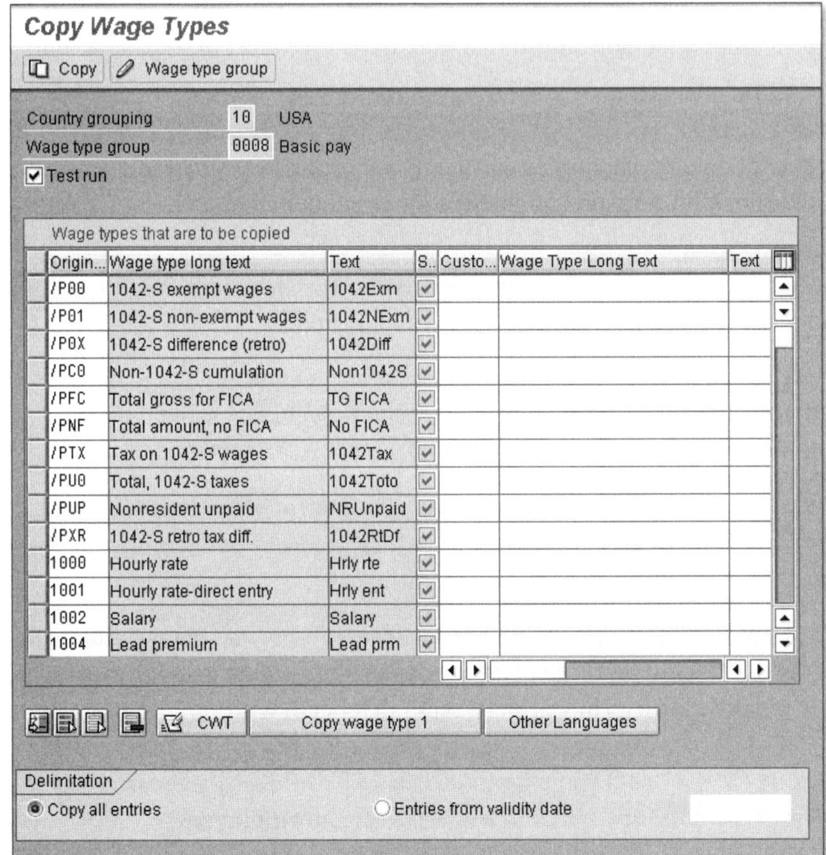

Figure 9.1 The Wage Types Copier (Transaction PU30)

- **Processing classes**
  Processing classes group wage types according to their characteristics. The characteristics of the processing classes of a wage type, rather than the wage type itself, are read from the payroll, and then the necessary processing steps are carried out. Abstracting a wage type itself offers more flexibility. The payroll does not have to have knowledge of every existing wage type. The characteristics of wage types can be easily changed. Processing Class 10, for example, controls whether and how a wage type is reduced in connection with unpaid absences (see Section 9.2.5). The accumulation of a wage type can be controlled by various additional processing classes. There, the time in the payroll at which the wage type is calculated determines the processing class to be used for accumulation. To avoid burdening payroll with unnecessary wage types, a wage type should be accumulated and shut down, i.e., transferred to the payroll account, as soon as a calculation is completed.
- **Evaluation classes**
  Characteristics of the wage types are determined in the evaluation classes for printing in the remuneration statement or in other statements.
- **Account assignment**
  Each wage type contains information on whether the wage type is to be posted to accounts and which accounts they are to be posted to.

You can analyze which wage types should have which characteristics using report RPDLGA20. Here, you can see that wage type 1212 is evaluated using the pay-scale group from the pay-scale table (see Figure 9.2).

We will now use an example to describe the valuation of wage types: Assuming an employee has done three hours overtime, which are to be paid out, regulations provide that he also receives an overtime bonus of 25%.

Wage type MM10 is entered manually or transferred from time management and its number field is filled with three hours. In the field valuation basis of wage type MM10 "01" is entered. All technical wage types that begin with "/0" are evaluation bases in SAP ERP HCM. This means that the relevant hourly wage can be found in wage type /001 ("/0" + "01").Wage type /001 in SAP ERP HCM standard delivery always contains the currently valid hourly wage for the employee.

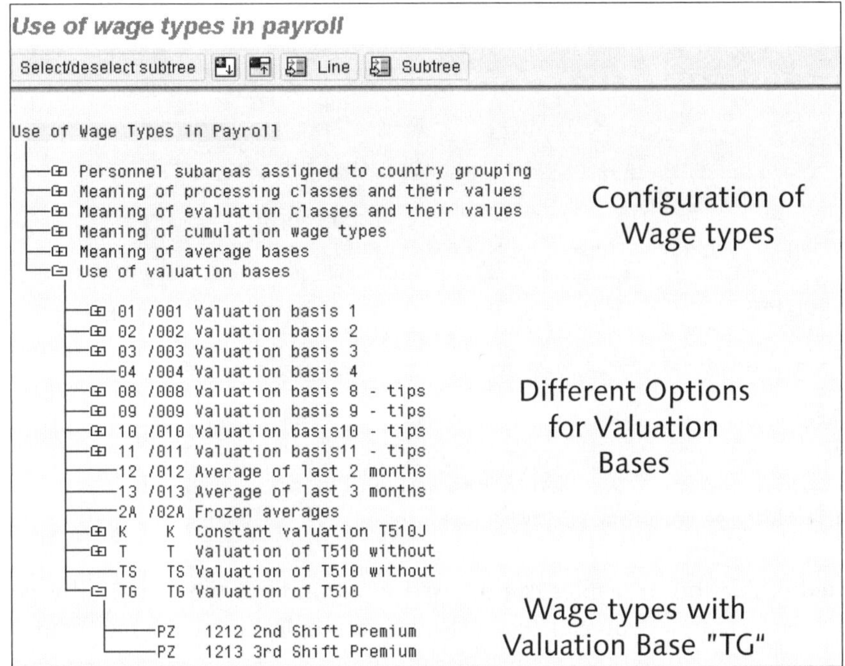

Figure 9.2 Distribution of Wage Types (RPDLGA20)

Now we must calculate the overtime bonus, which is 25% of the whole amount. To have a better basis for later evaluations, you should use two wage types here: one for the normal hourly wage (100%) and one for the overtime bonus (25%). Here we require derived wage types. The basic pay is mapped by wage type MM10. This wage type is supplemented by the percentage rate 100. A new wage type is entered for the overtime bonus, which is similarly valuated with the hourly wage of the employee (i.e. 01). However, you must change the percentage rate to 25%, which is the overtime bonus to be paid.

Through the derivation process, a wage type can generate up to two other wage types. However, this only works once; a derived wage type cannot create other derived wage types (see Figure 9.3).

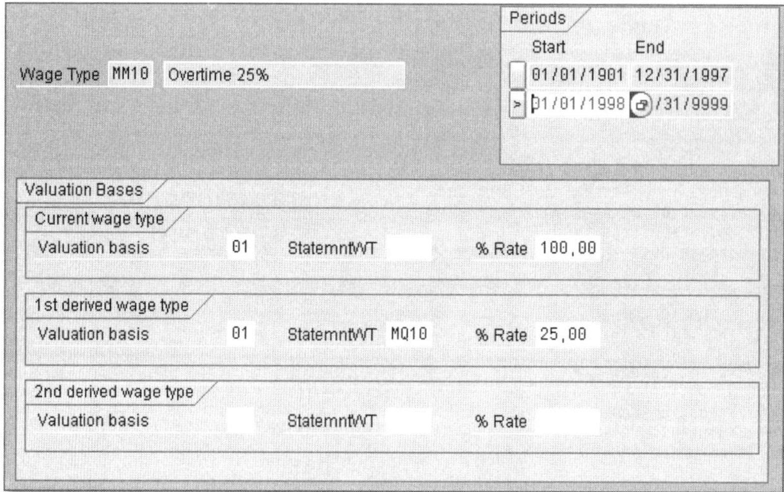

Figure 9.3 Evaluating a Wage Type (T512W)

Other fixed evaluation principles can be used in addition to the technical wage types /0**. For example, you can establish that an employee receives an hourly bonus of $1 U.S. for hazardous or unpleasant work. As shown in the previous example, the constant amount can be found on a cross-employee basis or in connection with pay-scale information in Infotype 0008 (Basic Pay) for the employee. Table 9.1 provides an overview of the possible valuation base of wage types.

Valuation base	The amount-per-unit field is transferred from:
nn	The amount-per-unit field of the wage type /0nn
K	Table T510J (constant value), employee independent
TS	Pay-scale table T510, which uses keys to search for pay-scale type, pay-scale area, pay-scale group, pay-scale level, and wage type (all from Infotype 0008 (Basic Pay), except for the wage type)
TG	Pay-scale table T510 is accessed just as TS, with the difference being that: pay-scale level = not filled
T	Pay-scale table T510 is accessed just as TG, with the difference being that: pay-scale group = not filled

Table 9.1 Possible Valuation Bases of a Wage Type

If a wage type is recorded in an infotype, it is referred to as a dialog wage type. For these types, additional information must be maintained (see Figure 9.4):

- Entries are permitted based on the enterprise and personnel structures
- Minimum and maximum values for the number and amount fields
- Several entries are permitted per month (time constraint)
- Indirect evaluation conducted by pay-scale tables

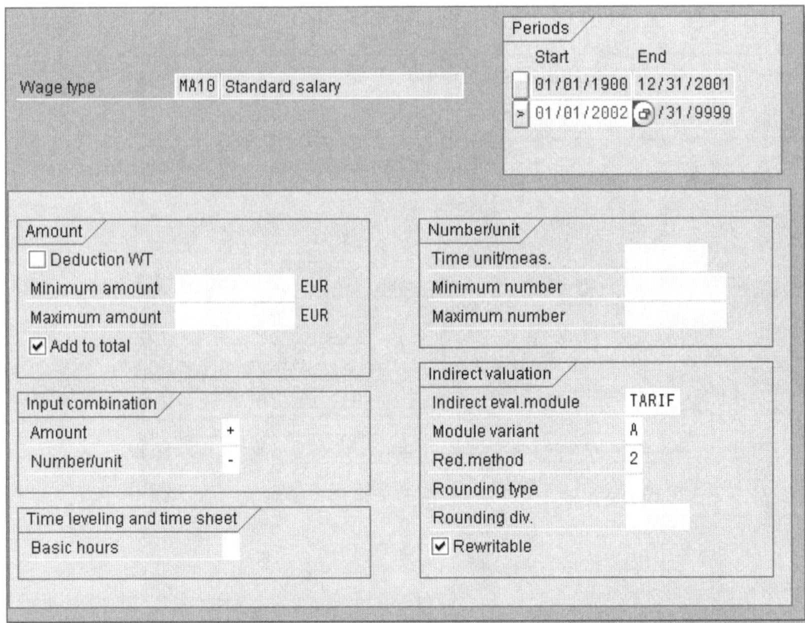

Figure 9.4 Dialog Characteristics of a Wage Type (T511)

Indirect Valuation

There is one basic issue to be dealt with in dialog wage types, i.e., whether or not these are to be valuated by entering a value manually, or if the valuation should occur indirectly by using a pay-scale table.

If a dialog wage type is indirectly valuated, this needs to be set in the dialog properties (see Figure 9.4). Here you work with modules and module variants. The combination describes the process according to which the relevant amount is transferred. Most processes work with the pay-scale table (see Figure 9.5). This is, however, not absolutely necessary.

If the amount of a wage type is automatically transferred to employee master data (Basic Pay) by an indirect valuation, other settings are required to make this powerful instrument suitable for actual practice. You must deal with the issue of what will happen if the employee works less or more than 100%.

How should this impact an employee's remuneration? A range of reduction methods is available, including rounding rules. The most useful reduction method provides the reduction by using the employment level from Infotype 0008 (Basic Pay).

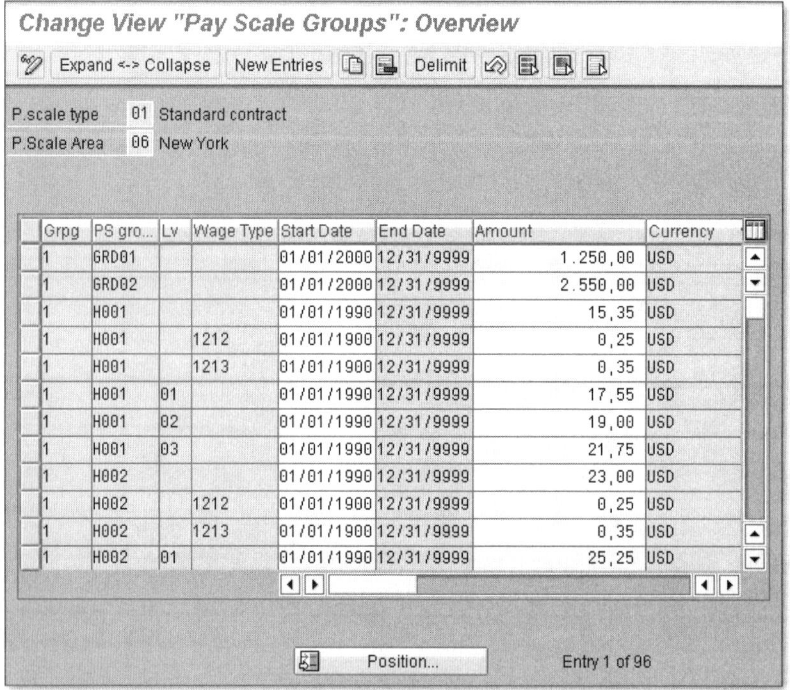

Grpg	PS gro...	Lv	Wage Type	Start Date	End Date	Amount	Currency
1	GRD01			01/01/2000	12/31/9999	1.250,00	USD
1	GRD02			01/01/2000	12/31/9999	2.550,00	USD
1	H001			01/01/1990	12/31/9999	15,35	USD
1	H001		1212	01/01/1900	12/31/9999	0,25	USD
1	H001		1213	01/01/1900	12/31/9999	0,35	USD
1	H001	01		01/01/1990	12/31/9999	17,55	USD
1	H001	02		01/01/1990	12/31/9999	19,00	USD
1	H001	03		01/01/1990	12/31/9999	21,75	USD
1	H002			01/01/1990	12/31/9999	23,00	USD
1	H002		1212	01/01/1900	12/31/9999	0,25	USD
1	H002		1213	01/01/1900	12/31/9999	0,35	USD
1	H002	01		01/01/1990	12/31/9999	25,25	USD

Figure 9.5 Pay-scale Table (T510)

For indirectly valuated wage types no amount is saved in the database. This value is usually recalculated by accessing infotypes, payroll, or reports. The disadvantage of the relatively complicated access to the concrete values is compensated for through simplifications during compilation and pay-scale increases. At the time of a pay-scale increase only the pay-scale table must be adjusted. The master data of all affected employees is automatically updated, because they have saved no values and instead have calculated these during runtime from the amended pay-scale table.

Split Indicators

If Infotype 0008 (Basic Pay), or the tax data (and other deduction data for that matter) change during a payroll period, several partial periods are created, and these must be taken into consideration separately during payroll.

Let's assume an employee who is paid monthly has a basic salary of $3,000 U.S. On 01/20/2008 he receives a salary increase so that his new salary is $3,500. Now there are two partial periods: one from 01/01/2008 to 01/19/2008 and the other from 01/20/2008 to 01/31/2008. The basic salary is mapped through wage type M003. The payroll creates two wage types M003, one for each partial period. To clearly assign the wage types to the corresponding partial periods, a split indicator is used. Payroll creates a table Work Place Basic Pay (WPBP) with the work center data according to Table 9.2.

WPBP split	From	To	Calendar days	Further identifiers
01	01/01/2008	01/19/2008	20	
02	01/20/2008	01/31/2008	10	

Table 9.2 WPBP After a Salary Increase on 01/20/2008

The wage types are created from Infotype 0008 (Basic Pay) according to Table 9.3.

Wage type	WPBP split	Amount
M003	01	$3,000
M003	02	$3,500

Table 9.3 WPBP Available Loan Types After a Salary Increase on 01/20/2008

Tables 9.2 and 9.3 are linked with each other via the split identifier. If the relevant calendar days are requested in the M003 wage type, they can be transferred using the WPBP split identifier from table WPBP (see Figure 9.6). To ensure that the employee does not receive $6,500, the amounts are reduced in the payroll at a later time so that in the precise calculations approximately $3,193 emerges as a weighted average value throughout the entire month (see Section 9.2.5).

Split identifiers are a technical utility to "attach" additional information to wage types.

Table WPBP

No	From	To	Action	ActionTxt	Cust.	Empl.
01	01/01/2004	01/19/2004	01	Hire		3
02	01/20/2004	01/31/2004	01	Hire		3

Table IT

A Wage type	APC1C2C3ABKoReBTAwvTvn One amount/one number	Amount
2 M003 Pay Period 01		3.000,00
2 M003 Pay Period 02		3.500,00

Figure 9.6 Wage Types with Split Identifiers

Retroactive Calculations

Retroactive calculations are always necessary if facts become known after the payroll process that necessitates a change to the payroll data. The payroll must therefore be repeated as it is no longer correct. What is problematic about this situation, however, is that the employee has already received payment, and the remuneration statement and the personnel costs for financial accounting (FI) and CO have been transferred, and the taxes and other deduction amounts have already been paid. A correction is therefore no longer possible. The error can be corrected, at the earliest, during the subsequent payroll.

How can you deal with this relatively frequent situation? This is an instance where SAP ERP HCM displays one of its greatest strengths. It has a complete retroactive calculation function. You only have to correct the incorrect entry in the appropriate master data infotype. The rest happens automatically when the next payroll is run.

The system recognizes that data has been changed in a period for which the payroll has already run. It marks these periods for correction. In the next payroll run, the payroll will be repeated for this period. A retroactive calculation takes place. The resulting difference is transferred to the current period, as the relevant period is in the past and therefore nothing can be changed in that past period.

If the system is capable of repeating payrolls for previous periods, this means that the entire Customizing of the payroll must be time-dependent. Each adjustment to the payroll, because of legal, pay-scale, or business reasons, must be integrated in a way so that it is becomes valid at a specific date. This is the only way of ensuring that in cases of a retroactive calculation the payroll logic did not change in the interim period and lead to misleading results. This is one of the reasons why the payroll component is so enormously complex.

For reasons of revision, the old result cannot just be changed. The retroactive calculation then creates an additional result for this period. So as to not lose the overview, we will work with the "for-period" and "in-period" concepts: In the case of an employee for whom retroactive calculation has been used, there are two payroll results for the same period, each of which has a different "in" period.

To better understand this complicated concept, let's look at another example: After a successful payroll for 01/2008, we find out that we forgot to pay an employee an allowance for special services of $100 for 01/2008. This is corrected, say, in Infotype 0015, and after the payroll run for 02/2008 the results can be found in the database (see Table 9.4, each row of the table represents a payroll result).

For period	In period	Description
01/2008	01/2008	Original payroll 01/2008 including the error, i.e., without the allowance for special services
01/2008	02/2008	Correction to the payroll for 01/2008 during the payroll run 02/2002 (with allowance for special services)
02/2008	02/2008	Original payroll 02/2008

Table 9.4 Payroll Results After Payroll 02/2008 with Retroactive Calculation for 01/2008

From a technical point of view, retroactive calculations can be carried out whenever necessary. It is a very powerful instrument for avoiding inconsistencies between the payroll and the parts of SAP ERP HCM that provide the required master data for payroll.

Payroll-Relevant Master Data

To ensure that master data changes trigger retroactive calculations for periods when a payroll already exists, a special check logic must be active. In Infotype 0003 (Payroll Status), the payroll saves the last date the employee has been accounted for (Accounted To field). In addition, it saves the latest date since the last payroll run on which a master data change to the payroll-relevant master data has been carried out (Earliest MD Change field). Using this field, the payroll determines the earliest period for which a retroactive calculation will be necessary. This field is always deleted by the productive payroll (see Figure 9.7).

The logic to fill the Earliest MD Change field is integrated in the processing logic of the infotypes. In the configuration of infotype characteristics, you only have to specify if the infotype is relevant for the payroll and must therefore trigger retroactive payroll calculation. In this context, either the entire infotype can be identified as completely relevant for payroll or just individual fields (see Figure 9.8). For example, the phone number of an employee is not payroll-relevant although his bank details would definitely be.

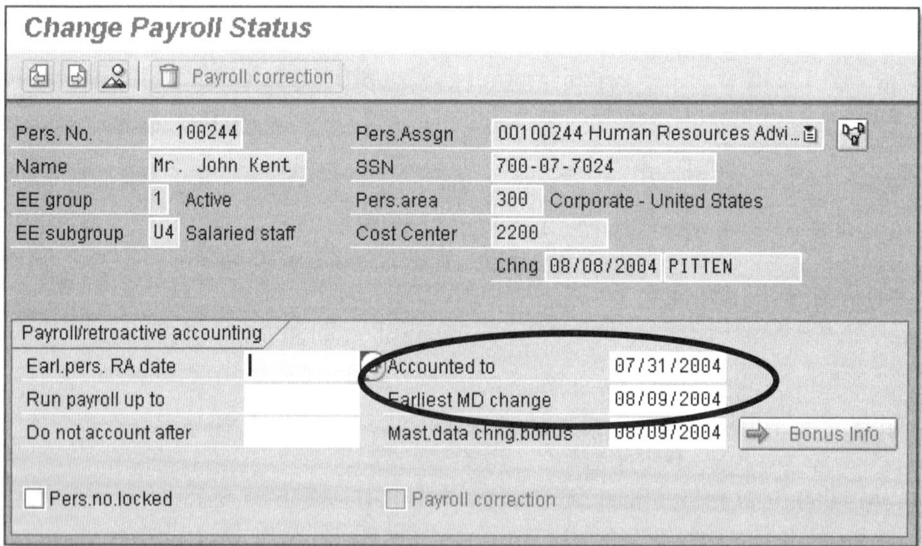

Figure 9.7 Infotype 0003 — (Payroll Status)

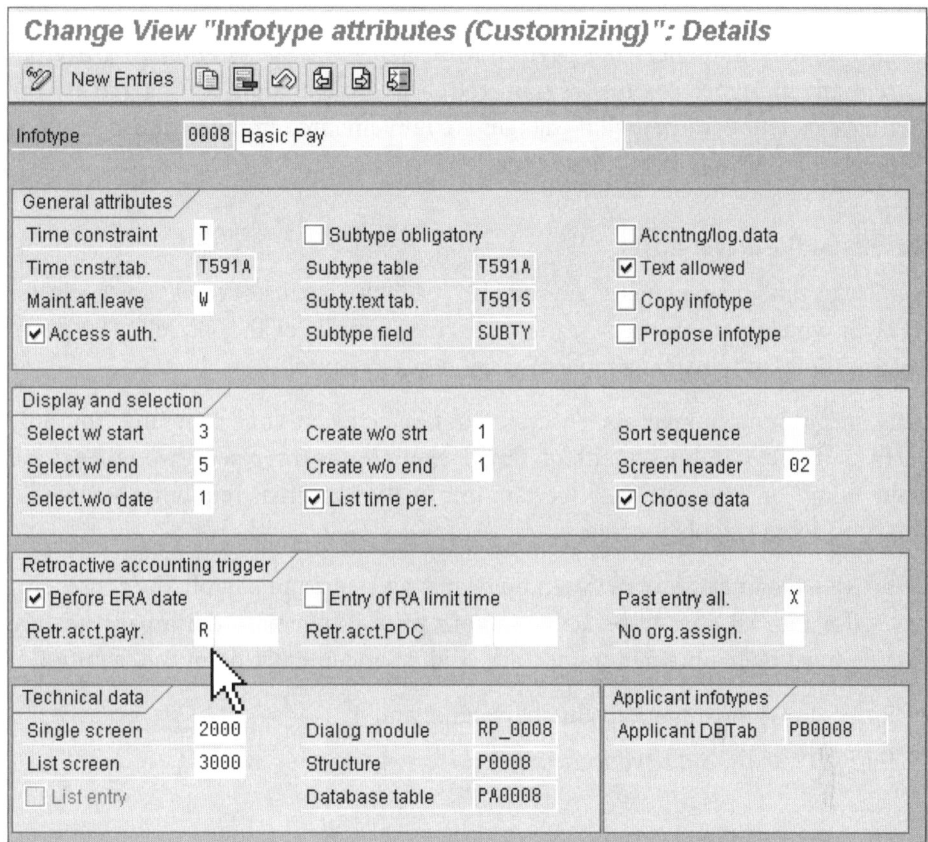

Figure 9.8 Characteristics of Infotypes

Results of Time Management

The results of the time evaluation (cluster B2) of the respective periods are read by payroll to receive the following data:

- The personal work schedule for the employee, including all attendances and absences. It contains, for example, the planned working time and paid and unpaid absences of the employee.
- A table with wage types, which generally contain time and shift bonuses, overtime, and time accounts paid out (and possibly deductions due to negative time accounts). The task of the payroll is to valuate these wage types that are provided in terms of hours.

- Because the results of the time evaluation are read by payroll, the time evaluation directly influences the payroll in the same way as an entry in a payroll-relevant infotype. For this reason, retroactive calculation is triggered by the time evaluation for payroll if changes are implemented in the periods for which payroll has already been carried out.

Results of the Travel Costs

Similar to time management, payroll also reads the results of travel costs (cluster TE/TX), which were created in the respective periods of the payroll. The travel costs settlement transfers a table of wage types to payroll.

This integration of Travel Expense may not be active at your company. You only need it if the reimbursement of travel expenses takes place through payroll accounting[3] or if payroll needs certain information, such as reimbursements that are considered taxable income.

To activate the integration between travel management and payroll, the subschema UREI (for the U.S.) has to be active in your payroll schema. Additionally, feature TRVPA must be maintained (refer to the online documentation of the feature):

- Entry "L+G" must have a value between 1 and 4
- Entry "PA3" should have the value 1

9.2.3 Payroll Process

The Payroll Control Record

Each payroll area has a payroll control record (Transaction PA03), which enables the task of performing lock administration. This lock administration ensures that all of the master data entries are considered in the payroll. To this end, you must work with the statuses Released for Payroll, Released for Correction, Exit Payroll, and Check Payroll Results. Apart from the status, a period counter is required to make it clear which period is being referred to. When you change the status from Exit Payroll to Released for Payroll (beginning of a new payroll run) the period

3 Alternatively, it can take place through accounts payable in financial accounting, by a special DME (Data medium exchange) or by check.

counter is automatically counted up one period. Apart from that, the period counter cannot be influenced.

The individual statuses affect the employees of the corresponding payroll areas, as shown in Table 9.5.

Status	Effect of master data	Effect on the payroll
released	The master data is locked for the current and previous periods. Maintenance for future periods is still possible.	Payroll is possible with the released period.
correction	A complete maintenance is possible. Payroll-relevant changes set the matchcode "W" for the employee (payroll correction).	No productive payroll is possible.
check	The master data is locked for the current and previous periods. Maintenance for future periods is still possible.	No productive payroll is possible.
ended	A complete maintenance is possible.	No productive payroll is possible.

Table 9.5 Status of the Payroll Control Record

If, according to the payroll control record, the status in the payroll run is "ended," it is completely finished and cannot be changed. All corrections are then carried out by retroactive calculation.

In addition, the earliest retroactive accounting period is saved in the payroll control record. This establishes to what extent a correction of master data is possible in the past and to what extent retroactive calculation can be carried out. This can only be changed in Transaction PA03 if the status of the payroll control record has just been set to Exit Payroll (see Figure 9.9).

At the same time, the earliest retroactive calculation determines the earliest retroactive accounting period for which retroactive calculation can be carried out. For this reason, it can only be changed if no retroactive accounting has been set for any employees. The only instance that guarantees this is the moment the Exit status is set.

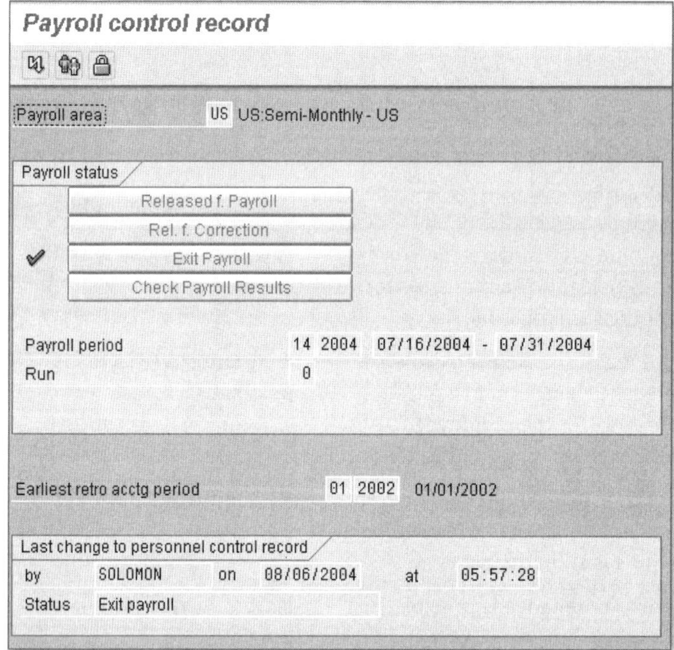

Figure 9.9 The Payroll Control Record (PA03)

The upper left corner of the payroll control record displays a range of icons, which can simplify the execution of the payroll run (see Figure 9.10). The user has the following options — restricted to the assigned payroll area:

Figure 9.10 Additional Icons of the Payroll Control Period

- Display matchcode "W" (employees whose payroll needs a correction before control record can be set to Exit)
- View the list of assigned employees
- Display the employees currently locked for processing via Infotype 0003

The payroll control record logs the history of the changes, so that you can see which user carried out which status change (see Figure 9.11).

Chngd on	Time	User Name	PP	PayY	Control record status...	SpRn
10/03/2003	21:35:14	PITTEN	14	2003	Exit payroll	
10/03/2003	21:04:58	PITTEN	14	2003	Released for payroll	
10/03/2003	18:46:17	PITTEN	13	2003	Exit payroll	
10/03/2003	15:39:19	PITTEN	13	2003	Released for payroll	
06/19/2003	18:12:52	HEATWOLE	12	2003	Exit payroll	
06/19/2003	18:12:46	HEATWOLE	12	2003	Released for payroll	
06/19/2003	18:12:40	HEATWOLE	11	2003	Created new	
06/19/2003	18:12:32	HEATWOLE	12	2003	Deleted	

Figure 9.11 Log of the Payroll Control Record

Payroll Run

The payroll run is started for a payroll control record (representing a payroll area), which establishes the period for which the payroll is performed. The assigned payroll area determines the employees for whom payroll is carried out. For each individual employee, it is then determined if retroactive calculation is necessary and if so for which period. This information is extracted from Infotype 0003 (Payroll Status). Payroll for an employee is chronologically implemented from the oldest to the newest period. Figure 9.12 shows the principle of the payroll program. The "basic version" RPCALCX0 displays an international template. The same principle is also used in the U.S. version RPCALCU0 and the other country versions. Some of these country versions (e.g., for the East European countries) are not delivered with the standard system but rather as add-ons.

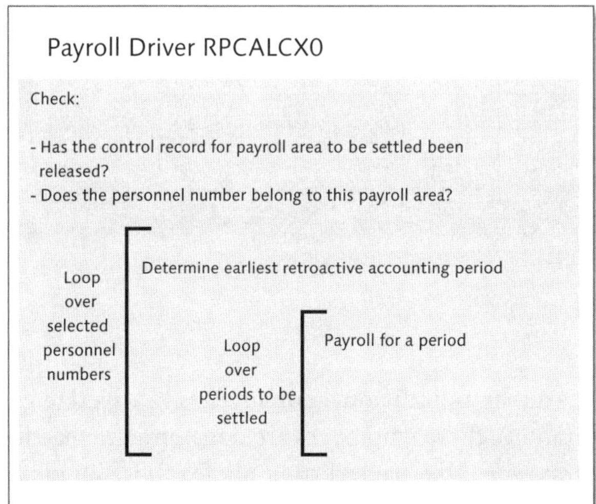

Figure 9.12 Payroll Structure

Payroll Cluster

The payroll calculates the gross components for all employees of a payroll area, while in the net payroll it calculates the relevant amounts to be paid out. These are saved in clusters. To avoid redundant data records and possible inconsistencies, all programs that require these results access them directly. In this context, the payroll results are stored according to the procedure described in Section 9.2.2 and can be displayed using report RPCLSTRU (U.S. version) (see Figure 9.13).

The payroll cluster then saves a multitude of data. In addition to a range of master data and data from time management, the calculated wage types are also saved (see Figure 9.14).

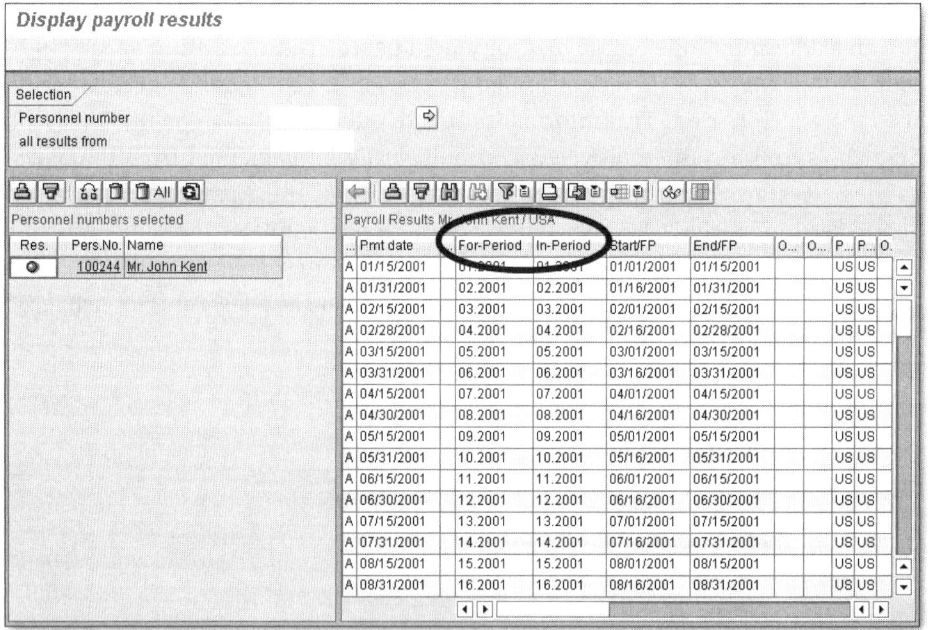

Figure 9.13 Payroll Results for an Employee

Matchcode "W"

If, during the payroll run, the payroll for an individual employee is canceled (e.g., due to errors in the basic remuneration), these employees are transferred to matchcode "W." This makes it possible to repeat the payroll run only for those employees for whom payroll was not carried out correctly. If payroll is carried out for an employee without any errors, the employee is removed from matchcode "W."

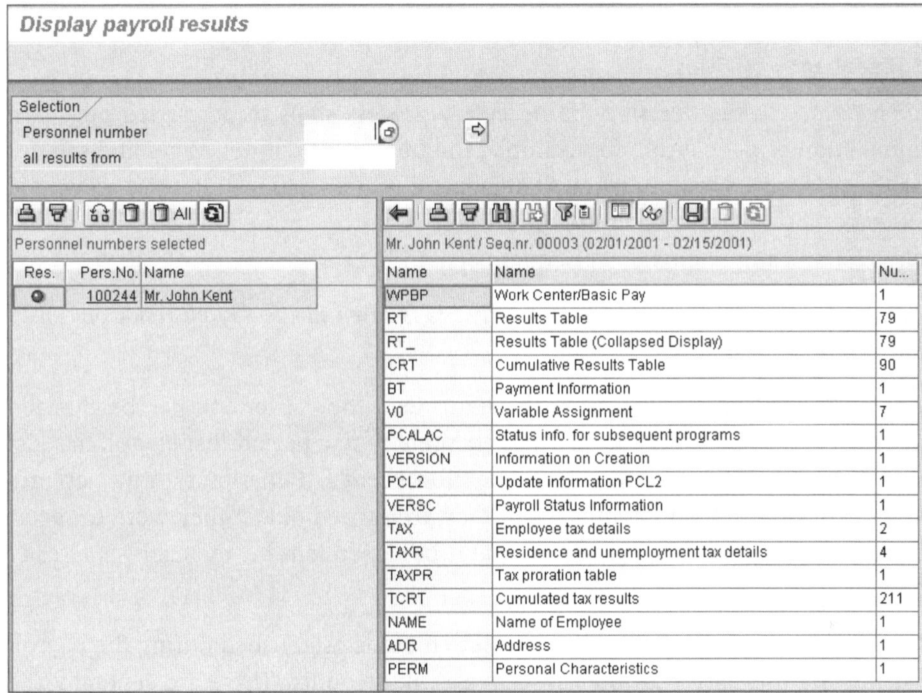

Figure 9.14 Payroll Result for a Period

Employees are also transferred to matchcode "W" if changes to the payroll-relevant master data have been implemented in periods for which payroll has already run. This is the case, for example, in the "correction" status of the payroll control record if the changes are not implemented for the future.

Thus, matchcode "W" ensures that in each case only the first payroll run for a period for all employees is performed. All other payroll runs can use matchcode "W." This saves time.

Matchcode "W" is visible as the Payroll Correction indicator in Infotype 0003 (Payroll Status) for an employee. However, from release 4.6x on, only the information from table T52MCW is displayed. It can be changed, however, via the maintenance screen of Infotype 0003 (which can be reached through the menu path UTILITIES • CHANGE PAYROLL STATUS from the master data maintenance) through the menu items EXTRAS • SET CORRECTION RUN OR EXTRAS • DELETE CORRECTION RUN. Employees of a payroll control record who are located in matchcode "W" can be seen using Transaction PA03 (see Figure 9.10).

Subsequent Activities

Subsequent activities describe the necessary process steps to be carried out upon completion of the payroll, for example, the transfer of the net wages and salaries or the printing of remuneration statements. From a technical point of view, you can carry this out at any point in time. There is, however, the following basic principle for all components of subsequent activities:

All necessary data for the subsequent activities is saved in the payroll result or can be retrieved from there.

As soon as the control record has the status Exit, the master data can be changed again. This also applies to master data that relates to a period that payroll has just been completed. The components of the subsequent activities must, however, provide identical results no matter when they are carried out. If they were to revert back to the master data, the result would be dependent on the changes already carried out.

With the bank transfer, all of the transfer amounts established during the payroll process are transferred to the respective bank accounts. These are generally the net wages and salaries and various local or country-specific transfers (in the U.S., for example, the company pension and garnishments). For this, not only the wage types but also the relevant bank details are saved in the payroll system.

The bank transfer itself is carried out in three steps:

1. In the first step, you create an extract of the transfer data through the so-called preliminary program. The extract is identified by the date and time of the program run where the last digit of the seconds is replaced with a "P." The preliminary program selects all of the transfers contained in the extract by supplementing the respective transfers in the payroll results with the program-run identification of the extract. This avoids transfers being carried out several times. In addition —by using the selection field "wage type, " — you can access the preliminary program so that the garnishments are transferred at a different time. You can then exclude the wage type for garnishment transfers so they can be written to another extract.

2. Next you must create the DME. The DME represents the nationally valid format for data to communicate with banks. For this reason, the program used for this comes from FI. It requires the program identification of the extract from the preliminary program. The "P" at the end of the program-run identification ensures that the individual transactions contained in the DME in FI cannot be seen.
3. In the last step, the newly created DME can be copied to a diskette and sent.

A separate payment run independent of the payroll can be implemented by using report RPCDTBU0. It reads data from Infotypes 0011, 0014, and 0015 and — as is the case with the normal preliminary program — provides these in an extract. The records thus created are locked against changes until the next payroll run and are integrated in the payroll results. A prerequisite for correct processing in the payroll is the relevant Customizing of the wage types used. By using this process, down payments between two payroll runs can be implemented.

Payroll posting runs in two steps. In the first step, all employees are checked to see if *debit = credit* is valid for the posting to be created. Only when this condition has been fulfilled are the posting dates of the employee transferred to the complete posting.

The posting program recognizes three types of posting runs:

- In the test run, only "T" is checked if the condition debit = credit is fulfilled for the employees.
- The simulation run "S" creates a simulation document for posting. Here, all warnings and errors emerge as they would at a later production run (e.g., locked cost centers or unavailable accounts).
- Production run "P" creates the same data as in the simulation run. The posting run, however, has the "productive" status and can therefore be released and posted (this is the second step). In addition, all employees for whom the necessary prerequisite *debit = credit* was fulfilled are provided with an indicator, so that multiple postings can be avoided. The production run can be repeated until no more employees exist with *debit = credit*. The frequent reason for such an inconsistency is that wage types were not accounted for.

The simulation and production runs can be seen using Transaction PCP0 (see Figure 9.15).

Display posting runs

Active filter using: Status

Typ Name								
Run number	**Run name**	**Run information**	**Sim**	**Status**	**St**	**User name**	**Created on**	**Time**
PP Payroll posting								
0000000113		PArea D2/11/2000	☑	Documents created	31	CORTADELLAS	2001.01.19	13:57:16
0000000112		PArea D2/12/2000	☑	Documents created	31	CORTADELLAS	2001.01.19	13:56:24
0000000111		PArea D1/07/2000	☑	Incorrect documents	90	CORTADELLAS	2000.08.01	14:11:37
0000000110		PArea D2/06/2000	☑	Documents created	31	BONIN	2000.07.28	12:19:39
0000000109		PArea D2/06/2000	☑	No documents created	30	BONIN	2000.07.28	12:17:29
0000000108		PArea J0/03/1999	☑	Documents created	31	NAGANOC	2000.03.03	17:06:10
0000000085		PArea D2/01/1999	☑	Documents created	31	BONIN	1999.06.11	11:01:23
0000000081		PArea D1/01/1999	☑	Documents created	31	BONIN	1999.06.10	16:29:27
0000000079		PArea D2/01/1999	☑	Documents created	31	BONIN	1999.06.10	16:20:37
0000000077		PArea D2/01/1999	☑	Incorrect documents	90	BONIN	1999.06.10	15:16:48
0000000076		PArea D2/01/1999	☑	Incorrect documents	90	BONIN	1999.06.10	15:15:25
0000000075		PArea D2/01/1999	☑	Incorrect documents	90	BONIN	1999.06.10	15:13:04
0000000074		PArea D2/01/1999	☑	Incorrect documents	90	BONIN	1999.06.10	13:49:12
0000000073		PArea D1/01/1999	☑	Documents created	31	BONIN	1999.06.10	13:43:09
0000000066		PArea D1/03/1999	☑	Documents created	31	BONIN	1999.06.10	11:40:29
0000000065		PArea G1/06/1997	☑	Incorrect documents	90	SPARKES	1998.11.04	08:54:35
0000000064		PArea G1/06/1995	☑	Incorrect documents	90	SPARKES	1998.11.04	08:54:02
0000000063		PArea G1/06/1995	☑	Incorrect documents	90	SPARKES	1998.11.04	08:53:11
0000000061		PArea G1/06/1995	☑	Incorrect documents	90	SPARKES	1998.11.03	16:58:52
0000000060		PArea G1/06/1995	☑	Incorrect documents	90	SPARKES	1998.11.03	16:54:14
0000000059		PArea G1/06/1995	☑	Incorrect documents	90	SPARKES	1998.11.03	16:47:07

Figure 9.15 Posting Runs (Transaction PCP0)

In the run history you can trace who carried out which steps (see Figure 9.16).

The run attributes display whether all employees have been transferred to FI (see Figure 9.17).

Run 0000000113: Display history

Status	User	Date	Time
new	CORTADELLAS	2001.01.19	13:57:16
Selection is running	CORTADELLAS	2001.01.19	13:57:16
Document creation initiated	CORTADELLAS	2001.01.19	13:57:17
Document creation is running	CORTADELLAS	2001.01.19	13:57:17
Documents created	CORTADELLAS	2001.01.19	13:57:19

Figure 9.16 Run History

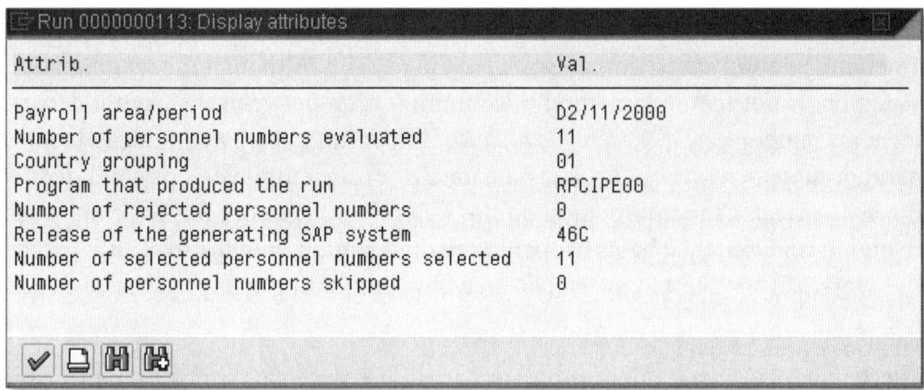

Figure 9.17 Run Attributes

Production runs must be released and posted for transfer into FI. It is not important at this point whether Human Resources (HR) and FI are located in two different systems. The payroll posting is Application Link Enabling (ALE) capable, i.e., the existing system landscape is not visible in the posting process.

If a production run is deleted, all of the flags set for the affected employees will be deleted again in the background so that a repetition of the production run is possible.

Warning

Deleting the flag takes place asynchronously to the dialog, i.e., it takes a few minutes until this process is completed by the system according to the amount of personnel numbers. Production runs that have already been booked can also be cancelled from here.

There are a range of evaluations that can read the payroll cluster and can display it in different processed forms (see Table 9.6).

Report	Technical Name	Period	Main focus
Payroll accounts	RPCKTOX0 (no U.S. version)	For Period	Employee
Payroll journal	RPCLJNU0	In Period	Employee
Wage-type reporter	H99CWTR0	Both	Wage type

Table 9.6 Evaluating the Payroll Results

Remuneration statement

The remuneration statement is also called the pay slip. Although the remuneration statement is not the only method of communication between the payroll department and employees, it certainly is the most important one. A well-designed remuneration statement clearly explains the details for the employee's pay and deductions. The clearer the information on the statement, the easier it is for employees to understand exactly what is happening to their payroll. It will also greatly reduce the workload for the payroll department by eliminating many queries on such issues.

The remuneration statement program has different versions for different countries and regions. The program name is RPCEDT<x>0, in which x stands for the country indicator (U for U.S., K for Canada, and X for international). This program reads employee master data and the payroll result cluster and prints that information in a predefined layout. The modifications to the remuneration statement do not have consequences for the generated payroll data. Sometimes it is necessary for the payroll data to be presented in a different way than the payroll result. For example, the amounts of some deduction wage types need to be grouped together and printed in one line item as a total. The layout of the remuneration statements is defined through forms. Figure 9.18 shows the selection screen of the remuneration statement program RPCEDTU0.

The parameters on the selection screen can control how the program runs. The following are some of the most important parameters:

The parameters in the field Print Retroactive Runs control whether retroactive runs are printed. There are three possible options:

- " " (space): Retroactive runs are never printed.
- "X": Retroactive runs are always printed.
- "L": Retroactive runs are only printed if a difference occurs with respect to the next-to-last payroll run for a wage type marked appropriately in table T512E in the field DIFAR.

As shown in Figure 9.19, in table T512E, the first three wage types are marked with R in column Dif, which is different from the last one. The changes can also be made within the Form Editor, through the path Window • Groups • DifRel field.

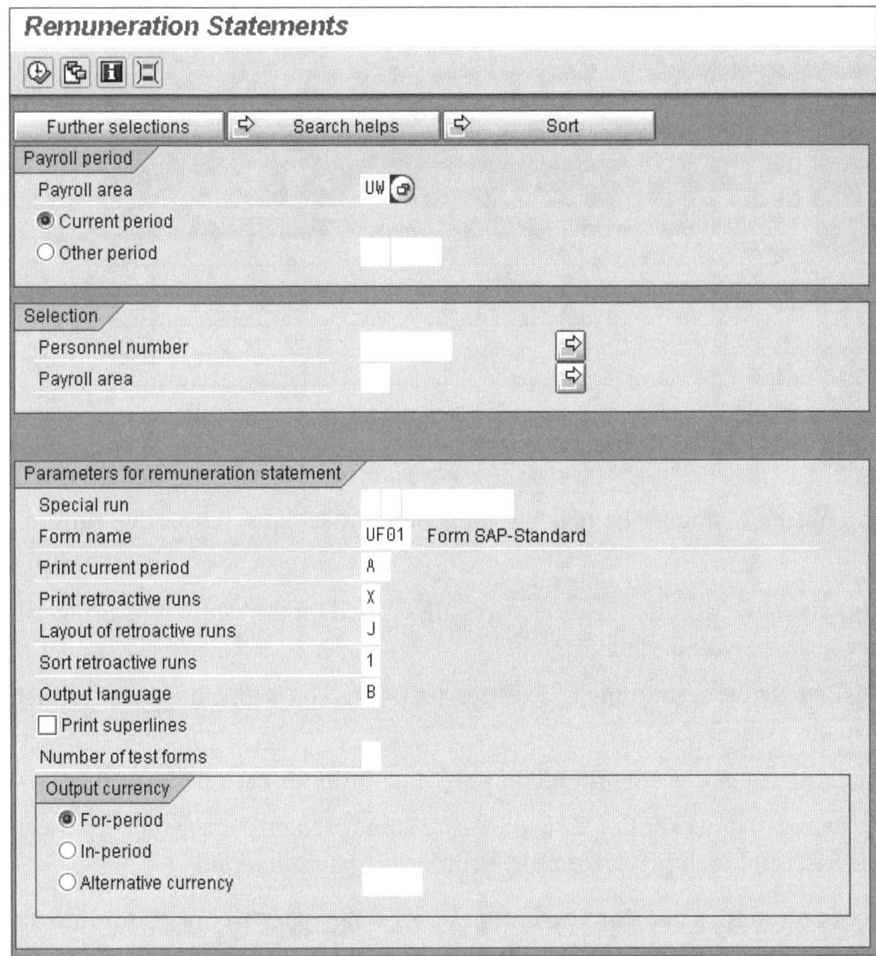

Figure 9.18 Run RPCEDTU0

During the program run, all wage types with this indicator are checked to see if there are changes to the "period's second-to-last payroll run." If a difference is found in at least one wage type, the form for retroactive accounting is printed. Those flags should be set only to the wage types for which changes are important (for example, insurance deductions). Changes to the rest of the wage types are ignored. Therefore, no retroactive statement will be printed out. This not only saves paper, it also decreases confusion among employees.

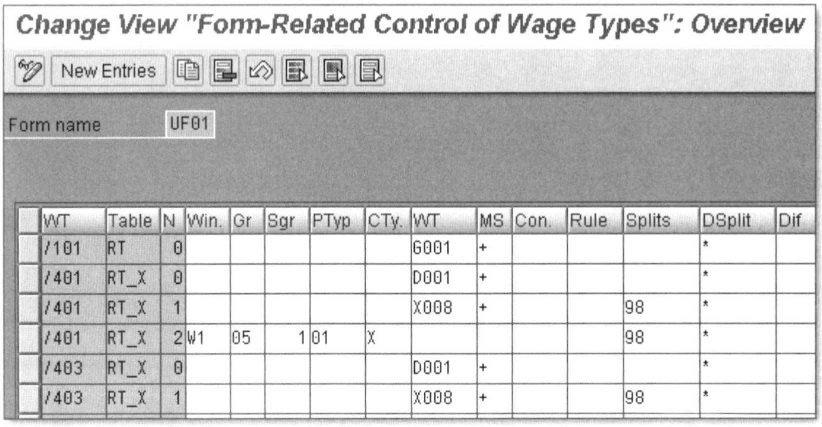

Change View "Form-Related Control of Wage Types": Overview

New Entries

Form name UF01

WT	Table	N	Win.	Gr	Sgr	PTyp	CTy.	WT	MS	Con.	Rule	Splits	DSplit	Dif
/101	RT	0						6001	+				*	
/401	RT_X	0						D001	+				*	
/401	RT_X	1						X008	+			98	*	
/401	RT_X	2	W1	05	1	01	X					98	*	
/403	RT_X	0						D001	+				*	
/403	RT_X	1						X008	+			98	*	

Figure 9.19 Print Control of Retroactive Run

The parameter Layout of Retroactive Runs determines how retroactive runs are printed:

- "A": Retroactive accounting differences are printed on the same form as the values for the payroll period
- "D": Retroactive accounting differences are printed on a separate form for each period
- "J": Retroactive runs are printed on a separate form for each period
- "S": Retroactive accounting differences are cumulated on a wage-type-by-wage-type basis and then printed on the form for the payroll period

The field Sort Retroactive Runs determines how wage types are sorted for retroactive accounting printouts. The detailed information for each program parameter can be displayed by pressing the key F1 while the cursor is put in the field. The control of retroactive payroll printouts significantly increased the complexity of the printing process of the remuneration statement, because it required special form-editing tools other than the standard SAPscript. The most commonly used tool is the Form Editor.

Form Editor

The Form Editor is a tool to modify forms used in HR. It can be accessed via Transaction code PE51 or the implementation guide (IMG) path Payroll: USA • Forms • Remuneration Statement • Setup Remuneration Statement.

Because the forms are processed by country-specific programs, such as remuneration statement printing program, a country grouping must be specified for each form. For each form, the following subobjects need to be maintained in the Form Editor.

- **Attributes**
  Attributes include the basic information of the form. The responsible person and maximum size can be maintained here.
- **Background**
  The background defines the information on the statement background.
- **Single fields**
  The single field refers to a field with value. The value can be a language-independent fixed text string, a language-dependent text module, or a variable value from a table field.
- **Window**
  A window is an area defined in the form. Fields can be located in any position within a window. For example, wage types to be printed on the remuneration statement can be printed in windows.
- **Line layout**
  A line layout defines how texts in one line are arranged for printing.
- **Cumulation IDs**
  Cumulation IDs are used to group together the same kinds of wage types, time quotas, or absence types so that their values can be summed up together. For example, a Cumulation ID can be created on the remuneration statement to show the total deduction of an employee, which may include wage types for benefit deduction, tax deduction, and all other deductions.
- **Text modules**
  Text modules contain texts for different languages. By using text modules, a text object can be defined to print at a specified position despite the text language.
- **Rules**
  Rules in the HR Form Editor refer to the logic that determines whether a field should be printed or not based on certain criteria.
- **Documentation**
  As with many other SAP objects, it is possible to store the documentation of the form together with the form itself.

Figure 9.20 shows the relationships between the form elements. Fields and groups in windows contain information to be printed on remuneration statements. The modularized structure makes it easier to change the layout. Only the position of each element needs to be adjusted; the definition of contents can remain the same.

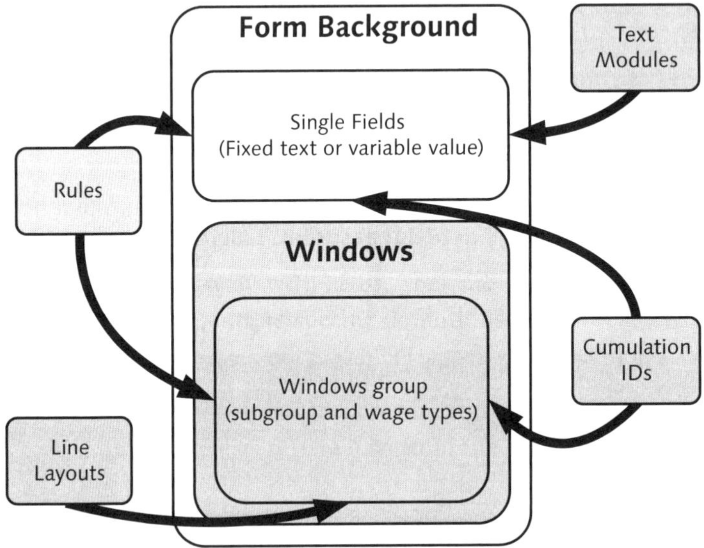

Figure 9.20 HR Form Editor

The adjustments to a single field, windows, and groups are described in detail in the following paragraphs. When you double-click on a field, a pop-up window appears with all attributes to be maintained for this field. Figure 9.21 shows the properties for the employee name field, whose value comes from employee master data table P0001. In the position information, you can also specify if this element is to be printed on every page or only on the first page or last page.

The print data section describes the source of the data for this field. The field value can be fixed as a constant or a text module that can be different for each language. It can also be a value from a table that can be determined only at run time. The pop-up window in Figure 9.21 shows some of the tables that can be used.

Tables RT, CRT, and SCRT are commonly used for wage-type-related information. If cumulation identifications are used, the table begins with Z, and contains the cumulation information. For example, ZRT contains information for cumulation wage types. You can get a full list of usable tables with possible entries with the (F4) function.

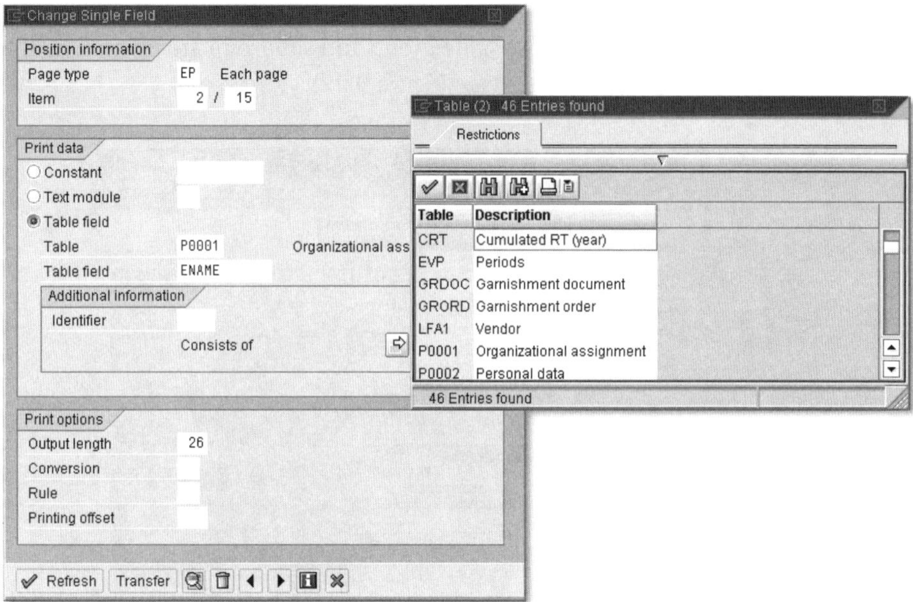

Figure 9.21 HR Form Single Field

There are two types of controls for the printing of wage types in the remuneration statement.

You can print out a wage type on the remuneration statement by maintaining evaluation class 02 in the table V_512W_D for the wage type. The IMG path for this is Payroll • Forms • Basic Settings • Maintain Evaluation Classes and Their Processing Class Values.

The value 01 to 03 determines which group in the windows the wage type is printed on forms. For example, if a wage type for state tax is to be printed, the value 02 is set for this wage type's evaluation class 2.

If the wage type is not to be printed, then value 00 should be assigned to the evaluation class for the wage type.

In the second type of control, you can use groups and subgroups of windows to directly include a wage type or cumulation identifier to be printed on the remuneration statement. The group and subgroup can be used to determine the sequence in which the wage types or cumulation identifier are printed. Giving group numbers to each wage type means that the wage types are printed in the ascending order of group numbers given. For wage types in the same group, the subgroup number is used. Wage types with the same group and subgroup are printed by the ascending order of wage-type names (see Figure 9.22).

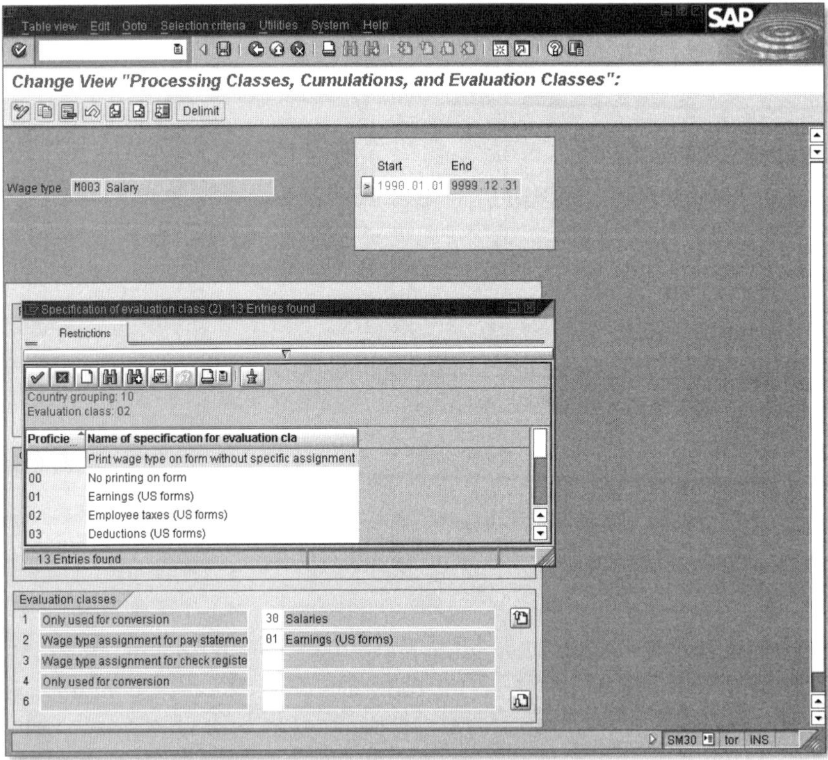

Figure 9.22 Printing Control for Wage Type by Evaluation Class 2

Double-clicking on the window area of the form triggers a pop-up window that shows all of the group definitions within the windows. Double-clicking on the group item again brings up another pop-up window for maintaining the detail of a group. Here you can maintain the wage types you want to print by referring to the wage-type table and the wage type directly. Subgroup (Sgr) is a mandatory field. You can also maintain other columns of the wage type as required, such as the condition rule for printing this element. For detailed meaning of each column, use F1 to get help information.

Because the elements within the group can only be displayed after double-clicking on the group entry, it is difficult to later find out the group with the wage type you want. Putting some quality summary information in the group text is a good way to help the search.

In Figure 9.23, all of the wage types have Ptyp 01 and Cty X. Those items are to be printed in the corresponding line layout shown in Figure 9.24.

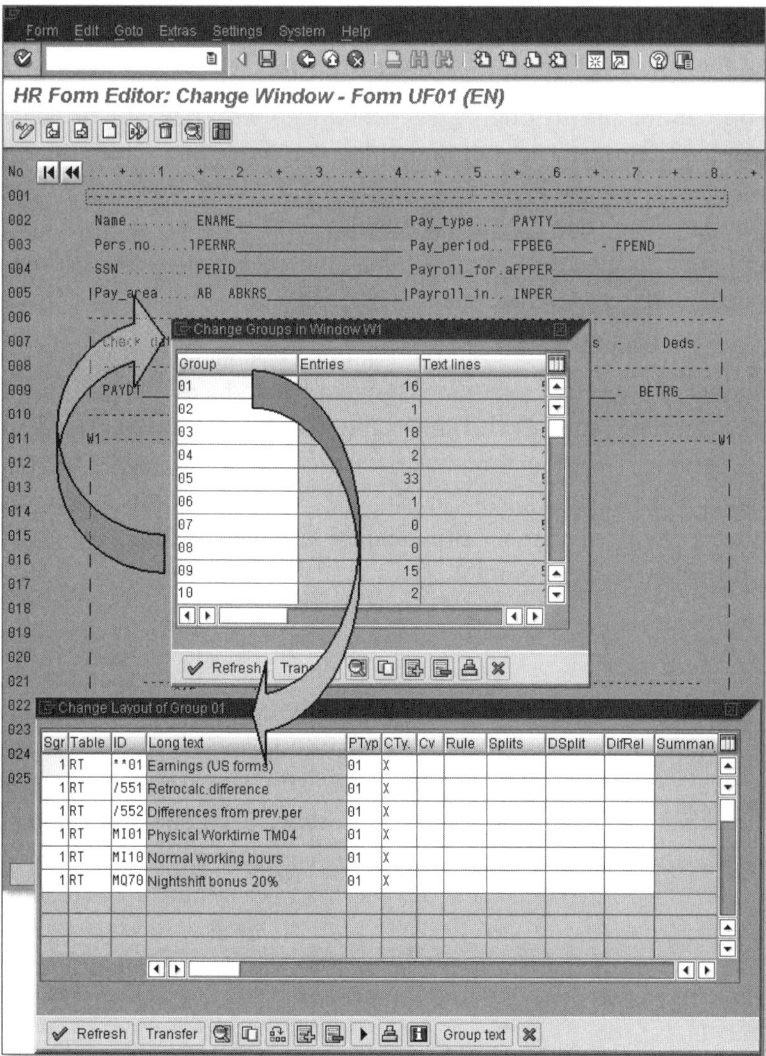

Figure 9.23 Form Window

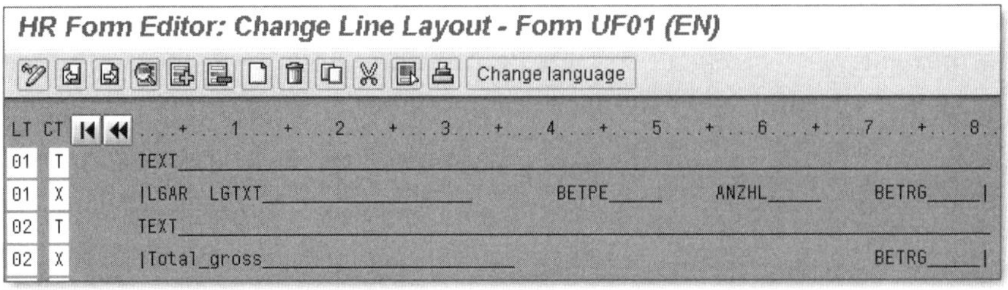

Figure 9.24 Line Layout in Form Editor

The settings for line layout are the same as those for single fields.

Although HR Form Editor already offers great flexibility, there could still be some requirement that cannot be met, such as information that has to be calculated from several fields. In that case, user exit RPCEDS29 can be used for enhancement. In this program, you can design your customized tables and fields, together with the logic to process them. However, before those tables and fields can be used in Form Editor, they must first be registered in table T514K and T514N.

All of the development effort devoted to the remuneration statement should be well documented. Usually, a remuneration statement has to be modified to meet legal and business requirements. At the same time, the documentation is crucial to understanding what was done before making new changes. We suggest that at least a text version of the documents be saved in the Form Editor with the documentation option. Thus, as long as the remuneration statement is there, the document can be easily found together with it.

HR Form Workplace

The remuneration statements printed from the Form Editor can only be text=based — the Form Editor supports neither the change of fonts nor any graphics. SAPscript can provide the rich format and graphics, but is not flexible enough for a complex remuneration-statement run logic. The HR Form Workplace is a newly developed tool from SAP to flexibly create and run various HR reports with advanced visual effects. From Enterprise HR Extension 2.00, the U.S. version of remuneration statement is supported (form name SAP_PAYSLIP_US). HR Form Workplace (Transaction code HRFORMS) is used to both define and execute the HR Smart Forms, including remuneration statement.

As shown in Figure 9.25, a remuneration statement in HR Form Workbench can have embedded graphics, different fonts, and shaded boxes. For more information about Smart Forms, please refer to the book SAP Smart Forms from SAP PRESS.

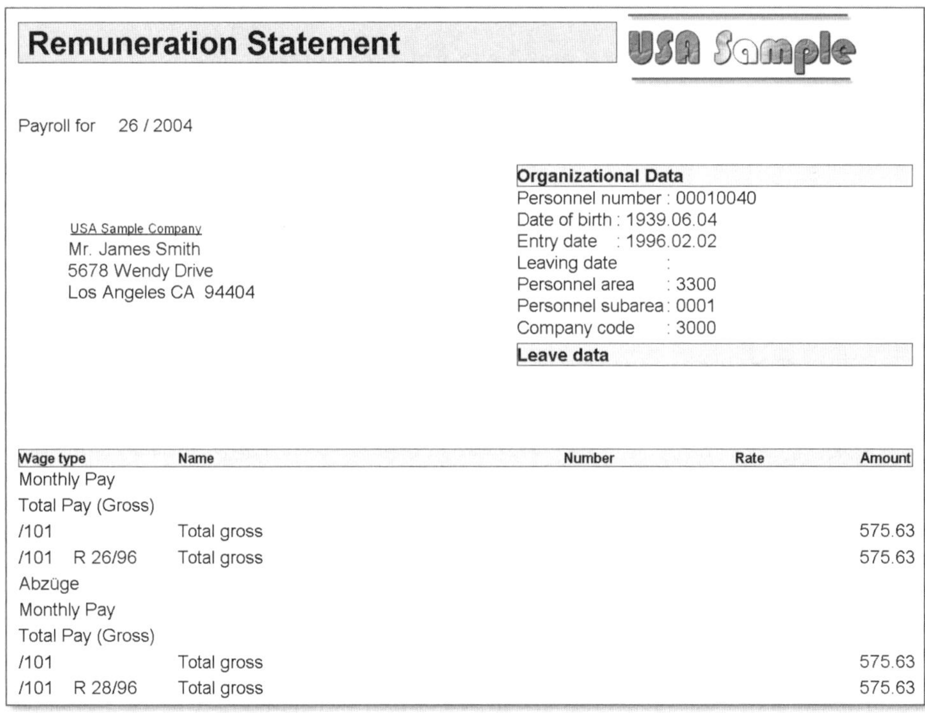

Remuneration Statement USA Sample

Payroll for 26 / 2004

USA Sample Company
Mr. James Smith
5678 Wendy Drive
Los Angeles CA 94404

Organizational Data
Personnel number : 00010040
Date of birth : 1939.06.04
Entry date : 1996.02.02
Leaving date :
Personnel area : 3300
Personnel subarea : 0001
Company code : 3000

Leave data

Wage type	Name	Number	Rate	Amount
Monthly Pay				
Total Pay (Gross)				
/101	Total gross			575.63
/101 R 26/96	Total gross			575.63
Abzüge				
Monthly Pay				
Total Pay (Gross)				
/101	Total gross			575.63
/101 R 28/96	Total gross			575.63

Figure 9.25 HR Form Workbench — Remuneration Statement

Tax Reporter

In the U.S., as a legal requirement, a company has to produce regular payroll tax reports to government authorities, which could involve a lot of work if done manually. SAP provides a tool for this called Tax Reporter (see Figure 9.26) that is closely integrated with payroll. The integration of the tax reporter with the payroll ensures the accuracy of the data on tax forms. You can use Tax Reporter to generate the following forms:

- Form 940 — Employer's Annual Federal Unemployment Tax Return
- Form 941 — Employer's Quarterly Federal Tax Return
- Form 941C — Supporting Statement to Correct Information

- Form W-2 — Wage and Tax Statement
- Form W-2C — Corrected Wage and Tax Statement
- 1099-R
- 1099-RC
- Multiple Worksite Report (Combined format for Bureau of Labor Statistics)
- Unemployment Insurance reports for all states

W-4 Withholding Allowance Report

W-4 Withholding Allowance Report

Tax Jurisdiction : CA
Allowance Threshold: 00

Per. no.	Employee name	Employee SSN	Effective date	Claimed Status	Claimed Allow	Mandated Status	Mandated Allow.
00010807	Natascha Pelster	777889999	1996.01.01	01	01	00	00
00010811	Milene Fisk	444332222	1996.01.01	01	01	00	00
00010812	Caroline Douglas	666443333	1996.01.01	01	01	00	00
00010813	Chris Zweber	666554444	1996.01.01	01	01	00	00
00010050	Matthew Stephens	777881234	1996.01.12	01	01	00	00
00010806	Bette Kay	666778888	1996.01.01	01	01	00	00
00010602	Carl Raymond	555221234	1995.05.18	01	01	00	00
00010603	Mary Ferguson	555998765	1996.01.01	01	01	00	00
00010604	Carl Jackson	555443333	1996.02.01	01	01	00	00
00010800	Frank Costello	556784567	1996.02.01	01	01	00	00
00010805	Butch Masters	555667777	1996.01.01	01	01	00	00
00010814	David Taylor	777665555	1996.01.01	01	01	00	00
00010009	Mike Eckert	555199991	1996.02.01	01	02	00	00
00010021	Anthony Benett	472998888	1996.01.04	01	05	00	00
00010817	Jane Simon	444335555	1996.01.01	01	01	00	00

Figure 9.26 Tax Reporter

When the tax reporting runs, it reads the payroll result from the payroll cluster tables and third-party remittance and generates the tax forms. The forms can be printed out or saved to disks, according to the setup of the output options.

After generating the Tax Reporter forms, all of the results for each employee and for the entire tax company are stored in the cluster PCL4 at field level. The advantage of storing the tax data in a cluster is obvious. This will allow the users to reproduce the forms already generated without repeating the calculation. When the retroactive payroll run is performed, you need to rerun the tax report to get the latest tax report result. The new result will be updated in PCL4 automatically when you rerun the Tax Reporter.

The menu path for running Tax Reporter is US PAYROLL • SUBSEQUENT ACTIVITIES • PERIOD-INDEPENDENT • PAYROLL SUPPLEMENT • TAX REPORTER, or Transaction Code PU19. Figure 9.26 shows the output screen for Tax Reporter.

The tax reports are generated based on the payroll results of the entire tax company, which is linked to the employee indirectly by personnel area and personnel subarea. You can define the tax company via IMG path PAYROLL • PAYROLL USA • TAX • TAX COMPANIES • ASSIGN TAX COMPANY TO PERSONAL AREA.

When running the tax reports for a tax company, especially when many employees are involved, we suggest running this report in the background to avoid timeout errors. Splitting the employee into batches by defining program variants for different selection ranges can also help to shorten the runtime.

Please note that legal requirements for the tax forms, including formula and layout, may change occasionally. SAP delivers the corresponding changes through HR support packages. Please make sure you have the correct packages installed before using the Tax Reporter.

Garnishment

Garnishment is a legal process to withdraw an employee's income directly from the employer to pay debts owned by the employee. SAP U.S. Payroll fully supports this functionality.

Garnishment can be processed only after a court order is issued requesting garnishment. The garnishment request information is stored in infotypes for later processing.

Several infotypes are used to support garnishment. Infotype 0194 (Garnishment Document) needs to be created for a garnishment request. Subsequently, Infotype 0195 (Garnishment Order) also needs to be created to store further detailed garnishment information, such as creditor information (as a vendor in the SAP FI component) and process information. These are the mandatory infotypes for the garnishment process. If an adjustment is required, such as a new balance or refund, the Infotype 0216 (Garnishment Adjustment) is created to reflect the change.

Figure 9.27 shows the garnishment process originated from a court order.

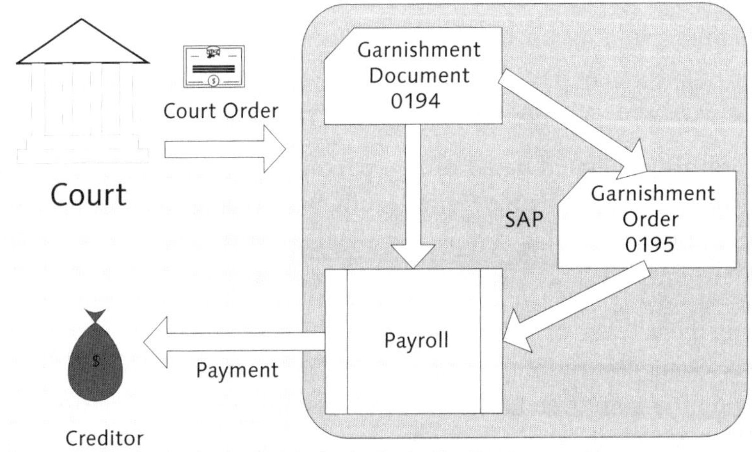

Figure 9.27 Garnishment Process

During the net-payroll processing, the garnishment infotypes are read and garnishment deductions are made to the employee's pay according to the Customizing.

To implement the garnishment functionality, the following settings are essential:

- Wage types have to be set up to represent the garnishments. Processing class 60 has to be set up for each wage type relevant to garnishment.
- Garnishment order types define the required fields and field rules for the garnishment document. They also define the priority for deduction when more than one garnishment deduction is needed.
- In SAP U.S. Payroll, schema UGRN is used to process garnishment. The concept of schema and payroll driver will be described in the following sections.

9.2.4 HR Process Workbench

The payroll run happens periodically and repeatedly for any organization. To finish one complete cycle, the payroll administrator has to run the payroll and all necessary subsequent activities, such as posting and check printing. If an error occurs during any step, the administrator has to fix the problem and then generally restart the whole payroll process. That's not all. If different groups of employees need to run payroll separately, a similar process has to be run again and again. Even for the most experienced payroll administrator, to execute all of these manually can be a challenging job.

It is a good idea to schedule parallel jobs for a payroll run to save some time. Report RPCSC000 can be used for parallel job scheduling. By defining different program variants with separate groups of employees, it is possible to run all of the jobs simultaneously.

But for the payroll run, subsequent steps and all dependencies also need to be considered. Some of these steps use the results from the previous steps. In the event of an error with some employees, the whole process must be able to either stop, or move forward with rest of the group. Those requirements are beyond the capacity of a simple job scheduler.

HR Process Workbench is an advanced tool to define, schedule, run, and monitor payroll run processes. Like program RPCSC000, it can schedule jobs in parallel to greatly speed up payroll calculation. From release 4.7, it also supports the job scheduling on separate servers to further enhance the performance.

To get benefits from the HR Process Workbench, process models must be defined. A process models is a sequence of elements that include programs that can be run one after another or in parallel.

Depending on the purpose of the process models, they must be given assignments, which can be regular payroll run, off-cycle payroll run, or interface toolbox. The system comes with predefined process models that are suitable for different assignments as templates. We recommend that you copy the predefined template process model to your own process models and apply your own changes.

The tool to define the process model is process model editor. The process model editor can be found via the path PEST. Human Resources • Payroll USA • Tools • Customizing Tools • Maintain Process Model.

There are three major areas on the process model editor's screen: Display Area, Navigation Area, and Insertable Object Area. As shown in Figure 9.28, the process model is displayed in the Display Area; the Navigation Area is used to control which part of the process model is displayed in the Display Area, and the Insertable Object Area provides the template of objects that can be used in the process model as steps.

Programs are the key elements for a process model. The programs used in the process model are exactly the same programs used for a manual run. To feed input such as selection criteria into the program while it is running in background, program variants are used.

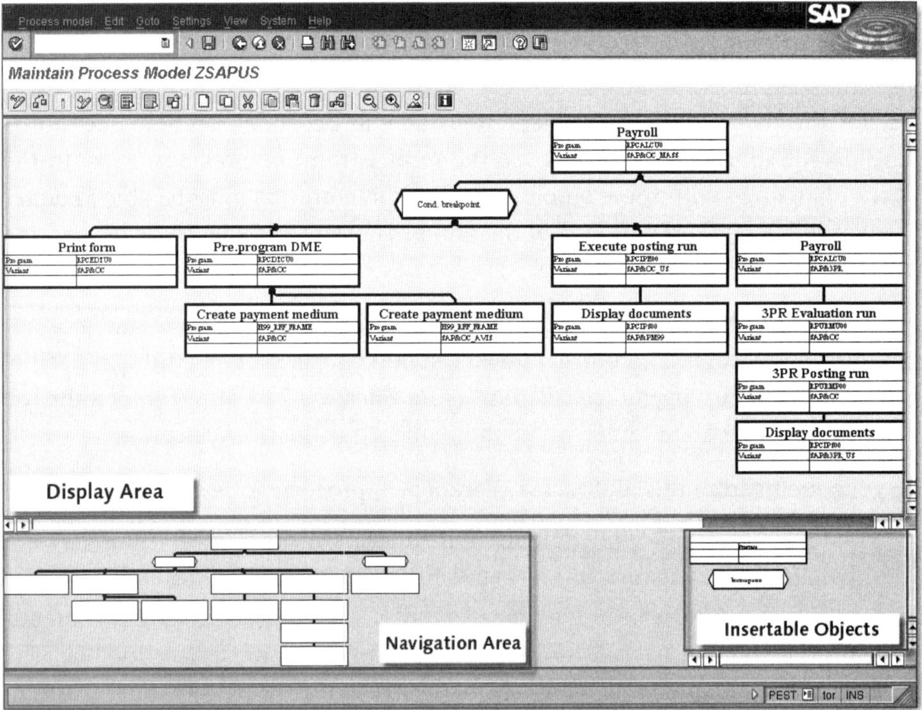

Figure 9.28 HR Process Workbench

Please note that it is very important that the correct variant is predefined and selected for a program element. This is especially true when a template process model is copied and modified. For example, if you copy a process model for production payroll run into a test-run model, you have to make sure the variant in the new process model includes the test flag checked.

Apart from the programs, a process model has to include a selection program that determines which employee numbers will be included in this process. The selection program defines the scope of the process run, so it must be defined at the creation of the process model. Please note that the selection program is not a step of the process, but an attached attribute of the whole process model.

A process workbench may also include breakpoints or wait points. A breakpoint is set where you want the process to stop with or without condition. Once the process is stopped, you can restart the process for the conditional breakpoint or continue to run the process from the steps after the unconditional breakpoint.

Wait points are always conditional. When a wait point is triggered, the process will go to "wait" status until a specified event occurs due to other HR activities in the system. The event can be a system event, workflow event, or simply the end of other steps within the process model. Once the specified event comes out (for example, an operation mode switch that indicates the time window for background processing to begin), the standby process will continue automatically. You cannot rerun the same process while it is at wait status.

The process models defined in the process workbench are also used on off-cycle workbench to perform post-payroll run activities, such as posting and check printing.

The Transaction PUST is used to run a process model. Each run of the process module is a process. SAP online help has detailed instructions on how to run a payroll process.

9.2.5 The Payroll Calculation

Payroll is a matter of getting correct numbers for employees' payments and deductions. All of the data and customizing are designed and maintained to support the calculation itself. A payroll calculation program is the core component of payroll.

For conversional software programs, any change in the logic requires a program change. The SAP system is designed as a standard system, which means it is designed to have common functionalities for all clients and, at the same time, the flexibility to be customized based on individual customer's needs. It is impossible to do this in a conversional way because programmers can not foresee all of the possibilities. To make the calculation logic easily customized without changing the calculation programs all of the time, SAP developed the concept of schemas and rules.

Concept

Unlike a conversional program that has all logic, including submodules in one program, SAP takes some of the logic controls out of its payroll program and makes those controls customizable. The core payroll calculation program is called payroll driver in SAP. The payroll driver contains only the commonly used program modules or subroutines for calculation. Schemas and rules are used to flexibly control how the payroll driver behaves in various circumstances.

The schema has a similar concept to that of a macro. It contains entries representing various pieces of code (submodules) within the payroll driver program. Reorganizing the entries in the schema has the same effect as rewriting the main program in a conversional program to include selected submodules in a specific order. After the payroll driver is triggered during the payroll run, the payroll driver refers to the schema and rules to decide which subroutines are called, in what sequence, and under what conditions.

By offering customizable schemas and rules, it is possible to change the payroll calculation process without having programming knowledge.

Figure 9.29 shows how the SAP payroll works differently from a conversional program.

Because legal requirements and business practices vary from country to country, SAP developed different standard versions of payroll calculation programs to reflect the various needs of different countries and regions. The payroll driver program name is RPCALC_0. The '_' represents a country indicator, e.g., U for U.S., K for Canada, and X for international payroll driver. The international payroll driver is used in regions that do not have a country-specific driver available, and it calculates only gross payroll. For U.S. payroll, the payroll driver program is RPCALCU0.

Schema

A personnel calculation schema consists of a number of functions in sequence. The term "function" in payroll means something different than it does in ABAP programming. A function in payroll schema is linked to a piece of ABAP code that will be called by the payroll driver when using the schema.

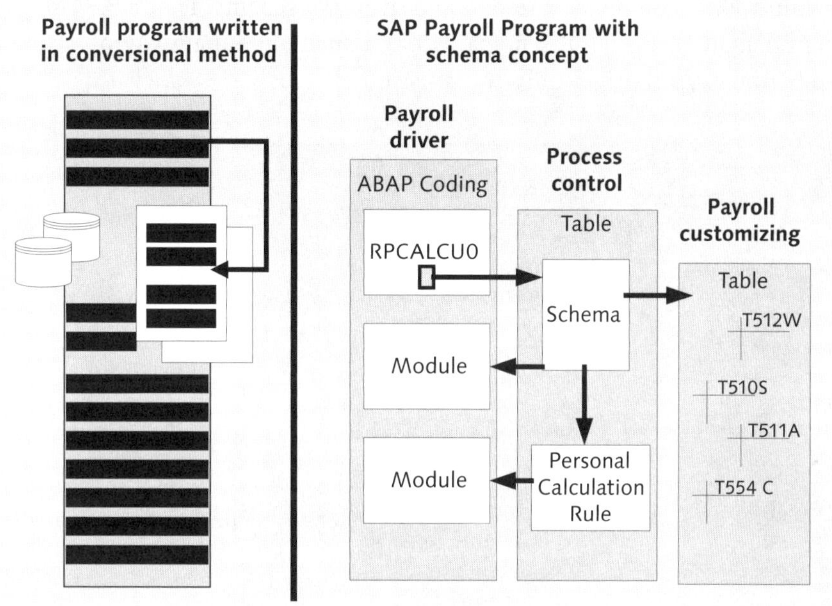

Figure 9.29 Schema Concept

A function may use a rule. Functions usually provide data and rules process them (see Figure 9.30). For example, function P0015 reads Infotype 0015 from employee master data. The rule following the function decides what's next.

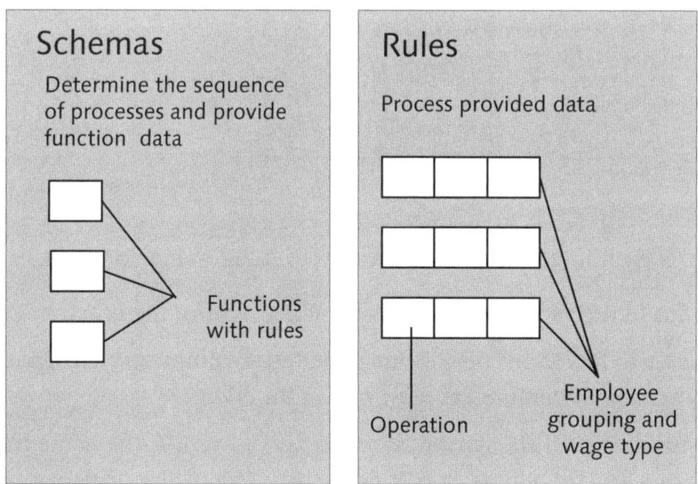

Figure 9.30 Schemas and Rules

Schema editor PE01 can be used to edit and display a schema. Figure 9.31 shows the system default U.S. payroll schema, U000. Usually, the main payroll schema executed by the payroll driver only contains subschemas.

	Func.	Par1	Par2	Par3	Par4	D	Text
000010	COPY	UIN0					US Payroll: Initialization of payroll
000020	COPY	UODP				*	On-demand regular (no need after 4.5A)
000030	COPY	UBD0					Basic data processing
000040	COPY	UPR0					Read previous result of current period
000050	COPY	ULR0					Import previous payroll results
000060	COPY	UMO0					Determine payroll modifiers
000070	COPY	UT00					Gross compensation and time evaluation
000080	COPY	UREI				*	Travel expense
000090	BLOCK	BEG					Gross cumulation and tax processing
000100	IF		NAMC				if non-authorized manual check (*)
000110	COPY	UMC0					Process Non authorized check (*)
000120	ELSE						else if non authorized manual check (*)
000130	COPY	UAP0					Process add. payments and deductions
000140	COPY	UAL0					Proration and cumulation gross
000150	COPY	UTBS					Save tables for iteration
000160	LPBEG						Begin of iteration
000170	COPY	UTBL					Load saved tables
000180	COPY	UDD0					Process deductions, Benefits
000190	COPY	UTX0					Calculate taxes
000200	COPY	UGRN					Calculate garnishments
000210	COPY	UNA0					Calculate net
000220	COPY	UDNT					Deductions not taken during loop ?
000230	LPEND						End of iteration
000240	ENDIF						to: if non authorized manual check (*)
000250	BLOCK	END					
000260	COPY	UGRR					Garnishment Retroactive
000270	COPY	URR0					Retroactive accounting
000280	COPY	UNN0					Net processing
000290	COPY	UAC0					Month end accruals
000300	COPY	UEND					Final processing

Figure 9.31 Schema U000

As shown in the Figure, each line of a schema includes the following columns:

- Line number to indicate the sequence of the current line within the schema.
- One Function column followed by up to four parameter columns, where you can put a function name and parameters used by the function.
- Column D is used to indicate if the current line is active or not. If the value in this column is * , it means the whole line is not active. When the driver program reads this line, it will simply be ignored.

- At the end of each line, a text can be maintained. This can be a note, comment, or anything you want to put.

Writing a schema is very much like writing a program. Schemas can be modularized for easy maintenance and reusability. There are several functions that are used for structuring the schemas.

Function COPY is used to include a subschema. This is just like an INCLUDE statement in ABAP programming. Whenever the payroll driver reads the function COPY, it jumps into the included schema and continues from there.

COM creates a comment line in the schema text. It can be put any where in a schema. A payroll driver always ignores these lines. However, they are not useless. It is very important to create short meaningful comment lines to briefly explain what the schema does.

BLOCK is another function used for structure control. The BLOCK BEGIN and BLOCK END are always a pair. They indicate the parts between those two lines as a block. In releases since 4.0, the schema logs are organized in a tree-like structure. With the block defined, the log information for a block will be displayed under one node. Blocks can be nested.

Function IF/ELSE/ENDIF provides a conditional route control for schema. There are two ways to set a condition: symbolic names or rules. Predefined symbolic names are populated automatically at certain points of the payroll run. A customer rule can also be used as condition, in which the operation SCOND is used to set the condition value. If the value to be set to **True, SCOND=T IF** should be included in the rule, **SCOND=F IF** is used to set the value to **False**. Nesting is also supported.

Loop functionality is implemented with LPBEG and LPEND. The LPBEG indicates the beginning of the loop and LPEND indicates the end. When the loop does not have a parameter, operation SCOND can be used in a rule within the loop to allow one more loop. To avoid a dead loop, the loop will stop by default.

Apart from the preceding structural control functions, there are three other types of commonly used functions in schema:

- Functions that read data from infotypes
- Functions that process data according to the Customizing
- Functions that update the wage types

Some of those functions will be explained later within the context of a schema. However, it's not possible to cover the use of all of those functions in this book. Details for a function can be displayed in schema editor PE01 by pressing the F1 key while placing the cursor on the function.

If the system-delivered schema cannot meet the requirements, you can make changes to it. We strongly suggest you do so in a customer client. Once you make changes to a standard schema in a customer client, a copy of the standard schema with your changes will form a new customer schema with the same name. The standard schema remains unchanged in client 000. Please note that the standard schemas may change during system upgrade or applying patches. Those SAP-delivered changes will not apply automatically to the customer schemas. It is important to manually compare the standard schema and customer schema after a system upgrade. If those changes reflect the latest legal requirements, you have to make corresponding changes to your customer schemas manually.

Due to the complexity and importance of the schema, only experts should be allowed to make changes.

Rules

Personnel calculation rules are used to process data made available by functions. A rule contains one or more operations. The operations define the value calculation statements in payroll and also the sequence of the statements.

Unlike the standard schemas and customer schemas, all rules can be modified the same way. You also can create your own rules in a suggested customer naming range. To modify a rule, you should do the following:

1. Copy the rule into a new one with the customer naming range (begins with Z or Y)
2. Only make changes to the new copy
3. Duplicate the line in the schema that calls the rule
4. Make the original line in the schema as comment (put a * in D column)
5. Change the new line to refer to the new rule name that was copied

The structure of rule is a decision tree. In the tool to edit rules (Transaction code PE02), a rule can be displayed either in a text table or in a tree-like structural graphic.

RPDASC00 is used to display a combined view of subschemas and rules within a main schema. It can expand and include all schema lines and rules detail into one continuous text while maintaining the sequence in which they are called by the payroll driver. Figure 9.32 shows an expanded view of schema U000 in report RPDASC00.

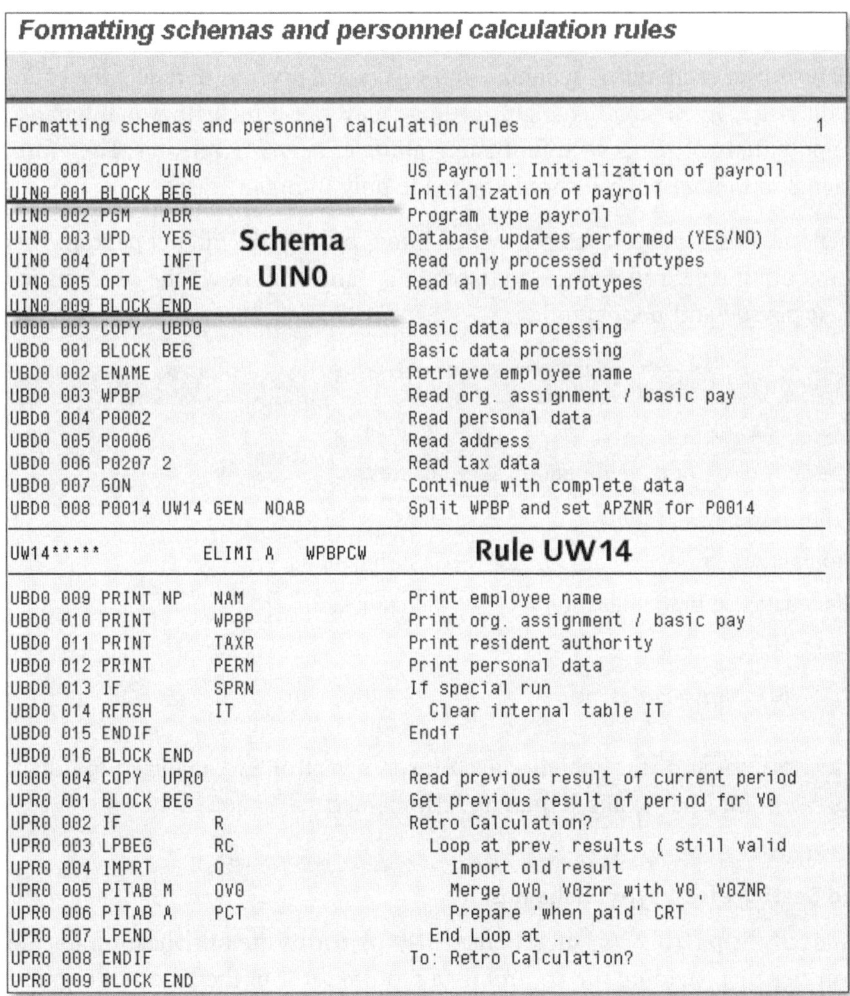

Figure 9.32 Schemas and Rules (RPDASC00)

For those special requirements in payroll calculation that have to be implemented with new operations in ABAP coding, SAP allows an enhancement to do it. New operations can be implemented in the reports and later used in the personnel-calculation rules. Report RPCBURZO is used for international customer operations, and RPCBURZ_O is for country-specific customer operations ("_" is the country indicator). After the enhancements for customer operations are done, the newly created operations need to be declared using Transaction PE04. You can also use this transaction to display ABAP codes related to existing functions and operations.

The SAP technical wage types, schemas, and rules are delivered to reflect the country-specific rules. Even small changes to those may cause recurring maintenance and also potential problems with future upgrading to new SAP releases. Therefore, adjustments to the net payroll should be made only in urgent cases.

The functionalities in payroll can be divided into gross payroll and net payroll. This applies to both the payroll driver and to schema. Table 9.7 shows the contents for both gross payroll and net payroll.

Gross Payroll (U.S.)	Net Payroll (U.S.)
Read basic data	Deductions
Read previous result of current period	Benefits
Import previous payroll results	Taxes
Gross compensation	Garnishment
Read time data and time evaluation	Net cumulation
Gross cumulation	

Table 9.7 Steps in Payroll Processing

In this section, some of the schemas used for U.S. payroll are analyzed in detail. The equivalent international schemas are also named.

Selected Settings for Payroll Schemas

At the start of the payroll run, subschema UINO performs the initialization for the payroll driver by providing the control data required to run the payroll program. For international payroll, XINO is the equivalent subschema.

A payroll program can be used to run payroll or do a postpayroll evaluation. The function PGM tells the payroll driver which type of program the schema will use.

To execute the payroll program, the function is set to parameter ABR. If this function is missing from the schema, the system will assume the program is for a payroll run. You can include more than one PGM function here, but only the value set by the last PGM function will be considered.

Function UPD is used to control the database update. Calling this function with parameter YES or NO controls whether the payroll results are updated into a database or only available during runtime. This applies only to a real payroll run. If the payroll run has been set to test run, function UPD will not update the database even when the parameter for UPD is set to "Yes."

Function OPT stands for optimize. This function is designed to enhance performance by reducing the infotypes to read during the payroll run. To import only the infotypes required in the functions within the schema, set the parameter to INFT. If the parameter TIME is set, all time infotypes are imported.

As shown in Figure 9.33, CHECK ABR is a function used to check the status of the employee's payroll area. When the function is used, only the employees in the payroll area with "released for payroll" status can be run. In a production client (for which client role T000-CCCATEGORY is set to "P"), this function is mandatory to keep the data consistency. For schemas used for test purposes, the status check for payroll control record is not necessary. To disable this check, this line should be changed to comment text.

	Func.	Par1	Par2	Par3	Par4	D	Text
000010	BLOCK	BEG					Initialization of payroll
000020	PGM	ABR					Program type payroll
000030	UPD	YES					Database updates performed (YES/NO)
000040	OPT	INFT					Read only processed infotypes
000050	OPT	TIME					Read all time infotypes
000060	OPT	DEC				*	Hourly rates with more than 2 decimals
000070	CHECK		ABR			*	Check over PA03
000080	OPT	BSI				*	Set switch BSI
000090	BLOCK	END					

Figure 9.33 Initializing Payroll Schema UINO

Note

CHECK ABR is deactivated by default (see Figure 9.33). Make sure it is activated before finalizing the payroll Customizing. If a test flag is marked for a payroll run, this check is disabled automatically. There is no need to keep a different version of a schema that has CHECK ABR deactivated in a production system.

Read Basic Data

Schema UBDO is a subschema used to read basic data for payroll. The basic data includes: employee name, event, scheduled work time, base pay, address, and relevant tax area data. The international equivalent schema is XBDO.

The function WPBP (work center basic pay) fills the employee master data, work center data, and basic pay data valid for the payroll period into the internal table WPBP. Function WPBP also fills internal table Information Technology (IT) with the basic pay wage types.

A function with name PXXXX where XXXX represents an infotype number is used to read and process infotype information. For example, P0002 reads personal data Infotype 0002, and P0014 reads and processes data from Infotype 0014. For some functions, rules can be used to further restrict the process of the infotype.

Time Matters in Payroll

When the SAP Time Management component is implemented, if the time evaluation for the payroll period has not been run, the payroll program can do the evaluation from a payroll perspective. In U.S. payroll schema U000, subschema UT00 is used to process time data, including the time evaluation. Within subschema UT00, function DAYPR calls the time evaluation schema for payroll TC00. The payroll schema for all regions shares the time evaluation schema XT00.

Both schema TC00 and TC04 can be used for time evaluation in payroll. TC00 deals with time data recorded in clock time format and full day records. TC04 only processes time data in an hourly format.

In the schema UT00, if the Plant Data Collection (PDC) is active for the payroll period being processed, the time wage types should already exist in table ZL of cluster B2. Then the system imports the cluster and only processes the days that have not been processed yet for the payroll period. The wage types that still have to be generated are formed according to the work schedule, which triggers retroactive accounting in the subsequent payroll period.

Time wage types are stored in internal table IT after the time data and employee remuneration information has been processed. Further process to the internal table IT is done using function PIT (process input table). Function PIT is widely used throughout the whole payroll schema. It reads personnel calculation rules to read Customizing table and process the internal table accordingly.

Like other wage types, time wage types are valuated using valuation bases. Based on the settings in view V_512W_B for each wage type, the valuation base can be one of the following:

- Valuation bases entered in a table as a constant
- Valuation bases calculated according to basic pay
- Valuation bases calculated as an average of several previous periods

Rule X015 checks whether each line in a wage-type internal table already has an amount. If this has not yet happened, then this rule tries to read table T512W to get the valuation base for the wage type. If the valuation base is set to K or TS, the constant from table T510 or T510J is used. If the valuation base is set to a number nn, the secondary wage type /0nn is used for the calculation. If no valuation base is found, X016 is called to evaluate the time wage type according to the principle of averages. X016 requires processing class 15.

The wage type that represents an element of the remuneration can follow different rules for different groups of employees. The Modifier is used to separate the different table entries in the Customizing tables. Function MOD is used to determine modifiers by calling a personnel calculation rule. The rule uses operation MODIF, which sets the modifier for table access. Table 9.8 shows the tables that a modifier can be set and the corresponding MODIF operations used.

Table	Function of the table	Operation
T510S	Wage type generation	MODIF 1=**
T510J	Constant valuations	MODIF 2=**
T510L	Levels table	MODIF 5=**
T599Y	Convert external wage types	MODIF 6=**
T599Z	Time wage types to external systems	MODIF 7=**
T554C	Absence valuation rule	MODIF A=**
T51D1	Limits for deductions	MODIF B=**

Table 9.8 Table of Modifier Assignment by MODIF

In schema UT00, the function ZLIT is used to valuate the absences. There are two basic principles for processing absences.

The first option is to valuate using an average or fixed amount. The other option is to valuate the absence as if the employee had worked. The function PAB processed the absences according to the settings for each absence wage type in V_T554C.

Factoring

The process of getting pro rata calculation of remuneration for a partial payroll period is called factoring. The process happens when the employee does not work for a complete payroll period, or during a period when the remuneration base for the work has changed, such as when salary has increased or scheduled working hours have been reduced.

When master data changes in the middle of a payroll period for an employee, the change may affect the gross payroll in such a way that the master data set before the change and after the change is used to calculate only remuneration for part of the payroll period. In this case, the calculation is done separately for each set of data and the prorated result is used to form the result for the whole pay period.

The payroll program checks the following infotypes to determine if factoring is needed:

- Infotype 0000 (Personnel Actions)
- Infotype 0001 (Organizational Assignment)
- Infotype 0007 (Planned Working Time)
- Infotype 0008 (Basic Pay)
- Infotype 0014 (Recurring Payments/Deductions)
- Infotype 0015 (Additional Payments)
- Infotype 2001 (Absences)

A factor with a value between 0 and 1 is required to calculate partial period amounts. The factor is determined based on the times obtained from employee's personal work schedule or absence data.

The formula used to calculate the factor has to be carefully selected according to needs. Because not all pay periods have the same length, it is possible that under certain circumstances a formula creates unwanted results. The commonly used formulas are:

- Deduction method — this method assumes the employee works for the whole period with the exception of the absences.

  Factor = 1 – absence/general period work time

You need an average working time for all periods as a calculation base. For example, 22 working days is used for general period work time for monthly payroll. This naturally causes problems when the pay period has different work time than the general period work time and the absence time is relatively big. An extreme example would involve absence for a whole period. If the period has 23 actual working days, then the factor becomes negative, while in a shorter period with only 20 working days, the factor is not zero and the employee gets paid even if he didn't work at all.

- Payment method — this method first assumes an employee does not work, and then gives payment to the employee according to the actual hours worked for the period.

  Factor = (planned working time – absence) / general period working time

Like the deduction method, this one does not suit all scenarios. For example, if an employee has one absence in a 23-day period, the factor is one, giving the employee a "free absence." On the other hand, if the same scenario happens in a short period with 20 actual working days, although the employee works 95% of the time, he gets paid only 83% of his monthly salary. This is obviously unfair.

- Personal Work Schedule method — this method uses the ratio of actual work time to "should work" time.

  Factor = 1 – absence / planned period working time

This seems fair, but there is a problem if the two periods have different scheduled working times. In that case, the same absence (e.g., one day) leads to different deductions from payment.

No method seems perfect, so during the implementation, the different scenarios need to be closely examined so that different methods are used for different circumstances.

In the payroll calculation, factors are stored in RTE fields of wage types from /801 to /816. The factor /801 to /809 can be freely used during the Customizing, while /810 to /816 has special meanings in the system. These wage types are generated by function GEN/8. The value is multiplied by 10,000 (KGENAU) to increase the accuracy of calculation.

In schema UALO (U.S. version of XALO), function PIT calls rules XPPF, XPPO, and XPP1 to calculate the factors. The actual formulas are maintained here. For example, in rule XPP1, the default rule reads:

RTE=TSSOLLRTE-TSAU** RTE*KGENAURTE/TSDIVIADDWT *

Here, TSSOLL stands for partial planned working hours, TSAU** stands for sum of all unpaid absence, and TSDIVI stands for the total working hours according to the employee's working schedule. So the formula means:

- Rate (the value of the factor) = Planned working hours
- Rate = Rate — Total of unpaid absences
- Rate = Rate * 10,000 (for accuracy)
- Rate = Rate / Total working hours according to the schedule
- Add the wage-type factor to wage-type table.

This is the personal work schedule method mentioned earlier. In default settings, it is used for factor wage type /801.

Note

Because a division operation is involved, make checks when writing formulas to make sure the divisor has a nonzero value to avoid an illegal operation.

Cumulation

During the payroll run, many wage types need to be cumulated, for example, the absence time and 401k contributions. The cumulation happens in different stages of the payroll run depending on the wage types' attributes. The following text shows the cumulation in U.S. payroll schema.

Personnel calculation rule X020 is used at the end of UTOO to cumulate the time-wage types based on the processing class 03. All time-wage types have already been valuated. Processing class 3 for each time wage type defines in which cumulation wage types it should be included, and how it is stored in the result table. The amounts of time wage types are cumulated to gross cumulation wage types /1nn and average base /2nn. Overtime hours can be cumulated into wage type /852.

In subschema UAL0, rule X023 is called to cumulate gross wage types. Processing class 20 is used to determine the cumulation wage type in which the basic pay wage type should be included and how the wage types are stored in the result table. The wage types are cumulated to wage types /1nn.

At the end of the payroll run, in subschema UEND, function ADDCU adds the wage types into annual result table CRT. Processing class 30 is used here to determine how the wage type is cumulated in the annual table.

Interface to Accounting

Different wage types and the amounts for each wage type represent the results for payroll. All of the dollars calculated by the payroll program have to have a source and destination in the accounting system. When SAP ERP HCM is integrated with the SAP FI and CO components, the expense and costs that occur during the payroll run can be posted to FI and CO. A symbolic account is the central concept for this posting process.

In payroll, a symbolic account is attached to the wage types whose amounts need to be posted. The account assignment type of the corresponding symbolic account determines the type of posting (for example, posting to expense accounts, debit posting, credit posting) and the process that the system uses in table T030 (Standard Account Table) to search for the assigned financial account. It also determines the source table for the item to be posted within the payroll. Figure 9.34 shows a list of account assignment types.

AA type	Name
C	Posting to expense account
CN	Posting to expense account(w/o quantity)
D	Posting to personal customer accounts
DF	Posting to fixed customers
F	Posting to balance sheet account
FL	Posting to check RA balance
FO	Posting to bal.sheet acc. in 0-per.only
K	Post to personal vendor accounts
KF	Posting to fixed vendor accounts
L	Posting to customer per loan
Q	Posting to bal.sheet acc. with pers.no.
R	Posting to expense account (for R/2)

Figure 9.34 Account Assignment Types for Symbolic Accounts

Each of the symbolic accounts is linked to an actual G/L account, so the posting program can post the amount placed on a symbolic account by payroll directly to the financial account.

A wage type can be assigned to more than one symbolic account if the wage types should be posted as both expenses and payables (for example, wage types for the employer's contribution for benefit plans). If the account in SAP ERP Financials is an expense account, it is usually assigned a cost element in CO. This is used for posting personnel costs.

Figure 9.35 illustrates the process of posting to FI via a symbolic account. Several symbolic accounts can be assigned to the same account in FI. The amounts that are posted via one symbolic account to FI can also be redirected to different financial accounts, based on the employee grouping for account determination (feature PPMOD).

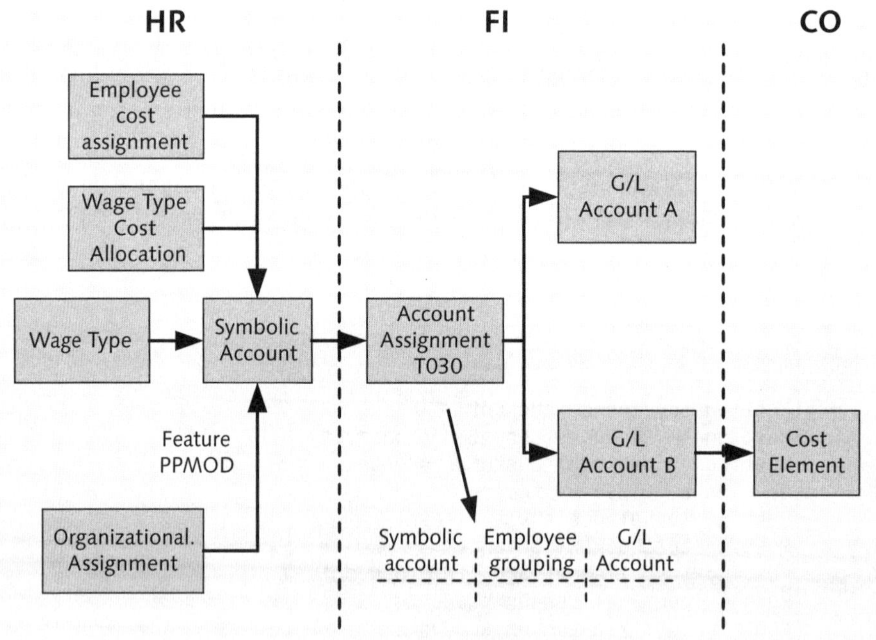

Figure 9.35 Symbolic Accounts

TaxFactory for U.S.

Unlike the net payroll programs for many countries, net payroll for the U.S. uses third-party software to calculate tax. The software product is TaxFactory, provided by a company named Business Software Inc. (BSI). The software needs to be installed separately and supports SAP payroll as a server. As a client, SAP connects to BSI TaxFactory via Remote Function Call (RFC) link. Though the TaxFactory does the actual tax calculation, SAP still performs all of the steps before and after calling the remote function. The payroll driver determines which taxes will be applied for each payment or deduction wage type. These steps depend largely on the configuration of wage types, tax types, tax authorities, and taxability models in the IMG.

For each wage type, the payroll driver reads its tax class (value of processing class 71). For example, the value of processing class 71 for wage type M003 (Salary) is 1 (Regular wages).

Based on the applicable tax area and tax authority read from the employee master data, the payroll driver selects a taxability model for this combination of tax class, tax area, and tax authority. Then the payroll driver determines which tax types must be applied to the wage type amount based on the model.

Wage type amount and the relevant tax types are then sent to BSI via RFC. The TaxFactory server decides which calculation formula to use based on the tax types passed and returns the result of tax calculation, including tax amounts for each wage type and tax type. The tax wage types determined in this process are stored in the payroll results cluster for the employee.

To use TaxFactory for tax calculation, the U.S.-specific schema for tax calculation must be correctly configured with TaxFactory information. UPAR1 BSI is used to indicate the correct version number for TaxFactory (see Table 9.9). For example, if TaxFactory version 7.0 is used for tax calculation, the following entry has to be maintained in UTX0.

Func.	Par1	Par2	Par3	Par4	D	Text
UPAR1	BSI	70				BSI Version Flag

Table 9.9 TaxFactory Version Check

Besides Customizing in payroll calculation, technical settings also need to be done, such as installation of BSI server and registration of an RFC link for TaxFactory in SAP. Report RPUBTCU0 can be used to check whether all of the technical settings have been done correctly.

9.3 Process Examples

9.3.1 Off-Cycle Workbench

Apart from regular payroll, there is the need to run payroll and other subsequent activities for individual employees. For example, if an employee is newly hired and the employee's personal information required for payroll cannot yet be updated in the system, a separate off-cycle payroll run is needed for this employee. Other examples include issuance of a replacement check after the original check is lost or damaged, running a payroll for a special bonus, or making corrections to previous payroll results.

All those off-cycle payroll activities can be performed in a dedicated tool in SAP payroll, Off-cycle Workbench. The SAP Easy Access Menu path to start this tool is HUMAN RESOURCES • PAYROLL • <COUNTRY> • OFF-CYCLE • OFF-CYCLE WORKBENCH. The corresponding Transaction code is PUOC_<nn> where <nn> represents the country grouping; for example, for the U.S., the Transaction code is PUOC_10.

After the Off-cycle Workbench is started, enter the personnel number for which the off-cycle activity will be performed. The search help is available for this field.

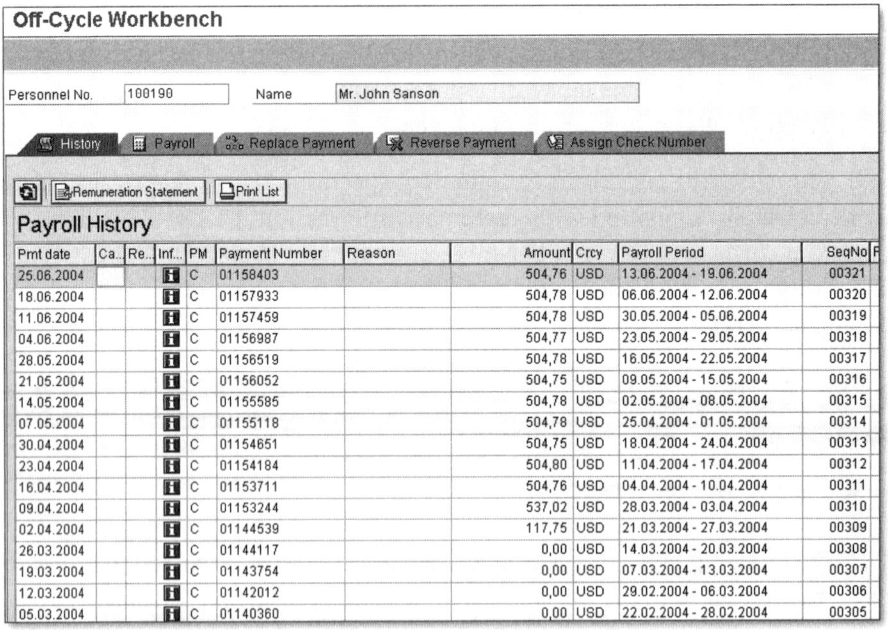

Off-Cycle Workbench

Personnel No. 100190 Name Mr. John Sanson

History | Payroll | Replace Payment | Reverse Payment | Assign Check Number

Remuneration Statement | Print List

Payroll History

Prmt date	Ca...	Re...	Inf...	PM	Payment Number	Reason	Amount	Crcy	Payroll Period	SeqNo
25.06.2004				C	01158403		504,76	USD	13.06.2004 - 19.06.2004	00321
18.06.2004				C	01157933		504,78	USD	06.06.2004 - 12.06.2004	00320
11.06.2004				C	01157459		504,78	USD	30.05.2004 - 05.06.2004	00319
04.06.2004				C	01156987		504,77	USD	23.05.2004 - 29.05.2004	00318
28.05.2004				C	01156519		504,78	USD	16.05.2004 - 22.05.2004	00317
21.05.2004				C	01156052		504,75	USD	09.05.2004 - 15.05.2004	00316
14.05.2004				C	01155585		504,78	USD	02.05.2004 - 08.05.2004	00315
07.05.2004				C	01155118		504,78	USD	25.04.2004 - 01.05.2004	00314
30.04.2004				C	01154651		504,75	USD	18.04.2004 - 24.04.2004	00313
23.04.2004				C	01154184		504,80	USD	11.04.2004 - 17.04.2004	00312
16.04.2004				C	01153711		504,76	USD	04.04.2004 - 10.04.2004	00311
09.04.2004				C	01153244		537,02	USD	28.03.2004 - 03.04.2004	00310
02.04.2004				C	01144539		117,75	USD	21.03.2004 - 27.03.2004	00309
26.03.2004				C	01144117		0,00	USD	14.03.2004 - 20.03.2004	00308
19.03.2004				C	01143754		0,00	USD	07.03.2004 - 13.03.2004	00307
12.03.2004				C	01142012		0,00	USD	29.02.2004 - 06.03.2004	00306
05.03.2004				C	01140360		0,00	USD	22.02.2004 - 28.02.2004	00305

Figure 9.36 Payroll History Displayed in Off-cycle Workbench

After filling in the employee number and hitting the enter key, the employee's name is displayed and all past payroll runs for this employee are listed in the history tab. The information listed includes payment date, payment method, payment number, and amount currency (see Figure 9.36).

To make a special payment to an employee, select the corresponding reason and the payment date for this special payment. The payment method also needs to be specified. In this example, a manual check will be issued (see Figure 9.37). After all of the information is in place, press the Start Payroll button.

An additional section called Payroll Result is displayed on the screen with a list of wage types and corresponding amount for each wage type (see Figure 9.38).

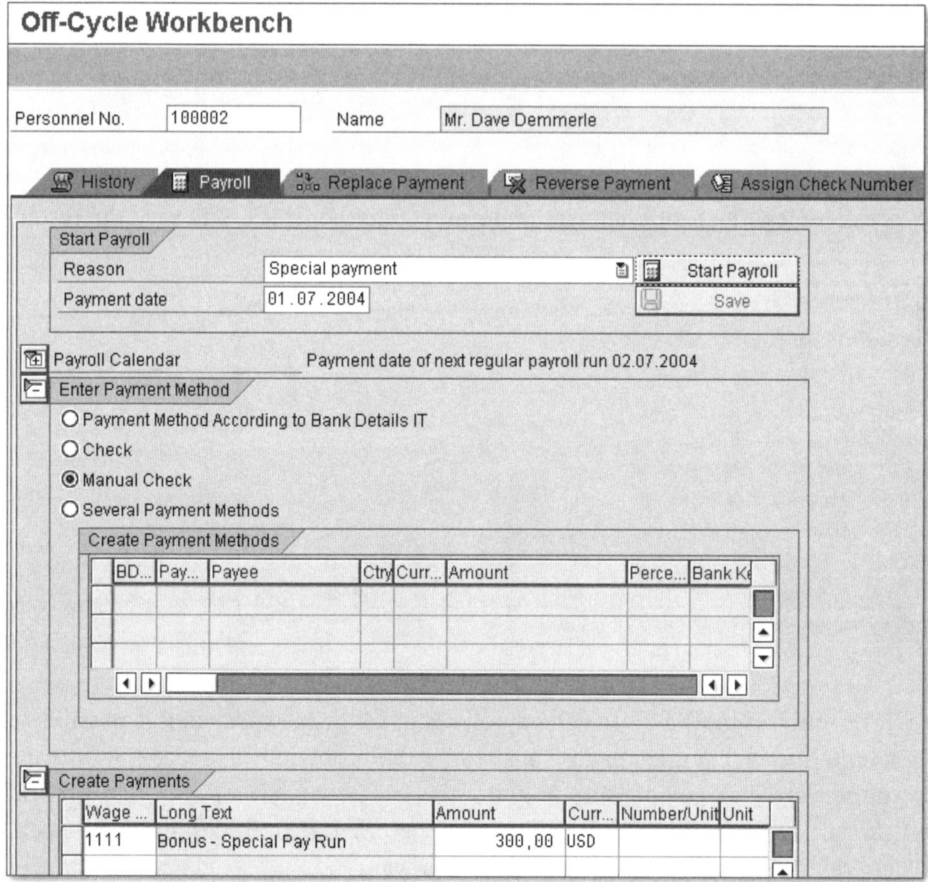

Figure 9.37 Special Payment

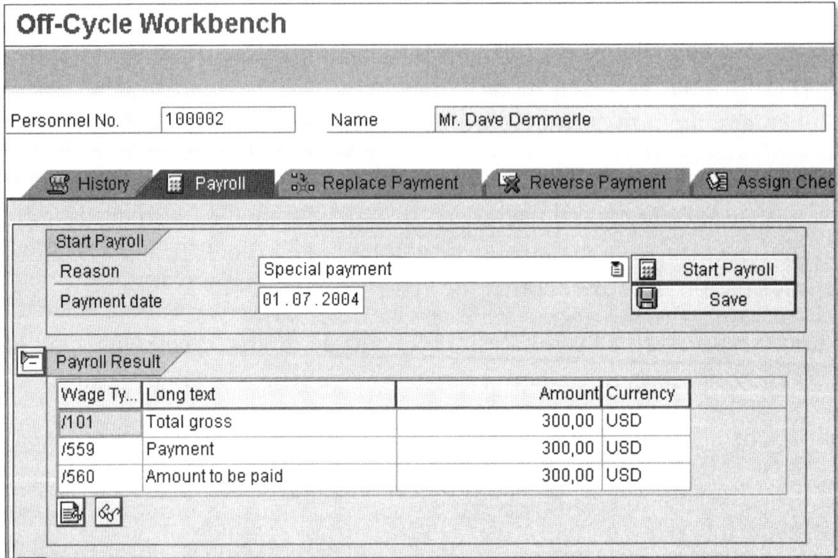

Figure 9.38 Off-cycle Payroll Result

You can review the result here and determine whether it is OK to save the result.

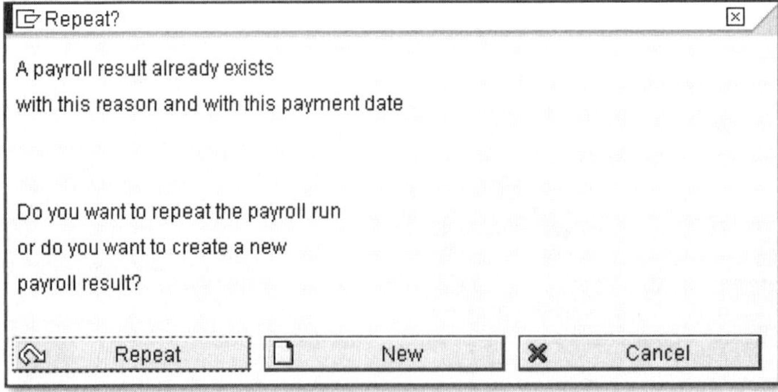

Figure 9.39 Confirmation to Repeat an Offline Payroll

If, for some reason, the displayed payroll result is not as expected, it is possible to rerun the special payment payroll again after the problem is fixed. At the time the rerun starts, a dialogue pops up asking if this is a new payroll run or just a repeat of the last run. For rerun, choose Repeat. The payroll continues and runs again. The rerun can be done as many times as you want.

The button in the payroll result area under the wage type is used to display the remuneration statement created for this special payment run (see Figure 9.40).

```
Remuneration Statement

Philadelphia                                    Check #    : <Not assigned>
123 Market Street                               Check Date: 01.07.2004
Philadelphia                   19111            Pay Period: 01.07.2004  -

Mr. Dave Demmerle          Tax Status       Add W/H   Gross              300,00
SSN.   445-55-5555                                    Taxes                0,00
Employee#.   100002                                   Deductions           0,00
Base Pay:                                             Net Retro            0,00
Cost Center:  4205
 Work scheduling                                      Net Pay            300,00

EARNINGS     HOURS        RATE      CURRENT              YTD

Bon-sp        0,00        0,00      300,00            300,00
Reg time      8,00        0,00        0,00         12.402,80
Holiday                                               614,00

Total         8,00        0,00      300,00         13.316,80
```

Figure 9.40 Remuneration Statement

After the work is done in the Off-cycle Workbench, subsequent processes are needed to finish the run. Depending on the requirements of different business scenarios for the off-cycle payroll, different subsequent activities may be required. For example, for a bonus payroll with check payment, the printing of the check and remuneration statements, and the posting to FI are all needed. In contrast, a check is issued to replace a lost paycheck may need no other steps but the check printing. All of those different scenarios need to be defined as process models in advance with HR Process Workbench.

The SAP menu path to start this tool is HUMAN RESOURCES • PAYROLL • <COUNTRY> • OFF-CYCLE • OC BATCH: FOLLOW-UP FOR PAYROLL. The Transaction code for this is PUOCBA (see Figure 9.41).

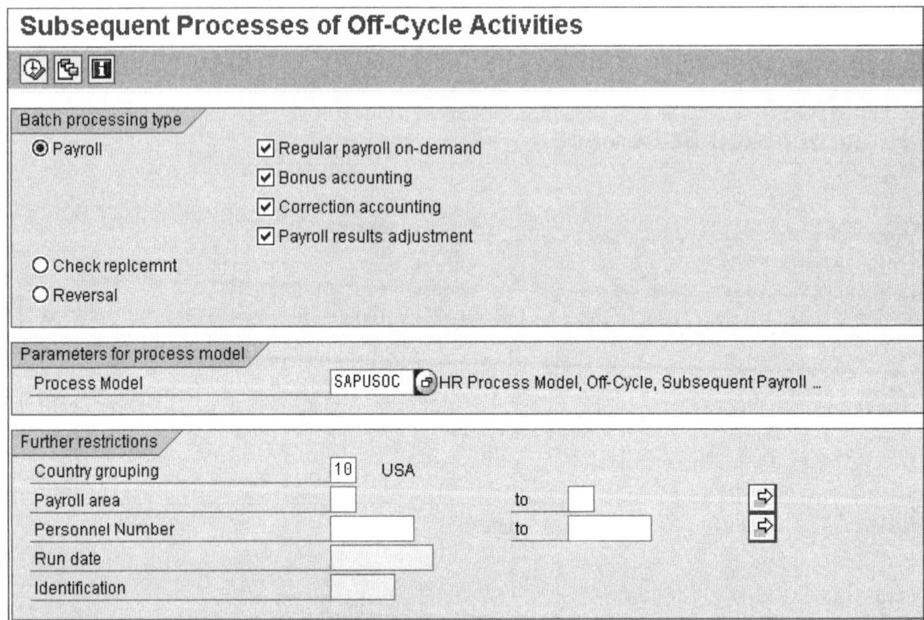

Figure 9.41 Post Process for Off-cycle Payment

This program then triggers the whole set of programs defined in process model to finish the rest of the tasks for a complete off-cycle payroll run.

Please note that the variant used in the process model steps has to be correctly defined to include the parameters needed to complete the tasks.

9.3.2 Samples of Personnel Calculation Rules

Process Wage Type in Internal Tables

Personnel calculation rules play very important roles in processing the wage types. The wage types are stored in various internal tables during the payroll run. When the rules that process the wage types are called, the internal table loops and puts every single line into a working area. Then the payroll driver checks if the rule applies to the wage type for this line. If it does, the processing steps defined in the rule are performed. When the processing is done, this line can be put back to the internal table from the working area.

We will use a sample rule to show how to create a rule to process the wage type. What this rule does is very simple: It uses wage type ZT01 to calculate wage type

ZT02 and stores the result to internal table. The value of ZT02 needs to be calculated as 85% of the amount of ZT02. The wage type ZT01 stays unchanged. The formula for calculation is as follows:

*Amount of ZT02 = Amount of ZT01 * 0.85*

First, go to Personnel Calculation Rule editor (Transaction PE02) to create a rule. Figure 9.42 shows the first screen of the rule editor.

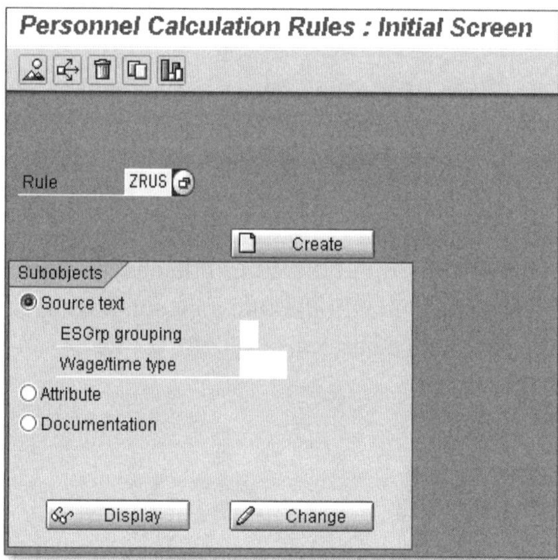

Figure 9.42 Post Process for Off-cycle Payment

After inputting the rule name, press the Create button, and the attribute screen for the rule shows up (see Figure 9.43).

The program class (rule for payroll or for time evaluation) and country grouping are mandatory. C means this rule will be used for payroll; 10 is the country grouping for the U.S. If the checkbox Changes only by person responsible is checked, the system prevents another user from changing the rule, even if the other user has the authorization to edit a rule. This helps keep the rule from being changed unexpectedly.

After inputting all of the information on the screen, save the attribute as shown in Figure 9.43 and go back to the first screen. Now the rule is created with empty source text.

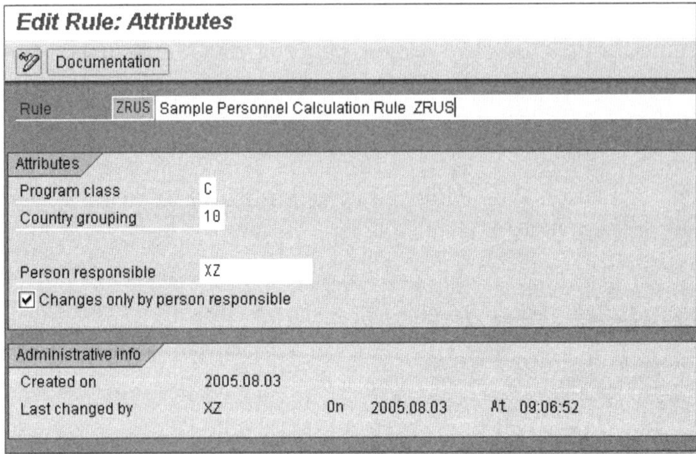

Figure 9.43 Edit Rule — Attributes

To make the rule process wage type ZT01 without affecting other wage types, the wage type has to be specified for the rule. To edit the rule logic for wage type ZT01, input the wage type and click the Change button (see Figure 9.44).

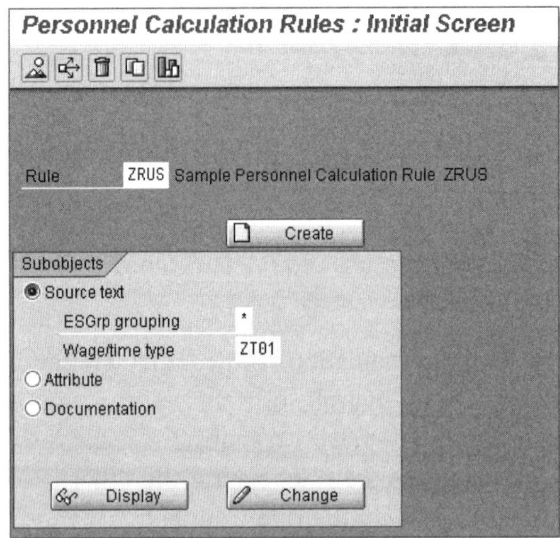

Figure 9.44 Specifying Wage Type for Rule

In the source text of rules, for each wage type, AMT, NUM, and RTE are used to represent the fields for amount, number, and rate. The calculation result is written back to those fields before the internal table is updated.

Operation ADDWT reads the wage type in the working area and appends it to an internal table. If a different wage type is specified after the ADDWT, the working area will be added as a new wage type entry in the internal table.

Operation MULTI is used to multiply values in any two fields (or one field with itself) of AMT, NUM, and RTE. The product is then put into one of the three. The initial character of each field is used to represent this field when used in the operation. For example, MULTI NRA means: Multiply N (number) and R (rate) and put the product into A (amount).

In this example, the requirement of the rule can be broken down into following:

1. Keep wage type ZT01, which means move wage type ZT01 into an output table without changing the number.
2. Use a temporary variant to store the factor 0.85. The NUM field can be used as the temporary variant.
3. Then multiply the amount of ZT02 by 0.85 and put the result back into the amount field.
4. Store the result as wage type ZT02.

So the preceding steps can be translated to:

1. ADDWT *
2. NUM=0.85
3. MULTI ANA
4. ADDWT ZT02

In the rule editor, the operations can be written in one line as shown in Figure 9.45.

```
Edit Rule: ZRUS ES Grouping * Wage Type/Time Type ZT01

Cmmnd                                                        Stack
Line    Var.Key  CL T Operation Operation Operation Operation Operation Operation *
                 -------------+---------+---------+---------+---------+---------+---------+
000010              ADDWT *   NUM=0.85  MULTI ANA ADDWTZT02
000020
000030
```

Figure 9.45 Sample Rule

Note

The first character of each operation must be aligned with the plus sign shown as a ruler. Unlike the schema, the rule does not need to be generated to get active. Once saved, it affects the payroll immediately.

The sample rule can also be written in several lines, as shown in Figure 9.46. An indicator must be placed to note there is a following line. The following lines also need to be numbered in sequence.

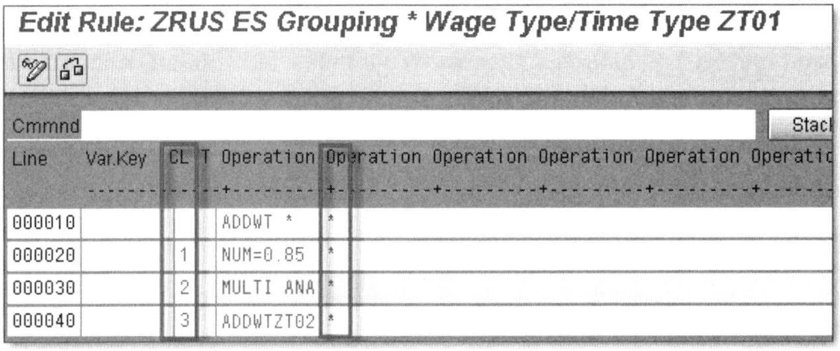

Edit Rule: ZRUS ES Grouping * Wage Type/Time Type ZT01

Cmmnd

Line	Var.Key	CL	T	Operation	Operation	Operation	Operation	Operation	Operatic
000010				ADDWT *	*				
000020		1		NUM=0.85	*				
000030		2		MULTI ANA	*				
000040		3		ADDWTZT02	*				

Figure 9.46 Rule with Multiple Lines

By running the payroll simulation with the schema that includes the rule, the contents of the internal table before and after the process of the rule can be displayed in the log. Figure 9.47 shows the time type ZT01 in the internal table before the rule is called.

Table IT

A	Wage type	APC1C2C3ABKoReBTAwvTvn	One amount/one number	Amount
2	ZT01	01		1.750,00

Figure 9.47 Internal Table Before the Rule Process

After the rule process, as shown in Figure 9.48, the ZT01 stays in the table unchanged; a new entry for wage type ZT02 is added. The number field is assigned with value 0.85 and the result is the product of the amount ZT01 and 0.85.

Table IT

A	Wage type	APC1C2C3ABKoReBTAwvTvn	One amount/one number	Amount
2	ZT01	01		1.750,00
2	ZT02	01	0,85	1.487,50

Figure 9.48 Internal Table After the Rule Process

Sample of Using Payroll Constant

Although the rule just discussed works, we strongly suggest that you do not hard-code any factor number into the personnel calculation rule. The reason is easier maintenance. If you do so, then each time the factor changes, someone has to go and make changes to the rule. If the same factor is used in many different rules, it is difficult to make sure it is correct in each and every place.

The correct approach is to create a constant in table V_511K. This table stores all constants that are used in payroll calculation. The constants defined in this table can be read by the payroll driver and be made available for rules to access.

To define a constant, call Transaction SM30 and edit the view V_T511K (see Figure 9.49).

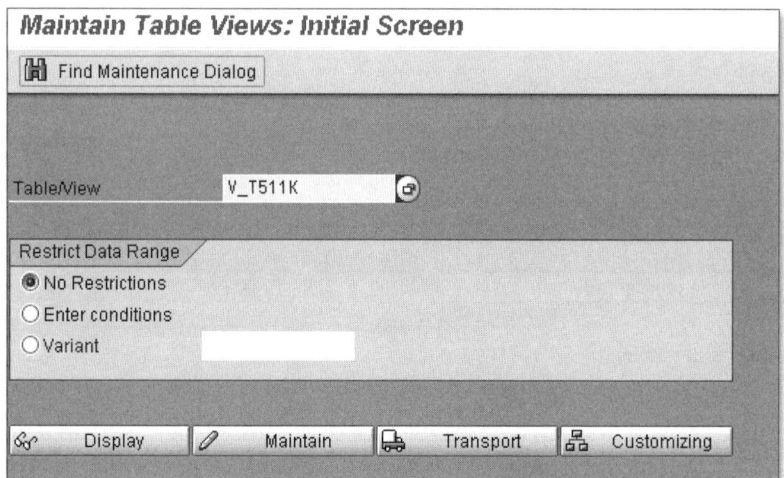

Figure 9.49 Maintenance of Constant Table

The constants are country-grouping specific, which means the same constant name may mean something different. Figure 9.50 shows the change screen for view V_T511W. Press the "New Entries" button to create new entries.

Give a name to the constant first. We suggest using a name beginning with Y or Z to avoid it being overwritten by later SAP upgrades. The constant also has a validation period, and we suggest that — unless there is a good reason — you use 99991231 as the end date. Last and most important, value has to be maintained.

Change View "Payroll Parameters": Overview

Expand <-> Collapse | New Entries | Delimit

Constant	Info	Payroll constant	Start Date	End Date	Value
A0168		GTL Absence exempt status	1900.01.01	9999.12.31	
ADIVP		Flat-rate working days/month	1985.01.01	9999.12.31	20.00
B0168		GTL Beneficiary exempt status	1900.01.01	9999.12.31	
BEGWW		Begin time for working week	1985.01.01	9999.12.31	12.00
CASUP		CA suppl tax indicator	2003.01.01	9999.12.31	1.00
DELIM		Delimiter for working time end	1985.01.01	9999.12.31	4.00
DYOFF		Overtime hours. for comp. day	1985.01.01	9999.12.31	6.50
EPSIL		Termin. criterion (iteration)	1985.01.01	9999.12.31	0.01

Figure 9.50 View V_T511W

For the same example, a new constant ZCLYR is created to replace the value 0.85 (see Figure 9.51).

New Entries: Overview of Added Entries

Delimit

Constant	Info	Payroll constant	Start Date	End Date	Value
ZCLYR		Sample constant factor	2005.01.01	9999.12.31	0.85

Figure 9.51 Edit Constant Value

Once the constant is defined, the rule in the earlier sample can be rewritten as shown in Figure 9.52. A letter K is added in front of the constant to indicate that the name following means a constant name in table T511W.

```
Line   Var.Key  CL T Operation Operation Operation Operation Operation Operation *
                ------------+---------+---------+---------+---------+---------+---------+
000010            ADDWT     NUM=KZCLYRMULTI ANA ADDWT ZT02
```

Figure 9.52 Rule Using Constant

This rule does the same job as the one with a hard-coded factor, but it is much easier to change the factor's value. Simply change the value in view V_T511W and the calculation will use the new value. Furthermore, by splitting the constant into different validation periods, the constant value can vary in different time periods. This makes it possible to have only one formula in the calculation rule, based on different constant values. For example, if the factor in the earlier example changes annually, the new values can be maintained in separate validation periods (see Figure 9.53). When the rule is called for calculation for 2006, the new value 0.88 will be used. If a retroactive payroll run occurs for a period in 2005, it is possible to use the value for 2005.

New Entries: Overview of Added Entries

Delimit

Constant	Info	Payroll constant	Start Date	End Date	Value
ZCLYR		Sample constant factor	2005.01.01	2005.12.31	0.85
ZCLYR			2006.01.01	2006.12.31	0.88
ZCLYR			2007.01.01	9999.12.31	0.88

Figure 9.53 Split Constant by Validation Period

9.4 Critical Success Factors

- The organizational structures must be clearly structured and verified. They must all conform to the relevant requirements in terms of master data, payroll, authorization concept, and personnel reporting, because a subsequent restructuring is very difficult.
- The wage-type catalog should be cleaned up before mapping it in SAP ERP HCM. And the concepts should consider technical wage types, evaluation, and accounting for wage types.
- For allocation of wage types, an early adjustment with accounting, and CO is necessary.

- A clean, permanent quality assurance is absolutely necessary. This is the only way of ensuring that requirements already realized deliver the expected results even after the mapping of additional requirements. Any automation tool that is available should be used here (e.g., Test Workbench).
- The net payroll should not be changed.
- Special cases frequently require extensive maintenance-intensive adjustments. In this case, you must check if they are actually mapped in this form.
- As the system permanently continues to develop even after a successful production start, the maintenance process must be clearly described.

SAP manages employee benefits based on plans and stores employees' benefit-related information in various infotypes. Benefits administration programs perform different activities according to the employees' master data and corresponding plan settings. Most of this chapter applies to all geographic regions, but at the end of this chapter, some U.S.-specific functionalities such as the Consolidated Omnibus Budget Reconciliation Act (COBRA) and Flexible Spending Accounts (FSAs) will be briefly introduced.

10 Benefits Administration

This chapter describes how information in the SAP ERP HCM Benefits Administration component is organized, how to perform the user setup, and how to run the component.

10.1 Business Principles

This section introduces the basic business concept behind SAP Benefits Administration. From here on, all implementation guide (IMG) paths described in the chapter can be found under PERSONNEL MANAGEMENT • BENEFITS.

The Human Resources (HR) system is mainly used to manage information for employees. For SAP Benefits Administration, the focus is on management of the properties and process rules for benefit packages and maintenance of relationships between employees and the packages.

Benefit packages are usually introduced to employees as plans, such as health plans, insurance plans, savings plans, or stock-purchase plans. To accurately describe a plan, many attributes of the plan have to be clearly defined. The following are very important attributes for benefit plan administration and therefore need to be set up and managed in any benefit management system.

- **Availability**
  Is the plan still available, yet to come, or obsolete?

- **Eligibility**
  Which employees can join the plan? The rules can be based on years of service, position level, location, and personal status, among other considerations.
- **Participation status**
  Who is in the plan, and who is not? During what period of time is the employee in the plan?
- **Beneficiaries and dependents**
  Who will get the benefit from this plan? Who is covered under the plan?
- **Cost**
  How much does the plan cost the employee and the employer?
- **Communication**
  What kind of communication is needed whenever an action is taken?

All of the information for each plan and each plan participant needs to be captured and organized by the benefits administrator. Apart from that, all communications such as letters to employees, statistic reports for management teams, payment deduction to payroll departments, and information exchanges between employer and benefit providers also need to be managed.

In later sections of this chapter, we will explain the SAP solution for all of the previously listed issues. At the end, a sample plan will be used to illustrate key settings and some commonly used operations.

Benefits administration is not a stand-alone activity. It is closely integrated with other SAP ERP HCM components that drive other HR processes, such as hiring, termination, and payroll processing. Information needs to be exchanged between different business divisions, employer and employee, and employer and benefit-service providers.

In the next section of this chapter, we will explain how the SAP Benefits Administration component integrates with other HCM components, how benefit data is transferred to service providers, and how benefit information is directed to employees via paper form or online.

10.2 Implementation in SAP ERP HR

In this section, we will cover the basic steps for implementing Benefits Administration.

10.2.1 Basic Conceptions

Benefit Area

The benefit area is the highest organizational data element in SAP ERP HCM Benefits Administration. It is used to administer use of different benefit options. For example, if a nationwide U.S. company offers one set of benefit plans for East Coast employees and a different set of plans for employees on the West Coast, a separate benefit area is created for each group of employees to enable different options.

Please note that only one currency can be used within one benefit area. In the preceding example, if this company opens another new office in Vancouver, Canada, even if all of the benefit packages offered are exactly the same for the rest of the employees living on the West Coast of the U.S., a separate benefit area has to be created because the Canadian dollar will be used for those plans.

The IMG path for defining a benefit area is Basic Settings • Define Benefit Area.

Plan Categories

SAP uses the following different plan categories:

- Health Plans
- Insurance Plans
- Savings Plans
- Stock Purchase Plans
- FSAs
- Credit Plans

Another category, Miscellaneous Plans, can be used for all plans not easily categorized into the preceding groups, such as employee-assistance programs, company car programs, or club memberships.

SAP ERP HCM is designed to handle benefits programs by processing different categories of plans in different ways. For example, if the plan in question is a health plan, the system will manage dependents and coverage. For an insurance plan, it will manage beneficiaries.

Because the processing logic for plan categories is built in standard SAP code, you cannot define new plan categories without changing the programs to make them recognizable by the system.

Plan Types

Unlike plan categories, plan types are left to the user to define, thus further reflecting the client's specific requirements. Please note that each plan type permits only one enrollment per employee. So if an employee must be enrolled simultaneously in multiple plans, those plans must belong to different plan types.

The IMG path for plan type definition is BASIC SETTINGS • PLAN ATTRIBUTES • DEFINE PLAN TYPES.

The plan type value is assigned to an individual plan when maintaining the general plan values. For example, to assign the plan type for a saving plan, the IMG path is PLANS • SAVING PLANS • DEFINE SAVING PLAN GENERAL DATA.

Group and Grouping

Both group and grouping are widely used in the SAP ERP HCM system. Both are used to organize objects with similar attributes into several circles for easier handling. Confusion results from the use of similar names (Aren't they the same thing? Why are two different words used?).

Generally speaking, group is used in most cases to combine objects with the same value or the same range of values in a certain field. Grouping is used to combine different objects that must be handled in the same way, no matter what attribute values they have. Grouping provides a more flexible way for the user to differentiate various business scenarios, while group is just a simple partition. Simply put — group is by value, and grouping is by action.

Example

If an employee age group contains all employees whose ages are in the same range then a cost grouping, by contrast, indicates employees who will use the same cost rule, regardless of their ages, salaries, or other attributes.

In some cases, features are used to check a combination of values to determine a new value for a group of objects that share the same logic.

Feature

A feature is a decision-tree object used by SAP programs. It can be used to determine certain values based on other field values already known within the HR data structure.

For example, after the cost groupings are defined, feature CSTV1 can be used to determine which cost grouping an employee belongs to (see Figure 10.1). If the CSTV1 definition shows that an employee belongs to EE group 1, EE subgroup U4, and his benefit area is the U.S., then the value for his cost grouping is set to SLRY.

A feature can be edited by using Transaction code PE03 and selecting the corresponding feature name.

> **Note**
>
> If a feature is changed after it has been used, the old value determined by the previous feature rule will not be updated automatically based on new rules. When changing the features, please remember that data inconsistency may exist.

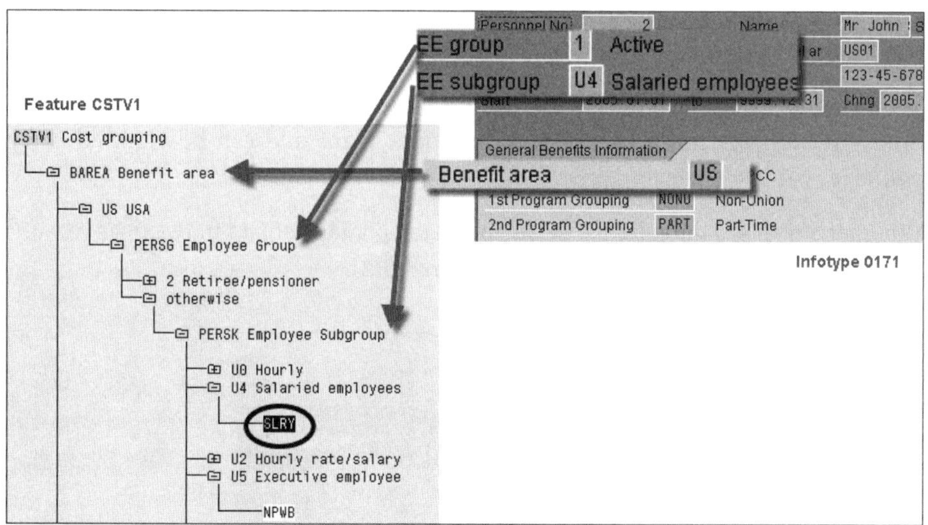

Figure 10.1 Use of Feature CSTV1

10.2.2 Benefit Plans

For plans in different plan categories, different settings have to be considered. Some settings are shared by more than one plan category. For example, both an insurance plan and a saving plan have beneficiary settings. Such settings exist under different IMG paths for different plan categories, but because they are the same, we will explain using them with only one IMG path as a detailed example.

Plan Status

By assigning the plan a plan status, you decide whether the plan should have active participants. You also define whether the plan can accept new enrollment.

The IMG path for plan status setting is Basic Settings • Plan Attributes • Define Benefit Plan Status.

Default Plans and Automatic Plans

There can be a gap between the time an event happens to an employee and the time an employee decides to participate in preferred plans. For example, a new hire needs several days to complete his benefit paperwork, due to communication within the organization. A default plan can be used as a temporary plan to provide minimal coverage to the employee. Usually, such a plan has very little flexibility regarding terms.

Some benefit plans are offered "as is," and do not need employees to make elections. Those plans can be defined as automatic plans and can be enrolled in by employees at any time.

Whether a plan is a default plan or an automatic plan is defined in Flexible Administration • Standard Selections (see Figure 10.2).

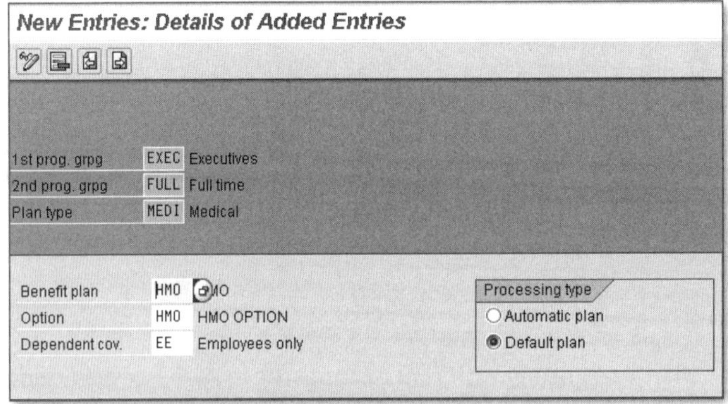

Figure 10.2 Standard Selection

Prerequisite Plans and C-requisite Plans

Both prerequisite plans and corequisite plans can be used to define dependencies between plans. However, there are differences between them.

If plan A is a prerequisite plan of plan B, the employee must have been enrolled into plan A on the date of enrolling to plan B; if plan A is corequisite with plan B, then plan A has to be enrolled in together with plan B.

The IMG path to set up the prerequisite plans and co-requisite plans is FLEXIBLE ADMINISTRATION • PREREQUISITES AND COREQUISITES.

Costs, Contributions, and Credits

Cost variants and cost-rule settings are used to determine the costs for a benefit plan. They work together to make the cost settings flexible and efficient. When costs are to be calculated, the cost variant that a user specifies will read an employee's master data to get all of the information needed to look up the predefined costs in a cost-rule table. Then, if such an entry is found, the cost details in this entry will be used as the employee's plan costs.

For example, Figure 10.3 shows that if the cost variant EE is selected for plan HMO by the employee, the costs are determined through cost variant and cost rules. First, according to the variant, the data to determine the costs comes from the employee master data. Then, because the cost grouping is flagged, the cost grouping value for the employee is set by feature CSTV1. (See Figure 10.1 for details on how the feature works.) When all of these steps are done, the system looks up the cost-rule table for the cost variant of the plan. The highlighted entry is the result, and the cost factors stored in this entry are used.

The IMG path for health plan cost variant and cost rule is PLANS • HEALTH PLANS • MAINTAIN COST VARIANT MAINTAIN COST RULES.

Similar IMG paths can be found under other plan categories' settings.

Contribution is used in most plan categories. It usually includes employee contribution and employer contribution. The way to set up a link between an employee and a certain contribution calculation rule is the same grouping-variant-rule mechanism. The IMG path for defining contribution groupings is under BASIC SETTINGS • DEFINE EMPLOYEE GROUPINGS.

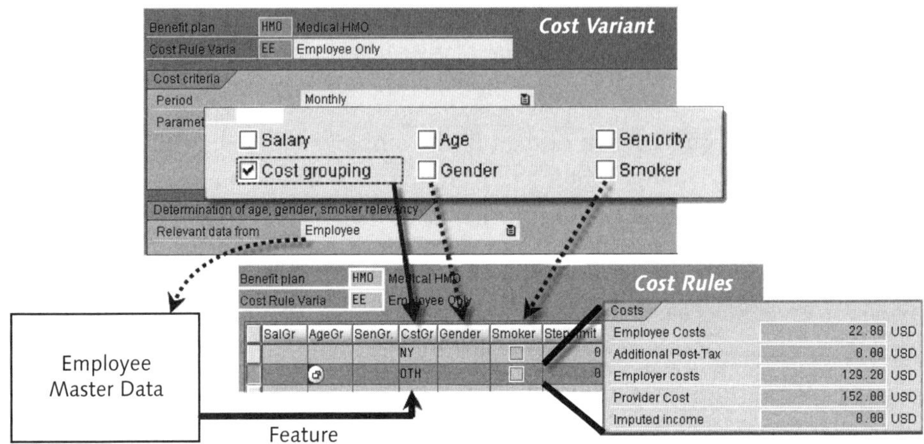

Figure 10.3 Usage of Cost Variant and Cost Rules

During the enrollment, contribution limits are copied to an employee's plan master data. If the limit rules change after the enrollment, the limit may no longer be valid. Report RPLBEN18 should be used to check those conflicts after each modification to the contribution rules.

The credits designation applies to credit plans and to some miscellaneous plans. The concept for credit can be seen as "negative cost." The setting is very much the same as that of a cost plan.

The IMG path for defining cost groupings is under BASIC SETTINGS • DEFINE EMPLOYEE GROUPINGS.

Evidence of Insurability (EOI)

For some health-plan and insurance-plan options, EOI needs to be presented before the coverage becomes effective.

Dependents and Beneficiaries

Dependent settings apply to health plans, and beneficiary settings apply to other plans.

All dependents used in plans must first be maintained in an employee's Infotype 0021 (Family/Related Person). In the dependents eligibility rule settings, the person who can participate in certain plans can be further restricted using a subtype of Infotype 0021, and even further using family member groupings (see Figure 10.4).

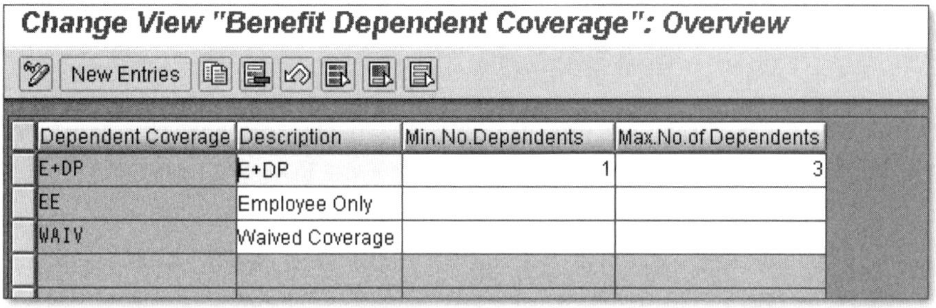

Change View "Benefit Dependent Coverage": Overview

New Entries

Dependent Coverage	Description	Min.No.Dependents	Max.No.of Dependents
E+DP	E+DP	1	3
EE	Employee Only		
WAIV	Waived Coverage		

Figure 10.4 Define Dependent Coverage Options

All of the characteristics ascribed to dependents also apply to beneficiaries with two exceptions: when the beneficiary is the employee himself, or when the beneficiary is an organization.

In the beneficiary-eligibility variant, you can set an indicator to allow the employee to be the beneficiary. For example, if it is necessary to have an employee as beneficiary for disability insurance.

When any eligibility rule is assigned to a plan, organizations are automatically eligible. No extra settings are needed. However, as with the use of Infotype 0021, external organizations need to be maintained in Infotype 0219 to be assigned as beneficiaries.

Via IMG path BENEFIT SETTINGS • DEPENDENT AND BENEFICIARIES, you can define which data stored in the related person infotypes can be displayed in the selection list of dependents and beneficiaries. In each of the plan settings the eligibility for dependents and beneficiaries can be further restricted. For example, in the IMG path PLANS • HEALTH PLANS • DEFINE DEPENDENT COVERAGE OPTIONS, the minimum and maximum number of dependents for each coverage option is defined (see Figure 10.4).

Coverage

Coverage applies to insurance plans and may also apply to some miscellaneous plans, depending on the plan settings.

Controlling coverage settings is similar to controlling cost. Here, we also use the variant and rule combination to direct the coverage that an employee should get for a particular plan.

Coverage grouping settings can be found under IMG path BASIC SETTINGS • DEFINE EMPLOYEE GROUPINGS.

The IMG paths for coverage settings are under each plan category, for example, for insurance plans, the IMG path is PLANS • INSURANCE PLANS • DEFINE COVERAGE RULES AND DEFINE COVERAGE VARIANTS.

10.2.3 Master Data

All employees' benefit-related information is stored in certain infotypes. The system will use such information to determine how to process a benefit of an employee.

Infotype 0171 (General Benefits Information)

Infotype 0171 is the most important infotype for Benefits Administration. An employee has to have this infotype created before enrolling in any benefit plan. Figure 10.5 shows the General Benefits Information display.

This infotype stores the Benefit area, 1st Program Grouping, and 2nd Program Grouping assignments of the employee.

The Benefit Area default value can be determined automatically using feature BAREA with reference to information in other basic Infotypes such as 0001 and 0002.

In Benefits Administration, 1st Program Grouping and 2nd Program Grouping are used to distinguish different employees using different sets of benefit programs.

Features BENGR and BSTAT are used to set default values for an employee's 1st Program Grouping and 2nd Program Grouping.

Note

The features only create default values. It is possible to override the default value manually by inputting a new value as an exception. However, if such exceptions happen too often you would do better to modify the feature and include the new rule.

Report RPLBEN13 can be used to display a report of all Infotype 0171 infotype records in which values maintained do not comply with the latest corresponding features.

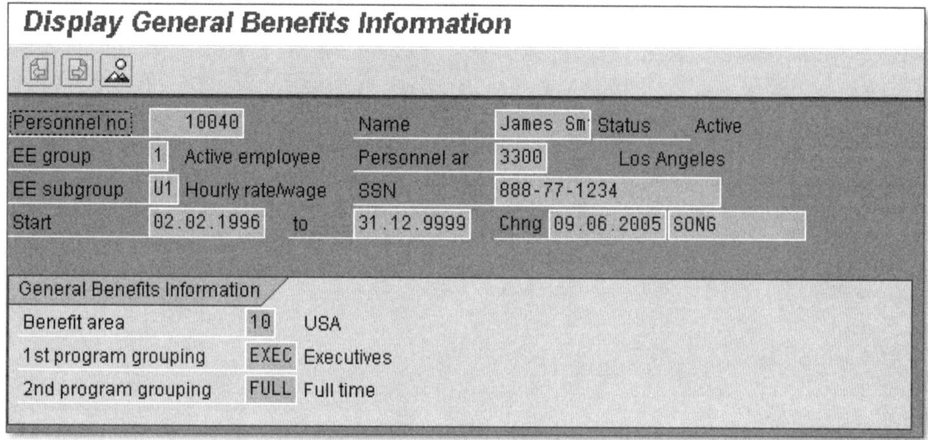

Figure 10.5 Infotype 0171 (General Benefits Information)

Plan Infotypes

After enrollment in a benefit plan, a plan infotype record is created automatically to store employee-specific information for this plan. For each benefit plan in which the employee participates, a separate record is used. The plan category determines which infotype to use for each plan. The plan type is the subtype of the infotype.

Following are the infotypes used to store plan data:

- Infotype 0167 (Health Plans); see Figure 10.6
- Infotype 0168 (Insurance Plans)
- Infotype 0169 (Savings Plans)
- Infotype 0236 (Credit Plans)
- Infotype 0379 (Stock Purchase Plans)
- Infotype 0377 (Miscellaneous Plans)

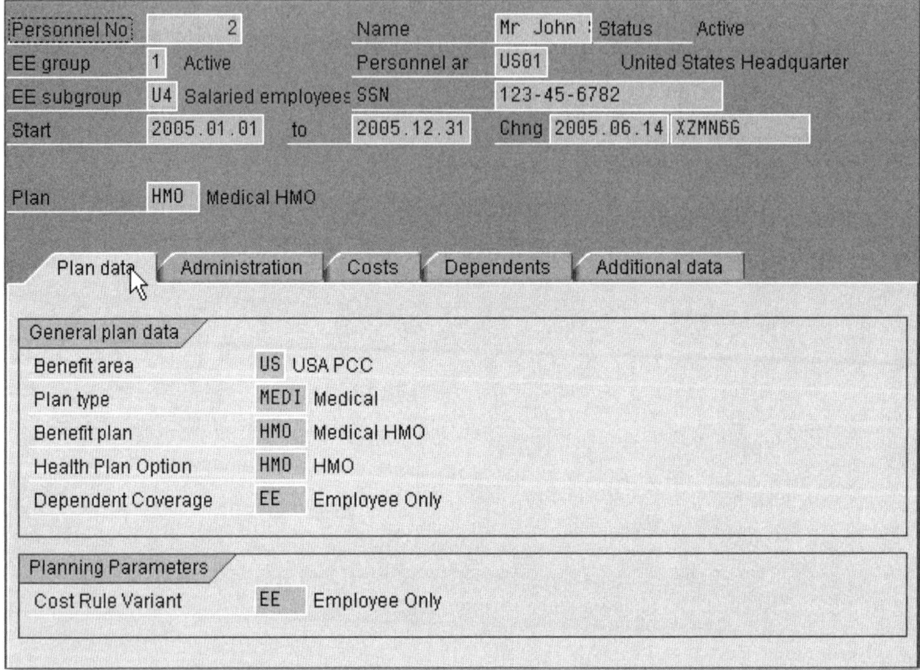

Figure 10.6 Infotype 0167 (Health Plan)

Depending on the setting of the benefit plan, some of the following information is stored in the infotype:

- Plan data, such as plan type, plan option, etc.
- Administration data
- Coverage
- Costs
- Credits
- Contributions
- Dependents
- Beneficiaries
- Vesting

- Investments
- Additional information

Although it is possible to create and maintain a plan infotype directly using Transaction PA30, we do not suggest doing so. Using only the benefit administration transactions, such as enrollment (HRBEN0001), can ensure that all plan rules, such as eligibility and cost-rule checks, are being carried out while processing the plans.

10.2.4 Enrollment

Enrollment is used to create a new benefit plan or to make changes to an existing plan for an employee. For example, if an employee gets married, then he needs to join a family medical insurance plan to have his family covered.

During the enrollment, the system will automatically check the master data against the predefined eligibility rules in customizing; if the conditions are met, then the offers containing plans available to the employee will be displayed (see Figure 10.7).

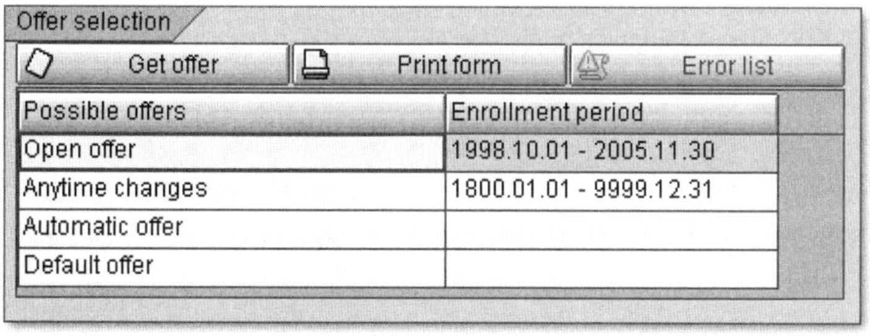

Offer selection

Get offer | Print form | Error list

Possible offers	Enrollment period
Open offer	1998.10.01 - 2005.11.30
Anytime changes	1800.01.01 - 9999.12.31
Automatic offer	
Default offer	

Figure 10.7 Enrollment Offer

Four types of offers are available:

- **Open offer**
  Offer contains all eligible plans that are currently in an open enrollment period.
- **Adjustment offer (Anytime changes)**
  Offer contains only plans for which an employee has a corresponding adjustment reason.

- **Automatic offer**
  Offer contains all plans flagged as automatic plans during customizing of the standard selection.
- **Default offer**
  Offer contains all plans flagged as default plans during customizing of the standard selection.

Adjustment offers displayed on the offer list appear under the corresponding adjustment reason names. The adjustment reason defines an event, such as a birth or a divorce, which may require an employee's benefit plans to change.

In the adjustment reason definition, the time period that the adjustment to the benefit plan has to take place has to be set. The adjustment reason can be defined as change at anytime, which means there is no time limit for the change. If not, an infotype record that stores such an adjustment reason (Infotype 0378) must be created before the offer can be taken.

During the enrollment process, the system checks whether the grouping the adjustment reason belongs to is permitted to make changes to certain plans.

The adjustment reasons can be defined via IMG path FLEXIBLE ADMINISTRATION • BENEFITS ADJUSTMENT REASONS • DEFINE BENEFIT ADJUSTMENT REASONS AND DEFINE BENEFIT ADJUSTMENT REASON GROUPINGS. The options under Define Adjustment Permissions are used to set the permitted adjustment reasons for each plan.

To enroll an employee in a benefit plan, in the backend SAP ERP HCM system, from the Easy Access Menu, select HUMAN RESOURCES • PERSONNEL MANAGEMENT • BENEFITS • ENROLLMENT.

- First, in the employee selection area, double-click on the employee in the selection list.
- Then, set the date for the enrollment.
- Next, select an offer that you want and click on the button Get Offer. Select the plan you would like to enroll this employee in, and a dialog window with detailed plan data will pop up (see Figure 10.8 and Figure 10.9).

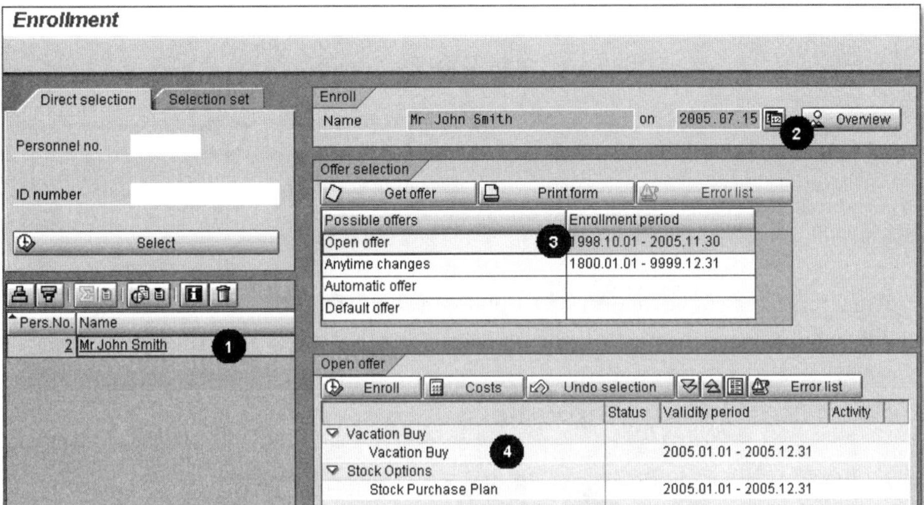

Figure 10.8 Enrollment

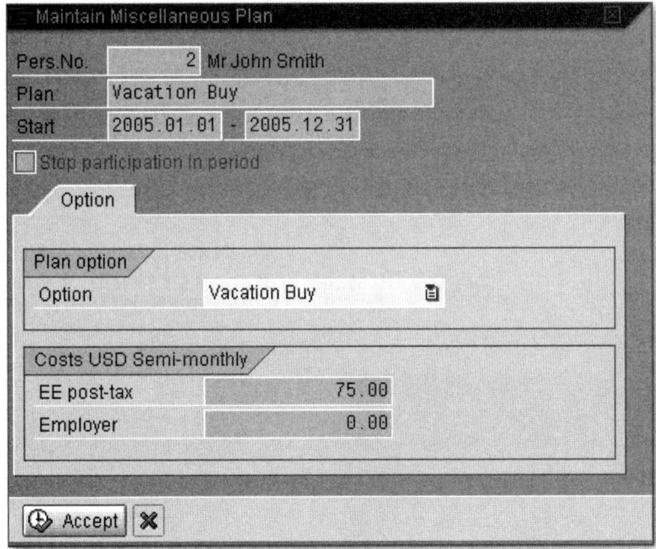

Figure 10.9 Enrollment — Plan Detail

- Go through the plan details. You can make changes to the default values. Click the Accept button to accept it. The accepted plan will have a green check next to it (see Figure 10.10).

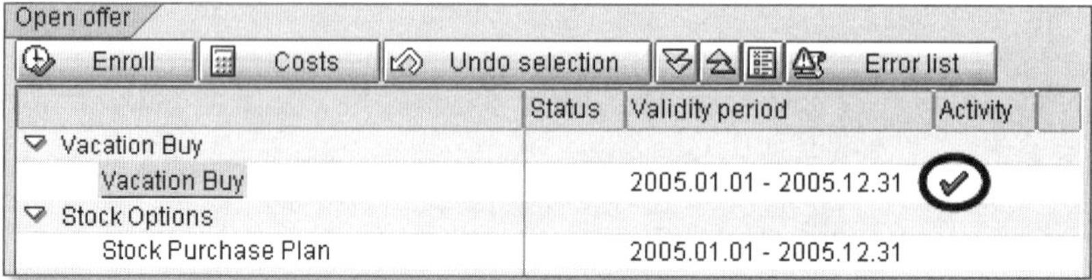

Figure 10.10 Enrollment — Plan Accepted

- After finishing the selection of all plans in the offer, click on the Enroll button. Another dialogue box will show up asking for the user's confirmation. It lists all of the actions to be taken. Here, you click on Enroll again and the actual enrollment will take place (see Figure 10.11).

Confirmation of Selected Actions

List of Plans

Activity	Plan	From	To
Create	Vacation Buy	2005.01.01	2005.12.31

Enroll Cancel

Figure 10.11 Confirmation of Selected Actions

- After the system finishes the enrollment, a message box shows up with a success message (see Figure 10.12).

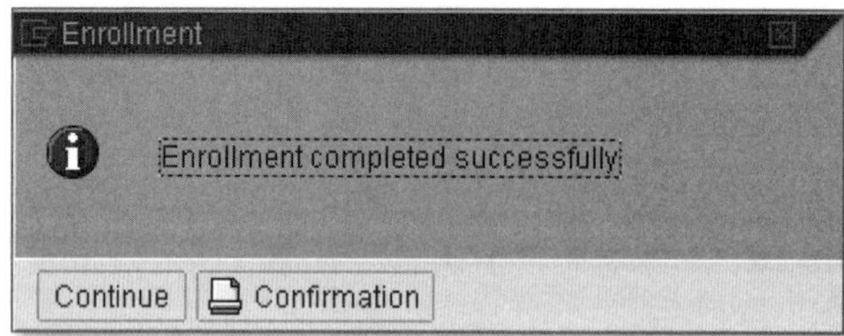

Figure 10.12 Enrollment Confirmation

- If you select the Confirmation button, a confirmation letter will be printed. The Continue button brings you back to the main enrollment screen. The enrollment is done.

Upon the completion of enrollment, the enrollment program creates an infotype for the corresponding benefit plan automatically. In this example, a miscellaneous plan Infotype 0337 is created. Now, go to PA20 to display Infotype 0337 for this employee, where a corresponding entry has been created (see Figure 10.13). The subtype of the infotype is the same as the plan name.

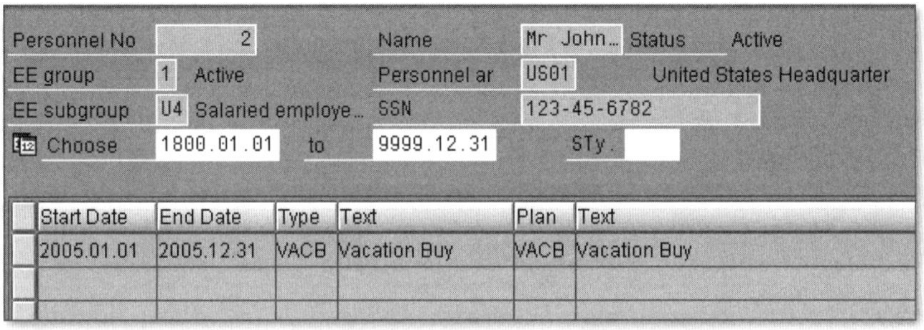

Personnel No 2 | Name Mr John... | Status Active
EE group 1 Active | Personnel ar US01 United States Headquarter
EE subgroup U4 Salaried employe... | SSN 123-45-6782
Choose 1800.01.01 to 9999.12.31 | STy.

Start Date	End Date	Type	Text	Plan	Text
2005.01.01	2005.12.31	VACB	Vacation Buy	VACB	Vacation Buy

Figure 10.13 Enrollment — Infotype Created

The plan information accepted during the enrollment is stored in the infotype. Figure 10.14 shows the cost data for the plan, the same as shown in Figure 10.9.

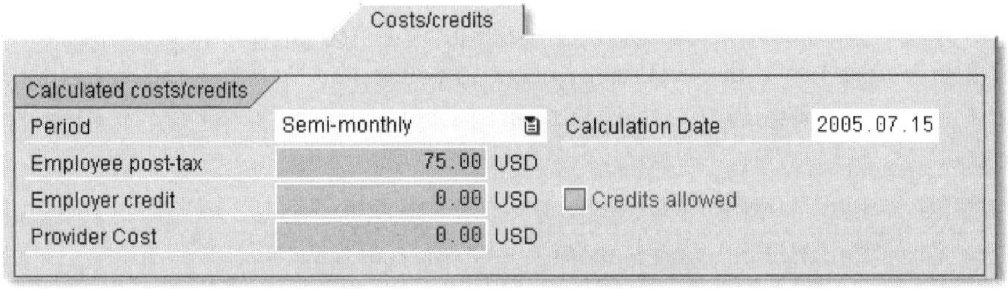

Costs/credits

Calculated costs/credits

Period	Semi-monthly	Calculation Date	2005.07.15
Employee post-tax	75.00 USD		
Employer credit	0.00 USD	Credits allowed	
Provider Cost	0.00 USD		

Figure 10.14 Plan Cost Information

10.2.5 Miscellaneous

Benefit Forms

Upon enrollment or changes to the plan, benefit forms are usually sent to employees for legal and information purposes. SAP can generate enrollment and confirmation forms using predefined form templates (see Figure 10.15).

Benefits - Enrollment

USA Sample, Benefits Dept., P.O. Box 112233, Anytown, CA 91234

Mr John Smith
Address Line
US city NY 11111

Type of offer	
Open enrollment	
Offer from	**To**
10/1/1998	11/30/2005

Personnel number	Name of employee	Social security number
00000002	John Smith	123456782

Personnel area	Personnel subarea
United States Headquarter	Administration

Employee group	Employee subgroup	Payroll area
Active	Salaried employees	Semi-monthly
Benefit area	**First program grouping**	**Second program grouping**
USA Sample	salary	Full-Time

Figure 10.15 Sample Benefit Enrollment Form (SAPscript)

You can set up the form template to be either a SAPscript form or a Word document template. Based on the setting, the system either triggers the SAPscript printing or brings up a Word document for users to print. The IMG path to determine which form print method to use is FLEXIBLE ADMINISTRATION • FORM SETUP (see Figure 10.16).

Change View "Benefit Forms for Benefit Administration": Details

New Entries

Form type: Enrollment form

Selection of document template

SAPscript
Form

Office integration
Document text: SAP Enrollment form 6.1
Version number: 00000001

Figure 10.16 Form Setup

Please note that using Word template forms requires the printing user to log on with a transactional session, and the frontend machine has to have the Microsoft Word application installed. Although there are other applications that can recognize Microsoft Word files, you must have the Microsoft Word application to run the macros defined in the templates. If you need to have forms printed in a background job, please choose the SAPscript method.

For enrollment and confirmation forms, Microsoft Word templates are both provided by SAP as standard. You can copy them and make changes according to your needs. You need SAPscript knowledge to modify a SAPscript form.

Note

In the Word templates provided by SAP, there are macros embedded that will get the data feed from Benefits Administration and put data into the correct fields in the Word file. When making changes to the Word template, always copy the SAP template and be careful not to damage the field definitions in the template file.

The transaction to copy and edit the Word templates for benefit forms is HRBEN0050. Figure 10.17 shows an embedded Word template for enrollment.

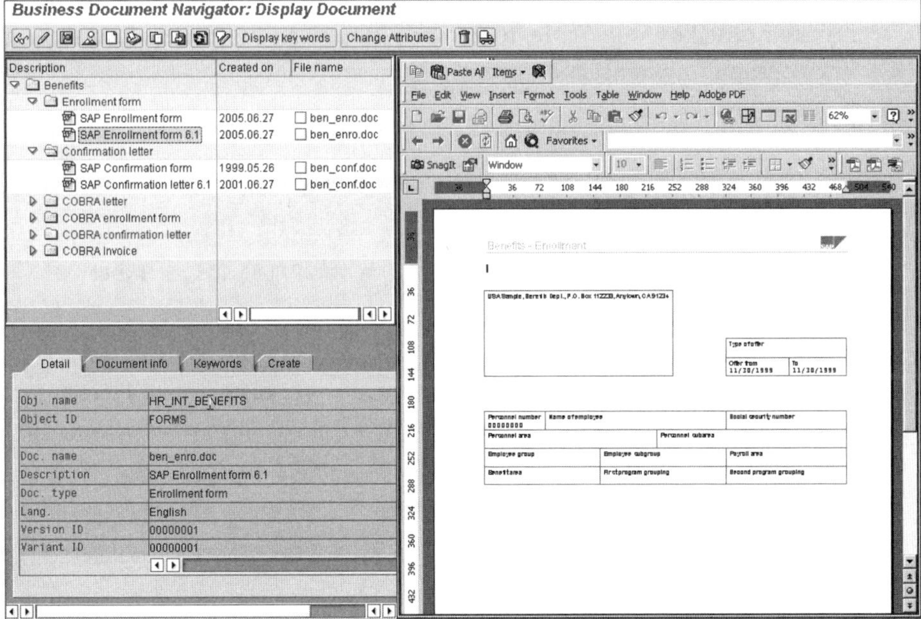

Figure 10.17 Enrollment Letter — Microsoft Word Template

Benefit Employee Self-Service (ESS)

To input plan data for many employees is a major effort. SAP ESS allows individual employees to be responsible for the benefit-data input. It gives employees the flexibility to update and monitor their own benefit plans.

The following ESS services are available with the Benefits Administration component, as shown in Table 10.1.

Service	Description
PZ14	Enrollment
PZ07	Participation Overview
PZ43	Retirement Benefits
PZ40	Spending Account Claims (U.S. only)

Table 10.1 ESS Services for Benefits Administration

Standard Benefit Reports

The SAP Benefits Administration component provides many standard reports for various functions, generally used by a Benefits specialist role and produced in the backed system, as shown in Table 10.2. The reports can be run via Transaction SA38 or corresponding transaction codes.

You can also define your own reports using standard reporting tools.

Report Category	Description	Report Name	Transaction Code
Participation analysis	Eligible Employees	RPLBEN01	HRBEN0071
	Benefit Plan Participation	RPLBEN02	HRBEN0072
	Changes in Benefit Elections	RPLBEN07	HRBEN0077
	Changes in Eligibility	RPLBEN09	HRBEN0079
	Changes in Default Values for General Benefits Information	RPLBEN13	HRBEN0083
Cost and contribution analysis	Health Plan Costs	RPLBEN03	HRBEN0073

Table 10.2 Standard Benefit Reports

Report Category	Description	Report Name	Transaction Code
	Insurance Plan Costs	RPLBEN04	HRBEN0074
	Savings Plan Costs	RPLBEN05	RPLBEN05
	Flexible Spending Account Contributions	RPLBEN08	HRBEN0078
	Stock Purchase Plan Contributions	RPLBEN16	HRBEN0083
	Costs/Contributions for Miscellaneous Plans	RPLBEN15	HRBEN0085
	Vesting Percentages	RPLBEN06	HRBEN0076
	Contribution Limit Check	RPLBEN18	HRBEN0088
Statistical analysis	Employee Demographics	RPLBEN11	HRBEN0081
	Benefits Election Analysis	RPLBEN17	HRBEN0087
	Enrollment Statistics	RPLBEN19	HRBEN0089
Customizing analysis	Plan Overview	RPUBEN09	HRBEN0009
	Benefit Customizing Consistency Check	RPUBEN42	HRBEN0042
	Plan Cost Summary	RPUBEN46	HRBEN0046

Table 10.2 Standard Benefit Reports (Cont.)

Integration

SAP Benefits Administration is closely integrated with other SAP ERP HCM components. For example, data from personnel management is used in the eligibility check and calculation. Deductions and taxable benefits can also be directly taken into consideration during payroll calculation, and the result can be reflected directly in an employee's pay slip. Employee time-management data, such as total hours worked during a given period of time, can also be used to decide if the employee is eligible for certain plan options.

Among all those, the payroll integration is the most important and will be discussed in more detail in the following section.

Payroll Integration

Benefits are closely integrated with payroll. Plans with associated costs, deductions, or contributions need to be taken into account when payroll is processed. By assigning wage types to each benefit plan, the deduction amount can be brought to payroll for calculation. Follow IMG path PAYROLL • US PAYROLL • BENEFIT INTEGRATION to make the payroll settings.

Note

If the costs or contributions are calculated during payroll runs, it is possible that the actual deduction for a pay period is different from the figure shown in the master data infotype for the plan, for which the costs or contributions are calculated upon enrollment.

After the U.S. payroll run, all accumulated benefit costs are stored in the following infotypes for reporting purposes (see Table 10.3).

Infotype	Description
0496	Benefits contributions/deductions: per payroll period
0497	Benefits contributions/deductions: monthly cumulations
0498	Benefits contributions/deductions: quarterly cumulations
0499	Benefits contributions/deductions: annual cumulations
0500	Benefits contributions/deductions: per payroll period from the arrears table
0501	Benefits contributions/deductions: per payroll period from the deductions not taken table

Table 10.3 Infotypes for Benefits Contribution and Deductions Cumulation

Benefit plan settings that are payroll related have to be set up correctly before running the payroll. For example, 401(K) plan deductions for an employee must not exceed the legal limits. To prevent that, you have to set up the contribution limits for the registered savings plans in contribution rules.

Enhancements

Each business is unique. In some cases, SAP standard systems cannot meet the special requirement of the logic for Benefit Administration. Enhancements then can be brought into the picture. Enhancements will not change existing SAP codes, but provide you an opportunity to create extra logic based on standard processes. The user exits available to use for customer-specific logic definition can be accessed by Transaction code SMOD.

For example, let us suppose that a company uses a formula to determine coverage amount of an employee's insurance plan. Usually, this is done by the standard SAP function HR_BEN_CALC_COVERAGE_AMOUNT based on the master data and plan settings. In this case, the company wants to take the employee's coverage during past years into account while calculating. This makes the formula too complex for the standard function to perform the required calculation; the user exit can be used to replace the function.

Another example is the replacement of a feature with a user exit to determine default values. Features can make decisions based on a certain field's value only if the value is directly available in a field. A feature cannot make a complex calculation to a field value before the field value is defaulted. In this case, a user exit can be used to take over the feature's work.

Table 10.4 shows a list of all available enhancements in Benefits Administration, and the corresponding standard features and functions they will replace once they are implemented.

User exit	Replaces
PBEN0001	Feature BAREA
PBEN0002	Feature BENGR
PBEN0003	Feature BSTAT
PBEN0004	Feature CSTV1
PBEN0005	Feature CRDV1
PBEN0006	Feature ELIGR
PBEN0007	Feature TRMTY
PBEN0008	Function HR_BEN_CALC_BENEFIT_COST
PBEN0009	Function HR_BEN_CALC_BENEFIT_CREDIT
PBEN0010	Function HR_BEN_CALC_BENEFIT_SALARY
PBEN0011	Function HR_BEN_CALC_COVERAGE_AMOUNT
PBEN0012	Form CALC_ELIG_DATE

Table 10.4 User Exits and Replacing Elements

User exit	Replaces
PBEN0013	Form CALC_TERM_DATE
PBEN0014	Function HR_BEN_CALC_SAVE_ER_CONTRIB
PBEN0015	Form CHECK_ELIG_SERVICE
PBEN0016	Function HR_BEN_CALC_PARTICIPATION_DATE
PBEN0017	Feature EVTGR
PBEN0018	Feature COVGR
PBEN0019	Feature EECGR
PBEN0020	Feature ERCGR
PBEN0021	Function HR_BEN_CALC_SPEN_ER_CONRIB
PBEN0022	Function HR_BEN_GET_PROCESS_DATES
PBEN0023	Function HR_BEN_CALC_CUTOFF_AGE
PBEN0024	Function HR_BEN_CALC_CUTOFF_LOS
PBEN0025	Function HR_BEN_CALC_CUTOFF_SAL
PCOB0001	COBRA Letter
PCOB0004	Form HR_BEN_COB_GET_TOTAL_COSTS

Table 10.4 User Exits and Replacing Elements (Cont.)

10.2.6 U.S.-Specific Benefits

The Benefits Administration subcomponent is designed to fit global needs; however, SAP also provides functionalities to administrate U.S.-specific benefit requirements such as COBRA plans, FSAs, and Tax-sheltered Annuity.

COBRA

COBRA requires most employers to provide employees the choice to continue the group health plan under certain circumstances so that they will not lose the group health plan coverage. The COBRA related plans are defined in IMG under COBRA • Choose COBRA Plans (see Figure 10.18).

There are eight legally defined event types (circumstances) for COBRA plans:

- Termination of employment
- Reduction in working hours

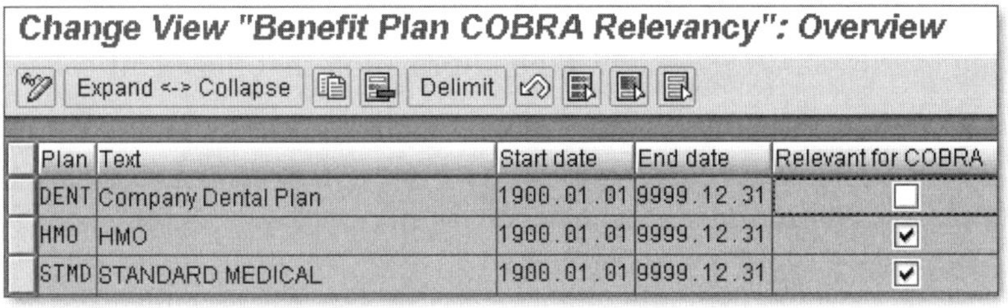

Change View "Benefit Plan COBRA Relevancy": Overview

Expand <-> Collapse | Delimit

Plan	Text	Start date	End date	Relevant for COBRA
DENT	Company Dental Plan	1900.01.01	9999.12.31	☐
HMO	HMO	1900.01.01	9999.12.31	☑
STMD	STANDARD MEDICAL	1900.01.01	9999.12.31	☑

Figure 10.18 COBRA Plan Selection

- Death of employee
- Entitlement to Medicare
- Divorce
- Legal separation
- Loss of dependent status
- Bankruptcy of employer

For each event type, the permitted coverage periods have to be defined. SAP standard settings fulfill the minimal legal requirements. The IMG path is COBRA • Define Qualifying Event Coverage Period.

Personnel actions in personnel administration can be linked with event type termination, death of employee, and reduction in hours. By establishing such a link, the event collection program can identify qualifying events by checking personnel actions. The IMG path for setting up the links is COBRA • Assign COBRA Events to Personnel Actions (see Figure 10.19).

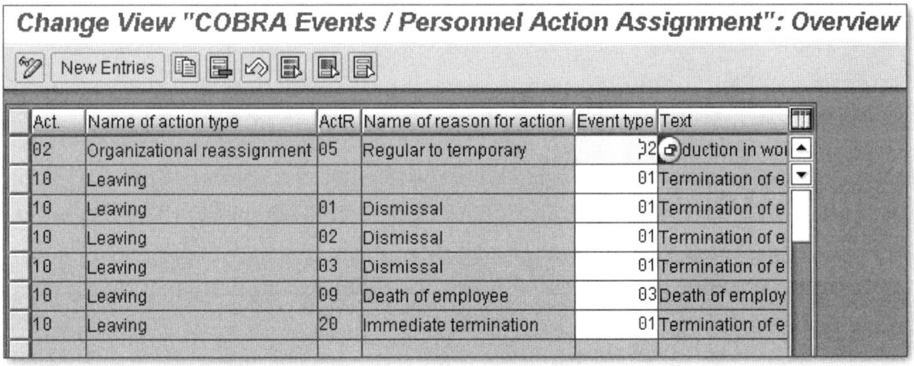

Change View "COBRA Events / Personnel Action Assignment": Overview

New Entries

Act.	Name of action type	ActR	Name of reason for action	Event type	Text
02	Organizational reassignment	05	Regular to temporary	02	duction in wor
10	Leaving			01	Termination of e
10	Leaving	01	Dismissal	01	Termination of e
10	Leaving	02	Dismissal	01	Termination of e
10	Leaving	03	Dismissal	01	Termination of e
10	Leaving	09	Death of employee	03	Death of employ
10	Leaving	20	Immediate termination	01	Termination of e

Figure 10.19 COBRA Event Settings

The event-collection program also checks the employee's master data to identify other qualifying events. Table 10.5 shows the information that the event collection program checks.

COBRA event	Personnel action	Other Infotype record
Termination	As defined, mandatory	-
Death of employee	As defined, mandatory	-
Reduction in hours	As defined, optional	New 0007
Medicare entitlement	-	New 0077, MEDIC = 'X'
Divorce	-	New 0021, SUBTY = 10
Separation	-	On 0021, SEPDT filled
Loss of dependent status	-	On 0021, over age limit
Bankruptcy	-	On 0000, status = retd.

Table 10.5 Master Data Checked During COBRA Event Collection

Note

COBRA event collection depends on actions performed within Personnel Administration. It is very important to perform the right activity in the system to ensure that the master data accurately reflect the facts of the employee. For example, suppose that an employee gets divorced. If the HR specialist simply deletes the employee's Infotype 0021 for the spouse rather than using a family-status change action to make sure a new Infotype 0021 for the ex-spouse is created, the event-collection program will not pick up this action as an event; therefore, the COBRA process will not start for this employee.

Once the event-collection program identifies events for employees, an Infotype 0211 is automatically created.

Transaction RBENUSCOB02 is used to generate COBRA letters. For the settings of a COBRA letter template, please refer to the form setting in Section 10.2.5.

After an employee accepts the offer within the permitted period, you can enroll the employee into COBRA plans using SAP Easy Access Menu COBRA • PARTICIPATION. Infotype 0212s and 0617 are created for each enrolled COBRA health plan and COBRA FSA plan. Infotype 0270 stores the COBRA plan participant's payment data.

If the employee declines the offer or his COBRA payment is overdue, termination will be carried out based on the settings.

FSAs

FSAs enable employees to fund their own benefit plans. Employees choose to set aside a certain amount of their pay in FSA accounts. Then, their FSA account reimburses them for qualifying expenses, such as childcare or eldercare and medical deductibles after they submit a valid claim.

The setup of an FSA plan is simple compared with other plans. Only employer-contribution variants and rules are defined when needed. Employee contribution is freely entered during enrollment as long as the total falls into the contribution range. Infotype 0170 stores details of each FSA in which the employee is enrolled.

FSA Claim

An employee submits the claim with a receipt. The claim is entered into the system using Transaction HRBENUS02. After entering the claim with all detailed information against the proper plan, the user assigns a status to the claim. There are four possible statuses for a claim:

- Not yet approved
- Approved
- Rejected
- Agreement given to rejection

For each claim the employee makes, a separate record of Infotype 0172 is created by the system. Only the claims with "approved" status are taken into account by payroll. Payments are made accordingly.

Infotype 0510 (Tax-Sheltered Annuity)

Infotype 0510 is used to store amounts contributed to employees' 403(b) savings plans, including contributions made by the employee, current employer, and the employee's previous employers. This infotype should be maintained before the employee has his first payroll run. The cumulation numbers will be updated by the system automatically.

10.3 Critical Success Factors

- We strongly recommend that you make a copy of the benefit area and make changes only in the copy. This ensures that a copy of the original reference model is always clean and unchanged so that if later other requirements come out, no previous changes are brought in as defaults. This practice is advisable even when all of the pre-defined plans and rules can be directly used without any modification. Thus, if there is a need of change in the future, the benefit area does not need to be switched.
- Try to avoid using very complex features. If too many value fields are to be checked in a feature, the complexity of the feature will become a challenge during testing.
- The eligibility and cost rules must be strictly defined, especially when ESS is used. The presence of incomplete or incorrect rules may allow unwanted plans to be created. It can be difficult to correct such defective plans, and they may lead to legal challenges for the company..
- The jobs of checking and updating the latest master data of employees should be scheduled to run automatically. It saves time if benefit administers are not running the jobs manually. It also helps protect the accuracy of the benefit information.

Human Resources (HR) reporting is often an important reason for implementing an integrated HR information system. However, its full potential is rarely realized. With the time constraints of implementation projects, HR reporting is usually not given sufficient consideration during the design phase.

11 HR Reporting

For the implementation or redesign of HR reporting it is necessary to harmonize the various requirements of reporting. For all reports, you must create a uniform data basis that is built on clear structures and provides coordinated key figures. For the provision of reports, you must consider the know-how of the recipient and the execution frequency.

11.1 Business Principles

HR reporting, or Personnel reporting, is a cross-application process that provides information from all processes. Reports can be restricted to information on individual processes, or they can combine the data from several processes.

The various chapters of this book mostly deal with process-specific reports. It is in personnel administration (and in organizational management) that you design organizational structures and master data to lay the foundations for most other reports. This way, you can also set up reports on personnel costs or working hours based on the structures from personnel administration, while also integrating some master data in most cases. For this reason, we will pay particular attention to reports in the area of master data.

This chapter uses extremely technical terms throughout. If you have little knowledge of reporting in ERP Central Component (ECC) or similar standard software systems, then you should only skim the technical passages at first. You are bound to read the same passages more carefully if the issues described occur while they are performing their everyday tasks.

11.1.1 Categorization of Personnel Reports

Personnel reports can be categorized according to different perspectives. When setting up reporting, you should also perform such a categorization and use it as a starting point when designing new reports:

- **Aggregated reports/Reports that are or can be specific to individual persons**
  Whether a report contains any data of individual persons is a very important consideration for data privacy and it often determines whether the report can be made available outside the HR department. The question of specificity to individual persons can be difficult to decide. On the one hand, prepared lists can contain aggregations on too detailed a level (e.g., total salaries per cost center, if there are cost centers with only one salaried employee). On the other hand, you should consider this question very carefully when you not only provide prepared lists but also the option to create reports in a decentralized manner. In this case, it is very difficult to avoid the creation of person-specific lists. It is more a question of restricting access for users outside the HR department, such as departmental managers, to information on their own employees and of training them in the responsible use of report generators.
- **Ad hoc reports/Recurring reports**
  Ad hoc reports are usually created for a specific purpose, and their concrete requirements cannot be predicted. It is a question of providing a defined information pool upon which the reports can be based. To ensure that reports can be compared, and to limit the workload, it is important in each case to assess the need for ad hoc reports and the habit of constantly making slight alterations to standard reports.
- **Personnel inventory reports/Personnel change reports**
  Personnel inventory reports generally refer to specific key dates and provide a snapshot (e.g., number of employees on January 1, 2007). Personnel change reports reflect changes (e.g., new employees or employees leaving in 2006). Personnel change reports have higher requirements, both for creation and interpretation.
- **Creation frequency**
  Recurring reports can be classified by their frequency, for example daily, weekly, and monthly.

- **Data sensitivity**
  Some HR data can be available across the company (name, location, internal phone number), while other data should only be available for the manager responsible or the relevant HR representative. This is particularly relevant for person-specific reports.
- **Recipient group**
  These can be public institutions, the executive board, employee representatives, managers, the HR department, all employees, etc.
- **Online reports/Paper lists**
  Online reports are preferable because they are more up-to-date, with better distribution processes and availability. Paper lists are, however, always useful if you require frozen information for reasons of data security or to compare data.

11.1.2 Requirements for Setting Up Reporting

The objective is to set up a comprehensive reporting system that meets external requirements (especially from public institutions), supplies employees with sufficient information, and provides a good foundation for qualified decisions for controlling the company. The following requirements must be met to achieve this goal:

- Inclusion of the recipient group when defining content, usability, and processes.
- Inclusion of employee representatives.
- Definition of authorizations.
- Structured definition of requirements and identification of redundancies, especially between different processes inside and outside of personnel management (e.g., controlling).
- Ensure standardized interpretation of report results.
- Question the need for traditional lists and layout requirements.
- Decentralization and use of online reports, as far as possible within the constraints of data security and complexity.
- Definition of a core of standard reports that all users know how to use and interpret, enabling comparisons over longer periods of time.

- Provision of a central area (e.g., HR services department) that deals with the creation of complex and sensitive reports, and ongoing quality assurance, ensuring standardized interpretation, disposal of obsolete reports, and training and ongoing support for decentralized recipient groups.
- Consolidation of information gained in a report hierarchy that provides the reports to more (for example, to all managers) or fewer (for example, to only three specialists within the HR department) people, based on data frequency, complexity, and sensitivity. Figure 11.1 illustrates the structure of a reporting hierarchy.

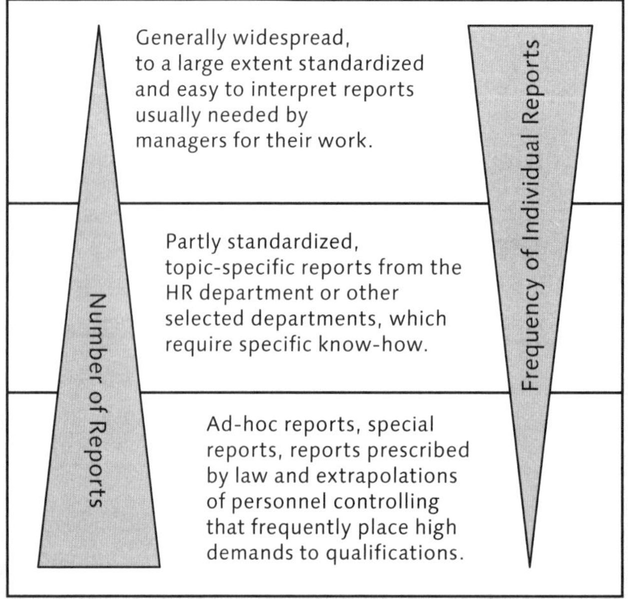

Figure 11.1 Reporting Hierarchy

11.1.3 Time Line for Reporting Data

This is ensured by clear data retrieval and maintenance processes, and by structuring reporting as described earlier. Even where these requirements are fully met, however, data stocks are still subject to changes in terms of quality and completeness. This means they become outdated over time, just as paper lists do from the moment they are printed.

An important aspect here is an awareness of the time line along which the report is moving. Both personnel inventory and personnel change reports are always characterized by the following three time specifications:

- Report creation time
- Reference point or period of time for which data is to be evaluated
- One (or usually several) point(s) in time at which the recipient views the report

As a rule, these are three different points in time. The three times only converge for online reports that have the current day as the key date.

Even if this fact appears to be obvious and trivial, failure to take it into account can often lead to communication problems. For example, users often make the incorrect assumption that sets of figures that have already been evaluated and presented no longer change. In HR, however, it is standard practice (ideally) to enter information into the data-processing system as it becomes known. Basically, this means data is entered before the fact (i.e., on May 15, the system already reflects the fact that a specific employee will leave the company on May 31). In many cases, however, data is entered retroactively. Retroactive transfers or changes to payments are everyday occurrences in the personnel departments of many companies.

Payroll systems are enabled for retroactive accounting to take this situation into account, thereby improving the quality of the results. In reporting (and this generally applies to processes that go beyond personnel management as well), users often try to ignore these retroactive data changes. The reason is often frighteningly simple: Nobody wants to explain to management why the last quarterly report was inaccurate.

The real explanation is quite clear. If you want to evaluate data for 4/1/2007, it is clear that the data will not be complete on 3/7/2007. The data used as the basis for the key date of 4/1/2007 is updated constantly as information is retrieved and maintained. New information can still become available on 4/10/2007, for example, even though the presentation to the board was made on 4/5/2007. Figure 11.2 represents an exemplary data-maintenance flow and the resulting ongoing improvement in data quality. HR reporting has the task of sensitizing the group that receives the report to this business reality. If you use "frozen data stocks" to avoid this problem, then you will be making decisions on the basis of reports that are of worse quality than those that could be based on the data actually available.

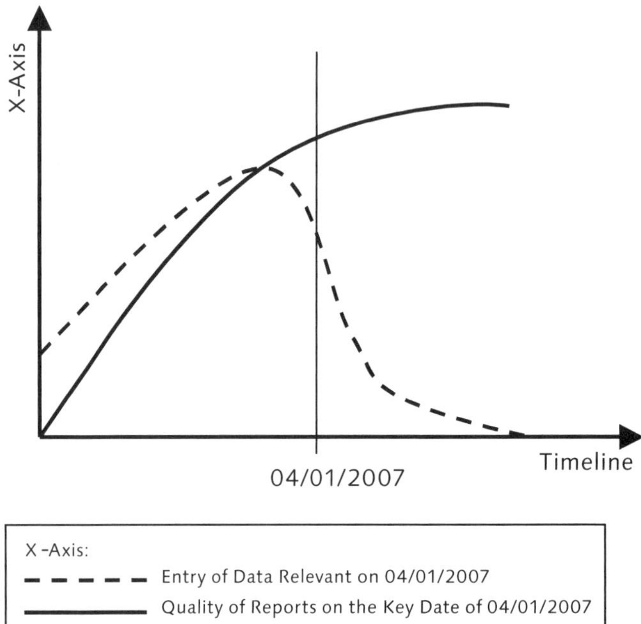

X -Axis:
- - - - - Entry of Data Relevant on 04/01/2007
——— Quality of Reports on the Key Date of 04/01/2007

Figure 11.2 Data Quality Over Time

Regardless of this, the objective is still to provide data as early as possible and at as high a level of quality as possible. This can be achieved with process changes to information distribution and authorization procedures, for example. The maintenance procedure in Figure 11.2, in particular, depends on other fixed dates. This means that users often work on a period-specific basis to guarantee the best possible data quality at the date of payroll settlement. Personnel HR reporting, requires continuously updated data maintenance.

Even with optimum processes, reporting still has its limits when it is restricted to the data stored as facts in the system. Future forecasts are often required to aid decision making. Reporting uses two methods to facilitate this:

- Extrapolation or estimation of future values based on past data
- Collection of planning data, requirements, or objectives from managers and employees

For the extrapolation method, personnel costs are calculated based on current costs for known new appointments, departures, and payment changes. An adjustment factor based on empirical values can also be used.

In data collection, managers specify the planned personnel changes, payment changes, and bonus payments. Here, too, prior experience shows that the value derived in this way also needs to be adjusted by a specific percentage.

Both methods have advantages and disadvantages. Data retrieval solely for report creation is extremely work intensive. It is also important to find out whether those specifying the information may have an interest in deliberately specifying false data (e.g., because they would rather fall below a high budget than exceed a low budget). The more dynamic the environment, including internal company structures and objectives, the less precise the values determined purely from extrapolation based on past data.

11.1.4 Counting Method

In HR statistics, two basic types of counting methods are possible: headcount or actual capacity. The latter can be counted in hours per week or as a percentage of the normal time worked per week. In both cases, it is also important to take unpaid absences into account.

If you want to define which tasks can be taken over by a given department, you should always consider the capacity as the full-time equivalent, i.e., 0.5 for a part-time worker working half the standard weekly hours. However, in an employee-turnover statistic, for example, the headcount might also be the appropriate method.

11.1.5 Special Case for Turnover Statistics

Turnover statistics are an important tool for HR-related work. For example, they are often used to solve the following problems:

- Recognition of problems with high turnover and the reasons for such problems
- Defining which channels are mainly used for recruitment
- Identifying channels via which personnel can be reduced

First, however, it is important to define the term turnover. In this context, the following questions need to be answered:

- Which employees are taken into account in the statistics?

- Will the system only consider external turnover, or also internal turnover?
- What counts as an employee departure? (for example, change within the corporation, change to inactive employment such as parental leave)
- What grouping should the statistics use? (for example, employer termination, employee termination, retirement, early retirement, inactivity period, death)

The final objective should be to identify the movements between the areas relevant to the problem, and movements into and out of the area considered. The company itself is generally the area considered. You must also decide whether to include temporary staff in the evaluation. Figure 11.3 displays a typical turnover overview, although it has been simplified by omitting some of the arrows. The lesson behind the graphic is clear: The company hardly ever recruits long-term employees directly —it first takes on interns and contract staff. Employees returning from an inactive employment are very important.

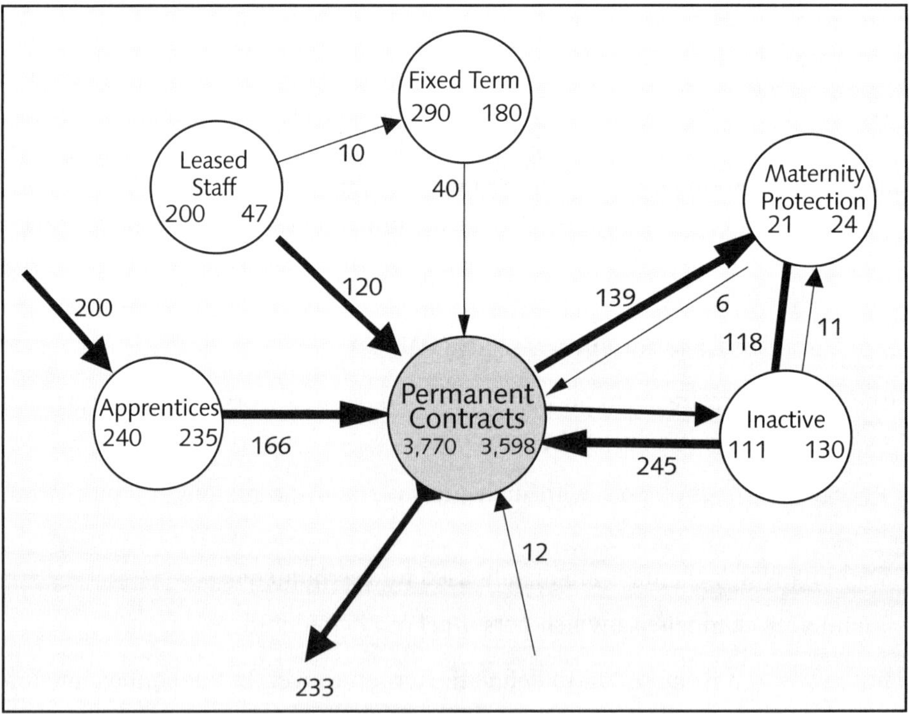

Figure 11.3 Example of a Turnover Overview (Simplified)

11.2 Implementation in SAP ERP HCM

For clear and meaningful HR reporting, clearly defined enterprise, personnel, and organizational structures are indispensable for the individual reports. This is the only way the reports can be compared with each other, making it possible to combine the information provided by the different reports.

11.2.1 Structures in HR Reporting

The SAP ERP HCM system provides different structures that were introduced in Section 4.2.5. When structuring the company, you generally use the company code, personnel area, personnel subarea, and cost center. These structure levels can also be used as the basis for reporting. It is often the case, however, that the criteria for forming these structures do not correspond to the requirements of reporting. The personnel area and personnel subarea, in particular, are meant to satisfy the requirements of payroll and time management.

For this reason, the use of organizational management is indispensable for efficient reporting in most companies. For some small companies, it might also be sufficient to use the Organizational unit, Position, and Job fields in Infotype 0001 without integration with Organizational Management.

Only the full implementation of Organizational Management, however, makes it possible to map an actual organizational structure for the company across any number of hierarchy levels. Also, different views of the organization (matrix organization) can be mapped and evaluated.

The fact that Organizational Management uses the general term organizational unit can often be problematic, however. While this guarantees maximum flexibility, it makes it more difficult to define an evaluation that needs to create subtotals at the division level, for example. You may therefore need to find a way of indicating the neutral objects.

One possible solution is to indicate the individual organizational levels, e.g., using a customer-specific infotype. You can find a detailed description of the organizational management in the book *HR Personnel Planning and Development Using SAP ERP HCM*.

The personnel structure presents a problem similar to that of the enterprise structure. The definition of employee groups and employee subgroups is also geared toward the requirements of payroll and time management. This is why there are employee subgroups such as Employees with 13-month salary, Industrial workers at old standard pay, etc. These criteria may be relevant for very specific evaluations, but they are generally not an appropriate basis for reporting.

On the other hand, in HR reporting you want to be able to make selections using criteria such as: inactive, semiretirement working phase, sick outside period of continued pay, part-time under 50 %, or fixed term. Some of these could also be represented as employee subgroups, but this is not recommended. First, these details are already entered in the master data and entering the data again in another way would be redundant. Second, this would quickly lead to an "explosion" in the number of employee subgroups (mainly because this would have a multiplying effect: for every employee subgroup, a "sick outside period of continued pay" version would have to be divided, for example).

Because all of the data is already stored in the master data, it can also be evaluated. The data is often not available as selection criteria, however. For this reason, users often perform different evaluations and then consolidate the results in a Microsoft Office product. Alternatively, using the Ad hoc Query's set operations or programming your own evaluations is an acceptable solution. At the same time, it is important that the underlying reporting structures are clearly defined on the basis of the system data. Only then is it possible to create reports that can be compared at a later date.

Another option is to use SAP NetWeaver Business Intelligence (BI) (see Section 11.2.2). This includes various options for combining different selection and aggregation criteria. A very flexible example for defining a clean reporting basis is the definition of a company-specific logical database (LDB).

11.2.2 Tools for HR Reporting

The requirements of reports can vary considerably with regard to content, layout, and execution frequency. Different tools are used to create reports as required.

Tools for Creating Evaluations

ECC provides various tools for creating evaluations. The main ones include:

- Standard reports
- Ad hoc Query

- SAP Query
- Programming individual customer-specific reports
- Programming a customer-specific reporting basis using your own LDB

The preceding options are listed in increasing order of flexibility and workload involved. For this reason, you should first clarify which requirements can be covered using standard reports and queries. It is, however, the norm to program additional reports to supplement the standard functionality. If the requirements of personnel HR reporting are not fully reflected in the standard, and a large number of new developments are required, then you should also consider the last alternative.

An LBD (see the following section) can encapsulate a large portion of the company-specific logic, so that it does not need to be reprogrammed for every single report. This makes the programming more efficient and also ensures consistency.

There are, however, reasons that this method is rarely used:

- This option is not well known.
- The workload of developing a company's own LDB is overestimated.
- Customers develop the additional evaluations individually as required, but do not realize the potential of consolidating them.
- It is easier to have a small budget assigned for specific requirements than make a one-time investment for the future. The investment is wasted, if—from a business perspective—no clear structure is defined on which to base the various reports.
- Customers do not want to take on the workload involved in defining a full HR reporting concept and a clean structure.
- Consulting companies earn money for every report programmed, and they therefore generate more revenue from individual reports than from a one-time development of an LDB that significantly reduces future development effort.

Even if these obstacles are often difficult to overcome, it can be worth the effort in our experience. You must have previously clarified that the standard solution is not sufficient in some places and that several reports need to be programmed in any case.

The following criteria apply when a company intends to create its own LDB:

- Complex personnel change statistics are required. In our experience, this logic can also be encapsulated very well in an LDB.
- Users constantly need aggregations at defined organizational levels that cannot be mapped using organizational criteria from Infotype 0001 and the neutral concept of the organizational unit in Organizational Management. Together with an indicator for the organizational units (e.g., as team, main department, or sales branch) this type of logic can also be mapped very well in an LDB. For the evaluations based on the LDB, it then appears as though every employee has a team key, a main department key, and a sales branch key.

Concept of the Logical Database (LDB)

ECC works intensively with LDBs. They are used to make the programmers' jobs easier and to concentrate specific definitions and structures in a central location.

An LDB used by a program (or query) behaves in almost the same way as a "real" database, even though it does not physically store data (hence the name). A program or query requests certain data from the LDB, which then only really reads the individual tables. This means that the programmer has far fewer things to worry about. The most important logical databases in HCM are the following:

- **PNP**: for HR master data
- **PNPCE**: for HR master data including concurrent employment (to remain future-oriented, you should work only with PNPCE after changing to R/3 Enterprise)
- **PAP**: for applicant master data
- **PCH**: for objects in personnel planning and development (also includes HR master data)

From this point on we will no longer use the term LDB PNP, but rather PNPCE. For release 4.6C and earlier, continue to use PNP.

The logical database PNPCE provides the familiar standard selection screen and its variants, for example. It also relieves programmers of the tasks of authorization checks, personnel number selection, and period selection. If the criteria for the standard selection screen are insufficient, then the company-specific LDB can be used to provide other selection criteria without the programmer having to check them.

BI and Strategic Enterprise Management (SEM)

Another tool that is increasingly important is *Business Intelligence*. The SAP NetWeaver BI solution is a separate system that extracts data from ECC and other systems, if necessary. Using *InfoCubes*, Business Warehouse (BW) provides the option of extremely flexible combination, selection, and aggregation of this data. For this reason, SAP NetWeaver BI represents an extremely powerful tool and is mainly needed for very large data stocks. It does, however, require additional work to configure and maintain—especially because it is an additional system. SAP's current strategy is strongly oriented toward SAP NetWeaver BI (i.e., little investment in reporting outside BI). You can find a detailed description on the use of SAP NetWeaver BI in SAP ERP HCM in the SAP PRESS book *HR Reporting with SAP*.

SEM is partly based on SAP NetWeaver BI. A core component is the *Balanced Scorecard (BSC)*, which can establish a relationship between aggregated key figures from different areas and trace those figures back to lower aggregation levels. The SEM principle is displayed in Figure 11.4.

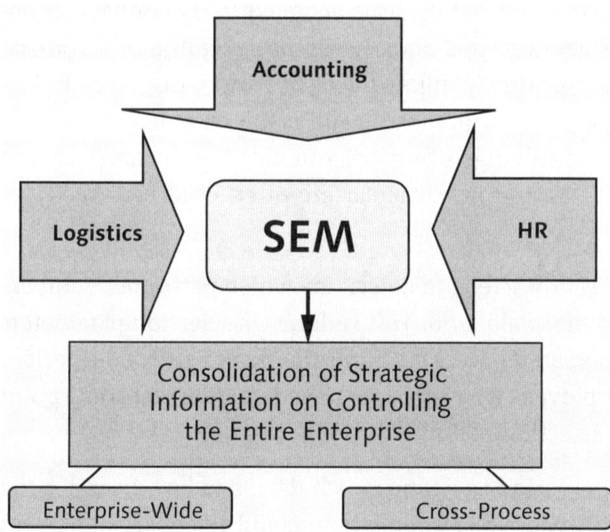

Figure 11.4 SEM as a Highly Aggregated Cross-Area Evaluation Tool

Tools for Accessing Evaluations

Apart from the individual evaluations, easy access is also an important factor. In ECC, and particularly in SAP ERP HCM, the following options are provided:

- Easy Access Menu
- Human Resources Information System (HIS) (see Section 11.2.7)
- Manager's Desktop (MDT) (see Section 2.5)
- Manager Self-Service (MSS) (see Section 2.4.6)

The last two tools are specifically tailored to the requirements of managers who want to run reports on their employees. HIS makes it possible to start evaluations based on the organization chart.

The Easy Access Menu is not restricted to evaluations. This is the normal menu with which SAP GUI users work. Every evaluation and every query infoset can, however, be included in the menu based on users' roles. This means that every user can be provided with the required evaluation options in the most ergonomic position in the menu.

11.2.3 Standard Reports

The reports of the SAP ERP HCM system must be assigned to individual components. In the processes considered in this book (with the exception of Organizational Management), evaluations usually follow the basic pattern displayed in Figure 11.5. Here, we explain the principle in more detail, as it is extremely important for the correct usage of the broad range of reports offered. The person-selection period and the data-selection period in particular are often used incorrectly — even by experienced users.

First, you use the report's selection screen to determine which personnel numbers will be taken into account in the evaluation. This is done via selection parameters (e.g., employee subgroup, personnel area, etc.) and the person-selection period. The system considers the employees who meet the selection criteria at some point during the specified person-selection period.

You can use the data-selection period to define which data is to be output for the persons already selected. This way, for example, you could select all employees that had been active in a specific personnel area at any time (leave the person-selection period empty) and have the system issue the current (data-selection period = current date) address for those employees.

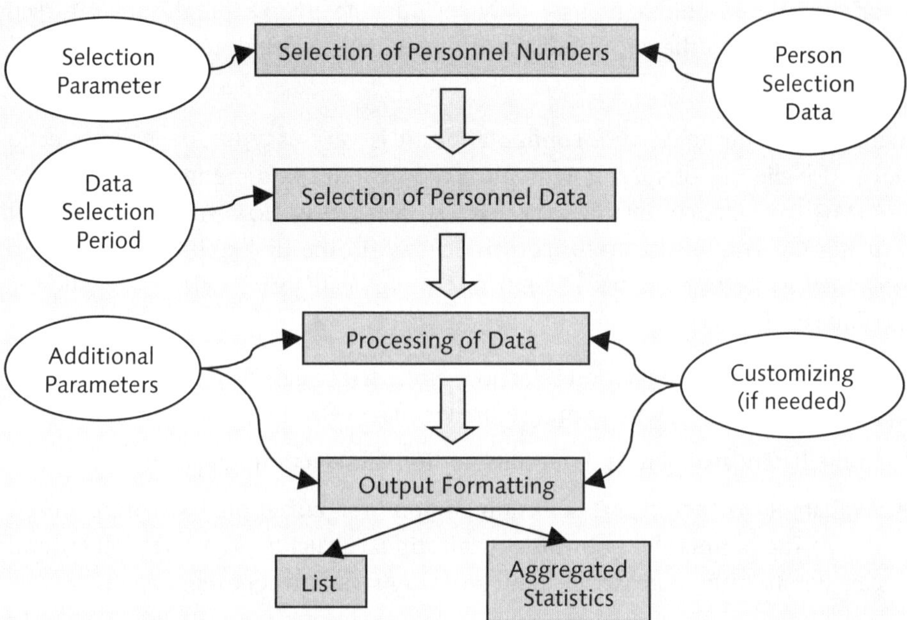

Figure 11.5 Basic Pattern for a Standard Report

Actual processing and output formatting for the data is report specific and is partly controlled via other parameters in the selection screen or in Customizing settings. See the online help regarding each specific report for more information (in the selection screen, follow the menu path HELP • APPLICATION HELP). The help field ((F1) help) may also provide information on any report-specific parameters of the selection screen.

The selection screens for the most commonly used standard reports are very similar. The standard selection screen from the PNPCE (PNP for older reports) logical database serves as the basis for these reports. It can and should also form the basis for individually programmed reports and SAP queries. It generally provides the following functionality:

- Period selection
- Selection parameters (can be enhanced using the Other selections button)
- Selection via matchcodes
- Selection via the organizational structure of Organizational Management. Remember that—depending on the configuration of your system—selecting an

organizational unit here may only include the people on the level directly below. To select the entire substructure, you must select it using the Select subtree.

Starting with the maximum configuration, it is very easy to adapt the selection screen for the use of specific individual reports. This is done in Customizing via the IMG path Personnel Management • HR Information System • Reporting • Adjusting the Standard Selection Screen. In the first step, you must create *report categories* (see Figure 11.6). These report categories define the following attributes:

- Selection options for period selection. Note that some evaluations only provide useful information when you use the key date selection.
- Immediately available and optional additional selection fields.
- Availability of additional selection options (organizational structure, matchcode). The permissibility of the organizational structure as a selection criterion can significantly increase the value of many standard reports.

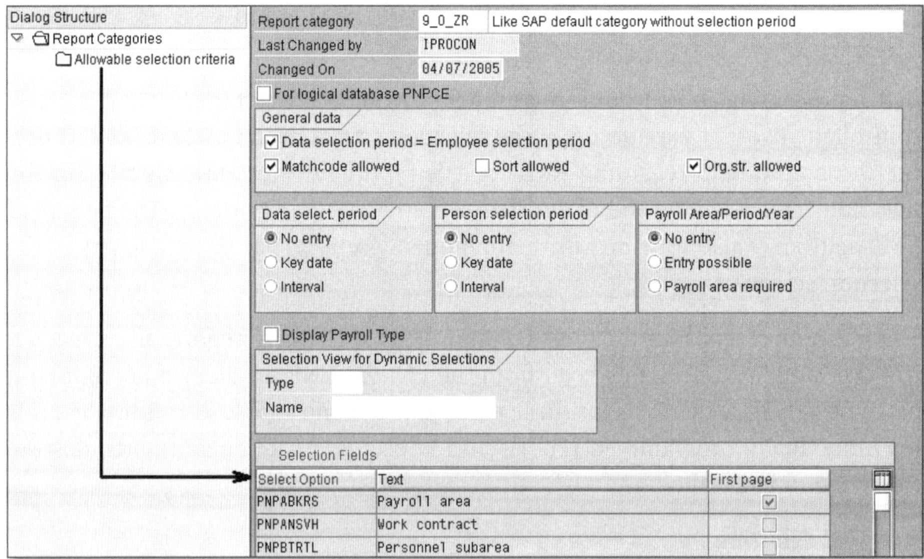

Figure 11.6 Defining a Report Category

When creating report categories, we recommend that you use an existing class as a copy template.

In the second step, these report categories are assigned to individual reports. When you assign report classes to standard reports, remember that enhanced options to the selection screen do not necessarily make sense. For example, a specific report only provides useful results on a key date.

The selection screens for most reports therefore provide many options. To avoid having to repeat the same entries each time you use the report, you should save frequently used selections as variants. This also ensures quality and ease of comparison for recurring evaluations.

When the structure is changed, you must also check and adapt variants. If, for example, a variant called Employee list, East Coast contains the personnel subareas Boston, MA; New York, NY; and Washington, DC the new location, Charleston, SC, can easily be overlooked. Variants that contain a selection across the entire organizational structure are particularly prone to errors.

Note

The Select subtree functionality selects all organizational units below the organizational unit East Coast for the current period. A new Team W4 set up in Washington must be maintained, as must a new personnel subarea in Charleston.

Examples

There is a very large supply of standard reports. Most of them are available via the menu. It is hardly possible to describe them all, and it is not necessary, as the online documentation is generally sufficient. We have, however, provided the following examples to give you an idea of the standard options. Additional standard reports can be found in the book *HR Reporting with SAP*.

The *employee list* is a very simple evaluation that you can access via the menu path Human Resources • Personnel Management • Administration • Info System • Reports • Employee • Employee list.

The system outputs a simple list of employees from the selected area (see Figure 11.7). In addition, the output screen provides the following possible options, for example:

- Sorting
- Filtering
- Print preview

- Transfer to a spreadsheet or word processor
- Save as local file
- Send as email in SAP Office
- Display as SAP business graphic (with no numeric values in this report, there is no point in using this option)
- Column selection in the layout

Employee List

Key date: 04/07/2005
Number of selected employees: 221
Number of selected cost centers: 86
Parameter KOSTLTXT only allowed in connection with KOSTL

CoCd	PA	Cost Center	Text	Pers.no.	PersIDNo.	Name	Name at birth	Job Title	Entry Date	Leaving
3000	3000	2130	Accounts Payable	00100206	589492934	Mr. Tom Hays		Manager (US)	01/01/1996	
3000	3000	9301	Production 1	00100208	222111111	Mrs Monette Collins		Technician (US)	12/31/1998	
3000	3000	2250	Payroll Admin.	00100209	376898766	Mr. Timmy Tabasco		Manager (US)	01/06/1997	
3000	3000	4130	Warehouse	00100227	198871123	Mr. George Metzger		QM Personnel (US)	01/01/1997	
3000	3000	2220	Labor Relations	00100230	174871124	Mrs Jennifer Esposito		Administration (US)	02/01/1997	
3000	3000	4120	IT Service	00100235	674012887	Mr. Peter Laursen		PC Service Technician (US)	09/24/1999	
3000	3000	2100	Finance & Admin.	00100245	321455030	Mrs Amy Sombat		Assistant (US)	08/01/1997	
3000	3000	4120	IT Service	00100246	990999993	Mrs Elizabeth Davis		Director	10/19/2000	

Figure 11.7 Example of a Standard Employee List

It makes sense to try out all of these options (see Figure 11.8). Using them is far easier than providing a written description. Note, however, that problems that occur when transferring data to other applications (such as Microsoft Excel) could also be due to authorization problems.

Figure 11.8 Options for Further Processing a Report Output

The employee list contains all of the options of the standard selection screen (sorting, matchcode selection (search help), selection via the organizational structure, and further selection fields) and report-specific selection fields. As a result, it is also possible to select by various characteristics such as nationality or gender (see Figure 11.9). These are not contained in the standard selection screen and are therefore not available with most of the other reports. Furthermore, because the report has the capability to display the cost-center text, it also provides an example of how the form of the output is controlled via the selection screen.

Apart from this, the employee list is simply provided as an example here.

You can access the report on *flexible employee data* via the menu path Human Resources • Personnel Management • Administration • Info System • Reports • Employee • Flexible Employee Data. Its extreme flexibility provides an extremely useful tool that can make it unnecessary to create a query or program a separate report.

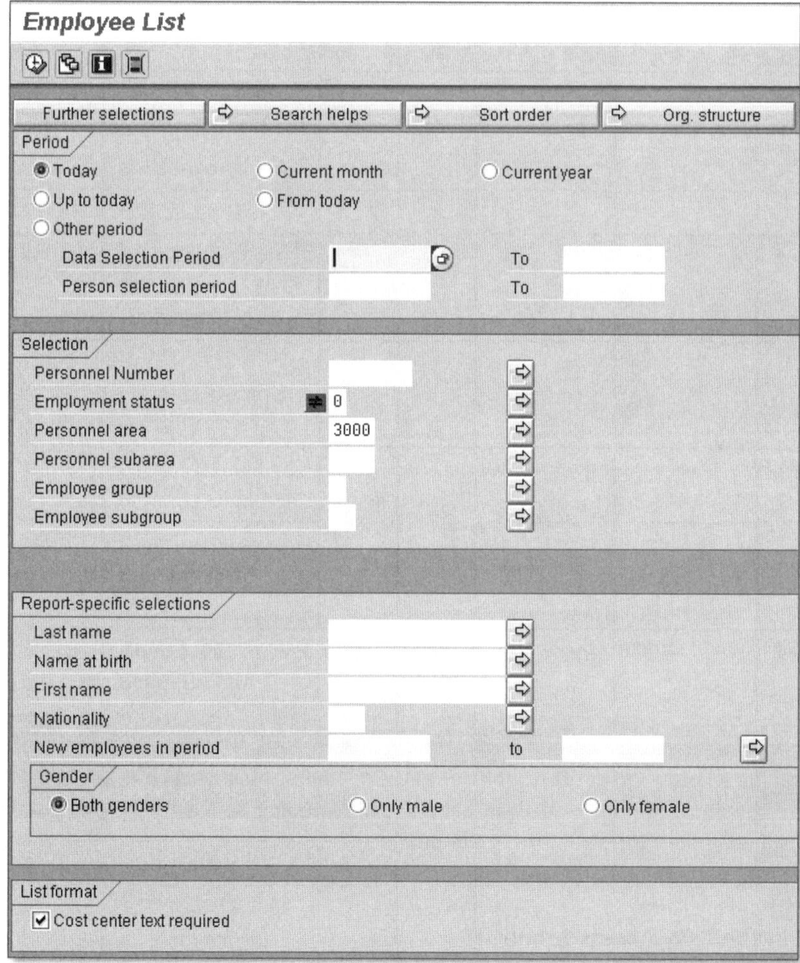

Figure 11.9 Selection Screen for the Standard Employee List

A total of 105 fields from different infotypes are available for output. These include some fields that are not saved in the database, but which are calculated dynamically (e.g., the age of an employee). Figure 11.10 displays the selection of output fields.

Because many of these fields are unequivocal only to given points in time, they can only be selected for key dates, not for periods. Using the filter function in the screen output, these 105 data fields can also be used to select employees.

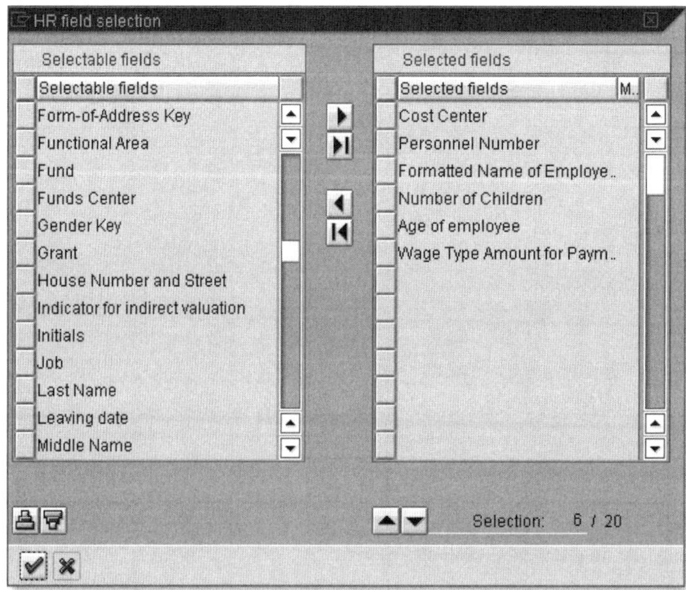

Figure 11.10 Selection of Output fields for the Flexible Employee Data Report

Important Note for Developers

It is worth taking a closer look at this report (RPLICO10) and possibly using it as a template for your own development. Due to generic programming, it is very easy to add further fields if you know the structure of the program.

Integration in the Easy Access Menu

Standard reports, customer-specific programmed reports, and even generated queries can easily be integrated in the Easy Access Menu using the role concept. You can maintain roles and collective roles via the menu path Tools • Administration

• User Maintenance • Role administration—Roles. This way, Reports can also be included in the roles, making them available via the Easy Access Menu. Role definition should, however, only be performed by suitably experienced administrators responsible for authorizations. For data-security reasons, other users should not be allowed to define roles!

11.2.4 SAP Query

SAP Query was originally a cross-application component. For this reason, we will not go into greater detail on this here; we will just present the basic options and special characteristics within the SAP ERP HCM system.

SAP Query is based on the same infosets and user groups as Ad hoc Query (see the following section).

Based on the defined infosets, the use of SAP Query can be organized in three different ways:

- Queries are defined at a central location and are then simply executed by transactional users or executives.
- Transactional users or executives create their own queries. In this case, clear conventions are needed.
- Transactional users or executives use centrally provided queries and create their own ad hoc queries (see the following section). Conventions are also needed here, although it is much easier to learn to use ad hoc queries. This variant is probably the most practical, because the number of available fields for ad hoc queries can significantly reduced in accordance with the wishes of the employee representatives.

SAP Query also provides Quick Viewer as an additional evaluation tool.

You can define an infoset via the following menu Human Resources • Information System • Reporting Tools • SAP Query • Environment • Infosets. First, however, you must select the correct query area (menu path Human Resources • Information System • Reporting Tools • SAP Query • Environment • Query Areas). In general, you work in the client-specific area (standard area). You must also define the user group to which you are going to assign the infoset (menu path Human Resources • Information System • Reporting Tools • SAP Query • Environment • User Groups).

When maintaining infosets, you must always bear in mind that they will be used in the future as the basis for many queries and ad hoc queries. For this reason, it is worth investing a little extra time when creating an infoset. The field names, in particular, should be self-explanatory. If they just have the name Wage Type, then it will be very difficult during query creation, and particularly during evaluation, to understand which wage type from which infotype was used. Changing an infoset for which queries already exist is restricted (in particular, you cannot remove fields used in queries). It is always possible to add new fields, however.

When the infoset has been created, it must be assigned to the user groups that will be allowed to access it. It is then possible to create a query based on the infoset. You can access the initial screen via the following menu path Human Resources • Information System • Reporting Tools • SAP Query.

11.2.5 Ad Hoc Query

Ad hoc Query (outside the SAP ERP HCM system, this tool is also referred to as the *Infoset Query*) is based on SAP Query. It is, however, significantly easier to use and can therefore be more widely used within departments and by managers and administrative staff. Just as with SAP Query, the Ad hoc Query is based on the definition of the infosets and user groups, as described in the previous section.

The Ad hoc Query allows easy (single-line) lists, based on an LDB. Using PNPCE as an example, the following data is available (this also applies to SAP Query):

- All infotypes in Personnel Administration and Time Management
- The Payroll results, provided they are stored in a Payroll results infotype
- The results from Time Management (although only daily balances and no monthly ones), provided they are included in Customizing for simulated infotypes
- Long texts for the most relevant keys stored in the infotypes that have already been named
- A comprehensive set of additional fields, e.g., of PD infotypes, where a reference can be created to an individual personnel number (e.g., manager)

You can access the Ad hoc Query via the following menu path Human Resources • Personnel Management • Administration • Info System • Reporting Tools • Ad-hoc Query. The menu item Reporting tools is also contained in other component infosystems and in cross-application infosystems. The Ad hoc Query can also be accessed via the normal SAP Query transaction using the Infoset query button.

Figure 11.11 displays the initial screen for the Ad hoc Query.

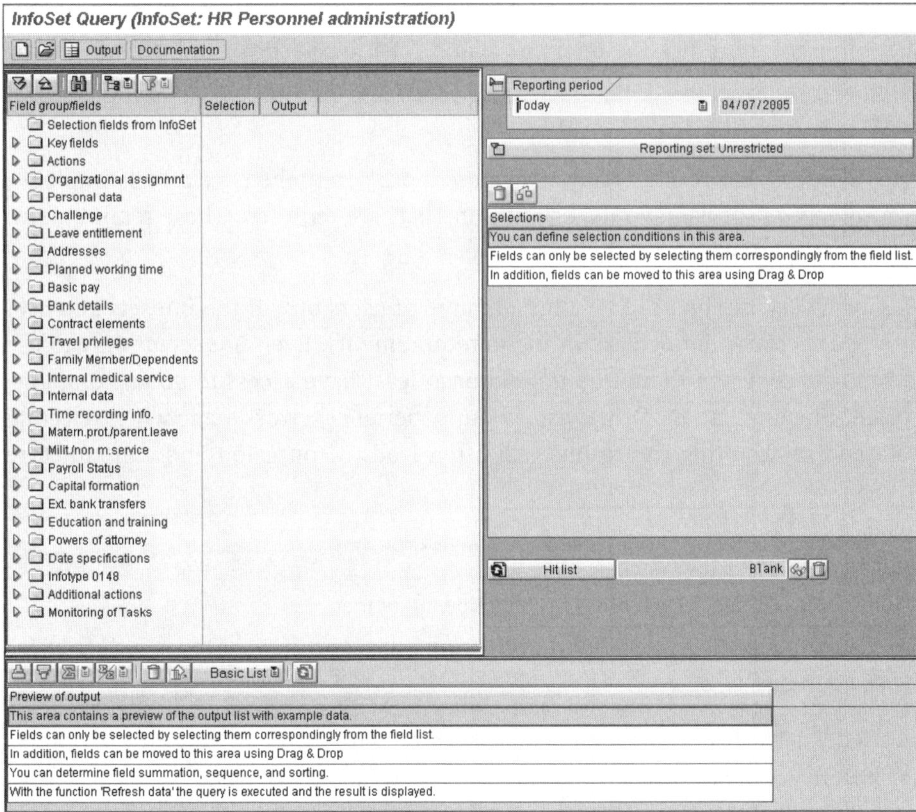

Figure 11.11 Initial Screen for the Ad hoc Query

The screen section at the top left displays the available field groups representing infotypes. The top right of the screen displays the Reporting period, the additional restriction of the Reporting set, and the selection screen. Restricting the reporting set is particularly useful. For example, you can define an additional restriction using the organizational structure. You can also use the Hit list to display the number of data records selected by the query. The bottom section of the initial screen displays the Preview of output. If you click on the Output button, the system displays the result of your Ad hoc Query.

The ability to link selection sets from several queries provides extreme flexibility. This makes it possible to map intersections, set unions, and exclude one set from another. The result of these set operations is then transferred for subsequent use to the resulting set. This means that in two steps it is possible, for example, to select all of the employees from a specific personnel area that do not have Infotype 0050.

It is often useful to use the query as an aid for pre-selection, and to forward the reporting set to another report via the *report-report interface*. To do this, select GOTO - START REPORT FROM THE MENU.

The Ad hoc Query reaches its limits where more comprehensive calculation logic, control levels, special layouts, or multiline lists are required. These requirements are at least partially covered by SAP Query.

Ad hoc Query can be used by a broad range of users only if the infosets and user groups are clearly defined according to requirements. Even if it seems easy to use at first glance, users should be trained or at least have access to good, company-specific documentation. Otherwise, in our experience, errors made when selecting data and interpreting the results will often lead to confusion and contradictory lists.

Note: Successful Use of Query Tools

You should pay special attention to the following points:

- Clarification of the terms used when naming fields (especially for terms such as *basic salary*, *variable salary*, *basic pay*, and *hourly rate*, which are often understood differently by employees in the payroll department than by managers. It is important to clearly define the composition of these aggregations.).
- Importance of the selection period (especially awareness that many reports only provide useful information when performed for a specific key date).
- Evaluation of actions (difference between Infotypes 0000 and 0302).
- Importance of object selection (HCM specific).

Using queries, you can evaluate not only infotypes, but also the payroll and time evaluation results saved in clusters. To learn more about this procedure refer to the SAP PRESS book *HR Reporting with SAP*. There, you can also learn how to create simple calculation fields in the SAP Query without programming.

We strongly recommend the broad use of Ad hoc Query within the framework of the restrictions imposed by data-security considerations and training costs. To ensure this, you must create a central concept (HR Reporting). You must have extensive knowledge of HCM data and functionality to succeed with this work.

11.2.6 Programming Customer-Specific Reports

If the standard reports provided by SAP do not meet the requirements of your organization, and the query options are not sufficient, you can program customer-specific reports. You should first check, however, whether the additional workload (both for creating and maintaining reports) is really justified:

- Can you get by with compromises to the layout of standard reports?
- Can you avoid the need for programming by switching from paper reports to completely online reports? Standard reports are often simply not suitable for central printing (e.g., insufficient options for controlling page breaks).
- Are the reports you usually use really better? The options in the standard reports reflect best-practice experience, which can also be applied in your company.

When creating your own reports, they should be based on the PNPCE (or other) logical database where possible, for the following reasons:

- Authorization checks have already been implemented, they would need to be programmed again in your own reports.
- It provides a comprehensive standard selection screen.
- It is easier to read personnel data.
- You can log the start of PNPCE reports via the implementation guide (IMG) menu path Personnel Management • Personnel Administration • Tools • Revision • Log Report Starts and evaluate them via report RPUPROTD.

In some cases however, there can be good reasons to develop customer ABAPs without using a logical database. Such as:

- As a rule of thumb, performance of a reasonably designed report that doesn't use an LDB is much better that that of an LDB-based report.
- LDBs are focused on a specific part of the data in the system. If you want to combine data, e.g., HR master data with data from SAP ERP Financial Cost Accounting (CO) and from travel management, you won't find it all in one LDB. Because one report can only use one LDB, there is no way to combine several LDBs within one report.

11.2.7 HIS

The HIS is based on the structural graphic from Organizational Management. It makes it possible to start a structured range of evaluations easily via a section of the organizational structure that can be selected graphically (see Figure 11.12).

You can access HIS via the menu path Human Resources • Information System • Reporting Tools • HIS.

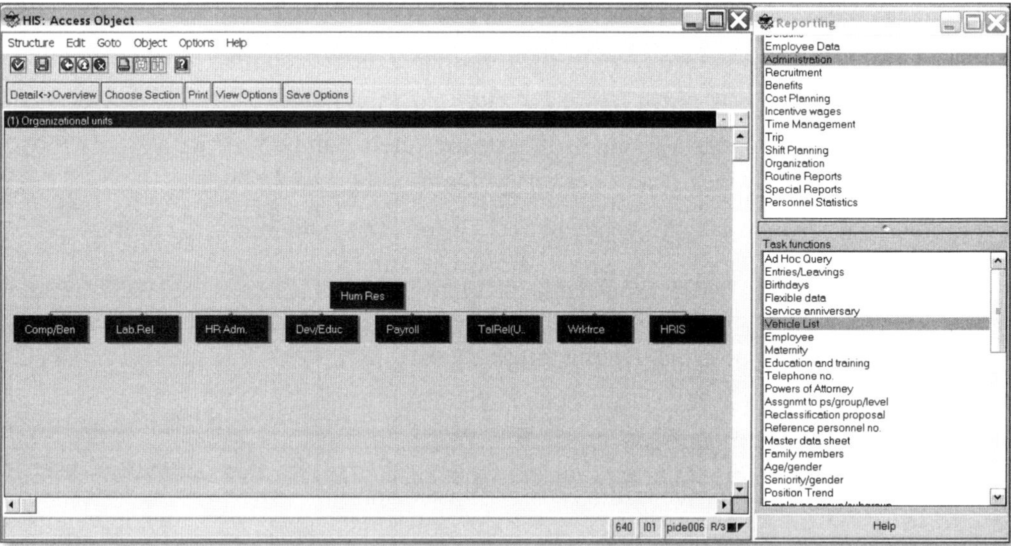

Figure 11.12 Example in HIS

11.2.8 Limits of HCM Reporting

All solutions for HR Reporting, no matter how technically perfect, reach their limits if the data quality and environment are not right. However, implementation in SAP ERP HCM also reveals shortcomings.

Shortcomings of the PNPCE Logical Database

The LDB PNPCE and its underlying data structures are an important basis for all of the forms of report creation described. Its shortcomings occur in nearly all reports. It should include:

- **Selection and aggregation via organizational structures is difficult.**
  The structure concepts in Infotype 0001 are generally not sufficient to map lower-level structures. The individual organizational levels are not sufficiently described. In addition to the department ID, HR controllers usually also like IDs for divisions, business areas, sub-departments, branch offices, teams, etc. A solution for this is to describe the organizational units using a company-specific infotype and possibly connect it to the selection of a company-specific logical database.
- **Organizational structures with several dimensions (matrix organization, project structure) are not considered in the selection.**
  A solution for this is the selection via PD structures and the transfer of the personnel numbers selected in this way to a PA report. In the standard version, this can be done by report RHPNPSUB. A more flexible solution, which also creates a higher workload, is to program a company-specific LDB that reflects these structures more closely.
- **Selection and aggregation via the personnel structure are not always sufficient.**
  Aside from the employee subgroups and positions, HR reporting also often requires a grouping of employees by more or less dynamic criteria. These can be criteria such as outside continued pay period, maternity leave, national service, or on night shift on this key date. It would be extremely time-consuming and redundant to change employee subgroups for every change to these characteristics to make clear selections in reports. Some possible solutions are: individual programming of selection and aggregation in every evaluation, preselection using more work-intensive ad hoc queries, and transfer of the selection set to the actual evaluation. This last approach only works partly and not for aggregation. Another way out is the creation of a company-specific LDB.

Limits to the Inclusion of Other Processes

Cross-process evaluations also often create problems. The inclusion of several of the processes described in this book is very well covered in the current release level. It is more difficult to include non-PA processes in PA evaluations, for example:

- **Processes for personnel planning and development are integrated very well up to this point.**
  SAP Query and Ad hoc Query already provide a significant amount of data, especially from Organizational Management. Furthermore, the PD LDB (PCH)

fully includes PA infotypes. The standard reports still represented a weak point, because they are seldom set up as cross-process reports. A possible solution is the use of PCH as the basis for queries or company-specific programming.

- **To evaluate the data of Travel Management with queries, the easiest way is to integrate it with an infoset.**
  At the current release level, travel management provides a good range of standard evaluations, and it can also be evaluated via SAP Query, now that travel cost infosets are provided. The inclusion of travel data in PA evaluations could be better, however. A solution to this could be to define your own infosets based on the database tables, avoiding the LDBs. SAP queries can then also be created on this basis. To do this, however, you should be very familiar with the data structures and SAP Query.
- **Cross-HCM data can be integrated with SAP NetWeaver BI with the most flexibility.**
  Evaluation of HCM data that is linked to data from SAP ERP Financials, Logistics, or industry solutions is not generally covered in the standard version. Very few standard reports are exceptions to this. This is to be expected, as the requirements of individual companies differ greatly in this area and there are many possible combinations. While certain special cases can only be covered using company-specific programming without LDB support (provided that you have good knowledge of the data structures for several processes), SAP NetWeaver BI does provide a comprehensive solution. It provides the opportunity to combine data from all SAP components and external systems. Based on the large data quantities, however, the system does not work with real-time data, but with extracted data stocks, to safeguard system performance. SAP NetWeaver BI is the most flexible and comprehensive evaluation tool, but it generates a heavy workload for implementation and maintenance.

11.3 Process Example: Company-Specific Reporting Concept

The process of HR reporting often lacks a clear strategy. The following sections provide an example of how HR reporting is set up with SAP ERP HCM. This reporting concept consists of the following components:

- Role distribution between the HR services or reporting t area and managers
- Inclusion of other report recipients

- Definition of standard reports available decentrally
- Definition of standard reports available centrally
- Procedure for implementing new standard reports
- Tools for ad hoc reports (centrally and decentrally)
- Tools for providing reports
- Authorization concept

Figure 11.13 displays the general structure of the reporting concept. At the same time, HR reporting supports various internal customers.

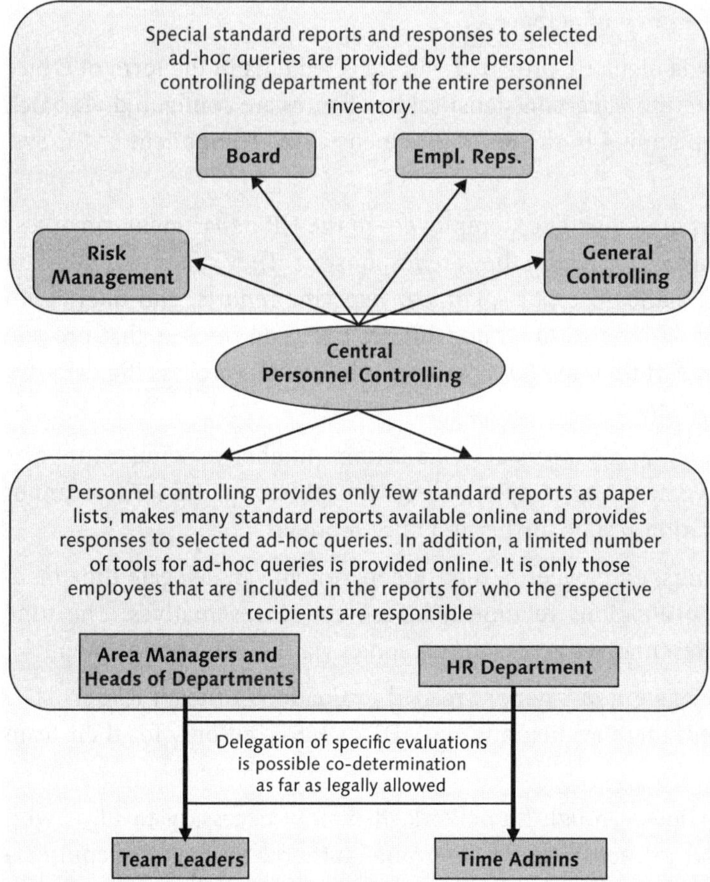

Figure 11.13 Recipients and Roles in HR Reporting

- The management board is provided with a few special standard reports and receives answers to ad hoc queries. These reports are provided in the form of Office documents or paper lists.
- In the system, the employee representatives can access many standard reports online. Some of these reports are legally required and some have been agreed upon within the framework of the reporting concept. They are also informed on all ad hoc queries and included in the definition of new standard reports, and new tools for ad hoc evaluations.
- Risk Management has online access to a few defined standard reports from HR Risk Management (turnover, age structure, remaining leave and time accounts, etc.). Risk Management can also create its own ad hoc queries within the boundaries of its own area of competence.
- General reporting is regularly provided with selected data in the form of Office documents. Furthermore, certain statistical key figures are configured via batch input or via cost-planning in the SAP ERP Financial CO component of the system.
- Within their areas of competence, employees in the HR department can access data on the employees for whom they are responsible. They can access this data in the system via standard reports, company-specific reports, and queries. In addition, they can also perform ad hoc queries based on infosets that provide very good coverage of their area of competence. They can process the data further in Office products.
- Area and departmental managers access a certain number of standard reports via MDT and have access to simple infosets for ad hoc queries. They cannot process the evaluation results further in Office products.
- Within certain limits, employees in the HR department can delegate time management–related evaluations to time management representatives. The time management representatives access these reports via the Easy Access Menu.
- Managers can delegate non-payment-related evaluations to team leaders. The team leaders access these evaluations via MDT or MSS, but only for their team members.
- This concept provides a rough framework. It is now necessary to fill it with actual reports and infosets, and to determine authorizations. This requires a certain amount of detailed work, but the process is not as work intensive as you may think. In our experience, this kind of solution creates a usable and fairly

stable HR reporting environment far more quickly than the habit of just skipping from one requirement to the next.

This concludes our review of HR Reporting. Because this is such a useful functionality and has many options available, we could not explain every detail here, but we hope you have a good overview of the possibilities.

11.4 Critical Success Factors

- When defining the HR Reporting strategy and the corresponding structures, internal customers must be included.
- The system must support the role of the HR department as a central framework, providing tools and advice for the interpretation of reports and creating more complex and wide-ranging evaluations.
- The system must support the role of managers who, with the support of the HR department, can create the reports they need online.
- The basis for high-quality HR reporting is high-quality and up-to-date data entry.
- The requirements of HR reporting should be included in the system design from the very start. They must definitely be regarded in a holistic way. Considering every single evaluation requirement in isolation rarely results in an ideal overall solution.
- Specific aspects of the authorization concept are relevant in HR reporting. A well-configured authorization check, in particular, can have an extremely positive effect on performance.
- Employee representatives should be included in the process.
- You must define evaluation requirements very precisely. A general, verbal description of the contents is not usually sufficient. You should clarify the following in particular: selection criteria, aggregation levels, numerical and non-numerical content, calculation formulae, layout, configurability, authorization check, and reusability of the results. Definitions must always clearly follow ECC terminology.

Quality has its price, especially if it is neglected. But with forward planning and discipline, a pragmatic and thorough quality-assurance (QA) strategy usually pays off very quickly.

12 Quality Assurance/Internal Control System

This chapter discusses both the cross-process QA measures and the measures for individual processes. However, this is not only about technical elements and tools as organization, documentation, and process design are important factors as well.

Besides the company-specific internal revision guidelines, legal guidelines such as Sarbanes-Oxley or Basel II also determine the requirements of QA. The QA elements we will discuss in this chapter will help support your SAP ERP HMC system implementation.

12.1 Quality in Software Projects

Implementation projects for Information Technology (IT) systems are often subject to extreme time and budget constraints. Even if the initial project planning is realistic, pressure can arise from the following factors:

- Late or drawn out project start
- Use of capacity elsewhere (especially if the workload for ongoing everyday tasks has been underestimated)
- Changes in membership of the project team during the project
- Changes in requirements

When projects are under pressure to meet a deadline or stay within a specific budget, QA is often neglected to save resources. This is a short-term approach, however. It may help you keep deadlines when running projects with short runtimes, but at the price of poorer quality. Targeted QA — provided it is not implemented for its own sake — generally reduces total costs.

Typical quality problems can be divided into four categories:

- **Incorrect definition of requirements**
  The first project phases are used to generate system requirements. Due to communication problems or the inclusion of the wrong group of people, the planned processes are often misunderstood. Just as frequently, individual processes or process variants are completely overlooked. In both cases, these mistakes may only come to light during end-user training or even during production operations.
- **Incorrect mapping of requirements**
  This is the classic "quality problem" that users often describe as a "program error," leading to incorrect system behavior. Along with a clear concept and a well-qualified project team, structured tests are indispensable.
- **Incorrect use of the system**
  System providers and consultants (even internal project teams) are often all too eager to call these problems "user errors," thereby removing them from their area of responsibility — even if users are not completely without responsibility in this situation. Change management in its broadest sense (including user-specific training) and optimal system support (e.g., via plausibility checks) can, however, significantly reduce these user errors during implementation.
- **The maintenance trap**
  Quality problems that occur only some time after production starts can also often be traced back to implementation. Missing documentation or badly structured customizing or program coding can make maintenance significantly more difficult.

These categories apply to IT projects of all kinds. Project owners should therefore remember that both internal and external project teams almost always try to save money at these areas when price is the main factor considered at the beginning of a project.

For the rest of this chapter, we will keep these four categories in mind when describing the use of QA in HCM projects. We will first consider some cross-process approaches and then individual subprocesses of the SAP ERP HCM system. We have omitted most general topics that do not have any special reference to

HCM. Figure 12.1 displays the listed quality-assurance fields and assigns the most important points to them.

Maintenance Trap	• Bear in Mind Strong Dynamics and Complex Customizing
Incorrect Use of the System	• User Guidance • Decentral Use
Incorrect Mapping of Requirements	• Test Helps, esp. for Time Evaluation and Payroll
Insufficient Definition of Requirements	• Include Decentral Institutions • Service Catalog • Process Definition

Figure 12.1 QA Fields

12.2 Cross-Process Quality Aspects in SAP ERP HCM

QA in and of itself is a critical success factor for a Human Resources (HR) project. It should, however, be based on a clear concept and not simply be implemented for its own sake. Projects can also be needlessly stifled in the name of QA.

12.2.1 Structured Procedure

There are many process models for implementing standard software products. Quality problems arise for the following three reasons:

- The selected process model is not used because it entails too great a workload.
- The selected process model is not used because it cannot be applied to the actual situation.
- The process model focuses on implementation and requires clear and sensible definition of the requirements.

An "off-the-rack" process model can only serve as a rough guide. One of the first tasks of a project team is to create a project-specific model from a general process model. The team must not only consider company-specific factors, but also the special characteristics of SAP ERP HCM. It is not enough for a technically oriented process to stipulate the definition of the most important structures. For an HCM project, the team must define the company and employee structure (see Chapter 4, "Personnel Administration"), and the use of Organizational Management.

It is even more important to find a structured procedure for defining requirements. It is not very helpful to start describing or modeling processes with no clear structure. In the HCM environment, in particular, the following dangers can arise:

- You concentrate too much on the HR department itself and forget other users or potential users.
- You concentrate too heavily on SAP ERP HCM terms. This means that processes that do not have their own modules in the system (e.g., personnel reporting, requirements planning, release, etc.) are often displaced.

A clear definition of requirements that clearly describes the planned processes is indispensable for QA. The planned processes are, after all, the means for measuring the success and therefore the quality of the project.

There are varying opinions on the necessary formats for the requirements documentation or process documentation. The following points should, however, be clearly documented in some form:

- What services should the SAP ERP HCM system support?
- How are the individual processes reflected in the most important variants?
- Which exceptions should you be aware of?
- What technical and organizational interfaces are provided?

These points should be supplemented with a detailed description of the data and interfaces that can be refined over the course of the project.

The service specifications, in particular, represent a useful guideline for QA. It is important to ensure that the processes listed in the service specifications are supported and that additional functionalities aren't included merely because the system provides them.

12.2.2 Documentation and Customizing

Because the SAP ERP HCM system is constantly changing, the changes in Customizing and programming are not only driven by real process improvements, but also by work agreements, wage agreements, and regulatory changes. Another measure of the HCM dynamic is the number of support packages delivered by SAP. Between the appearance of release 4.6C in the middle of 2000 until the middle of February 2003, 66 HR packages were delivered, as opposed to a total of 40 for all other R/3 modules. We strongly recommend a clean structure and ongoing cleanup of Customizing entries and report variants.

Also, easy-to-use documentation is very important for ongoing maintenance. It is important to document the frequent small changes as quickly as possible. The implementation guide (IMG) (see Appendix A) is a useful documentation tool in this area. There are other documentation tools, but IMG documentation is unbeatable, because it can be called directly from the Customizing screens of the IMG. The ease of simply clicking on the documentation button increases the likelihood that smaller changes will be documented immediately. However, you shouldn't succumb to the temptation of simply repeating the contents of the Customizing table in the documentation. Instead, you should concentrate on the following points:

- Reasons for certain settings
- Reference to laws, works agreements, process descriptions, or other documentation
- Naming conventions
- Modifiers or groupings (especially in SAP ERP HCM)

The IMG can rarely replace the comprehensive documentation of cross-application processes and concepts. It is, however, very helpful for documenting individual settings.

In addition, there is a newer tool available called the SAP Solution Manager. The Solution Manager is a tool for managing the entire spectrum of SAP (and non-SAP) solutions within a company's IT landscape. It provides the tool, content, and gateway to create, operate, manage, and monitor solutions over time. For more detailed information on the Solution Manager, refer to the Recommended Reading List in Appendix D.

12.2.3 Clear and Transparent Customizing

Clear Customizing in both the implementation and maintenance phases represents a significant contribution to QA.

During implementation, clear conventions are very important, especially when structuring tables that contain many entries. In the HCM system, this applies when defining wage types or time types, for example. Also, the relationships between the different Customizing tables are often extremely complicated and multilayered (e.g., absence valuation, Time Manager's Workplace (TMW), Manager's Desktop (MDT), etc.). It is precisely these relationships that are rarely clearly described in the standard documentation. Before you start making your settings in Customizing, you should first graphically display the dependencies for the area you work in and create a configuration design with easy-to-use naming conventions. Every time a subsequent change is made to the settings, you will be rewarded for the initial time invested.

Many of the settings in HCM are subject to extreme changes, so you should make sure that Customizing entries that are no longer required are time restricted. It usually makes little sense to delete obsolete entries, because this then restricts the system's ability to do retroactive accounting and the option for displaying past data. The practice of time restriction also gives you a better overview of the current entries. During system checks, we often work with tools that search for entries that are no longer required (e.g., time types, time models). These tools are very easy to create yourself.

Unfortunately, some table entries cannot be time restricted, because they are not stored with start and end dates. These include personnel areas and subareas, and employee groups and subgroups, for example. While most users do not seem to view this as a problem, it can often become one after several years of production-system operation. In Customizing, there is a way to improve input help for end users and to indicate obsolete entries. If you add ZZ to the beginning of the text description (not the key), then the corresponding settings can be recognized immediately. Because most input help programs sort the entries by text, rather than by the key, these obsolete entries will appear at the end of the list. (Note that in other input help programs, there is still the option to sort by text after calling the help.) Figure 12.2 displays an example of this solution as applied to a personnel subarea. Although the offices in Houston and Jackson would appear in the middle of the list according to their keys, when the input help sorts the entries by long text, they appear at the end of the list. This makes it easier for the user when working with very long selection lists.

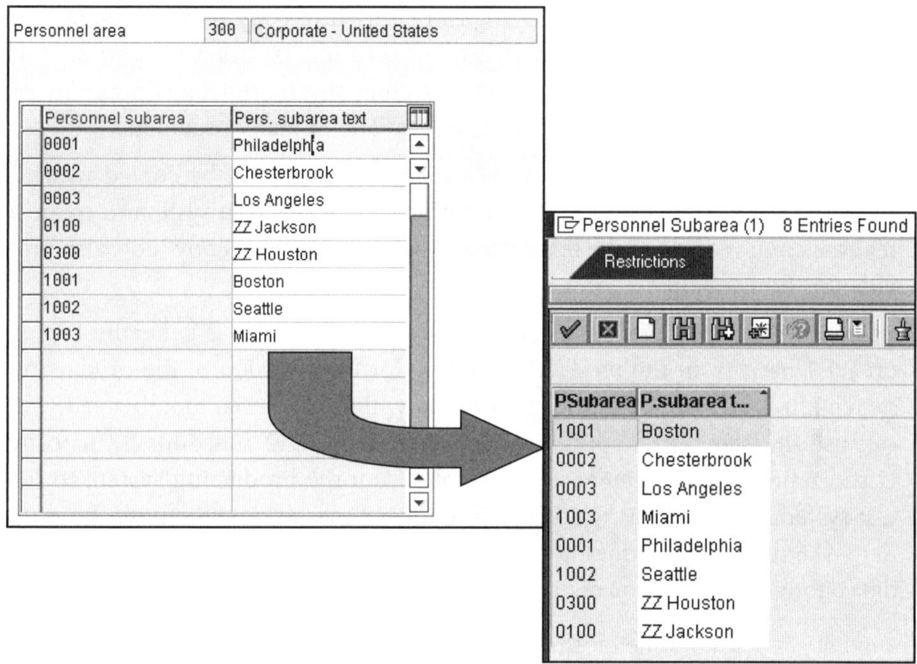

Figure 12.2 Placing Old Customizing Entries at the End

12.2.4 Test Concept

Tests in the SAP ERP HCM system often focus on the correct calculation in the areas of Time Management, Remuneration Payroll, and the company pension plan. While there is no doubt that these areas require the heaviest testing, it is important not to forget the tests for more dialog-oriented processes and evaluations. To test dialog applications, CATT processes can be used, just as they can be outside of HCM.

HCM is characterized by strong relationships between individual components and changes to planned results over time. For this reason, it is particularly important to document the test cases in a structured way and to set up a lasting test dataset.

Setting up test data can be time-consuming and labor intensive. You have to take into account very different configurations and many exceptions. It is, however, possible to reduce the workload involved in setting up test data:

- Personnel data (HR master, including payroll results, travel expenses, etc.) can be copied if you use the right programs. This can be done within a system and across systems. Cross-system copying can be used to copy new configurations from the production system to test systems on a regular basis, to keep the test dataset up-to-date. You can either create a company-specific copy program, or purchase a ready-made tool or template from one of many providers.

- Objects in personnel planning and development can also be copied using a similar process. This means that you can use the production system to create a realistic environment in the test system. Some providers of copy tools also provide this functionality.
- Because test data in personnel planning and development is generally copied on a 1:1 basis from the production system (or for a section of the production system), it is also possible to copy the data without a special tool. Instead, you can use the standard Application Link Enabling (ALE) functionality to copy Organizational Management, for example, from the production system to the test system. Usually, this is not possible for HR master data, because the standard ALE functionality does not include all personnel data and does not render data anonymously during distribution.

Anonymity is probably the most critical factor when copying test data from a production system. Usually, for data-security reasons, it is not possible to use original data in the test system. Some companies deal with this problem by setting up the test environment within a QA system, in which the use of original data is not critical. This means, however, that the QA system would have to be subject to the same access authorization restrictions that apply to the production system.

Usually, the test environment is created using anonymous data (i.e., with data that cannot be traced back to a real person). This applies both to the permanent test dataset, and to individual cases that are copied due to specific errors or Customizing changes.

The copy tools available on the market generally allow this kind of anonymity. However, the option to configure these on a company-specific basis is often extremely restricted. The scope depends heavily on specific requirements. For example:

- When testing age-dependant remuneration components, it makes no sense to assign a standard birth date to all test cases. At best — depending on the rule used — it can be set to 01.01 of the respective year.
- A company might enter the number of a company cell phone in a customer-specific subtype of Infotype 0040 (Objects on Loan). In this case, this field must also be made anonymous.

- If data that can identify an individual person has been entered in a customer-specific infotype, then this infotype must also be linked with an anonymization process.

For these reasons, a ready-made tool must also provide corresponding options that allow it to be adjusted to meet company-specific requirements. One alternative is to program the tool yourself, or to have one created based on a template. In the latter case, your own programming personnel should be included in the process so that they can make future changes themselves.

The following points list criteria that may be relevant when choosing a copy tool:

- Is cross-system copying also possible?
- Is data security guaranteed during cross-system copying?
- Is there an anonymization option?
- Is it possible to adapt the range of data to be copied and the anonymization process to your company-specific requirements?
- Apart from the HR master data, which data can also be copied (payroll results, business trips, applicant data, etc.)?
- How is the pricing, including maintenance (can it be adapted to new releases)?
- Can several people be copied in one run? What is the selection process and how long is the runtime?
- Is there a log that allows tracking of copy actions?

12.2.5 Authorization Concept

In HCM, the authorization check is often seen as particularly critical. This is due to the sensitivity of HR data and the importance that employee representatives (rightly) place on this topic. Furthermore, the authorization concept of the SAP ERP HCM system is extremely complicated. In a strongly decentralized implementation of the system, creating, implementing, and testing of authorizations are often extremely labor-intensive tasks.

The following points list some aspects of HCM authorizations that can lead to quality problems in practical project experience:

- HCM contains many different authorization objects, some of which refer to the same data (HR master). Interaction between the different objects is often not taken into account. There are checks that are connected with AND and checks connected with OR operations.
- The default values of the profile generator (Transaction PFCG) are not always appropriate in the standard version. Authorization object P_ABAP, in particular, is often proposed although it is not always required. Also, users often misunderstand the way that this object works: It is not necessary for running a report; rather it fully or partially deactivates the master data authorization check for a report.
- The authorization check display behaves in a similar manner (Transaction SU53). When authorization problems arise, this check is intended to display the authorizations that are missing for a user. This check often displays the object P_ABAP unnecessarily. Also, up to and including release 4.6C, this check could not be used in the area of structured authorizations. Where problems arise in this area, it often incorrectly indicates authorization object P_PERNR. However, after release 4.6C, this is no longer an issue.
- Structural authorization, especially context-dependent variants from release 4.7 onward, is particularly time-consuming to test. In this case, we recommend that you use report RHAUTH00, which displays the authorized objects per profile and/or per user.

Because the authorization concept as such is not dealt with in this book[1], we will finish the topic with these warnings. Above all, it is important to be aware that this area can easily become a minefield, and you cannot put off dealing with it until just before production starts. It is much more important to include the authorization concept from the very beginning of an HCM project. In many cases, you can reduce the workload simply through early planning. Even if your budget for external consultants is tight, this subproject is the one area in which you should try to avoid making savings your top priority. It is also important that the consultants working on the project have a broad range of experience both in HCM authorizations and the HCM application, rather than just authorizations in general.

1 See the following titles on this subject: Brochhausen, Kielisch, Schnerring, Staeck: mySAP HR—Technical Principles and Programming, SAP PRESS 2005; IBM Business Consulting Services: SAP Authorization System, SAP PRESS 2003

12.2.6 Decentralized Use of the System

SAP ERP HCM is increasingly decentralized (i.e., implemented outside of the HR department). This is the best way to support HR processes while not being limited only to HR *department* processes.

This decentralized development can, however, create some quality problems. Aside from the special requirements for the authorization concept, it is also important to bear the following points in mind:

- For medium-sized companies, in particular, definition of processes is often implicit, as long as there are a limited number of system users within the HR department. With decentralized implementation, user numbers quickly rise to larger numbers, which means that process changes can no longer be made at will. Processes must be clearly defined *and* understood.
- Decentralized users only spend a small part of their working time in the HCM system. Furthermore, it is generally not possible to give these users time-intensive training for this part-time job. For this reason, the complexity of the application must be kept at a much lower level than for users in the HR department. This is done by efficiently using specific interfaces such as MDT, Manager Self-Service (MSS), Employees Self-Service (ESS), and TMW. You shouldn't forget, however, that it is not only the interface that can complicate the process. Long-winded rules, overloaded evaluations, and personnel-specific technical terminology can also make life difficult for users.
- The interfaces provided to decentralized users may be easier to use, but the users within the HR department are often unaware of them. This can lead to misunderstandings when users in the HR department have to answer questions from decentralized users. For this reason, it is important for employees in the HR department who are constantly in contact with decentralized users to also be familiar with the relevant interfaces, such as TMW, MSS, etc.
- While it is important for all users, it is crucial for users outside the HRdepartment to adapt the user interface to the particular requirements as efficiently as possible. It is a bad habit to have screens with various fields or buttons the users do not need at all. In most cases this can be avoided by customizing (e.g., table T555m for infotypes) GUIXT screen variants. These techniques also allow you to make fields obligatory or to determine default values.
- To make processes more efficient and secure, process automation is especially useful when many users outside the HR department are involved. Back in Chap-

ter 4, Section 4.4.2 shows how to use dynamic actions for this purpose. Other options are workflows or the generation of emails by custom ABAP development. The latter is not as difficult as it may seem at first sight. The automatic generation of straightforward emails (going to MS Outlook or Lotus Notes) can easily be implemented within one or two days; such as, for example,

- Missing clock-in or clock-out stamps
- Missing travel expense records
- Birthday or anniversary mails
- Records in Infotype 0019 when the due date is reached

12.2.7 Setting Up Your QM Project

Whether you have just completed the implementation of SAP HR and you want to start a quality initiative as part of the continuous improvement process or your system is running for several years and you feel you urgently need to improve usability and data quality, before going into the details you should build a framework, set up an action plan, and decide about the priorities of each issue. The good news is that this project can be spread over a longer period of time with low intensity. Once the framework and action plan are established, the project can be broken down into many small pieces of work, with each of them delivering some value of its own.

We recommend a methodology called the HR process check. This is based on four steps and can be used in a similar way for all projects that require an efficient analysis of the HR processes of your organization. When reading through these four steps, it may look like an unbearable workload. As a matter of fact, the structured procedure allows you to get through it quite swiftly. If you get the right people involved, it will probably take between 4 and 10 one-day workshops to get the whole framework and action plan set up. But focusing on a single process will make it even faster.

The four steps for setting up your quality management project are:

1. Decide which parts of the HR function to analyze. For example, if there are parts that are not supported by SAP HR you don't have to invest any effort there.

2. Now you must go into detail. You need a catalogue of each service or function within the scope of your project on a very detailed level. The authors use a reference model containing more than 600 typical functions within HR, because many organizations find it very difficult to tell right away which functions are performed within their HR.[2] This is something you have to build – no matter whether based on your process documentation or on some reference model. At the end of this step, you'll have a catalogue with all of the relevant functions that are supported by SAP HR. To give you a benchmark: When you are focusing on personnel administration, payroll, and time management, you'll probably end up with about 150 to 400 functions.
3. Now, each function in your framework has to be assessed according to the criteria that tell you whether there is a need for action. These are the Key Performance Indicators (KPIs) for your QM project. To decide if any effort has to be invested into a specific function, you may want to know:
   - How often is the function performed per year?
   - How much time is spend on it?
   - Is it seen as critical?
   - How do users assess usability and the potential for improving quality?
   - Where is it supported within SAP HR (e.g., transaction, report, infotype)?
   - Who is responsible?
4. For some functions, you might need a detailed process description because they are very complex or contain an important interface between departments or IT systems. However, this will be a minority of the functions involved. So, although the methodology is process oriented, it avoids creating a huge workload in process modelling.

Now that your framework is built up, the fun part of the project can start. With the information gathered, you can check out all of the possibilities to improve quality that are outlined in this book and in other sources.[3] This provides you with your action plan and you can implement it step by step, some of which will only take an hour. Each step will improve your HR processes by some degree.

---

2 For more information about using a template see *http://www.iprocon.de/referencemodel*

3 For example, in the free newsletter all readers of this book are invited to subscribe to. See chapter "Invitation."

However, you must not think that the mission is over once your action plan is completed. Processes and systems change with time and new technical options may allow you to tackle a problem that seemed unsolvable two years ago. So, make sure that your framework is kept up-to-date by adding new functions or removing old ones. Regular meetings between users and SAP HR administrators have proven to be a key element of continuous improvement. It is a good idea to establish a monthly meeting with those who rely on the system for their daily work and those who do the customizing and programming. When there are too many users to take part at the same time, let a group of 5 or 10 users join each meeting. It is astonishing how easily some problems can be solved once those involved are discussing them directly without any managers standing between them.

12.2.8 Auditing tools

If your HR system is subject to an audit, the advice given in this chapter will definitely help you to get good rates. After all, the whole chapter is aimed at avoiding wrong procedures, wrong data, and miscalculations based on wrong configuration.

However, our approach is not so much that of an auditor as that of a business process engineer. We want to avoid mistakes in the first place, whereas, from an auditor's point of view, mistakes (often equated with fraud) must be detected and the responsible person must be found. If you can prove to an auditor that it is impossible to enter wrong data into the system (a probably impossible task), he will be satisfied. Otherwise, he will probably request a system that can trace any mistake or fraud. This approach, which focuses more on the end of the process, is what auditing tools are doing.

Basically, the auditing tool allows you:

1. To define rules about what situations are considered an exception, which leads to a warning message or an error.
2. To identify all exceptions with a reporting tool that allows you to deal with each exception (e.g., by approving it or by correcting the data). The tool will keep a track record of each exception and the way it was dealt with, so that the auditor can assess the whole process.

A very sophisticated tool is Accenture Audit and Compliance. Besides audits focused on master data and payroll, it supports some other areas such as authorizations and system parameters, with other areas to follow soon. Figure 12.3 shows the customizing for a simple exception rule, which will cause an error when wage type M120 in Infotype 0015 is above 10,000. Besides checks based on master data, it is also possible to refer to payroll results.

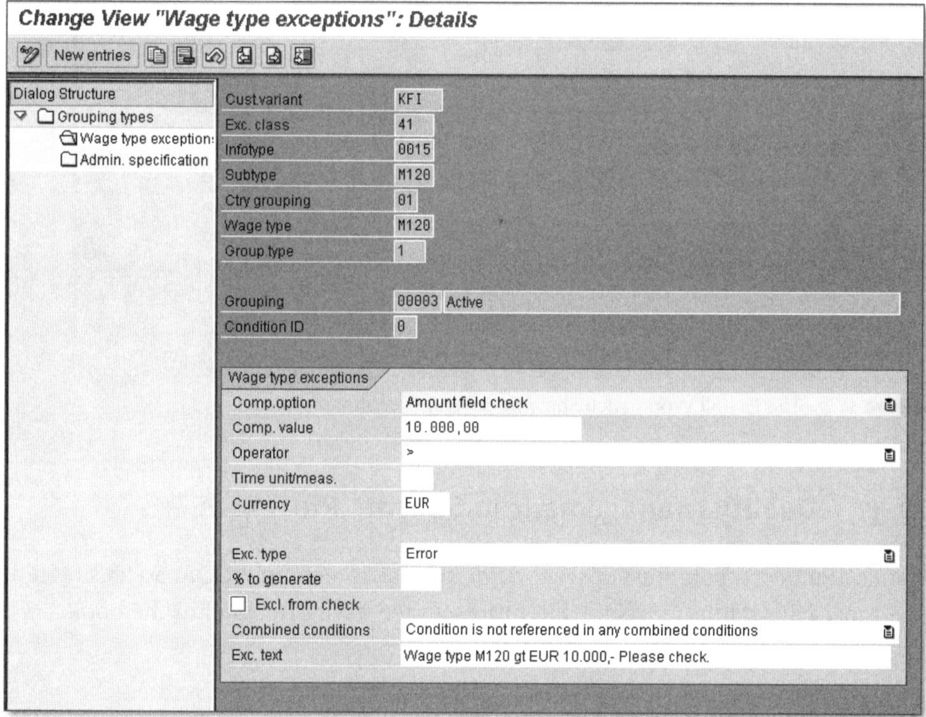

Figure 12.3 Exception Rule in The Accenture Audit and Compliance

Figure 12.4 shows the payroll workbench. The exceptions are selected, categorized (left-hand side of the screen), and can be analyzed in detail and dealt with on the right-hand side of the screen.

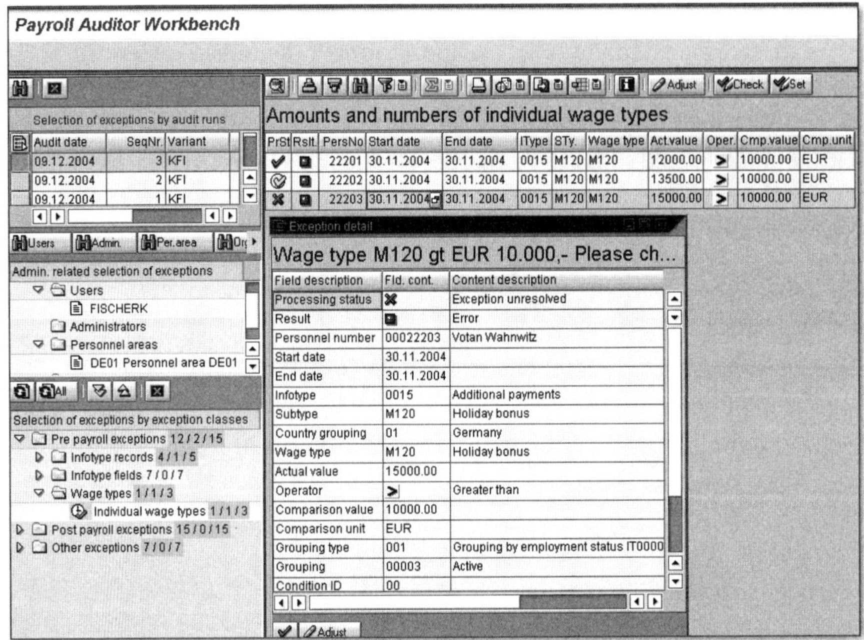

Figure 12.4 The Payroll Workbench Showing Several Exceptions

12.3 Quality Management in Specific Processes

For each process, you must observe some special aspects about QA. So let's review the most important aspects for the processes we have discussed in the book.

12.3.1 QA in Organizational Management

Organizational Management represents the basis for many different processes. You must be aware of the fact that incorrect or obsolete data here leads to errors in the following areas:

- The wrong access rights are assigned via the structural authorization check.
- The wrong roles are assigned to users.
- MSS, MDT, or TMW assign the wrong employees to managers or time-management representatives.
- Cost centers are assigned incorrectly in the HR master, causing personnel costs to be posted incorrectly.

- Workflows flow to the wrong people.
- The wrong compensation components are assigned via compensation management.
- Too many or too few vacancies are specified in recruitment. In the worst case, job advertisements are started even though there are no open positions.
- Many of the evaluations provide incorrect results.
- Personnel cost planning provides incorrect results.

These examples should be motivation enough to make sure that you keep Organizational Management carefully maintained and up-to-date. The availability of information is often a big problem. Those responsible for entering data often receive information too late or only unofficially. In the latter case, they usually cannot make any data changes (e.g., because the employee representatives have not yet given authorization), although the new situation is effectively already in place.

This is essentially an organizational problem. There are different methods for improving information flow. In practice, sticking to official information and up-to-date maintenance often improves discipline if Organizational Management is broadly implemented and applied decentrally. If managers themselves receive incorrect evaluations online, if the organizational chart is incorrect on the Internet, or if cost centers are debited with personnel costs that are too high, then the communication process between the affected parties often changes quickly. It is important that these "educational measures" have the backing of top management. This should not be a problem if you can calculate the very high process costs due to insufficient communication.

12.3.2 QA in Recruitment

In recruitment, you often have to deal with very poor data quality. This is because the only data that is entered carefully is the data required for processing day-to-day activities. To process an immediate rejection, for example, you do not necessarily require data such as date of birth, nationality, or assignment to a publication. This only becomes a problem if you need to evaluate this data later on.

For this reason, you must be clear about the evaluation requirements from the very beginning and make sure that users are aware of the importance of the additional data. Recruitment is often implemented as part of the SAP ERP system due to its evaluation options, and it replaces the sort of application management that merely consisted of processing correspondence with applicants within Microsoft Office applications. The changeover often means that significantly more data needs to be maintained. You should factor in the fact that this also impacts processing time. In no other process are such simple rules as the following so often misunderstood:

- You can only evaluate data that you have entered into the system.
- You cannot wait until the end of the year to retroactively define the data that you want to enter.
- Standard software only has a limited stock of standard reports (in recruitment of the SAP ERP system, this stock is unfortunately very restricted indeed). Reports that you will need regularly should be defined early. More complex ad-hoc reports create a high one-time workload.
- The system is not aware of processes that take place outside the system (handing over a paper file or sending a letter) unless you enter these processes in a previously defined manner.

If you feel it is not necessary to formulate these statements, you should count yourself lucky. Otherwise, you should prepare to treat them as company policy.

The following are some tips on quality in recruitment:

- There are often communication problems between representatives in application management and personnel administration. This leads to the creation of new HR masters based on the file without reference to the applicant. On an organizational level, you should ensure that the file always contains the applicant number and that HR masters are only created in exceptional circumstances without transferring the applicant.
- The list of incomplete planned processes needs to be checked regularly. By correctly configuring process controls in Customizing, you can also use this list to prevent applicant documents from being mislaid.
- The PACTV feature, with its subfeatures and the action types, activity types, and text documents that it refers to, control the core of the application-management process. These relationships should be clearly documented.

12.3.3 QA in Personnel Administration

Personnel administration suffers from similar problems as those of Organizational Management. Because HR master data forms the basis for many other processes, quality problems here often have wide-ranging consequences.

Along with documentation and training, plausibility checks and sensible default values lead to an improvement in data quality. The following sections describe various options.

Plausibility Check via Customizing

For a great many infotypes, plausibility checks can be defined in Customizing. For example, consider the permissibility of wage types for employee groups and subgroups, and for personnel areas and sub-areas. This is controlled via View V_511_B. Figure 12.5 displays an example in which wage type 1602 is only permitted for employees in employee Subgrouping 6 and personnel subareas in Groupings 1 to 4. It is also permitted with a warning message for employee subgroups in Grouping 5. The groupings used are those for primary wage types. For employee subgroups, for example, this is maintained in View V_503_ALL. For personnel subareas, it is maintained in View V_001P_ALL.

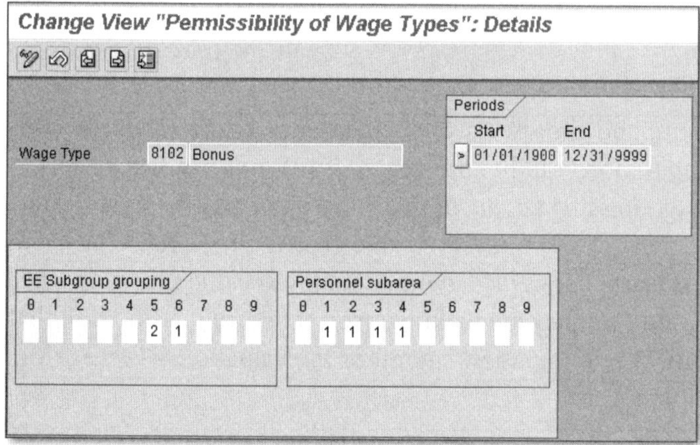

Figure 12.5 V_511_B — Permissibility of Wage Types

Similar checks that are often also controlled via groupings are also provided for the following:

- Wage types per infotype
- Work schedule rules
- Attendance types and absence types
- Pension plans

Other checks can also be based purely on the permissibility of keys, such as:

- Minimum and maximum amount of a wage type (e.g., in Infotype 0015 – Additional Payments and Deductions) via View V_511
- Minimum and maximum duration of attendances via View V_554S_B

These options are often used only to a very limited extent, either because not enough time is spent during the planning stage, or because users do not want to "break" anything. When a change is made, these settings are very easy to adjust.

Plausibility Checks via Programming

Customizing options are not always sufficient. Companies often need company-specific checks. This can be done with very little additional labor. You can use the function module exits for SAP enhancement PBAS0001 to store almost any number of checks (see Section 4.2.4). From release 4.7, Business Add-In (BAdI) HRPAD00INFTY is also available (see Section 4.2.4).

"Emergency Brake" in Payroll

In some cases, we recommend the use of the "emergency brake" concept. This means that certain configurations can be intercepted in payroll to trigger a termination. In many cases (e.g., missing tax data), this is already part of standard functionality. In other cases, these checks still have some gaps in the standard version. Also, software publishers cannot always plan for company-specific configurations. Users may then be unaware that they are making incorrect entries, a situation that leads to unwanted results in remuneration payroll or in evaluations. These errors may take a long time to uncover.

This concept primarily offers a way of finding missing infotypes. Because the checks listed earlier only work on the basis of the data in an infotype, they cannot be applied if the corresponding infotype has not been created.

To avoid missing infotypes from the very beginning, you should configure Customizing for the optimum use of personnel actions and dynamic actions.

12.3.4 QA in Time Management

Most of the information on plausibility checks in personnel administration also applies to time management. In addition to the individual infotypes, you should also configure TMW (see Chapter 8, "Time Management") for optimum performance with plausibility checks.

Test Procedures

A specific problem when maintaining data for time management is caused by intended or unintended changes that reach too far back into the past. This can be restricted by limiting retroactive accounting relevance. There are often situations where it should be possible to make corrections that extend one or two years into the past, but not every time-management representative should have the authorization to make such corrections.

This can be reflected using Infotype 0130 (Test Procedures). You can also use it outside of time management, but this is an area where it is frequently used. To configure this in Customizing, go to PERSONNEL MANAGEMENT • PERSONNEL ADMINISTRATION • TOOLS • AUTHORIZATION MANAGEMENT • TEST PROCEDURES. You can define one or more *test procedures* here. You then assign a number of infotypes and subtypes to each test procedure (see Figure 12.6).

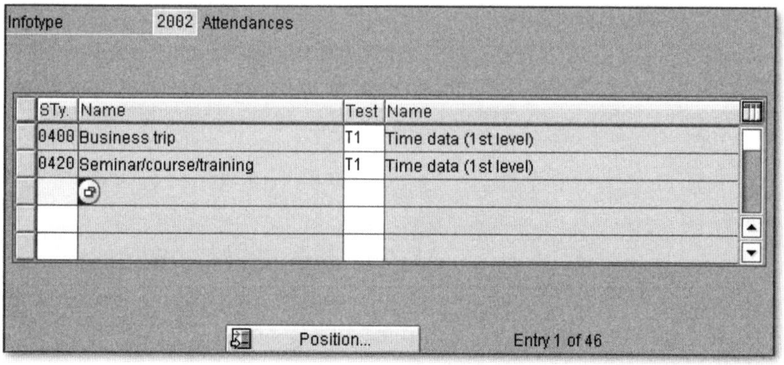

Infotype 2002 Attendances

STy.	Name	Test	Name
0400	Business trip	T1	Time data (1st level)
0420	Seminar/course/training	T1	Time data (1st level)

Position... Entry 1 of 46

Figure 12.6 Assigning Subtypes to a Test Procedure

For each test procedure defined this way (number of infotypes or subtypes), you can now define the point in the past to which data can be changed retroactively. This way, every test procedure represents a subtype of Infotype 0130. Figure 12.7 shows that data in test procedure T1 for personnel number 1000 can only be changed retroactively up to 2/1/2003.

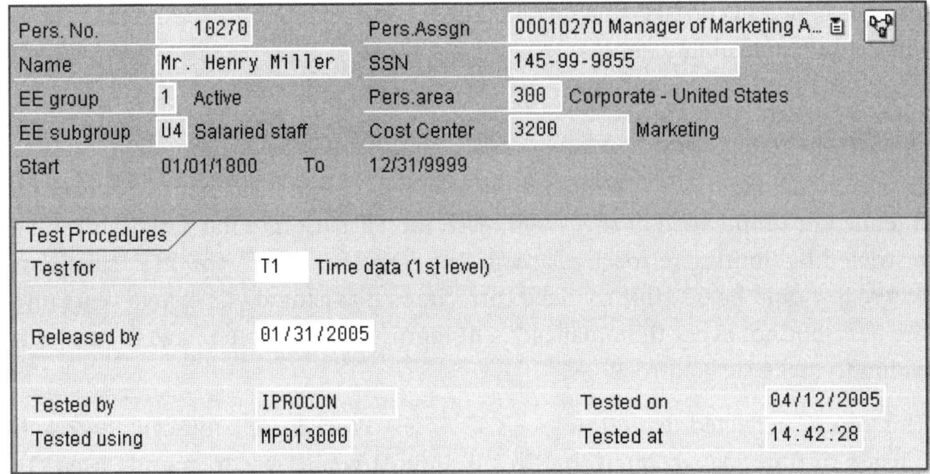

Figure 12.7 Infotype 0130 (Test Procedures)

In this context, the term *released by* often causes confusion. It means that the data is checked up to this point in time and is released as correct, and therefore no more changes are allowed. Because no individual data-checking and maintenance are required for Infotype 0130, it is generally maintained automatically via a program. The following exception applies: Users who have maintenance authorization for the corresponding subtype of Infotype 0130 can also maintain the corresponding data in the past.

Automating Tests

Depending on the company, very complicated rules can underlie the time evaluation process. It is also very difficult to configure Customizing via schemas and rules. This makes testing very important and particularly difficult. A serious problem is created by the fact that when a particular rule is changed (or a specific error is corrected) — although the directly affected areas are tested — there are often unexpected consequences in completely different areas. It is not possible, however, to test the entire test database on every occasion.

This problem can be solved by partially automating the test. There are tools available on the market that compare the results of copied personnel numbers with those of the original in the production system. In many projects, it has proved worthwhile to set up successive, comprehensive test datasets (see section 12.2.4) that are tested automatically at every change.

To do this, you need a program that stores reference results for all test cases. These reference results only need to be checked and declared correct once. Then, every time a change is made, the program can determine where the new results differ from the reference results. This kind of program is called a *test workbench*. Figure 12.8 illustrates the QA process when using a test workbench and a copy tool.

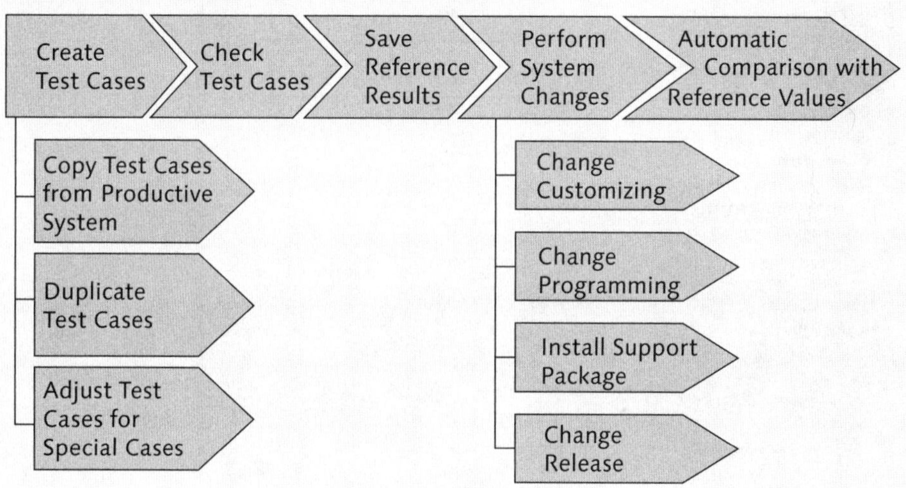

Figure 12.8 QA Process with Test Workbench and Copy Tool

We will use a specific example to demonstrate how this works. Figure 12.9 displays the selection screen for a simple test workbench that we (the authors) use in time management. Similar tools with different functional scope from different providers are available on the market for time management and for payroll. It is possible to select the personnel numbers and the periods to be tested. It is also possible to restrict the test to specific time types and time-wage types. The tool in the example does not compare quota types. If these are not reflected in time types, then they must also be included. The most important selection option is the indicator Update with New Results. This saves the current results as the new reference results. This is necessary, for example, if you want to include new test cases (new personnel numbers or new periods), or if a new rule means that a changed result is actually the correct version (e.g., a change to the flextime upper limit).

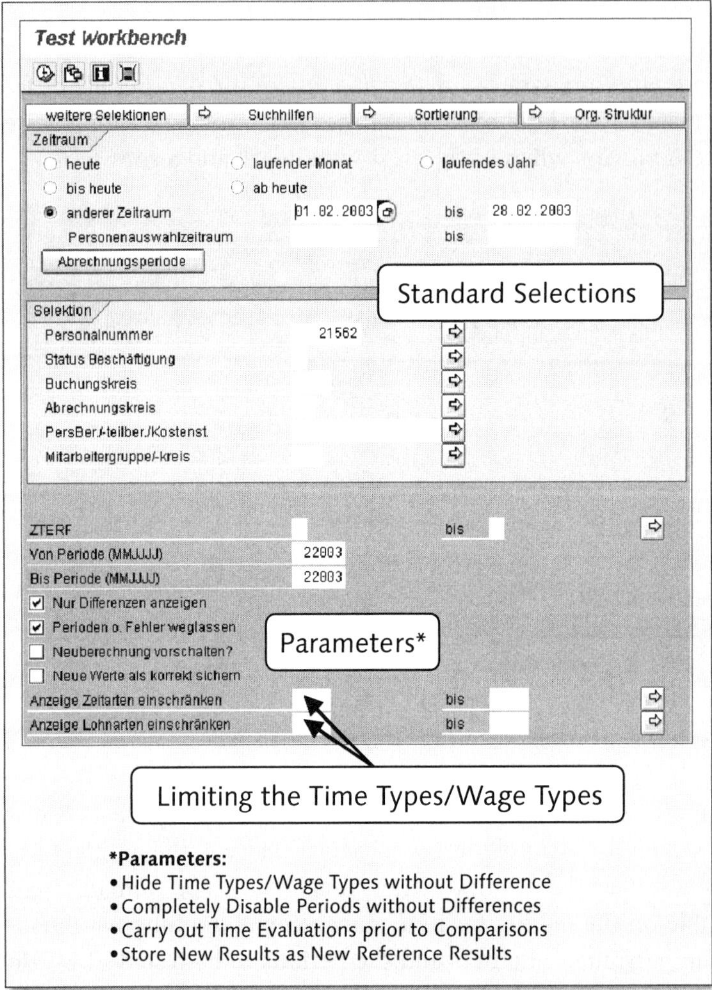

Figure 12.9 Selection Screen for a Test Workbench for Time Management

The result returned by the test workbench consists of the personnel numbers for which a difference compared to the reference result has been identified. Figure 12.10 displays a difference of three hours in several time types and three time-wage types for a personnel number. You must now check whether there is really an error in Customizing, or whether the change was deliberate. It is also possible that the test case data was changed. This should be avoided wherever possible, however.

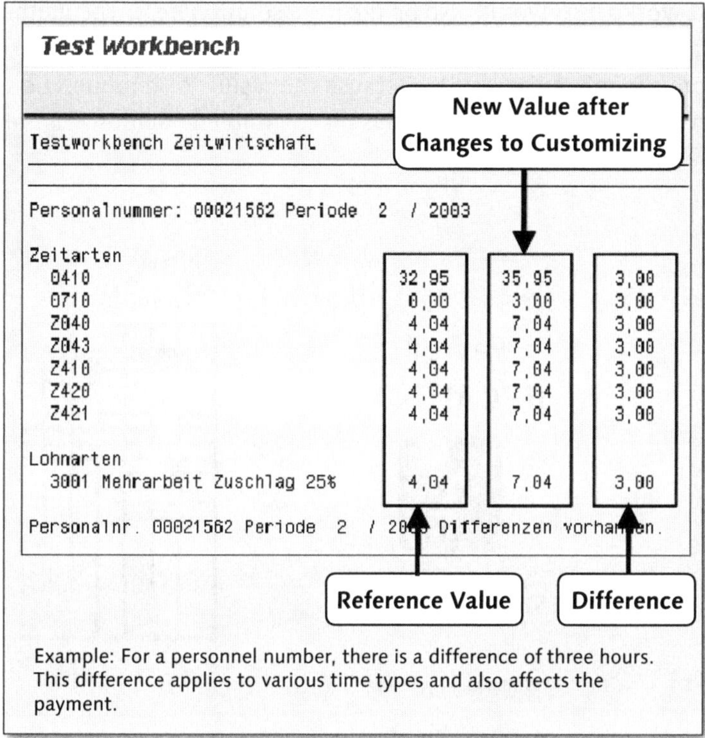

Figure 12.10 List of Differences from the Test Workbench

It is still possible to make the automated test help even more comprehensive and easy to use, depending on individual company requirements. The basic model presented here significantly improves quality and can be used in the following activities:

- Error correction
- Customizing change due to new regulations
- Importing support packages
- Release upgrade

12.3.5 QA in Payroll

The testing problems for remuneration payroll are the same as those for time management. They just seem more serious due to the greater complexity of Customizing in this area.

For this reason, a test workbench would also be the ideal solution here. The methodology is the same as for time management, except that you do not need to worry about where you store the reference results. Because the results of remuneration payroll use version management, you can use this during implementation. Figure 12.11 provides an overview.

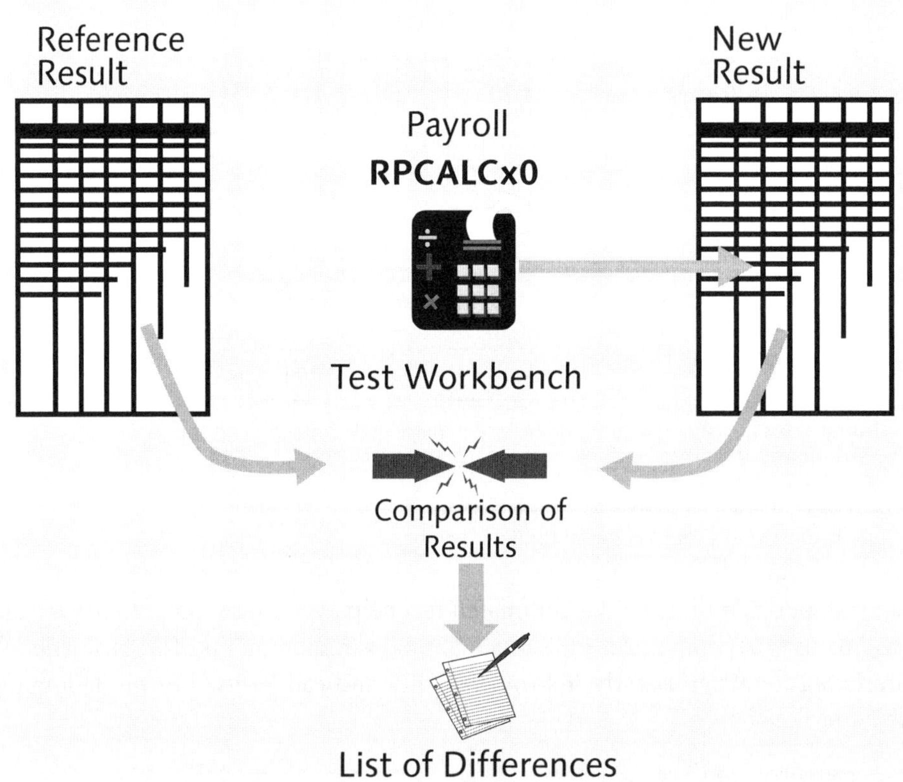

Figure 12.11 Using a Test Workbench

12.3.6 QA in Pension Scheme

The pension scheme must be dealt with similar to payroll. Initially, the quality of the basic data is important which must guarantee the QA measures of personnel administration. For the calculations within the CPS module it may be necessary to use an automatic test workbench.

The pension scheme area is particularly tricky in that some errors aren't noticed immediately. Because not all of the results are printed on the remuneration statement, some are stored in the CPS database and/or are posted in financial accounting, the employees concerned don't recognize the errors. Moreover, the values are usually difficult to understand. Therefore, an extensive QA must be maintained in the pension scheme area, especially because systematic errors can easily incur high costs.

12.3.7 QA in Reporting

The quality of reporting mainly depends on the quality of the upstream processes. The evaluation is only useful if these processes can guarantee data that is up-to-date and of good quality.[4]

Here are a few tips on improving quality within reporting:

- If reports (paper or online) are provided decentrally, then it is important to ensure that recipients can also interpret the data. Too much HR background knowledge is often required.
- If reports are being compared, it is important to know how those reports were generated. This is often not the case when decentralized users are using flexible evaluation options. Users will often, for example, try to compare a staffing report that has been developed based on headcount with one based on full-time capacity. In this case, it is helpful if you add a selection log to printed reports. This displays exactly what has been included in the report and which parameters were set.
- Using the simplest possible report call with the fewest possible influencing factors will also make it easier to compare with other reports. You can achieve this using the MDT, for example, which includes reports with fixed variants.
- When creating SAP Queries or Ad-hoc Queries, it is very important to make the infosets user-friendly and easy to understand. This means that you should remove unnecessary fields and possibly replace standard texts with more meaningful terms.

4 Frustrated controlling professionals responsible for reporting based on poor data quality coined the expression: "Garbage in, garbage out."

12.4 Set up of an Internal Control System

The internal control system combines technical and organizational QA elements to a consistent overall system.

12.4.1 Integration of Processes Outside the System

Up to now, we only covered elements within SAP ERP HCM. However, one single data-processing system can't be the answer to all quality issues. An essential prerequisite is the clear definition of processes, including their documentation beyond system boundaries.

We only want to mention some aspects that are outside the system and should be observed within the framework of an Internal Control System:

- Simplification of processes
- Clear definition and communication of processes
- Checklists
- Leeway for exceptions
- Responsibilities
- Use of tools outside of SAP ERP HCM
- Traceability/auditability (signatures, storage, electronic archiving with digital signature)

12.4.2 Merging all the Elements to Build an Internal Control System

These constitute most of the possible elements of an internal control system. But prior to defining an Internal Control System, you should be aware of its tasks and goals, because this term may be used in different ways. You should consider the following questions:

- Is the system supposed to respond to only one audit report?
- Is it only about reducing the number of errors in payroll?
- Will the real company risks arising in HR processes be managed?

  In this case, payroll may not be relevant at all, and the focus is primarily on recruiting, skills management, and succession planning.
- Which capacity restrictions exist?

It is recommended to create a main document based on these goals in which all essential elements of an Internal Control System are documented:

- Which processes are contained?
- How must they be described and where can you find this documentation?
- How do exceptions have to be handled?
- How does the IT system support the quality of the processes?
- How are system changes made and documented?
- How must test procedures be described?
- How are tests and other test-relevant facts documented in a revision-proof form?
- Which checks are implemented periodically?

Keep this central document as short as possible and refer to the respective documentation for details. This facilitates the overview and the further development of the system. The Internal Control System document serves as a framework for all relevant QA elements within SAP ERP HCM (Customizing, programming) and the elements outside the system (process descriptions, checklists, etc.) and can particularly be used as the basis for checks.

Note that if an Internal Control System is not adapted to the actual requirements continuously, the employees are bound to work around it.

Always keep the following two principles in mind:

- The system compliance must be possible with the available capacity. The intelligent use of the system, checklists, etc., facilitates the employees' work.
- The system must be maintainable. Definitions that are too specific require permanent adjustments.

12.5 Critical Success Factors

QA in and of itself is a critical success factor for an HR project. It should, however, be based on a clear concept and not simply be implemented for its own sake. Projects can also be needlessly stifled in the name of QA.

SAP ERP HCM provides a high degree of integration, so it is important to completely understand the interrelationships between individual processes in terms of both their content and technology. Even though the administrative processes can be easily separated from planning processes, there are many interdependencies between them.

13 Integration with Personnel Planning

Implementation projects often initially focus on administrative processes, so it is critical to know the interdependencies of the personnel planning and development processes to ensure that they are considered in your design right from the start.

13.1 General Remarks on Integration

In some areas, the integration can be technically switched off. This is, for instance, the case in the integration of personnel administration with organizational management or skills. Interdependencies in terms of content still remain, however. If the system doesn't permit a highly integrated work process, it is particularly important to make every employee fully aware of their responsibility in the overall process.

Once SAP ERP HCM has been implemented, users often regard the high degree of integration as very challenging, because the legacy system (frequently consisting of several standalone solutions for different HCM areas) allowed employees to work in ways that were isolated from the overall process.

Surprisingly, the problem of data inconsistency and high redundancy caused by this did not really bother the users; on the contrary, they considered it very convenient to be able to work without having to take upstream or downstream processes into account. It is only a comprehensive overview that demonstrates the advantage of a high degree of integration, which in turn also requires more attention from the users. Despite the initial effort, a highly integrated system promotes a holistic way of thinking and working in the minds of users. However, the system cannot solve this problem by itself, so this process should be accompanied by appropriate change management.

Basically, the interdependencies between the various processes of the personnel administration among each other are critical, but based on the scope of components utilized within the company, the interdependencies between the processes of the personnel administration and the processes of the personnel planning and development are just as key. In this chapter we will briefly describe the integration aspects relevant to the processes of personnel administration we have covered in the book, particularly with regard to the essential processes in personnel planning and development.

13.1.1 Organizational Management

Organizational management can serve as a basis for each HCM implementation, or even for that of the administrative processes. This was described in more detail in Chapter 5, "Organizational Management in SAP ERP HCM."

13.1.2 Training and Event Management

- HR master data and applicant master data are required for scheduling training. Additionally, the HR master data is also used for assigning internal instructors.
- The master cost center from Infotype 0001 is the default for the activity allocation.
- Attendances from Infotype 2002 are integrated for training participation or for the instructor function. Absences and public holiday calendars can be considered.
- Numerous values from HR master data are used for automatic correspondence.

13.1.3 Personnel Development

- Employee master data and applicant master data serve as a basis for the allocation of qualifications profiles.
- In addition to the qualifications profile, the selection of employees for succession planning also requires data from administration, such as age and gender.

- The applicant selection is generally based on data from personnel development.
- The maintenance of profiles can be called via Infotype 0024 within administration.

13.1.4 Compensation Management/Cost Planning

- In addition to the basic master data, such as names and organizational assignments, numerous payroll-relevant infotypes are included in cost planning:
  - Infotype 0008 (Basic pay)
  - Infotype 0010 (Capital formation savings payment)
  - Infotype 0014 (Recurring payments and deductions)
  - Infotype 0015 (Additional payments)
  - Infotype 0521 (Semiretirement)
  - Other infotypes from customer-specific data collection methods
- The results from payroll and their future projections are also an important basis for personnel cost planning.
- The pay data from the administration infotypes directly affects compensation management.
- The defaults of compensation management can be included in administration (particularly Infotypes 0008 and 0015) or used as a validation basis.
- A cost planning scenario data can be integrated into compensation management as a budgeted amount for compensation plans.
- The pay-scale customizing can represent the basis for the projected pay.
- The results from payroll that have been transferred to cost accounting (CO) can be compared with the results from personnel cost planning transferred earlier in the form of a target-actual analysis.

13.1.5 Performance Management

Performance management with employee appraisals and objective settings has a rather low degree of integration with the personnel administration – particularly because appraisal results or the attainment of objectives cannot be directly included in payroll-relevant data. This can only be done via compensation management or through manageable, customer-specific programming. However, there are key integration points between performance management and compensation management, qualifications, and specific talent management processes, such as development and succession planning.

Like the other personnel development processes, performance management also uses some basic personal data, such as names and organizational assignments.

13.1.6 Workforce Planning/Shift Planning

By its very nature, shift planning is closely related to time management because the times recorded and managed in time management are used in shift planning in terms of both quantity and quality. At this point, however, it won't be helpful to provide a list of all of the individual integration aspects.

13.1.7 Cross-Component Aspects

- Workflow, authorization concepts, and reporting structures apply to all processes. This allows for a consistency that is very difficult to achieve when using different systems.
- Infotype 0105 (Communication) is the basis for all Employee Self-Service (ESS) applications, including those in personnel planning and development.
- The communication language maintained in Infotype 0002 (Personal Data) can be used in all components.

Appendices

A Cross-Process Customizing Tools

This appendix briefly describes the most important customizing tools used in the various components of SAP ERP HCM. This presentation cannot replace practical experience or training on the system. Because the Implementation Management Guide (IMG), in particular, has a considerable range of customer-defined functions, it would scarcely even be possible.

The Features Editor

Features are used in all processes of SAP ERP HCM to control system behavior in various respects. Basically, a feature represents a decision tree that arrives at a result in several branches. This result is referred to as the return value.

An example of this is the ABKRS feature that branches out to include the transaction class (personnel administration or recruitment), the country grouping (MOLGA), the employee group, and the employee subgroup. Finally, as a return value it provides the payroll area that is predefined as a default value in Infotype 0001.

Therefore, the most important consideration in maintaining a feature is the structure of the decision tree. In this respect it is essential to know which decision criteria are available to create branches. The structure of the feature can give you a clue to this (see Figure A.1) as the available criteria are highlighted here. Highlighting additional criteria doesn't necessarily mean that these will also function. For this reason, you should restrict the selection to those criteria that are active by default.

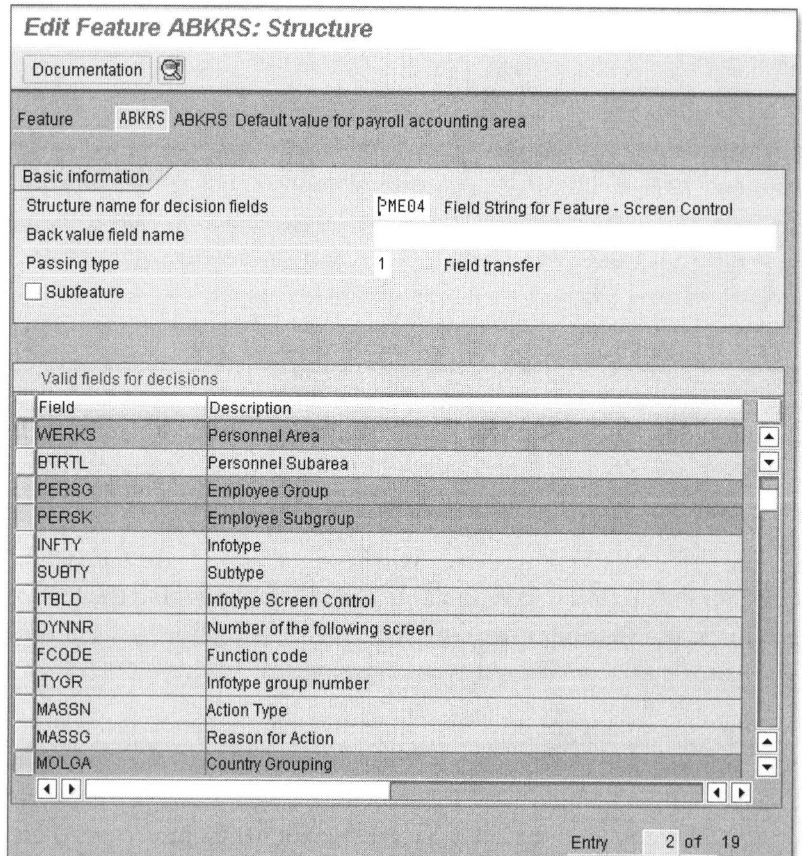

Figure A.1 Structure of a Feature

There are two possible ways to maintain a feature. At first glance the *table view* may appear complex (see Figure A.2), with syntax that looks cryptic. However, an experienced user can quickly handle it and will soon find out that this table actually provides a good overview of complex features.

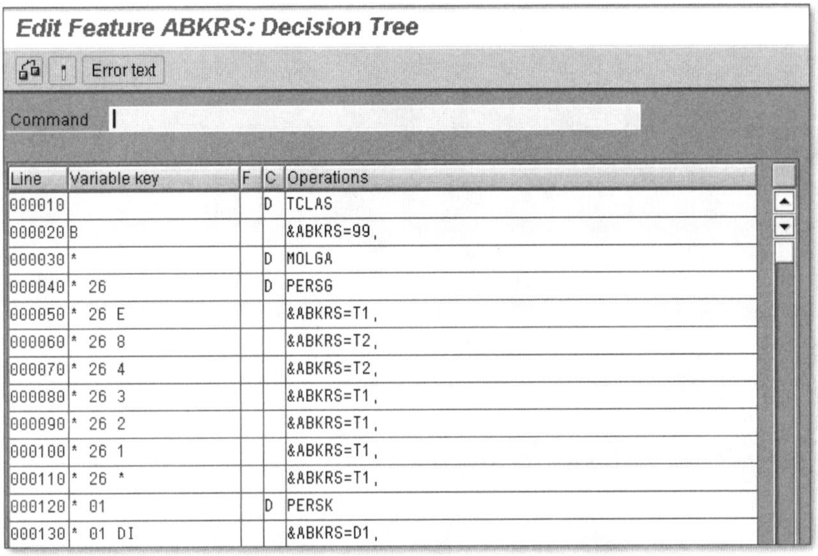

Edit Feature ABKRS: Decision Tree

Error text

Command

Line	Variable key	F	C	Operations
000010			D	TCLAS
000020	B			&ABKRS=99,
000030	*		D	MOLGA
000040	* 26		D	PERSG
000050	* 26 E			&ABKRS=T1,
000060	* 26 8			&ABKRS=T2,
000070	* 26 4			&ABKRS=T2,
000080	* 26 3			&ABKRS=T1,
000090	* 26 2			&ABKRS=T1,
000100	* 26 1			&ABKRS=T1,
000110	* 26 *			&ABKRS=T1,
000120	* 01		D	PERSK
000130	* 01 DI			&ABKRS=D1,

Figure A.2 Feature Maintenance: Table View

The tree view (see Figure A.3) clearly displays the effectiveness of the decision tree. It is very useful to understand the structure of an unknown feature and to check features you created by yourself.

You can navigate to the feature maintenance via Transaction PE03 or using the menu path Human Resources • Time Management • Administration • Tools • Maintain Features.

We don't need to describe the exact syntax of features at this point, because the system itself provides sufficient guidance for this. It is more important to draw your attention to the following basic items:

- If the branching possibilities are insufficient due to the width of the variable argument, you can use the FLDID command to branch to a subfeature.
- Checking and generating of features and their corresponding subfeatures always happen simultaneously.
- Subfeatures have to be identified as such in the attributes.
- Features are assigned to certain SAP ERP HCM components and countries via their attributes.

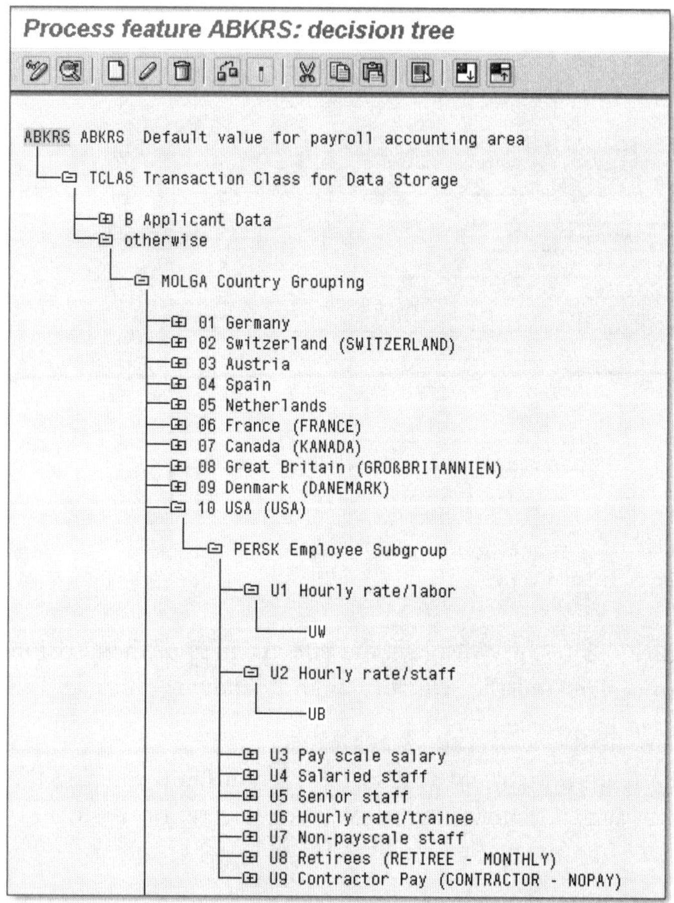

Figure A.3 Feature Maintenance: Tree View

- If you have modified an SAP feature in your client and want to reset it to the original status, you can simply delete it. In this case the system will automatically revert to Client 000, which contains the original status.
- Comprehensive decision trees should first be designed outside the system because you can then define a division into subfeatures that makes sense for your requirements.
- Not only must changes to features be saved, but they must also be generated before they can take effect. It is a popular pastime, even among experts, to search for alleged errors in a feature. However, the system behavior often

doesn't meet expectations because the feature in question simply hasn't been generated.

View Maintenance

Most Customizing settings are made in what is known as view maintenance. This offers a particular view of one or more tables, which are then used to control system performance.

You can access view maintenance using Transaction SM31 or with the menu path SYSTEM • SERVICES • TABLE MAINTENANCE • EXTENDED TABLE MAINTENANCE.

In addition to directly maintaining the settings, the system also allows you to branch to IMG using the Customizing button (see Figure A.4). This is generally useful because it offers the possibility of using or adjusting the documentation of a project IMG.

In the actual maintenance, the following options are available:

- Change existing entries (Note: The grayed key fields cannot be changed. To do this, you would have to copy the entry.)
- Copy existing entries
- Create new entries
- Delete existing entries
- Admit entries in a transport request

If you have to process very extensive tables, the following functions are particularly helpful (see Figure A.5):

- You can use the menu path SELECTION • BY CONTENTS... to select specific table rows, for example, all those with an end date before December 31, 2007.
- You can use the menu path EDIT • CHANGE FIELD CONTENTS... to make batch changes. You must have previously flagged all of the entries to be changed prior to making these batch changes. Then you can change a certain field in all of the marked entries in just one step. For example, you might use this option if you want to change working times. You could select all of the work schedule rules with 38.5 hours per week and in one step change them all to 36 hours per week.

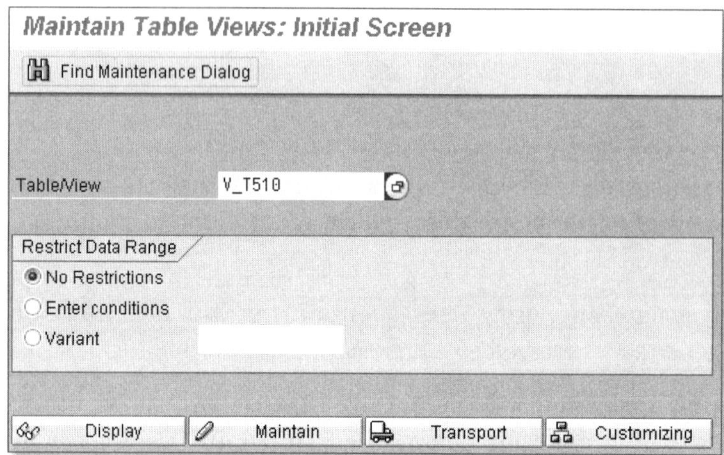

Figure A.4 Initial Screen of View Maintenance

Change View "Pay Scale Groups": Overview

Expand <-> Collapse | New Entries | Delimit

P.scale type 01 Standard contract

P.Scale Area 06 New York

Grpg	PS group	Lv	Wage Type	Start Date	End Date	Amount	Currency
1	GRD01			01/01/2000	12/31/9999	1.250,00	USD
1	GRD02			01/01/2000	12/31/9999	2.550,00	USD
1	H001			01/01/1990	12/31/9999	15,35	USD

Figure A.5 Maintaining a Table View

The IMG

The IMG contains all customizing activities, organized according to component; it can be accessed using Transaction SPRO. In addition to the Reference IMG, which contains all activities, you can also create any number of project IMGs to support specific projects (for example, Implementation of SAP ERP HCM in France and Switzerland).

The use of the IMG in general and the project IMGs in particular, offers the following advantages:

- It is easier to find the required activities because of clear structuring.
- You can use the documentation prepared by SAP for the individual steps.
- You can store enterprise-specific documentation for the individual steps.
- Project management is supported by status administration, time scheduling, and resource allocation.

Figure A.6 shows an example of a project IMG. On the left-hand side of the screen, you can see the component structure. The status, schedule, and resource allocation are maintained at the top right of the screen, and customer-specific documentation is stored below that in the form of notes.

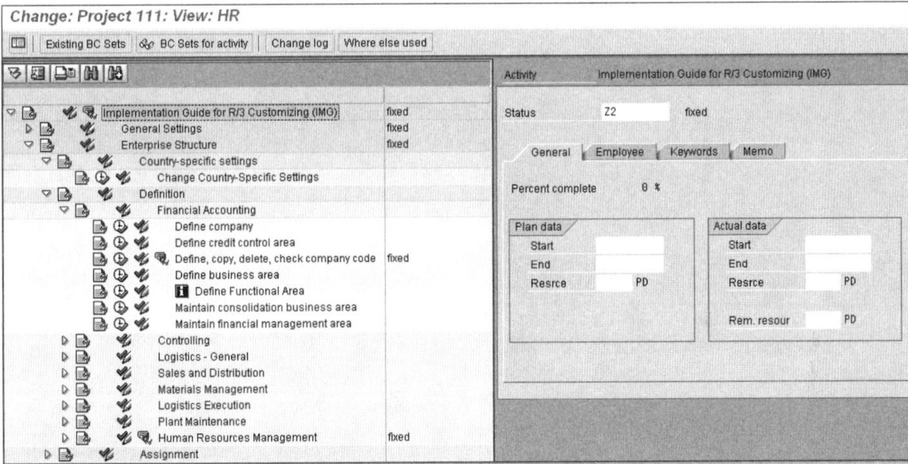

Figure A.6 Sample Project IMG

B Infotypes in SAP ERP HCM

In Table B.1, you will find nearly all the Human Resource (HR) infotypes that are used to keep data for employees or applicants. The exceptions are those infotypes that have no description in English or that are not part of the SAP standard delivery (for example, infotypes for Central and Eastern Europe are only available via add-on solutions).

For each infotype, the table provides the following information:

The third column (RA PY) tells you if this infotype triggers a retroactive calculation in payroll.

The forth column (RA TIM) does the same for time management.

The fifth and sixth columns tell you if the infotype is used for employees, applicants, or both.

The seventh column (TC) contains the time constraint of the respective infotype.

Finally, the column Country names the country the infotype is used for, providing it is only allowed for one country. If the infotype can be used for more than one country, the column is blank. In most cases, the content of this column depends on the standard customizing, which may sometimes be inaccurate.

All of these settings can be changed via Customizing. Thus, this table does not necessarily reflect the usage of infotypes in your organization.

IT	Description	RA PY	RA TIM	Employee	Applicant	TC	Country
0000	Actions	X		X		1	
0001	Organizational Assignment		X	X	X	1	
0002	Personal Data			X	X	1	
0003	Payroll Status			X		A	
0004	Challenge			X		2	

Table B.1 HR Infotypes

IT	Description	RA PY	RA TIM	Employee	Applicant	TC	Country
0005	Leave Entitlement			X		2	
0006	Addresses		X	X	X	T	
0007	Planned Working Time		X	X		1	
0008	Basic Pay	X		X		T	
0009	Bank Details	X		X	X	T	
0010	Capital Formation		X	X		T	Germany
0011	External Transfers	X		X		T	
0012	Fiscal Data D		X	X		2	Germany
0013	Social Insurance D		X	X		2	Germany
0014	Recurring Payments/ Deductions	X		X		T	
0015	Additional Payments and Deductions	X		X		T	
0016	Contract Elements		X	X		1	
0017	Travel Privileges			X		2	
0019	Monitoring of Tasks			X		2	
0020	DEUEV	X		X		1	Germany
0021	Family Member/ Dependents		X	X		T	
0022	Education			X	X	3	
0023	Other/Previous Employers			X	X	3	
0024	Qualifications			X	X	3	
0025	Appraisals	X		X		2	
0026	Company Insurance		X	X		T	Germany
0027	Cost Distribution	X		X		T	

Table B.1 HR Infotypes (Cont.)

IT	Description	RA PY	RA TIM	Employee	Applicant	TC	Country
0028	Internal Medical Service			X		T	
0029	Workers' Compensation			X		2	Germany
0030	Powers of Attorney			X		3	
0031	Reference Personnel Numbers			X		B	
0032	Internal Data		X	X		2	
0033	Statistics			X		2	
0034	Corporate Function			X		T	
0035	Company Instructions			X		T	
0036	Social Insurance CH		X	X		1	Switzerland
0037	Insurance			X		3	
0038	Fiscal Data CH		X	X		1	Switzerland
0039	Add. Org. Assignment CH		X	X		1	Switzerland
0040	Objects on Loan			X		3	
0041	Date Specifications			X		2	
0042	Fiscal Data A		X	X		1	Austria
0043	Family Allowance A		X	X		2	Austria
0044	Social Insurance A		X	X		1	Austria
0045	Loans	X		X		2	
0046	Company Pension Fund CH		X	X		2	Switzerland
0048	Residence Status			X		2	Switzerland

Table B.1 HR Infotypes (Cont.)

IT	Description	RA PY	RA TIM	Employee	Applicant	TC	Country
0049	Red. Hrs./Bad Weather	X		X		T	Germany
0050	Time Recording Info			X		2	
0051	ASB/SPI Data	X		X		1	Germany
0052	Wage Maintenance	X		X		2	
0053	Company Pension			X		3	Germany
0054	Works Councils	X		X		2	
0055	Previous Employer A			X		2	Austria
0056	Sickness Certificates A			X		T	Austria
0057	Membership Fees	X		X		T	
0058	Commuter Rate A		X	X		2	Austria
0059	Social Insurance NL	X		X		1	Netherlands
0060	Fiscal Data NL	X		X		1	Netherlands
0061	Social Insurance S	X		X		1	Spain
0062	Fiscal Data S	X		X		1	Spain
0063	Social Ins. Funds NL			X		T	Netherlands
0064	Social Insurance F	X		X		1	France
0065	Tax Data GB			X		1	U.K.
0066	Garnishment/ Cession CA	X		X		2	Canada
0067	Garnishment: Claim CA	X		X		2	Canada
0068	Garnishment: Compensation CA	X		X		2	Canada
0069	National Ins. GB		X	X		1	U.K.

Table B.1 HR Infotypes (Cont.)

IT	Description	RA PY	RA TIM	Employee	Applicant	TC	Country
0070	Court Orders GB		X	X		3	U.K.
0071	Pension Funds GB	X		X		T	U.K.
0072	Fiscal Data DK	X		X		1	Denmark
0073	Private Pension DK			X		3	Denmark
0074	Leave Processing DK			X		T	Denmark
0075	ATP Pension DK			X		1	Denmark
0076	Workers' Compensation NA	X		X		T	
0077	Additional Personal Data			X		1	
0078	Loan Payments	X		X		3	
0079	SI Additional Ins. D	X		X		T	Germany
0080	Maternity Protection/ Parental Leave	X		X		3	
0081	Military Service			X		3	
0082	Additional Abs. Data			X		T	
0083	Leave Entitlement Compensation	X		X		3	
0084	SSP Control GB	X		X		1	U.K.
0085	SSP1(L) Form Data GB		X	X		2	U.K.
0086	SSP/SMP Exclusions GB	X		X		3	U.K.
0087	WFTC/DPTC GB	X				2	U.K.
0088	SMP/SAP/SPP GB	X		X		2	U.K.

Table B.1 HR Infotypes (Cont.)

IT	Description	RA PY	RA TIM	Employee	Applicant	TC	Country
0090	Additional Income E			X		3	Spain
0092	Seniority E			X		3	Spain
0093	Previous Employers D			X		2	Germany
0094	Residence Status			X		1	
0095	Tax data CAN			X		T	
0098	Profit Sharing F			X		2	France
0100	Social Insurance B	X		X		1	Belgium
0101	Fiscal Data B	X		X		1	Belgium
0102	Grievances NA			X		3	
0103	Bond Purchases			X		2	
0104	Bond Denominations			X		3	
0105	Communication			X		T	
0106	Family/Related Person			X			
0107	Working Time B			X			Belgium
0108	Personal Data B			X			Belgium
0109	Contract Elements B			X			Belgium
0110	Pensions NL	X		X		2	Netherlands
0111	Garnishment/ Cession D	X		X		2	Germany
0112	Garnishment Claim D	X		X		2	Germany
0113	Garnishment Interest D	X		X		2	Germany
0114	Garnishment Amount D	X		X		2	Germany

Table B.1 HR Infotypes (Cont.)

IT	Description	RA PY	RA TIM	Employee	Applicant	TC	Country
0115	Garnishment Wages D	X		X		2	Germany
0116	Garnishment Transfer D	X		X		2	Germany
0117	Garnishment Compensation D	X		X		2	Germany
0118	Child Allowance		X	X		2	Germany
0119	Definition of Child Allowance (pre-1996)			X		2	Germany
0120	Company Pension Fund Transaction CH			X		3	Switzerland
0121	RefPerNo Priority	X		X		1	
0124	Disruptive Factor D	X				3	Germany
0125	Garnishment B		X	X		T	Belgium
0126	Supplemental Pension D		X	X		T	Germany
0127	Commuter Traffic NL	X		X		2	Netherlands
0128	Notifications			X		T	
0130	Test Procedures			X		B	
0131	Garnishment/ Cession	X		X		2	Austria
0132	Garnishment Claim A	X		X		2	Austria
0133	Garnisment Interest A	X		X		2	Austria
0134	Garnishment Amount A	X		X		2	Austria

Table B.1 HR Infotypes (Cont.)

IT	Description	RA PY	RA TIM	Employee	Applicant	TC	Country
0135	Special Garnishment Cond. A	X		X		2	Austria
0136	Garnishment Transfer A	X		X		2	Austria
0137	Garnishment Compensation A	X		X		2	Austria
0138	Family/Related Person B			X			Belgium
0139	EE's Applicant Number			X		B	
0140	SI Basic Data JP			X		T	Japan
0141	SI Premium Data JP			X		T	Japan
0142	Residence Tax JP			X		2	Japan
0143	Life Insurance Ded. JP			X		T	Japan
0144	Property Accum. Sav. JP			X		T	Japan
0145	Personnel Tax Status JP		X	X		1	Japan
0146	Y.E.A. Data JP			X		2	Japan
0147	Pers. Appraisals JP			X		T	Japan
0148	Family JP			X			Japan
0149	Taxes SA		X	X		1	South Africa
0150	Social Insurance SA		X	X		1	South Africa
0151	External Insurance SA	X		X		T	South Africa
0154	Social Security Data (IT)	X				1	Italy

Table B.1 HR Infotypes (Cont.)

IT	Description	RA PY	RA TIM	Employee	Applicant	TC	Country
0155	Additional Administrative Data (IT)			X		1	Italy
0156	Tax Deductions (IT)					1	Italy
0157	User Administration Data (IT)					1	Italy
0158	Amounts Paid by Third Parties (IT)					2	Italy
0159	Seniority (IT)					1	Italy
0160	Family Allowance (IT)	X				T	Italy
0161	IRS Limits USA			X		2	USA
0162	Insurance Y.E.T.A. Data JP			X		T	Japan
0165	Deduction Limits	X		X		3	
0167	Health Plans		X	X		2	
0168	Insurance Plans		X	X		2	
0169	Savings Plans		X	X		2	
0170	Flexible Spending Accounts	X		X		2	
0171	General Benefits Information	X		X		1	
0172	Flexible Spending Account Claims	X		X		3	
0173	Tax Card Information (Norway)	X		X		1	Norway
0177	Registration of Country of Birth NL			X		2	Netherlands

Table B.1 HR Infotypes (Cont.)

IT	Description	RA PY	RA TIM	Employee	Applicant	TC	Country
0179	Tax SG		X	X		1	Singapore
0181	Additional Funds SG		X	X		1	Singapore
0182	Alternatative Names Asia			X		T	
0183	Awards			X		3	
0184	Resume Texts			X		2	Singapore
0185	Personal IDs		X	X		2	
0186	CPF		X	X		1	Singapore
0187	Family Add. (TH)			X			Thailand
0188	Tax Australia	X		X		1	Australia
0189	Construction Pay: Funds Procedure	X		X		2	Germany
0190	Construction Pay: Previous ER	X		X		2	Germany
0191	Construction Pay: Expenses	X		X		2	Germany
0192	Construction Pay: Assignment	X		X		2	Germany
0194	Garnishment Document	X		X		2	USA
0195	Garnishment Order	X		X		2	USA
0196	Employees Provident Fund			X		1	Malaysia
0197	Employees' Social Security			X		2	Malaysia
0198	Schedular Deduction Tax			X		T	Malaysia
0199	Additional Tax Deduction			X		2	Malaysia
0200	Garnishments DK			X		3	Denmark

Table B.1 HR Infotypes (Cont.)

IT	Description	RA PY	RA TIM	Employee	Applicant	TC	Country
0201	Basic Pension Payments CPS	X				T	Germany
0202	Entitlements CPS		X			2	Germany
0203	Pension/Valuation Status BAV					A	Germany
0204	DA/DS Statistics DK			X		T	Denmark
0205	Tax Card Information Finland	X				2	Finland
0206	Social Insurance Information Finland	X				2	Finland
0207	Residence Tax Area	X		X		1	USA
0208	Work Tax Area	X		X		2	USA
0209	Unemployment State	X		X		2	USA
0210	Withholding Info W4/W5 U.S.	X		X		2	USA
0211	COBRA-Qualified Beneficiary	X		X		T	USA
0212	COBRA Health Plans	X		X		2	USA
0213	Additional Family Info			X			
0214	Loan Supplement, Denmark						
0215	CP: Transaction Data	X		X		T	Germany
0216	Garnishment Adjustment	X		X		2	USA

Table B.1 HR Infotypes (Cont.)

IT	Description	RA PY	RA TIM	Employee	Applicant	TC	Country
0217	Employment Contract: Additional Data			X		2	France
0218	Membership to Insurance			X		3	France
0219	External Organizations		X	X		T	
0220	Superannuation Aust.	X		X		T	Australia
0221	Payroll Results Adjustment	X		X		3	
0222	Company Cars GB		X	X		2	U.K.
0225	Company Car Unavailable GB	X		X		2	U.K.
0227	TFN Australia		X	X		1	Australia
0228	Garnishments Finland	X				2	Finland
0229	Value Types BAV					2	Germany
0230	Supplement to P0008 PSG			X			Germany
0231	Supplement to P0001 PSG			X			Germany
0232	Child Allowance D		X	X		2	Germany
0233	Bilan social (Social survey)			X		1	France
0234	Additional Withholding Info. U.S.	X		X		2	USA
0235	Other Taxes U.S.	X		X		2	USA
0236	Credit Plans		X	X		2	

Table B.1 HR Infotypes (Cont.)

IT	Description	RA PY	RA TIM	Employee	Applicant	TC	Country
0237	Supplement to P0052 PSG			X			Germany
0241	Tax Data Indonesia		X	X		1	Indonesia
0242	Jamsostek Insurance Indonesia		X	X		2	Indonesia
0261	Loading Leave Aust.	X		X		3	Australia
0262	Retroactive Accounting					T	
0263	Salary Conversion	X				2	Germany
0264	Family NL						Netherlands
0265	Special Regulations	X		X		2	Germany
0266	Supplement to P0027 PSG			X			Germany
0267	Additional Off-Cycle Payments	X		X		T	
0268	Company Loans JP						Japan
0270	COBRA Payments	X		X		3	USA
0271	Statistics, Public Sector Germany						Germany
0272	Garnishment (F)			X		3	France
0273	Taxes SE	X		X		T	Sweden
0275	Garnishments SE	X		X		T	Sweden
0277	Exceptions SE	X		X		T	Sweden
0278	Basic Data Pension Fund			X		2	
0279	Individual Values Pension Fund	X		X		2	

Table B.1 HR Infotypes (Cont.)

IT	Description	RA PY	RA TIM	Employee	Applicant	TC	Country
0280	View for Contractual Elements GB						U.K.
0281	View for Beneficial Loans GB						U.K.
0283	Archived Objects			X		T	
0288	Family CH						Switzerland
0302	Additional Actions	X				3	
0303	Premium Reduction NL	X		X		2	Netherlands
0304	Additional Basic Pay Information	X		X		2	Germany
0305	Previous Employers (IT)					3	Italy
0306	Family Addition						
0309	IRD Nbr New Zealand		X	X		1	
0310	Superannuation NZ	X		X		T	
0311	Leave Balance Adj	X		X		3	
0312	Leave History Adj	X		X		3	
0313	Tax NZ	X		X		1	
0315	Time Sheet Defaults			X		2	
0317	Special Provisions NL	X		X		T	Netherlands
0318	Family View Indonesia			X			Indonesia
0319	Private Insurances Indonesia		X	X		T	Indonesia

Table B.1 HR Infotypes (Cont.)

IT	Description	RA PY	RA TIM	Employee	Applicant	TC	Country
0320	Official Housing	X		X		2	Germany
0321	Employee Accommodations	X		X		2	Germany
0322	Pension Payments	X				T	Germany
0323	Entitlement Group Type CPS					2	Germany
0326	Imputation of Pension		X			T	Germany
0329	Sideline Job					2	Germany
0330	Nonmonetary Remuneration	X				2	
0331	Tax PT	X				1	Portugal
0332	Social Security PT	X				1	Portugal
0333	Disability PT	X				2	Portugal
0334	Supplemental it0016 (PT)						Portugal
0335	Supplemental it0021 (PT)						Portugal
0336	SupplEmental it0002 (PT)						Portugal
0337	Prof.Classification PT	X				2	Portugal
0338	Absence Payment Clearing PT	X				2	Portugal
0341	DEUEV Start			X		B	Germany
0342	Personal Data HK			X			Hong Kong
0343	Contract Elements HK			X			Hong Kong
0344	Additional Family HK			X			Hong Kong
0345	General Tax HK		X	X		1	Hong Kong

Table B.1 HR Infotypes (Cont.)

IT	Description	RA PY	RA TIM	Employee	Applicant	TC	Country
0346	Contribution Plan HK	X		X		2	Hong Kong
0347	Entitlement Plan HK	X		X		2	Hong Kong
0348	Appraisal & Bonus HK			X		2	Hong Kong
0349	Cont./Ent. Eligibility HK			X		2	Hong Kong
0351	Country Information			X		T	
0352	Additional Family Information (TW)			X			Taiwan
0353	Income Tax (TW)	X		X		1	Taiwan
0354	Labor Insurance (TW)		X	X		1	Taiwan
0355	National Health Insurance (TW)		X	X		1	Taiwan
0356	Employee Stab. Fund (TW)	X		X		2	Taiwan
0357	Saving Plan (TW)	X		X		T	Taiwan
0358	EE Welfare Fund (TW)	X		X		2	Taiwan
0359	Tax Data Ireland	X				1	Ireland
0360	PRSI Ireland	X				1	Ireland
0361	Pensions Ireland	X				0	Ireland
0362	Membership View Indonesia			X			Indonesia
0363	Previous Employment Period			X		T	
0364	Tax TH	X		X		1	Thailand
0365	Social Security TH			X		T	Thailand

Table B.1 HR Infotypes (Cont.)

IT	Description	RA PY	RA TIM	Employee	Applicant	TC	Country
0366	Provident Fund TH			X		2	Thailand
0367	SI Notification Supplements A			X		T	Austria
0369	Social Security Data	X		X		1	Mexico
0370	INFONAVIT Loan	X		X		T	Mexico
0371	Retenciones en otros empleos	X		X		T	Mexico
0372	Integrated Daily Wage	X				3	Mexico
0373	Loan Repayment JP						Japan
0374	General Eligibility					T	
0375	HCE Information			X		2	USA
0376	Benefits Medical Information			X		2	
0377	Miscellaneous Plans	X		X		2	
0378	Adjustment Reasons			X		2	
0379	Stock Purchase Plans		X			2	
0380	Compensation Adjustment			X			
0381	Compensation Eligibility			X			
0382	Award			X		3	
0383	Compensation Component					2	
0384	Compensation Package					1	

Table B.1 HR Infotypes (Cont.)

IT	Description	RA PY	RA TIM	Employee	Applicant	TC	Country
0386	Health Insurance Ireland	X				0	Ireland
0387	Starters Details Ireland	X				2	Ireland
0388	Union Due Deadline JP			X		2	Japan
0389	Impuesto a las Ganancias AR			X		1	Argentina
0390	Impto.Ganancias: Deducciones AR			X		T	Argentina
0391	Impto.Ganancias: Otro empleador AR			X		3	Argentina
0392	Seguridad Social AR			X		1	Argentina
0393	Datos familia: Ayuda escolar AR			X		2	Argentina
0394	Datos familia: información adic. AR			X			Argentina
0395	External Organizational Assignment	X				3	
0396	Expatriation	X				3	
0397	Dependents BR						Brazil
0398	Contractual Elements BR						Brazil
0399	Income Tax	X		X		1	Venzuela
0400	Social Insurance	X		X		1	Venzuela
0401	Prestaciones/ Antigüedad	X		X		1	Venzuela
0402	Payroll Results					3	

Table B.1 HR Infotypes (Cont.)

IT	Description	RA PY	RA TIM	Employee	Applicant	TC	Country
0403	Payroll Results 2					3	
0404	Military Service (TW)			X			Taiwan
0405	Absence Event	X		X		2	Germany
0406	Pension Information	X				T	Germany
0407	Absences (Additional Information)	X				Z	Italy
0408	CBS NL					2	Netherlands
0409	Execution of Employee Insurances					2	Netherlands
0411	Taxation Philippines	X				1	Philippines
0415	Export Status					B	
0416	Time Quota Compensation	X				3	
0419	Additional Tax Statement Info (NO)					2	Norway
0421	Special Remunerations (IT)	X				2	Italy
0422	Social Security Philippines	X				1	Philippines
0423	HDMF Philippines	X				1	Philippines
0424	Work Stopped (F)	X				2	France
0425	IJSS Summary (F)	X				2	France
0426	Orden jurídica México	X		X		2	Mexico

Table B.1 HR Infotypes (Cont.)

IT	Description	RA PY	RA TIM	Employee	Applicant	TC	Country
0427	Deudas por órden jurídica México	X		X		2	Mexico
0428	Additional Data on Beneficiary						
0429	Position in PS		X			T	
0430	Fam. Allowance for Processing		X			T	
0431	View: Basic Pay	X				T	
0432	View: Type of Employment	X				2	
0433	GB View for Bank Details						U.K.
0434	GB view for External Transfers						U.K.
0435	ITF ADP 309 Free Format	X				3	France
0436	ITF ADP 409 Free Format	X				3	France
0438	Annual Tax Additions SE					2	Sweden
0439	Data Transfer Information					B	
0440	Receipts & Misc. Information HK					T	Hong Kong
0442	Company Car	X				3	
0446	Payroll U.S. Federal Taxes			X		3	USA
0447	Payroll U.S. Federal Taxes MTD			X		3	USA
0448	Payroll U.S. Federal Taxes QTD			X		3	USA

Table B.1 HR Infotypes (Cont.)

IT	Description	RA PY	RA TIM	Employee	Applicant	TC	Country
0449	Payroll U.S. Federal Taxes YTD			X		3	USA
0450	Payroll U.S. State Taxes			X		3	USA
0451	Payroll U.S. State Taxes MTD			X		3	USA
0452	Payroll U.S .State Taxes QTD			X		3	USA
0453	Payroll U.S. State Taxes YTD			X		3	USA
0454	Payroll U.S. Local Taxes			X		3	USA
0455	Payroll U.S. Local Taxes MTD			X		3	USA
0456	Payroll U.S. Local Taxes QTD			X		3	USA
0457	Payroll U.S. Local Taxes YTD			X		3	USA
0458	Monthly Cumulations					3	
0459	Quarterly Cumulations					3	
0460	Annual Cumulations					3	
0461	Tax Assignment CA	X				1	Canada
0462	Provincial Tax CA	X				1	Canada
0463	Federal Tax CA	X				1	Canada
0464	Additional Tax Data CA	X				2	Canada
0465	Documents					T	Brazil

Table B.1 HR Infotypes (Cont.)

IT	Description	RA PY	RA TIM	Employee	Applicant	TC	Country
0467	Add'l SI Notif. Data f.Comp. Agts A			X		T	Austria
0468	Travel Profile (not specified)					2	
0469	Travel Profile (not specified)					2	
0470	Travel Profile					2	
0471	Flight Preference					2	
0472	Hotel Preference					2	
0473	Rental Car Preference					2	
0474	Train Preference					2	
0475	Customer Program					3	
0476	Garnishments: Order	X				2	
0477	Garnishments: Debt	X				2	
0478	Garnishments: Adjustment	X				2	
0480	Enhancement: Contracts Processing						
0482	Additional Data Family/Related Person						
0483	CAAF Data Clearing (IT)					2	Italy
0484	Taxation (Enhancement)					T	
0485	Stage					2	

Table B.1 HR Infotypes (Cont.)

IT	Description	RA PY	RA TIM	Employee	Applicant	TC	Country
0486	Military Service (PS-SG)						Singapore
0487	Security/Medical Clearance					3	Singapore
0488	Leave Scheme					2	Singapore
0489	Voluntary Service/ ECA					3	Singapore
0490	Staff Suggestion					3	Singapore
0491	Payroll Outsourcing					2	
0493	Education (PS-SG)						Singapore
0494	Staff Suggestion Scheme—Evaluator					3	Singapore
0495	Retirement Benefits/Death Gratuity					1	
0496	Payroll U.S. Benefits Data			X		3	USA
0497	Payroll U.S. Benefits Data MTD			X		3	USA
0498	Payroll U.S. Benefits Data QTD			X		3	USA
0499	Payroll U.S. Benefits Data YTD			X		3	USA
0500	Statistical Data			X		3	USA
0501	Other Social Insurance Data			X		3	USA
0502	Letter of Appointment					2	Singapore

Table B.1 HR Infotypes (Cont.)

IT	Description	RA PY	RA TIM	Employee	Applicant	TC	Country
0503	Pensioner Definition		X			2	
0504	Pension Advantage	X				3	
0505	Holiday certificate (B)		X			3	Belgium
0506	Tip Indicators	X		X		2	USA
0507	Superannuation						
0508	Prior Service					2	
0509	Activity with Higher Rate of Pay	X				2	
0510	Tax-Sheltered Pension (U.S.)	X		X		3	USA
0511	Cost-of-Living Allowance/ Amount		X			1	Switzerland
0521	Semiretirement D	X				2	Germany
0525	Child Care	X				2	Netherlands
0526	Work & Remuneration Confirmation A					3	Austria
0527	Payment Upon Leaving A	X				2	Austria
0528	Additional Family Information (CN)						China
0529	Additional Personal Data for (CN)					1	China
0530	Public Housing Fund (CN)	X				1	China
0531	Income Tax (CN)	X				1	China

Table B.1 HR Infotypes (Cont.)

IT	Description	RA PY	RA TIM	Employee	Applicant	TC	Country
0532	Social Insurance (CN)	X				T	China
0533	Personal File Management (CN)					1	China
0534	Party Information (CN)					1	China
0535	Project & Achievement (CN)					T	China
0536	Administration Information (CN)						China
0537	Going Abroad Information (CN)						China
0538	Separation Payment					2	South Korea
0539	Personal Data						
0540	Family/Related Person						
0541	Personnel Tax Status	X				2	South Korea
0542	Year-End Adjustment Data					2	South Korea
0543	Social Insurance	X				T	South Korea
0544	Social Insurance Premium					T	South Korea
0545	Disciplinary Measure					3	South Korea
0546	Termination Data		X			2	
0547	BIK(TAX) Infotype for Malaysia					3	Malaysia

Table B.1 HR Infotypes (Cont.)

IT	Description	RA PY	RA TIM	Employee	Applicant	TC	Country
0548	Supplementary Pension Funds (IT)					2	Italy
0551	Termination: General Data					2	Argentina
0552	Time Specification/ Employ. Period					2	
0553	Calculation of Service			X		2	USA
0554	Hourly Rate per Assignment	X				T	
0555	Military service					2	South Korea
0556	Tax Treaty	X		X		2	USA
0557	Additional Personal Data					2	South Korea
0559	Commuting Allowance Info JP		X			3	Japan
0560	Overseas Pay JP	X				2	Japan
0561	Tax Data	X				2	Mexico
0565	Retirement Plan Valuation Results					2	
0566	U.S. Pension Plan QDRO Information			X		3	USA
0567	Data Container					B	
0568	Anniversary Date History		X			2	
0569	Additional Pension Payments	X				3	
0570	Offshore Tax GB					2	U.K.

Table B.1 HR Infotypes (Cont.)

IT	Description	RA PY	RA TIM	Employee	Applicant	TC	Country
0571	Offshore Social Security GB					2	U.K.
0572	Absence Scheme Override	X				2	
0573	Absence Infotype for Australia PS					2	Australia
0574	Contract Elements Austria PS						Austria
0576	Seniority for Promotion					3	
0578	PBS Accumulator Correction					3	Denmark
0579	External Wage Components						
0580	Previous Employment Tax Details					A	India
0581	Housing (HRA/ CLA/COA)		X			1	India
0582	Exemptions		X			3	India
0583	Car & Conveyance	X				1	India
0584	Income From Other Sources					T	India
0585	Section 80 Deductions					2	India
0586	Investment Details (Sec88)					2	India
0587	Provident Fund Contribution		X			1	India
0588	Other Statutory Deductions		X			T	India
0589	Individual Reimbursements					1	India

Table B.1 HR Infotypes (Cont.)

IT	Description	RA PY	RA TIM	Employee	Applicant	TC	Country
0590	Long-Term Reimbursements					2	India
0591	Nominations					2	India
0592	Public Sector—Foreign Service		X			2	
0593	Rehabilitants		X			2	
0595	Family-Related Bonuses		X			2	Germany
0596	PhilHealth Philippines	X				1	Philippines
0597	Part-Time Work During Parental Leave	X				Z	
0600	Employer Statement					2	Switzerland
0601	Absence History	X				2	
0602	Retirement Plan Cumulations					3	
0611	Garnishments: Management Data						
0612	Garnishments: Interest	X					
0613	Absence Donation/ Withdraw (U.S.)			X		3	USA
0614	HESA Master Data					2	
0615	HE Contract Data					2	
0616	HESA Submitted Data					2	
0617	Clinical Details					2	

Table B.1 HR Infotypes (Cont.)

IT	Description	RA PY	RA TIM	Employee	Applicant	TC	Country
0618	Academic Qualification					3	
0619	Equity and Diversity					2	
0622	Contract Elements (Public Sector BE)						Belgium
0623	Career History (Public Sector BE)					2	Belgium
0624	HE Professional Qualifications					3	
0626	Payment Summary					3	Australia
0632	Semiretirement A		X			2	Austria
0633	EEO/ Grievance Case Management			X		3	USA
0634	Other/Previous Employers					3	Philippines
0646	FVP					2	Netherlands
0647	GBA					T	Netherlands
0648	Bar Point Information					2	
0649	Social Insurance (Public Sector BE)						Belgium
0650	BA Statements					2	
0651	SI Carrier Certificates					2	
0652	Certificates of Training					2	
0653	Certificates to Local Authorities					2	

Table B.1 HR Infotypes (Cont.)

IT	Description	RA PY	RA TIM	Employee	Applicant	TC	Country
0655	ESS Settings Remuneration Statement					2	
0656	Nature of Actions			X		T	USA
0662	Semiretirement A—Notification Supplements					2	Austria
0665	External Pension Rights					T	Netherlands
0666	Planning of Pers. Costs					3	
0671	COBRA Flexible Spending Accounts			X		2	USA
0672	FMLA Event			X		3	USA
0694	Previous Employment Details	X				2	
0696	Absence Pools					T	
0697	Drug Screening			X		T	USA
0698	Loan Master to Supplement for KR						
0699	Pension Provision Act	X				2	Germany
0701	End Point Australia					2	Australia
0702	Documents					3	
0703	Documents on Dependants					T	
0704	Information on Dependants					T	

Table B.1 HR Infotypes (Cont.)

IT	Description	RA PY	RA TIM	Employee	Applicant	TC	Country
0705	Information on Checklists					3	
0706	Compensation Package Offer					3	
0707	Activation Information					2	
0708	Details on Global Commuting					2	
0709	Person ID					A	
0710	Details on Global Assignment					2	
0711	Employer Number					1	Netherlands
0712	Main Personnel Assignment	X				2	
0713	Termination	X				2	
0715	Status of Global Assignment					T	
0717	Benefit Point Account					2	South Korea
0718	Benefit Request		X			3	South Korea
0722	Payroll for Global Employees	X				2	
0723	Payroll for GE: Retroactive Accounting					B	
0724	Financing Status					1	
0725	Taxes SA					3	South Africa
0734	View for IT Basic Pay Brasil						Brazil
0736	Alimony Brasil	X				2	Brazil
0737	Alimony Debt Brasil	X				2	Brazil

Table B.1 HR Infotypes (Cont.)

IT	Description	RA PY	RA TIM	Employee	Applicant	TC	Country
0738	Alimony Adjustment Brasil	X				2	Brazil
0739	Stock Option (Singapore)					3	Singapore
0742	HDB Concession					2	
0743	Discipline					3	
0744	Blacklist					2	
0745	HDB Messages in Public Sector					2	
0748	Command and Delegation					T	
0751	Company Pension Plan AT	X				T	Austria
0752	Declaration of Land/Houses/ Property					3	
0753	Declaration of Shares					3	
0754	Declaration of Interest in Business					3	
0755	Declaration of Non-Indebtedness					3	
0758	Compensation Program					2	
0759	Compensation Process					3	
0760	Compensation Eligibility Override					3	
0761	LTI Granting					2	
0762	LTI Exercising	X				3	

Table B.1 HR Infotypes (Cont.)

IT	Description	RA PY	RA TIM	Employee	Applicant	TC	Country
0763	LTI Participant Data					2	Netherlands
0764	Permanent Invalidity Benefit Act Netherlands					2	
0780	HR Pension Administration (PADM)					3	
0781	HR Pension Administration (PADM)					3	
0782	HR Pension Administration (PADM)					3	
0783	Job Title					2	
0784	HR Pension Administration (PADM)					3	
0785	HR Pension Administration (PADM)					3	
0786	HR Pension Administration (PADM)					3	
0787	HR Pension Administration (PADM)					3	
0788	HR Pension Administration (PADM)					3	
0789	HR Pension Administration (PADM)					3	

Table B.1 HR Infotypes (Cont.)

IT	Description	RA PY	RA TIM	Employee	Applicant	TC	Country
0790	HR Pension Administration (PADM)					3	
0793	Payment Made in Error GB	X				2	U.K.
0815	Multiple Check in One Cycle					3	
0900	Sales Data			X		2	
0901	Purchasing Data			X		2	
2001	Absences	X		X		Z	
2002	Attendances	X		X		Z	
2003	Substitutions	X		X		Z	
2004	Availability	X		X		Z	
2005	Overtime	X		X		Z	
2006	Absence Quotas			X		Z	
2007	Attendance Quotas			X		Z	
2010	Employee Remuneration Info	X		X		T	
2011	Time Events			X		Z	
2012	Time Transfer Specifications			X		Z	
2013	Quota Corrections			X		Z	
3003	Materials Management			X		1	
4000	Applicant Actions				X	1	
4001	Applications				X	3	
4002	Vacancy Assignment				X	2	

Table B.1 HR Infotypes (Cont.)

IT	Description	RA PY	RA TIM	Employee	Applicant	TC	Country
4003	Applicant Activities				X	3	
4004	Applicant Activity Status				X	A	
4005	Applicant's Personnel Number				X	B	

Table B.1 HR Infotypes (Cont.)

C Explanations for Process Models

To understand the process examples in the various chapters, you should know the meaning of the following symbols. Readers with ARIS© skills can skip this section.

For reading the process examples you must know the meaning of the following symbols.

Events

Figure C.1 ARIS Symbol: Event

Events are starting points for processes; in other words, a process is started because "something has happened." In Recruitment, for example, there is the event applicant to be hired. For the hiring process, this means that a trigger event occurs and the process is started.

Events can also be the results of decision-making processes. For example, after an interview, a decision must be made as to whether the candidate will be hired. Possible results of this decision-making process can be applicant to be hired or applicant to be rejected.

Functions

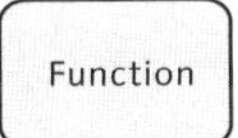

Figure C.2 ARIS Symbol: Function

Functions present activities. An example is "interview." In accordance with general ARIS convention, an event must be set after each function (see Figure C.3). Due to the lack of space in process models, the use of this "trivial event" is waived in this book.

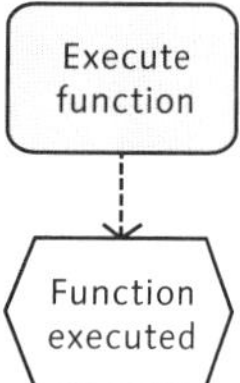

Figure C.3 Function and Event

The relationships between functions, events, and the *connectors* are called *connections*.

System Functions

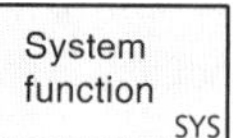

Figure C.4 ARIS Symbol: System Function

Actions carried out by the system — SAP in this case — are presented in *system functions*. These are actions that are run from the system without any user intervention.

Process Interfaces

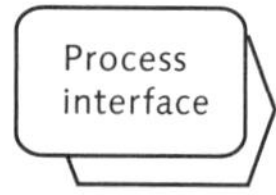

Figure C.5 ARIS Symbol: Process Interface

Process interfaces create a connection between two processes. For example, the recruitment process ends with the event candidate to be hired, and then proceeds to the process hiring (see Figure C.6).

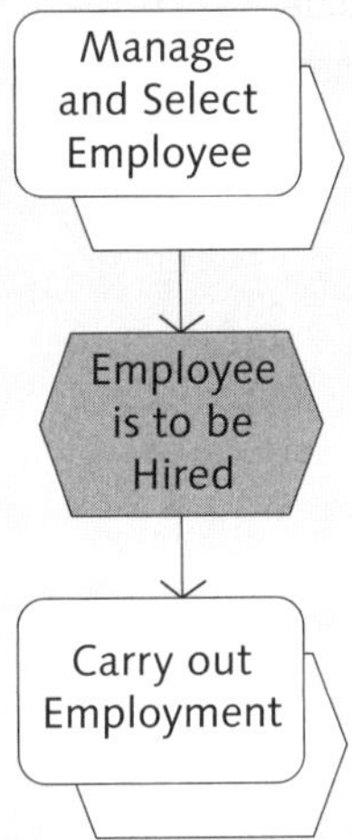

Figure C.6 Example of a Process Interface

Jobs and Organizational Units

Jobs and organizational units are linked to functions. They indicate who carries out the functions in question or in which organizational unit they are carried out (see Figure C.7).

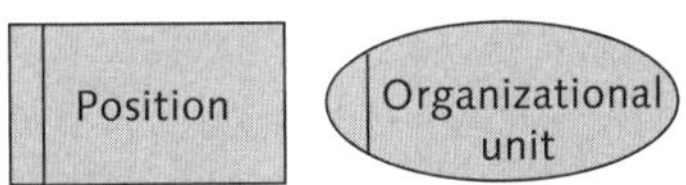

Figure C.7 ARIS Symbols: Job and Organizational Unit

Connector

Connectors represent logical links between functions containing decisions and the results of these decisions. The relationship between an event and the functions resulting from it is also represented by connectors. The connectors, AND, AND/OR, and XOR, are used in the process examples shown (see Figures C.8-C.10).

Figure C.8 ARIS Symbol: AND Connector

The AND connector means that after an event or a function, several functions are executed in parallel. It is used if *all* functions that emerge after an event or function *must* be carried out.

Figure C.9 ARIS Symbol: AND/OR Connector

If, on the other hand, not all functions that crop up after another function always need to be carried out, then the AND/OR connector is used.

Figure C.10 ARIS Symbol: XOR Connector

The XOR connector is used to show that decisions must be made in a function. Figure C.11 shows an example of how the XOR connector is used.

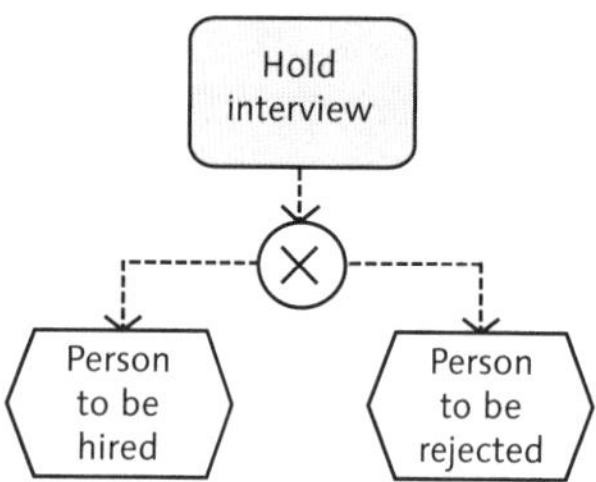

Figure C.11 Example of a Process Interface

D Recommended Reading

In the following list, you can find some publications that provide detailed information about the topics discussed or contain further topics of the SAP ERP environment that were mentioned within the framework of integration aspects in this book.

- Badgi, Satish: *Practical SAP US Payroll*. SAP PRESS, Boston 2008.
- Becker, Brian; Huselid, Mark; Ulrich, Dave: *HR Scorecard. Linking People, Strategy and Performance*. SAP PRESS, Boston 2001.
- Brochhausen, Kielisch, Schnerring, Staeck: *mySAP HR—Technical Principles and Programming*. SAP PRESS, Bonn 2005.
- Chaudoir, Sylvia: *Mastering SAP ERP HCM Organizational Management*. SAP PRESS, Boston 2008.
- Esch, Martin; Junold, Anja: *Authorizations in SAP ERP HCM*. SAP PRESS, Boston 2008.
- Figaj, Hans-Jürgen; Haßmann, Richard; Junold, Anja: *HR-Reporting With SAP*. SAP PRESS, Boston 2007.
- Gallardo, Manuel: *Configuring and Using CATS*. SAP PRESS, Boston 2008.
- Gillet, Martin: *Integrating CATS*. SAP PRESS, Boston 2008.
- HaÐmann, Richard; Krämer, Christian, *Personnel Planning and Development Using SAP ERP HCM*. SAP PRESS, Boston 2009
- IBM Business Consulting Services: *SAP Authorization System*. SAP PRESS 2003.
- Jung, Thomas; McKellar, Brian: *Advanced BSP Programming*. SAP PRESS, Bonn 2006.
- Masters, Jeremy: *SAP ERP HCM Performance Management*. SAP PRESS, Boston 2007.
- Masters, Jeremy; Kotsakis, Christos: *Implementing Employee and Manager Self-Services in SAP ERP HCM*. SAP PRESS, Boston 2008.
- Melich, Matthias; Schafer, Marc O.: *SAP Solution Manager*. SAP PRESS, Boston 2008.

- Newman, Greg: *Discover SAP ERP HCM*. SAP PRESS, Boston 2009.
- Schaer, Brian: *Time Management in SAP ERP HCM*. SAP PRESS, Boston 2008.

D.1 Web Sites

- *help.sap.com* (Note: Don't use the prefix www)
  Help portal of SAP AG; contains help files for all SAP products in different releases (free of charge, navigation in English, documentation available in multiple languages).
- *www.admanus.de/english-newsletter*
  Newsletter for SAP ERP HCM and Human Resources (HR) processes (free of charge).
- *www.asug.com*
  Home page of the American SAP user group. News materials for download, event calendar (most parts are only accessible to members — requires membership fee).
- *www.hrexpertonline.com*
  Online database of the HREXPERT newsletter, expert articles on SAP ERP HCM (fee required).
- *www.iproconhcm.co.uk/knowledge*
  Free articles, white papers and case studies around Human Capital Management, alignment with business strategy, HR-IT strategy, and right-sourcing. Also information available through free newsletter or RSS feed.
- *www.sap.com*
  Corporate web site of SAP. A wide variety of documentations, whitepapers, live demos, newsletters, links, support pages, and so on. (Some parts are publicly available, some are only available for sale.)
- *www.sap.info*
  Online version of the *SAP INFO* magazine. Articles about all kinds of topics on SAP AG (free of charge).
- *www.sapusers.org*
  Home page of the SAP UK & Ireland user group. News, materials for download, event calendar (most parts are only accessible to members — requires membership fee).

- *www.sd-solutions.com/documents/KnowledgeBase.html*
  Free and very comprehensive online information on SAP HCM, reporting and data migration tools.
- *www.sdn.sap.com*
  SAP community network. Huge amount of information, though not always neutral or high quality. Still great value particularly from discussion forums, where peers help each other to solve problems. (Registration required, but free of charge)

E Authors

This book is the result of a team effort. The authors are grateful to the following contributors, without whom this project would never have attained its current standard of quality.

- Our friends at the AdManus network (*www.admanus.de*) and iProCon GmbH, most notably Anja Junold and Christian Lübke who added valuable insights as well as screenshots and moral support.
- The many helpful members of the staff at SAP, who contributed very detailed information, particularly in the area of new developments.
- The technical support team at PIKON International Consulting Group (*www.pikon.com*), who ensured that we always had access to the IDES system and to SAP NetWeaver Portal, which were used as a source of numerous examples.
- And last but not least, we want to thank the team at Galileo Press and SAP PRESS. They not only put up a brave fight against the dreaded typo monster. They also supported the authors in the conception of this book and contributed to closing the gap swiftly after the second edition sold so well.

We shall now briefly introduce the authors themselves (in an "age before beauty" order):

Sven Ringling has worked as a consultant with organizations in 8 countries and various industries on improving their Human Capital. In SAP ERP HCM his focus recently was on performance management, quality assurance (QA), and international rollouts. He co-founded iProCon GmbH in Germany in 2000 and was a managing director until 2008, when he co-founded iProCon HCM Ltd. in the UK. He is now Senior Partner and heads the people strategy practice. His latest projects comprise HR-IT strategy, rightsourcing, change management, and innovation culture.

Jörg Edinger has joined iProCon GmbH in 2002 and became a Managing Director in 2009. He attends to customers of SAP ERP HCM with a focus on payroll, pension schemes, personnel controlling, personnel cost planning and ESS/MSS. In addition, he supports enterprises in the design of HR metrics outside of the SAP system. Prior to joining iProCon GmbH, he was controller at the German health insurance company Barmer Ersatzkasse. He has many years of practical experience in payroll, pension schemes, and controlling.

iProCon Group

Since early 2000, iProCon GmbH (*www.iprocon.com*) has set for itself the mission of optimizing HR processes through redesign and better use of technology. In addition to process-oriented consulting, the implementation of modern HR systems, most notably SAP ERP HCM, forms the core of its business. iProCon HCM Ltd. (*www.iproconhcm.co.uk*) was set up in 2008 as a strategy consultancy to help organizations to align their people management (incl. HR-IT) with business strategy. The idea of allowing requirements to flow directly from business requirements through processes to the Information Technology (IT) implementation is a cornerstone of this book.

Janet McClurg has been working for 12 years at SAP as an HCM consultant, the last 9 as a Platinum Consultant. She has worked on several dozen implementation projects in this time, most of them being global in scope. Her areas of expertise are Enterprise Compensation Management (ECM), personnel development (including performance management and succession planning), organizational management, and personnel administration. She is a frequent contributor to the industry newsletter for SAP HCM users: *HR Expert*.

Index

A

B

C

D

E

F

G

H

I

J

L

M

N

O

P

Q

R

S

T

U

V

W

Y

Z

Develop your own enterprise services

Benefit from in-depth descriptions of standard services usage

Increase your knowledge through recommendations on service enabling

Martin Huvar, Timm Falter, Thomas Fiedler, Alexander Zubev

Developing Applications with Enterprise SOA

With this book, application developers and software architects finally have at their disposal a thorough introduction to software development with SAP's enterprise service-oriented architecture (enterprise SOA).
The book provides an in-depth description of all enterprise SOA components and methodologies, as well as the metadata model, and it explains how to develop your own enterprise services, and combine them into applications in different scenarios (service consumer). The book covers user interface scenarios as well as process and integration scenarios.

329 pp., 2008, 69,95 Euro / US$ 69.95, ISBN 978-1-59229-178-6

>> www.sap-press.de/1604

Planning and implementing new, self-contained SAP applications

Developing flexible application architectures with SAP NetWeaver Application Server ABAP

Best practices for optimum usage of all potentials in an existing infrastructure

Thorsten Franz, Tobias Trapp

ABAP Objects: Application Development from Scratch

Developing completely new ABAP applications – separate from the SAP standard – represents a very challenging task even for experienced developers. To help you master this challenge, this comprehensive programming guide for ABAP Objects provides an overview of the overall software development process. It describes the basic principles of designing and implementing an application in ABAP Objects, and how you can ensure that the application remains extensible for customer processes and sufficiently flexible for further development. The book describes from scratch all process steps to be carried out during programming, and illustrates these steps with numerous code examples and screenshots.

505 pp., 2008, 69,95 Euro / US$ 69.95
ISBN 978-1-59229-211-0

>> www.sap-press.de/1790

Master the installation, administration, and programming of SAP NetWeaver Portal

Efficiently navigate portal content, user administration, roles, transports, and externally facing portal

Learn from workshops on SAP NetWeaver Developer Studio, Web Page Composer, SAP Interactive Forms by Adobe, and much more

Marcus Banner, Berthold Latka, Michael Spee, Roland Schroth

Developer's Guide to SAP NetWeaver Portal Applications

From a strategic perspective, SAP NetWeaver Portal is perhaps the most important product of the SAP NetWeaver family of products. In fact, the Portal is essential to all processes within SAP NetWeaver. It serves as the fundamental platform that provides a condensed overview of all information and enables central access to all applications in the enterprise. In addition, the Portal provides the infrastructure for cooperation within and across company borders. This book provides the highly advanced functional knowledge required to correctly set up, operate, administer, and program the SAP NetWeaver Portal.

423 pp., 2008, 79,95 Euro / US$ 79.95
ISBN 978-1-59229-225-7

>> www.sap-press.de/1847

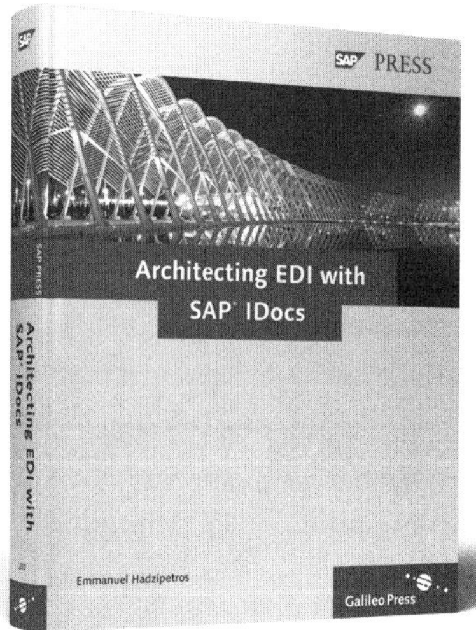

Covers the requirements, standards, and capabilities of EDI and IDocs

Teaches how to design the architectural blueprint of the EDI systems

Provides a sample scenario for implementing order-to-cash in a real-world project

Emmanuel Hadzipetros

Architecting EDI with SAP IDocs

This book is your project-based guide to architecting Enterprise Data Interchange (EDI) with SAP IDocs. Following a large sample scenario of an order-to-cash process from blueprint to code, you'll get an A-to-Z explanation of what an EDI system or architecture looks like. The book explains the basics of the process, shows a real-life implementation, and introduces utilities, test strategies, monitoring and troubleshooting activities. Following the sample project, you'll learn everything you need to know about SAP EDI.

approx. 600 pp., 69,95 Euro / US$ 69.95
ISBN 978-1-59229-227-1, July 2009

>> www.sap-press.de/1850